# CORPORATE
# ACCOUNTING in AUSTRALIA

# CORPORATE ACCOUNTING in AUSTRALIA

MICHAEL GAFFIKIN

RON DAGWELL

GRAEME WINES

ROB SMITH

JULIE WALKER

UNSW PRESS

A UNSW Press book

*Published by*
University of New South Wales Press Ltd
University of New South Wales
Sydney 2052 Australia

The authors & University of New South Press Ltd

National Library of Australia
Cataloguing-in-Publication entry:

Corporate accounting in Australia

Includes index
ISBN 0 86840 528 0.

1. Corporations-Australia-Accounting. L. Gaffikin, M.
J.R. (Michael John Renny). 1944–

657.950994

Cover Design: Di Quick
Editor: Robyn Flemming
Managing Editor: Nada Madjar
Printer: South China Printing
Production Manager: Di Quick
Publisher: Derelie Evely
Text Design & Formatting: Dizign Pty Ltd

# Contents

# Preface

Strong winds of change are sweeping through accounting education. Technology, globalisation and the increasing sophistication of business are continuously changing the role of the accountant. Accounting education has to reflect the different demands being placed on its 'products' — the accountants that are going to take the profession into the next century. Not only will these accountants have to have technical skills, they will also have to be skilled in many other areas not previously the typical domain of the accountant. The obvious impact of information technology has been that many of the procedural, mechanical tasks performed by the accountants of the past can now be done more quickly and efficiently by electronic means. An equally obvious implication of this is that it frees up the accountant to take a more active role in analysing information and advising on the implications of it. The accounting education program will reflect these demands being placed on its graduates by allocating more time, in the limited programs, to developing the necessary additional skills.

For a variety of reasons, many accounting students have found the subject or subjects that included corporate accounting difficult. One of the major reasons has been the highly technical nature of the subject and the almost infinite number of intricacies that can be introduced to challenge the students' comprehension of the subject. Much of these technical minutiae would rarely be encountered in practice by a few and never by most. However, it is vital that students fully comprehend the principles and concepts underlying the practice so that they can meet the technical challenges if and when they occur.

It is on this understanding that we have developed this book. Our guiding principle has been to develop a book that provides a comprehensive coverage of company accounting principles and issues in a very 'user-friendly' manner. Any corporate accounting text that provided less than a comprehensive treatment of the subject would fail to meet the students' need for a full appreciation of a very significant subject.

However, a recognition of the complexity of the subject can be inferred from the legislators' actions to simplify the law relating to corporations in Australia. We are firmly of the opinion that this is pedagogically desirable as well. Where students feel less threatened and daunted by the enormity of the subject, they will respond more positively: familiarity and security enhance the learning situation.

In writing the book we have incorporated recent changes brought about through the enactment of the *First Corporations Law Simplification Act 1995*, and those changes proposed in the Second Corporate Law Simplification Bill 1996. In some cases this has inevitably involved our making assessments of the likely or potential implications of the legislation, some of which are far-reaching but not necessarily capable of unambiguous interpretation.

The chapters have been arranged in what we believe to be the most logical sequence, given our guiding principle of user-friendliness. Review questions and exercises are provided at the end of each chapter to reinforce the material covered. The review questions are intended to reinforce the basic principles, procedures and conceptual issues. The exercises provide more extended problems for students and are graded according to the level of difficulty.

In preparing the material for the text we have been assisted by several friends and colleagues. We acknowledge are gratitude to these people who include Robyn Cook, Connie Spasich and Cynthia Nicholson of the University of Wollongong, and Jenny Waters, Preethi Weerasinghe and Amanda Zuttion of Griffith University.

We are also grateful to those who gave permission to reproduce material; they include Duncan Craig and Robert Harley of the *Australian Financial Review*, the Australian Society of Certified Practising Accountants, the Institute of Chartered Accountants of Australia and Amcor Ltd.

Michael Gaffikin
Ron Dagwell
Graeme Wines

chapter *1*

# COMPANY FORMATION, SHARE CAPITAL AND DEBT SECURITIES

# introduction

There are many different forms of business organisation, including sole proprietorships, partnerships, trusts and companies. Of the several forms of business organisation in developed economies the company is the most common. This book is concerned with the accounting that is followed within and by companies. This chapter serves as an introduction to companies and describes what they are, how they are formed and the accounting that is used for their formation. Companies are separate legal entities, so the accounting for their creation involves the setting up of a new 'set of books' – the double entry process creates a new accounting system. Because of their nature, this accounting system must conform to certain legal requirements as well as normal accounting conventions and practices.

# What is a company?

A company is an entity created by law with many of the same privileges and responsibilities enjoyed by individuals. In order to be able to effectively account for companies it is important to know just what a company is. There are many angles from which the company can be viewed — there are different perspectives on companies, namely, legal, economic, financial, political and sociological, all of which overlap to some extent.

**different perspectives on companies**

## A LEGAL PERSPECTIVE

Legally a company in Australia is a body incorporated, or taken to be incorporated, under the Australian Corporations Law.[1] The Corporations Law is one of the biggest and most complex statutes in the country, so it is not easy to summarise it in a few sentences. However, in so far as this book is concerned with company accounting, it is only important to be aware of certain provisions of the Corporations Law. These relate to the formation, the winding up and the reorganisation of companies, the need to maintain accounting records, and the extent to which the company must present financial information to various interested parties. Even this is complicated. For example, there are different types and classes of companies, with a variety of ways in which they can be formed. Thus, accounting for their formation, unfortunately, is not simple. Nevertheless, there are certain common principles to be borne in mind and it is to these that attention will be directed in this book. As indicated, a company is created by the law to have similar rights and responsibilities to individuals. The law is designed to protect all those dealing with the company — the owners or investors, the suppliers of credit, its customers, the employees, and the state generally. Recognising its complexity there have been, to date, three attempts to simplify the legal requirements (the Corporate Law Simplification Acts). These have had or will have some impact on procedures for accounting for companies.

From a legal perspective a company is an artificially created entity which needs a body of regulation to control its creation and operation. Those involved in the formation and management of a company must conform to this body of law in order that all other entities dealing with the company are offered some protection. Part of this regulation or law is concerned with the establishment and maintenance of financial records and with the financial reporting that the company is obliged to undertake. This is the subject of company accounting.

## AN ECONOMIC PERSPECTIVE

Societies have designed laws to enable the creation of companies because they have felt it desirable to do so. That is, companies are seen as desirable entities within societies and this is mainly because they can facilitate economic activity which will benefit the community. Thus, companies have the capacity to engage in economic activity that individuals acting as sole traders or small groups of individuals working in partnerships cannot. Essentially this is the capacity to serve as the collecting point of large quantities of resources — capital. These large amounts of capital can then be employed in activities that require large-scale investment — for example, the construction of large (or even small) factories, the purchase of expensive equipment or the operation of a large number of geographically spread-out activities. However, there are also many small companies, so there are other advantages in the company form of business organisation. One of the more important of these is the limiting of the potential liability of the owners or investors. Therefore, a group of investors investing $100 000 will have their liability, if the need ever arises (that is, the company fails), limited to their original investment (or commitment to invest). This limited liability provision in companies has long been viewed as the major reason for the growth in the company form of business organisation over the last 150 or so years.

**limited liability**

From an economic perspective a company is a facilitator of economic activity. As a legal entity a company can engage in most of the economic activities any individual can. That is, it can borrow, own resources and generally trade in its own right. A major objective of company accounting is to record and report on the economic actions taken by the company; to indicate the resources owned by the economic entity, its commitments to providers of equity; and to report on the success of its operations over a given period.

## A FINANCIAL PERSPECTIVE

The ownership of most companies is reflected in their share capital. That is, most companies are formed with a number of ownership units called shares owned by shareholders. The share capital contributed on the formation of a company enables it to then undertake economic activity. However, once issued by the company, these ownership rights, the shares, can usually be transferred, and formal markets exist for the selling and buying of the shares — stock exchanges. In addition, a company can issue other types of securities when it raises funds in the economy. That is, it borrows and issues documentary evidence of the debt. Like shares, these are issued in units which are normally transferable. In recent years, other types of financial securities concerning companies have developed. Formal securities markets, such as stock exchanges, have evolved for trading and investing in company securities. Investors are interested in companies in so far as they can have these avenues of investment. They are not so much interested in the everyday economic activities of the company other than the extent to which they affect the prices other investors are willing to pay for the securities. For example, they are concerned with what their shares are worth in the financial market. These securities markets have become an important part of the economic activity of most developed countries as is evidenced, for example, in the fact that the daily television news will indicate the general level or trend of prices for that day (in Australia it is referred to as the All Ordinaries Index). They are important because companies can only operate if there are sufficient numbers of entities willing to invest in the securities markets and provide them with the necessary capital.

**shares**
**shareholders**

**securities**

Company accounting from a financial perspective is important for it provides investors and potential investors with information on the financial stability, liquidity and operating potential of companies. This information is useful to those making investment decisions. Investment and efficient securities or financial markets are crucial to the well-being of companies, as it is only through investment in them that companies can undertake economic activity.

## A POLITICAL PERSPECTIVE

The well-being of individuals in particular parts of an economy depends on the level of economic activity that is undertaken. Some towns are called 'company towns'. That is, the town survives because of the presence of a company. The company provides employment for the community which in turn necessitates services such as retail shops, educational and medical facilities, and so on. Therefore, companies are important politically, and often policies need to be implemented to encourage them to locate in certain areas and their closure causes severe social problems not only for small communities but also in large metropolitan cities. Governments, then, will implement policies that induce companies to operate in certain locations. One of the major goals of developing economies is to encourage investment and this is often done by international or multinational companies. In Australia there is considerable competition between the states to encourage companies to set up business in their states. Investment brings employment, which is a fundamental part of economic activity and the economic wealth of a community.

Company accounting is important to political decision makers as it provides a guide to the contribution companies are making to the well-being of the community and even the whole economy. Sometimes companies making losses are subsidised in order to enable them to continue operations, as their closure would result in a significant social cost to the community through the loss of employment and other derived economic activities. Sometimes there needs to be state investment or economic cooperation in order that the company remain economically viable. Therefore, decisions to provide state support for companies are based on political considerations, such decisions being affected by the operation of companies.

## A SOCIOLOGICAL PERSPECTIVE

Societies create laws to regulate their operation. Some activities are encouraged through regulation, while some are discouraged. Thus, it is considered desirable to have some types of economic activity, such as the creation of employment mentioned above, but not others, such as the selling of narcotic drugs. The fact that companies have been created by law indicates that they are considered as desirable. Yet their activities must be controlled to avoid hurting those dealing with them. Historically, company law has increased significantly, reflecting the expansion and increasing sophistication of business and economic activity over the years. In fact, as a result of the increasing complexity of economic activity and business ownership, the original concept of a company (150 years ago) no longer exists. The sheer size of some companies, the international activities of many and the increasingly complex ownership structures have been major forces in the changing nature of companies. Some sections of societies are demanding more from companies than before. For example, they argue that if a company is going to exploit the country's economic resources it must be able to demonstrate benefits and not costs that flow to the society from its operation. A good example is the effect the operations have on the environment, such as the mining of natural resources and pollution. Our economic system is open to the abuses of privileges and the law has attempted to restrict such abuses. No society is perfect and will always contain those who try to take unfair advantage. There have been some well-publicised recent law cases in Australia (and other parts of the world) concerning the 'undesirable activities' of those in charge of companies which are evidence of the existence of those who attempt to manipulate situations to their own advantage. The costs of bringing (and attempting to bring) these people to justice are often enormous and are borne by societies generally. The costs of a large-scale company failure inevitably trickle through to the rest of the economy.

The law requires most large companies to publish financial statements in their annual reports. The accounting information then becomes public information. Announcements of profits (and losses) often attract the attention of the news media. In cases where these results are seen to be 'unfair', considerable pressure is placed on the regulators to remedy the perceived ills. For example, where banks report unusually large profits there will be public pressure for a decrease in bank charges or rates of interest charged to customers.

## Accountability

As indicated above, there is considerable overlapping in the perspective of companies. While all views are important, this book is concerned mainly with the economic and legal perspectives. However, also as already indicated, the legal aspects of companies are complex. Thus, when learning company accounting it is only those legal aspects that impinge on the accounting process that are significant and that is the principle adopted here. The primary aim is to account for an **economic entity** and satisfy the financial reporting obligations of that entity. Investment is made on the basis that there be some **accountability** in the form of information. You deposit your savings in a bank — your investment — on the understanding that you will receive a bank statement indicating the extent of your investment (and, hopefully, any interest you have earned). Investors in companies, whether they be the shareholders, the providers of loan capital or suppliers of assets, expect some accountability: published company financial reports provide a significant part of this accountability.

There are a large number of companies in Australia, by far the majority of them being small companies. Such companies usually are not required to publish their financial reports. However, it is the larger companies that have the most significant impact on the economy — investment in them far exceeds the investment in the smaller companies. The fundamental company accounting is the same for both small and large companies, but the form will differ in the degree of detail and complexity. One advantage of the company form of business organisation is that it has permitted specialist managers to administer the day-to-day operations of the company. This is especially true of larger companies, as smaller companies are invariably managed by their owners. For example, a small retail store may be a family company — family members are the only shareholders — many of whom work in the business. Yet this is not possible for a large industrial company with a very large number of shareholders living in different parts of the country or the world. These companies are **directors** administered by directors who are then accountable to the shareholders, and this is one of the reasons why company law requires companies to provide annual reports containing financial statements.

The Corporations Law imposes strict obligations on directors so that the interests of investors (and others) are protected. As there has been the separation of owners from managers, one view of directors is that they act as stewards for the shareholders, **stewardship** protecting their investment; there is a stewardship relationship so that they must act in the best interests of the shareholders. However, others argue that the directors **agent** have their own interests and personal aspirations and they are simply agents for the shareholders (and other investors), so there must be a system of rewards for them to ensure that their interests coincide with the investors so that all parties benefit from the decisions they make in operating the company.

# The development of companies

The company form of business organisation has been around for 400 years, but the modern form of company emerged in Britain in the middle of the 19th century. It is no coincidence that it grew with the increasing industrialisation of the period, as the company was seen as a convenient form of organisation for the accumulation of capital. Thus, in the 17th century when European traders were making ventures to newly 'discovered' parts of the world, there was a need for sufficient capital to fund the venture that exceeded the amounts that could be raised by one or two partners. There was also, of course, considerable risk in investing in these ventures as the ships may never return! Many companies were formed to gather together the different levels of funds contributed by many investors. Some famous companies such as the Dutch East Indies Company in the Netherlands and the East India Company of Great Britain were formed in this period.

In the 19th century the industrial revolution and the expansion of the railway networks usually required very large amounts of capital, amounts beyond the means of a few investors, and it is generally believed that this provided the impetus for the growth in the company form of organisation. However, this was accompanied by the growth in company legislation and one of the most important elements in this new law was the notion of limited liability — limiting the liability of investors to the extent of their investment. This meant that individuals could invest their savings in a company in the knowledge that they would only lose their investment if the company failed. In other forms of business organisation such as partnerships, the investors — the partners — are personally liable for the debts of the business. Thus, while the *company is responsible for all its debts*, if it has insufficient resources to meet them the private resources of the shareholders are not available.

Other legal provisions facilitated the growth of the company form of organisation, such as the requirement of **audit** — the independent investigation of and report on the company's financial affairs — and the possibility of **transfer of ownership interests**. A partnership ceases to exist on the death (or withdrawal) of one of the partners. However, the shares owned by a shareholder may be sold or transferred (for example, as a gift or bequest) to others. Thus, the company, unless otherwise designed, has a potentially **unlimited life**. The capacity of transfer of ownership has transformed the modern company this century. As legal entities, companies can hold shares in other companies and, today, the major shareholders in companies are in fact companies themselves. As the shareholders can direct the operation of a company through their voting at meetings, any entity holding a majority of the shares and voting rights can **control** the company. Attaining such control is a strategy of many companies — to obtain a **controlling interest** in other companies through, for example, buying a majority of their shares. This relationship affects the accounting of such economic entities and that is the subject of many of the later chapters of this book. There are other means of controlling an entity, but the most common is through ownership rights. This process of control and cross-ownership has changed companies from the 19th century view of them and made them extremely important economic and social institutions in modern developed economies.

In Australia the regulation of companies has always been the responsibility of the states and initially this caused considerable confusion. More recently the states have agreed to a common source of regulation in the form of the Corporations Law, uniform legislation adopted by all the states. The Law is divided into chapters and most of the accounting provisions are contained in Chapter 3, part 3.6. Note that the terms '**company**' and '**corporation**' are often used interchangeably. The term 'corporation' includes some incorporated bodies which are subject to the same law but are not usually considered as companies. Thus, the word 'corporation' has a broader meaning than 'company' (see s 57A of the Corporations Law) but the terms are often used interchangeably. Because it is so complex, there have recently been moves to rewrite and simplify the Corporations Law (through a series of Corporate Law Simplification Acts) which have greatly affected the way companies are created and administered.

# Types of company

## LIMITED LIABILITY COMPANIES

Although it has been seen as one of the most attractive features of the company form of organisation, not all companies have the liability of members limited. There are a number of different types of company permitted under the Corporations Law, but the main one discussed in this book will be those which have a share capital with the liability of the members limited. There are two broad types of such companies — **proprietary companies** and **public companies**. A company which has its liability limited must contain the word 'Limited', often abbreviated to 'Ltd', as part of its name, indicating to all who deal with it that the liability of the members is limited.

A proprietary company must also have the word 'Proprietary' (or the abbreviation 'Pty') included in its title. A proprietary company is usually smaller than a public company and can be formed by one or more (but not more than 50) persons and must have a share capital. There are restrictions on some activities of a proprietary company, such as it is not able to raise money from the public and there are restrictions on the transfer of shares. Proprietary companies are further classified as being either a *large proprietary company* or a *small proprietary company*. A large proprietary company is one that satisfies at least two of the following three tests. It has:

1  a consolidated annual gross operating revenue of at least $10 million;
2  end of financial year consolidated gross assets of at least $5 million;
3  more than 50 full-time employees (or their part-time equivalent) of the company and the entities it controls (if any) at the end of the financial year.

**Australian Securities Commission**

A large proprietary company is required to lodge audited accounts each year with the body charged with the responsibility of administering companies, the Australian Securities Commission (ASC), while the small proprietary company has no obligation to even prepare annual accounts.

Traditionally, small proprietary companies have been more suited to small operations, often family-controlled businesses, but which wish to have the advantages of being a company.

Public companies used to have to have a minimum of five members but now, with recent changes in the law in respect of proprietary companies, a public company is any other company that is not a proprietary company (and, therefore, may have only one member). Public companies have the advantage of being able to invite the public to invest in them through the subscription to share or debt capital (these terms will be more fully explained later). The large companies that are discussed in the news and which have become familiar names are public companies. However, some of Australia's well-known public companies started as proprietary companies and grew and were converted to public companies — for example, some of the large retail store companies such as David Jones Ltd and Grace Brothers (now part of a larger group).

**company limited by guarantee**

There is a less common form of company with limited liability: a company limited by guarantee. The liability of the members is limited to a prearranged amount similar to any type of guarantee. Trading companies usually do not adopt this form and such companies are often encountered as clubs, non-profit charitable organisations or schools. It used to be possible for a company to be limited by shares and guarantee, but these too are rare and no new such companies can be formed.

## UNLIMITED LIABILITY COMPANIES

Companies may also be formed without the protection of limited liability for their shareholders. Because it does not have what has been viewed as one of the most beneficial advantages, namely limited liability for members, this type of company is rare. The advantage of unlimited liability is that there are fewer legal restrictions on the issue and redemption (in effect, buying back or cancelling) of shares.

## SPECIAL COMPANIES

There are a variety of other types of companies involved in special industries — usually the service industries — which have special conditions applying to them. Usually these companies are subject to special companies legislation relating to their industry. For example, banking companies are subject to the Commonwealth's banking legislation. In addition, companies incorporated outside Australia but which trade in the country are recognised as foreign companies and have certain legal obligations in Australia, such as registering with the ASC.

This book is concerned with the general principles involved in accounting for companies, so we will direct attention to companies with a share capital and limited liability. Only slight modifications to the procedures described would be necessary to account for the extra conditions imposed by special industry legislation.

# Forming a company

The administration of the Corporations Law is the responsibility of the ASC. In order to form a company, those who are promoting (organising) it must submit an application to the ASC. The application must include certain information (as set out in s 117 of the Corporations Law) such as the name of the company, the names and

**certificate of registration**
**Australian Company Number**

addresses of the original subscriber(s), the address of the business, etc. If satisfied that the application contains the necessary information the ASC will issue a certificate of registration and a registration number — an Australian Company Number (abbreviated to ACN) which must appear on certain company documents.

**constitution**

Another legal document which can be prepared and attached to the application is the company's constitution. This contains the rules for managing the internal affairs of the company, the responsibilities of the directors and their relationship to the shareholders. A company need not include a constitution, in which case the

**replaceable rules**

replaceable rules in the Corporations Law will apply. However, a company can replace or discard any of the replaceable rules by passing a special resolution at a general meeting of the company. The replaceable rules will not apply to a small proprietary company with one member who is the sole director.

Until recently a company needed to have a *memorandum* to lodge with the application for registration and could also have *articles of association* which contained the day-to-day management rules of the company. The requirement for these has been removed (simplification) and much of the information they included is now found in the application and the constitution (or replaceable rules).

**prospectus**

Once registered, the company, if it is a public company, can issue an invitation to the public to subscribe to its shares. This invitation is called a prospectus and, because it is inviting investment from the public, there are strict legal requirements that must be adhered to. Such regulation tries to ensure that prospective shareholders are not misled.

# Financing a company

Before a company can commence operations it must have the funds to do so. Similarly, if an existing company wishes to expand its operations it needs to finance this expansion. An existing company can borrow from a lending institution in the same way as any individual can. A new company will have to raise funds through issuing securities to investors, more particularly issuing shares. Generally speaking, those investors who purchase the shares become the **members** or shareholders (the terms are mostly used interchangeably) of the company: they provide the **equity capital** of the company and, as part owners of it, are entitled to a share in the future profits and a voice in the management of the company. For public companies these shares are transferable — that is, the owner may sell them to a third party. This is usually done through the medium of the **Australian Stock Exchange** (ASX) and this concerns the financial perspective of companies discussed earlier. When the company issues the shares, it receives the funds. When the shares are traded on the ASX it is the owner of the shares who receives the proceeds. However, companies tend to want to have their shares listed on a stock exchange— that is, have them officially recognised as tradable on the stock exchange. In order for companies to have this privilege they must comply with various regulations and rules imposed by the stock exchange; these are referred to as the **listing requirements**. The benefits to the company arise from the fact that listing provides a 'market incentive' in the finance market — investors are aware of the company and will be prepared to invest in any future issues of securities by the company, reducing the cost of any additional finance.

There are other forms of securities which a company can issue and these are usually referred to as **debt capital**. These other securities include **debentures**, convertible notes or other units of prescribed interest (for example, the right to purchase shares at some future date). Providers of debt capital do not form part of the owners of the company but they are important to the financing of company operations. In order to facilitate this investment the Corporations Law has the underlying principle of enhanced disclosure (or continuous disclosure). This is the principle that as the company wishes to raise money from the public it should keep the public informed of events that could affect the price of the company's securities. It is an example of how the financial perspective of companies is seen as important and is especially relevant to companies with securities listed on the ASX. Basically it involves the lodgment of half-yearly reports and any price-sensitive information with the ASX (for listed companies) and the ASC.

Margin terms: members, equity capital, Australian Stock Exchange, share listing, listing requirements, debt capital, debenture

# Issuing of shares

Before any securities such as shares, debentures or prescribed interest can be issued for public subscription the company must issue a prospectus. The strict legal requirements of prospectuses are designed to protect prospective investors. Throughout history there have been many instances of dishonest offers of investment and the subsequent financial distress — or even ruin— of investors as their companies failed and they lost their investment. Unfortunately, no law will stop the unscrupulous, but prospectuses are in line with the enhanced disclosure idea that providing as much reliable information as possible will avoid investors being financially hurt. Recent legislation has adopted the principles of solvency, fairness and disclosure: keeping the company in a sound financial position so that it can continue operating, being fair to all who deal with it, and providing all the relevant information on the company that the investors need to make their decisions. Prospectuses must not only be *lodged* with the ASC; they usually must be *registered* with the ASC, an extra step involving the ASC scrutinising the prospectus before it is issued.

A share is defined in the Corporations Law (s 9) as a share in the share capital of a body, but it can more appropriately be viewed as a right to a specified amount of the share capital of a company with rights and liabilities in respect to that company. The share represents a share in the net worth of the company in proportion to the amount of share capital the company issues. A company may, in its constitution, limit the number of shares the directors can issue.

The capital may be divided into different types of shares each with different rights.

**ordinary shares**
The most common types of shares are called ordinary shares (they are called common stock in the United States). Many companies, especially proprietary companies, will only have this class of share. They form the basic 'ownership' units for which members subscribe. For example, if a company is formed with a capital of 1 000 000 shares, each share will represent one millionth ownership of the company. Alternatively, the company may have a capital of 750 000 ordinary shares and 250 000 preference shares. In both cases the number of shares is the same — 1 000 000. In the second situation the shares have been divided into two types of shares. The 750 000 will be ordinary shares with the usual rights attaching to ordinary shares, such as entitlement to shares in any profit but only in so far as a

**preference shares**
profit has been made. The preference shares will have some preferential right. For example, they could be entitled to a fixed amount of return (dividend) each year irrespective of whether or not a profit has been earned. If the company does not have the cash to pay these amounts, then it assumes a liability for the amounts due. Or they could be preferential as to return of capital in preference to (that is, before) the ordinary shareholders in the event that the company ceases to operate (is wound up). Or they could be both preferential as to income and capital return. They may be participating, which means that they are entitled to a fixed income return and they share with the ordinary shares in any remaining distributable profit. Sometimes preference shares are issued for a set period and on the expiration of this period the shareholders are paid back their capital or are able to convert their shares into ordinary shares. These shares are called redeemable preference shares. Because of their preferential rights, preference shares may have restricted voting rights.

Ordinary shares are nowadays the most common type of shares, but over the years many companies have issued some form of preference shares. There may be many other types of shares, but we will be mostly concerned with those two types. For example, the promoters of a company may be entitled to promoters' or founders' deferred shares, employees entitled to employee shares, and so on.

**application**
**allotment**

Investors apply for shares, and this application in contractual terms is treated as an offer. When the application is successful, the shares are allotted, the allotment or the notice of acceptance of the application being the acceptance. As with most contracts, there must be both offer and acceptance for the contract to be binding.

**issued capital**

Once the shares are allotted, this becomes the company's issued capital. The shareholders will receive from the company a share certificate indicating the number of the shares held and the company will keep a register of all shareholders, a share register.

# Accounting for the share issue

It is usual for an application for shares to require some payment, either full payment for the shares applied for or a proportion as a 'deposit'. For example, a company may decide to issue 500 000 ordinary shares at $1 and require applicants to pay 25 cents for each share applied for on application. The money so received does not belong to the company as there is no contract until the offer has been accepted. Therefore, the company must keep the money received for applications in a special trust bank account. If the company received applications for all these shares, it would record in its books the receipt of this money with the following general journal entry:

|  | Debit | Credit |
|---|---|---|
| Bank Trust | 125 000 |  |
| Application |  | 125 000 |
| (cash received on application, 25 cents on 500 000 shares) | | |

At this stage the company has no assets and no capital which can be accounted for because the money received for applications does not legally belong to the company but is held in trust for the applicants. Once the closing date for applications is reached, the directors will meet and allot the shares and send allotment letters to the successful applicants. Now the money belongs to the company and the company has a paid-up capital of $125 000. It will need to record this in the general journal.

|  | Debit | Credit |
|---|---|---|
| Application | 125 000 |  |
| Paid-up Capital |  | 125 000 |
| (application money of 25 cents due on 500 000 allotted shares) | | |
| Bank | 125 000 |  |
| Bank Trust |  | 125 000 |
| (transfer of money received on application) | | |

At this stage the company has an

| | |
|---|---|
| Issued capital | $500 000 |
| *of which* | |
| Paid-up capital is | $125 000 |
| and an Asset: | |
| Bank | $125 000 |

Note that the issued capital is *not* recorded in the general journal, so a balance sheet as at this date would only comprise the last two items.

|  | $ |
|---|---|
| *Shareholders' equity* | |
| Paid-up capital | 125 000 |
| *Asset* | |
| Bank | 125 000 |

In a *published* balance sheet the issued capital would be disclosed, as that is required by law, but it would not be added in with the other shareholders' equity items.

The company may well require the shareholders (successful applicants) to pay a further 50 cents per share on receipt of the allotment letter. This would be recorded in the general journal as:

|  | Debit | Credit |
|---|---|---|
| Allotment | 250 000 | |
| Paid-up Capital | | 250 000 |
| (being 50 cents per share due on allotment) | | |

When the cash is received from all shareholders, a summary general journal entry would record this.

|  |  |  |
|---|---|---|
| Bank | 250 000 | |
| Allotment | | 250 000 |
| (being amount received on allotment) | | |

The balance sheet as at this date (assuming no other transactions) would now appear as follows:

|  | $ |
|---|---|
| *Shareholders' equity* | |
| Paid-up capital | 375 000 |
| *Asset* | |
| Bank | 375 000 |

Note that the company has an

|  |  |
|---|---|
| Issued capital | $500 000 |
| of which | |
| Paid-up capital is | $375 000 |

The remaining 25 cents per share that is as yet not paid may be outstanding by the company to a later date when the directors feel the money would be needed for a second or later stage in the set-up or the expansion of the business. Thus, it could be due a year later, so when the directors resolve that this is due they make a call. The entry in the general journal would be:

**call**

|  | Debit | Credit |
|---|---|---|
| Call | 125 000 | |
| Paid-up Capital | | 125 000 |
| (amount of 25 cents per share due on call) | | |

and when the money is all received a general journal entry would record:

|  | Debit | Credit |
|---|---|---|
| Bank | 125 000 |  |
| Call |  | 125 000 |
| (cash received for payment of call) |  |  |

The balance sheet at this date would include the shareholders' equity item of paid-up capital of $500 000.

Note that the receipt of money would be over a period of time. The company would maintain a cashbook or cash journal that would record the receipt of the cash separately, and the above journal entry would be for the total amounts received.

## OVER- AND UNDERSUBSCRIPTION

The success of a share issue will depend on the economic conditions of the time. In a buoyant, confident economic climate it is likely that there would be applications for more shares than were available (being issued). In such a case, there is an **oversubscription**, in which case the shares would be allotted on some basis the directors had decided on. In accounting terms, the cash received would be in excess of that due so some would have to be returned or, if the terms of the issue permit (indicated in the prospectus), be used to pay the amounts that became due on allotment and/or calls.

Thus, if in our example there were applications for 600 000 shares, the general journal entry would be:

|  | Debit | Credit |
|---|---|---|
| Bank Trust | 150 000 |  |
| Application |  | 150 000 |
| (cash received on application, 25 cents on 600 000 shares) |  |  |

If the amount received for the oversubscribed shares was to be returned to the unsuccessful applicants, a general journal entry to record this would be:

|  |  |  |
|---|---|---|
| Application | 25 000 |  |
| Bank Trust |  | 25 000 |
| (amounts refunded to unsuccessful applicants) |  |  |

This could be combined with the entry to transfer the money for the successful applications.

|  |  |  |
|---|---|---|
| Application | 25 000 |  |
| Bank | 125 000 |  |
| Bank Trust |  | 150 000 |
| (transfer and refund of amounts received for application) |  |  |

If everyone who applied for shares were allotted some and the terms of issue permitted it, the extra money received on oversubscription could be used to pay amounts due on allotment. Using the same illustrative information as above, the general journal entries would be:

| | Debit | Credit |
|---|---|---|
| Bank Trust | 150 000 | |
|     Application | | 150 000 |
| (cash received on application, 25 cents on 600 000 shares) | | |
| | | |
| Bank | 150 000 | |
|     Bank Trust | | 150 000 |
| (transfer of amount received on application) | | |
| | | |
| Application | 150 000 | |
|     Paid-up Capital | | 125 000 |
|     Allotment | | 25 000 |
| (amounts received on application transferred to capital and allotment amounts due) | | |

and when allotment is made:

| | | |
|---|---|---|
| Allotment | 250 000 | |
|     Paid-up Capital | | 250 000 |
| (amount due on allotment) | | |

and when amounts due on allotment are received:

| | | |
|---|---|---|
| Bank | 225 000 | |
|     Allotment | | 225 000 |
| (amounts received in settlement of that owing on allotment) | | |

At this stage the assets and equities are the same as where there was no oversubscription and would include:

| | |
|---|---|
| Paid-up capital of | $375 000 |
| Bank | 375 000 |

**undersubscription**<br>**underwriter** Where the directors have misread the economic climate and there are too few applicants, there has been an undersubscription. Often this situation is avoided by the use of an underwriter (a broking firm, a financial institution, etc). The underwriter undertakes to take up any undersubscribed shares in return for an underwriting commission. In such situations there are no complications in respect of the accounting for the share issue. Where the underwriter takes up part of the issue the share issue will be accounted for as a full issue (as above). Where there is an undersubscription the amount received (bank trust) will simply be a lower figure.

## ISSUE FOR PAYMENT IN FULL

In the above examples it has been assumed that shares are issued requiring payment in instalments — that is, part on application, part on allotment and part as a call. However, the shares may have been issued requiring payment in full on application. In this situation the full amount will be recorded in the first general journal entry. Using the same information as in the above examples the entries would be:

| | Debit | Credit |
|---|---|---|
| Bank Trust | 500 000 | |
|     Application | | 500 000 |
| (amounts received on application for 500 000 ordinary $1 shares) | | |

and then:

|  | Debit | Credit |
|---|---|---|
| Bank | 500 000 | |
|     Bank Trust | | 500 000 |
| (transfer of money received on application) | | |
|  | | |
| Application | 500 000 | |
|     Paid-up Capital | | 500 000 |
| (amount due on application for shares issued) | | |

## ILLUSTRATIVE EXAMPLE 1.1

# BASIC SHARE ISSUE

Ariel Ltd was formed on 1 July 20X1 with a clause in its constitution limiting the number of shares to 1 000 000. The directors decide to issue 600 000 shares at $1 each with the terms being that 50 cents is payable on application by 31 July, allotments to be made on 1 August with 25 cents on allotment and due by 30 September, and a first and final call of 25 cents to be made on 30 November and due by 31 December 20X1. The issue is fully subscribed and all amounts due are received by the specified dates.

### General journal

| 20X1 | | Debit $ | Credit $ |
|---|---|---|---|
| July 31 | Bank Trust | 300 000 | |
| |     Application | | 300 000 |
| | (amounts received on application of 50 cents on 600 000 ordinary shares) | | |
| Aug 1 | Bank | 300 000 | |
| |     Bank Trust | | 300 000 |
| | (transfer of amounts received on application) | | |
| | Application | 300 000 | |
| |     Paid-up Capital | | 300 000 |
| | (amounts due on application for shares allotted) | | |
| | Allotment | 150 000 | |
| |     Paid-up Capital | | 150 000 |
| | (amounts due on allotment) | | |
| Sept 30 | Bank | 150 000 | |
| |     Allotment | | 150 000 |
| | (amounts received for allotment) | | |
| Nov 30 | Call | 150 000 | |
| |     Paid-up Capital | | 150 000 |
| | (first and final call of 25 cents per share) | | |
| Dec 31 | Bank | 150 000 | |
| |     Call | | 150 000 |
| | (amounts received for call) | | |

## General ledger

| 20X1 | | Debit $ | Credit $ | Balance $ | |
|------|--|---------|----------|-----------|--|
| **Application** | | | | | |
| July 31 | Bank Trust | | 300 000 | 300 000 | Cr |
| Aug 1 | Paid-up Capital | 300 000 | | – | |
| **Bank Trust** | | | | | |
| July 31 | Application | 300 000 | | 300 000 | Dr |
| Aug 1 | Bank | | 300 000 | – | |
| **Bank** | | | | | |
| Aug 1 | Bank Trust | 300 000 | | 300 000 | Dr |
| Sept 30 | Allotment | 150 000 | | 450 000 | Dr |
| Dec 31 | Call | 150 000 | | 600 000 | Dr |
| **Allotment** | | | | | |
| Aug 1 | Paid-up Capital | 150 000 | | 150 000 | Dr |
| Sept 30 | Bank | | 150 000 | – | |
| **Call** | | | | | |
| Nov 30 | Paid-up Capital | 150 000 | | 150 000 | Dr |
| Dec 31 | Bank | | 150 000 | – | |
| **Paid-up Capital** | | | | | |
| Aug 1 | Application | | 300 000 | 300 000 | Cr |
| | Allotment | | 150 000 | 450 000 | Cr |
| Nov 30 | Call | | 150 000 | 600 000 | Cr |

In Illustrative example 1.1 there were no complications with the share issue. Often, however, this is not the case. A company may have different types of shares and if they were to be issued at the same time there needs to be an entry for each type. For example, if a company were to issue 500 000 ordinary shares at $1 and 300 000 preference shares at $2, payable in full on application, the company would have recorded the cash received for applications as:

| | Debit | Credit |
|--|-------|--------|
| Bank Trust | 1 100 000 | |
|     Application – Ordinary | | 500 000 |
|     Application – Preference | | 600 000 |
| (amounts received on application for shares) | | |
| | | |
| Application – Ordinary | 500 000 | |
| Application – Preference | 600 000 | |
|     Paid-up Capital – Ordinary | | 500 000 |
|     Paid-up Capital – Preference | | 600 000 |
| (amounts due on application for ordinary $1 shares and preference $2 shares) | | |
| | | |
| Bank | 1 100 000 | |
|     Bank Trust | | 1 100 000 |
| (amounts received on share issues transferred) | | |

If the issue was to be by instalments the entries would be similar to those in the illustrative example except there would be an entry for each type of share affected — for example, Allotment — Ordinary, Allotment — Preference, and so on.

There may be other 'complications'. As indicated above, there may be an oversubscription with the need for some money to be returned to unsuccessful applicants, some money transferred to offset amounts due on allotment, and/or the call. Some successful applicants may pay the call amounts when they pay the amounts due on allotment. When amounts are received before they are due and the company keeps them, they are described as **calls in advance** and are in effect a 'liability' of the company similar to revenue received in advance. This is an instance when the law becomes complicated and care should be exercised when dealing with calls in advance. Sometimes calls are not received by the due dates, in which case they become **calls in arrears**. These will be reflected in any debit balance in a call account. For example, if Ariel Ltd only received for the call $145 000 by 31 December there would be a debit balance in the Call account, implying that there were calls in arrears of $5000 (meaning that holders of 20 000 shares had not yet paid the 25 cents due on the call).

*Margin terms:* calls in advance; calls in arrears

# Forfeiture of shares

An advantage of issuing shares by instalment is that investors can purchase a large number without having to pay the full amount up front — as with the purchase of many other assets by instalments. However, there is a legally binding commitment to pay the calls the company makes. When an investor does not pay the calls by the due dates the company, if its constitution so authorises, may forfeit the shares. When it does this *the issue of the shares* that have been forfeited is in effect 'cancelled'. (In fact, the company can formally cancel the forfeited shares.) That is, those shares no longer form part of the company's issued capital. In accounting terms, all the entries in respect of the shares forfeited have to be reversed and any amounts received for those shares are transferred to a Forfeited Shares account.

**ILLUSTRATIVE EXAMPLE 1.2**

## FORFEITURE OF SHARES

Using the same information as in Illustrative example 1.1 except that by 31 December $5000 remains outstanding on the call. The directors, in accordance with the company's constitution, resolve on 15 January 20X2 to forfeit the shares on which calls remain unpaid.

Working:

Number of shares forfeited is 5000/.25 = 20 000

| | | |
|---|---|---|
| Amounts paid are | Application – 20 000 @ 50 cents = | $10 000 |
| | Allotment – 20 000 @ 25 cents = | 5 000 |
| | | $15 000 |
| Amount not paid | Call – 20 000 at 25 cents | $5 000 |

### General journal

| | | Debit | Credit |
|---|---|---|---|
| | | $ | $ |
| 20X2 | | | |
| Jan 15 | Paid-up Capital | 20 000 | |
| | Call | | 5 000 |
| | Forfeited Shares Account | | 15 000 |
| | (forfeiture of 20 000 shares for non-payment of call) | | |

### General ledger (extract)

| | | Debit | Credit | Balance | |
|---|---|---|---|---|---|
| | | $ | $ | $ | |
| | **Call** | | | | |
| 20X1 | | | | | |
| Nov 30 | Paid-up Capital | 150 000 | | 150 000 | Dr |
| Dec 31 | Bank | | 145 000 | 5 0000 | Dr |
| 20X2 | | | | | |
| Jan 15 | Paid-up Capital | | 5 000 | – | |
| | **Paid-up Capital** | | | | |
| 20X1 | | | | | |
| Aug 1 | Application | | 300 000 | 300 000 | Cr |
| | Allotment | | 150 000 | 450 000 | Cr |
| Nov 30 | Call | | 150 000 | 600 000 | Cr |
| 20X2 | | | | | |
| Jan 15 | Call & Forfeited Shares Account | 20 000 | | 580 000 | Cr |
| | **Forfeited Shares Account** | | | | |
| Jan 15 | Paid-up Capital | | 15 000 | 15 000 | Cr |

## REISSUE OF FORFEITED SHARES

Although the company can formally cancel the forfeited shares, it may want to reissue shares that have been forfeited. Accounting for the reissue will be the same as for the issue. However, the conditions of the reissue will most likely be different. For example, the shares forfeited by Ariel Ltd in Illustrative example 1.2 may be issued for a single payment of $1 per share rather than by instalments, in which case the general journal entry would be:

| | Debit | Credit |
|---|---|---|
| Bank | 20 000 | |
| Paid-up Capital | | 20 000 |
| (reissue of forfeited shares) | | |

When dealing with forfeited shares and their reissue, it is advisable to bear in mind the number of shares involved and the desired effect on the paid-up capital. Thus, in the simple situation above, it is clear that the reissue brings the issued shares back to 600 000 and the paid-up capital to $600 000, which is what the balance would have been had all shares been paid for without any forfeiture. Note that the company still retains the amounts received from the previous shareholders from whom the shares were forfeited. The constitution will indicate what should be done with that amount. At present it is indicated by the balance in the Forfeited Shares account (also called Forfeited Shares Reserve). It is usual for the constitution to state that the amount be returned to those from whom the shares were forfeited after deducting any expenses or loss incurred in reissuing the shares.

# Share premiums and discounts

**par value**

**premium**

Until the recent changes to the Corporations Law, when formed, a company was required to have a stated amount of capital and how it was comprised in respect of types of shares. This was referred to as the company's authorised capital, and the company could not issue capital in excess of that. In addition, each share had to be of a stated amount. This was the par value or nominal value of a share and was the value stated on the shares at the date of incorporation (most commonly $1 or 50 cents). The only funds a company receives from a share issue are those from the initial issue. It is the owners of the shares that receive any benefit from a subsequent increase in the value of those shares. Where the market value of shares is above the par value the company will want to take advantage of this and issue the shares for a price in excess of the par. This was referred to as issuing shares at a premium. However, the law no longer requires companies to have an authorised capital or shares to have a par value. The company, if permitted by its constitution, can issue additional shares and at a price it considers the market can bear. The changes to the law were not retrospective so there are many companies that will still have in their accounts amounts referred to as the Share Premium account (or Share Premium Reserve). These represent the amounts in excess of the par values that the company received from share issues and will be kept separate from the issued and paid-up capital. As shares now have no par values, the amount received from future share issues will simply increase the paid-up capital. Thus, if a company, which had previously issued shares at $1 each, were to make a new issue of 1 000 000 ordinary shares at $1.50 cents per share, amounts to be fully paid on application, anyone wishing to invest in the issue would have to pay $1.50 for each share. If all shares are subscribed, the general journal entries to record the applications received would be:

|  | Debit | Credit |
|---|---|---|
| Bank Trust | 1 500 000 | |
|     Application | | 1 500 000 |
| (amounts received on application for shares) | | |

and then when the allotment is made —

|  | Debit | Credit |
|---|---|---|
| Application | 1 500 000 | |
|     Paid-up Capital | | 1 500 000 |
| (issue of shares at $1.50 per share) | | |
| | | |
| Bank | 1 500 000 | |
|     Bank Trust | | 1 500 000 |
| (transfer of amounts received on share issue) | | |

Previously, if the shares had a par value of $1 the company would have to have shown the extra 50 cents per share in a Share Premium account; many companies had such accounts prior to the law change and may still have such an account.

When deciding at what price to issue shares, the directors would have to be careful as any new shares will affect the market price of the existing shares. However, there are many compounding influences on the share price.

In the past, if a company issued shares for less than the par value, then it was said **discount** to have issued shares at a discount.

# Other aspects of share issues

## RIGHTS ISSUES

In Illustrative example 1.1 the directors of Ariel Ltd did not issue all the shares its constitution permitted it to — the limit on the capital was 1 000 000 shares, yet they only issued 600 000 shares. This is common, as the directors could have anticipated some expansion at a later date for which the company would need funds. These funds could come from a further issue. It is usual for the constitution to contain a provision that any additional shares be first offered to the existing shareholders before being offered to the public — the existing shareholders have first right of refusal, so such **rights issues** issues are called rights issues. The shareholders would be entitled to a number of shares in proportion to their existing shareholdings — for example, a one for six rights issue means that the existing shareholders have rights to purchase an additional share for each six held. The new issue may be at the original price but would more likely be at a greater price in order to take advantage of any increased market price of the issued shares. The price would likely be a little less than the market price of the shares so as to encourage subscription. The new shares are in effect 'allotted' to the existing shareholders, so the accounting entries are slightly simpler than the initial issue. The rights issue may be by payment in full or by instalments.

For example, a company with an issued and paid-up capital of 600 000 ordinary $1 shares decides to make a one for six rights issue at $1.30 per share and all shareholders subscribe.

|  | Debit | Credit |
|---|---|---|
| Bank | 130 000 | |
| Paid-up Capital | | 130 000 |
| (a 1 for 6 rights issue fully subscribed at $1.30 per share) | | |

In this example it is assumed that the entry is made after the cash has been received. It would have been possible to make an entry at the date of the resolution to issue the shares using an allotment account, but this seems to be unnecessary work. **renounceable rights** Sometimes the rights are renounceable — that is, the shareholders are permitted to sell their rights to purchase the shares in the new issue. Thus, a market has arisen whereby rights can be sold and bought.

## PRIVATE ISSUES

*private issue*

Proprietary companies cannot offer shares to the public — they are sold privately. A public company, where authorised by its articles, can also offer shares for sale privately. The shares may be sold to a large institutional investor to avoid the cost and time involved in a full public issue. The ASX usually prohibits listed public companies from issuing more than 10% of its shares in this manner: a private issue.

## SHARE OPTIONS

*call option*

A company may sell the right to buy a certain number of shares in the company at some fixed time in the future. This right is called a company-issued call option. Where the company issues options for some valuable consideration the amount received will increase the shareholders' equity. For example, a company may issue options over 100 000 shares to purchase shares in the company at the price of $2.10 after one year's time for a cash payment now of 30 cents. When the cash is received the general entry would be:

|  | Debit | Credit |
|---|---|---|
| Bank | 30 000 | |
| Options | | 30 000 |
| (issue of options at 30 cents over a potential future issue of 100 000 shares) | | |

The company may also issue options for no valuable consideration — for example, to its employees. As no valuable consideration is received, there is no entry in the company's books.

## BONUS ISSUES

A company can also issue shares to existing shareholders for no cost. The company uses past profits (or gains) to make the issue as a bonus issue to existing shareholders in proportion to their current shareholding. The next chapter will indicate how this is entered in the books.

# Shareholders' equity

*shareholders' equity*

As the name implies, the shareholders' equity in the balance sheet represents the owners' equity in a company. As such it will include all equity attributable to the shareholders. This will not only be the paid-up capital but also many of the items discussed above, as well as undistributed past profits. Therefore, a company could have a shareholders' equity that includes several items (assumed figures for illustrative purposes only):

| | $ | $ |
|---|---|---|
| *Shareholders' equity* | | |
| Paid-up capital | | |
| 1 000 000 ordinary shares at $1 paid to 80 cents | 800 000 | |
| 500 000 preference shares at $1 fully paid | 500 000 | 1 300 000 |
| Forfeited Shares account | 30 000 | |
| Options | 20 000 | |
| Retained profits | 123 897 | 173 897 |

**ILLUSTRATIVE EXAMPLE 1.3**

# SHARE ISSUES (COMPREHENSIVE)

On 2 January 20X0, Ptolemy Ltd was registered as a public company with an established share capital of 5 000 000 ordinary shares and 1 000 000 preference shares. At the same date the company published a prospectus for an issue of shares on the following terms:

- 3 000 000 ordinary shares at $1 with 50 cents payable on application by 31 January, 30 cents payable on allotment due by 28 February; and
- 1 000 000 preference shares at $1 payable in full on application by 31 January.

By 31 January all the preference shares had been subscribed and applications for 3 600 000 ordinary shares received. On 1 February the directors made a pro rata allotment to all applicants and, in terms of the prospectus, excess application monies were used as part payment of allotment money due.

On 28 February the directors made a first and final call of 20 cents on the ordinary shares, payable by 31 March.

By 31 March all call money had been received except for that on 50 000 shares which the directors resolved to forfeit for non-payment of call in accordance with the constitution. At the same date they reissued these shares as fully paid for a payment of 60 cents per share due by 21 April.

On 31 August the directors resolved to make a rights issue of one for three ordinary shares at $1.30 per share. Application amounts payable were due by 30 September and the issue was fully subscribed.

On 30 November the directors resolved to make a private issue to the underwriting firm of Steeple Insurance Ltd of 500 000 ordinary shares for a single payment of $1.40 per share.

On 1 December the directors decided to make a call option on the remaining 500 000 unissued ordinary shares of 25 cents per share, the option to be taken up after 30 November 20X1 at $2 per share. The call closed on 15 December, by which time all options had been sold.

## General journal

| | | | Debit | Credit |
|---|---|---|---|---|
| 20X0 | | | $ | $ |
| Jan 31 | Bank Trust | | 2 800 000 | |
| | | Application – Ordinary | | 1 800 000 |
| | | Application – Preference | | 1 000 000 |
| | (cash received on application for shares) | | | |
| Feb 1 | Application – Ordinary | | 1 500 000 | |
| | Application – Preference | | 1 000 000 | |
| | | Paid-up Capital – Ordinary | | 1 500 000 |
| | | Paid-up Capital – Preference | | 1 000 000 |
| | (amounts due on application for shares issue) | | | |
| | Allotment – Ordinary | | 900 000 | |
| | | Paid-up Capital – Ordinary | | 900 000 |
| | (amount due on allotment – 30 cents per share) | | | |
| | Application – Ordinary | | 300 000 | |
| | | Allotment – Ordinary | | 300 000 |
| | (transfer of oversubscription amounts received) | | | |

| | | Debit | Credit |
|---|---|---|---|
| 20X0 | | $ | $ |
| Feb 1 | Bank | 2 800 000 | |
| | Bank Trust | | 2 800 000 |
| | (transfer of amounts received on issue of shares) | | |
| Feb 28 | Bank | 600 000 | |
| | Allotment – Ordinary | | 600 000 |
| | (amounts due on allotment received) | | |
| | Call | 600 000 | |
| | Paid-up Capital – Ordinary | | 600 000 |
| | (first and final call made 20 cents per share) | | |
| Mar 31 | Bank | 590 000 | |
| | Call | | 590 000 |
| | (amounts due on call received) | | |
| | Paid-up Capital – Ordinary | 50 000 | |
| | Call | | 10 000 |
| | Forfeited Shares Account | | 40 000 |
| | (forfeiture of 50 000 shares for non-payment of call) | | |
| Apr 21 | Bank | 30 000 | |
| | Forfeited Shares Account | 20 000 | |
| | Paid-up Capital – Ordinary | | 50 000 |
| | (amounts received on reissue of forfeited shares) | | |
| Sept 30 | Bank | 1 300 000 | |
| | Paid-up Capital – Ordinary | | 1 300 000 |
| | (amounts received on rights issue) | | |
| Nov 30 | Bank | 700 000 | |
| | Paid-up Capital – Ordinary | | 700 000 |
| | (private issue of 500 000 shares at $1.40 cents per share) | | |
| Dec 15 | Bank | 125 000 | |
| | Options | | 125 000 |
| | (options issued on 500 000 shares at 25 cents) | | |

## General ledger

| | | Debit | Credit | Balance | |
|---|---|---|---|---|---|
| 20X0 | | $ | $ | $ | |
| | **Application – Ordinary** | | | | |
| Jan 31 | Bank Trust | | 1 800 000 | 1 800 000 | Cr |
| Feb 1 | Paid-up Capital – Ordinary | 1 500 000 | | 300 000 | Cr |
| | Allotment – Ordinary | 300 000 | | – | |
| | **Application – Preference** | | | | |
| Jan 31 | Bank Trust | | 1 000 000 | 1 000 000 | Cr |
| Feb 1 | Paid-up Capital – Preference | 1 000 000 | | – | |
| | **Bank Trust** | | | | |
| Jan 31 | Application – Ordinary | 1 800 000 | | 1 800 000 | Dr |
| | Application – Preference | 1 000 000 | | 2 800 000 | Dr |
| Feb 1 | Bank | | 2 800 000 | – | |

| 20X0 | | Debit $ | Credit $ | Balance $ | |
|---|---|---|---|---|---|
| | **Bank** | | | | |
| Feb 1 | Bank Trust | 2 800 000 | | 2 800 000 | Dr |
| Feb 28 | Allotment – Ordinary | 600 000 | | 3 400 000 | Dr |
| Mar 31 | Call | 590 000 | | 3 990 000 | Dr |
| Apr 21 | Paid-up Capital – Ordinary | 30 000 | | 4 020 000 | Dr |
| Sept 30 | Paid-up Capital – Ordinary | 1 300 000 | | 5 320 000 | Dr |
| Nov 30 | Paid-up Capital – Ordinary | 700 000 | | 6 020 000 | Dr |
| Dec 15 | Options | 125 000 | | 6 145 000 | Dr |
| | **Allotment – Ordinary** | | | | |
| Feb 1 | Paid-up Capital – Ordinary | 900 000 | | 900 000 | Dr |
| | Application – Ordinary | | 300 000 | 600 000 | Dr |
| Feb 28 | Bank | | 600 000 | – | |
| | **Call** | | | | |
| Feb 28 | Paid-up Capital – Ordinary | 600 000 | | 600 000 | Dr |
| Mar 31 | Bank | | 590 000 | 10 000 | Dr |
| | Paid-up Capital – Ordinary | | 10 000 | – | |
| | **Paid-up Capital – Ordinary** | | | | |
| Feb 1 | Application – Ordinary | | 1 500 000 | 1 500 000 | Cr |
| | Allotment – Ordinary | | 900 000 | 2 400 000 | Cr |
| Feb 28 | Call | | 600 000 | 3 000 000 | Cr |
| Mar 31 | Forfeited Shares Account | 50 000 | | 2 950 000 | Cr |
| Apr 21 | Bank | | 50 000 | 3 000 000 | Cr |
| Sept 30 | Bank | | 1 300 000 | 4 300 000 | Cr |
| Nov 30 | Bank | | 700 000 | 5 000 000 | Cr |
| | **Paid-up Capital – Preference** | | | | |
| Feb 1 | Application – Preference | | 1 000 000 | 1 000 000 | Cr |
| | **Options** | | | | |
| Dec 15 | Bank | | 125 000 | 125 000 | Cr |
| | **Forfeited Shares Account** | | | | |
| Mar 31 | Paid-up Capital – Ordinary | | 40 000 | 40 000 | Cr |
| Apr 21 | Paid-up Capital – Ordinary | 20 000 | | 20 000 | Cr |

**Ptolemy Ltd**
**Balance Sheet (extract) as at 31 December 20X0**

| | $ | $ |
|---|---|---|
| *Shareholders' equity* | | |
| Issued and paid-up capital | | |
| 4 500 000 ordinary shares | 5 000 000 | |
| 1 000 000 preference shares | 1 000 000 | 6 000 000 |
| Forfeited Shares account | 20 000 | |
| Options | 125 000 | 145 000 |
| | | $6 145 000 |
| *Assets* | | |
| Bank | | $6 145 000 |

# Debt securities

The distinction was made above between equity capital and debt capital as methods by which a company can be financed. So far we have been examining equity capital — that relating to the issue of shares. Debt capital is simply a term for long-term debt (borrowing) incurred by the company and includes debentures, convertible notes, unsecured notes, mortgages and leases. It is usual for the company to issue evidence of the debt and this is referred to as debt securities. Similar legal principles are involved with debt capital as with equity capital — namely, the protection of those dealing with the company — so care should be exercised when dealing with debt capital. The concern here, however, is with the accounting treatment.

**convertible note**
**unsecured note**
**mortgage**
**lease**

## DEBENTURES

A debenture is merely an acknowledgment of a debt. However, debentures are usually issued in units similar to shares (but usually larger). By doing this the company is able to borrow funds from a number of investors (in a manner similar to a new share issue). Those who invest in the debentures issued by a company are lending the company money. This 'loan' will be for a period of time and attracts a rate of interest. The debenture holders will have their investment protected in at least two ways. First, the debenture will be secured by a charge over some of the company's assets. This charge will be fixed — relating to specific assets — or floating — relating to the assets generally. Secondly, there will be (unless exempted by law) an entity which serves as the trustee for the debenture holders — a person or an institution appointed to act on behalf of the debenture holders to protect their interests.

**debenture holder**
**charge**
**fixed charge**
**floating charge**
**trustee**

The accounting for a debenture issue is similar to that for a share issue — a prospectus is issued inviting offers (applications) which are then accepted (or not) by the company, at which stage a binding contract exists requiring the company to protect the debentures, pay interest, and repay them at the stated date. So, if a company were to issue a prospectus inviting investors to subscribe to an issue of 5000 debentures of $100 and the issue is fully taken up, the general journal entry would be:

|  | Debit | Credit |
|---|---|---|
| Bank Trust | 500 000 |  |
|     Debenture Application |  | 500 000 |
| (amount received from an issue of 5000 $100 debentures) |  |  |

and when the directors accept the debenture subscriptions:

|  | Debit | Credit |
|---|---|---|
| Bank | 500 000 |  |
|     Bank Trust |  | 500 000 |
| (transfer of amount received from debenture issue) |  |  |
| Debenture Application | 500 000 |  |
|     Debentures |  | 500 000 |
| (acceptance of debenture applications) |  |  |

The company now has a non-current liability (assuming maturity is more than 12 months away) for the debentures, and will have each year of the debenture issue, and will incur an expense for the interest.

The debentures can be issued at a *premium* or a *discount*. Opinion is divided as to how to account for the debenture premium and debenture discount. However, as the premium has been received for debentures which have been issued for a period of time, the gain (that is, the premium) should be regarded as being earned over the period of the debentures as it probably reflects the interest rate on the debentures. Alternatively, a simpler approach is to treat the premium as income in the year it is received. An issue at a discount has been made to attract investors to take up the debentures. Therefore, the discount should be amortised over the life of the debentures as it is a cost of raising the funds. Once again, some accountants argue for the simpler treatment of expensing the discount in the year of issue.

redemption

The redemption (repaying) of the debentures when they fall due will require a large amount of funds, so it is wise to set aside an amount each year. When redeemed the general journal entry will simply reflect the payment of cash (bank) and a reduction in the liability (debentures).

## CONVERTIBLE NOTES

Convertible notes are a form of debenture which can be converted to shares after a set period of time. They are now not commonly found in Australia, although they were once a popular method of raising funds.

## UNSECURED NOTES

As their name implies, these are a form of debt for which there is no charge over the company's assets — they are unsecured.

## MORTGAGES

mortgagee
mortgagor

A mortgage is a form of charge over property to secure a loan from a mortgagee (lender) to a mortgagor (borrower — the company).

Accounting for notes and mortgages is similar to that for debentures. Funds are received from the lenders and a liability is incurred. Accounting for leases is more complicated and not appropriately discussed here. Nevertheless, it is viewed as an important method of financing the acquisition of assets.

# Review

This chapter has introduced companies (corporations): what they are, how they are formed and the accounting for their formation. Companies are separate legal entities, having been created by law to undertake many of the activities individuals can. An appreciation of the law relating to corporations is necessary in learning how to account for companies. However, this law is complex so this chapter has restricted discussion of it to those aspects that need to be understood in accounting for the formation of companies. The chapter has concentrated on the accounting for share issues and discussed some of the complications that may arise in share issues and how they are accounted for. The share capital is considered a company's owners' equity — it is the shareholders' equity in the company. Companies also issue securities other than those relating to the shareholders' equity, and this chapter has introduced some of these debt securities and discussed how they are treated in the accounting system.

# Endnote

1  There are many good texts on the law of companies which can be referred to by those wishing to know more detailed legal information. An excellent one, very suitable for accountants, is *Australian Corporations Law Guide* (Sydney: CCH, annual), edited by Brian Burnett.

## KEY TERMS

accountability

agent

allotment

application

audit

Australian Company Number

Australian Securities Commission

Australian Stock Exchange

call

call option

calls in advance

calls in arrears

certification of registration

charge

company

company limited by guarantee

constitution

control

controlling interest

convertible note

corporation

debenture

debenture holder

debt capital

different perspectives on companies

directors

discount

economic entity

equity capital

fixed charge

floating charge

issued capital

lease

limited liability

listing requirements

members

mortgage

mortgagee

mortgagor

ordinary shares

oversubscription

par value

preference shares

premium

private issue

proprietary company

prospectus

public company

redemption

renounceable rights

replaceable rules

rights issues

securities

shareholders

shareholders' equity

share listing

shares

stewardship

transfer of ownership interests

trustee

undersubscription

underwriter

unlimited life

unsecured note

# REVIEW QUESTIONS

**1.1** What are the different views of a company and in what ways do these views differ?

**1.2** What are some of the reasons generally believed to account for the growth of the joint stock company form of business organisation?

**1.3** What is meant by the expression 'investment is made on the basis that there be some accountability'?

**1.4** Why is the distinction made between a public company and a proprietary company?

**1.5** What is the function of the 'replaceable rules' of the Corporations Law?

**1.6** In accounting for share issues, one of the first accounts involved is a Bank Trust account. Why is this so?

**1.7** Distinguish between calls in arrears and calls in advance.

**1.8** What is a rights issue and why are such issues made?

**1.9** Why does the price at which a company issues shares vary over time?

**1.10** What is meant by debt capital and what common forms does it take?

# EXERCISES

**Exercise 1.11** **Accounting for share issue**

Sprague Ltd was formed on 1 January 20X1 with a clause in its constitution limiting the number of shares that it could issue to 1 000 000. The directors resolved to issue 500 000 shares at $1. The terms of the issue are that 50 cents be payable on application and 50 cents on allotment. By 28 February applications had been received for all 500 000 shares with the required application amounts. The directors met on 5 March and allotted the shares to the applicants, and the company issued notices of allotment indicating that all amounts due were to be paid by 31 March. By 31 March, allotment amounts had been received on 450 000 shares.

*Required*
Prepare general journal entries to record the above.

**Exercise 1.12** **Accounting for share issue by instalments**

On 1 July 20X1, Hatfield Ltd was formed. On that date the directors resolved to issue 1 000 000 ordinary shares at $1 and the prospectus that had been prepared was duly published. It indicated that 50 cents was to accompany applications for each share with the remainder to be paid, 25 cents on notice of allotment and 25 cents at a call to be made by the directors at a later date. The date set for all applications for shares to be made was 15 August 20X1 and applications for all shares were received by that date. The directors met on 24 August and duly resolved to issue the shares to applicants and indicated that allotment amounts due were to be paid by 30 September 20X1. All amounts due were received by the due date. The directors concluded that the call should be made to enable the company to purchase extra buildings. This call was made on 1 November with amounts due by 1 December. Amounts due on the call were received on all but 5000 shares.

*Required*
Prepare general journal entries to record the above in the books of Hatfield Ltd.

**Exercise 1.13** **Accounting for share issue — ordinary and preference**
W Paton & Son Ltd was registered on 1 February 20X8. The directors of the company resolved that the promoters were to be issued 500 000 preference shares issued at $1 each, amounts to be paid by 15 February and all amounts were received by that date. They also resolved to make a public issue of 2 000 000 ordinary shares at $1.75 each to be paid in full on application. The closing date for applications was 31 March 20X8, by which time amounts had been received with applications for 2 300 000 shares. The directors met on 5 April and issued the shares pro rata to applicants, with any amounts in excess of that due being returned to applicants.

*Required*
Prepare general journal entries to record the above in the books of the company and show the accounts in the general ledger.

**Exercise 1.14** **Accounting for share issue including an oversubscription**
The constitution of Henrietta Sweeney Ltd indicated that the company could issue up to 5 000 000 ordinary shares and 1 000 000 preference shares. Prospectuses had been published offering 1 000 000 preference shares at $1.50 payable in full on application by 31 March 20X9 and 2 000 000 ordinary shares at $1.20 with 50% due on application by 31 March 20X9, 25% on allotment, and 25% on a call to be made by the directors at a later date. By 31 March amounts due on 800 000 of the preference shares had been received and on applications for 2 400 000 ordinary shares. The directors met on 10 April and resolved to issue the preference and ordinary shares. The ordinary shares were allotted to applicants on a pro rata basis and the amounts received in excess of that due were to be credited against amounts due on allotment. The amount due on the allotment of the ordinary shares was due by 15 May 20X9 and this was received on all shares. The directors made the call on the ordinary shares on 31 August 20X9, with amounts due by 30 September. By this date, amounts due on 1 997 000 ordinary shares had been received.

*Required*
Show how the above would be recorded in the general journal of the company and the general ledger.

**Exercise 1.15** **Share issue with a forfeiture**
The constitution of Stephens & Gillman Ltd indicated that the directors could forfeit shares for the non-payment of calls. On 31 July 20X8 the directors decided to forfeit 4000 ordinary shares of $1 held by George O May upon which the application of 15 cents and the allotment of 40 cents per share had been paid but the first call of

20 cents had not been received. The directors also resolved to reissue the forfeited shares to William Ripley, credited as paid to 75 cents per share for a payment in cash of 80 cents per share.

*Required*
Show how the above would be recorded in the general journal of the company.

**Exercise 1.16**  **Share issue with a forfeiture**
Montgomery Ltd had issued 2 000 000 ordinary $1 shares on which 75 cents per share had been called. The holder of 6000 shares had failed to pay the second call of 25 cents per share and another shareholder had failed to pay the second call and the first call of 10 cents per share on 4000 shares. In accordance with the provisions of the company's constitution, the directors resolved on 31 May 20X7 to forfeit the shares of both shareholders. On 28 June 20X7 the forfeited shares were reissued for a single payment of 70 cents as being paid to 75 cents.

*Required*
Prepare general journal entries to record the above transactions.

**Exercise 1.17**  **Share issue including an issue not for cash**
Canning & Co Ltd was registered on 1 January 20X2 to operate and trade as manufacturers of a newly invented mass data storage medium. The directors issued 40 000 000 ordinary shares at $2.10, with $1.50 due with applications due 28 February 20X2 and the remainder on allotment. The directors met on 3 March and allotted shares to applicants for all the shares. In fact, applications had been received for 45 000 000 shares and the amounts received in excess of that due were returned to the unsuccessful applicants. All amounts due on allotment were received by the due date of 31 March 20X2. On 17 March the directors purchased a lease on a factory at a cost of $35 000 and purchased plant for $30 000 on 31 March. The company was most successful and it became obvious that it would need to expand within the next two years. The directors, on 31 August 20X2, issued a call option for 30 cents per share to a group of potential investors for one year to purchase 10 000 000 shares at $4. They also issued an ex gratia option to the employees to participate in that future issue for an additional 5 000 000 shares.

*Required*
Show how the above would be recorded in the general journal of the company.

**Exercise 1.18**  **Debenture issue**
The directors of Vatter Brothers Ltd resolved to issue 100 000 debentures of $100, with $50 being payable on application and $50 being paid on allotment, and a prospectus was duly published indicating that the final date for applications was 20 September 20X5. By this date, applications had been received for 130 000 debentures together with the appropriate application amounts. The directors met on 30 September and accepted on a pro rata basis the applications of applicants for 115 000 debentures. The amounts received with these applications in excess of that due were used to apply to sums due on allotment. The unsuccessful debenture applicants had their applications amounts returned on 4 October.

*Required*
Show general journal entries to record the above transaction.

**Exercise 1.19** **Accounting for debenture issue**
In 20X0, Sprouse and Moonitz Ltd issued 100 000 ten-year 8% debentures of $100 at $95. The issue was fully subscribed and all amounts were received by 1 January 20X1. The directors resolved to amortise any discount over the life of the debentures.

*Required*
Show general journal entries that relate to the above transactions for the period 1 January 20X1 to 31 December 20X2, assuming that the financial year of the company ends 31 December.

**Exercise 1.20** **Initial and rights share issues**
On 2 January 20X4, Mattessisch Ltd decided to issue 3 000 000 ordinary shares at $1.80 and 1 000 000 8% preference shares at $2 each. The terms of the issue were that $1 per share was to accompany applications for the ordinary shares, while applications for the preference shares were to be with the full amount. The date 28 February was set as the last day for applications for both classes of shares. On 31 January the directors resolved to issue 1 000 000 ordinary shares to Paul Grady for the purchase of his business which had net assets at the agreed value of $2 000 000. By 28 February, applications had been received for 3 100 000 ordinary shares and 950 000 preference shares. The directors met and allotted the ordinary shares on a pro rata basis, applying the extra amounts received on application to that due on allotment which was to be by 25 March 20X4. They also allotted the preference shares. All allotment amounts due were received by the due date.

On 31 August the directors made a one for four rights issue of ordinary shares at $2.50 per share. The issue date was to be 30 September 20X4 payable in full. All the rights were taken up and amounts received by the due date.

*Required*
Show general journal entries to record the above share issues transactions. (Show the purchase of Grady's business as net assets.) Also show the balances that would appear in the balance sheet of Mattessisch Ltd at 31 December 20X4, assuming no other transactions had taken place.

**Exercise 1.21** **Share issues and options**
RJ Chambers & Co Ltd was formed with the constitution limiting the shares that could be issued to 5 000 000 ordinary A shares and 2 000 000 non-voting ordinary B shares on 5 January 20X3. The company decided to offer to the public 3 000 000 of the ordinary A shares at a price of $2.50. The shares were to be offered from 20 February, with the closing date for applications being 31 March 20X3 and with $1 required with the applications, and $1 due on allotment with the remaining 50 cents to be called within four months of allotment.

The directors also decided that 1 000 000 of the ordinary B shares were to be issued as fully paid to the promoters for a payment of $2 per share by 31 January and the remaining B shares were to be part of an employee incentive scheme.

By 31 March, applications for 3 500 000 shares had been received. The directors met and allotted the shares, with $150 000 being returned to unsuccessful shareholders and any other excess application amounts received being transferred to amounts due on allotment. Allotment amounts were due by 15 April and by that date all amounts due were received.

The call on the A shares of 50 cents was made on 30 June and due by 31 July 20X3. All call money was received except for that owing on 20 000 shares. On 6 August the directors met and forfeited these shares. They were then reissued to Will Baxter as fully paid for a payment of $2.75 per share, with the amounts that had been paid by the previous shareholder being returned less $2000 for reissue costs.

On 8 September the directors announced that they were to make a further issue of 1 000 000 ordinary A shares in 11 months' time for $4 per share and issued a call option on these shares at 30 cents payable by 30 September. All the options were sold.

*Required*
Show general journal entries to record the above share issues transactions and indicate what the balance in the Cash at Bank account would be assuming that no other transactions had taken place.

**Exercise 1.22** **Issue of shares in consideration for going concern**
G & G Ltd was a public company formed to acquire the businesses of L Goldberg Pty Ltd and R Gynther Pty Ltd. It was agreed that the businesses were to be valued at $1 500 000 for L Goldberg Pty Ltd and $1 000 000 for R Gynther Pty Ltd and that the shareholders of these two companies were to be allotted 750 000 and 500 000 ordinary shares respectively in G & G Ltd for their companies' net assets. These shares were to be allotted on 1 February 20X8. On 15 January a prospectus was published offering 3 000 000 ordinary shares for $3 per share. The closing date for applications for the shares was 31 March 20X8, with $2 per share due with the application and $1 per share on allotment. The public offering was oversubscribed by 500 000 shares. The allotment was made and allotment amounts were due by 30 April 20X8. Amounts received on oversubscription were returned to the unsuccessful applicants. All allotment amounts were received by the due date.

On 30 September the company made a further issue of 1 000 000 shares at $3.50 to the public, payable in full on application by 31 October 20X8. The issue was fully subscribed.

*Required*
Prepare general journal entries to record the above transactions to 1 November and show the amount that would be included in the shareholders' equity section of a balance sheet if one were to be prepared at that date.

chapter 2

# RESERVES AND PROFITS DISTRIBUTION

# introduction

As indicated in the previous chapter, one of the main principles of the Corporations Law has been the protection of those dealing with the company – the shareholders, the creditors, the employees and other bodies. Behind this has been the principle of the preservation of the company's capital, and up until now it has been fairly difficult for a company to reduce its capital. Recent changes in the Corporations Law have made this easier, but the principle still remains. Previously a company needed the 'approval' of the court to reduce its capital, and while this is no longer necessary any capital reduction must, amongst other things,

• be fair and reasonable to all shareholders
• not materially prejudice the company's ability to pay its creditors.

In order to preserve this 'doctrine of capital maintenance', companies have only been permitted to distribute to their shareholders profits earned, so it has been important for accountants to distinguish that which formed capital (and had to be maintained) from that which could be regarded as income (and which could be distributed). This is the subject matter of this chapter.

# Shareholders' equity

The owners' equity in a company is usually described as shareholders' equity or shareholders' funds. This equity is a residual and, as with other forms of business ownership, it is the owners' interest in the assets of the entity after the external or outside interests have been taken care of. This is indicated in Statement of Accounting Concepts No. 4 (SAC 4), which defines equity as 'the residual interest in the assets of the entity after deduction of its liabilities'.

Thus, equity is represented by the net assets of the entity — the company. In a company it will comprise the capital subscribed by the shareholders, undistributed past profits, and reserves. It is important to appreciate that the assets and liabilities of a company are owned and owed *by the company*, not the shareholders. The shareholders have the residual equity in the assets — as indicated above, an interest in the net assets of the company. As with other forms of business ownership, as owners the shareholders from time to time can lay claim to some of the net assets as part satisfaction of their equity claims. That is, they can expect distributions from the profits earned by the company. These distributions are the dividends the shareholders receive. The directors can distribute as dividends all profits the company has earned, but prudent management holds that they will only distribute some of the profits. The undistributed profits can be maintained as retained profits or transferred to reserves.

**dividends**

**retained profits**

**reserves**

# Reserves

Although the term 'reserve' is referred to many times in the Corporations Law, accounting standards and other professional statements, it is not precisely defined anywhere. It is best seen as a division of the owners' equity and therefore is part of the total residual interest in the net assets of the company. In the past, reserves were divided into capital reserves and revenue reserves. The latter emerged from past profits earned by the company (and therefore were distributable as dividends), and capital reserves referred to various reserves that resulted from complying with statute or other regulation and which were of a capital nature (and usually not distributable). However, this is too simplistic as the definition of what can be classified as the company's profits has changed over the years. In addition, revenue reserves could be capitalised and thus reclassified. Therefore, it is appropriate to see the types of reserves as those arising from regulation and those from prudent management practices.

## REGULATORY RESERVES

### Statutory reserves

Until recently, shares were issued with a par value — that is, the shares were created for a stated amount, often $1. As indicated in chapter 1, this, on the face of it, prevented the company taking advantage of a high market price for their shares when making a subsequent issue. For example, a company may wish to make an additional share issue of its $1 ordinary shares when the market price for its shares was far in excess of $1. In fact, this would be a good time for the company to raise additional capital as it indicates a favourable demand for its shares. So, if it needed extra capital for expansion, or whatever, it could issue previously unissued shares. The only way the company could benefit from the high price would have been to issue the shares at a premium. For example, if the shares were selling in the market for $3.40, the company could issue the $1 shares at a premium of $2 so that anyone wishing to subscribe would have to pay $3 per share. It would be unlikely that the premium would be the full difference between the par value and the market value, as the new share issue would impact on the market value — there would now be more shares, so the market value would most likely decrease. And a price lower than the market would act as an incentive for potential subscribers. In accounting for the share issue the company would have recorded an increase in the paid-up capital (the $1 per **share premium reserve** share) and an amount described as the share premium reserve (the $2 per share). The amount so received — the $3 per share — increased the shareholders' equity, part being described as paid-up capital and part as a reserve. The Corporations Law required the premium to be credited to the share premium reserve, hence it was a statutory reserve. The law placed restrictions on the reserve such that it was non-distributable (as dividends). In effect, the law recognised that it was in effect part of the 'contributed capital' and if it were to be distributed it would violate the doctrine of capital maintenance as the capital would be reduced.

**no par value** Recent changes in the law have resulted in shares having no par value, meaning that any new share issue the company makes can be at a price the directors determine, so there is no share premium. Therefore, there will also be no share premium reserve. However, companies formed prior to the law change may well still have share premium reserves. The general rule is that such reserves are non-distributable and remain part of the company's capital.

When a company issued redeemable preference shares, it did so with the intention of redeeming the shares at some future date — that is, 'buying' them back from the shareholders. In the past the company when redeeming these shares (and not **capital redemption reserve** replacing them with a new share issue) had to create a capital redemption reserve. The legal drafters obviously considered the redemption a reduction in the company's capital, so they added the requirement for a statutory reserve to be created. There were similar restrictions placed on this reserve to those on the share premium reserve. The recent changes in the Corporations Law have removed the requirement for the creation of the capital redemption reserve but, once again, companies formed prior to the law change may have such reserves and they too form part of the capital of the company and, in general, are not distributable.

As detailed in chapter 1, in the past companies were required to have and register a memorandum of association. They were also required to have articles of association (or to adopt the 'model articles' in Table A in the Corporations Law) which provided the day-to-day rules for managing the company. Companies are now no longer required to have a memorandum or articles, but they should have a constitution; if not, the Corporations Law contains a set of replaceable rules with a similar function to that which Table A had. Existing companies have had either to adopt their memorandum and articles as their constitution or to repeal them and create a new constitution (or accept the replaceable rules). The constitution (in the past, the articles) will contain the rules for share issues and may empower the directors to forfeit shares for non-payment of calls. Any amounts received on the forfeited shares are credited to the forfeited shares reserve (as indicated in chapter 1). Although not a statutory reserve like the share premium and the capital redemption reserves, the forfeited shares reserve has been created by the rules governing the day-to-day management of the company. There will be restrictions placed on the use of this reserve and they will be found in the company's constitution.

**forfeited shares reserve**

### Reserves required by accounting standards

The constitution may also require other reserves to be created, but this is now increasingly rare as the day-to-day management is left to the directors who may see fit to create reserves as part of prudent management. However, some accounting standards require reserves to be set up and amounts transferred to them.

### Asset revaluation reserve

One of the most important reserves required by accounting standards is the asset revaluation reserve in AASB 1010: Accounting for the Revaluation of Non-current Assets. The requirements of this standard are a good illustration of accounting conservatism: downward revaluations (decrements) are recognised as losses in the period in which the revaluation is made, but upward revaluations (increments) are to be held 'in reserve' until actually realised. Thus, usually no increment can be recognised as profits and distributed as dividends until the asset is disposed of. The standard refers to revaluations of classes of assets. The process is fairly straightforward but is complicated by the definition of assets, the accumulated depreciation on the assets, and the subsequent sale or later revaluation of part or all of the class of assets.

Where the revaluation is straightforward, the journal entry would debit the asset and credit the reserve. For example, if land recorded in the books at $300 000 were to be revalued at $400 000, a journal entry would be needed to increase the asset balance to reflect the revaluation; this entry would be:

|  | Debit | Credit |
|---|---|---|
| Land | 100 000 | |
| Asset Revaluation Reserve | | 100 000 |
| (to record new increased fair value of land held) | | |

If one-quarter of this land is then sold for cash of $120 000, the entries would be:

|  | | |
|---|---|---|
| Bank | 120 000 | |
| Land | | 120 000 |
| (sale of land for cash) | | |

Logic and consistency with accounting principles would suggest that one-quarter of the revaluation has now been realised and should be recognised as revenue in the period. However, Australian accounting standards do not permit the transfer of amounts from the reserve to current profits (AASB 1010, para .18). Therefore, the only gain on sale recognised will be that received in excess of the carrying amount of

**carrying amount**

the asset. The carrying amount is defined in AASB 1010 as 'the amount at which the asset is recorded in the accounting records as at a particular date'. This is, in effect, what as known as the net book value of the asset, so it will be the amount recorded in the asset account less any accumulated depreciation relating to that asset. Consequently, in the example, the entry needed to record the gain on sale will be:

|  | Debit | Credit |
|---|---|---|
| Land | 20 000 | |
| Gain on Sale of Land | | 20 000 |
| (realisation of asset revaluation on sale) | | |

Had the revaluation entry not been made, the gain on sale would have been $45 000 (one-quarter of $300 000 is $75 000, but the sale price was $120 000). However, the revaluation had been recorded, so the extra $25 000 (that is, one-quarter of the revaluation of $100 000) is already recorded in the reserves of the company — it is in the Asset Revaluation Reserve and, therefore, part of the shareholders' equity.

The revaluation is made on classes of assets and there is likely to be accumulated depreciation relating to the assets. A class of assets is a category of non-current assets having a similar nature or function in the operations of the entity. Revaluations refer to each class, and any differences between classes should not be offset — that is, an increment in one class cannot be offset against a decrement in another class. However, *within* classes such offsets are acceptable. Any revaluation of assets should

**recoverable amount**

not exceed their recoverable amount, defined in AASB 1010 as the 'net amount that is expected to be recorded through the cash inflows and outflows arising from its continued use and subsequent disposal' (para .09). This means that, as assets are future economic benefits, any revaluation should not exceed the amount of future benefits expected to be recovered for those assets. Accumulated depreciation on a class of assets is offset against any revaluation of that class of assets. Where there are subsequent revaluations in which a decrement follows an increment, the downward revaluation can be offset against the original increment amount that has been credited to an asset revaluation reserve. Any excess decrement can be charged to a Loss on Revaluation account and expensed in the period of the later revaluation. The converse applies where an increment follows a decrement — namely, income can be credited to the amount of earlier loss recognised and any excess increment credited to an Asset Revaluation Reserve.

Where the revaluation of assets affects assets on which there is accumulated depreciation, the balance of the accumulated depreciation is credited to the asset account (AASB 1010, para .17). This applies irrespective of whether the revaluation is an upward or downward one. In the above example there was no depreciation, as the asset involved was land. However, had it been an asset on which there was a related balance of accumulated depreciation, the balance in the Accumulated Depreciation account would have been transferred to the asset account first. It is important to note that where there is a downward revaluation the accumulated depreciation must still be credited to the asset account prior to the revaluation and not simply credited with the net amount of the downward revaluation.

While all this may seem rather convoluted, as long as the basic principles are remembered then the process is straightforward — that is, recognising revaluation losses immediately but retaining in reserves any increment until it is realised so that distributions are not made from profits that might not eventuate.

## ILLUSTRATIVE EXAMPLE 2.1

## ASSET REVALUATION

Ashley Ltd had the following non-current assets in its books at 1 July 20X0:

|  | Asset balance | Accumulated depreciation | Carrying amount |
|---|---|---|---|
|  | $ | $ | $ |
| Land | 200 000 | – | 200 000 |
| Buildings | 500 000 | 100 000 | 400 000 |
| Equipment | 400 000 | 120 000 | 280 000 |
| Motor vehicles | 120 000 | 60 000 | 60 000 |

The directors, on that date, decided to revalue the assets to:

| | |
|---|---|
| Land | $300 000 |
| Buildings | 650 000 |
| Equipment | 450 000 |
| Motor vehicles | 40 000 |

The general journal entries to reflect this would have been:

|  |  | Debit | Credit |
|---|---|---|---|
| 20X0 |  | $ | $ |
| July 1 | Accumulated Depreciation – Buildings | 100 000 |  |
|  | Accumulated Depreciation – Equipment | 120 000 |  |
|  | Accumulated Depreciation – Motor Vehicles | 60 000 |  |
|  |     Buildings |  | 100 000 |
|  |     Equipment |  | 120 000 |
|  |     Motor Vehicles |  | 60 000 |
|  | (write-off of depreciation on revaluation) |  |  |
|  | Loss on Revaluation of Motor Vehicles | 20 000 |  |
|  |     Motor Vehicles |  | 20 000 |
|  | (loss on revaluation) |  |  |
|  | Land | 100 000 |  |
|  | Buildings | 250 000 |  |
|  | Equipment | 170 000 |  |
|  |     Asset Revaluation Reserve |  | 520 000 |
|  | (revaluation of assets) |  |  |

Eleven months later the directors were aware that the economic climate had changed considerably, so the assets were again revalued. For simplicity, assume that at the date of revaluation no depreciation need be charged on these assets for the year and the assets were to be revalued to:

| | |
|---|---|
| Land | $350 000 |
| Buildings | 800 000 |
| Equipment | 350 000 |
| Motor vehicles | 70 000 |

The general journal entries to record this would be:

## General journal

| | Debit<br>$ | Credit<br>$ |
|---|---|---|
| **20X1** | | |
| May 30 Land | 50 000 | |
| Buildings | 150 000 | |
| Asset Revaluation Reserve | | 200 000 |
| (incremental revaluation of assets) | | |
| | | |
| Asset Revaluation Reserve | 100 000 | |
| Equipment | | 100 000 |
| (decremental revaluation of assets) | | |
| | | |
| Motor Vehicles | 30 000 | |
| Gain on Revaluation of Motor Vehicles | | 20 000 |
| Asset Revaluation Reserve | | 10 000 |
| (incremental revaluation of assets) | | |

## General ledger (extract)

| | Debit<br>$ | Credit<br>$ | Balance<br>$ | |
|---|---|---|---|---|
| **Land** | | | | |
| **20X0** | | | | |
| July 1 Balance | | | 200 000 | Dr |
| Asset Revaluation Reserve | 100 000 | | 300 000 | Dr |
| **20X1** | | | | |
| May 30 Asset Revaluation Reserve | 50 000 | | 350 000 | Dr |
| **Buildings** | | | | |
| **20X0** | | | | |
| July 1 Balance | | | 500 000 | Dr |
| Accumulated Depreciation | | 100 000 | 400 000 | Dr |
| Asset Revaluation Reserve | 250 000 | | 650 000 | Dr |
| **20X1** | | | | |
| May 30 Asset Revaluation Reserve | 150 000 | | 800 000 | Dr |
| **Equipment** | | | | |
| **20X0** | | | | |
| July 1 Balance | | | 400 000 | Dr |
| Accumulated Depreciation | | 120 000 | 280 000 | Dr |
| Asset Revaluation Reserve | 170 000 | | 450 000 | Dr |
| **20X1** | | | | |
| May 30 Asset Revaluation Reserve | | 100 000 | 350 000 | Dr |

|  | Debit | Credit | Balance |  |
|---|---|---|---|---|
|  | $ | $ | $ |  |
| **Motor Vehicles** |  |  |  |  |
| 20X0 |  |  |  |  |
| July 1 Balance |  |  | 120 000 | Dr |
| Accumulated Depreciation |  | 60 000 | 60 000 | Dr |
| Loss on Revaluation |  | 20 000 | 40 000 | Dr |
| 20X1 |  |  |  |  |
| May 30 Gain on Revaluation | 30 000 |  | 70 000 | Dr |
| **Asset Revaluation Reserve** |  |  |  |  |
| 20X0 |  |  |  |  |
| July 1 Land/Buildings/Equipment |  | 520 000 | 520 000 | Cr |
| 20X1 |  |  |  |  |
| May 30 Land/Buildings |  | 200 000 | 720 000 | Cr |
| Equipment | 100 000 |  | 620 000 | Cr |
| Motor Vehicles |  | 10 000 | 630 000 | Cr |

Note that as a $20 000 loss on the first revaluation of motor vehicles had been recorded, only a $20 000 gain on the second revaluation could be included in the current period's profits, with the extra $10 000 being credited to the reserve as required by AASB 1010. Although the example may be a little unrealistic, it illustrates how the revaluations are treated in varying circumstances. In the case of the motor vehicles, as both the loss and the gain are recorded in one accounting period they will be offset against each other.

### Foreign currency translation reserve

Transactions that involve different currencies often give rise to gains or losses resulting from movements in the exchange rates (the rate of exchange of one currency for another). The accounting standard AASB 1012: Foreign Currency Translation requires non-realised gains, in some circumstances, to be maintained in a foreign currency translation reserve. Once again, the principle is that distributions not be made from unrealised profits in case such profits are ultimately not realised. Foreign currency translation is the subject of chapter 14 and will be discussed there.

## OTHER RESERVES

Included in the reserves of many companies are those that do not arise from some regulatory requirement but rather from the practices of prudent management. A survey of financial reporting by the largest 150 Australian companies in 1994 showed that there were 500 reserves disclosed by these companies, with 51 different names.[1] Of these the most common were the regulatory reserves — share premium, asset revaluation, foreign currency translation and capital redemption — which accounted for more than 70%. A variety of other reserve names existed, but the most common were a general reserve and a capital profits reserve. These (and many of the other) reserves are created by the transfer of undistributed profits to the reserves. That is, they are appropriations of retained profits, indicating that they are not intended to be distributed as dividends for the time being. It is important to

general reserve

capital profits reserve

43

remember that as part of the shareholders' equity they represent residual claims against the assets of the company. That is, the reserves do not mean that there are specific assets (such as cash) set aside for some future contingency but that a part of the residual claim in the assets of the company is not to be used for dividends. This, of course, is a fundamental aspect of double entry accounting, of which anyone with accounting knowledge should be aware. However, those without an accounting knowledge sometimes act as though reserves indicate specifically earmarked funds available to the entity. Where there are specifically earmarked funds, the fund is

**reserve fund** referred to as a reserve fund — for example, funds set aside and invested in order to be able to repay debentures or a term loan. These are not what is commonly meant by the term 'reserve'. The Reserve Fund Equity account should have a corresponding Reserve Fund Investment (Asset) account.

The transfer of retained profits to a general reserve is straightforward and the journal entry is (for example):

|                                        | Debit   | Credit  |
| -------------------------------------- | ------- | ------- |
| Transfer to General Reserve            | 500 000 |         |
| General Reserve                        |         | 500 000 |
| (appropriation to general reserve)     |         |         |

The Transfer to General Reserve account will be closed off against retained profits, as are other appropriations at year end.

Whereas non-regulatory reserves are created from appropriations of profit, companies sometime earmark future funds through a charge against current profits

**provisions** (as expenses). These are referred to as provisions and they are very different to reserves. The practice of creating provisions is sometimes confusing to non-accountants, as originally they were intended always to be associated with specific assets. Older books referred to them as 'contra assets' and they would be disclosed in the balance sheet as deductions from the assets to which they referred. For example, Accounts Receivable would have a deduction for a Provision for Doubtful Debts (now often referred to as 'Allowance for Doubtful Debts'). Even non-current assets would have a deduction for a Provision for Depreciation (now usually referred to as 'Accumulated Depreciation'). However, practices change and some provisions exist that cannot be regarded as contra assets but are merely recognition of a liability. (For example, the next chapter will discuss a provision for deferred tax.) However, one thing that is certain is that provisions are not reserves and should never be disclosed as part of the shareholders' equity.

# Dividends

A dividend is an appropriation of profits to satisfy the shareholders' entitlement to receive a portion of the profits. The company's constitution will usually determine the matters dealing with the payment of the dividends. But this may not always be the case, so that directors can pay a dividend without authorisation from the constitution. However, normally a replaceable rule will allow the company to limit this right of the directors. The Corporations Law contains some general principles, the main one being that the company will not be able to pay a dividend if to do so would leave it unable to pay its debts as they fall due. Where directors do pay a dividend in such circumstances, then they may be liable to pay the amount of the dividend to the company. Similarly, if the directors pay a dividend otherwise than out of profits, they may be liable for the extent of the reduction in capital that eventuates. A legal debt for a dividend arises from the due date for payment, so, if circumstances change from when a dividend is declared to when it is due for payment, the directors may cancel the dividend but unless they do so a debt for the dividend then arises at the date fixed for paying the dividend.

Thus, the laws relating to the declaration and payment of a dividend are strict in order to preserve the doctrine of capital maintenance, especially in so far as it affects the company's responsibility to pay its debts. Dividends are usually recommended by the directors. If the recommendation is confirmed by the shareholders at the company's annual general meeting (they may also reduce it or reject the recommendation but not increase it), the dividend is declared. The shareholders do not have the right to demand a dividend but have to rely on the directors' recommendation. In most cases the directors' recommendation is automatically approved by the shareholders. As indicated above, a date is set for payment of the dividend and from that date the company has a *legal* liability to pay it. Despite this it has been the practice of most companies to report the recommended dividend as a current liability in its balance sheet. (This is discussed in chapter 11.)

## INTERIM AND FINAL DIVIDENDS

The company's constitution will usually allow the directors during the year to declare a 'part dividend' in anticipation of profits being made, without the approval of the shareholders. This is referred to as an interim dividend. As with all dividends the declaration of an interim dividend by the directors does not create a liability for the company and the decision may be revoked or amended before it is paid; the legal liability arises at the date set for payment. At the end of the year, if the directors recommend a further dividend, that dividend becomes the final dividend. It is common for the final dividend to be declared for the full amount of dividends for the year, with any interim dividend being subtracted from the amount of final dividend to be paid. Note that the shareholders determine the final dividend but not the interim dividend.

In the past, when ordinary shares were issued with a par value, dividends were declared as a percentage of the par value of the shares. However, with shares having no par value, dividends are declared as an amount per share. The situation is less clear with preference shares. Although not common nowadays, preference shares were issued with a stated dividend percentage. Thus, companies that were formed prior to the changes in the Corporations Law may still have preference shares stated at a percentage — for example, cumulative 8% $1 preference shares. In this case, the shareholders are entitled to receive 8 cents per share each year, irrespective of whether profits are made. Thus, if there are no profits in one year, such amounts are added to the subsequent year's dividend (unless the company is in liquidation).

*interim dividend*

*final dividend*

When dividends are declared, a date is set for payment. Those shareholders who are the registered shareholders at that date are entitled to receive the dividend. However, shareholders may sell their shares at this time. Where the shares are sold with the purchaser entitled to the dividend, the shares are sold *cum dividend*; where the dividend is to be paid to the seller, the shares are sold *ex dividend*.

## ACCOUNTING FOR CASH DIVIDENDS

As dividends are appropriations of profits, at the end of the year all dividend accounts will be closed to the Retained Profits account (or the Profit and Loss Appropriation account). For example, if an interim dividend has been declared and paid during the year, the following entries would have been made:

when declared —

|  | Debit | Credit |
|---|---|---|
| Interim Dividend | 50 000 | |
|     Interim Dividend Payable | | 50 000 |
| (interim dividend declared) | | |

when paid —

| | | |
|---|---|---|
| Interim Dividend Payable | 50 000 | |
|     Bank | | 50 000 |
| (interim dividend paid) | | |

Therefore, at the end of the financial year the Interim Dividend balance is closed to the Retained Profits account:

| | | |
|---|---|---|
| Retained Profits | 50 000 | |
|     Interim Dividend | | 50 000 |
| (to close and transfer balance) | | |

A similar accounting entry will be necessary for the final dividend, except that the payable account will most likely not have been paid at balance date and will show in the balance sheet as a current liability. Note that this is an economic liability rather than a legal liability at balance date because, as indicated above, the Corporations Law states that the liability for a dividend does not exist until the due date for payment is reached. However, for accounting purposes, the liability is recognised as existing as there is a high degree of certainty involved and it is expected that a dividend be paid (a constructive obligation).[2]

## ILLUSTRATIVE EXAMPLE 2.2

# ACCOUNTING FOR DIVIDENDS

Burrowes Ltd earned a profit for the year ended 30 June 20X1 of $3 000 000. During the year the directors had declared an interim dividend on ordinary shares which amounted to $200 000. The interim dividend was declared on 30 November 20X0 and paid on 24 December 20X0. At the end of the financial year there was an obligation for a payment of 10 cents per share on the 1 000 000 preference shares (which had also been paid last year) and the directors recommended a final dividend on the 2 000 000 ordinary shares of 18 cents per share, this amount to include any interim dividend paid during the year. In addition, the directors decided to transfer $1 000 000 to the general reserve.

The general journal of Burrowes Ltd would include the following entries:

| | | Debit $ | Credit $ |
|---|---|---|---|
| **20X0** | | | |
| Nov 30 | Interim Dividend | 200 000 | |
| |     Interim Dividend Payable | | 200 000 |
| | (interim dividend declared) | | |
| | | | |
| Dec 24 | Interim Dividend Payable | 200 000 | |
| |     Bank | | 200 000 |
| | (interim dividend paid) | | |
| | | | |
| **20X1** | | | |
| June 30 | Preference Dividend | 100 000 | |
| |     Preference Dividend Payable | | 100 000 |
| | (preference dividend payable) | | |
| | | | |
| | Final Dividend | 160 000 | |
| |     Final Dividend Payable | | 160 000 |
| | (final dividend recommended) | | |
| | | | |
| | Transfer to General Reserve | 1 000 000 | |
| |     General Reserve | | 1 000 000 |
| | (transfer to reserve) | | |
| | | | |
| | Retained Profits (Profit & Loss Appropriation) | 1 460 000 | |
| |     Interim Dividend | | 200 000 |
| |     Preference Dividend | | 100 000 |
| |     Final Dividend | | 160 000 |
| |     Transfer to General Reserve | | 1 000 000 |
| | (to transfer and close accounts) | | |

In the above example, accounts have been used for Preference Dividend, the Final Dividend and the Transfer to General Reserve. Sometimes an entry is simply made debiting the Retained Profits account and crediting the Dividend Liabilities and the Reserve(s) account(s), making the opening of the individual accounts unnecessary. However, the extra step has been employed in this example to clearly indicate the appropriations. Therefore, at year end, these accounts will have to be closed, as indicated by the last general journal entry. A closing entry transferring the net profit ($3 000 000) from the Income account to the Retained Profits account would also have been made.

The Retained Profits (Profit and Loss Appropriation) account will appear in the general ledger thus (assuming it had an opening balance of $500 000):

| Retained Profits | Debit $ | Credit $ | Balance $ |
|---|---|---|---|
| 20X0 | | | |
| July 1  Balance | | | 500 000 Cr |
| 20X1 | | | |
| June 30  Income Account (net profit) | | 3 000 000 | 3 500 000 Cr |
| Interim Dividend | 200 000 | | 3 300 000 Cr |
| Preference Dividend | 100 000 | | 3 200 000 Cr |
| Final Dividend | 160 000 | | 3 040 000 Cr |
| Transfer to General Reserve | 1 000 000 | | 2 040 000 Cr |

The balance sheet for Burrowes Ltd will show the *increase* of $1 000 000 in the general reserve and an *increase* in retained profits of $1 540 000 (both part of the shareholders' equity section). It will also show current liabilities for the preference dividend payable of $100 000 and the final dividend recommended of $160 000. The total dividend paid and payable to the ordinary shares for the year is 18 cents per share for 2 000 000 shares, or $360 000.

The Retained Profits account will indicate the undistributed profits (or accumulated losses) of the company. Its function is to indicate the amount of profits that have been accumulated yet remain undistributed to shareholders or not transferred to other reserves. It, too, is a reserve account. In the general ledger it will be a separate account. However, in companies' published financial statements it is usual to see the appropriations that have been made (or recommended) by the directors in the lower part of the profit and loss account. (This is discussed in greater detail in chapter 11.)

## ACCOUNTING FOR BONUS SHARES ISSUES

The above examples have shown how dividends that are paid or payable in cash are accounted for. However, a company may decide to capitalise some of its retained profits. This is done by issuing shareholders with fully paid bonus shares instead of paying a cash dividend. The journal entries to record this are straightforward. For example:

capitalisation

| | Debit | Credit |
|---|---|---|
| Bonus Dividend | 100 000 | |
| Paid-up Capital | | 100 000 |
| (bonus dividend of 1 for 5 declared) | | |
| | | |
| Retained Profits | 100 000 | |
| Bonus Dividend | | 100 000 |
| (to close and transfer account) | | |

In the example, the narration in the first entry indicates a one for five bonus share issue. This means that the dividend was declared such that the shareholders received one bonus share for every five they held. A bonus dividend may be to satisfy uncalled portions of shares, but it is more common to see them issued for fully paid shares. Although two entries were made, it is possible to simply have one entry for the transaction by combining the above entries, omitting the Bonus Dividend account.

When a bonus issue is made, the company, in increasing the number of shares on issue, is increasing potential future cash dividends since companies try to maintain dividends per share at the same level over several years. Therefore, when this action is taken it is an indication that the company is confident of the future — that there will be future profits to support any additional cash dividends. There may be other reasons for the company capitalising its profits in this way. For example, the company may have a current cash shortage but expect this situation to turn around and improve in the future. Therefore, in making the bonus issue it has avoided the immediate commitment of cash outflows, thus protecting its current liquidity. It may be that there are profitable uses for the cash at present. Issuing bonus shares is sometimes used as a defence against unwanted takeover bids. Increasing the number of shares may make the prospect unattractive to a would-be takeover bidder — knowing that they will have to service extra shares and possibly have to pay for more shares than they had originally intended.

A bonus issue may be made from sources other than retained earnings. A company can capitalise part or all of its reserves. For older companies, a common source was the Share Premium account or the capital redemption reserve. It is apparent that in 'converting' these reserves to paid-up capital the company is not reducing its capital at all. A company can also utilise its asset revaluation reserve in issuing bonus shares. Or it could use its general reserve. Once again, there are many reasons for making the bonus share issue and they are similar to the above suggested reasons. However, there may be additional reasons. For example, it 'tidies up' the company's shareholders' equity using reserves that have existed for some time. It could be made from the asset revaluation reserve after assets have been revalued prior to an unwelcome (or even welcome) takeover offer, thus increasing the 'value' of the company (in so far as the existing shareholders are concerned) or the price a successful takeover bidder would have to meet.

Accounting for bonus share issues made from sources other than retained profits is equally straightforward. There is some uncertainty about the permitted expression to describe the shares issued, but the expression 'bonus dividend' seems legally acceptable. Thus, the account debited will be the source of the 'dividend', with the credit (obviously) still to paid-up capital. If the asset revaluation reserve has been used and there is a subsequent decrement of that reserve required as a result of a revaluation, then only the amount of reserve left can be used, with the remainder of the decrement having to be charged against current profits. This, in effect, means that the dividend was partly funded by profits. However, this is an uncommon complication.

# Review

We have considered in this chapter the uses to which profits of the company can be put. It seems an obvious comment to make, but the directors can either distribute the profits the company makes or retain them within the company. Most commonly there will be a combination and the directors will distribute a proportion of the profits and retain the rest. In doing so, they may have determined some percentage of profits that they will distribute each year and this becomes a 'rule of thumb' so that, unless there are special considerations, it is that percentage of profits which the company distributes each year. It is important to know what the directors do with the profits retained. By not distributing them, they are leaving net assets in the company which can be used for growth, expansion or to increase profitability. Profits not distributed usually become part of the reserves of the company and, as such, form a major part of the shareholders' equity. A combination of prudent management practices and legal obligations has determined the appropriate accounting and this has been the subject of this chapter.

# Endnotes

1  JB Ryan & CT Heazlewood, *Australian Company Financial Reporting: 1995* (Australian Accounting Research Foundation, Accounting Research Study 13, 1995), pp 265–66.
2  This is consistent with Statement of Accounting Concepts  No. 4.

# KEY TERMS

| | | |
|---|---|---|
| capital profits reserve | forfeited shares reserve | reserve fund |
| capital redemption reserve | general reserve | reserves |
| capitalisation | interim dividend | retained profits |
| carrying amount | no par value | share premium reserve |
| dividends | provisions | |
| final dividend | recoverable amount | |

# REVIEW QUESTIONS

**2.1**  What are the three major divisions of the shareholders' equity of a company?

**2.2**  What is a reserve and what is its major function?

**2.3**  What were the two main statutory reserves and why were they necessary?

**2.4**  What are the replaceable rules of the Corporations Law?

**2.5**  AASB 1010 requires an asset revaluation reserve to be created in certain circumstances. What are these circumstances and why does the standard require the reserve to be created?

**2.6**  How does a reserve fund differ from a reserve (if at all)?

**2.7**  Why are provisions not disclosed within the shareholders' equity section in a company's balance sheet?

**2.8**  Distinguish between an interim dividend and a final dividend.

**2.9**  In what sort of situations would a company issue a bonus share dividend?

**2.10**  Why would a company not usually pay out all its profits as dividends?

**2.11**  Creation of a general reserve implies that the company has assets set aside equal to the reserve balance — is this true?

# EXERCISES

**Exercise 2.12** **Single asset revaluation**

Included in its assets, Alpha Ltd has land in Brisbane, Sydney and Melbourne recorded in the accounts at $350 000, $1 200 000 and $600 000 respectively. The company directors believe the Brisbane property is undervalued and that $550 000 would better reflect its value, and this is consistent with recent valuers' reports. On 1 April 20X2 the company receives an offer of $500 000 for the Brisbane land, so the directors resolve on 5 April to revalue the Brisbane land.

*Required*
1  Prepare the general journal to revalue the land.
2  Explain the basis for determining the figure to be used for the revaluation.

**Exercise 2.13** **Asset revaluation**

Beta Ltd had the following non-current assets in its books at 1 January 20X8:

|  | Asset balance | Accumulated depreciation | Net book value |
|---|---|---|---|
|  | $ | $ | $ |
| Motor vehicles | 240 000 | 120 000 | 120 000 |
| Plant & equipment | 800 000 | 240 000 | 560 000 |
| Land | 1 000 000 |  | 1 000 000 |
| Buildings | 1 000 000 | 200 000 | 800 000 |

On that date the directors resolve to revalue the assets according to a valuation report which indicated the following values:

| | |
|---|---|
| Motor vehicles | $80 000 |
| Land | 1 500 000 |
| Buildings | 1 300 000 |
| Plant & equipment | 800 000 |

*Required*
Prepare general journal entries to record the revaluation.

**Exercise 2.14** **Asset revaluation over more than one year**

The following information relates to the non-current assets of Gamma Ltd as at 30 June 20X8:

|  | Cost | Accumulated depreciation | Revaluation (as at 30 June 20X8) |
|---|---|---|---|
|  | $ | $ | $ |
| Plant & equipment | 320 000 | 80 000 | 200 000 |
| Motor vehicles | 300 000 | 100 000 | 240 000 |
| Land | 500 000 |  | 800 000 |

The amounts indicated as revaluation were those that the directors had obtained from a recent valuation. They had decided to revalue the assets to those valuations. The cost of motor vehicles was written off over three years and the plant and equipment over four years. The company used the straight-line depreciation method.

A year later, on 30 June 20X9, the directors decided the carrying values of the assets should be:

| | |
|---|---|
| Plant & equipment | $280 000 |
| Motor vehicles | 150 000 |
| Land | 1 000 000 |

*Required*
Prepare general journal entries for the above revaluations and show the Asset Revaluation Reserve account for the two years.

**Exercise 2.15**  **Asset revaluation over several years**
On 1 January 20X1, Delta Ltd purchased, for cash, a computer lathe for $1 500 000. It was planned to last ten years and to have no residual scrap value. The machine proved most useful and was revalued on 1 July 20X3 to $1 600 000, but by 20X6 technology had changed and the machine was revalued again — on 1 January 20X6 it was revalued at $500 000. The company's financial year is 1 January to 31 December.

*Required*
Prepare general journal entries to record:
(a) the purchase of the asset and the depreciation for 20X1;
(b) the sale of the asset on 1 January 20X3 for $1 800 000; and
(c) the sale of the asset on 1 January 20X7 for $300 000.

**Exercise 2.16**  **Deciding on revaluation measure**
The directors of a scientific consulting company, Epsilon Ltd, were in disagreement over the value to place on some of the company's scientific equipment. The equipment was highly specialised and had cost $2 000 000 and, at that date, 30 June 20X9, had accumulated depreciation of $800 000. The company had recently had a valuation of the equipment, and the valuer's report indicated the equipment to be worth $1 500 000. However, one director pointed out that the equipment had been superseded and the recent offer of $300 000 from another company was about all they could ever hope to get. But, another director argued, the equipment could be shipped overseas and probably fetch $1 400 000. The marketing director pointed out that the machine was still useful to the company and she was extremely confident that the discounted cash flows generated by it would be at least $2 100 000; thus, in accordance with AASB 1010, it should be revalued to that amount, as the accountant had told her that assets should be measured at their expected future economic benefits and had confirmed her calculations.

*Required*
Prepare the general journal entry that you believe is most appropriate to record the revaluation of the asset (if any) and provide an explanation for your decision.

**Exercise 2.17**  **Payment of a dividend**
Iota Ltd earned a profit for the year ended 30 June 20X9 of $2 500 000. During the year, the company had declared an interim dividend on ordinary shares which amounted to $450 000. This had been declared on 3 January and was paid on 31

January 20X9. At year end, 30 June 20X9, the company had an obligation to pay a dividend of 10 cents per share on 2 000 000 cumulative preference shares and declared a final dividend on the 5 000 000 ordinary shares of 30 cents per share. This dividend was to include any interim dividend. It was also decided to transfer $100 000 to the general reserve.

*Required*
Prepare general journal entries to record the appropriations and the interim dividend.

**Exercise 2.18**  **Cash dividend and retained profits account**
Omicron Ltd earned a profit for the year ended 31 December 20X7 of $4 500 000. During the year the company had declared an interim dividend on ordinary shares which amounted to $450 000. This had been declared on 3 July and was paid on 31 July 20X7. At year end, 31 December 20X7, the company declared a final dividend on the 6 000 000 ordinary shares of 40 cents per share. This dividend was to include any interim dividend. The company was also required to pay a dividend of 11 cents per share on 2 500 000 cumulative preference shares. The directors had resolved to transfer $100 000 to a dividend equalisation reserve and a further $100 000 to the general reserve.

*Required*
Prepare general journal entries to record the appropriations and the interim dividend and the Retained Profits account, assuming there was an opening balance of accumulated profits of $2 000 000, as it would appear in the general ledger.

**Exercise 2.19**  **Cash and share dividend**
Rho Ltd earned a profit for the year ended 30 June 20X6 of $3 000 000. It had a balance in the Retained Profits account of $8 000 000 and a paid-up capital of $10 000 000, which comprised 5 000 000 ordinary shares which had been issued at $2 per share. The directors resolved to recommend:
(a) a cash dividend of 30 cents per share (issued as at 1 July 20X5);
(b) capitalisation of a portion of the retained profits by making a two for five bonus share dividend of $2 fully paid ordinary shares; and
(c) transfer to the general reserve of $1 000 000.

*Required*
Prepare general journal entries to record the appropriations and the interim dividend and the Retained Profits account, as it would appear in the general ledger.

**Exercise 2.20**  **Cash and share dividend**
Mu Ltd earned a profit for the year ended 31 December 20X4 of $3 000 000. It had a balance in the Retained Profits account of $1 500 000 and in the General Reserve account a balance of $8 000 000. The company had a paid-up capital of $10 000 000, which comprised $1 ordinary shares. The directors resolved to recommend:
(a) a cash dividend of 30 cents per share (issued as at 1 January 20X4);
(b) transfer to the general reserve of $1 000 000; and
(c) capitalisation of a portion of the general reserve by making a one for five bonus share dividend of $1 fully paid ordinary shares.

*Required*

Prepare general journal entries to record the appropriations and the interim dividend and the Retained Profits account, as it would appear in the general ledger.

**Exercise 2.21** Comprehensive — appropriations and revaluations

The summary balance sheet of Sigma Ltd as at 31 December 20X8 was as follows:

**Sigma Ltd**
**Balance Sheet as at 31 December 20X8**

| | Cost | Accumulated depreciation | Net book value | $000 | $000 |
|---|---|---|---|---|---|
| *Assets* | | | | | |
| Current assets | | | | | |
| Cash | | | | 450 | |
| Accounts receivable | | | | 560 | |
| Inventories | | | | 400 | 1 410 |
| | | | | | |
| Non-current assets | | | | | |
| Plant & equipment | 3 800 | 800 | 3 000 | | |
| Motor vehicles | 500 | 310 | 190 | | |
| Land | 1 000 | | 1 000 | | |
| Buildings | 5 400 | 1 300 | 4 100 | | 8 290 |
| | | | | | $9 700 |
| | | | | | |
| *Liabilities* | | | | | |
| Current liabilities | | | | | |
| Accounts payable | | | | 400 | 400 |
| | | | | | |
| Non-current liabilities | | | | | |
| Debentures | | | | 800 | 800 |
| | | | | | |
| *Shareholders' equity* | | | | | |
| Paid-up capital (5 000 000 ordinary shares) | | | | 5 000 | |
| Retained profits | | | | 1 400 | |
| General reserve | | | | 2 100 | 8 500 |
| | | | | | $9 700 |

The directors resolve the following, and all resolutions are approved at the annual general meeting on 20 January 20X9:
(a) declare a cash dividend of 10% to be paid on 10 February 20X9;
(b) revalue the assets in accordance with a recent valuation — namely, revalue to:

| | |
|---|---|
| Plant & equipment | $4 000 000 |
| Motor vehicles | 100 000 |
| Land | 1 300 000 |
| Buildings | 4 500 000 |

(c) declare a two for five bonus share dividend, using the asset revaluation reserve and, if insufficient, any extra amount needed from retained profits; and

(d) transfer the balance in the retained profits to the general reserve.

*Required*

Prepare general journal entries to record the above and, assuming, for simplicity, no other transactions, a balance sheet as at 31 January 20X9 after the journal entries had been posted.

**Exercise 2.22**  **Comprehensive — appropriations and revaluations**

The balance sheet of Theta Ltd as at 30 June 20X3 appeared as follows:

### Theta Ltd
### Balance Sheet as at 30 June 20X3

|  | $ | $ | $ |
|---|---|---|---|
| *Shareholders' equity* | | | |
| Issued and paid-up capital | | | |
| 40 000 7% cumulative preference shares at $5 | | | 200 000 |
| *Shareholders' equity* | | | |
| Issued and paid-up capital | | | |
| 40 000 7% cumulative preference shares at $5 | | | 200 000 |
| 1 000 000 ordinary $1 shares | | 1 000 000 | |
| *Less* Uncalled capital of 50 cents per share | | 500 000 | 500 000 |
| Paid-up capital | | | 700 000 |
| Retained profits | | | 300 000 |
| | | | 1 000 000 |
| *Current liabilities* | | | |
| Accounts payable | | | 88 000 |
| | | | $1 088 000 |
| *Non-current assets* | | | |
| Plant & equipment | 500 000 | | |
| Accumulated depreciation | 120 000 | 380 000 | |
| Motor vehicles | 120 000 | | |
| Accumulated depreciation | 80 000 | 40 000 | |
| Land | | 300 000 | |
| Buildings | 300 000 | | |
| Accumulated depreciation | 60 000 | 240 000 | 960 000 |
| *Current assets* | | | |
| Bank | | 45 000 | |
| Accounts receivable | | 35 000 | |
| Inventories | | 48 000 | 128 000 |
| | | | $1 088 000 |

The following resolutions have been passed:

(a) On 1 August 20X3, the declaration of a final dividend of 4% on the preference shares which together with an interim dividend of 3% paid on 25 February 20X3 made a total of 7% for the year.

(b) On 1 August 20X3, the declaration of a final dividend of 6% on the paid-up value of the ordinary shares which together with an interim dividend of 4% paid on 25 February 20X3 made a total of 10% for the year.

(c) On 1 August, a call of 25 cents per share on all the ordinary shares to be paid by 10 September 20X3. All amounts due were received except on 5000 shares, so these shares were forfeited on 30 September 20X3.

(d) On 1 August, the revaluation of the non-current assets to:

| | |
|---|---|
| Plant & equipment | $300 000 |
| Motor vehicles | 30 000 |
| Land | 150 000 |
| Buildings | 400 000 |
| (No depreciation was to be charged since the balance date.) | |

(e) The issue of a debenture of 10 000 units at $100 payable in full on application by 30 September 20X3. All amounts were received.

(f) On 10 October 20X3, the purchase of land ($200 000) and buildings ($800 000) for cash.

*Required*

Prepare general journal entries for the above and then, assuming for simplicity that there were no other transactions, prepare a balance sheet as at 31 October 20X3.

# chapter 3

ACCOUNTING FOR COMPANY INCOME TAX

# introduction

This chapter examines the payment of income taxes by companies and its accounting treatment. The applicable accounting standard is AASB1020: Accounting for Income Tax (Tax-effect Accounting). The standard became operative for financial years ending on or after 31 December 1989 and applies to all companies that are reporting entities and all parent entities of an economic entity that is a reporting entity (AASB 1025, para .11). In addition, a number of state governments have introduced legislation requiring public sector business undertakings to pay income tax expense substantially equivalent to what they would be required to pay if they were subject to the *Income Tax Assessment Act 1936*. Therefore, these organisations are also subject to AASB 1020.

The purpose of the standard is to prescribe the method for calculating, recording and disclosing income tax expense and related items. AASB 1020 (AAS 3 is identical) requires the use of a modified comprehensive liability method of tax-effect accounting in preference to the deferral method and the net of tax method. Under the liability method, income tax expense is accrued in the same way as other expenses incurred in earning revenue.

**liability method**

Before AAS 3 became operative in October 1974, the tax payable method was used when accounting for company income tax. The latter will be explained as it is still applicable in certain circumstances. The major thrust of this chapter will be tax-effect accounting. Experience shows that accounting students often have difficulty in applying tax-effect accounting principles; hence the material presented in this chapter is graduated from simple to more complex issues. Worksheets will be used to assist in explanations.

The principles underlying the payment of income tax are the same for companies as for individuals. Most individual tax payers have tax deducted from their wages and salaries at each pay period and these amounts are remitted to the Australian Taxation Office (ATO) under the Pay-As-You-Earn (PAYE) system. Companies do not pay tax on current income as individuals do, but pay taxes after the end of the financial year based on their self-assessed taxation liability. For both individuals and companies, taxation returns are required to be lodged each financial year. Under the current self-assessment system a formal notice of assessment is not normally issued. The Commissioner of Taxation is deemed to have made an assessment on the date the return is lodged. Unlike individuals, companies are not subject to provisional tax.

# Tax payments

taxable income   Income tax payable is assessed on taxable income (assessable income less allowable deductions) as determined under the *Income Tax Assessment Act 1936*. Company tax is payable by quarterly instalments. The instalment dates (depending on the amount of tax payable) are, for example, 1 June, 1 September and 1 December, with the final payment due on 1 March. A variation exists for companies with estimated taxation liabilities of less than $8000. In that case the applicable tax is to be paid in full by 1 December following the year of income.

# Tax payable method

tax payable method   The tax payable method requires a balance day adjustment to record a liability for income tax based on the estimate of taxation liability at the end of the financial year. For example, assume A Ltd has estimated taxable income for the financial year ended 30 June 20X2 at $500 000 and the income tax rate is 33%. Income tax payable is then $500 000 × 33%, or $165 000.

The journal entries are as follows (note the date of each entry as discussed above):

| 20X2 | | Debit | Credit |
|---|---|---|---|
| June 1 | Provision for Income Tax Payable | 41 250 | |
| | Cash | | 41 250 |
| | (first quarterly instalment) | | |
| June 30 | Income Tax Expense | 165 000 | |
| | Provision for Income Tax | | 165 000 |
| | (estimated tax liability) | | |
| Sept 1 | Provision for Income Tax Payable | 41 250 | |
| | Cash | | 41 250 |
| | (second quarterly instalment) | | |
| Dec 1 | Provision for Income Tax Payable | 41 250 | |
| | Cash | | 41 250 |
| | (third quarterly instalment) | | |
| 20X3 | | | |
| Mar 1 | Provision for Income Tax Payable | 41 250 | |
| | Cash | | 41 250 |
| | (final instalment) | | |

These entries assume that the estimated income tax liability equals the income tax payable as per the ATO assessment notice. Therefore, the income tax expense equals the provision for income tax payable. Where this is not the case, the under/overprovision of income tax payable must be accounted for.

For example, in the above case of A Ltd, assume that $5000 more than the original estimate of $165 000 is to be paid. The journal entry is:

| 20X3 | | Debit | Credit |
|---|---|---|---|
| Mar 1 | Provision for Income Tax Payable | 41 250 | |
| | Underprovision of Income Tax Payable | 5 000 | |
| | Cash | | 46 250 |

If the income tax assessed is less than the estimate of $165 000, the final payment for tax is reduced. The journal entry is:

| 20X3 | | Debit | Credit |
|---|---|---|---|
| Mar 1 | Provision for Income Tax Payable | 41 250 | |
| | Overprovision of Income Tax Payable | | 5 000 |
| | Cash | | 36 250 |

AASB 1018: Profit and Loss Accounts requires the prior period adjustment to be passed through the profit and loss statement and not taken directly to retained profits. Therefore, the Underprovision for Income Tax Payable account of $5000 (above) is treated as an expense in the current period even though it relates to the previous period. The Overprovision for Income Tax Payable account is treated in the same way; the only difference is that it is a revenue item.

# Accounting profit and taxable income

The tax payable method has the advantage of being easy to understand and the accounting treatment is relatively simple. However, proponents of tax-effect accounting maintain that income tax should be treated as an expense and matched against the accounting profit earned in a particular year. That is, income tax expense should be calculated using accounting principles (proper matching), whereas the provision for income tax payable is calculated using taxation principles. This means that the two amounts will usually differ as the rules for calculation are different.

Under generally accepted accounting principles, the determination of income for financial statement purposes is based on revenues being recognised when the criteria for revenue recognition are met (the revenue recognition principle) and expenses should be charged to the period in which related revenues are recognised (the matching principle). In this framework, income tax is considered a cost or expense incurred in the process of earning income.

In comparison, the determination of taxable income is based on the objective of minimising income taxes paid over the life of the company whilst adhering to the rules and regulations of taxation legislation. This simply means that the rules for calculating accounting income are different from the rules for calculating assessable/taxable income.

# Tax-effect accounting

income tax expense
accounting profit
permanent differences
provision for income
tax payable

Using tax-effect accounting, the income tax expense (ITE, a debit) is calculated by applying the current tax rate for companies to the accounting profit determined in accordance with accounting principles after allowing for permanent differences. In contrast, the provision for income tax payable (PITP, a credit) is calculated by applying the current tax rate to taxable income (assessable income less allowable deductions) determined in accordance with taxation legislation.

These two amounts, income tax expense and provision for income tax payable, usually differ because the rules for calculating accounting profit and taxable income are different. It follows that the difference between the two amounts must be reconciled. ITE shows as a debit in the profit and loss statement and represents the income tax expense associated with the current financial period. PITP is shown as a credit in the balance sheet and represents the amount the company has estimated it owes in taxes payable.

The reconciliation between ITE (based on accounting profits *after* allowing for permanent differences) and PITP is achieved by accounting for what represents the difference, timing differences and tax losses carried forward. Tax losses will be discussed later in this chapter.

Whilst the term 'accounting profit' has been used in this discussion, it should be noted that accounting profit is the result of adding/subtracting extraordinary items to/from the operating profit. That is:

Operating profit (includes abnormal items)
+/− Extraordinary items
= Accounting profit (before tax)

Under the disclosure requirements of AASB 1018 the income tax expense attributable to both operating profit and extraordinary items is to be disclosed separately.

## PERMANENT DIFFERENCES

These differences are items of revenue or expense that are included in either taxable income or accounting profit but are *never* included in *both*. For example, tax-exempt revenue will form part of accounting profit but will never be assessed for income tax purposes because it is exempt from taxation. Amortisation of goodwill is an accounting expense but is not an allowable taxation deduction. Research and development expenditure may qualify for a 150% allowable deduction for taxation purposes but only for a 100% deduction as an accounting expense. Other examples include depreciable asset revaluations, entertainment expenses, dividends received and capital gains. To calculate taxable income, the permanent differences, depending on their nature, must be added to or subtracted from accounting profit before tax. This is the starting point in the reconciliation process for the calculation of PITP. Refer to the worksheet on the following page.

## TIMING DIFFERENCES

These differences are defined as items of revenue or expense that enter into the calculation of *both* accounting profit and taxable income but in different accounting periods. Timing differences will reverse in future accounting periods. That is, the total amount recorded as revenue or expense is treated by the ATO as assessable or

**allocation**  deductible. However, the allocation to each relevant period is different. For example, a company pays $100 000 for an item of plant. For accounting purposes it uses a depreciation rate of 20% straight line but is allowed depreciation at 25% prime cost (similar to the straight-line method) for taxation purposes. Only $100 000 may be written off over the life of the asset, but the amount allowed for accounting purposes will be $20 000 per annum whilst $25 000 per annum will be allowed for taxation purposes. Clearly this is a timing difference, not a permanent difference.

To illustrate:

| Year | Accounting depreciation $ | Tax depreciation $ | Difference $ |
|---|---|---|---|
| 1 | 20 000 | 25 000 | (5 000) |
| 2 | 20 000 | 25 000 | (5 000) |
| 3 | 20 000 | 25 000 | (5 000) |
| 4 | 20 000 | 25 000 | (5 000) |
| 5 | 20 000 | – | 20 000 |
| Total | $100 000 | $100 000 | – |

**future income**
**tax benefit**
**provision for deferred**
**income tax**

Timing differences are recorded as either a future saving in income tax, called a future income tax benefit (FITB), shown as an asset in the balance sheet, or a deferral of income tax called a provision for deferred income tax (PDIT), shown as a liability in the balance sheet. Timing differences that have to be accounted for include depreciation, bad and doubtful debts, long service and annual leave, instalment sales, rent received in advance, and profit or loss on sale of assets.

| PERMANENT DIFFERENCES | TIMING DIFFERENCES |
|---|---|
| Exempt income | Depreciation |
| Goodwill amortisation | Bad and doubtful debts |
| Franked dividends | Long service and annual leave |
| Capital gains | Prepaid revenue (eg rent received in advance) |
| | Instalment sales |
| ↓ | ↓ |
| A revenue or expense item included in either taxable income or accounting profit but NEVER in both. | A revenue or expense item that enters into the calculation of BOTH accounting profit and taxable income but in different accounting periods. |

\* For further examples see AASB 1020.

The above is now illustrated in a worksheet format.

**Worksheet**

| Reconciliation | Tax rate xx% | ITE Debit | FITB Debit | PDIT Credit | PITP Credit |
|---|---|---|---|---|---|
| Accounting profit before tax | | | | | |
| +/− **Permanent differences:** | | | | | |
| = **Adjusted accounting profit** | | x tax rate | | | |
| +/− **Timing differences** | | | | | |
| Accounting | | | | | |
| Tax | | | x tax rate | x tax rate | |
| = **Taxable income** | | | | | x tax rate |

Note that where a FITB is reversing (eg bad and doubtful debts) a credit entry is required in the FITB column, and where a PDIT item is reversing (eg depreciation) a debit entry is required in the PDIT column.

### Summary

It is not easy at times to determine if a timing difference leads to a FITB or a PDIT. The following four cases cover all situations.

1   Where revenues are recognised more quickly for accounting purposes than for tax purposes, a PDIT arises — for example, instalment sales and accrued income. It means that this revenue is included in accounting profit before it is included in taxable income. Therefore, less tax is payable initially but this will reverse in the future. Hence a PDIT arises which will be debited in the future when this revenue is included in taxable income. This difference is only due to timing, so less tax is payable now but more will be payable in the future when the difference reverses.

2   Where revenues are recognised more slowly for accounting purposes than for tax purposes, a FITB arises — for example, rent received in advance. This is the opposite of (1), above. That is, the revenue is included in taxable income before it is included in accounting profit. Hence a FITB will arise, a future saving in income tax, which reverses in the future when the revenue is included in accounting profit. Again this difference is only due to timing, so more tax is payable now but less will be payable in the future when the difference reverses.

3   Where expenses are written off more quickly for accounting purposes than for tax purposes, a FITB arises — for example, bad debts expense, and long service and annual leave. Hence the expense reduces accounting profit before it reduces taxable income. Here a FITB arises which reverses in the future when the expense reduces taxable income. As the difference is only due to timing, more income tax will be paid now but less will be payable in the future when the difference reverses.

4   Where expenses are written off more slowly for accounting purposes than for tax purposes, a PDIT arises — for example, depreciation, and research and development expenditure when it is capitalised for accounting purposes. This is the opposite of (3), above. More expense is claimed for taxation purposes than for accounting purposes. Therefore, less tax is payable initially but this will reverse in the future. Hence a PDIT arises which will be debited in the future when this expense is included in accounting profit. This difference is only due to timing, so less tax is payable now but more will be payable in the future when the difference reverses.

The nature of the account cannot change when it reverses — that is, a FITB is of a debit nature, and when it reverses it must be credited. A PDIT is of a credit nature, and when it reverses it must be debited. Positive timing differences give rise to debits — that is, additions to the adjusted accounting profit — and negative timing differences give rise to credits — that is, subtractions from the adjusted accounting profit.

**ILLUSTRATIVE EXAMPLE 3.1**

# SINGLE PERMANENT AND TIMING DIFFERENCE

Assume B Ltd supplies the following information as at 30 June 20X1:

| | |
|---|---|
| Accounting profit before tax | $500 000 |
| Goodwill amortised during year | $20 000 |
| Plant purchased 1 July 20X0 (cost) | $100 000 |
| Depreciation – accounting purposes (straight line) | 10% |
| Depreciation – tax purposes (prime cost) | 20% |
| Income tax rate | 33% |

*Required*
Prepare the tax-effect accounting journal entry for the year ended 30 June 20X1.

**Worksheet**

| Reconciliation | Tax rate 33% | ITE Debit | FITB Debit | PDIT Credit | PITP Credit |
|---|---|---|---|---|---|
| Accounting profit before tax | 500 000 | | | | |
| **Permanent differences** | | | | | |
| + Goodwill amortisation | 20 000 | | | | |
| **Adjusted accounting profit** | 520 000 | 171 600 | | | |
| **Timing differences** | | | | | |
| Depreciation | | | | | |
|   Accounting    10 000 | | | | | |
|   Tax    (20 000) | (10 000) | | | 3 300 | |
| **Taxable income** | 510 000 | 171 600 | | 3 300 | 168 300 |

The journal entry is:

| | | Debit $ | Credit $ |
|---|---|---|---|
| 20X1 | | | |
| June 30 | Income Tax Expense | 171 600 | |
| | Provision for Deferred Income Tax | | 3 300 |
| | Provision for Income Tax Payable | | 168 300 |

Note the following:
1. Permanent differences are simply added to or subtracted from accounting profit, depending on their effect on taxable income. Here, goodwill amortisation is not an allowable deduction for tax purposes. Therefore, it is a part of taxable income and must be added back to accounting profit. There is no necessity to calculate the tax effect of permanent differences.

2. The timing difference in this example relates to depreciation. Here the plant is being written off *faster* for tax purposes than for accounting purposes. Therefore, initially *less* tax is being paid and this leads to a provision for deferred income tax (PDIT). This account has a credit nature. When the account reverses, it must be debited.

# Treatment of permanent differences

Using accounting profit before tax as a starting point in calculating taxable income, all permanent differences must be added/subtracted to arrive at the adjusted accounting profit. The following section illustrates how some permanent differences are treated. This list is not intended to be exhaustive.

### Exempt income

Any exempt income will be included in accounting profit before tax. Therefore, to arrive at taxable income, always subtract it from accounting profit before tax as no tax is paid on exempt income.

### Goodwill amortisation

This expense is included in the calculation of accounting profit before tax but is not an allowable deduction for tax purposes. Therefore, it is added back to accounting profit before tax.

### Research and development

To encourage research and development, governments at times allow a company to claim 150% of its expenditure on research and development in the year of payment. If $100 000 is spent on research and development, the accounting expense is $100 000 but $150 000 for taxation purposes. The additional $50 000 is a permanent difference which will reduce taxable income and is therefore subtracted from accounting profit before taxation.

### Franked dividends

Dividends received are similar to exempt income, as they are revenue and included in the calculation of accounting profit. The difference between dividends and exempt income is that dividends are not actually exempt from tax but are subject to a tax rebate. That is, franked dividends received are included in assessable income for income tax purposes but the company is then entitled to a rebate of income tax for the full amount of the tax payable on that dividend (assuming that the dividend is fully franked). The rebate fully offsets the amount of tax otherwise payable on the dividend received. Using tax-effect accounting, the dividend received is shown in the worksheet at the bottom of the reconciliation because it is subject to a rebate of income tax and therefore no tax is payable on this item of income. The rebate gives rise to a permanent difference which is only available where the company has taxable income. A dividend rebate reduces the company's income tax expense for the period, as well as the income tax payable. If there is insufficient taxable income to claim the rebate, it is lost as it cannot be carried forward (see the example on page 71). Note that AASB 1020 and AAS 3 do not deal with rebates.

### Depreciation on asset revaluations

It is common practice to revalue non-current assets. AASB 1010: Accounting for the Revaluation of Non-current Assets and AASB 1021: Depreciation of Non-current Assets stipulate that where a non-current asset is revalued, future depreciation charges must be based on the new carrying amount of the asset. If the asset is revalued upwards, the future depreciation charges will cause a permanent difference to arise. This occurs because for tax purposes only the original cost of the asset may be claimed as an allowable deduction via depreciation expenses. For example, if a building originally cost $300 000, and was subsequently revalued upwards by $200 000, the additional depreciation charges on the $200 000 would not qualify as an allowable deduction for taxation purposes. However, for accounting purposes this additional depreciation is included as an expense. The additional depreciation is a permanent difference and must be added back to accounting profit before taxation. (Note that there is also a timing difference based on the original cost of $300 000 if the accounting rate of depreciation differs from the rate allowed for tax purposes.)

### Capital gains

The calculation of a capital gain for accounting purposes and for tax purposes creates a difference, because the two methods of calculation differ and this difference is permanent in nature. For accounting purposes the calculation is as follows:

Capital gain = Sale proceeds − Original cost (or revalued amount) of asset

For tax purposes it is:

Capital gain = Sale proceeds − Indexed cost (adjusted for inflation) of asset

Clearly the difference will be equal to the adjusted (or indexed) original cost minus the original cost (as the sale proceeds are common to both calculations). This represents a permanent difference, as it is not assessable income but is included in accounting profit before taxation.

# Treatment of timing differences

### Depreciation

To recap, a timing difference occurs when an item of revenue or expense enters into the calculation of both taxable income and accounting profit but in different accounting periods. For example, assume an item of plant cost $100 000 and for accounting purposes the depreciation rate is 25% straight line and for tax purposes it is 50% prime cost. (Recall that the straight-line depreciation method allocates an equal amount of depreciation to each accounting period. The amount of depreciation for each period is the cost of the asset less any estimated residual value, divided by the asset's useful life. The prime cost depreciation method allocates the acquisition cost (residual values are ignored) as per the percentage allowed — for example, 50% prime cost means an equal amount of depreciation is charged each year for two years.)

| Year | Accounting depreciation $ | Tax depreciation $ | Difference $ |
|------|---------------------------|--------------------|--------------|
| 1 | 25 000 | 50 000 | (25 000) |
| 2 | 25 000 | 50 000 | (25 000) |
| 3 | 25 000 | | 25 000 |
| 4 | 25 000 | | 25 000 |
| Total | $100 000 | $100 000 | − |

In years 1 and 2, $25 000 more per year is allowed in depreciation expenses for taxation purposes than for accounting purposes. That is, the company is paying less tax in these first two years. This means a provision for deferred tax is created and is a credit item. In each of years 1 and 2, $25 000 is multiplied by the tax rate to ascertain the PDIT. In years 3 and 4, this process reverses; hence a debit to PDIT is required. Note that once a PDIT is established initially (and it is always a credit), the only way to reverse it is with a debit entry. It cannot change to a FITB.

A PDIT arises whenever an item of revenue is recognised for accounting purposes before being included in taxable income, or when an item of expense is deducted for taxation purposes prior to being deducted for accounting profit. Examples include instalment sales on the revenue side and depreciation on the expense side.

## Bad and doubtful debts

Most companies use the indirect method when accounting for bad and doubtful debts (as opposed to the direct method, where there is no provision for doubtful debts created and bad debts are written off directly against accounts receivable). This means that an *estimate* is made of the expected level of doubtful debts. The journal entry is:

|  | Debit | Credit |
|---|---|---|
| Doubtful Debts Expense | XXX |  |
| Allowance for Doubtful Debts |  | XXX |

The above debit reduces accounting profit. When an account receivable proves to be uncollectable, a debit is made to the provision for doubtful debts. The journal entry is:

|  | | |
|---|---|---|
| Allowance for Doubtful Debts | XXX |  |
| Accounts Receivable |  | XXX |

When a bad debt is written off, it is an expense allowable as a deduction for taxation purposes (subject to certain conditions). That is, the accounting expense estimate for calculating accounting profit is not allowed as a deduction for taxation purposes; it is only allowed when the debt proves to be 'bad'.

Assume Company C had a doubtful debts expense of $4000 for accounting purposes, but $2000 was actually written off as bad debts for taxation purposes. That is, an expense is being written off more quickly for accounting purposes than for taxation purposes. This means the company is paying more tax this period, or it may be said that the company has a future saving in income tax. This leads to a FITB, which is always a debit item.

If the above situation were reversed and the company had a bad debts expense of $2000 for accounting purposes and in the same year wrote off $4000 in bad debts for tax purposes, this represents a reversal. This means FITB would be credited for $2000 × the tax rate. The nature of FITB cannot be changed; it is a debit and when it reverses (as above), FITB is credited. This treatment assumes that the write-off is against a provision created in an earlier period.

## Long service and annual leave

These items (plus provisions for warranty expenses) always lead to a FITB because for accounting purposes the expenses are being written off more quickly than for tax purposes. The treatment and explanation is the same as that for bad and doubtful debts (as above). The *Income Tax Assessment Act 1936* only allows for actual payments to be deductible, not the amount provided for in the accounting process.

## Prepaid revenue

Prepaid revenue is recognised for taxation purposes as soon as it is received. For accounting purposes, prepaid revenue is treated as a liability until it is earned. The journal entry is:

|  | *Debit* | *Credit* |
|---|---|---|
| Cash | XXX |  |
| Revenue Received in Advance |  | XXX |

When the prepaid revenue is earned, the journal entry is:

|  | | |
|---|---|---|
| Revenue Received in Advance | XXX |  |
| Revenue Earned |  | XXX |

This means that for accounting purposes the revenue is being recognised more slowly than for tax purposes. That is, tax is being prepaid, leading to a FITB. Because FITB is a debit, it must be credited when this process reverses.

## Research and development

As noted above, when additional write-offs of research and development are allowed (say, 150%) and the entire payment occurs in one financial year, this leads to a permanent difference. There will also be a timing difference when the expenditure is capitalised as an asset and amortised over the period of time that it provides economic benefits.

For example, Stricker Ltd spent $200 000 on research and development on 1 July 20X0. This amount was capitalised as an asset and amortised at 25% straight line. For tax purposes the company claimed 150% of amounts spent on research and development as an allowable deduction. Assume that accounting profit before taxation for the year ended 30 June 20X1 was $750 000 and the tax rate is 33%.

The total expenditure on research and development is $200 000, but as a 150% allowable deduction is being claimed, the total claim for tax purposes is $300 000 ($200 000 × 150 ÷ 100). This results in a *permanent* difference of $100 000.

For accounting purposes the amortised amount in the first year is $50 000 ($200 000 × 25%). For tax purposes the allowable deduction is $200 000, the actual expenditure. This is the same as the discussion above regarding depreciation. A PDIT always arises when an item of expense is deducted for taxation purposes prior to being deducted in the determination of accounting profit. Here there is a timing difference of $150 000 ($200 000 − $50 000). Therefore, a PDIT arises of $49 500 ($150 000 × 33%). In summary, assuming accounting profit before tax is $750 000:

**Worksheet**

| Reconciliation | Tax rate 33% | ITE Debit | FITB Debit | PDIT Credit | PITP Credit |
|---|---|---|---|---|---|
| Accounting profit before tax | 750 000 | | | | |
| **Permanent differences** | | | | | |
| — Research & development | 100 000 | | | | |
| **Adjusted accounting profit** | 650 000 | 214 500 | | | |
| | | | | | |
| **Timing differences** | | | | | |
| Research & development | | | | | |
| Accounting     50 000 | | | | | |
| Tax           (200 000) | (150 000) | | | 49 500 | |
| **Taxable income** | 500 000 | 214 500 | | 49 500 | 165 000 |

The journal entry is:

| | Debit | Credit |
|---|---|---|
| Income Tax Expense | 214 500 | |
| Provision for Deferred Income Tax | | 49 500 |
| Provision for Income Tax Payable | | 165 000 |

## ILLUSTRATIVE EXAMPLE 3.2

# MULTIPLE TIMING DIFFERENCES

This and Illustrative example 3.3 illustrate the principles discussed to this point. Kenny Ltd presents the following information for the year ended 30 June 20X1.

| | Debit $ | Credit $ |
|---|---|---|
| Accounting revenue | | 400 000 |
| *Includes:* | | |
| Foreign exchange gain | 10 000 | |
| Rent earned | 4 000 | |
| Accounting expenses total | | 150 000 |
| *Includes:* | | |
| Amortisation of goodwill | 1 000 | |
| Depreciation of vehicles | 1 000 | |
| Depreciation of plant | 4 000 | |
| Doubtful debts expense | 4 000 | |
| *Tax information* | | |
| Rent received and assessable | 10 000 | |
| Depreciation on vehicles | — | |
| Depreciation on plant | 6 000 | |
| Bad debts written off | 3 000 | |

The foreign exchange gain is a permanent difference and the tax rate is 33%.

*Required*

Prepare a worksheet using the principles of tax-effect accounting and the journal entry for the year ended 30 June 20X1.

**Worksheet**

| Reconciliation | Tax rate 33% | ITE Debit | FITB Debit | PDIT Credit | PITP Credit |
|---|---|---|---|---|---|
| Accounting profit before tax | 250 000 | | | | |
| **Permanent differences** | | | | | |
| + Goodwill amortisation | 1 000 | | | | |
| − Foreign exchange gain | (10 000) | | | | |
| **Adjusted accounting profit** | 241 000 | 79 530 | | | |
| **Timing differences** | | | | | |
| Rent income | | | | | |
|   Accounting        (4 000) | | | | | |
|   Tax               10 000 | | 6 000 | 1 980 | | |
| Bad & doubtful debts | | | | | |
|   Accounting        4 000 | | | | | |
|   Tax               (3 000) | | 1 000 | 330 | | |
| Depreciation – vehicle | | | | | |
|   Accounting        1 000 | | | | | |
|   Tax               – | | 1 000 | | dr 330 | |
| Depreciation – plant | | | | | |
|   Acccounting       4 000 | | | | | |
|   Tax               (6 000) | | (2 000) | | 660 | |
| **Taxable income** | 247 000 | 79 530 | 2 310 | 330 | 81 510 |

The journal entry is:

| | Debit $ | Credit $ |
|---|---|---|
| 20X1 | | |
| June 30  Income Tax Expense | 79 530 | |
|              Future Income Tax Benefit | 2 310 | |
|                    Provision for Deferred Income Tax | | 330 |
|                    Provision for Income Tax Payable | | 81 510 |

Note the following:

1  The first step is to adjust for permanent differences. The $10 000 in foreign exchange gain is included in accounting revenue, but as it is not taxable it is deducted from accounting revenue. Recall that this is a reconciliation process – that is, starting with accounting profit before tax, various additions and subtractions are made to arrive at taxable income.

2  Recall the four combinations of timing differences:
   (a)  Where revenue is recognised more quickly for accounting purposes than for tax purposes, a PDIT arises. It means that this revenue is included in accounting profit *before* it is included in taxable income. Therefore, less tax is payable initially but this will reverse in the future. Hence a PDIT arises which will be debited in the future when this revenue is included in taxable income. This difference is only due to timing, so less tax is payable now but more will be payable in the future when the difference reverses.

(b) Where revenue is recognised more slowly for accounting purposes than for tax purposes, a FITB arises. This is the case above for rent received. This is the opposite of (a), above. That is, the revenue is included in taxable income before it is included in accounting profit. Hence a FITB will arise, a future saving in income tax, which reverses in the future when the revenue is included in accounting profit. Again this difference is only due to timing, so more tax is payable now but less will be payable in the future when the difference reverses.

(c) Where expenses are written off more quickly for accounting purposes than for tax purposes, a FITB arises. This is the case above for bad debts expense. Hence the expense reduces accounting profit before it reduces taxable income. Here a FITB arises which reverses in the future when the expense reduces taxable income. As the difference is only due to timing, more income tax will be paid now but less will be payable in the future when the difference reverses.

(d) Where expenses are written off more slowly for accounting purposes than for tax purposes, a PDIT arises. This is the case above for depreciation on plant. This is the opposite of (c), above. More expense is claimed for taxation purposes than for accounting purposes. Therefore, less tax is payable initially but this will reverse in the future. Hence a PDIT arises which will be debited in the future when this expense is included in accounting profit. This difference is only due to timing, so less tax is payable now but more will be payable in the future when the difference reverses.

(e) In the case of depreciation on vehicles ((d), above), the vehicle has been written off for tax purposes, but *not* for accounting purposes. Therefore, a PDIT arises but it is reversing and requires a debit entry.

3  Positive timing differences always give rise to debits – that is, additions to the adjusted accounting profit. Negative timing differences always give rise to credits – that is, subtractions from the adjusted accounting profit.

**ILLUSTRATIVE EXAMPLE** 3.3

## MULTIPLE TIMING DIFFERENCES, DIVIDENDS RECEIVED

Perry Ltd presents the following information for the year ended 30 June 20X1. Accounting profit before tax is $400 000. This figure included the following items:

| | |
|---|---|
| Exempt income received | $100 000 |
| Doubtful debts expense | 10 000 |
| Depreciation on plant | 5 000 |
| Dividends received (fully franked) | 5 000 |
| Goodwill amortisation | 12 000 |
| Loss on sale of equipment | 8 000 |
| Rent income | 15 000 |
| Long service leave | 14 000 |

*Additional information for tax purposes is as follows:*

| | |
|---|---|
| Depreciation on plant | $16 000 |
| Profit on sale of equipment | 2 000 |
| Long service leave payment | 6 000 |
| Bad debts expense | 17 000 |
| Rent received and assessable | 25 000 |

Assume a tax rate of 33%.

*Required*

Prepare a worksheet using the principles of tax-effect accounting and the journal entry for the year ended 30 June 20X1.

**Worksheet**

| Reconciliation | Tax rate 33% | ITE Debit | FITB Debit | PDIT Credit | PITP Credit |
|---|---|---|---|---|---|
| Accounting profit before tax | 400 000 | | | | |
| **Permanent differences** | | | | | |
| — Exempt income | (100 000) | | | | |
| + Goodwill amortisation | 12 000 | | | | |
| **Adjusted accounting profit** | 312 000 | 102 960 | | | |
| **Timing differences** | | | | | |
| Bad & doubtful debts | | | | | |
|   Accounting  10 000 | | | | | |
|   Tax  (17 000) | (7 000) | | cr 2 310 | | |
| Depreciation plant | | | | | |
|   Accounting  5 000 | | | | | |
|   Tax  (16 000) | (11 000) | | | 3 630 | |
| Rent received | | | | | |
|   Accounting  (15 000) | | | | | |
|   Tax  25 000 | 10 000 | | 3 300 | | |
| Long service leave | | | | | |
|   Accounting  14 000 | | | | | |
|   Tax  (6 000) | 8 000 | | 2 640 | | |
| Sale of asset | | | | | |
|   Accounting loss  8 000 | | | | | |
|   Tax profit  2 000 | 10 000 | | | dr 3 300 | |
| **Taxable income** | 322 000 | | | | |
| Dividends received | (5 000) | cr 1 650 | | | |
| **Taxable income after rebate** | 317 000 | 101 310 | 3 630 | 330 | 104 610 |

The journal entry is:

| | | Debit $ | Credit $ |
|---|---|---|---|
| 20X1 | | | |
| June 30 | Income Tax Expense | 101 310 | |
| | Future Income Tax Benefit | 3 630 | |
| |   Provision for Deferred Income Tax | | 330 |
| |   Provision for Income Tax Payable | | 104 610 |

Notes:

1 The fully franked dividends received are included in the calculation of accounting profit, but rather than being non-taxable (like exempt income) they give rise to a *rebate of tax* (s 46 of the *Income Tax Assessment Act 1936*). This then is a permanent difference, but it must be subtracted from taxable income at the bottom of the worksheet to ensure that there is sufficient taxable income to take advantage of the rebate. In the worksheet, both income tax expense and provision for income tax payable will be reduced as shown.

2   A loss on sale of plant – in this case, $8000 for accounting purposes and a $2000 profit on sale for tax purposes – results in $10 000 being added to accounting profit before tax to calculate taxable income. As the taxable income has increased, the amount of tax payable must also increase. The debit side of the entry is a reversal caused by the asset being written off more quickly for tax purposes than for accounting purposes, which would have led to a credit to PDIT up until the point of sale of the asset. Therefore, a debit must be made to PDIT to make the reversal. Another way of viewing the sale of an asset which has been depreciated for tax and accounting purposes at different rates is that its sale must completely reverse all remaining timing difference accruals. Since these will have been credited to PDIT in past years, the debit of $3300 must be made to PDIT when the asset is sold.

# Other issues

## LEASING

AASB 1008: Accounting for Leases describes two types of leases and their prescribed accounting treatment. The first type is an operating lease. This is the simplest type of leasing arrangement. Here the lessee pays a predetermined amount for the use of the asset for a specified period. The amount paid is shown as an expense in the lessee's profit and loss statement. For tax purposes this expense is an allowable deduction. Since both occur in the same accounting period, there are no timing differences.

The second type of lease is a finance lease. Here the lessee must record an asset and a liability equal to the fair value of the leased asset. The asset is then amortised over the term of the lease. (If it is intended to acquire the asset at the end of the lease, the asset is amortised over its useful life.) The lease payment consists of a principal and an interest component. For accounting purposes the asset amortisation amount and the interest expense component of the lease payment are both deducted as expenses. For tax purposes the lease payment is an allowable deduction, just the same as for operating leases. The difference with finance leases is that a timing difference occurs that has to be accounted for under tax-effect accounting.

This timing difference is the same principle underlying timing differences with asset depreciation. That is, over the life of an asset the *total* amount of depreciation for accounting and tax purposes is the same, but the amounts for each will be different in each accounting period. At the end of the term of a finance lease the total of interest expense and asset amortisation will equal total lease payments. The former are expenses for accounting purposes; the latter are deductible for tax purposes. The only difference will be the periods in which the expenses and lease payments were recognised for accounting and tax purposes.

## SECTION 59(2A) ELECTIONS

This section of the *Income Tax Assessment Act 1936* provides for an election to be made regarding the use of taxable profits on the sale of depreciable assets. Such an election will result in a timing difference. The election simply enables a company to use any taxable profit made on the sale of an asset to reduce the depreciable amount of the replacement asset. This will reduce the taxable depreciation allowed on the replacement asset. The original tax payable on the profit from the sale is deferred and then recognised over the life of the replacement asset in the form of reduced deductions for allowable depreciation on the replacement asset. The deferral of tax payable results in a timing difference because any accounting profit on the sale will be recognised when the asset is sold.

## CHANGES IN COMPANY TAX RATE

AASB 1020 requires the liability method of accounting for timing differences between accounting profit and taxable income. One of the implications of using this method is that the PDIT and FITB account balances must be measured using the current rate of income tax. When there is a change in the rate of company income tax, existing balances in these two accounts must be adjusted. There are two ways to make this adjustment, both of which give the same result.

1  Adjustment = Existing account balance $-$ $\dfrac{\text{[Existing account balance} \times \text{New tax rate]}}{\text{Old tax rate}}$  OR

2  Adjustment = Existing account balance $\times$ Percentage change in tax rate.

For example, assume the following opening balances in the books of E Ltd for the current year beginning 1 July.

|      | $      |
|------|--------|
| FITB | 12 000 |
| PDIT | 7 500  |

On 30 September the company tax rate was reduced from 39% to 33%. When the tax rate decreases, there must be a downward adjustment (decrease) in FITB and PDIT. When the tax rate increases, there is an upward adjustment (increase) in FITB and PDIT. The adjustment to the existing account balances is calculated as follows:

- FITB balance $12 000

$$= 12\,000 - \frac{[12\,000 \times 33\%]}{39\%}$$

$$= 12\,000 - 10\,154$$

$$\text{Adjustment} = 1846$$

OR

$$= 12\,000 \times \frac{6}{39}$$

$$\text{Adjustment} = 1846$$

- PDIT balance $7500

$$= 7500 - \frac{[7500 \times 33\%]}{39\%}$$

$$= 7500 - 6346$$

$$\text{Adjustment} = 1154$$

OR

$$= 7500 \times \frac{6}{39}$$

$$\text{Adjustment} = 1154$$

This means that the asset account FITB, which represents future tax savings, is reduced by $1846. PDIT, representing deferred tax payable in the future, is reduced by $1154. The reduction in FITB results in an operating loss for the period (asset reduced), and the reduction in PDIT (liability reduced) results in an operating gain. Combining these two reductions results in an overall operating loss of $692 ($1846 loss − $1154 gain).

The journal entry is:

|  | Debit | Credit |
|---|---|---|
| Provision for Deferred Income Tax | 1154 | |
| Loss from Change in Tax Rate (P & L) | 692 | |
| Future Tax Benefit | | 1846 |

At the end of the current year, the loss of $692 is included in the operating profit for the year. It represents a permanent difference between accounting profit and taxable income when calculating the current year's journal entry for taxation expense using tax-effect accounting.

# Tax losses

**virtual certainty test**

Where a company incurs a tax loss, it may claim the loss as an allowable deduction in future years (s 80 of the *Income Tax Assessment Act 1936*). If the company is virtually certain it will claim the loss as a tax deduction in future periods — that is, earn future taxable income sufficient to cover the loss — a FITB is raised equal to the tax loss × tax rate.

**beyond any reasonable doubt test**

AASB 1020 makes a distinction between a FITB arising from timing differences and a FITB arising from a tax loss. A FITB arising from timing differences may only be recognised as an asset where it is assured beyond any reasonable doubt that the benefits will be realised. Such realisation will be dependent on:
- the company deriving future assessable income of a nature and amount sufficient to enable the benefit to be realised;
- the company continuing to comply with the conditions for deductibility imposed by law; and
- there being no changes in tax legislation which adversely affect the company realising the benefit.

A FITB arising from a tax loss may only be recognised if realisation of the benefit is virtually certain. It should be noted that s 79E of the *Income Tax Assessment Act 1936* now allows a tax loss to be carried forward as a deduction against assessable income with no time limit. Previously there was a seven-year limitation clause.

## ILLUSTRATIVE EXAMPLE 3.4

# VIRTUAL CERTAINTY

Assume D Ltd supplies the following information as at 30 June 20X2:

| | |
|---|---|
| Operating loss for the year | $(50 000) |
| Depreciation on machinery for accounting purposes | 40 000 |
| Depreciation on machinery for taxation purposes | 65 000 |

The worksheet would appear as follows:

**Worksheet**

| Reconciliation | Tax rate 33% | ITE Debit | FITB Debit | PDIT Credit | PITP Credit |
|---|---|---|---|---|---|
| Accounting loss | (50 000) | *cr 16 500 | | | |
| **Timing differences** | | | | | |
| Depreciation – machinery | | | | | |
|   Accounting     40 000 | | | | | |
|   Tax        (65 000) | (25 000) | | | 8 250 | |
| **Tax loss** | (75 000) | *cr 16 500 | | 8 250 | *dr 24 750 |

\* The debit in the PITP column translates to a FITB based on the tax loss ($75 000 x .33 = $24 750). Further, because there is an operating loss of $50 000, there is no debit to the income tax expense column but a credit of $16 500 ($50 000 x .33) which becomes an income tax benefit. In effect, the income tax benefit is a negative income tax expense.

**income tax benefit**

At balance date the amount of the income tax benefit is credited to the profit and loss account, as shown below. This results in a reduction of $16 500 in the operating loss for the year.

| | Debit $ | Credit $ |
|---|---|---|
| Future Income Tax Benefit (tax loss) | 24 750 | |
| Provision for Deferred Income Tax | | 8 250 |
| Income Tax Benefit | | 16 500 |

The profit and loss account for the year would show as:

| | |
|---|---|
| Operating loss before income tax | $(50 000) |
| Income tax benefit | 16 500 |
| Operating loss after income tax | (33 500) |

Tax-effect accounting shows the income tax benefit reducing the operating loss from $50 000 to $33 500. Further, the tax loss $75 000 $\times$ .33, or $24 750, results in a FITB. The income tax benefit is based on accounting measurement of loss, whereas the tax loss of $24 750 is based on the measurement of taxable income.

If in the following year D Ltd made a profit of $100 000 and this was equal to taxable income:

#### Worksheet

| Reconciliation | Tax rate 33% | ITE Debit | FITB Debit | PDIT Credit | PITP Credit |
|---|---|---|---|---|---|
| Accounting profit | 100 000 | 33 000 | | | |
| **Timing difference** | | | | | |
| Tax loss recovered | (75 000) | | cr 24 750 | | |
| **Taxable income** | 25 000 | 33 000 | cr 24 750 | | 8 250 |

The journal entry is:

| | Debit $ | Credit $ |
|---|---|---|
| Income Tax Expense | 33 000 | |
| Future Income Tax Benefit | | 24 750 |
| Provision for Tax Payable | | 8 250 |

Therefore, the FITB of $24 750 raised in the previous year is now reversed and is credited for the same amount. Note also that D Ltd must have met the criterion of 'virtual certainty' in 20X2, as it raised a FITB of $24 750. If the virtual certainty test is not met, any existing balance in FITB should be debited to the profit and loss account and a FITB based on the tax loss would not be raised.

## ILLUSTRATIVE EXAMPLE 3.5

# PAST LOSSES UNCERTAINTY AND NO PDIT

Assume that D Ltd supplies the following information as at 30 June 20X1.

| | |
|---|---|
| Accounting profit for the year | $250 000 |
| Goodwill amortisation | 10 000 |
| Past tax losses (no FITB raised) | 100 000 |
| Doubtful debts expense (accounting) | 40 000 |
| Bad debts expense (taxation) | 20 000 |

The tax rate is 33%.

#### Worksheet

| Reconciliation | Tax rate 33% | ITE Debit | FITB Debit | PDIT Credit | PITP Credit |
|---|---|---|---|---|---|
| Accounting profit before tax | 250 000 | | | | |
| **Permanent differences** | | | | | |
| + Goodwill amortisation | 10 000 | | | | |
| **Adjusted accounting profit** | 260 000 | 85 800 | | | |
| **Timing differences** | | | | | |
| Tax loss recovered | (100 000) | | *cr 33 000 | | |
| Bad & doubtful debts | | | | | |
| Accounting 40 000 | | | | | |
| Tax (20 000) | 20 000 | | | 6 600 | |
| **Taxable income** | 180 000 | | 6 600 | | 59 400 |

* Credited to Income Tax Benefit.

Therefore, the journal entry is:

|  | Debit $ | Credit $ |
|---|---|---|
| Income Tax Expense | 85 800 | |
| Future Income Tax Benefit | 6 600 | |
| Income Tax Benefit | | 33 000 |
| Provision for Income Tax Payable | | 59 400 |

Note that the tax losses recovered of $100 000 did not result in a prior FITB of $33 000 being raised, but it will be included in the current period's profit and loss account as shown in the above journal entry.

## FURTHER ASPECTS OF TAX LOSSES

Where a company is not virtually certain of recovering the FITB attributable to a tax loss, AASB 1020 (para .13) prescribes that FITBs attributable to tax losses and timing differences should not be raised. The exception (para .14) to this is: where a PDIT exists, the FITB attributable to the tax loss should be brought to account as a reduction of the PDIT.

Further, AASB 1020 does not indicate whether a company should discontinue tax-effect accounting in the situation where it cannot meet the test of virtual certainty. This means that if an existing PDIT is larger than the tax effect of a tax loss, a company could maintain a PDIT in its balance sheet and therefore comply with AASB 1020. It is maintained by the authors that where a company is unable to meet the virtual certainty test, the tax payable method should be adopted and the balance of the PDIT account is closed to profit and loss.

## ILLUSTRATIVE EXAMPLE 3.6

# TAX LOSS AND EXISTENCE OF PDIT

The following example illustrates the issue of certainty and uncertainty regarding realisation of tax loss benefits with reference to AASB 1020 (para .14).

Assume that on 1 July 20X0, D Ltd purchased an item of plant for $240 000 with an estimated residual value of $10 000. Depreciation for accounting purposes was charged at 20% straight line, and for tax purposes at 33 1/3% prime cost. For the year ended 30 June 20X4, D Ltd incurred an operating loss of $100 000 and in the following year made a profit of $220 000. The tax rate is 33%.

*Required*
Prepare tax-effect accounting journal entries for the years ended 30 June 20X4 and 30 June 20X5 where there is:
• virtual certainty of realisation of the tax loss benefit; and
• uncertainty of realisation of the tax loss benefit.

The first step is to compare the depreciation charges to ascertain the effects of timing differences.

| Year | Accounting depreciation | Tax depreciation | Difference | Cumulative difference | PDIT × 33% |
|---|---|---|---|---|---|
| | $ | $ | $ | $ | |
| 20X0/X1 | 46 000* | 80 000** | (34 000) | (34 000) | 11 200 |
| 20X1/X2 | 46 000 | 80 000 | (34 000) | (68 000) | 22 440 |
| 20X2/X3 | 46 000 | 80 000 | (34 000) | (102 000) | 33 660 |
| 20X3/X4 | 46 000 | – | 46 000 | (56 000) | 18 480 |
| 20X4/X5 | 46 000 | – | 46 000 | (10 000) | 3 300 |

\* [240 000 − 10 000] ÷ 5
\*\* 240 000 ÷ 3

### Virtual certainty case – year to 30 June 20X4
**Worksheet**

| Reconciliation | Tax rate 33% | ITE Debit | FITB Debit | PDIT Credit | PITP Credit |
|---|---|---|---|---|---|
| Accounting loss | (100 000) | cr 33 000 | | | |
| **Timing differences** | | | | | |
| Depreciation – machinery | | | | | |
| Accounting 46 000 | | | | | |
| Tax – | 46 000 | | | dr 15 180 | |
| **Tax loss** | (54 000) | cr 33 000 | 17 820 | dr 15 180 | |

**Certainty**

| | Debit | Credit |
|---|---|---|
| | $ | $ |
| Future Income Tax Benefit | 17 820 | |
| Provision for Deferred Income Tax | 15 180 | |
| Income Tax Benefit | | 33 000 |

The tax loss of $54 000 results in a FITB of $17 820. The depreciation timing difference (now reversing) requires a debit of $15 180 to the PDIT account. Instead of an entry to ITE, an account called Income Tax Benefit is credited with $33 000 and the operating loss for the year (after tax) becomes $67 000 ($100 000 − $33 000). The balance in the PDIT account is now $18 480 ($102 000 − $46 000 = $56 000 × .33).

**Uncertainty**

| | Debit | Credit |
|---|---|---|
| | $ | $ |
| Provision for Deferred Income Tax | 33 660 | |
| Income Tax Benefit | | 33 660 |

The balance in the PDIT account before the current year's adjustment is $102 000 × .33 – that is, $33 660. This amount will not become payable (that is, reverse) while the tax loss remains as a deduction. AASB 1020 requires this amount to be disclosed in the profit and loss account as an income tax benefit called 'provision for deferred income tax no longer required'. The write-off of the PDIT of $33 660 is consistent with the discussion in AASB 1020 (para .14) that tax loss benefits can be recognised where the virtual certainty criterion has not been met, provided that there exists a PDIT which will reverse during the time the company is eligible to benefit from its current tax loss. No other journal entry is required for the year.

## Virtual certainty case – year to 30 June 20X5

### Worksheet

| Reconciliation | Tax rate 33% | ITE Debit | FITB Debit | PDIT Credit | PITP Credit |
|---|---|---|---|---|---|
| Accounting profit before tax | 220 000 | 72 600 | | | |
| **Timing differences** | | | | | |
| Tax loss recovered | (54 000) | | cr17 820 | | |
| Depreciation – machinery | | | | | |
|   Accounting    46 000 | | | | | |
|   Tax        – | 46 000 | | | dr15 180 | |
| **Taxable income** | 212 000 | 72 600 | cr17 820 | dr15 180 | 69 960 |

### Certainty

| | Debit $ | Credit $ |
|---|---|---|
| Income Tax Expense | 72 600 | |
| Provision for Deferred Income Tax | 15 180 | |
|   Future Income Tax Benefit | | 17 820 |
|   Provision for Income Tax Payable | | 69 960 |

The FITB raised in the previous year is now reversed, hence the credit of $17 820 to the FITB account. The credit balance remaining in the PDIT account, $3300 ($10 000 × .33), is closed to profit and loss.

### Uncertainty

| | Debit $ | Credit $ |
|---|---|---|
| Income Tax Expense | 18 480 | |
|   Provision for Deferred Income Tax | | 18 480 |

AASB 1020 (paras .15 and .16) requires the reinstatement of the PDIT which was reduced in the previous period to the extent of the timing differences which were still to reverse in relation to the depreciation charges – that is, $102 000 − $46 000 = $56 000 × .33 = $18 480. This is a prior period adjustment which is shown in the current period's profit and loss account.

| | Debit $ | Credit $ |
|---|---|---|
| Income Tax Expense | 72 600 | |
| Provision for Deferred Income Tax | 15 180 | |
|   Provision for Income Tax Payable | | 69 960 |
|   Income Tax Benefit | | 17 820 |

The debit to the PDIT account is the reversal of this year's depreciation timing difference. The credit to the Income Tax Benefit account of $17 820 represents the realised benefit of the tax loss in the current year.

## SUMMARY

1 Where the virtual certainty criterion is satisfied, a company may recognise a FITB attributable to a tax loss as an asset. When the resulting FITB is realised, the FITB account is reduced by the amounts realised.

2 Where there is uncertainty and no PDIT account balance exists, no tax benefit of the loss is recognised. If such losses are subsequently recouped, the tax benefit is recognised in the profit and loss account as an income tax benefit (a credit to ITE).

3 Where there is uncertainty and a PDIT account exists, the realisation of the future benefit from the tax loss is regarded as virtually certain to the extent of the balance in the PDIT account.

## DISCLOSURE

AASB 1020 contains specific disclosure requirements about tax:
* Paragraph .10: If permanent differences are material, a note to the accounts should state their general nature and the extent to which they have affected the amount of income tax expense.
* Paragraph .13: Where any part of a future income tax benefit carried forward is attributable to tax losses, that part should be disclosed by way of a note to the accounts.
* Paragraph .14: Any reduction in a provision for deferred income tax caused by a future income tax benefit arising from a tax loss should be disclosed and referred to as a 'provision for deferred income tax no longer required'.
* Paragraph .15: If a future income tax benefit attributable to a tax loss has not been recognised in the accounts and there is a possibility that the tax losses will be recouped in accordance with tax legislation, a note should be included in the financial report specifying certain details as set out in para .15.
* Paragraph .40: If an adjustment caused by a change in income tax rates is material, the amount of the adjustment should be disclosed.

AASB 1018, paras .13, .15 and .17, prescribe that the profit and loss account is required to contain disclosure of a company's:
* income tax expense/benefit attributable to operating profit/loss;
* income tax in relation to each abnormal item; and
* income tax attributable to any extraordinary profit or loss.

Future tax benefit may be shown as an intangible current or non-current asset, although the usual presentation is non-current. Also, provision for deferred tax is shown as a current or non-current liability.

# Proposed international accounting standard

Both AASB 1020 and International Accounting Standard 12 (IAS 12): Accounting for Taxes on Income require a profit and loss statement approach to accounting for income taxes. As discussed in this chapter, this approach recognises and discloses the expected tax effects of timing differences as a FITB or a PDIT in a reporting entity's balance sheet.

Interestingly, a balance sheet approach when accounting for income tax has been required in the United States since Statement of Financial Accounting Standards 109 (SFAS 109): Accounting for Income Taxes was first issued in 1992. This balance sheet approach is the basis of Proposed International Accounting Standard (E49): Income Taxes. It was issued by the International Accounting Standards Committee (IASC) in October 1994. E49 represents a fundamental change to the method of accounting for income taxes.

If E49 is issued in the future as an international accounting standard to replace IAS 12, then AASB 1020 would have to be reviewed. If this were to occur, it would be a lengthy process to replace AASB 1020.

# Review

This chapter has examined accounting for company income tax. Both the tax payable and tax-effect accounting methods were discussed, with emphasis on the latter. Perhaps the critical section of the area is the reconciliation from accounting profit to taxable income. Remember that the worksheet starts with accounting profit before tax and adds/subtracts permanent and timing differences to arrive at taxable income. Hence, when deciding if a particular item should be added or subtracted, think about the effect it will have on taxable income.

Tax-effect accounting is used in subsequent chapters and hence an understanding of its application is critical. This especially applies in the chapters on consolidation.

## KEY TERMS

| | | |
|---|---|---|
| accounting profit | income tax expense | payable |
| allocation | liability method | taxable income |
| beyond any reasonable doubt test | permanent differences | tax payable method |
| future income tax payable | provision for deferred income tax | virtual certainty test |
| income tax benefit | provision for income tax | |

## REVIEW QUESTIONS

**3.1** Discuss the differences between the tax payable method and the tax-effect method of accounting for a company's income tax liability.

**3.2** Why are there differences between taxable income and accounting profit?

**3.3** Explain permanent and timing differences and how they are treated in a tax-effect accounting worksheet. Give three examples of each.

**3.4** Discuss a situation, with an example, where an item of expense can lead to both a permanent and a timing difference.

**3.5** What are the criteria for determining virtual certainty when dealing with tax losses? In your opinion, how much subjectivity is involved when applying the criteria?

**3.6** From the viewpoint of a user of financial statements, explain why (or why not!) tax-effect accounting is more useful than the tax payable method.

**3.7** How does a timing difference 'reverse' over its life? Give two examples.

# EXERCISES

**Exercise 3.8** **Single timing difference**

Swim Ltd purchased an item of equipment on 1 July 20X1 at a cost of $120 000. For accounting purposes the equipment is estimated to have a useful life of three years and a zero residual value. Swim Ltd uses the straight-line method to calculate accounting depreciation. For tax purposes the equipment is depreciated at 50% of prime cost.

Accounting profits before income tax earned by Swim Ltd are provided below. Exempt income has been included in the determination of accounting profit. Assume the company tax rate is 33%.

| Year ended 30 June | Operating profit | Exempt income |
|---|---|---|
| | $ | $ |
| 20X2 | 80 000 | 1 000 |
| 20X3 | 60 000 | 2 000 |
| 20X4 | 70 000 | 1 500 |

*Required*

Prepare a tax-effect worksheet and the journal entries for each of the above years.

**Exercise 3.9** **Simple tax-effect worksheet**

Chandler Ltd purchased an item of equipment on 1 July 20X1 for $96 000. For accounting purposes, equipment is depreciated at 25% straight-line method and at 50% prime cost method for tax purposes. Accounting profits and other related items are as follows:

| Year ended 30 June | Accounting profit before tax | Amount provided for long service leave | Actual payments for long service leave |
|---|---|---|---|
| | $ | $ | $ |
| 20X2 | 150 000 | 30 000 | 20 000 |
| 20X3 | 170 000 | 30 000 | – |
| 20X4 | 190 000 | 30 000 | 40 000 |

The company tax rate is 39%.

*Required*

Prepare a tax-effect worksheet and the journal entries for each of the above years.

**Exercise 3.10**  **Tax-effect journal entries**

Pain Ltd commenced business on 1 July 20X0. The following reconciliations of accounting profits and taxable income were prepared by the accountant and included in the company work files for 20X1 and 20X2.

| | 20X1 $ | 20X2 $ |
|---|---|---|
| Accounting profit before tax after including: | 100 000 | 100 000 |
| **Permanent differences** | | |
| Goodwill amortisation | 20 000 | 20000 |
| Political donation | 5 000 | – |
| **Accounting profit after permanent differences** | 125000 | 120 000 |
| **Timing differences** | | |
| Depreciation | | |
| Tax | 30 000 | 30 000 |
| Accounting | 20 000 | 20 000 |
| Research & development expenditure | | |
| Tax | 10 000 | 10 000 |
| Accounting | – | – |
| Prepaid rent | | |
| Tax | 2 000 | – |
| Accounting | – | 2 000 |
| Increase in provision for doubtful debts | 8 000 | – |
| Bad debts written off | – | 6 000 |
| Warranty expense accrued | 5 000 | – |
| Warranty expenses paid | – | 5 000 |
| **Taxable income** | $116 000 | $91 000 |

The company tax rate is 40%.

*Required*

Prepare the tax-effect journal entries for the years ended 30 June 20X1 and 20X2.
*[The authors wish to thank Dr Richard Morris, Senior Lecturer in Accounting, University of NSW, for this question.]*

**Exercise 3.11**  **Tax-effect worksheet**

After recognising all items of revenue and expenses, the accounting profit before tax of Sansby Ltd for the year ended 30 June 20X2 was calculated to be $100 000. The following items were included in the calculation of accounting profit:

| | |
|---|---|
| Depreciation of equipment | $18 000 |
| Rental revenue | 4 000 |
| Goodwill amortisation | 3 000 |

Assume the company tax rate is 33% and that in the preparation of the tax return of the company the accountant included the following items:

| | |
|---|---|
| Depreciation of equipment | $27 000 |
| Rentals received | 6 000 |
| Investment allowance – equipment | 5 000 |

*Required*

Prepare a tax-effect worksheet and the relevant journal entries for the year.

**Exercise 3.12**  **Tax-effect worksheet with dividend rebate**

The accounting profit before tax of Loren Ltd was determined to be $250 000 for the year ended 30 June 20X0. Selected items included in the calculation were as follows:

| | |
|---|---|
| Non-deductible foreign exchange loss | $25 000 |
| Franked dividend received (s 46) | 100 000 |
| Amortisation of research and development (deducted for tax purposes when paid) | 5 000 |
| Increase in the balance of the provision for doubtful debts account | 8 000 |

The following items which were deducted for tax purposes did not affect the accounting profit. The company tax rate is 36%.

| | |
|---|---|
| Bad debts written off (against the provision) | $4 000 |
| Annual leave paid (previously provided for) | 7 000 |
| Excess of tax depreciation on plant over accounting depreciation | 35 000 |

*Required*

Prepare a tax-effect worksheet and the relevant journal entries for the year.

**Exercise 3.13**  **Tax rate change**

The general ledger of Appleby Ltd disclosed the following account balances as at 30 June 20X2:

| | |
|---|---|
| Future tax benefit | $24 000 |
| Provision for deferred tax | 56 000 |

On 15 March 20X3 the company rate of tax was reduced from 36% to 33%.

*Required*

Prepare the 30 June 20X3 journal entry to record the effect of the change in tax rate.

**Exercise 3.14**  **Tax-effect worksheet with tax rate change**

Accounting profit before tax for Cherry Ltd amounted to $350 000 for the year ended 30 June 20X1. Details of selected expense items included in the total operating costs and charged against revenue to determine accounting profit are provided below.

| | |
|---|---|
| Depreciation of plant | $30 000 |
| Amortisation of goodwill | 25 000 |
| Legal expenses (not an allowable tax deduction) | 8 000 |

Additional information:

(a) Analysis of the general ledger provision accounts provides the following information:

| | Long service leave | Annual leave | Doubtful debts |
|---|---|---|---|
| | $ | $ | $ |
| Balance 1 July 20X0 | 30 000 | 20 000 | 15 000 |
| Increase in provision | 35 000 | 15 000 | 5 000 |
| | 65 000 | 35 000 | 20 000 |
| Paid during year | 20 000 | 15 000 | – |
| Balance 30 June 20X1 | $45 000 | $20 000 | $20 000 |

ORPORATE ACCOUNTING IN AUSTRALIA

(b) The balances in the Provision for Deferred Income Tax and the Future Income Tax Benefit accounts at 30 June 20X0 were $12 000 and $28 000 respectively.

(c) The company income tax rate was reduced from 40% to 35% during the year ended 30 June 20X1, but no entry had yet been made to accounting profit to adjust for this change.

(d) Depreciation for tax purposes was $60 000.

*Required*

1  Prepare a tax-effect worksheet and the relevant journal entries for the year, including an entry to adjust the accounts to reflect the new company tax rate.

2  Illustrate in T-account format the entries in the Provision for Deferred Tax and Future Income Tax Benefit accounts.

3  Prepare the profit and loss statement for the year ended 30 June 20X1.

**Exercise 3.15**  **Tax loss and virtual certainty — single year**

For the year ended 30 June 20X1, Michelson Ltd recorded an accounting loss of $70 000 after receipt of exempt income of $24 600. The loss was calculated after inclusion of the following expense items:

|  | Accounting expense | Allowable deduction |
|---|---|---|
|  | $ | $ |
| Depreciation on plant | 16 800 | 28 400 |
| Doubtful debts | 8 000 | 10 000 |
| Long service leave | 12 000 | 7 200 |
| Goodwill | 9 000 |  |

The company tax rate is 33%.

*Required*

Prepare a tax-effect worksheet and relevant journal entries for the year ended 30 June 20X1. Assume that Michelson's tax losses are virtually certain of realisation in the future.

**Exercise 3.16**  **Tax losses, virtual certainty, multiple periods and disclosure**

Aqua Ltd has the following history of accounting profits:

| Year ended 30 June | Profit/(Loss) |
|---|---|
|  | $ |
| 20X2 | (50 000) |
| 20X3 | 25 000 |
| 20X4 | 30 000 |

In each of the above years, the company recognised goodwill amortisation of $10 000 per annum. Aqua Ltd advised the following tax-effect timing differences:

(a) On 1 July 20X1 an item of equipment was purchased for $60 000. For accounting purposes the straight-line method is used. The useful life is estimated to be four years and the residual value zero. The equipment is depreciated at 50% prime cost for tax purposes.

(b) Aqua Ltd makes a provision for deferred maintenance expenses. A summary of the transactions to the provision account is provided:

|  | 20X2 $ | 20X3 $ | 20X4 $ |
|---|---|---|---|
| Beginning balance | 40 000 | 20 000 | 30 000 |
| Increase in provision | 15 000 | 20 000 | 20 000 |
|  | 55 000 | 40 000 | 50 000 |
| Warranty expenses | 35 000 | 10 000 | – |
| Ending balance | $20 000 | $30 000 | $50 000 |

The company tax rate is 40%.

*Required*

1  Prepare a tax-effect worksheet and journal entries for each of the years ending 30 June 20X2, 20X3 and 20X4. Assume virtual certainty of recovery of tax losses.
2  What additional information about the future income tax benefit should Aqua Ltd disclose in each of the three years (AASB 1020, para .13)? Assume the balance of FITB as at 1 July 20X1 was $10 000.

**Exercise 3.17**  **Tax losses, uncertainty, treatment of FITB, multiple periods**
Refer to Exercise 3.16. For this exercise, assume:

(a) At the end of the 20X2 financial year the directors of Aqua were doubtful whether the company would be able to generate sufficient profits to recoup the tax loss in future years. The existing balance in the FITB account relates to timing differences associated with the provision for deferred maintenance which have not been reversed.
(b) The purchase of the equipment on 1 July 20X1 had not taken place. Therefore, Aqua will not have an existing provision for deferred income tax, as all other timing differences relating to depreciable assets had reversed.

*Required*
Prepare a tax-effect worksheet and journal entries for each of the years ending 30 June 20X2, 20X3 and 20X4.

**Exercise 3.18**  **Tax losses, uncertainty, treatment of PDIT, multiple periods**
The following tax-effect reconciliations were extracted from the 20X2 and 20X3 work papers for Fast Ltd.

|  | 20X2 $ | 20X3 $ |
|---|---|---|
| Accounting profit | (65 000) | 25 000 |
| **Permanent difference** |  |  |
| Amortisation of goodwill | 15 000 | – |
| **Accounting profit adjustment for permanent differences** | (50 000) | 25 000 |
| **Timing differences** |  |  |
| Amortisation of research & development costs | 20 000 | 20 000 |
| Tax loss recovered |  | (30 000) |
| **Taxable income** | $(30 000) | $15 000 |

A provision for deferred income tax was created when expenditure of $100 000 for research and development was capitalised at 30 June 20X0. The capitalised research and development expenditure is amortised to accounting expenses evenly over the next five-year period.

All other timing differences of Fast Ltd have been reversed; therefore, the balance in the Provision for Deferred Income Tax account relates only to the treatment of the research and development expenditure.

At the financial year end in 20X2 the directors of Fast Ltd believed there was a possibility that the tax loss would be recouped in future years, but they were not sufficiently confident to claim virtual certainty. The company tax rate is 40%.

*Required*
Prepare the tax-effect journal entries for 20X2 and 20X3.

chapter

*4*

ACQUISITION OF ASSETS

# introduction

When a company acquires an individual asset, the accounting treatment is usually straightforward. For example, when purchasing items such as furniture or equipment for cash consideration, a debit to the relevant asset account and a credit to the cash account are the only entries required to record the transaction. However, complications can arise when it is a group of assets, perhaps representing an existing business operation or entity, that is acquired or where another company is indirectly acquired by purchasing a controlling interest in its issued share capital. Further complications can arise where consideration comprises an issue of shares or the transfer of assets other than cash.

AASB 1015: Accounting for the Acquisition of Assets and AAS 21: Accounting for the Acquisition of Assets (including Business Entities) discuss the accounting principles applicable to the acquisition of assets. These standards aim to ensure that the economic substance of the exchange transactions leading to an acquisition of assets is reflected in the accounts (AASB 1015, para .03). An acquisition of assets means 'undertaking the risks, and receiving the rights to future benefits, as would be conferred with ownership, in exchange for valuable consideration' (AASB 1015, para .06). Hence, the standard does not apply to situations involving the receipt of assets involving no cost of acquisition – for example, by donation, gift or bequest.

In addition to AASB 1015, the provisions of AASB 1013/AAS 18: Accounting for Goodwill are applicable to circumstances involving the acquisition of another entity where the cost of acquisition is greater or less than the fair value of the identifiable net assets acquired. Further, if the acquisition results in control and a parent entity–subsidiary entity relationship, the provisions of AASB 1024: Consolidated Accounts and AAS 24: Consolidated Financial Reports will apply. If acquisition results in the acquirer gaining not control but significant influence over the associated company, the provisions of AASB 1016: Disclosure of Information about Investments in Associated Companies and AAS 14: Equity Method of Accounting will apply. These latter standards will be discussed in later chapters.

# Date and cost of acquisition

AASB 1015, para .10 requires acquired assets to be recorded at cost of acquisition as at the date of acquisition. The date of acquisition is 'the date on which the risks and rights to future benefits, as would be conferred with ownership, pass to the acquiring company', while the cost of acquisition 'means the purchase consideration plus any costs incidental to the acquisition' (AASB 1015, para .06).

Purchase consideration is defined as 'the fair value of assets given or share capital issued, liabilities undertaken, and other securities given by the purchaser, in exchange for assets (net where applicable) or shares of another entity' (AASB 1015, para .06). The important aspect of this definition is that the cost of any acquisition is calculated by reference to the value of the consideration given up by the company, rather than by determining the value of the assets received in exchange. Also, incidental costs of acquisition are to be added to the purchase consideration in determining the total acquisition cost. Examples given in AASB 1015 of costs that relate directly to acquisition are legal fees, stamp duty and other government charges, and professional fees in the nature of feasibility tests and investigations preceding an acquisition (commentary, para (xi)).

AASB 1015 notes that purchase consideration may include cash, other monetary assets, non-monetary assets, securities issued or liabilities undertaken (or any combination of these), and requires that the purchase consideration be valued at fair value as at the date of acquisition (commentary, paras (vi) to (viii)). Fair value is defined in both AASB 1013, para 13.1 and AASB 1015, para .06 as 'the amount for which an asset could be exchanged between a knowledgeable, willing buyer and a knowledgeable, willing seller in an arm's length transaction'. Any incidental costs such as transfer fees, registration fees, or any applicable brokerage, underwriting, or other costs of issuing securities or liabilities representing purchase consideration should be included in the cost of acquisition. It is important to determine the acquisition's cost as at the date of acquisition to ensure the economic reality of the acquisition transaction is properly reflected in the financial statements.

# Acquisition of a single asset

The recording of the purchase of a single asset is relatively straightforward, in that the asset is recorded at its individual cost of acquisition as at the date of acquisition. As an example of a simple acquisition, consider a situation involving the purchase of a new motor vehicle by ABC Ltd for cash consideration of $59 200. This consideration comprises the base cost of the vehicle ($55 000), dealer delivery charges ($700), stamp duty ($2500), registration ($450) and insurance ($550). In recording this acquisition, ABC must distinguish between items which represent incidental costs of purchase (to be included in the cost of the vehicle) and those which represent expense items. In this example, the dealer delivery charges and stamp duty represent incidental costs of purchase, whereas registration and insurance represent annual running costs to be expensed. To record the acquisition, ABC would record the following journal entry (shown in general journal format).

|  | Debit | Credit |
|---|---|---|
| Motor Vehicle (asset) | 58 200 | |
| Registration (expense) | 450 | |
| Insurance (expense) | 550 | |
| Cash at Bank | | 59 200 |
| (acquisition of motor vehicle) | | |

Consider an identical situation to that above with the exception that part of the purchase consideration involves the trade-in of a truck. The truck has a written-down value as at date of acquisition of the new vehicle of $20 000 ($40 000 cost less $20 000 accumulated depreciation). ABC is allowed a trade-in allowance of $25 000, this being the fair value of the truck. The balance of the consideration, $34 200, is in the form of cash. As recording of the acquisition of the new vehicle must recognise the fair value of the purchase consideration, a $5000 profit on trade-in of the truck must be recognised. That is, it is not appropriate to consider the cost of the new motor vehicle as amounting to $53 200 (the $20 000 written-down value of the trade-in plus the cash consideration, net of registration and insurance, of $33 200), as this would not represent the fair value of the purchase consideration. To record the acquisition of the new vehicle, the following journal entry would be recorded.

|  | Debit | Credit |
|---|---|---|
| Motor Vehicle | 58 200 | |
| Registration | 450 | |
| Insurance | 550 | |
| Accumulated Depreciation – Truck | 20 000 | |
| Truck | | 40 000 |
| Profit on Disposal | | 5 000 |
| Cash at Bank | | 34 200 |
| (acquisition of motor vehicle) | | |

# Acquisition of multiple assets (not being a business entity)

A further issue which arises concerning the acquisition of assets is the method of recording a single transaction involving the acquisition of multiple assets. AASB 1015 requires that, where more than one asset is acquired (and that acquisition does not constitute the acquisition of a business entity), the aggregate acquisition cost should be apportioned to the individual assets acquired in proportion to their fair values as at the date of acquisition (commentary, para (xii)). For example, consider that, for cash consideration of $60 000, a company acquires three items of office equipment. The fair values for each of the individual items are assessed at $28 000, $24 000 and $12 000 respectively (ie $64 000 in total). The following calculation illustrates the apportionment of the $60 000 total cost of acquisition to each of the individual items.

| | Fair value of assets acquired | Proportion of fair value | Apportionment of cost of acquisition |
|---|---|---|---|
| | $ | % | $ |
| Item A | 28 000 | 43.75 | 26 250 |
| Item B | 24 000 | 37.50 | 22 500 |
| Item C | 12 000 | 18.75 | 11 250 |
| | $64 000 | 100.00 | $60 000 |

The journal entry to record the acquisition would therefore appear as follows:

| | Debit | Credit |
|---|---|---|
| Office Equipment – Item A | 26 250 | |
| Office Equipment – Item B | 22 500 | |
| Office Equipment – Item C | 11 250 | |
| Cash at Bank | | 60 000 |
| (acquisition of office equipment) | | |

# Alternative forms of consideration

As noted earlier, the purchase consideration for the acquisition of an asset may be in the form of cash, other monetary assets, non-monetary assets, securities issued or liabilities undertaken, or any combination of these. In many cases the fair value of these forms of consideration will be obvious or readily determinable. However, in other cases, some degree of judgment and estimation will be required. The general principles are outlined below.

- **Cash and other monetary assets**
  In the case of cash consideration, the determination of fair value does not present any problems. For other monetary assets, the fair value will usually be readily determinable as the equivalent amount of cash foregone. For example, if all or part of the consideration for an acquisition involves the assignment of amounts due from the company's debtors, the fair value would be the amount that would have been received from those debtors. Where all or part of any cash settlement is deferred, Urgent Issues Group Abstract 6: Accounting for Acquisitions — Deferred Settlement of Cash Consideration requires the future amount payable to be discounted to present value as at the date of acquisition.

- **Non-monetary assets**
  Non-monetary assets include items such as inventory, investments, plant and equipment, land and buildings, and trademarks and patents. AASB 1015 states that the fair value of non-monetary assets needs to be ascertained by reference to existing markets for such assets (commentary, para (viii)). In the case of assets such as motor vehicles or listed share investments where active markets exist, fair value can be readily determined. In other cases where an active market does not exist, it may be possible to estimate fair value by reference to markets for similar items. For example, it may be possible to estimate the fair value of a rare historic building on the basis of recent sale prices of historic buildings in other geographical locations. Alternatively, it may be necessary to engage experts such

as registered valuers to obtain valuations for specific assets. This could particularly be required for unique intangible assets such as licences, trademarks, copyrights and patents.

- **Securities issued**

  A company may issue equity securities, such as ordinary or preference shares, in consideration for an acquisition of assets. If the company's shares are listed on a stock exchange, then the prevailing market price can serve as a starting point for the determination of fair value. If a large number of shares are issued in consideration, the current market price may require discounting to determine fair value, reflecting the fact that any large new issue may have to be made at a price below current market value to induce investors to subscribe for the shares. If the company's shares are unlisted, the use of an expert valuer or financial valuation techniques may be required to estimate fair value.

- **Liabilities undertaken**

  A company may issue debt securities, such as debentures or unsecured notes, or incur other liabilities in consideration for an acquisition. The liability incurred may be in the form of a loan owing to the entity from which the assets are acquired or may involve taking over loan repayments or other debts of the vendor. The fair value will often be the face value of the debt security issued or the liability undertaken. However, an adjustment for such factors as current market interest rates may be required in other cases to establish fair value.

## ILLUSTRATIVE EXAMPLE 4.1

## COST OF ACQUISITION

DEF Ltd, a listed public company, acquires plant and equipment from Seller Pty Ltd. In consideration, DEF issues 100 000 new shares in the company to Seller. DEF's shares, at the date of acquisition, were trading on the Australian Stock Exchange at $1.10 per share. DEF incurs solicitor's legal costs of $1500 for the issue of these new shares. In further consideration, DEF also agrees to transfer to Seller 50 000 shares it holds in Radmill Ltd, another listed public company. Radmill shares, as at the date of acquisition, were trading at a price of $1.50 per share. These shares had originally cost DEF $1.20 each. DEF also agrees to reimburse Seller the amount of $2500 for brokerage and stamp duty payable on the transfer of the Radmill shares.

In the above situation, the cost of acquisition of the plant and equipment amounts to $189 000, calculated as follows:

|  | $ | $ |
|---|---|---|
| *Purchase consideration* | | |
| New shares issued – 100 000 × $1.10 | 110 000 | |
| Shares in Radmill Ltd – 50 000 × $1.50 | 75 000 | 185 000 |
| *Incidental costs* | | |
| Legal costs applicable to new share issue | 1 500 | |
| Cash reimbursement to Seller Ltd | 2 500 | 4 000 |
| Cost of acquisition | | $189 000 |

To record the acquisition, DEF would post the following journal entry.

| | Debit $ | Credit $ |
|---|---|---|
| Plant & Equipment | 189 000 | |
| Paid-up Capital | | 110 000 |
| Shares in Radmill (at cost) | | 60 000 |
| Profit on Sale of Radmill Shares | | 15 000 |
| Creditor – Solicitor's Costs | | 1 500 |
| Cash at Bank (reimbursement to Seller) | | 2 500 |
| (acquisition of plant and equipment) | | |

# Direct acquisition of assets or net assets of an existing entity

direct acquisition

indirect acquisition

The principles for asset acquisition discussed in the chapter to this point have related to single assets or to multiple assets not constituting a business entity. The third category of asset acquisition recognised by AASB 1015, for which particular rules are specified, is the acquisition of an entire entity or part of an entity. The acquisition of assets or net assets of an entity directly is outlined in this section, while the situation of an indirect acquisition of a corporate entity or part thereof, through the purchase of that entity's equity, is discussed in the following section.

In the case of the purchase of an entity or part of an entity, the same general principles as outlined previously apply when determining the cost of acquisition. That is, the cost of acquisition is calculated as at the date of acquisition by reference to the fair value of the purchase consideration plus any incidental costs. The potential complicating factor arising is that the total cost of acquisition relates to an entire bundle or package of assets. Hence, the individual assets acquired must be valued for recording purposes at their separate costs.

## GOODWILL

goodwill

The assets acquired may be identifiable assets such as cash at bank, debtors, inventory, plant and equipment, land and buildings, and trademarks and patents. However, the acquiring company may be prepared to pay more than the fair value of the identifiable assets when acquiring the net assets of an existing entity due to such factors as the established customer base, operations and market share of the entity, or the synergistic benefits which the acquiring company believes will flow from the acquisition. These unidentifiable assets are termed purchased goodwill. Goodwill is defined in AASB 1013, para 13.1 and AASB 1015, para .06 as 'the future benefits from unidentifiable assets'. Provided certain conditions specified in AASB 1013 are met, the purchased goodwill is recorded as a non-current asset in the books of the acquiring company.

AASB 1015, para .20 requires any goodwill on acquisition to be 'determined and brought to account in accordance with the requirements of AASB 1013: Accounting for Goodwill'. AASB 1013 requires the identifiable net assets of the entity acquired to be measured at their fair value (para 5.6). Fair value, as defined earlier, is the amount for which the assets could be exchanged between knowledgeable, willing buyers and sellers in an arm's length transaction. Goodwill is the amount by which the total cost of acquisition incurred by the company exceeds the fair value of the identifiable net assets acquired, provided it is considered that future benefits will arise from the unidentifiable asset. AASB 1013 requires goodwill to be brought to account as a non-current asset in the books of the acquiring company (para 5.1). If the excess of the cost of acquisition over the fair value of the identifiable net assets acquired is not considered to constitute goodwill (that is, if it is considered that future benefits will not arise from this amount), the difference must be recognised immediately as an expense in the profit and loss account (AASB 1013, para 5.8).

## ILLUSTRATIVE EXAMPLE 4.2

# PURCHASED GOODWILL

GFG Ltd purchases the net assets of HGH Ltd for cash consideration of $800 000 on 30 June 20X1. The identifiable net assets acquired, valued at fair value at date of acquisition, comprise the following:

|  | $ | $ |
|---|---|---|
| *Assets acquired* | | |
| Cash on deposit | 30 000 | |
| Debtors | 75 000 | |
| Inventory | 100 000 | |
| Plant & equipment | 200 000 | |
| Land & buildings | 400 000 | |
| Patents | 100 000 | 905 000 |
| *Liabilities acquired* | | |
| Creditors | 65 000 | |
| Bank loan | 140 000 | 205 000 |
| *Net assets acquired (fair value)* | | $700 000 |

We have assumed that GFG is willing to pay $800 000 for the net assets of HGH. This suggests GFG is willing to pay $100 000 more than the fair value of the identifiable net assets, as it believes that future benefits from unidentifiable assets (goodwill) also exist, stemming from the fact that it is acquiring the assets of an existing entity. The goodwill acquired in this situation ($100 000) is calculated as the cost of acquisition ($800 000) less the fair value of the net assets acquired ($700 000). The following journal entry would be required on 30 June 20X1 to record the acquisition.

|  | Debit $ | Credit $ |
|---|---|---|
| Cash on Deposit | 30 000 | |
| Debtors | 75 000 | |
| Inventory | 100 000 | |
| Plant & Equipment | 200 000 | |
| Land & Buildings | 400 000 | |
| Patents | 100 000 | |
| Goodwill | 100 000 | |
| Creditors | | 65 000 |
| Bank Loan | | 140 000 |
| Cash at Bank (cost of acquisition) | | 800 000 |
| (acquisition of net assets of HGH Ltd) | | |

## ACCOUNTING FOR GOODWILL SUBSEQUENT TO ACQUISITION

Once the $100 000 has been recorded by GFG in the accounts as a non-current asset, the question arises as to the subsequent accounting treatment for this purchased goodwill. AASB 1013 requires purchased goodwill to be amortised to the profit and loss account on a straight-line basis (ie an equal amount each period) over the period of time during which benefits are expected to arise, subject to a maximum amortisation period of 20 years (para 5.2). Assuming that GFG believes the benefits of the goodwill will arise over a ten-year period, the following journal entry will be required at 30 June 20X2 (and, assuming no change in circumstances, for each of the following nine years).

amortisation
straight-line method

|  | Debit | Credit |
|---|---|---|
| Amortisation of Goodwill (expense) | 10 000 | |
| Accumulated Amortisation | | 10 000 |
| (annual goodwill amortisation) | | |

The AASB 1013 requirement for straight-line amortisation has been subject to some controversy and debate. Prior to 1 July 1996, the operative date for the straight-line amortisation requirement, goodwill was to be systematically amortised over the expected period of benefits, subject to the 20-year maximum. Using the systematic amortisation requirement, a number of companies employed methods such as the inverted sum of the years' digits method under which a smaller portion of goodwill was amortised in the earlier years, hence having less of an impact on the net profit figure.[1] The requirement for straight-line amortisation was introduced to disallow this practice.

AASB 1013 requires the unamortised balance of goodwill to be reviewed at each reporting date and expensed to profit and loss to the extent that future benefits are no longer probable (para 5.4). Purchased goodwill cannot be revalued in any other way (para 5.5). Returning to the GFG example, the unamortised balance of goodwill as at 30 June 20X3 (ie two years after acquisition) will amount to $80 000 (calculated as $100 000 cost less $20 000 accumulated amortisation). If GFG believes at that point in time that $30 000 of the future benefits are no longer probable, the following journal entry will be required to record the write-off.

|  | Debit | Credit |
|---|---|---|
| Goodwill Write-off (expense) | 30 000 | |
| Goodwill | | 30 000 |
| (goodwill write-off) | | |

The unamortised balance of goodwill at 30 June 20X3 will then amount to $50 000. If the original ten-year amortisation period continues to be considered appropriate, the annual amortisation charge commencing in the year ending 30 June 20X4 will become $6250 (ie $50 000 amortised over the remaining eight years). The unamortised balance of goodwill at 30 June 20X4 will then amount to $43 750.

AASB 1013 also requires the time period over which goodwill is to be amortised to be reviewed at each reporting date (para 5.3). If necessary, the time period should be adjusted to reflect the amount and timing of expected future benefits (but still subject to the 20-year maximum period). In the GFG example, assume that an assessment is made at 30 June 20X5 that the benefits from the goodwill will only arise over an eight-year period rather than over the ten years originally estimated. Hence, the $43 750 unamortised goodwill balance as at 30 June 20X4 will be amortised over a further five years following this review (ie $8750 per annum).

To summarise the above circumstances and reassessments, the following table indicates the accounting periods in which GFG charges the $100 000 goodwill on acquisition to profit and loss.

| Year ended | Opening balance $ | Annual amortisation $ | Write-off $ | Closing balance $ |
|---|---|---|---|---|
| 30/6/X1 | – | – | – | 100 000 |
| 30/6/X2 | 100 000 | (10 000) | – | 90 000 |
| 30/6/X3 | 90 000 | (10 000) | (30 000) | 50 000 |
| 30/6/X4 | 50 000 | (6 250) | – | 43 750 |
| 30/6/X5 | 43 750 | (8 750) | – | 35 000 |
| 30/6/X6 | 35 000 | (8 750) | – | 26 250 |
| 30/6/X7 | 26 250 | (8 750) | – | 17 500 |
| 30/6/X8 | 17 500 | (8 750) | – | 8 750 |
| 30/6/X9 | 8 750 | (8 750) | – | – |
| | | $(70 000) | $(30 000) | |

## DISCOUNT ON ACQUISITION

In contrast to the goodwill situation, it is possible in some circumstances for the total cost of an acquisition to be less than the fair value of the identifiable net assets acquired. Such a purchase involves discount on acquisition. AASB 1013 defines **discount on acquisition** as 'the saving or allowance in the cost of acquisition that flows to the purchaser on acquiring shares or other identifiable net assets at less than their fair value' (para 13.1). Discount on acquisition may represent a bargain purchase, perhaps because the selling entity wishes to realise the value of its assets quickly in a single sale transaction. Alternately, the discount may reflect such factors as 'compensation in anticipation of temporary future losses or inadequate future profits' (AASB 1013, para 8.1.1).

To recognise the discount, AASB 1013 requires the fair values of the non-monetary assets acquired to be reduced proportionately until the discount is eliminated (para 8.1). If the non-monetary assets' values are decreased to zero and a discount on acquisition still remains, this remaining balance must be recognised as an item of revenue in the profit and loss account. Non-monetary assets are not defined in AASB 1013. However, a separate statement, SAP 1: Current Cost Accounting, defines non-monetary assets as 'all assets which are not monetary assets' (para 49). Monetary assets comprise cash and other claims of a fixed monetary amount, including money on deposit, accounts receivable, bills receivable and prepayments. Examples of non-monetary assets include investments in listed shares, inventory, plant and equipment, land and buildings, and intangibles.

ILLUSTRATIVE EXAMPLE **4.3**

# DISCOUNT ON ACQUISITION

We will return to GFG Ltd's acquisition of the net assets of HGH Ltd depicted in Illustrative example 4.2, but now assume that the total cost of acquisition is $650 000 rather than $800 000. It will be recalled that the fair values of the net assets acquired at the date of acquisition were as follows:

|  | $ | $ |
|---|---|---|
| *Assets acquired* | | |
| Cash on deposit | 30 000 | |
| Debtors | 75 000 | |
| Inventory | 100 000 | |
| Plant & equipment | 200 000 | |
| Land & buildings | 400 000 | |
| Patents | 100 000 | 905 000 |
| *Liabilities acquired* | | |
| Creditors | 65 000 | |
| Bank loan | 140 000 | 205 000 |
| Net assets acquired (fair value) | | $700 000 |

In this case, the discount on acquisition amounts to $50 000, calculated as the amount by which the fair value of the identifiable net assets ($700 000) exceeds the cost of acquisition ($650 000). The non-monetary assets in this example comprise inventory, plant and equipment, land and buildings, and patents, the fair values of which total $800 000. The table below illustrates how the $50 000 discount on acquisition is allocated to reduce proportionately the fair values of the non-monetary assets from $800 000 to $750 000.

| Non-monetary asset | Fair value $ | Proportion % | Allocation of discount $ | Adjusted cost $ |
|---|---|---|---|---|
| Inventory | 100 000 | 12.5 | (6 250) | 93 750 |
| Plant & equipment | 200 000 | 25.0 | (12 500) | 187 500 |
| Land & buildings | 400 000 | 50.0 | (25 000) | 375 000 |
| Patents | 100 000 | 12.5 | (6 250) | 93 750 |
| | $800 000 | 100.0 | $(50 000) | $750 000 |

The following journal entry would record the acquisition of assets by GFG in this situation. This entry results in the monetary assets and liabilities being recorded at their monetary value, while the non-monetary assets are stated at their adjusted cost, as calculated above.

| | Debit $ | Credit $ |
|---|---|---|
| Cash on Deposit | 30 000 | |
| Debtors | 75 000 | |
| Inventory | 93 750 | |
| Plant & Equipment | 187 500 | |
| Land & Buildings | 375 000 | |
| Patents | 93 750 | |
| Creditors | | 65 000 |
| Bank Loan | | 140 000 |
| Cash at Bank (cost of acquisition) | | 650 000 |
| (acquisition of net assets of HGH Ltd) | | |

## DISCLOSURE REQUIREMENTS

Where a company acquires an entity, or part of an entity, through acquisition of its assets, AASB 1015, para .40 requires, for material acquisitions, the following to be disclosed:

- name of the entity acquired;
- date of acquisition;
- cost of acquisition; and
- description of purchase consideration, including any contingent consideration and the proposed accounting treatment thereof.

# Indirect acquisition by purchase of an entity's shares

Rather than acquiring another entity by purchasing its assets and liabilities directly, it is possible to gain control of a corporate entity by purchasing its entire issued share capital or a controlling interest in its share capital. That is, the equity of the company, rather than its individual assets and liabilities, can be acquired. This is achieved by purchasing the shares held by the individual shareholders. This may involve acquiring shares from a small number of shareholders holding all or a substantial proportion of the company's issued shares, or it may involve purchasing shares from a large number of shareholders (possibly thousands, in the case of a large public company). The object is to acquire a large enough proportion of the issued shares to gain control of the target company. In a broad sense, control means 'the capacity of an entity to dominate decision-making, directly or indirectly, in relation to the financial and operating policies of another entity so as to enable that other entity to operate with it in pursuing the objectives of the controlling entity' (AASB 1024, para 9). This is usually achieved by gaining sufficient voting power to be able to dominate the composition of the board of directors or the casting of a majority of the votes at a meeting of the board of directors or a company general meeting. It should be noted, though, that it may be possible to gain control with less than a majority of the issued share capital of a company. This will particularly be the case where the issued shares are widely dispersed over a large number of shareholders.

In the case of an indirect acquisition by purchase of an entity's shares, it is not necessary to identify and record the individual assets and liabilities acquired for the purpose of recording the acquisition. The investment in the company's shares is simply recorded at cost price, being the fair value of the purchase consideration plus any incidental costs (such as brokerage and stamp duty). This accounting treatment for recording the acquisition of shares means that there is no attempt to recognise any goodwill or discount on acquisition implicit in the transaction. This is because there is only one asset, the shares themselves, being acquired. The purchase consideration, plus any incidental costs, therefore represents the cost of acquisition for the purpose of recording the purchase of the shares.

**control**

However, we will see in the following chapters that any goodwill or discount on acquisition implicit in the purchase of shares will be relevant where it is necessary for consolidated, or group, accounts to be prepared. AASB 1013, para 9.1 states:

> On acquisition of a subsidiary, the accounting treatment for goodwill which is purchased by the entity (including any amortisation thereof) and discount on acquisition must be effected as an adjustment in the consolidated accounts and not in the subsidiary's or parent entity's accounts.

Consolidated accounts involve combining the accounts of each of the entities comprising an economic entity. An economic entity means a group of entities made up of the parent (holding) entity and any subsidiary (controlled) entities. The consolidated financial statements present the accounts of the group, comprising two or more entities, as one aggregated set of financial statements. However, consolidation is not simply a case of adding together the individual accounts of the entities comprising the group. In aggregating the accounts of the individual entities, various adjustments are required.

While the accounting concepts involved in the preparation of consolidated accounts are relatively detailed, it is sufficient to reiterate at this point that the initial recording of an acquisition of a company's shares in the books of the acquiring company simply involves recording the single asset account at the cost of acquisition as at the date of acquisition.

## ILLUSTRATIVE EXAMPLE 4.4

# INDIRECT ACQUISITION

JGG Ltd, a listed public company, wishes to acquire the business operations of KMM Pty Ltd. KMM has four shareholders, each of whom holds 25% of the company's issues shares. These shareholders, each owning 2000 shares, agree to sell their shares to JGG. The terms of the sale are that each KMM share will be exchanged for two JGG shares plus $20 cash. JGG incurs legal costs of $1000 for the issue of the new shares and stamp duty of $500 on the transfer of the KMM shares. JGG shares are trading on the Australian Stock Exchange at a price of $12.50 each on the date of acquisition.

In this example, the cash portion of the purchase consideration amounts to $160 000 (ie 8000 KMM issued shares multiplied by $20 per share). The share portion of the purchase consideration will involve JGG issuing 16 000 shares to the KMM shareholders (ie two JGG shares for each of KMM's issued shares). For the purpose of determining the cost of acquisition, each of these JGG shares must be valued at its fair value of $12.50 as at the date of acquisition, implying a total value of $200 000. The legal costs and stamp duty, representing incidental costs, must also be included in the cost of acquisition. Accordingly, the total cost of acquiring the 8000 KMM shares from the four shareholders amounts to $361 500, calculated as follows:

| *Purchase consideration* | $ | $ |
|---|---|---|
| New shares in JGG issued — 16 000 × $12.50 | 200 000 | |
| Cash — 8 000 × $20.00 | 160 000 | 360 000 |
| *Incidental costs* | | |
| Legal costs applicable to issue of new JGG shares | 1 000 | |
| Stamp duty on transfer of KMM shares | 500 | 1 500 |
| *Cost of acquisition* | | $361 500 |

The following journal entry would be required to record the acquisition.

|  | Debit | Credit |
|---|---|---|
|  | $ | $ |
| Shares in KMM Pty Ltd | 361 500 |  |
| Cash at Bank |  | 160 000 |
| Paid-up Capital |  | 200 000 |
| Accrued Legal Costs |  | 1 000 |
| Accrued Stamp Duty |  | 500 |
| (acquisition of shares in KMM Pty Ltd) |  |  |

The Shares in KMM Pty Ltd account would be classified in JGG's balance sheet as a current or non-current asset, depending on the circumstances. In the majority of cases, acquiring a controlling shareholding in another company would usually represent a long-term investment, suggesting classification as a non-current asset.

## DISCLOSURE REQUIREMENTS

Where a company acquires an investment in a subsidiary, AASB 1015, para .41 requires, for material investments, the following to be disclosed:
- name of the company acquired;
- date of acquisition;
- cost of acquisition;
- description of purchase consideration, including any contingent consideration and the proposed accounting treatment thereof;
- percentage of voting shares acquired; and
- date from which operating results of acquired subsidiary are included in the profit and loss account.

# A comprehensive example

This section provides a comprehensive example of the acquisition of an existing entity. The example involves Investor Ltd acquiring the net assets of Seller Pty Ltd and illustrates alternative scenarios involving (a) direct acquisition of the net assets involving goodwill on acquisition, (b) direct acquisition of the net assets involving discount on acquisition, and (c) indirect acquisition by purchase of shares in Seller Pty Ltd.

## DIRECT ACQUISITION

### Goodwill

The balance sheet of Investor Ltd immediately prior to the acquisition of the net assets of Seller Pty Ltd is shown on the following page.

**Investor Ltd**
**Balance Sheet as at 1 January 20X2**

| Assets | $ | Liabilities | $ | $ |
|---|---|---|---|---|
| Cash at bank | 10 000 | Creditors | 90 000 | |
| Debtors | 65 000 | Provisions | 10 000 | |
| Inventory | 80 000 | Bank loans | 355 000 | 455 000 |
| Investments (cost) | 100 000 | | | |
| Art collection (cost) | 40 000 | Shareholders' equity | | |
| Plant & equipment (net) | 350 000 | Paid-up capital | 500 000 | |
| Land & buildings (net) | 450 000 | Retained earnings | 140 000 | 640 000 |
| | $1 095 000 | | | $1 095 000 |

The identifiable net assets of Seller Pty Ltd acquired by Investor Ltd, valued at fair value at the date of acquisition, comprise the following:

| | $ | $ |
|---|---|---|
| Assets acquired | | |
| Debtors | 10 000 | |
| Inventory | 25 000 | |
| Plant & equipment | 100 000 | |
| Land & buildings | 200 000 | 335 000 |
| Liabilities acquired | | |
| Bank overdraft | 30 000 | |
| Creditors | 40 000 | 70 000 |
| Net assets acquired (fair value) | | $265 000 |

The following outlines the terms of the acquisition.

- Cash consideration amounting to $140 000 is to be paid to Seller Pty Ltd. This amount is to be raised by way of a new bank loan.
- The investments owned by Investor Ltd, which have a fair market value of $90 000, are to be transferred to Seller Pty Ltd.
- The art collection held by Investor Ltd, which has a fair market value of $70 000, is also to be transferred to Seller Pty Ltd.
- Investor Ltd incurs solicitor's costs of $3000. These are to be paid immediately from the company's existing cash balances.

Under the above scenario, the cost of acquisition of the net assets of Seller Pty Ltd amounts to $303 000, calculated as follows:

| | $ | $ |
|---|---|---|
| Purchase consideration | | |
| Cash | 140 000 | |
| Investments (fair market value) | 90 000 | |
| Art collection (fair market value) | 70 000 | 300 000 |
| Incidental costs | | |
| Solicitor's costs | | 3 000 |
| Cost of acquisition | | $303 000 |

Goodwill in this situation amounts to $38 000, calculated as the cost of acquisition ($303 000) less the fair value of the identifiable net assets acquired ($265 000). Also to be recorded is a loss on disposal of the investments amounting to $10 000 ($100 000 cost less $90 000 fair value) and a profit on disposal of the art collection of $30 000 ($70 000 fair value less $40 000 cost).

To record the above fact situation, Investor Ltd would record the following journal entries (shown in general journal format).

| | Debit $ | Credit $ |
|---|---|---|
| Cash at Bank | 140 000 | |
|   Bank Loan | | 140 000 |
| (proceeds from bank loan) | | |
| | | |
| Debtors | 10 000 | |
| Inventory | 25 000 | |
| Plant & Equipment | 100 000 | |
| Land & Buildings | 200 000 | |
| Goodwill | 38 000 | |
| Loss on Disposal of Investments | 10 000 | |
|   Bank Overdraft | | 30 000 |
|   Creditors | | 40 000 |
|   Cash at Bank | | 140 000 |
|   Investments (at cost) | | 100 000 |
|   Art Collection (at cost) | | 40 000 |
|   Profit on Disposal of Art Collection | | 30 000 |
|   Creditor – Solicitor's Costs | | 3 000 |
| (acquisition of net assets from Seller Pty Ltd) | | |
| | | |
| Creditor – Solicitor's Costs | 3 000 | |
|   Cash at Bank | | 3 000 |
| (payment of legal costs) | | |

Immediately after recording the above journal entries related to the acquisition, the balance sheet for Investor Ltd would appear as follows:

**Investor Ltd**
**Balance Sheet (immediately subsequent to acquisition)**

| Assets | $ | Liabilities | $ | $ |
|---|---|---|---|---|
| Cash at bank | 7 000 | Bank overdraft | 30 000 | |
| Debtors | 75 000 | Creditors | 130 000 | |
| Inventory | 105 000 | Provisions | 10 000 | |
| Plant & equipment (net) | 450 000 | Bank loans | 495 000 | 665 000 |
| Land & buildings (net) | 650 000 | *Shareholders' equity* | | |
| Goodwill | 38 000 | Paid-up capital | 500 000 | |
| | | Retained earnings | 160 000 | 660 000 |
| | $1 325 000 | | | $1 325 000 |

Examination of the balance sheet subsequent to acquisition reveals that the assets and liabilities acquired from Seller Pty Ltd, including the goodwill of $38 000, have now been included in Investor Ltd's balance sheet, together with the new bank loan of $140 000. The retained earnings figure, amounting to $160 000, comprises the opening balance of $140 000, the loss on disposal of the investments of $10 000 and the profit on disposal of the art collection of $30 000.

## Discount on acquisition

Assume the same facts as outlined above with the exception that the cash portion of the consideration, to be raised by the new bank loan, amounts to $90 000 instead of $140 000. In this situation, the cost of acquisition of the net assets of Seller Ltd amounts to $253 000, calculated as follows:

|  | $ | $ |
| --- | --- | --- |
| *Purchase consideration* | | |
| Cash | 90 000 | |
| Investments (fair market value) | 90 000 | |
| Art collection (fair market value) | 70 000 | 250 000 |
| *Incidental costs* | | |
| Solicitor's costs | | 3 000 |
| *Cost of acquisition* | | $253 000 |

Discount on acquisition in this case amounts to $12 000, calculated as the amount by which the fair value of the identifiable net assets acquired ($265 000) exceeds the cost of acquisition ($253 000). The non-monetary assets acquired from Seller Pty Ltd comprise inventory, plant and equipment, and land and buildings. The table below illustrates how the $12 000 discount on acquisition is allocated to reduce proportionately the fair values of the non-monetary assets acquired.

| Non-monetary asset | Fair value | Proportion | Allocation of discount | Adjusted cost |
| --- | --- | --- | --- | --- |
| | $ | % | $ | $ |
| Inventory | 25 000 | 7.69 | (923) | 24 077 |
| Plant & equipment | 100 000 | 30.77 | (3 692) | 96 308 |
| Land & buildings | 200 000 | 61.54 | (7 385) | 192 615 |
| | $325 000 | 100.00 | $(12 000) | $313 000 |

To record the above situation, Investor Ltd would record the following journal entries.

|  | Debit $ | Credit $ |
|---|---|---|
| Cash at Bank | 90 000 | |
|    Bank Loan | | 90 000 |
| (proceeds from bank loan) | | |
| | | |
| Debtors | 10 000 | |
| Inventory | 24 077 | |
| Plant & Equipment | 96 308 | |
| Land & Buildings | 192 615 | |
| Loss on Disposal of Investments | 10 000 | |
|    Bank Overdraft | | 30 000 |
|    Creditors | | 40 000 |
|    Cash at Bank | | 90 000 |
|    Investments (at cost) | | 100 000 |
|    Art Collection (at cost) | | 40 000 |
|    Profit on Disposal of Art Collection | | 30 000 |
|    Creditor – Solicitor's Costs | | 3 000 |
| (acquisition of net assets from Seller Pty Ltd) | | |
| | | |
| Creditor – Solicitor's Costs | 3 000 | |
|    Cash at Bank | | 3 000 |
| (payment of legal costs) | | |

Immediately after recording the above journal entries related to the acquisition, the balance sheet for Investor Ltd would appear as follows:

### Investor Ltd
### Balance Sheet (immediately subsequent to acquisition)

| Assets | $ | Liabilities | $ | $ |
|---|---|---|---|---|
| Cash at bank | 7 000 | Bank overdraft | 30 000 | |
| Debtors | 75 000 | Creditors | 130 000 | |
| Inventory | 104 077 | Provisions | 10 000 | |
| Plant & equipment (net) | 446 308 | Bank loans | 445 000 | 615 000 |
| Land & buildings (net) | 642 615 | Shareholders' equity | | |
| | | Paid-up capital | 500 000 | |
| | | Retained earnings | 160 000 | 660 000 |
| | $1 275 000 | | | $1 275 000 |

## INDIRECT ACQUISITION

Instead of directly acquiring the assets and liabilities, Investor Ltd could gain control of Seller Pty Ltd by acquiring its issued share capital. Assume that Seller Pty Ltd has two shareholders owning 5000 shares each and that both shareholders are willing to sell their shares to Investor Ltd. The terms of the sale are that each Seller Pty Ltd share will be exchanged for three Investor Ltd shares plus $10 cash. The cash portion of the purchase consideration is to be raised by a new bank loan. Investor Ltd also incurs legal costs amounting to $2000 for the issue of the new shares and stamp duty amounting to $400 on the transfer of the Seller Pty Ltd shares. These amounts are paid immediately from the company's cash balances. Investor Ltd is a listed public company, and its shares are trading on the Australian Stock Exchange at a price of $6.10 each on the date of acquisition.

In this example, the cash portion of the purchase consideration amounts to $100 000 (ie 10 000 Seller issued shares multiplied by $10 per share). The share portion of the purchase consideration will involve Investor Ltd issuing 30 000 shares to the Seller Pty Ltd shareholders (ie three Investor shares for each of Seller's 10 000 issued shares). For the purpose of determining the cost of acquisition, each of these Investor shares must be valued at their fair value of $6.10, implying a total value of $183 000 (ie 30 000 shares multiplied by $6.10 per share). The legal costs and stamp duty, representing incidental costs, must also be included in the cost of acquisition. Accordingly, the total cost of acquiring the 10 000 Seller shares from the two shareholders amounts to $285 400, calculated as follows:

|  | $ | $ |
|---|---|---|
| *Purchase consideration* | | |
| New shares in Investor issued | | |
|   – 30 000 × $6.10 | 183 000 | |
| Cash – 10 000 × $10.00 | 100 000 | 283 000 |
| *Incidental costs* | | |
| Legal costs applicable to issue | | |
|   of new Investor shares | 2 000 | |
| Stamp duty on transfer of Seller shares | 400 | 2 400 |
|    *Cost of acquisition* | | $285 400 |

To record the above situation, Investor Ltd would record the following journal entries.

|  | Debit $ | Credit $ |
|---|---|---|
| Cash at Bank | 100 000 | |
|   Bank Loan | | 100 000 |
| (proceeds from bank loan) | | |
| | | |
| Shares in Seller Pty Ltd | 285 400 | |
|   Paid-up Capital | | 183 000 |
|   Cash at Bank | | 100 000 |
|   Accrued Legal Costs | | 2 000 |
|   Accrued Stamp Duty | | 400 |
| (acquisition of shares in Seller Pty Ltd) | | |
| | | |
| Accrued Legal Costs | 2 000 | |
| Accrued Stamp Duty | 400 | |
|   Cash at Bank | | 2 400 |
| (payment of legal costs and stamp duty) | | |

Immediately after recording the above journal entries related to the acquisition, the balance sheet for Investor Ltd would appear as follows:

**Investor Ltd**
**Balance Sheet (immediately subsequent to acquisition)**

| Assets | $ | Liabilities | $ | $ |
|---|---|---|---|---|
| Cash at bank | 7 600 | Creditors | 90 000 | |
| Debtors | 65 000 | Provisions | 10 000 | |
| Inventory | 80 000 | Bank loans | 455 000 | 555 000 |
| Shares in Seller Pty Ltd | 285 400 | | | |
| Investments (cost) | 100 000 | Shareholders' equity | | |
| Art collection (cost) | 40 000 | Paid-up capital | 683 000 | |
| Plant & equipment (net) | 350 000 | Retained earnings | 140 000 | 823 000 |
| Land & buildings (net) | 450 000 | | | |
| | $1 378 000 | | | $1 378 000 |

Examination of the above balance sheet indicates that the assets of Investor Ltd are as they were prior to the acquisition except that the Shares in Seller Pty Ltd account is now included and the bank balance is lower due to payment of the legal costs and stamp duty. On the other side of the balance sheet, the Bank Loan account has increased by the amount of the new loan ($100 000) and the Paid-up Capital account has increased by the fair value of the new shares issued ($183 000).

# Further issues

## POOLING-OF-INTERESTS METHOD

*purchase method*

The accounting treatment for the acquisition of entities outlined in the previous sections is referred to as the cost, or purchase, method. For the direct acquisition of the assets or net assets of an existing entity, the purchase method requires the fair values of all assets and liabilities to be recorded. This requires the fair value of the purchase consideration to be ascertained and any goodwill or discount on acquisition to be taken into account. For indirect acquisitions by purchase of an entity's shares, the investment is valued by reference to the fair value of the purchase consideration.

*pooling-of-interests method*

An alternative accounting treatment to the purchase method is the pooling-of-interests, or merger, method. The pooling-of-interests method considers that the two entities involved are amalgamating, or merging, their businesses into a single economic entity, almost as if a single entity had always existed. AASB 1015 (commentary, para (xv)) states that the objective of the method is 'to account for the merger as if the separate businesses were continuing as before, though now jointly owned and managed'.

For direct acquisitions of the assets or net assets of an existing entity, the pooling-of-interests method results in the values of the individual assets and liabilities being valued at their pre-acquisition book values and goodwill not being recognised. Hence, the cost of acquisition is not calculated by reference to the fair value of the purchase consideration but to the book values of the net assets of the merging entity. For indirect acquisitions by purchase of an entity's shares, the cost of acquisition under pooling-of-interests would generally be calculated by reference to the existing book values of the merging entity, again ignoring the fair value of the purchase consideration.

While the pooling-of-interests method is allowed in some countries for true merger situations, AASB 1015 (commentary, paras (xv) and (xvi)) considers that the method does not reflect the negotiation process between the parties to the acquisition or the economic substance of the transaction, nor does it measure the cost to the acquiring company of giving up the purchase consideration in exchange for the shares or other assets of the other entity. Accordingly, the method is not allowed in Australia.

## ISSUES FOR THE SELLING ENTITY

In outlining the principles applicable to the acquisition of assets, this chapter has focused on the issues facing the entity acquiring the assets. However, there are also various issues applicable to the entity disposing of the assets.

The obvious principle from the selling entity's viewpoint is that any profit or loss on disposal of the applicable asset(s) must be brought to account. This involves the application of normal accounting principles. These principles are straightforward in the case of an entity disposing of a single asset or a small number of assets, and where that entity continues in operation after the sale of the asset or assets.

However, complications may arise in the case of a company disposing of its entire net assets. For example, a company may have been forced to dispose of its entire net assets, due to severe financial difficulties, which would allow settlement of its legal obligations. This may then result in the liquidation of the company. Alternatively, a company may voluntarily sell the net assets of its existing business for various reasons. These reasons can include the retirement of the owners, a need to rationalise the company's activities, or a decision to undertake a major expansion of activities. This may also result in a reorganisation of the company's share capital, such as through a major new share issue, the return of capital to owners, or other alterations to the structure of shareholders' equity. These types of issues are discussed in chapters 12 and 13.

In the case of an indirect acquisition by purchase of a company's shares, there are no entries required in the selling company's books of account. The sale transaction is between the acquiring company and the selling company's shareholders, and not with the selling company itself. The effect is that the selling company has the same shareholders' equity as before the transaction. All that has changed is the identity of the individual shareholders. This does necessitate an update of the company share register.

# Review

The material in this chapter has provided a broad overview of the accounting principles applicable to the acquisition of assets, with particular reference to accounting standard AASB 1015. The chapter concentrated on issues facing the entity acquiring assets, with particular reference to principles for transactions involving the acquisition of single and multiple assets, the direct acquisition of the net assets of an existing entity, and the indirect acquisition of an entity by purchase of its issued shares.

# Endnote

1 Assuming amortisation over a 20-year period, amortisation expense under the inverted sum of the years' digits method in the first year would be 1/210 of the cost of goodwill, 2/210 in the second year and 3/210 in the third year. In years 19 and 20, amortisation would be 19/210 and 20/210 of the goodwill cost. Hence, only a very small proportion of goodwill is amortised in the early years using this method.

## KEY TERMS

| | | |
|---|---|---|
| acquisition of assets | discount on acquisition | non-monetary assets |
| amortisation | economic entity | parent entity |
| consolidated accounts | fair value | pooling-of-interests method |
| control | goodwill | purchase consideration |
| cost of acquisition | incidental costs | purchase method |
| date of acquisition | indirect acquisition | straight-line method |
| direct acquisition | monetary assets | subsidiary entity |

## REVIEW QUESTIONS

4.1 How does AASB 1015 define an acquisition in relation to assets? Why is an acquisition defined in this way?

4.2 Outline the different forms that an acquisition of assets by a company may take.

4.3 How does AASB 1015 define the term 'date of acquisition'? Why is the term defined in this way?

4.4 What are the components of the cost of acquisition? Provide some examples.

4.5 Explain the concept of fair value as it applies to the acquisition of assets.

4.6   Contrast the method of recording the acquisition of a single asset with the recording of a single transaction involving the purchase of multiple assets (not constituting a business entity).

4.7   Contrast the accounting principles for the direct acquisition of an existing entity's assets with an indirect acquisition by purchase of the entity's shares.

4.8   Under what circumstances are the provisions of AASB 1013: Accounting for Goodwill applicable to situations involving the acquisition of assets?

4.9   Outline the principles prescribed in AASB 1013 for the initial recognition of, and subsequent accounting treatment for, goodwill on acquisition.

4.10   Explain the meaning of, and the accounting treatment for, discount on acquisition.

# EXERCISES

**Exercise 4.11**    **Basic acquisition**

A property is acquired by ZAB Ltd for cash consideration of $256 000. Part of this consideration includes the amount of $1500 in respect of council rates. It is estimated that the land on which the building is situated, and furniture and fittings included with the property, have a fair value of $120 000 and $14 500 respectively.

*Required*

Prepare the journal entry to record the acquisition of the property by ZAB Ltd.

**Exercise 4.12**    **Basic acquisition**

BAZ Ltd acquires a new motor vehicle for cash consideration of $41 100 plus a trade-in allowance amounting to $20 000. The consideration comprises the base cost of the vehicle ($56 900), dealer delivery charges ($650), stamp duty ($2400), registration ($500) and insurance ($650). The trade-in allowance relates to an old vehicle which had an original cost of $35 000 and a current written-down value of $25 000. The trade-in allowance represents the fair value of this vehicle.

*Required*

Prepare the journal entry to record the acquisition of the motor vehicle by BAZ Ltd.

**Exercise 4.13**    **Acquisition of multiple assets**

CAB Pty Ltd attends an auction and, for cash consideration of $79 000, acquires one lot comprising four unregistered ex-government motor vehicles. The fair values for each of the four motor vehicles are independently assessed at $25 000, $22 000, $20 000 and $15 000 respectively.

*Required*

Prepare the journal entry to record the acquisition of these vehicles by CAB Ltd.

**Exercise 4.14** **Acquisition of multiple assets**

DAG Ltd attends an art auction at which two paintings completed by a well-known local artist comprise one lot. Before the auction, it is estimated that the fair value of painting A is $150 000 and of painting B is $100 000. After spirited bidding at the auction, DAG acquires these paintings for a cash outlay of $275 250. In addition, a bidding fee of $100 was required to be paid by all bidders at the auction. The paintings were the only items acquired by DAG.

*Required*
Prepare the journal entry to record the acquisition of these paintings by DAG Ltd.

**Exercise 4.15** **Alternative forms of consideration**

GEG Ltd, a listed public company, acquires land from Vendor Ltd. In consideration, GEG issues 200 000 new shares in the company to Vendor. GEG's shares, as at the date of acquisition, were trading at $2.30 per share. GEG incurs solicitor's legal costs of $3000 for the issue of these new shares. GEG also agrees to transfer to Vendor 30 000 shares it holds in Carlin Ltd. Carlin's shares are listed on the Australian Stock Exchange and at the date of acquisition were trading at a price of $4.50 per share. These shares had an original cost to GEG of $5 each.

*Required*
Calculate the cost of acquisition of the land and prepare the journal entry to record the acquisition by GEG Ltd.

**Exercise 4.16** **Direct acquisition of net assets**

PBL Ltd acquires the net assets of TZE Pty Ltd for cash consideration of $175 000 on 30 June 20X2. The identifiable net assets acquired, valued at fair value at this date, comprise the following:

| | $ | $ |
|---|---|---|
| *Assets acquired* | | |
| Debtors | 15 000 | |
| Inventory | 31 000 | |
| Plant & equipment | 130 000 | 176 000 |
| *Liabilities acquired* | | |
| Bank overdraft | 10 500 | |
| Creditors | 20 500 | 31 000 |
| Net assets acquired (fair value) | | $145 000 |

*Required*
Prepare the journal entry to record PBL's acquisition of the net assets of TZE Pty Ltd.

**Exercise 4.17** **Goodwill subsequent to acquisition**

Assume for the fact situation outlined in Exercise 4.16 above that PBL's directors, at the date of acquisition (30 June 20X2), expect that the benefits from the goodwill on acquisition should arise over a period of 30 years. However, the directors subsequently make an assessment on 30 June 20X4 that the benefits of the goodwill will only arise over the following 14 years.

*Required*
Calculate the amount of goodwill amortisation for the financial years ending 30 June 20X3 and 20X4 in accordance with AASB 1013.

**Exercise 4.18** **Direct acquisition of net assets and goodwill subsequent to acquisition**
PDD Ltd acquires the net assets of CBR Pty Ltd for cash consideration of $390 000 on 30 June 20X3. The identifiable net assets acquired, valued at fair value at this date, comprise the following:

|  | $ | $ |
|---|---|---|
| *Assets acquired* | | |
| Debtors | 35 000 | |
| Inventory | 60 000 | |
| Plant & equipment | 120 000 | |
| Land & buildings | 210 000 | |
| Brandnames | 70 000 | 495 000 |
| *Liabilities acquired* | | |
| Bank overdraft | 25 000 | |
| Creditors | 45 000 | |
| Bank loan | 100 000 | 170 000 |
| Net assets acquired (fair value) | | $325 000 |

PDD's directors make an assessment at 30 June 20X4 that, considering the expected future benefits, goodwill is overvalued by $35 000. The directors also estimate that the benefits from the goodwill should arise over a period of ten years subsequent to acquisition.

*Required*
1 Prepare the journal entry, in accordance with AASB 1013, to record PDD's acquisition of the net assets of CBR Pty Ltd at 30 June 20X3.

2 Prepare any journal entries required for the year ending 30 June 20X4, and calculate the goodwill balance as at that reporting date.

**Exercise 4.19** **Discount on acquisition**
Assume the same fact situation as outlined in Exercise 4.18 above, except that PDD Ltd acquires the net assets of CBR Pty Ltd for cash consideration of $285 000.

*Required*
Prepare the journal entry to record the acquisition in accordance with AASB 1013.

**Exercise 4.20** **Indirect acquisition by purchase of shares**
Assume the same fact situation as outlined in Exercise 4.18 above, except that PDD Ltd, instead of directly acquiring the net assets of CBR Pty Ltd, undertakes an indirect acquisition by acquiring all of CBR's issued shares.

*Required*
Prepare the journal entries to record the acquisition, assuming:
(a) $390 000 cash consideration to shareholders of CBR plus $2500 in legal costs and stamp duty paid in cash; and

(b) consideration in the form of the issue of PDD Ltd shares having a fair market value at date of acquisition amounting to $390 000 (plus the $2500 in legal costs and stamp duty paid in cash).

**Exercise 4.21**  **Comprehensive**

Bradfield Ltd acquires the net assets of an existing business, Enfield Pty Ltd, on 1 January 20X3. The balance sheet of Bradfield Ltd immediately prior to the acquisition is shown below.

**Bradfield Ltd**
**Balance Sheet as at 1 January 20X3**

| Assets | $ | Liabilities | $ | $ |
|---|---|---|---|---|
| Cash at bank | 20 000 | Creditors | 110 000 | |
| Debtors | 80 000 | Provisions | 35 000 | |
| Inventory | 105 000 | Debentures | 450 000 | 595 000 |
| Shares in Amcor Ltd | 110 000 | | | |
| Motor vehicles (net) | 140 000 | *Shareholders' equity* | | |
| Plant & equipment (net) | 500 000 | Paid-up capital | 800 000 | |
| Land & buildings (net) | 750 000 | Retained earnings | 310 000 | 1 110 000 |
| | $1 705 000 | | | $1 705 000 |

The identifiable net assets of Enfield Pty Ltd acquired by Bradfield Ltd, valued at fair value at date of acquisition, comprise the following.

| | $ | $ |
|---|---|---|
| *Assets acquired* | | |
| Debtors | 20 000 | |
| Inventory | 55 000 | |
| Plant & equipment | 175 000 | |
| Land & buildings | 280 000 | |
| Trademarks | 200 000 | 730 000 |
| *Liabilities acquired* | | |
| Bank overdraft | 30 000 | |
| Creditors | 80 000 | |
| Bank loan | 120 000 | 230 000 |
| *Net assets acquired (fair value)* | | $500 000 |

The terms of the acquisition are as follows:
- Cash consideration amounting to $310 000 is to be paid to Enfield. This amount is to be raised by way of a new bank loan.
- The shares in Amcor Ltd held by Bradfield, which have a fair market value (at date of acquisition of Enfield's net assets) amounting to $180 000, are to be transferred to Enfield.
- A motor vehicle owned by Bradfield, which has a fair market value of $30 000, is also to be transferred to Enfield. This motor vehicle has a book value of $40 000 (cost of $50 000 and accumulated depreciation of $10 000).
- Bradfield Ltd incurs solicitor's costs of $5000. These are to be paid immediately from the company's existing cash balances.

*Required*
Prepare the journal entries to record the acquisition and prepare Bradfield's balance sheet immediately subsequent to the acquisition.

**Exercise 4.22** **Comprehensive**
Assume the same fact situation as outlined in Exercise 4.21 above, but with the exception that the cash portion of the consideration, to be raised by the new bank loan, amounts to $265 000.

*Required*
Prepare the journal entries to record the acquisition and prepare Bradfield's balance sheet immediately subsequent to the acquisition.

**Exercise 4.23** **Comprehensive**
Assume the same fact situation as outlined in Exercise 4.21 above, except that Bradfield Ltd, instead of directly acquiring the net assets of Enfield Pty Ltd, acquires the company's issued shares. Enfield has four shareholders, each of whom owns 3000 shares. The terms of the sale are that each Enfield share will be exchanged for four Bradfield shares plus $20 cash. The cash portion of the purchase consideration is to be raised by a new bank loan. Legal costs amount to $2500 for the issue of the new shares and stamp duty of $500 on the transfer of the Enfield shares. These amounts are paid immediately from Bradfield's existing cash balances. At the date of acquisition, Bradfield Ltd's shares are trading on the Australian Stock Exchange at a price of $5.95 each.

*Required*
Prepare the journal entries to record the acquisition and prepare Bradfield's balance sheet immediately subsequent to the acquisition.

chapter 5

PRINCIPLES OF CONSOLIDATION

# introduction

A business can be structured in a number of forms, and it is not unusual for the operations of a business to be conducted through holdings in separate entities which collectively represent a group structure. In Australia, one of the most important and widely used group structures occurs where a group of companies or entities is controlled by a company or other type of entity. Such controlled entities are known as subsidiaries. The focus of this and the following three chapters is the preparation of the consolidated accounts, the financial statements pertaining to a group of entities. This chapter introduces the basic principles of consolidations in the context of wholly-owned subsidiaries.

Group structures arise for a number of reasons. For example, a company may take over its competitors (horizontal integration) or its suppliers or clients (vertical integration), or it may diversify by taking over companies in other types of businesses. Another reason is that the company may establish or separate out a part of its business into a controlled limited liability company as a means of reducing its exposure to risk in a particular business venture. To provide more complete financial information about the overall group, a set of consolidated accounts is prepared.

The process of consolidation involves adding together the accounts of the controlling entity and the entities being controlled, after eliminating any inter-entity holdings and inter-entity transactions. The resulting consolidated accounts provide the operating results and financial position of the entities as a single unit in their trading and dealings with entities outside the group.

This chapter first considers the legislative requirements for preparing consolidated accounting information for group structures and the information to be disclosed in general purpose financial reports as set out in ss 295A and 295B of the Corporations Law[1] and accounting standards AASB 1024: Consolidated Accounts and AASB 1013: Accounting for Goodwill. The chapter then commences a discussion of the consolidation process in detail. This discussion of consolidation is continued in chapters 6 to 8.

# Definitions

Before proceeding, we need to review some definitions of the term 'entity' as used in consolidations:

**entity**    *Entity*    'Any legal, administrative or fiduciary arrangement, organisational structure or other party ... having the capacity to deploy scarce resources in order to achieve objectives.' This includes companies, partnerships, trusts and persons. (AASB 1024, para 9)

**parent entity**    *Parent entity*    'An entity which controls another entity.' (AASB 1024, para 9)

**subsidiary**    *Subsidiary*    'An entity which is controlled by another entity.' A parent entity may also be a subsidiary of another entity. (AASB 1024, para 9)

**chief entity**    *Chief entity*    'The ultimate parent entity in an economic entity which must be a reporting entity.' (Corporations Law, s 295(2))

**economic entity**    *Economic entity*    'A group of entities made up of the parent entity and one or more subsidiaries.' (AASB 1024, para 9)

**reporting entity**    *Reporting entity*    'An entity (including an economic entity) which is required to prepare general purpose financial reports.' (SAC 1, para 40 and AASB 1024, para 9)

AASB 1024 uses the entity approach to consolidations. This requires the inclusion of all assets and liabilities of a parent entity and its subsidiaries in the consolidated accounts for the economic entity together with the operating results of the group's transactions with other entities outside the group. Total equity of the **consolidated accounts** consolidated entity is shown in the consolidated accounts and is provided by the members (shareholders) of the parent and any equity holders of a subsidiary which is not wholly owned by the parent. The equity of a subsidiary not owned by the parent **outside equity interest** is known as outside equity interest.

Figure 5.1 sets out a simple group structure with two entities which together make up an economic entity.

**Figure 5.1**
Two-entity group structure

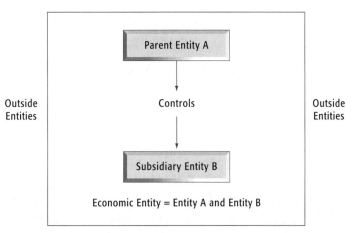

Group structures are frequently more complex than the simple two-entity example shown in Figure 5.1. For example, Coles Myer Ltd disclosed over 90

controlled entities in its 1996 annual report. The Coles Myer economic entity therefore consists of the ultimate parent entity (Coles Myer Ltd) and the 90 or so entities that it controls. The more complex group structure illustrated in Figure 5.2 provides an example of the situation where the ultimate parent controls a number of subsidiary entities.

**Figure 5.2**

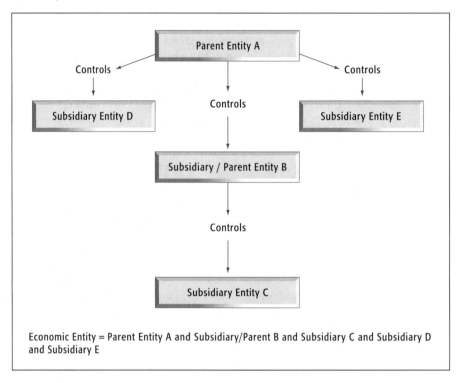

Economic Entity = Parent Entity A and Subsidiary/Parent B and Subsidiary C and Subsidiary D and Subsidiary E

Note that in Figure 5.2, entity B is *both* a parent and a subsidiary entity. This is because entity B is a subsidiary entity of the ultimate parent (chief) entity A, as well as being parent entity to subsidiary C by virtue of its control over entity C.

Sections 295(1), 295A and 295B of the Corporations Law require that an economic entity which is a reporting entity must prepare consolidated accounts. In Figure 5.2, consolidated accounts would be prepared for the economic entity consisting of A, B, C, D and E if the economic entity is also a reporting entity.

# Rationale for the preparation of consolidated accounts

AASB 1024 states that the purpose of the consolidated accounts of an economic entity is to allow users of general purpose financial reports to 'assess the performance, financial position and financing and investing of an economic entity, rather than relying solely on individual accounts' of the entities that make up the economic entity (commentary, para (xxvii)). It is only in the consolidated accounts that the effects of inter-entity (intra-group) transactions are eliminated. For example, if a parent and subsidiary entity frequently transact with sales of inventory to one another, any profit or loss on these intra-group transactions is unrealised from the economic entity's point of view and is eliminated in the consolidated accounts. In contrast, profits or losses on such intra-group transactions are recognised in the accounts of the individual entities that comprise the group. It would be extremely difficult to obtain an accurate picture of the results and financial position of an economic entity by trying to amalgamate the accounts of individual entities in a group without access to the full information on inter-company transactions and balances.

Further, the accounts for any single entity within the group will not reflect the total resources available to, and used by, the economic entity. For example, since control of one entity by another implies that the parent entity can control the disposition of profits or losses earned by the subsidiary entity, the subsidiary's profits (adjusted for intra-group transactions) are fully brought to account in the consolidated statements. Information on dividends received by the parent will not alone provide sufficient information on the amount of earnings available to the *economic entity* because it is possible for the parent to manipulate the timing and amount of dividends paid by a subsidiary.

Similarly, the ability of entities within the group to transfer assets to one another at other than arm's-length prices suggests that creditors, as well as shareholders, find the consolidated statements useful for monitoring purposes. It is only in the consolidated accounts that the effect of such intra-group transactions are eliminated.

# The concept of control

Prior to the introduction of AASB 1024 and the amendment of the Companies legislation to include entities other than companies in consolidated accounts, essentially only subsidiary companies in which the holding company (now known as the parent entity) held more than a 50% ownership interest were required to be consolidated. Since the legislation applied only to incorporated entities and the major test for control hinged on percentage ownership, it was possible for holding companies to structure groups as vehicles for off balance sheet financing (whereby the liability for certain borrowings did not appear in the consolidated balance sheet).

**control** Under AASB 1024, control, and not percentage ownership, is the sole criterion for determining when a parent/subsidiary relationship exists. For there to be more than one entity within an economic entity, one of the entities must control each of the other constituent entities. Control is defined in para 9 of AASB 1024 as:

> ... the capacity of an entity to dominate decision-making, directly or indirectly, in relation to the financial and operating policies of another entity so as to enable that other entity to operate with it in pursuing the objectives of the controlling entity.

AASB 1024 (commentary, paras (xv) to (xxiv)) provides details on the components of the definition of control and factors to be considered in determining whether control exists.

Only one parent can exercise control at any one time, and consolidation is not permitted if joint control is exercised over an entity. An example of joint control was the joint ownership (50% each) and joint control exercised over the Ansett Airlines partnership by TNT Ltd and News Ltd. There is currently no accounting standard which requires full consolidation of entities over which joint control is exercised. Later in this text, we will look at accounting for associated companies, where significant influence, but not control, is held (chapter 9), as well as at accounting for unincorporated joint ventures (chapter 10).

If a parent does not control an entity when consolidated accounts are prepared but has controlled an entity for a part of the year, then it must include the operating results for the subsidiary in the consolidated accounts for the part of the year during which control existed (AASB 1024, paras 26 and 27, and s 295A of the Corporations Law).

The decision as to whether control exists should be a matter of substance over form in all cases and this requires the exercise of professional judgment (AASB 1024, commentary, para (xv)). The key points in the AASB 1024 definition of control are:

- domination of decision making;
- capacity to dominate decision making;
- direct or indirect domination;
- domination of both financial and operating policies; and
- pursuit of objectives of controlling entity.

## DOMINATION OF DECISION MAKING

AASB 1024 (commentary, para (xvi)) gives examples of indicators of the existence of control. These include situations where control does not hinge on ownership interests. For example, one entity can control another via its capacity to dominate the composition of the board of directors or governing body of that other entity. It is not necessary for a minimum level of ownership of an entity to exist to establish domination of decision making. Indeed, one entity may dominate another without having an equity interest.

## CAPACITY TO DOMINATE DECISION MAKING

A parent need only have the capacity to dominate the decision making of another entity for control to exist. It may not actually be exercising dominance. For example, consider the case where a corporation holds convertible notes in another entity and that those notes, if converted into ordinary shares, would give the holder a majority shareholding in the other entity. In such a case, the holder of the convertible notes has the capacity to control the other entity but does not actually do so. Under the provisions of AASB 1024, the holder of the notes should consolidate the issuing entity because it has the capacity to control it, even if it does not actually do so. This is, of course, subject to the establishment of the other limbs in the AASB 1024 definition of control.

## DIRECT OR INDIRECT DOMINATION

Domination of decision making need not be direct. Figure 5.2 above illustrates a situation where indirect control is exercised by parent entity A over subsidiary entity

C by virtue of the intermediate entity B. Entity A has no direct control of entity C. However, because entity A controls entity B, which in turn controls entity C, entity A has *indirect* control over entity C.

## DOMINATION OF BOTH FINANCIAL AND OPERATING POLICIES

Before control can exist, the parent must dominate *both* the financial and operating policies of the subsidiary. Dominance over only one of the policies would not satisfy the requirements for control and, in fact, if one entity dominates operating policies while another dominates financial policies, then joint control would exist.

## PURSUIT OF OBJECTIVES OF CONTROLLING ENTITY

For control to exist, the subsidiary should also be operating in a way which contributes to the objectives of the parent. Capacity to control may be established, but this will imply consolidation only if such control involves the subsidiary in the pursuit of the objectives of the controlling entity. Hence, the definition of control contained in AASB 1024 would normally exclude a lender and borrower relationship and a receiver relationship (commentary, para (xxxiii)).

# Single set of consolidated accounts

Prior to the introduction of AASB 1024 and changes in the Corporations Law, it was possible to prepare consolidated accounts in the following combinations:
- a full set of consolidated accounts for the group;
- two or more sets of consolidated accounts for the entire group;
- separate accounts for each company in the group; and
- one or more sets of consolidated accounts and one or more separate accounts for each company.

It was argued by some reporting entities that some subsidiaries should not be included because their business was significantly different from the business of the rest of the group and would give a skewed view of the group accounts. For example, the inclusion of finance subsidiaries in the group accounts would significantly increase the debt-to-equity ratio of the entire group.

AASB 1024, para 11 and ss 295A and 295B of the Corporations Law permit only one set of accounts for the entire economic entity. AASB 1024 states that complete consolidated accounts 'are the only presentation format which satisfies the objective of reporting for the economic entity as a single reporting entity' (commentary, para (xxvii)). A full set of consolidated accounts gives an overall view of the entire economic entity. Any perceived problems in including information from different activities with varying risk can be overcome, in part, by the requirement of AASB 1005: Financial Reporting by Segments to disclose some summary information for each industrial and geographical segment of an economic entity. Note also that there is nothing to prevent the economic entity from making additional disclosures above those required by the regulations to mitigate any perceived shortcomings in the statutory consolidated accounts.

# The process of consolidation

In this chapter and the next, we will cover the process of preparing consolidated accounts for a simple economic entity consisting of a parent entity and a wholly-owned single subsidiary entity, as represented in Figure 5.3.

**Figure 5.3**

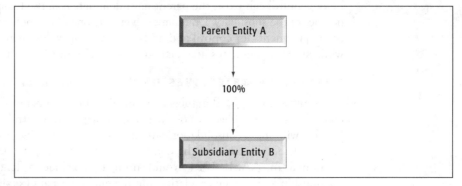

In chapter 7 we will introduce partly-owned subsidiaries, and chapter 8 will deal with multiple subsidiaries.

When a parent entity acquires a 100% interest in a subsidiary, the components of the balance sheets of both entities can be represented as shown in Figure 5.4 on the next page.

During the financial year, both entities continue to keep their own individual accounts. At the date of acquisition, Parent A will complete the following *general journal* entry to account for the acquisition (assuming the acquisition was for cash consideration of $10 000).

## General journal

|  | Debit | Credit |
|---|---|---|
| Investment in Subsidiary B | 10 000 | |
|    Cash | | 10 000 |
| (acquisition of shares in B) | | |

Subsidiary B would take no accounting action on the date of acquisition. However, it would amend its share register to reflect the fact that Parent A is now the owner of 100% of its issued capital. During the financial year, both A and B will continue to keep their accounts as individual entities and will record any transactions with one another in exactly the same way as they would for any transactions with parties external to the economic entity. At the end of the reporting period, the consolidated accounts must be prepared and it is at this point that the two sets of accounts are added together and any necessary consolidated adjustments made.

The parent company's asset, Investment in Subsidiary, gives the parent ownership of the assets and liabilities of the subsidiary by way of its ownership of the equity of the subsidiary. Before the accounts of the parent and subsidiary can be added together to give the total net assets under the control of the economic entity, it is necessary to eliminate the parent's Investment in Subsidiary asset account and the equity in the subsidiary which the investment represents. This avoids the double counting of assets and equity. These are the shaded components shown in Figure 5.4.

**Figure 5.4**
Elimination of investment in subsidiary and equity in wholly-owned subsidiary at date of acquisition

| | Net assets | | | = Owners' equity |
|---|---|---|---|---|
| Parent: | (Other assets – Liabilities) + | Investment in subsidiary | | = Owners' equity |
| Subsidiary: | (Assets – Liabilities) | | | = Owners' equity |
| Consolidation: | (Other assets – Liabilities) of Parent + (Assets – Liabilities) of Subsidiaries | | | = Consolidated owners' equity |

As a simple example, assume that Parent A and Subsidiary B have balance sheets immediately after acquisition of B by A as follows:

| | Parent A $ | Subsidiary B $ |
|---|---|---|
| Inventory | – | 20 000 |
| Plant | 140 000 | – |
| Investment in Subsidiary B | 10 000 | – |
| *Total assets* | 150 000 | 20 000 |
| Liabilities | 40 000 | 10 000 |
| *Net assets* | $110 000 | $10 000 |
| Owners' equity | $110 000 | $10 000 |

Substituting this information into Figure 5.4 gives:

| | Net assets | | | = | Owners' equity |
|---|---|---|---|---|---|
| Parent: | (140 – 40) | + | 10 | = | 110 |
| Subsidiary: | (20 – 10) | | | = | 10 |
| Consolidation: | 110 | | | = | 110 |

In other words, since Parent A has acquired 100% of the owners' equity of Subsidiary B, it owns 100% of the residual value of Subsidiary B, as represented by its net assets. In the consolidated accounts, we include 100% of B's assets and liabilities and eliminate B's owners' equity at acquisition against A's Investment in Subsidiary B account.

If a consolidated balance sheet for the economic entity was prepared at this point, it would appear as below:

| | $ |
|---|---|
| Inventory | 20 000 |
| Plant | 140 000 |
| *Total assets* | 160 000 |
| Liabilities | 50 000 |
| *Net assets* | $110 000 |
| Owners' equity | $110 000 |

In the simple example shown above, the cost of the investment by Parent A is exactly equal to the book value of the net assets acquired. That is, no goodwill or discount on acquisition has arisen. Often this is not the case and there is a residual amount to be accounted for.

The steps in the process of consolidation can be summarised as follows:

1 Complete an acquisition analysis calculation (taking into account the fair value of the assets and liabilities of the subsidiary at the date of acquisition).

2 Prepare the elimination of investment in subsidiary journal entry following this calculation. This entry should include any required revaluations of subsidiary assets.

3 Prepare entries for the elimination of inter-entity transactions and balances, eliminating the effects of these in full (discussed in chapter 6).

4 Post these journals to the consolidation worksheet and complete the worksheet.

5 Calculate and prepare outside equity adjustments (discussed in chapters 7 and 8).

6 Prepare the consolidated financial statements using the worksheet and the outside equity adjustments.

AASB 1024 (commentary, para (xxix) and paras 16 and 17) and s 290 of the Corporations Law require that the accounts of the parent and the subsidiary must have been prepared to the same balance date and using the same accounting policies before consolidation can proceed. In steps 1, 2 and 3, the accounts of the parent and subsidiary are added together after eliminating the Investment in Subsidiary item and the equity of the subsidiary which this represents at the date of acquisition and eliminating any inter-entity transactions (see AASB 1024, paras 18 and 23).

The next section illustrates steps 1 and 2 of the consolidation process for a parent company and one wholly-owned subsidiary company.

## ELIMINATION OF INVESTMENT IN SUBSIDIARY
### Entries at date of acquisition where purchase price equals fair value of assets acquired

The concept of fair value is very important in the analysis of the assets and liabilities which the parent indirectly purchases by acquiring the shares of the subsidiary. The principles covered by AASB 1015: Accounting for Acquisitions of Assets and AASB 1013: Accounting for Goodwill have been covered in detail in chapter 4. The fair value of an asset is defined in AASB 1015 as 'the amount for which an asset could be exchanged between a knowledgeable, willing buyer and a knowledgeable, willing seller in an arm's length transaction' (para .06).

AASB 1015 requires that the identifiable net assets resulting from any acquisition be recorded at fair value. AASB 1024 requires that this approach apply to net assets acquired in a subsidiary at the date of acquisition of the subsidiary (para 21 and commentary, para (xxxiii)). That is, the net assets resulting from the acquisition are required to be recorded in the consolidated accounts at fair value. The simplest situation is where the net assets in the books of the subsidiary are recorded at their fair value and the consideration given is equal to the fair value of the subsidiary's identifiable net assets. We will consider this situation first.

Assume that two independent companies, P Ltd and S Ltd, have the following balance sheets.

|  | P Ltd | S Ltd |
|---|---|---|
|  | $ | $ |
| Paid-up capital | 40 000 | 20 000 |
| General reserve | – | 5 000 |
| Retained profits | 15 000 | 5 000 |
| Liabilities | 15 000 | 10 000 |
|  | $70 000 | $40 000 |
| Cash | 30 000 | 5 000 |
| Other assets | 40 000 | 35 000 |
|  | $70 000 | $40 000 |

At this stage, the net assets under the control of P Ltd amount to $55 000 (ie $70 000 assets less $15 000 liabilities).

Assume that the net assets of S Ltd are recorded in its books at fair value and that P Ltd purchases all (100%) of the issued capital of S Ltd for $30 000 cash, this being equal to the fair value of S's net assets. The cash of P Ltd will be replaced by an account, Investment in S Ltd, which is now a subsidiary of P Ltd. The individual balance sheets of the two companies immediately after the acquisition will be:

|  | P Ltd | S Ltd |
|---|---|---|
|  | $ | $ |
| Paid-up capital | 40 000 | 20 000 |
| General reserve | – | 5 000 |
| Retained profits | 15 000 | 5 000 |
| Liabilities | 15 000 | 10 000 |
|  | $70 000 | $40 000 |
| Investment in S Ltd | 30 000 | – |
| Cash | – | 5 000 |
| Other assets | 40 000 | 35 000 |
|  | $70 000 | $40 000 |

Following the acquisition, the total net assets controlled by P Ltd are still $55 000 — that is, they have not changed. The account Investment in S Ltd represents P Ltd's ownership of the net assets of S Ltd through its ownership of the owners' equity in S Ltd. Before the two sets of accounts can be aggregated, it is necessary to post an elimination entry to remove the account Investment in S Ltd and the equity in S Ltd which this ownership represents as at the date of acquisition.

The consolidation process does not involve entries in the books of the parent entity or any of the subsidiaries being consolidated. Each entity still maintains its own accounts as an entity separate from the 'group'. The consolidated statements are prepared from the accounts of each individual entity, but the eliminations and other consolidation adjustments are made only in consolidation working papers. Thus, the adjustments made to prepare consolidated accounts are notional entries in that they appear only on the consolidated worksheet. Further, the process must be repeated each year as no consolidation entries are carried forward in the accounts of any of the individual legal entities making up the group.

AASB 1024 requires that the fair value of identifiable net assets acquired in buying the shares of the subsidiary be compared with the cost of acquisition (para 19 and commentary, para (xxxii)). Any difference between the two amounts will represent either goodwill or discount on acquisition and must be accounted for in accordance with AASB 1013 and AASB 1015. Accounting for goodwill and discount on acquisition will be discussed in detail later in this chapter.

The value of the net assets of the subsidiary can be measured using the value of equity of the subsidiary. As it is the parent's interest in the subsidiary's equity that needs to be eliminated on consolidation, it is easier to represent the fair value of identifiable net assets in the acquisition analysis by using the subsidiary's equity at time of acquisition. Recall that in our example above of P Ltd and S Ltd, the net assets of S Ltd are recorded in the books of S Ltd at fair value. Therefore, the acquisition analysis would be:

## Acquisition analysis

| | | $ | |
|---|---|---|---|
| Fair value of identifiable net assets acquired | = | 20 000 | Capital |
| | | 5 000 | Retained profits |
| | | 5 000 | General reserve |
| | | $30 000 | |
| Cost of acquisition | = | $30 000 | |
| Excess/(deficiency) of cost of acquisition over the fair value of net assets acquired | = | Nil | |

Presenting an acquisition analysis in this form reinforces the accounts and amounts which must be considered when eliminating the investment and the equity of the subsidiary that it represents.

At the time of acquisition, the Elimination of Investment in Subsidiary entry is:

## Consolidation journal

| | Debit | Credit |
|---|---|---|
| Paid-up Capital | 20 000 | |
| Retained Profits | 5 000 | |
| General Reserve | 5 000 | |
| Investment in S Ltd | | 30 000 |

The necessary consolidation adjustments and aggregation of the accounts are carried out in a consolidation worksheet. The worksheet to consolidate the accounts of P Ltd and S Ltd at the date of acquisition is shown on the next page.

## Consolidation worksheet — balance sheet at date of acquisition

| Account | P Ltd | S Ltd | Eliminations Debit | Eliminations Credit | Consolidation |
|---|---|---|---|---|---|
| | $ | $ | $ | $ | $ |
| Paid-up capital | 40 000 | 20 000 | 20 000 | | 40 000 |
| Retained profits | 15 000 | 5 000 | 5 000 | | 15 000 |
| General reserve | – | 5 000 | 5 000 | | – |
| Liabilities | 15 000 | 10 000 | | | 25 000 |
| | $70 000 | $40 000 | | | $80 000 |
| Investment in S Ltd | 30 000 | – | | 30 000 | – |
| Cash | – | 5 000 | | | 5 000 |
| Other assets | 40 000 | 35 000 | | | 75 000 |
| | $70 000 | $40 000 | $30 000 | $30 000 | $80 000 |

Each entity's individual accounts are listed in the consolidation worksheet in single columns, while the eliminations are in the debit and credit (eliminations) columns. Therefore, it is important that you recognise whether the normal balance of an account is a debit or a credit before adding or subtracting the elimination adjustment to arrive at the final consolidated figure in the far right-hand (consolidation) column.

### Consolidation entries in the periods following acquisition

Following the acquisition of S Ltd, both companies will continue with their normal operations, earning profits (hopefully) in the process. Assume that the shares in S Ltd were purchased on 30 June 20X0 and it is now a year later. Assume that the full sets of accounts for both companies, shown in vertical form, are as follows:

| | P Ltd | S Ltd |
|---|---|---|
| | $ | $ |
| Revenues | 100 000 | 40 000 |
| Expenses | 80 000 | 30 000 |
| Operating profit before tax | 20 000 | 10 000 |
| Income tax expense | 8 000 | 4 000 |
| Operating profit after tax | 12 000 | 6 000 |
| Retained profits 1 July 20X0 | 15 000 | 5 000 |
| Retained profits 30 June 20X1 | 27 000 | 11 000 |
| Paid-up capital | 40 000 | 20 000 |
| General reserve | – | 5 000 |
| Liabilities | 18 000 | 9 000 |
| | $85 000 | $45 000 |
| Investment in S Ltd | 30 000 | – |
| Cash | 10 000 | 5 000 |
| Other assets | 45 000 | 40 000 |
| | $85 000 | $45 000 |

The retained profits as at the date of acquisition become the opening retained profits for the period. The acquisition analysis and the elimination entry are the same, except that the entry to retained profits has to be made against retained profits at 1 July 20X0 in the profit and loss account section of the financial statements. This is the account which now contains the retained profits as at the date of acquisition. The retained profits amount at 30 June 20X1 is the result of adding together retained profits at 1 July 20X0 and operating profit after tax for the year.

The worksheet to complete a consolidation for the two companies at 30 June 20X1 is shown below.

## Consolidation worksheet – profit and loss and balance sheet as at 30 June 20XI

| Account | P Ltd | S Ltd | Eliminations Debit | Eliminations Credit | Consolidation |
|---|---|---|---|---|---|
|  | $ | $ | $ | $ | $ |
| Revenue | 100 000 | 40 000 |  |  | 140 000 |
| Expenses | 80 000 | 30 000 |  |  | 110 000 |
| Operating profit before tax | 20 000 | 10 000 |  |  | 30 000 |
| Income tax expense | 8 000 | 4 000 |  |  | 12 000 |
| Operating profit after tax | 12 000 | 6 000 |  |  | 18 000 |
| Retained profits 1 July 20X0 | 15 000 | 5 000 | 5 000 |  | 15 000 |
| Retained profits 30 June 20X1 | 27 000 | 11 000 |  |  | 33 000 |
| Paid-up capital | 40 000 | 20 000 | 20 000 |  | 40 000 |
| General reserve | – | 5 000 | 5 000 |  | – |
| Liabilities | 18 000 | 9 000 |  |  | 27 000 |
|  | $85 000 | $45 000 |  |  | $100 000 |
| Investment in S Ltd | 30 000 | – |  | 30 000 | – |
| Cash | 10 000 | 5 000 |  |  | 15 000 |
| Other assets | 45 000 | 40 000 |  |  | 85 000 |
|  | $85 000 | $45 000 | $30 000 | $30 000 | $100 000 |

Note the way in which the worksheet is constructed. The individual accounts add and subtract across to the Consolidation column (ie add the individual entity account balances and subtract any consolidation eliminations), while the results of the consolidation add and subtract down the Consolidation column. For example, retained profits at 30 June 20X1 is the result of adding the consolidated amounts for operating profit after tax and retained profits at 30 June 20X0.

The consolidated equity of the economic entity ($73 000) now includes all of the equity of P Ltd (ie $67 000) plus the post-acquisition equity of S Ltd (ie $6000 profit earned in the current year). As there have been no dividends paid during the year, we would expect that the total net assets of the economic entity will have increased by the amount of profit earned by the economic entity for the year, this being $18 000. This can be proved by:

|  |  | $ |
|---|---|---|
| Consolidated net assets at 30 June 20X1: | | |
| 85 000 + 15 000 − 27 000 | = | 73 000 |
| Consolidated net assets at 1 July 20X0: | | |
| 75 000 + 5000 − 25 000 | = | 55 000 |
| Change for the year | | $18 000 |

## Dividends from pre-acquisition profits

So far we have assumed that nothing has happened to the retained profits and general reserve existing in S Ltd's books at the time of its acquisition by P Ltd. However, this may not always be the case. There may be transfers of this pre-acquisition equity between retained profits and general reserve, and there may also be a dividend payment by S Ltd to P Ltd from pre-acquisition retained profits. If there is any movement in the pre-acquisition equity, this must be adjusted on consolidation.

To give you an understanding of accounting for pre-acquisition dividends, the following dividend situations will be reviewed:
- dividend declared, but not paid by the subsidiary at the date of acquisition; and
- dividend declared and paid from pre-acquisition profits after the date of acquisition.

*Dividend declared but not paid by the subsidiary at date of acquisition*
If there is a dividend payable by the subsidiary at the time of acquisition and the parent purchases the shares of the subsidiary with the dividend payable to the purchaser, the dividend payable is a part of the parent's ownership of the net assets of the subsidiary. That is, in the simple example used so far, P Ltd has purchased 100% of the net assets of S Ltd. This is represented by the shareholders' equity of S Ltd at the date of acquisition, including retained profits. Any dividends payable at date of acquisition will be sourced from the retained profits (or other similar reserves) of the subsidiary.

Payment of a dividend from pre-acquisition profits is therefore in substance a return of a portion of the purchase price to the acquiring entity. AASB 1015 requires that such dividends from pre-acquisition profits 'shall be accounted for by the acquiring company as a reduction in the carrying amount of the investment in the acquired entity' (para .30).

Assume that, in the case of our example of P Ltd and S Ltd, S Ltd had declared a dividend of $2000 prior to P Ltd acquiring the shares of S Ltd. Assume also that P Ltd recognises dividends as revenue on receipt of the dividend payment, not on declaration, and that it purchased the shares in S Ltd cum dividend. Cum dividend

**cum dividend**

means that P Ltd has purchased the shares in S Ltd with the right to receive the dividend declared by S Ltd when it is paid. This situation can be contrasted with shares that are ex dividend, where the previous owner(s) of the shares have the right to receive the dividend.

Under the above circumstances, the acquisition analysis would appear as follows. (Note that, at this point in time, S Ltd has provided for the dividend in its accounts but P Ltd has not recognised, as revenue or as a receivable, the dividend to be received.)

### Acquisition analysis

|  |  | $ |  |
|---|---|---|---|
| Fair value of identifiable net assets acquired | = | 20 000 | Capital |
|  |  | 5 000 | General reserve |
|  |  | 3 000 | Retained profits |
|  |  | 2 000 | Dividend payable |
|  |  | $30 000 |  |
| Cost of acquisition | = | $30 000 |  |

At the date of acquisition, the consolidation elimination entry is:

### Consolidation journal

|  | Debit | Credit |
|---|---|---|
| Retained Profits | 3 000 |  |
| Paid-up Capital | 20 000 |  |
| General Reserve | 5 000 |  |
| Dividend Payable | 2 000 |  |
| Investment in S Ltd |  | 30 000 |

The dividend payable represents a part of the pre-acquisition equity and is not payable outside the economic entity. Therefore, it must be removed in the elimination entry. When S Ltd pays the dividend, the transactions recorded in the individual accounts of both companies are:

### General journal of S Ltd

|  | Debit | Credit |
|---|---|---|
| Dividend Payable | 2000 |  |
| Cash |  | 2000 |
| (dividend paid) |  |  |

### General journal of P Ltd

|  | Debit | Credit |
|---|---|---|
| Cash | 2000 |  |
| Investment in S Ltd |  | 2000 |
| (reduction in investment for dividend from pre-acquisition profits) |  |  |

The Dividends Payable account has now been cleared in S Ltd's books and the Investment in S Ltd account has been reduced to $28 000 in P Ltd's books, as required by AASB 1015. The elimination of investment entry made after the payment of the dividend (ie in subsequent years), and assuming no other movements in the pre-acquisition equity, will be:

## Consolidation journal

| | Debit | Credit |
|---|---|---|
| Retained Profits 1 July 20X0 | 3 000 | |
| Paid-up Capital | 20 000 | |
| General Reserve | 5 000 | |
| Investment in S Ltd | | 28 000 |

Both the pre-acquisition equity of S Ltd and the value of the investment which P Ltd holds have been reduced permanently by the amount of dividend paid to P Ltd from pre-acquisition profits.

*Dividend declared and paid from pre-acquisition profits after the date of acquisition*
Assume again that the cost of acquisition of S Ltd by P Ltd was $30 000 and that the equity of S Ltd (fair value of identifiable net assets) at the time of acquisition was:

| | $ |
|---|---|
| Paid-up capital | 20 000 |
| Retained profits | 5 000 |
| General reserve | 5 000 |
| | $30 000 |

Assume that S Ltd declared and paid a dividend of $1000 from pre-acquisition profits during a year subsequent to its acquisition by P Ltd. The journal entries completed by S Ltd to account for declaration and payment are:

## General journal of S Ltd

| | Debit | Credit |
|---|---|---|
| Dividend | 1000 | |
| Dividend Payable | | 1000 |
| (declaration of dividend from pre-acquisition profits) | | |
| Dividend Payable | 1000 | |
| Cash | | 1000 |
| (payment of dividend) | | |
| Dividend Paid (P & L) | 1000 | |
| Dividend | | 1000 |
| (to close and transfer balance) | | |

## General journal of P Ltd

| | Debit | Credit |
|---|---|---|
| Cash | 1000 | |
| Investment in S Ltd | | 1000 |
| (reduction in investment for dividend from pre-acquisition profits) | | |

The dividend paid will be displayed as a reduction in retained profits in the profit and loss account of S Ltd. The simplest approach to carrying out the elimination of investment entry is to eliminate the investment account and equity in S Ltd at their original values and then eliminate the pre-acquisition dividend separately.

The Dividend Paid account must also be eliminated on consolidation, as the dividend is not payable outside the group. Removing the dividends paid also ensures that the amounts included in the consolidated profit and loss account are applicable only to the post-acquisition situation. Consolidation journal entries for the year in which the dividend from pre-acquisition profits is declared and paid are:

### Consolidation journal

|  | Debit | Credit |
|---|---|---|
| Retained Profits (opening) | 5 000 | |
| Paid-up Capital | 20 000 | |
| General Reserve | 5 000 | |
|     Investment in S Ltd | | 30 000 |
| | | |
| Investment in S Ltd | 1 000 | |
|     Dividend Paid (P & L) | | 1 000 |

The closing pre-acquisition retained profits of S Ltd are now $4000 (ie $5000 – $1000). This is consistent with the concept of the pre-acquisition dividend being a return of part of the acquisition cost to P Ltd. The pre-acquisition elimination entries in *future years*, assuming no other changes to the pre-acquisition equity of S Ltd, will be:

### Consolidation journal

|  | Debit | Credit |
|---|---|---|
| Retained Profits (opening) | 5 000 | |
| Paid-up Capital | 20 000 | |
| General Reserve | 5 000 | |
|     Investment in S Ltd | | 30 000 |
| | | |
| Investment in S Ltd | 1 000 | |
|     Retained Profits (opening) | | 1 000 |

This approach to removing the effect of the pre-acquisition dividend writes back the dividend paid and removes from the Retained Profits (at the start of the year) and Investment in S Ltd accounts the net amounts applicable to the pre-acquisition equity. After the entries are completed, the Investment in S Ltd account will be reduced to zero. The adjustment for the pre-acquisition dividend is a permanent entry and must continue to be made each year, along with the rest of the elimination of investment in subsidiary entry.

## GOODWILL AND DISCOUNT ON ACQUISITION

In the chapter to this point, we have considered the simple situation where the cost of the shares purchased by the parent is exactly equal to the fair value of the identifiable net assets of the subsidiary acquired. This will quite often not be the case.

**purchased goodwill**

**discount on acquisition**

When the cost of acquisition exceeds the fair value of identifiable net assets acquired, purchased goodwill is created (AASB 1013, para 5.7) and must be recognised in the consolidated accounts. When the cost of acquisition is less than the fair value of the identifiable net assets acquired, a discount on acquisition arises. AASB 1024 (para 19 and commentary, para (xxxii)) requires that goodwill and discount on acquisition resulting from the acquisition of a subsidiary be accounted for in accordance with AASB 1013 and AASB 1015. AASB 1013 allows only purchased goodwill to be recorded in an entity's books and specifically disallows the recording of internally generated goodwill that has been built up within the company by its day-to-day activities (para 4.1).

## Goodwill on acquisition

To illustrate the measurement and accounting treatment of goodwill on acquisition, assume that Parent Ltd acquires all of the issued shares of Subco Ltd on 1 July 20X0 for $80 000 cash. Subco Ltd has all of its identifiable net assets recorded in its books at fair value. At the time of acquisition on 1 July 20X0, the fair value of the identifiable net assets of Subco Ltd, as represented by its shareholders' equity, is:

|  | $ |
|---|---|
| Retained profits | 20 000 |
| Paid-up capital | 50 000 |
|  | $70 000 |

The acquisition analysis in this case is:

## Acquisition analysis

|  |  | $ |  |
|---|---|---|---|
| Fair value of identifiable net assets acquired | = | 50 000 | Capital |
|  |  | 20 000 | Retained profits |
|  |  | $70 000 |  |
| Cost of acquisition | = | $80 000 |  |
| Goodwill ($80 000 − $70 000) | = | $10 000 |  |

This purchased goodwill does not appear in either of the individual companies' accounts. However, it is recognised as an asset in the consolidated accounts by including it as an asset in the elimination of investment in subsidiary entry. Note that purchased goodwill is defined as an unidentifiable intangible asset and that the excess of the purchase consideration over the fair value of the net assets acquired must represent genuine goodwill (ie expected future benefits). If the acquiring firm simply paid too much for the net assets of the subsidiary, the excess of the purchase price over the fair value of the net assets acquired does *not* represent goodwill and should be immediately written off to profit and loss. In this case, we will assume that the $10 000 excess *does* represent genuine goodwill. The elimination of investment entry at the date of acquisition on 1 July 20X0 is as follows:

## Consolidation journal

|  | Debit | Credit |
|---|---|---|
| Retained Profits | 20 000 |  |
| Paid-up Capital | 50 000 |  |
| Goodwill | 10 000 |  |
| Investment in S Ltd |  | 80 000 |

As discussed in chapter 4, goodwill must be amortised against future income over a period not exceeding 20 years (AASB 1013, para 5.2). Effective from 30 June 1996, AASB 1013 specifies the straight-line method for amortisation for goodwill, although prior to this certain other methods were allowable by the standard. The amortisation of goodwill is also recorded, along with the elimination of investment consolidation journal entry, in periods after the acquisition.

For the example above, assume that a decision has been taken by management to amortise goodwill over five years (ie $2000 per annum) and that consolidated accounts are being prepared as at 30 June 20X1 (ie 12 months after the date of acquisition).

An amortisation expense will need to be created in the consolidation journal entries for $2000 per annum. As AASB 1013 (para 10.1) only requires the unamortised balance of goodwill to be disclosed, this can be offset against the goodwill created on consolidation. The net goodwill in the consolidated accounts will now be $8000, represented by the original amount of $10 000 less the first year's amortisation charge of $2000.

The elimination entries one year after acquisition at 30 June 20X1 will be:

### Consolidation journal

|  | Debit | Credit |
|---|---|---|
| Retained Profits 1 July 20X0 | 20 000 | |
| Paid-up Capital | 50 000 | |
| Goodwill | 10 000 | |
| Investment in Subco Ltd | | 80 000 |
| Amortisation Expense | 2 000 | |
| Goodwill | | 2 000 |

At 30 June 20X2, two years after acquisition, allowance must be made for two years' amortisation of goodwill. There will still be amortisation expense for the current year, and the effect of amortisation expense for the previous year must be introduced as a debit to opening retained profits, as expenses for a previous year decrease retained profits brought forward. Goodwill to be introduced is now $6000 ($10 000 – (2 × 2000)). The elimination entries at 30 June 20X2 are:

### Consolidation journal

|  | Debit | Credit |
|---|---|---|
| Retained Profits 1 July 20X1 | 20 000 | |
| Paid-up Capital | 50 000 | |
| Goodwill | 10 000 | |
| Investment in Subco Ltd | | 80 000 |
| Amortisation Expense | 2 000 | |
| Retained Profits 1 July 20X1 | 2 000 | |
| Goodwill | | 4 000 |

The amortisation of goodwill will continue each year until all of the goodwill created by the acquisition is expensed. Six years after acquisition (at 30 June 20X6), all the goodwill will have been amortised and the elimination entry will become:

|  | Debit | Credit |
|---|---|---|
| Retained Profits 1 July 20X5 | 20 000 | |
| Paid-up Capital | 50 000 | |
| Goodwill | 10 000 | |
| Investment in Subco Ltd | | 80 000 |
| Retained Profits 1 July 20X5 | 10 000 | |
| Goodwill | | 10 000 |

Note that at 30 June 20X6, there is no charge to current period amortisation expense because all the goodwill has been amortised over the previous five years. However, we must adjust prior period retained profits for the amortisation of goodwill. This adjustment for the amortisation of goodwill is a permanent entry and must continue to be made each year, along with the rest of the elimination of investment entry.

### Discount on acquisition

As discussed in chapter 4, AASB 1013 (para 8.1) requires that a discount on acquisition, which is the excess of the fair value of identifiable net assets over the cost of acquisition, be applied proportionately against the non-monetary assets acquired. Only after the value of all acquired non-monetary assets has been written down to zero can any balance of the discount be recorded as a gain. A definition of monetary assets is provided by Statement of Accounting Practice SAP 1: Current Cost Accounting. Paragraph 49 of SAP 1 defines monetary assets as 'currency units or claims to determined numbers of such units of currency'. Examples of monetary assets include cash held or at bank, accounts receivable, bills receivable and prepayments. Non-monetary assets are then defined as 'all assets which are not monetary assets'. Examples of non-monetary assets include inventory, investments in listed shares, plant and equipment, land and buildings, and intangibles.

The requirement to write down the value of non-monetary assets acquired by the amount of any discount on acquisition is logical if you consider the economics of the acquisition transaction. Discount on acquisition arises only because the acquisition price of a subsidiary is lower than the fair value of the net identifiable assets acquired. Under what circumstances is such a discount on acquisition likely to arise? AASB 1013 suggests that discount on acquisition 'may reflect a bargain purchase and/or compensation in anticipation of temporary future losses or inadequate future profits' (para 8.1.1). Under these circumstances, the net non-monetary assets held by the subsidiary are written down to reflect such a bargain price/future losses to be consistent with the cost method of accounting for investments. Since monetary assets are stated on the balance sheet in currency units, they cannot be overvalued and any adjustments to balance sheet values must be made to the non-monetary assets.

The following example demonstrates the accounting treatment for a discount on acquisition. Assume that on 1 July 20X0, A Ltd acquired all of the issued shares of B Ltd for $40 000. At the date of acquisition all of B Ltd's identifiable net assets were recorded at fair value. The balance sheet of B Ltd on 1 July 20X0 was:

| | $ | | $ |
|---|---|---|---|
| *Assets* | | *Liabilities* | 10 000 |
| Current assets (monetary only) | 35 000 | *Shareholders' equity* | |
| Non-current assets | | Paid-up capital | 20 000 |
| Land | 12 000 | Retained profits | 25 000 |
| Plant (net) | 8 000 | | |
| *Total* | $55 000 | *Total* | $55 000 |

The plant has a further life of five years, with benefits being received evenly over that period. Hence, depreciation charged by B will be $1600 per annum.

The acquisition analysis is:

## Acquisition analysis

|  |  |  |  |
|---|---|---|---|
|  |  | $ |  |
| Fair value of identifiable net assets acquired | = | 20 000 | Capital |
|  |  | 25 000 | Retained profits |
|  |  | $45 000 |  |
| Cost of acquisition | = | $40 000 |  |
| Discount on acquisition | = | $5 000 |  |

The discount on acquisition is allocated proportionately against the fair value of non-monetary assets at the time of acquisition, as follows:

| Asset | Fair value | Proportion | Allocation of discount | Economic entity cost |
|---|---|---|---|---|
|  | $ | % | $ | $ |
| Land | 12 000 | 60.0 | (3 000) | 9 000 |
| Plant | 8 000 | 40.0 | (2 000) | 6 000 |
|  | $20 000 | 100.0 | $(5 000) | $15 000 |

From the viewpoint of the economic entity, the land and plant are overstated in the books of B Ltd. Therefore, these non-monetary assets must be reduced in the elimination of investment entry by the amount of the discount allocated to arrive at the economic entity value in the consolidated accounts.

An implication of writing down the value of depreciable assets is that an adjustment is required, from the economic entity's viewpoint, to the depreciation charged on the plant by B Ltd. That is, B Ltd is overdepreciating the plant because it is basing its depreciation charge on the book value of the plant, this being overstated from the economic entity point of view. In this case, an adjustment of $400 per annum (20% of $2000) is required as the plant has a further life of five years.

The elimination of investment in subsidiary entry at 1 July 20X0 is:

|  | Debit | Credit |
|---|---|---|
| Retained Profits | 20 000 |  |
| Paid-up Capital | 25 000 |  |
| Land |  | 3 000 |
| Plant |  | 2 000 |
| Investment in B Ltd |  | 40 000 |

One year later, on 30 June 20X1, assuming no other movements in pre-acquisition equity, the consolidation entries are:

|  | Debit | Credit |
|---|---|---|
| Retained Profits 1 July 20X0 | 20 000 |  |
| Paid-up Capital | 25 000 |  |
| Land |  | 3 000 |
| Plant |  | 2 000 |
| Investment in B Ltd |  | 40 000 |
| Accumulated Depreciation – Plant | 400 |  |
| Depreciation Expense |  | 400 |

Two years after acquisition, on 30 June 20X2, assuming no other movements in the pre-acquisition equity, the elimination entries will be:

|  | Debit | Credit |
|---|---|---|
| Retained Profits 1 July 20X1 | 20 000 | |
| Paid-up Capital | 25 000 | |
| Land | | 3 000 |
| Plant | | 2 000 |
| Investment in B Ltd | | 40 000 |
| Accumulated Depreciation – Plant | 800 | |
| Depreciation Expense | | 400 |
| Retained Profits 1 July 20X1 | | 400 |

The adjustments to non-monetary assets and consequent adjustments to depreciation expense will be continued every year as a consolidation elimination entry.

## ILLUSTRATIVE EXAMPLE 5.1

## CONSOLIDATION USING ADJUSTMENTS FOR GOODWILL AND DIVIDENDS FROM PRE-ACQUISITION PROFITS

On 1 July 20X0, C Ltd gained control of D Ltd when it purchased 100% of the issued capital of D Ltd for $120 000 cash. At that date the shareholders' equity of D Ltd was:

|  | $ |
|---|---|
| Paid-up capital | 80 000 |
| General reserve | 10 000 |
| Retained profits | 20 000 |
|  | $110 000 |

All of D Ltd's identifiable assets were recorded at fair value.

In September 20X1, D Ltd paid a dividend of $6000 from pre-acquisition profits. This dividend had been provided for in the previous year's accounts of D Ltd. C Ltd recognises dividends as revenue only when payment is received.

The abbreviated financial statements for C Ltd and D Ltd at 30 June 20X2 are as follows:

| Profit and Loss Accounts for the year ended 30 June 20X2 | | |
|---|---|---|
|  | C Ltd | D Ltd |
|  | $ | $ |
| Revenue | 80 000 | 50 000 |
| Expenses | 30 000 | 20 000 |
| Operating profit before income tax | 50 000 | 30 000 |
| Income tax expense | 20 000 | 12 000 |
| Operating profit after income tax | 30 000 | 18 000 |
| Retained profits 1 July 20X1 | 70 000 | 25 000 |
|  | 100 000 | 43 000 |
| Dividend proposed | 10 000 | 5 000 |
| Retained profits 30 June 20X2 | $ 90 000 | $ 38 000 |

## Balance Sheets as at 30 June 20X2

| | C Ltd $ | D Ltd $ |
|---|---|---|
| *Assets* | | |
| Current assets | 40 000 | 25 000 |
| Non-current assets | | |
| Investment in D Ltd | 114 000 | – |
| Other non-current assets | 161 000 | 163 000 |
| *Total non-current assets* | 275 000 | 163 000 |
| *Total assets* | 315 000 | 188 000 |
| *Liabilities* | | |
| Current liabilities | | |
| Dividend payable | 10 000 | 5 000 |
| Other current liabilities | 30 000 | 20 000 |
| *Total current liabilities* | 40 000 | 25 000 |
| Non-current liabilities | 60 000 | 35 000 |
| *Total liabilities* | 100 000 | 60 000 |
| *Net assets* | $215 000 | $128 000 |
| *Shareholders' equity* | | |
| Paid-up capital | 100 000 | 80 000 |
| General reserve | 25 000 | 10 000 |
| Retained profits | 90 000 | 38 000 |
| *Total shareholders' equity* | $215 000 | $128 000 |

Additional information:
(a) The dividend proposed by D Ltd at 30 June 20X2 is from pre-acquisition profits.
(b) Goodwill is amortised straight line over five years.

*Required*
Prepare the consolidation journal entries and consolidation worksheet to enable the preparation of consolidated accounts at 30 June 20X2 (ie two years after acquisition).

**Solution**
Acquisition analysis at date of acquisition on 1 July 20X0:

**Acquisition analysis**

| | | $ | |
|---|---|---|---|
| Fair value of identifiable net assets acquired | = | 80 000 | Capital |
| | | 10 000 | General reserve |
| | | 20 000 | Retained profits |
| | | $110 000 | |
| Cost of acquisition | = | $120 000 | |
| Goodwill on acquisition | = | $10 000 | |
| Amortisation of goodwill | = | $2 000 per annum | |

Consolidation journal entries at 30 June 20X2 are:

## Consolidation journal

|  | Debit $ | Credit $ |
|---|---|---|
| (1) Elimination of investment in subsidiary. | | |
| Retained Profits 1 July 20X1 | 20 000 | |
| Paid-up Capital | 80 000 | |
| General Reserve | 10 000 | |
| Goodwill 10 000 | | |
| Investment in S Ltd | | 120 000 |
| (2) Adjustment for amortisation of goodwill. | | |
| Amortisation Expense | 2 000 | |
| Retained Profits 1 July 20X1 | 2 000 | |
| Goodwill | | 4 000 |
| (3) Adjustment for dividend paid in September 20X1. | | |
| Investment in D Ltd | 6 000 | |
| Retained Profits 1 July 20X1 | | 6 000 |
| (4) Adjustment for dividend from pre-acquisition profits proposed at 30 June 20X2. | | |
| Dividend Payable | 5 000 | |
| Dividend Proposed (P&L) | | 5 000 |

The consolidation worksheet at 30 June 20X2 follows.

## Consolidation worksheet

| Account | P Ltd | S Ltd | Eliminations Debit | Eliminations Credit | Consolidation |
|---|---|---|---|---|---|
|  | $ | $ | $ | $ | $ |
| Revenue | 80 000 | 50 000 | | | 130 000 |
| Expenses | 30 000 | 20 000 | 2 000 (2) | | 52 000 |
| Operating profit before tax | 50 000 | 30 000 | | | 78 000 |
| Income tax expense | 20 000 | 12 000 | | | 32 000 |
| Operating profit after tax | 30 000 | 18 000 | | | 46 000 |
| Retained profits 1 July 20X1 | 70 000 | 25 000 | 20 000 (1) 2 000 (2) | 6 000 (3) | 79 000 |
|  | 100 000 | 43 000 | | | 125 000 |
| Dividends proposed | 10 000 | 5 000 | | 5 000 (4) | 10 000 |
| Retained profits 30 June 20X2 | 90 000 | 38 000 | | | 115 000 |
| Paid-up capital | 100 000 | 80 000 | 80 000 (1) | | 100 000 |
| General reserve | 25 000 | 10 000 | 10 000 (1) | | 25 000 |
| Non-current liabilities | 60 000 | 35 000 | | | 95 000 |
| Other current liabilities | 30 000 | 20 000 | | | 50 000 |
| Dividend payable | 10 000 | 5 000 | 5 000 (4) | | 10 000 |
|  | $315 000 | $188 000 | | | $395 000 |
| Current assets | 40 000 | 25 000 | | | 65 000 |
| Other non-current assets | 161 000 | 163 000 | | | 324 000 |
| Investment in D Ltd | 114 000 | | 6 000 (3) | 120 000 (1) | – |
| Goodwill | | | 10 000 (1) | 4 000 (2) | 6 000 |
|  | $315 000 | $188 000 | $135 000 | $135 000 | $395 000 |

## SUBSIDIARY'S ASSETS NOT RECORDED AT FAIR VALUE AT DATE OF ACQUISITION

As discussed earlier in this chapter, AASB 1024 (para 19) requires that any difference between the cost of the investment in the subsidiary and the fair value of the identifible net tangible assets acquired shall be accounted for in accordance with AASB 1013 and AASB 1015. AASB 1013 also requires that the identifiable net assets of the entity acquired be measured at their fair values (para 5.6).

In discussions on consolidation to this point, the assumption has been made that the net assets held by the subsidiary have been recorded in the books of the subsidiary at their fair value. In this case, the equity of the subsidiary acquired will represent the fair value of the cost of investment.

However, if the net assets of the subsidiary are not all recorded at fair value, the acquisition analysis will need to be adjusted to reflect all identifiable assets at fair value and the assets will need to be revalued to fair value in the consolidated accounts. AASB 1024 points out that this revaluation of assets held in the subsidiary can be achieved in either of two ways: (a) revalue the identifiable assets in the books of the subsidiary; or (b) revalue the identifiable assets in the consolidation entry (commentary, para (xxxiii)). In both cases, the revaluation would be accounted for in accordance with AASB 1010: Accounting for the Revaluation of Non-current Assets.

For a wholly-owned subsidiary, the asset revaluation reserve created by either of these revaluation methods will be eliminated against the investment account in the elimination of investment in subsidiary entry. The same final result will be obtained in the consolidated accounts irrespective of whether the revaluation is effected in the books of the subsidiary or as part of the consolidation process.

If depreciable assets are revalued and the revaluation is effected in the books of the subsidiary, then additional depreciation or amortisation expense will be recorded by the subsidiary. This additional expense will be reflected in the reported profits of the subsidiary. Where the revaluation of depreciable assets is carried out as part of the consolidation entries, consolidation adjustments must be made to correctly account for any change in depreciation or amortisation arising because of the revaluation (AASB 1024, para 21). This will also necessitate an adjustment for any profit or loss on subsequent disposal of the asset.

From the discussion above it can be seen that the simplest approach to revaluation of assets not stated at fair value at time of acquisition is to have the assets revalued to fair value in the books of the subsidiary immediately after acquisition. This obviates the need to make the attendant depreciation and amortisation adjustments discussed above. However, revaluation in the subsidiary's accounts is not always carried out in practice.

### Revaluation in subsidiary's accounts

Assume that, on 1 July 20X0, E Ltd purchases 100% of the issued capital of F Ltd for $320 000. At the date of acquisition, the equity of F Ltd consisted of:

| | |
|---|---|
| Paid-up capital | $200 000 |
| Retained profits | 20 000 |
| General reserve | 30 000 |

All of the identifiable net assets of F Ltd were recorded at fair value with the exception of land, which had a book value of $120 000 and a fair value of $160 000. Immediately after acquisition, F Ltd revalued the land to fair value with the following journal entry.

## General journal of F Ltd

| | Debit | Credit |
|---|---|---|
| Land | 40 000 | |
| Asset Revaluation Reserve | | 40 000 |
| (revaluation of land) | | |

Consolidation is now being carried out for the financial year ended 30 June 20X1 (ie 12 months after acquisition), and the land is still held by F Ltd. Under these circumstances, the acquisition analysis appears as follows (assuming any goodwill is to be amortised over a ten-year period).

## Acquisition analysis

| | | $ | |
|---|---|---|---|
| Fair value of identifiable net assets acquired | = | 200 000 | Paid-up capital |
| | | 20 000 | Retained profits |
| | | 30 000 | General reserve |
| | | 40 000 | Revaluation of land |
| | | $290 000 | |
| Cost of acquisition | = | $320 000 | |
| Goodwill on acquisition | = | $30 000 | |
| Amortisation of goodwill | = | $3 000 per annum | |

The above acquisition analysis recognises that, while the revaluation of the land was made in F Ltd's accounts immediately after the acquisition, the revaluation reserve is effectively part of F's equity which is being acquired by E Ltd. Hence, it must be eliminated against the investment in subsidiary account on consolidation. If the revaluation reserve relating to the land was not taken into account as part of pre-acquisition equity to be eliminated on consolidation, goodwill would be incorrectly calculated as $70 000 rather than as $30 000.

Consolidation journal entries at 30 June 20X1 would be as follows:

## Consolidation journal

| | Debit | Credit |
|---|---|---|
| Retained Profits 1 July 20X0 | 20 000 | |
| Paid-up Capital | 200 000 | |
| General Reserve | 30 000 | |
| Asset Revaluation Reserve | 40 000 | |
| Goodwill | 30 000 | |
| Investment in F Ltd | | 320 000 |
| | | |
| Amortisation Expense | 3 000 | |
| Goodwill | | 3 000 |

## Revaluation on consolidation

Assume the same acquisition situation and information as in the previous example, but with the exception that the subsidiary does not revalue the land to fair value after acquisition. In this case, the revaluation adjustment must be made in a consolidation journal entry as part of the consolidation process.

Consolidation journal entries at 30 June 20X1 would then be as follows:

**Consolidation journal**

| | Debit | Credit |
|---|---|---|
| Land | 40 000 | |
|     Asset Revaluation Reserve | | 40 000 |
| | | |
| Retained Profits 1 July 20X0 | 20 000 | |
| Paid-up Capital | 200 000 | |
| General Reserve | 30 000 | |
| Asset Revaluation Reserve | 40 000 | |
| Goodwill | 30 000 | |
|     Investment in F Ltd | | 320 000 |
| | | |
| Amortisation Expense | 3 000 | |
|     Goodwill | | 3 000 |

As can be seen from these entries, the only additional entry required, compared to the case where the subsidiary revalues the land in its own accounts, is the first entry relating to the revaluation.

## ILLUSTRATIVE EXAMPLE 5.2

## CONSOLIDATION USING ADJUSTMENTS FOR GOODWILL, DIVIDENDS FROM PRE-ACQUISITION PROFITS AND REVALUATION OF SUBSIDIARY'S ASSETS

To reinforce the principles covered in this chapter, the following is a comprehensive illustration of the consolidation process for a wholly-owned subsidiary where the net assets of the subsidiary are not all stated at fair value and the revaluation entry is made as part of the consolidation journal entries. The example also illustrates dividends from pre-acquisition profits where the dividend has been declared but not paid at the date of acquisition.

On 1 July 20X1, G Ltd acquired control of H Ltd by purchasing 100% of its issued capital for $240 000. At the date of acquisition, the equity of H Ltd consisted of:

| | |
|---|---|
| Paid-up capital | $100 000 |
| Retained profits | 20 000 |
| General reserve | 30 000 |

At 30 June 20X2, 12 months after acquisition, the profit and loss accounts and balance sheets for G Ltd and H Ltd were as follows:

| Profit and Loss Accounts for the year ended 30 June 20X2 | | |
|---|---|---|
| | G Ltd | H Ltd |
| | $ | $ |
| Operating revenue | 522 500 | 245 000 |
| Cost of goods sold | | |
| Opening stock 1 July 20X1 | 110 000 | 20 000 |
| Purchases | 350 000 | 160 000 |
| | 460 000 | 180 000 |

| | G Ltd $ | H Ltd $ |
|---|---|---|
| Closing stock 30 June 20X2 | 120 000 | 55 000 |
| Cost of goods sold | 340 000 | 125 000 |
| Gross profit | 182 500 | 120 000 |
| Administrative expenses | 24 000 | 18 000 |
| Financial expenses | 23 000 | 25 000 |
| Selling expenses | 23 000 | 29 000 |
| Total expenses | 70 000 | 72 000 |
| Operating profit before tax | 112 500 | 48 000 |
| Income tax expense | 50 000 | 18 000 |
| Operating profit after tax | 62 500 | 30 000 |
| Retained profits 1 July 20X1 | 50 000 | 20 000 |
| | 112 500 | 50 000 |
| Dividend proposed | 50 000 | 15 000 |
| Retained profits 30 June 20X2 | $62 500 | $35 000 |

## Balance Sheets as at 30 June 20X2

| | G Ltd $ | H Ltd $ |
|---|---|---|
| Shareholders' equity | | |
| Paid-up capital | 400 000 | 100 000 |
| General reserve | 10 000 | 30 000 |
| Retained profits | 62 500 | 35 000 |
| Total shareholders' equity | $472 500 | $165 000 |
| Assets | | |
| Current assets | | |
| Cash | 10 000 | 5 000 |
| Receivables | 40 000 | 20 000 |
| Inventory | 120 000 | 55 000 |
| Other current assets | 5 000 | 10 000 |
| Total current assets | 175 000 | 90 000 |
| Non-current assets | | |
| Investment in H Ltd | 230 000 | – |
| Plant & machinery | 320 000 | 110 000 |
| Accumulated depreciation | (180 000) | (20 000) |
| Land | 140 000 | 100 000 |
| Other non-current assets | 10 000 | 5 000 |
| Total non-current assets | 520 000 | 195 000 |
| Total assets | 695 000 | 285 000 |
| Liabilities | | |
| Current liabilities | | |
| Creditors | 35 000 | 40 000 |
| Provision for income tax payable | 45 000 | 15 000 |
| Dividend payable | 50 000 | 15 000 |
| Total current liabilities | 130 000 | 70 000 |
| Non-current liabilities | | |
| Bank loan | 92 500 | 50 000 |
| Total liabilities | 222 500 | 120 000 |
| Net assets | $472 500 | $165 000 |

Additional information:

(a) At the date of acquisition, the identifiable net assets of H Ltd were recorded at fair value with the exception of land, which had a book value of $100 000 and a fair value of $150 000. This land has not been revalued by H Ltd during the year ended 30 June 20X2 and is still held by the company at balance date.

(b) On 16 August 20X1, H Ltd paid a dividend of $10 000 to G Ltd. This dividend had been provided for in the prior financial year's accounts.

(c) The dividend of $15 000 provided in H Ltd's accounts for the current year is to be paid from pre-acquisition profits.

(d) Any goodwill on acquisition is to be amortised over a 15-year period.

*Required*

1 Prepare an acquisition analysis.

2 Prepare the consolidated profit and loss and balance sheet for the year ending 30 June 20X2.

**Solution**
**Acquisition analysis**

| | $ | |
|---|---|---|
| Fair value of identifiable net assets acquired = | 100 000 | Paid-up capital |
| | 20 000 | Retained profits |
| | 30 000 | General reserve |
| | 10 000 | Dividend payable |
| | 50 000 | Revaluation of land |
| | $210 000 | |
| Cost of acquisition = | $240 000 | |
| Goodwill on acquisition = | $30 000 | |
| Amortisation of goodwill = | $2 000 | per annum |

**Consolidation journal**

| | Debit $ | Credit $ |
|---|---|---|
| (1) Revaluation of land. | | |
| Land | 50 000 | |
| Asset Revaluation Reserve | | 50 000 |
| (2) Elimination of investment in subsidiary. | | |
| Retained Profits 1 July 20X1 | 20 000 | |
| Paid-up Capital | 100 000 | |
| General Reserve | 30 000 | |
| Asset Revaluation Reserve | 50 000 | |
| Goodwill | 30 000 | |
| Investment in H Ltd | | 230 000 |
| (3) Amortisation of goodwill. | | |
| Amortisation Expense | 2 000 | |
| Goodwill | | 2 000 |
| (4) Adjustment for dividend from pre-acquisition profits proposed at 30 June 20X2. | | |
| Dividend Payable | 15 000 | |
| Dividend Proposed (P&L) | | 15 000 |

The consolidation worksheet at 30 June 20X2 follows.

| Account | P Ltd | S Ltd | Eliminations Debit | Eliminations Credit | Consolidation |
|---|---|---|---|---|---|
| | $ | $ | $ | $ | $ |
| Operating revenue | 522 500 | 245 000 | | | 767 500 |
| Opening stock 1 July 20X1 | 110 000 | 20 000 | | | 130 000 |
| Purchases | 350 000 | 160 000 | | | 510 000 |
| | 460 000 | 180 000 | | | 640 000 |
| Closing stock 30 June 20X2 | 120 000 | 55 000 | | | 175 000 |
| Cost of goods sold | 340 000 | 125 000 | | | 465 000 |
| Gross profit | 182 500 | 120 000 | | | 302 500 |
| Administrative expenses | 24 000 | 18 000 | | | 42 000 |
| Financial expenses | 23 000 | 25 000 | | | 48 000 |
| Selling expenses | 23 000 | 29 000 | | | 52 000 |
| Amortisation expense | – | – | 2 000 (3) | | 2 000 |
| Total expenses | 70 000 | 72 000 | | | 144 000 |
| Operating profit before tax | 112 500 | 48 000 | | | 158 500 |
| Income tax expense | 50 000 | 18 000 | | | 68 000 |
| Operating profit after tax | 62 500 | 30 000 | | | 90 500 |
| Retained profits 1 July 20X1 | 50 000 | 20 000 | 20 000 (2) | | 50 000 |
| | 112 500 | 50 000 | | | 140 500 |
| Dividend proposed | 50 000 | 15 000 | | 15 000 (4) | 50 000 |
| Retained profits 30 June 20X2 | 62 500 | 35 000 | | | 90 500 |
| Paid-up capital | 400 000 | 100 000 | 100 000 (2) | | 400 000 |
| General reserve | 10 000 | 30 000 | 30 000 (2) | | 10 000 |
| Asset revaluation reserve | – | – | 50 000 (2) | 50 000 (1) | – |
| Total shareholders' equity | $472 500 | $165 000 | | | $500 500 |
| Cash | 10 000 | 5 000 | | | 15 000 |
| Receivables | 40 000 | 20 000 | | | 60 000 |
| Inventory | 120 000 | 55 000 | | | 175 000 |
| Other current assets | 5 000 | 10 000 | | | 15 000 |
| Investment in H Ltd | 230 000 | – | | 230 000 (2) | – |
| Plant & machinery | 320 000 | 110 000 | | | 430 000 |
| Accumulated depreciation | (180 000) | (20 000) | | | (200 000) |
| Land | 140 000 | 100 000 | 50 000 (1) | | 290 000 |
| Goodwill | – | – | 30 000 (2) | 2 000 (2) | 28 000 |
| Other non-current assets | 10 000 | 5 000 | | | 15 000 |
| Total assets | 695 000 | 285 000 | | | 828 000 |
| Creditors | 35 000 | 40 000 | | | 75 000 |
| Provision for income tax | 45 000 | 15 000 | | | 60 000 |
| Dividend payable | 50 000 | 15 000 | 15 000 (4) | | 50 000 |
| Bank loan | 92 500 | 50 000 | | | 142 500 |
| Total liabilities | 222 500 | 120 000 | | | 327 500 |
| Net assets | $472 500 | $165 000 | $297 000 | $297 000 | $500 500 |

# Review

This chapter has introduced the basic principles of the consolidation process for wholly-owned subsidiary entities. Chapter 6 builds on this material and focuses on the elimination of inter-entity transactions for the purpose of consolidated reporting. Chapters 7 and 8 discuss further aspects of the consolidation process relating to subsidiaries that are not wholly owned.

# Endnote

1  The chapters in this text concerning consolidation refer to the existing Corporations Law provisions. The Second Corporate Law Simplification Bill 1996 will require a consolidated profit and loss statement, balance sheet and statement of cash flow to be prepared where this is required by accounting standards (s 295(2)(d)). This is essentially identical to the existing Corporations Law.

## KEY TERMS

| | | |
|---|---|---|
| chief entity | economic entity | outside equity interest |
| consolidated accounts | entity | parent entity |
| control | ex dividend | purchased goodwill |
| cum dividend | monetary assets | reporting entity |
| discount on acquisition | non-monetary assets | subsidiary |

## REVIEW QUESTIONS

**5.1** Define the terms *entity*, *parent entity* and *subsidiary entity*.

**5.2** Define the terms *chief entity, economic entity, reporting entity* and *general purpose financial reports*.

**5.3** Define the term *consolidated accounts*. What is the rationale for the preparation of consolidated accounts?

**5.4** How does AASB 1024 define *control*? What are the essential aspects of this definition?

**5.5** Is it possible for one entity to control another entity without an equity interest in the subsidiary entity? If so, under what circumstances might this occur?

**5.6** What are the advantages and disadvantages of requiring the accounts of a group of entities to be presented only as a single set of consolidated accounts?

**5.7** What are the essential steps and entries involved in preparing consolidated accounts for a group comprising a parent entity and a single wholly-owned subsidiary?

5.8 Outline the rationale for the consolidation journal entry eliminating a parent entity's investment in a subsidiary.

5.9 How do the requirements of AASB 1013 and AASB 1015 impact on the AASB 1024 requirements for the preparation of consolidated accounts?

5.10 Explain the accounting treatment required for dividends of a subsidiary paid from pre-acquisition profits. What is the rationale for this requirement?

5.11 What is goodwill on acquisition? How should it be accounted for in accordance with AASB 1024?

5.12 What is discount on acquisition? How should it be accounted for in accordance with AASB 1024?

5.13 What are the alternative accounting treatments allowable under AASB 1024 where assets of a subsidiary are not recorded at fair value in the accounts as at the date of acquisition?

# EXERCISES

**Exercise 5.14** **Simple consolidation — balance sheet**

Buckley Ltd acquired 100% of the issued capital of Carlos Ltd on 1 July 20X1 for $70 000 cash. The balance sheets of both companies immediately prior to the acquisition were as follows. (All assets were stated at their fair values.)

| Balance Sheets as at 30 June 20X1 | | |
|---|---|---|
| | Buckley Ltd | Carlos Ltd |
| | $ | $ |
| Shareholders' equity | | |
| Paid-up capital | 170 000 | 50 000 |
| Retained profits | 30 000 | 20 000 |
| Total shareholders' equity | $200 000 | $70 000 |
| Assets | | |
| Cash | 80 000 | 1 000 |
| Other current assets | 30 000 | 19 000 |
| Non-current assets | 200 000 | 85 000 |
| Total assets | 310 000 | 105 000 |
| Liabilities | | |
| Creditors & borrowings | 110 000 | 35 000 |
| Net assets | $200 000 | $ 70 000 |

*Required*

1 Prepare the balance sheet for Buckley Ltd as it would appear immediately after the acquisition.

2 Prepare an acquisition analysis and the consolidation journal entry as at the date of acquisition.

3 Prepare the consolidated balance sheet as at 1 July 20X1 (immediately after the acquisition).

**Exercise 5.15**  Simple consolidation — balance sheet

Wilson Ltd acquired 100% of the issued capital of Morrison Ltd on 1 July 20X2 for $240 000. The balance sheets of both companies immediately after the acquisition were as follows. (All assets were stated at their fair values.)

| Balance Sheets as at 1 July 20X2 | | |
|---|---|---|
| | Wilson Ltd | Morrison Ltd |
| | $ | $ |
| *Shareholders' equity* | | |
| Paid-up capital | 600 000 | 200 000 |
| Retained profits | 80 000 | 40 000 |
| Total shareholders' equity | $680 000 | $240 000 |
| | | |
| *Assets* | | |
| Current assets | 200 000 | 90 000 |
| Investment in Morrison Ltd | 240 000 | – |
| Other non-current assets | 550 000 | 270 000 |
| Total assets | 990 000 | 360 000 |
| *Liabilities* | | |
| Current liabilities | 140 000 | 50 000 |
| Non-current liabilities | 170 000 | 70 000 |
| Total liabilities | 310 000 | 120 000 |
| Net assets | $680 000 | $240 000 |

*Required*

1  Prepare an acquisition analysis and the consolidation journal entry as at the date of acquisition.

2  Prepare the consolidated balance sheet as at 1 July 20X2 (immediately after the acquisition).

**Exercise 5.16**  Simple consolidation — profit and loss and balance sheet

Refer to Exercise 5.14.  At 30 June 20X2, 12 months after acquisition, the profit and loss accounts and balance sheets for Buckley Ltd and Carlos Ltd appeared as below.

| Profit and Loss Accounts for the year ended 30 June 20X2 | | |
|---|---|---|
| | Buckley Ltd | Carlos Ltd |
| | $ | $ |
| Revenues | 210 000 | 55 000 |
| Expenses | 187 000 | 48 000 |
| Operating profit before tax | 23 000 | 7 000 |
| Income tax expense | 8 000 | 2 000 |
| Operating profit after tax | 15 000 | 5 0000 |
| Retained profits 1 July 20X1 | 30 000 | 20 000 |
| Retained profits 30 June 20X2 | $45 000 | $25 000 |

| Balance Sheets as at 30 June 20X2 | | |
|---|---|---|
| | Buckley Ltd $ | Carlos Ltd $ |
| *Shareholders' equity* | | |
| Paid-up capital | 170 000 | 50 000 |
| Retained profits | 45 000 | 25 000 |
| Total shareholders' equity | $215 000 | $75 000 |
| | | |
| *Assets* | | |
| Current assets | 60 000 | 25 000 |
| Investment in Carlos Ltd | 70 000 | – |
| Non-current assets | 225 000 | 90 000 |
| Total assets | 355 000 | 115 000 |
| *Liabilities* | | |
| Creditors & borrowings | 120 000 | 35 000 |
| Provisions | 20 000 | 5 000 |
| Total liabilities | 140 000 | 40 000 |
| Net assets | $215 000 | $75 000 |

*Required*

1 Prepare the consolidated profit and loss and balance sheet for the year ending 30 June 20X2.

2 Explain the composition of the consolidated shareholders' equity balance as at 30 June 20X2.

**Exercise 5.17** Simple consolidation — profit and loss and balance sheet

Refer to Exercise 5.15. At 30 June 20X3, 12 months after acquisition, the profit and loss accounts and balance sheets for Wilson Ltd and Morrison Ltd appear as below.

| Profit and Loss Accounts for the year ended 30 June 20X3 | | |
|---|---|---|
| | Wilson Ltd $ | Morrison Ltd $ |
| Revenues | 620 000 | 255 000 |
| Less Cost of goods sold | 340 000 | 125 000 |
| Gross profit | 280 000 | 130 000 |
| Administrative expenses | 90 000 | 27 000 |
| Financial expenses | 75 000 | 36 000 |
| Selling expenses | 55 000 | 43 000 |
| Total expenses | 220 000 | 106 000 |
| Operating profit before tax | 60 000 | 24 000 |
| Income tax expense | 28 000 | 8 000 |
| Operating profit after tax | 32 000 | 16 000 |
| Retained profits 1 July 20X2 | 80 000 | 40 000 |
| | 112 000 | 56 000 |
| Dividend declared | 20 000 | – |
| Retained profits 30 June 20X3 | $92 000 | $56 000 |

| Balance Sheets as at 30 June 20X3 | | |
|---|---|---|
| | *Wilson Ltd* | *Morrison Ltd* |
| | $ | $ |
| *Shareholders' equity* | | |
| Paid-up capital | 600 000 | 200 000 |
| Retained profits | 92 000 | 56 000 |
| Total shareholders' equity | $692 000 | $256 000 |
| | | |
| *Assets* | | |
| Current assets | 225 000 | 101 000 |
| Investment in Morrison Ltd | 240 000 | – |
| Other non-current assets | 612 000 | 290 000 |
| Total assets | 1 077 000 | 391 000 |
| *Liabilities* | | |
| Current liabilities | 180 000 | 65 000 |
| Non-current liabilities | 205 000 | 70 000 |
| Total liabilities | 385 000 | 135 000 |
| Net assets | $692 000 | $256 000 |

*Required*

1 Prepare the consolidated profit and loss and balance sheet for the year ending 30 June 20X3.

2 Explain the composition of the consolidated shareholders' equity balance as at 30 June 20X3.

**Exercise 5.18**

## Dividend from pre-acquisition profits

Waters Ltd acquired 100% of the issued capital of Cale Ltd on 15 June 20X0 for $200 000. At the date of acquisition, Cale Ltd's shareholders' equity comprised paid-up capital amounting to $130 000, retained profits of $40 000 and general reserve of $30 000. All assets of Cale Ltd were stated at fair value.

On 30 June 20X0, the directors of Cale Ltd declared a dividend of $15 000 from the prior year's profits. The dividend was subsequently paid on 30 September 20X0. No other dividends were declared or paid during the year.

At 30 June 20X1, the balance sheets for Waters Ltd and Cale Ltd appeared as below.

| Balance Sheets as at 30 June 20X1 | | |
|---|---|---|
| | *Waters Ltd* | *Cale Ltd* |
| | $ | $ |
| *Shareholders' equity* | | |
| Paid-up capital | 800 000 | 130 000 |
| General reserve | 50 000 | 30 000 |
| Retained profits | 145 000 | 50 000 |
| Total shareholders' equity | $995 000 | $210 000 |

|  | Waters Ltd $ | Cale Ltd $ |
|---|---|---|
| *Assets* |  |  |
| Current assets | 515 000 | 104 000 |
| Investment in Cale Ltd | 185 000 | – |
| Other non-current assets | 720 000 | 286 000 |
| Total assets | 1 420 000 | 390 000 |
| *Liabilities* |  |  |
| Current liabilities | 250 000 | 95 000 |
| Non-current liabilities | 175 000 | 85 000 |
| Total liabilities | 425 000 | 180 000 |
| Net assets | $995 000 | $210 000 |

*Required*

1  Prepare an acquisition analysis.
2  Prepare the consolidation journal entries required as at 30 June 20X1.
3  Prepare the consolidated balance sheet as at 30 June 20X1.

**Exercise 5.19  Dividend from pre-acquisition profits**

Walsh Ltd acquired 100% of the issued capital of Frey Ltd on 30 June 20X1 for $150 000. At the date of acquisition, Frey Ltd's balance sheet appeared as below. (All assets were recorded at fair value.)

| **Frey Ltd** Balance Sheet as at 30 June 20X1 | |
|---|---|
|  | $ |
| *Shareholders' equity* |  |
| Paid-up capital | 80 000 |
| General reserve | 20 000 |
| Retained profits | 30 000 |
| Total shareholders' equity | $130 000 |
| *Assets* |  |
| Current assets | 125 000 |
| Non-current assets | 195 000 |
| Total assets | 320 000 |
| *Liabilities* |  |
| Current liabilities |  |
| Creditors | 100 000 |
| Dividend payable | 20 000 |
| Total current liabilities | 120 000 |
| Non-current liabilities |  |
| Bank loan | 70 000 |
| Total liabilities | 190 000 |
| Net assets | $130 000 |

The dividend provided in Frey's accounts at 30 June 20X1 was paid on 15 August 20X1.  At 30 June 20X2, the profit and loss accounts and balance sheets for Walsh Ltd and Frey Ltd appeared as below.

### Profit and Loss Accounts for the year ended 30 June 20X2

|  | Walsh Ltd $ | Frey Ltd $ |
|---|---|---|
| Revenues | 580 000 | 260 000 |
| *Less* Cost of goods sold | 300 000 | 130 000 |
| *Gross profit* | 280 000 | 130 000 |
| Administrative expenses | 90 000 | 30 000 |
| Financial expenses | 75 000 | 36 000 |
| Selling expenses | 55 000 | 43 000 |
| *Total expenses* | 220 000 | 109 000 |
| *Operating profit before tax* | 60 000 | 21 000 |
| Income tax expense | 28 000 | 8 000 |
| *Operating profit after tax* | 32 000 | 13 000 |
| Retained profits 1 July 20X1 | 43 000 | 30 000 |
|  | 75 000 | 43 000 |
| Dividend declared | 30 000 | 10 000 |
| Retained profits 30 June 20X2 | $45 000 | $33 000 |

### Balance Sheets as at 30 June 20X2

|  | Walsh Ltd $ | Frey Ltd $ |
|---|---|---|
| *Shareholders' equity* |  |  |
| Paid-up capital | 300 000 | 80 000 |
| General reserve | – | 20 000 |
| Retained profits | 45 000 | 33 000 |
| *Total shareholders' equity* | $345 000 | $133 000 |
| *Assets* |  |  |
| Current assets | 245 000 | 132 000 |
| Investment in Frey Ltd | 130 000 | – |
| Other non-current assets | 230 000 | 196 000 |
| *Total assets* | 605 000 | 328 000 |
| *Liabilities* |  |  |
| Current liabilities |  |  |
| Creditors | 55 000 | 105 000 |
| Provisions | 35 000 | 10 000 |
| Dividend payable | 30 000 | 10 000 |
| *Total current liabilities* | 120 000 | 125 000 |
| Non-current liabilities |  |  |
| Bank loan | 90 000 | 70 000 |
| Debentures | 50 000 | – |
| *Total non-current liabilities* | 140 000 | 70 000 |
| *Total liabilities* | 260 000 | 195 000 |
| *Net assets* | $345 000 | $133 000 |

*Required*

1 Prepare an acquisition analysis.
2 Prepare the consolidated profit and loss and balance sheet for the year ending 30 June 20X2.
3 Explain the composition of the consolidated shareholders' equity balance as at 30 June 20X2.

**Exercise 5.20** Goodwill

Joplin Ltd acquired 100% of the issued capital of Hendrix Ltd on 1 July 20X0 for $290 000. The balance sheets of both companies immediately after the acquisition were as follows. (All assets were stated at their fair values.)

| Balance Sheets as at 1 July 20X0 | | |
|---|---|---|
| | Joplin Ltd | Hendrix Ltd |
| | $ | $ |
| *Shareholders' equity* | | |
| Paid-up capital | 400 000 | 200 000 |
| General reserve | 40 000 | 20 000 |
| Retained profits | 120 000 | 30 000 |
| Total shareholders' equity | $560 000 | $250 000 |
| | | |
| *Assets* | | |
| Current assets | 130 000 | 55 000 |
| Investment in Hendrix Ltd | 290 000 | – |
| Other non-current assets | 455 000 | 310 000 |
| Total assets | 875 000 | 365 000 |
| *Liabilities* | | |
| Current liabilities | 145 000 | 35 000 |
| Non-current liabilities | 170 000 | 80 000 |
| Total liabilities | 315 000 | 115 000 |
| Net assets | $560 000 | $250 000 |

*Required*

1 Prepare an acquisition analysis and the consolidation journal entry as at the date of acquisition.
2 Prepare the consolidated balance sheet as at 1 July 20X0 (immediately after the acquisition).

**Exercise 5.21**  Goodwill

Refer to Exercise 5.20. At 30 June 20X1, 12 months after acquisition, the profit and loss accounts and balance sheets for Joplin Ltd and Hendrix Ltd were as follows.

### Profit and Loss Accounts for the year ended 30 June 20X1

|  | Joplin Ltd $ | Hendrix Ltd $ |
|---|---|---|
| Revenues | 475 000 | 295 000 |
| *Less* Cost of goods sold | 215 000 | 135 000 |
| *Gross profit* | 260 000 | 160 000 |
| Administrative expenses | 64 000 | 39 000 |
| Financial expenses | 73 000 | 43 000 |
| Selling expenses | 65 000 | 49 000 |
| *Total expenses* | 202 000 | 131 000 |
| *Operating profit before tax* | 58 000 | 29 000 |
| Income tax expense | 22 000 | 10 000 |
| *Operating profit after tax* | 36 000 | 19 000 |
| Retained profits 1 July 20X0 | 120 000 | 30 000 |
| Retained profits 30 June 20X1 | $156 000 | $49 000 |

### Balance Sheets as at 30 June 20X1

|  | Joplin Ltd $ | Hendrix Ltd $ |
|---|---|---|
| *Shareholders' equity* | | |
| Paid-up capital | 400 000 | 200 000 |
| General reserve | 40 000 | 20 000 |
| Retained profits | 156 000 | 49 000 |
| *Total shareholders' equity* | $596 000 | $269 000 |
| | | |
| *Assets* | | |
| Current assets | 130 000 | 83 000 |
| Investment in Hendrix Ltd | 290 000 | – |
| Other non-current assets | 455 000 | 321 000 |
| *Total assets* | 875 000 | 404 000 |
| *Liabilities* | | |
| Current liabilities | 185 000 | 40 000 |
| Non-current liabilities | 94 000 | 95 000 |
| *Total liabilities* | 279 000 | 135 000 |
| *Net assets* | $596 000 | $269 000 |

*Required*

Prepare the consolidated profit and loss and balance sheet for the year ending 30 June 20X1. Assume that goodwill on acquisition is to be amortised over a ten-year period.

**Exercise 5.22** **Discount on acquisition**
Gates Ltd acquired 100% of the issued capital of Chapin Ltd on 30 June 20X1 for $200 000. The balance sheets of both companies immediately after the acquisition were as follows. (All assets were stated at their fair values.)

| Balance Sheets as at 30 June 20X1 | | |
| --- | --- | --- |
| | Gates Ltd | Chapin Ltd |
| | $ | $ |
| *Shareholders' equity* | | |
| Paid-up capital | 600 000 | 150 000 |
| General reserve | – | 40 000 |
| Retained profits | 75 000 | 40 000 |
| Total shareholders' equity | $675 000 | $230 000 |
| | | |
| *Assets* | | |
| Current assets | | |
| Cash at bank | 5 000 | 2 000 |
| Debtors | 65 000 | 38 000 |
| Inventory | 70 000 | 40 000 |
| Total current assets | 140 000 | 80 000 |
| Non-current assets | | |
| Investment in Chapin Ltd | 200 000 | – |
| Office furniture & fittings (net) | 160 000 | 80 000 |
| Plant & equipment (net) | 225 000 | 140 000 |
| Land | 240 000 | 120 000 |
| Total non-current assets | 825 000 | 340 000 |
| Total assets | 965 000 | 420 000 |
| *Liabilities* | | |
| Current liabilities | 130 000 | 65 000 |
| Non-current liabilities | 160 000 | 125 000 |
| Total liabilities | 290 000 | 190 000 |
| Net assets | $675 000 | $230 000 |

*Required*
1 Prepare an acquisition analysis and the consolidation journal entry as at the date of acquisition.
2 Prepare the consolidated balance sheet as at 30 June 20X1 (immediately after the acquisition).

**Exercise 5.23** **Discount on acquisition**
Page Ltd acquired 100% of the issued capital of Plant Ltd on 30 June 20X2 for $250 000. The balance sheets of both companies immediately after the acquisition were as follows. (All assets were stated at their fair values.)

| Balance Sheets as at 30 June 20X2 | | |
|---|---|---|
| | Page Ltd | Plant Ltd |
| | $ | $ |
| *Shareholders' equity* | | |
| Paid-up capital | 550 000 | 250 000 |
| General reserve | 40 000 | 10 000 |
| Retained profits | 20 000 | 40 000 |
| *Total shareholders' equity* | $610 000 | $300 000 |
| | | |
| *Assets* | | |
| Current assets | | |
| Cash at bank | 10 000 | 5 000 |
| Debtors | 80 000 | 20 000 |
| Inventory | 100 000 | 20 000 |
| Other current assets (monetary) | 60 000 | 5 000 |
| *Total current assets* | 250 000 | 50 000 |
| Non-current assets | | |
| Investment in Plant Ltd | 250 000 | – |
| Office furniture & fittings (net) | 100 000 | 80 000 |
| Plant & machinery (net) | 100 000 | 140 000 |
| Land & buildings (net) | 220 000 | 210 000 |
| Patents | – | 100 000 |
| *Total non-current assets* | 670 000 | 530 000 |
| *Total assets* | 920 000 | 580 000 |
| *Liabilities* | | |
| Current liabilities | 150 000 | 90 000 |
| Non-current liabilities | 160 000 | 190 000 |
| *Total liabilities* | 310 000 | 280 000 |
| *Net assets* | $610 000 | $300 000 |

*Required*

1 Prepare an acquisition analysis and the consolidation journal entry as at the date of acquisition.

2 Prepare the consolidated balance sheet as at 30 June 20X2 (immediately after the acquisition).

**Exercise 5.24** **Revaluation of subsidiary's assets**

Jagger Ltd acquired 100% of the issued capital of Richards Ltd for $260 000 on 30 June 20X3. The balance sheets of both companies immediately after the acquisition were as follows.

| Balance Sheets as at 30 June 20X3 | | |
|---|---|---|
| | Jagger Ltd | Richards Ltd |
| | $ | $ |
| *Shareholders' equity* | | |
| Paid-up capital | 350 000 | 100 000 |
| General reserve | 10 000 | 10 000 |
| Retained profits | 40 000 | 40 000 |
| *Total shareholders' equity* | $400 000 | $150 000 |
| | | |
| *Assets* | | |
| Current assets | | |
| Cash | 10 000 | 5 000 |
| Receivables | 60 000 | 30 000 |
| Inventory | 50 000 | 30 000 |
| *Total current assets* | 120 000 | 65 000 |
| Non-current assets | | |
| Investment in Richards Ltd | 260 000 | – |
| Plant & machinery | 400 000 | 135 000 |
| Accumulated depreciation | (280 000) | (40 000) |
| Land | 120 000 | 90 000 |
| *Total non-current assets* | 500 000 | 185 000 |
| *Total assets* | 620 000 | 250 000 |
| *Liabilities* | | |
| Current liabilities | | |
| Creditors | 40 000 | 35 000 |
| Provision for income tax payable | 35 000 | 15 000 |
| Dividend payable | 25 000 | – |
| *Total current liabilities* | 100 000 | 50 000 |
| Non-current liabilities | | |
| Bank loan | 120 000 | 50 000 |
| *Total liabilities* | 220 000 | 100 000 |
| *Net assets* | $400 000 | $150 000 |

Additional information:
(a) At the date of acquisition, the identifiable net assets of Richards Ltd were recorded at fair value with the exception of land, which had a book value of $90 000 and a fair value of $160 000.
(b) Any goodwill on acquisition is to be amortised over a 20-year period.

*Required*
1 Prepare an acquisition analysis and consolidation journal entries as at the date of acquisition.
2 Prepare the consolidated balance sheet as at 30 June 20X3 (immediately after the acquisition).

**Exercise 5.25** **Comprehensive**

On 1 July 20X1, Lennon Ltd acquired control of McCartney Ltd by purchasing 100% of its issued capital for $160 000. At the date of acquisition, the equity of McCartney Ltd consisted of:

| | |
|---|---:|
| Paid-up capital | $80 000 |
| Retained profits | 15 000 |
| General reserve | 10 000 |

At 30 June 20X2, 12 months after acquisition, the profit and loss accounts and balance sheets for Lennon Ltd and McCartney Ltd were as follows.

| Profit and Loss Accounts for the year ended 30 June 20X2 | | |
|---|---:|---:|
| | *Lennon Ltd* | *McCartney Ltd* |
| | $ | $ |
| Operating revenue | 285 000 | 130 000 |
| *Cost of goods sold* | | |
| Opening stock 1 July 20X1 | 60 000 | 10 000 |
| Purchases | 160 000 | 80 000 |
| | 220 000 | 90 000 |
| Closing stock 30 June 20X2 | 70 000 | 25 000 |
| *Cost of goods sold* | 150 000 | 65 000 |
| *Gross profit* | 135 000 | 65 000 |
| Administrative expenses | 13 000 | 8 500 |
| Financial expenses | 13 500 | 15 000 |
| Selling expenses | 15 000 | 14 500 |
| *Total expenses* | 41 500 | 38 000 |
| *Operating profit before tax* | 93 500 | 27 000 |
| Income tax expense | 29 000 | 8 000 |
| *Operating profit after tax* | 64 500 | 19 000 |
| Retained profits 1 July 20X1 | 15 000 | 15 000 |
| | 79 500 | 34 000 |
| Dividend proposed | 35 000 | 10 000 |
| Retained profits 30 June 20X2 | $44 500 | $24 000 |

| Balance Sheets as at 30 June 20X2 | | |
|---|---|---|
| | Lennon Ltd | McCartney Ltd |
| | $ | $ |
| *Shareholders' equity* | | |
| Paid-up capital | 250 000 | 80 000 |
| General reserve | – | 10 000 |
| Retained profits | 44 500 | 24 000 |
| Total shareholders' equity | $294 500 | $114 000 |
| | | |
| *Assets* | | |
| Current assets | | |
| Cash | 5 000 | 2 000 |
| Receivables | 15 000 | 12 000 |
| Inventory | 70 000 | 25 000 |
| Other current assets | 5 000 | 10 000 |
| Total current assets | 95 000 | 49 000 |
| Non-current assets | | |
| Investment in McCartney Ltd | 145 000 | – |
| Plant & machinery | 130 000 | 120 000 |
| Accumulated depreciation | (95 000) | (45 000) |
| Land | 120 000 | 80 000 |
| Other non-current assets | 15 000 | 5 000 |
| Total non-current assets | 315 000 | 160 000 |
| Total assets | 410 000 | 209 000 |
| *Liabilities* | | |
| Current liabilities | | |
| Creditors | 17 000 | 28 000 |
| Provision for income tax payable | 28 500 | 7 000 |
| Dividend payable | 35 000 | 10 000 |
| Total current liabilities | 80 500 | 45 000 |
| Non-current liabilities | | |
| Bank loan | 35 000 | 50 000 |
| Total liabilities | 115 500 | 95 000 |
| Net assets | $294 500 | $114 000 |

Additional information:
(a) At the date of acquisition, the identifiable net assets of McCartney Ltd were recorded at fair value with the exception of land, which had a book value of $80 000 and a fair value of $105 000. This land has not been revalued by McCartney Ltd during the year ended 30 June 20X2 and is still held by the company at balance date.
(b) On 15 July 20X1, McCartney Ltd paid a dividend of $15 000 to Lennon Ltd. This dividend had been provided for in the prior financial year's accounts.
(c) The dividend of $10 000 provided in McCartney Ltd's accounts for the current year is to be paid from pre-acquisition profits.
(d) Any goodwill on acquisition is to be amortised over a ten-year period.

*Required*

1  Prepare an acquisition analysis.
2  Prepare the consolidated profit and loss and balance sheet for the year ending 30 June 20X2.

**Exercise 5.26**  **Comprehensive**

Harrison Ltd acquired 100% of the issued capital of Starr Ltd for $210 000 on 1 July 20X2.  At the date of acquisition, the equity of Starr Ltd consisted of:

| | |
|---|---|
| Paid-up capital | $120 000 |
| Retained profits | 25 000 |
| General reserve | 15 000 |

At 30 June 20X3, 12 months after acquisition, the profit and loss accounts and balance sheets for Harrison Ltd and Starr Ltd were as follows.

**Profit and Loss Accounts for the year ended 30 June 20X3**

| | Harrison Ltd $ | Starr Ltd $ |
|---|---|---|
| Operating revenue | 470 000 | 260 000 |
| Cost of goods sold | 225 000 | 110 000 |
| *Gross profit* | 245 000 | 150 000 |
| Depreciation | 42 000 | 35 000 |
| Interest expense | 17 000 | 10 000 |
| Office expenses | 19 500 | 17 000 |
| Salaries | 39 000 | 39 000 |
| Selling expenses | 17 000 | 8 000 |
| *Total expenses* | 134 500 | 109 000 |
| *Operating profit before tax* | 110 500 | 41 000 |
| Income tax expense | 39 500 | 14 000 |
| *Operating profit after tax* | 71 000 | 27 000 |
| Retained profits 1 July 20X2 | 30 000 | 25 000 |
| | 101 000 | 52 000 |
| Dividends paid | 50 000 | 20 000 |
| Retained profits 30 June 20X3 | $51 000 | $32 000 |

**Balance Sheets as at 30 June 20X3**

| | Harrison Ltd $ | Starr Ltd $ |
|---|---|---|
| *Shareholders' equity* | | |
| Paid-up capital | 350 000 | 120 000 |
| General reserve | 30 000 | 15 000 |
| Retained profits | 51 000 | 32 000 |
| *Total shareholders' equity* | $431 000 | $167 000 |

|  | Harrison Ltd $ | Starr Ltd $ |
|---|---|---|
| *Assets* | | |
| Current assets | | |
| Cash | 8 000 | 3 000 |
| Receivables | 38 000 | 40 000 |
| Inventory | 34 000 | 34 000 |
| Other current assets | 15 000 | 5 000 |
| *Total current assets* | 95 000 | 82 000 |
| Non-current assets | | |
| Investment in Starr Ltd | 190 000 | – |
| Office equipment | 140 000 | 84 000 |
| Accumulated depreciation | (40 000) | (36 000) |
| Plant & machinery | 170 000 | 160 000 |
| Accumulated depreciation | (70 000) | (95 000) |
| Land | 160 000 | 120 000 |
| Other non-current assets | 16 000 | 2 000 |
| *Total non-current assets* | 566 000 | 235 000 |
| *Total assets* | 661 000 | 317 000 |
| *Liabilities* | | |
| Current liabilities | | |
| Creditors | 37 000 | 53 000 |
| Provision for income tax payable | 42 000 | 12 000 |
| Other current liabilities | 16 000 | 5 000 |
| *Total current liabilities* | 95 000 | 70 000 |
| Non-current liabilities | | |
| Bank loan | 135 000 | 80 000 |
| *Total liabilities* | 230 000 | 150 000 |
| *Net assets* | $431 000 | $167 000 |

Additional information:
(a) At the date of acquisition, the identifiable net assets of Starr Ltd were recorded at fair value with the exception of land, which had a book value of $120 000 and a fair value of $150 000. This land has not been revalued by Starr Ltd during the year ended 30 June 20X3 and is still held by the company at balance date.
(b) On 19 August 20X2, Starr Ltd declared a dividend of $20 000 from pre-acquisition profits. This dividend was subsequently paid to Lennon Ltd on 30 September 20X2.
(d) Any goodwill on acquisition is to be amortised over a ten-year period.

*Required*
1 Prepare an acquisition analysis.
2 Prepare the consolidated profit and loss and balance sheet for the year ending 30 June 20X3.

# chapter 6

CONSOLIDATION: INTER-ENTITY
TRANSACTIONS

# introduction

This chapter discusses the third step in the consolidation process introduced in chapter 5 – that is, the preparation of consolidation journal adjustment entries to eliminate, when preparing consolidated accounts, the effect of any inter-entity transactions and balances between members of the economic entity.

It is common for separate entities in an economic entity to have transactions with each other. Examples of these transactions are the supply of raw materials, finished goods and services by one entity to another in the group. Entities of the group may also borrow from others in the economic entity and pay dividends from post-acquisition profits to parent entities within the group.

An economic entity cannot boost its profits or asset values by way of group members trading with each other. As explained in the previous chapter, the purpose of consolidated accounts is to show the operating result and financial position of the economic entity in its dealings with entities outside the group. To show these results, AASB 1024 specifies that the effects of inter-entity transactions between group members must be removed in full (para 23). As an entity cannot transact with itself, this elimination of transactions and balances between individual group entities is required if the economic entity is to be reflected, for financial reporting purposes, as a single reporting entity (AASB 1024, commentary, para (xxxvii)). Under the entity approach of AASB 1024, all inter-entity transactions are removed in full, regardless of whether the parent entity owns all or only some of the equity of a subsidiary.

# Inter-entity (intra-group) transactions

**inter-entity transactions**

**intra-group transactions**

The term *inter-entity transactions* refers to the transactions that have taken place between individual entities of an economic entity and that are reported in the financial statements of those individual entities. As the parties to these transactions are members of the same group, such transactions are also referred to as intra-group (within the group) transactions. The terms *inter-entity* and *intra-group* are used interchangeably in this chapter.

Transactions between entities in an economic entity are recorded in the accounts of the separate entities of the group as they occur. AASB 1024 requires any amounts owing and receivable between members of an economic entity, and any inter-entity transactions which create a profit or loss not realised by the economic entity, to be eliminated when preparing consolidated accounts (commentary, para (xxxviii)). This elimination of intra-group transactions and balances is achieved by preparing consolidation journal entries for processing in the consolidation worksheet.

**unrealised profit or loss**

The elimination of intra-group transactions may result in timing differences for income tax purposes arising between the recognition of profit or loss in an individual entity and the recognition of that profit or loss by the economic entity. If this is the case, AASB 1024 (commentary, para (xxxix)) requires adjustments also to be made to the economic entity's Income Tax Expense and Future Income Tax Benefit and Deferred Income Tax Liability accounts, as appropriate, in accordance with AASB 1020: Accounting for Income Tax (Tax-Effect Accounting).

This chapter will discuss and demonstrate the specific elimination entries for intra-group transactions relating to:

- services;
- sale of inventory;
- sale of depreciable assets;
- borrowings; and
- payment of inter-entity dividends from post-acquisition profits.

# Intra-group services

**intra-group services**

Intra-group services are the simplest type of inter-entity transaction. They create items of service revenue and service expense in the accounts of the respective separate entities of the group. Examples of these transactions are rental of premises and equipment, management fees, and the provision of specialist services to one entity by staff from another entity. While the revenue of one entity balances out the expenses of the other entity, and hence does not have an effect on the amount of group profit, failure to remove the applicable revenue and expense items from the consolidated accounts would result in the actual amount of revenue and expense being overstated in the accounts of the economic entity.

For example, assume that subsidiary S Ltd rents premises from parent P Ltd, with P Ltd recording rental income of $30 000 in its accounts and S Ltd recording rental expense of $30 000 in its accounts. The consolidation elimination journal entry in this situation is:

### Consolidation journal

| | Debit | Credit |
|---|---|---|
| Rental Income | 30 000 | |
|     Rental Expense | | 30 000 |

Likewise, if S Ltd pays management fees of $25 000 to P Ltd (or vice versa), the consolidation elimination journal entry is:

### Consolidation journal

| | Debit | Credit |
|---|---|---|
| Management Fees Income | 25 000 | |
|     Management Fees Expense | | 25 000 |

Note that, for service transactions, the direction of the transaction has no effect on the consolidation elimination entry. That is, in the above examples of intra-group sales and management fees, it makes no difference whether P Ltd or S Ltd has derived the revenue. The consolidation journal entry simply eliminates the amount of revenue and expense, without any consideration required of which individual entity has derived the revenue and which individual entity has incurred the expense.

There is also no tax-effect adjustment required in these cases because no adjustment has been made to the amount of consolidated operating profit.

Inter-entity services may also result in account balances existing in the balance sheets of the individual entities at reporting date. For example, it is common for rent to be paid in advance. Assume that S Ltd prepaid rent of $2000 to P Ltd. In this case, the accounts of P Ltd would include a liability 'Unearned Rental Income' for $2000 while the accounts of S Ltd would record an asset 'Prepaid Rent' of $2000. As this amount does not represent an asset/liability owing from/to other entities outside the economic entity, the amount of inter-entity prepaid rent recorded in the accounts must be eliminated with the following consolidation journal entry.

### Consolidation journal

| | Debit | Credit |
|---|---|---|
| Unearned Rental Income (Liability) | 2000 | |
|     Prepaid Rent (Asset) | | 2000 |

# Intra-group sale of inventory

### SALES AND PURCHASES

**intra-group inventory sales**

Any intra-group inventory sales will result in the individual entities recording sales and purchases, respectively, for the amount of the transaction. Failure to eliminate these sales and purchases in preparing the consolidated accounts will result in the turnover of the economic entity being overstated with respect to dealings with entities outside the group.

For the purposes of the discussion in this chapter, the periodic system of accounting for inventory will be assumed. As an example of the intra-group sale of inventory, assume that, during the period, S Ltd sold inventory to P Ltd for $10 000 and P Ltd sold inventory to S Ltd for $5000. As with intra-group services, it makes no difference which way the sales were made. They are simply intra-group sales and purchases that must be eliminated from the consolidated accounts. In this example, the intra-group sales and purchases amount to $15 000. The consolidation elimination entry is therefore:

**Consolidation journal**

|  | Debit | Credit |
|---|---|---|
| Sales | 15 000 | |
| Purchases | | 15 000 |

It can be seen that the effect of this consolidation entry is identical to that of the elimination of intra-group services discussed in the previous section. That is, the relevant revenue item is debited and the relevant expense item is credited in the consolidation worksheet.

## UNREALISED PROFIT IN CLOSING INVENTORY

While it would be simpler from a consolidation point of view for inventory to be transferred between entities in a group at cost, this is not normally the case. Rather, because the separate entities operate with their own performance measures, inventory will usually be sold at a profit.

If any inventory is sold at a profit between individual entities in a group and remains on hand within the group at the end of the accounting period (i.e. it is still held by one of the entities within the group at reporting date), its cost to the economic entity will be overstated. For example, assume that S Ltd buys inventory from outside the group for a cost of $4000. This inventory is then sold to P Ltd for $6000 and remains on hand at the end of the accounting period. This situation is depicted in Figure 6.1.

**Figure 6.1**
Cost of closing inventory to economic entity

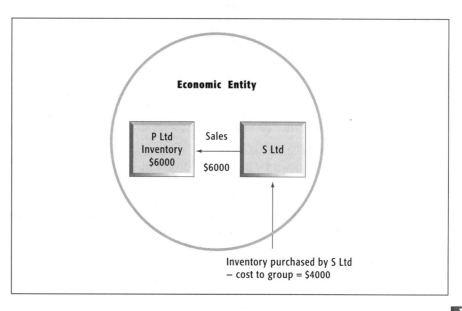

In this case, the inventory entered the group at a cost of $4000 and, from the economic entity's point of view, must be recorded at the lower of cost or net realisable value (i.e. $4000). Two adjustments are required in the preparation of the consolidated accounts in this situation. The sale by S Ltd and the purchase by P Ltd is an intra-group sale of inventory transaction and must be eliminated on consolidation, as discussed in the previous section. Also, the profit on this transaction recorded by S Ltd must be eliminated in preparing the consolidated accounts, as this profit has not been earned from entities outside the group (i.e. it is unrealised from the economic entity viewpoint). The consolidation elimination is achieved by adjusting for the overvaluation of inventory, from the group viewpoint, recorded by P Ltd in its accounts. A record of the journal entries recorded in the individual accounts of S Ltd and P Ltd will help in understanding this consolidation adjustment.

The transactions recorded in the accounts of S Ltd during the period, shown in general journal format and assuming the transactions were for cash, would have been:

### General journal of S Ltd

|  | Debit | Credit |
| --- | --- | --- |
| Purchases | 4000 | |
|     Cash | | 4000 |
| (purchase of inventory) | | |
| | | |
| Cash | 6000 | |
|     Sales | | 6000 |
| (sale of inventory) | | |

The entries recorded in the accounts of P Ltd during the period would have been:

### General journal of P Ltd

|  | Debit | Credit |
| --- | --- | --- |
| Purchases | 6000 | |
|     Cash | | 6000 |
| (purchase of inventory) | | |
| | | |
| Inventory (Balance Sheet) | 6000 | |
|     Closing Stock (P&L) | | 6000 |
| (closing inventory) | | |

In discussing inventory adjustments for consolidated accounts, a distinction between whether an asset or cost of goods sold account is being affected will be made by using the account title 'Inventory' to indicate an asset and 'Opening Stock' and 'Closing Stock' to indicate cost of goods sold accounts in the profit and loss statement.

*Consolidation adjustments*
In this example, the closing inventory should be valued at $4000 original cost from an economic entity viewpoint. S Ltd has recorded a profit of $2000 and, as a separate entity, pays tax on this profit. However, from an economic entity point of view, no profit has yet been made but, rather, will only be made when P Ltd resells the inventory outside the group. Because this is a timing difference, an adjustment is required to the income tax expense of the group. The recording and payment of income tax expense by S Ltd creates a future income tax benefit from the economic entity point of view. Also, as the gross amount of the profit on the intra-group sale must be eliminated in preparing the consolidated accounts, so too must the income tax expense related to that profit.

In this example, the consolidation adjusting journal entries relating to the inter-entity transfer of inventory, assuming a tax rate of 40%, are:

## Consolidation journal

|  | Debit | Credit |
|---|---|---|
| Sales | 6000 |  |
| Purchases |  | 6000 |
|  |  |  |
| Closing Stock (P&L) | 2000 |  |
| Inventory (Balance Sheet) |  | 2000 |
|  |  |  |
| Future Income Tax Benefit | 800 |  |
| Income Tax Expense |  | 800 |

The consolidated accounts will now show purchases of $4000 and inventory of $4000 for this stock purchased by the group during the period and which remains on hand at the end of the period. The $2000 profit recorded in the accounts of S Ltd, and the $800 income tax expense applicable to this profit, will also have been eliminated with the above consolidation journal entries.

If all of the inventory sold by S Ltd to P Ltd had been resold outside the group by P Ltd, there would be no unrealised profit in closing stock and all profit would have been realised by the group. Part of the profit would be recognised in the accounts of S Ltd and part in the accounts of P Ltd. In this situation, the only consolidation entry required is for the elimination of the gross amount of the inter-entity sale. However, if only some of the inventory sold to P Ltd by S Ltd had been sold outside the group by P Ltd during the period, the only amount relevant for consolidation adjustment purposes (apart from the gross amount of the inter-entity sale) is the cost of the proportion of inventory still held by P Ltd at the end of the period.

Assume that one-half of the inventory purchased by S Ltd and sold to P Ltd has been sold by P Ltd outside the economic entity. This situation is depicted in Figure 6.2.

**Figure 6.2**
Cost of closing inventory to economic entity

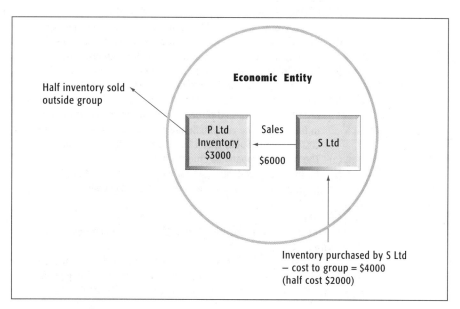

As one-half of the inventory has been resold outside the group, no consolidation adjustment is required for this portion of the profit on the sale of inventory that was originally the subject of the inter-entity sale. However, the remaining portion of inventory is still held by P Ltd. While this one-half portion had a cost to the group of $2000, it is now recorded in P Ltd's accounts at $3000. Hence, a consolidation adjustment is required for this $1000 unrealised profit and the $400 tax expense applicable to this profit. The full set of consolidation adjustment entries relating to this inventory, assuming a tax rate of 40%, is:

### Consolidation journal

| | Debit | Credit |
|---|---|---|
| Sales | 6000 | |
|     Purchases | | 6000 |
| | | |
| Closing Stock (P&L) | 1000 | |
|     Inventory (Balance Sheet) | | 1000 |
| | | |
| Future Income Tax Benefit | 400 | |
|     Income Tax Expense | | 400 |

## ILLUSTRATIVE EXAMPLE 6.1

# CONSOLIDATION USING INTRA-GROUP SERVICES AND SALE OF INVENTORY

Kay Ltd is a wholly-owned subsidiary of Jay Ltd. An extract of the accounts of the two companies for the year ending 30 June 20X3 is shown in the worksheet below.

Additional information:
(a) During the accounting period, Kay Ltd paid management fees of $15 000 to Jay Ltd. This expense appears in Kay's accounts under the 'Financial expenses' heading.
(b) Jay paid $10 000 to Kay for laboratory testing services during the period. This expense appears in Jay's accounts under the 'Other expenses' heading.
(c) Kay sold inventory to Jay for $15 000 during the period. All of this inventory was sold by Jay to parties external to the group during the period.
(d) Jay sold inventory to Kay for $40 000 during the period. This inventory had originally cost Jay $20 000. Kay sold three-quarters of this inventory during the period to parties external to the group. The remaining one-quarter (i.e. with a cost to Kay of $10 000 and an original cost to Jay of $5000) is still held by Kay at the end of the period.
(e) The rate of company income tax is 36%.
(f) All other consolidation journal entries (i.e. other than those required for the above intra-group transactions) have no effect on the calculation of group profit.

*Required*
1 Prepare the consolidation elimination journal entries required for the above intra-group transactions.
2 Complete the consolidation worksheet (extract) below for the year ending 30 June 20X3.
3 Provide an explanation of the difference between the aggregate of operating profit after tax for the two individual entities compared to consolidated operating profit after tax.

**Solution**

**1 Consolidation journal entries**

## Consolidation journal

|  | Debit $ | Credit $ |
|---|---|---|
| (1) Elimination of intra-group management fees. | | |
| Management Fees Income | 15 000 | |
| Financial Expenses | | 15 000 |
| (2) Elimination of intra-group laboratory service fees. | | |
| Laboratory Services Income | 10 000 | |
| Other Expenses | | 10 000 |
| (3) Elimination of intra-group sales and purchases of inventory. | | |
| Sales | 55 000 | |
| Purchases | | 55 000 |
| (4) Elimination of unrealised profit in closing inventory. | | |
| Closing Stock (P&L) | 5 000 | |
| Inventory (Balance Sheet) | | 5 000 |
| (5) Elimination of income tax expense on unrealised profit. | | |
| Future Income Tax Benefit | 1 800 | |
| Income Tax Expense | | 1 800 |

**2 Consolidation worksheet (extract)**

| Account | Jay Ltd | Kay Ltd | Eliminations Debit | Eliminations Credit | Consolidation |
|---|---|---|---|---|---|
|  | $ | $ | $ | $ | $ |
| Sales | 380 000 | 250 000 | 55 000 (3) | | 575 000 |
| Opening stock 1 July 20X2 | 20 000 | 10 000 | | | 30 000 |
| Purchases | 190 000 | 115 000 | | 55 000 (3) | 250 000 |
|  | 210 000 | 125 000 | | | 280 000 |
| Closing stock 30 June 20X3 | 25 000 | 20 000 | 5 000 (4) | | 40 000 |
| Cost of goods sold | 185 000 | 105 000 | | | 240 000 |
| Gross profit | 195 000 | 145 000 | | | 335 000 |
| Administrative expenses | 36 000 | 35 000 | | | 71 000 |
| Financial expenses | 34 000 | 30 000 | | 15 000 (1) | 49 000 |
| Selling expenses | 40 000 | 35 000 | | | 75 000 |
| Other expenses | 30 000 | 25 000 | | 10 000 (2) | 45 000 |
| Total expenses | 140 000 | 125 000 | | | 240 000 |
|  | 55 000 | 20 000 | | | 95 000 |

**(continued)**

| Account | Jay Ltd | Kay Ltd | Eliminations Debit | Eliminations Credit | Consolidation |
|---|---|---|---|---|---|
| | $ | $ | $ | $ | $ |
| *Other revenue* | | | | | |
| Laboratory services income | – | 10 000 | 10 000 (2) | | – |
| Management fees income | 15 000 | – | 15 000 (1) | | – |
| Interest revenue | 10 000 | 5 000 | | | 15 000 |
| *Total other revenue* | 25 000 | 15 000 | | | 15 000 |
| *Operating profit before tax* | 80 000 | 35 000 | | | 110 000 |
| Income tax expense | 25 000 | 10 000 | | 1 800 (5) | 33 200 |
| *Operating profit after tax* | $55 000 | $25 000 | | | $76 800 |
| | | | | | |
| *Assets* | | | | | |
| Inventory | 25 000 | 20 000 | | 5 000 (4) | 40 000 |
| Future income tax benefit | 10 000 | 5 000 | 1 800 (5) | | 16 800 |
| | | | $86 800 | $86 800 | |

### 3 Explanation of group operating profit after tax

The aggregate of the operating profit after tax for the individual entities totals $80 000 (i.e. $55 000 for Jay Ltd plus $25 000 for Kay Ltd). However, consolidated operating profit after tax amounts to $76 800. The difference of $3200 represents the gross amount of unrealised profit on the intra-group sale of inventory ($5000) less the income tax applicable to this profit ($1800). It should be noted that the consolidation entries for the elimination of management fees ($15 000), laboratory service fees ($10 000) and the gross amount of intra-group inventory sales/purchases ($55 000) has had no effect on the actual amount of consolidated operating profit after tax, as the relevant revenue and expense items for these intra-group transactions offset each other.

## UNREALISED PROFIT IN OPENING INVENTORY

The closing inventory held by an entity at the end of one period becomes the opening stock in the profit and loss summary for the next period. Any inventory transferred between entities in a group at a profit in a prior period, and not resold by the receiving entity at the end of the prior period, will remain recorded in the accounts of that individual entity at cost. That cost will include the unrealised profit on the earlier intra-group sale. Accordingly, from a group viewpoint, the opening stock of the economic entity will be overstated if a consolidation adjustment is not made.

Assume the same situation as in the immediately preceding example relating to P Ltd and S Ltd (i.e. unrealised profit of $1000 in closing inventory), but that it is now the following accounting period. The opening inventory of P Ltd has been recorded in its accounts at a cost of $3000. However, the original cost of this inventory to the group was $2000, and this was the value recorded for this inventory in the prior year's consolidated accounts after the elimination of the $1000 unrealised profit.

From a group point of view, the opening retained profits and the opening stock of P Ltd will be overstated by $1000 before tax. The opening retained profits of P Ltd will be overstated as the $1000 unrealised profit in the prior year was only eliminated in the consolidated accounts via the consolidation worksheet, and not in P Ltd's individual accounts. Hence, a consolidation journal entry to eliminate this unrealised profit in opening inventory is required in the current period.

A tax-effect adjusting entry will also be required as tax was paid by P Ltd last year but was not due, from an economic entity viewpoint, until this year when the inventory is sold outside the group. The result of income tax expense for a prior period is reflected in opening retained profits for the current period. Hence, the consolidation adjustment entries required, again assuming a 40% tax rate, are:

## Consolidation journal

|  | Debit | Credit |
|---|---|---|
| Retained Profits (Beginning of Period) | 1000 | |
| Opening Stock (P&L) | | 1000 |
| Income Tax Expense | 400 | |
| Retained Profits (Beginning of Period) | | 400 |

The effect of these adjustments is to move the profit on the sale of this inventory, in the consolidated accounts, from the previous accounting period to the current period. These adjustments for unrealised profit in opening inventory would also be required in the following accounting period if this inventory was not sold in the current period. The fact that the inventory would still be on hand at the end of the current period will be accounted for in the consolidated accounts when adjustments for unrealised profit in closing inventory are made.

It should be remembered that consolidated accounts are notional accounts prepared each period on the basis of the individual accounts of the group entities. Therefore, when preparing the accounts in the current period, the Future Income Tax Benefit account raised in the previous period in adjusting for the tax effect on closing stock of that period will not be in the accounts of either P Ltd or S Ltd, and therefore does not come into account when making the tax-effect adjustments for the current period. The after-tax profit on opening stock is simply shifted, by way of the consolidation adjustment entries outlined above, from the previous period to the current period.

# Intra-group sale of depreciable assets

**intra-group non-current asset sales**

Similar consolidation principles as were discussed for the intra-group sale of inventory are also applicable to intra-group non-current asset sales. The intra-group sale of depreciable assets, such as plant and equipment, will be discussed in this section, as additional consolidation adjustments arise due to depreciation effects.

If a non-current asset is sold between two entities in a group, a consolidation adjustment is required to return the value of the asset and any accumulated depreciation to that recorded in the selling entity at the time of transfer. Also, any gain or loss on sale must be eliminated from the consolidated accounts. From a group viewpoint, there has not been any gain or loss on sale of the asset as there has been no transaction with an external party. Rather, the asset has simply moved from one entity to another within the group.

The consolidation journal entry will also include a tax-effect adjustment because of a timing difference arising from the group point of view, and this will also be discussed in detail below.

Assume that P Ltd sold an item of equipment to S Ltd for $12 000 on 1 July 20X0. The equipment had originally been acquired by P Ltd five years previously at a cost of $20 000. P Ltd has been charging depreciation on this equipment at 10% straight line. Accordingly, accumulated depreciation of $10 000 had been recorded as at the date of sale. On acquiring the asset, S Ltd assessed that the equipment still had a remaining useful life of five years and therefore commenced depreciating the equipment at 20% per annum straight line.

### ADJUSTMENTS FOR PROFIT OR LOSS ON SALE

Immediately after the sale, the equipment is recorded in S Ltd's accounts at $12 000. P Ltd has recorded a profit of $2000 on the sale of the asset, being the difference between the sale price of $12 000 and the written-down value of $10 000. For consolidation purposes, this unrealised profit of $2000 must be eliminated. Also, the equipment asset account must be returned to original cost of $20 000 and accumulated depreciation on this equipment amounting to $10 000 must be reinstated. At 30 June 20X1, the financial year in which the transfer was made, the consolidation adjustment required is:

**Consolidation journal**

|  | Debit | Credit |
|---|---|---|
| Profit on Sale of Equipment | 2 000 | |
| Equipment | 8 000 | |
|     Accumulated Depreciation – Equipment | | 10 000 |

The tax effect of the elimination of the profit on sale must also be considered. A timing difference has arisen from the viewpoint of the economic entity. P Ltd has recorded and paid tax on a profit of $2000. However, from an economic entity point of view, there is no profit and hence no income tax expense applicable to this profit. Because P Ltd has recorded and paid income tax expense on the profit, a future income tax benefit must be created with respect to the economic entity. This future income tax benefit will be reversed as S Ltd depreciates the asset at 20% per annum on $12 000 over the asset's life and thus records less profit and therefore less income tax expense each year than is applicable from a group point of view. (This point will become clearer when depreciation adjustments are discussed in the next section.) The tax effect consolidation adjustment applicable to the profit on sale at 30 June 20X1, assuming a tax rate of 40%, is:

**Consolidation journal**

| | Debit | Credit |
|---|---|---|
| Future Income Tax Benefit ($2000 × 40%) | 800 | |
|    Income Tax Expense | | 800 |

Because consolidated accounts are notional accounts prepared each year from the individual accounts of the subsidiaries, consolidation adjustment entries for the asset must continue to be made while the asset remains within the economic entity. For example, the consolidation adjusting entries at 30 June 20X2, two years after the transfer of the equipment, will be:

**Consolidation journal**

| | Debit | Credit |
|---|---|---|
| Retained Profits 1 July 20X1 | 2 000 | |
| Equipment | 8 000 | |
|    Accumulated Depreciation – Equipment | | 10 000 |
| | | |
| Future Income Tax Benefit | 800 | |
|    Retained Profits 1 July 20X1 | | 800 |

If a loss was recorded on the intra-group sale, the same principles discussed above apply. From an economic entity point of view, no loss would be incurred and the income tax deduction for the loss would not be applicable to the group at the time of transfer of the asset.

Assume that, in the example above, the inter-entity sale price of the equipment was $9000, resulting in a loss on sale of $1000. The consolidation journal entries in the year of the sale would be:

**Consolidation journal**

| | Debit | Credit |
|---|---|---|
| Equipment | 11 000 | |
|    Loss on Sale of Equipment | | 1000 |
|    Accumulated Depreciation – Equipment | | 10 000 |
| | | |
| Income Tax Expense | 400 | |
|    Provision for Deferred Income Tax | | 400 |

## DEPRECIATION ADJUSTMENTS

When a depreciable asset is transferred between entities in an economic entity, the acquiring entity depreciates the asset based on its cost (i.e. the sale price) over the expected remaining life of the asset. If there is an intra-group sale of an asset at a gain or loss, the depreciation applied by the acquiring entity will not be that applicable to the economic entity. Therefore, adjustments will be required to restate the depreciation charged in the consolidated accounts, and income tax expense, to the amount applicable had the sale not taken place, as this is the amount applicable to the economic entity.

For example, assume the earlier information where equipment was sold from P Ltd to S Ltd at a profit of $2000 and S Ltd assessed the further life of the equipment as five years. S Ltd will charge depreciation of $2400 per annum (20% of $12 000). However, from an economic entity viewpoint, depreciation should be charged at 10% of the $20 000 original cost to P Ltd, or $2000 per annum. From the group point of view, depreciation is being overcharged by $400 per annum. The consolidation adjustment entry required at 30 June 20X1 is:

**Consolidation journal**

| | Debit | Credit |
|---|---|---|
| Accumulated Depreciation – Equipment | 400 | |
| Depreciation Expense | | 400 |

An adjustment to depreciation expense results in an adjustment to operating profit. Thus, an income tax timing difference arises. As S Ltd depreciates the asset based on its cost of $12 000 ($2400 per annum) and claims a tax deduction for this amount, the future income tax benefit created by the tax-effect entry on the adjustment for the profit on sale of the asset (discussed in the previous section) is now being received by the economic entity. The future income tax benefit created for the economic entity in the current example will be completely reversed after five years. The tax-effect consolidation adjustment entry at 30 June 20X1 is:

**Consolidation journal**

| | Debit | Credit |
|---|---|---|
| Income Tax Expense ($400 × 40%) | 160 | |
| Future Income Tax Benefit | | 160 |

Continuing consolidation adjustments are required each year while the transferred asset remains within the economic entity. When preparing consolidated accounts in periods after the transfer of the asset, the consolidation adjustment must take into account the depreciation adjustment applicable to both prior periods and the current period. The effects of adjustments for depreciation expense applicable to prior years are made against the opening balance of retained profits. In the example above, the consolidation adjustment entries at 30 June 20X2, in the second financial year after transfer of the asset, are:

**Consolidation journal**

| | Debit | Credit |
|---|---|---|
| Accumulated Depreciation – Equipment | 800 | |
| Retained Profits 1 July 20X1 | | 400 |
| Depreciation Expense | | 400 |
| | | |
| Income Tax Expense | 160 | |
| Retained Profits 1 July 20X1 | 160 | |
| Future Income Tax Benefit | | 320 |

If the equipment was sold from P Ltd to S Ltd at a sale price of $9000, a loss on sale of $1000 would be recorded in P Ltd's accounts. S Ltd, in its accounts, would be charging annual depreciation of $1800 per annum (20% of $9000). This compares to depreciation of $2000 per annum from the economic entity viewpoint (i.e. had the sale not taken place). Hence, depreciation is being undercharged by the amount of $200 per annum from a group viewpoint. The tax effect of this amounts to $80 per annum (40% of $200). The consolidation adjustment entries required for depreciation at 30 June 20X1 are therefore:

### Consolidation journal

| | Debit | Credit |
|---|---|---|
| Depreciation Expense | 200 | |
|     Accumulated Depreciation – Equipment | | 200 |
| | | |
| Provision for Deferred Income Tax | 80 | |
|     Income Tax Expense | | 80 |

The consolidation adjustment entries for depreciation at 30 June 20X2, in the second year after the transfer, would be:

### Consolidation journal

| | Debit | Credit |
|---|---|---|
| Depreciation Expense | 200 | |
| Retained Profits 1 July 20X1 | 200 | |
|     Accumulated Depreciation – Equipment | | 400 |
| | | |
| Provision for Deferred Income Tax | 160 | |
|     Retained Profits 1 July 20X1 | | 80 |
|     Income Tax Expense | | 80 |

# Intra-group borrowings

**intra-group borrowings**

It is common for individual entities in an economic entity to have amounts owing between them and for interest to be charged and paid on these amounts. Examples of these amounts owing include trade debtors and trade creditors created as a result of intra-group trading and loan account balances resulting from borrowings made between group members.

As these amounts owing do not represent borrowings with parties external to the economic entity, and because interest paid on these borrowings does not represent a transaction with external parties, they must be eliminated when preparing consolidated accounts.

To eliminate amounts owing between group members, the consolidation journal entry will credit the relevant asset account and debit the relevant liability account. For example, assume that S Ltd has loaned the amount of $25 000 to P Ltd. S Ltd's accounts will record a debtors account (loan asset) for the amount owing from P Ltd, while P Ltd's accounts will record a creditors account (loan liability) for the amount payable to S Ltd. To eliminate these balances owing when preparing consolidated accounts, the consolidation journal entry is:

### Consolidation journal

| | Debit | Credit |
|---|---|---|
| Creditors (Loan Liability) | 25 000 | |
| Debtors (Loan Asset) | | 25 000 |

If S Ltd had charged P Ltd interest of $2000 on this loan during the year, this transaction must also be eliminated on consolidation in the same way as for intra-group services and intra-group sales of inventory. The consolidation elimination entry is:

### Consolidation journal

| | Debit | Credit |
|---|---|---|
| Interest Revenue | 2000 | |
| Interest Expense | | 2000 |

To further illustrate the consolidation entries required for intra-group borrowings, the example of the intra-group issue of debentures will be demonstrated in the following section.

## INTRA-GROUP DEBENTURES

Assume that, on 1 July 20X0, S Ltd issued 1000 five-year debentures of $100 each (i.e. $100 000 in total). Interest on the debentures is 12% per annum, payable half-yearly on 31 December and 30 June each year. Assume that the interest is actually paid in early January and July respectively. P Ltd purchased one-quarter ($25 000) of these debentures.

It is necessary to trace the inter-entity holdings and interest payments to ensure that the consolidation eliminations are complete. The liability account 'Debentures' in S Ltd's accounts amounts to $100 000, of which $25 000 relates to the debentures issued to P Ltd. This is matched by the asset account 'Debentures in S Ltd' amounting to $25 000 in the accounts of P Ltd. These intra-group balances must be eliminated on consolidation.

The interest expense relating to the debentures will be recorded in the accounts of S Ltd as follows (note that P Ltd receives only one-quarter of this interest):

### General journal of S Ltd

| | | Debit | Credit |
|---|---|---|---|
| **20X0** | | | |
| Dec 31 | Interest Expense ($100 000 × 6%) | 6000 | |
| | Interest Payable | | 6000 |
| | (interest payable on debentures) | | |
| | | | |
| **20X1** | | | |
| Jan 4 | Interest Payable | 6000 | |
| | Cash | | 6000 |
| | (debenture interest paid) | | |
| | | | |
| June 30 | Interest Expense | 6000 | |
| | Interest Payable | | 6000 |
| | (interest payable on debentures) | | |

The interest revenue relating to the debentures will be recorded in the accounts of P Ltd as follows:

## General journal of P Ltd

|  |  | Debit | Credit |
|---|---|---|---|
| 20X0 |  |  |  |
| Dec 31 | Interest Receivable ($25 000 x 6%) | 1500 |  |
|  | Interest Revenue |  | 1500 |
|  | (interest receivable on debentures) |  |  |
|  |  |  |  |
| 20X1 |  |  |  |
| Jan 4 | Cash | 1500 |  |
|  | Interest Receivable |  | 1500 |
|  | (debenture interest received) |  |  |
|  |  |  |  |
| June 30 | Interest Receivable | 1500 |  |
|  | Interest Revenue |  | 1500 |
|  | (interest receivable on debentures) |  |  |

These transactions indicate that the inter-entity interest expense for the financial year amounted to $3000 ($25 000 $\times$ 12%). At 30 June 20X1, there is also an inter-entity asset account (interest receivable) amounting to $1500 recorded in P Ltd's accounts and an inter-entity liability account (interest payable) in S Ltd's accounts.

*Consolidation adjustments*
Based on the analysis above, the consolidated elimination entries at 30 June 20X1 are:

## Consolidation journal

|  | Debit | Credit |
|---|---|---|
| Debentures (Liability) | 25 000 |  |
| Debentures in S Ltd (Asset) |  | 25 000 |
| Interest Revenue | 3 000 |  |
| Interest Expense |  | 3 000 |
| Interest Payable (Liability) | 1 500 |  |
| Interest Receivable (Asset) |  | 1 500 |

Tax-effect consolidation journal entries are not required as the adjustments to interest revenue and interest expense have not affected consolidated operating profit. Hence, the elimination entries have had no effect on economic entity income tax expense.

These consolidation journal entries will be carried out each year while the debentures are on issue. In the financial year ended 30 June 20X5, the year in which the debentures are redeemed by S Ltd, there will be no asset and liability amount owing between S Ltd and P Ltd. However, it should be remembered that it will still be necessary to eliminate the intra-group interest revenue and expense for that year.

# Intra-group dividends from post-acquisition profits

**intra-group dividends**

The treatment of dividends paid from pre-acquisition profits was covered in chapter 5. This discussion now addresses consolidation elimination entries applicable to dividends paid by a subsidiary to a parent entity from profits earned subsequent to acquisition.

Dividends paid between entities from post-acquisition profits are a transfer of profits between members of the group and are recorded as revenue by the receiving entity. However, all dividends paid or proposed between entities within an economic entity are not transactions with parties outside the economic entity. The process of preparing consolidation journal entries involves identifying transactions relating to dividends recorded in the accounts of the individual entities, including any payables and receivables. These transactions are then eliminated by reversing them.

In the examples discussed in this section, it will be assumed that the subsidiary paying the dividend is wholly owned by the parent entity. Later, chapter 7 will introduce partly-owned subsidiaries where some of the dividend is paid to shareholders outside the economic entity.

## INTERIM DIVIDEND DECLARED AND PAID DURING THE CURRENT PERIOD

Assume that, during the current period, S Ltd declared and paid to P Ltd an interim dividend of $5000 from post-acquisition profits. The journal entries recorded in S Ltd's accounts are:

### General journal of S Ltd

|  | Debit | Credit |
|---|---|---|
| Interim Dividend Declared (P&L) | 5000 | |
|    Interim Dividend Payable (Liability) | | 5000 |
| (declaration of interim dividend) | | |
| Interim Dividend Payable | 5000 | |
|    Cash | | 5000 |
| (payment of interim dividend) | | |

P Ltd will record the following journal entry in its own accounts.

### General journal of P Ltd

|  | Debit | Credit |
|---|---|---|
| Cash | 5000 | |
|    Dividend Revenue (P&L) | | 5000 |
| (receipt of dividend) | | |

*Consolidation elimination*

After the posting of the above journal entries, the two accounts relating to these dividends with balances remaining in the individual entity's books are S Ltd's Interim Dividend Declared (Profit and Loss Appropriation) account and P Ltd's Dividend Revenue account. The dividend revenue is not revenue from outside the group and the interim dividend declared as an appropriation from S Ltd's profit was not paid to parties external to the group. The consolidation elimination entry to remove the effects of the dividend transactions is therefore:

**Consolidation journal**

| | Debit | Credit |
|---|---|---|
| Dividend Revenue | 5000 | |
| Interim Dividend Declared (P&L) | | 5000 |

## FINAL DIVIDEND DECLARED BUT NOT PAID DURING THE CURRENT PERIOD

### Dividend not recognised prior to receipt

Assume that, during the current period, S Ltd declared from post-acquisition profits a final dividend of $10 000. This dividend will be paid to P Ltd in the following period and has not been recorded as revenue in the books of P Ltd at balance date.

In this situation, the only journal entry relating to the dividend recorded in the accounts of the separate entities will be that recorded in the books of S Ltd as follows:

### General journal of S Ltd

| | Debit | Credit |
|---|---|---|
| Final Dividend Proposed (P&L) | 10 000 | |
| Dividend Payable (Liability) | | 10 000 |
| (declaration of final dividend) | | |

*Consolidation elimination*

The consolidation elimination entry to remove the effect of declaration of the inter-entity dividend is a reversal of the declaration as follows:

### Consolidation journal

| | Debit | Credit |
|---|---|---|
| Dividend Payable (Liability) | 10 000 | |
| Final Dividend Proposed (P&L) | | 10 000 |

### Dividend recognised prior to receipt

While a final dividend is not legally payable until sanctioned by the annual general meeting, approval of payment is generally a formality given that the parent entity has control of the subsidiary. In these circumstances, a parent may recognise as revenue a dividend proposed by a subsidiary prior to its receipt.

In addition to the journal entries recorded by S Ltd and discussed above, P Ltd would record the following journal entry if it wished to recognise the dividend as revenue prior to its receipt.

### General journal of P Ltd

| | Debit | Credit |
|---|---|---|
| Dividend Receivable (Asset) | 10 000 | |
| Dividend Revenue (P&L) | | 10 000 |
| (dividend receivable) | | |

*Consolidation elimination*

When a dividend proposed by a subsidiary in the current period is recognised by a parent prior to payment, the complete consolidation entries to remove the effect of the inter-entity dividend, using the present example, are:

### Consolidation journal

|  | Debit | Credit |
|---|---|---|
| Dividend Payable (Liability) | 10 000 | |
|     Final Dividend Proposed (P&L) | | 10 000 |
| | | |
| Dividend Revenue | 10 000 | |
|     Dividend Receivable (Asset) | | 10 000 |

## DIVIDENDS DECLARED IN A PRIOR PERIOD AND PAID IN THE CURRENT PERIOD

If the parent entity had recognised, prior to receipt, a dividend proposed by a subsidiary in a previous period, no consolidation elimination entry would be required. To illustrate this, assume that the dividend information is that used in the previous section and that it is now the following financial year. The entries recorded in the accounts of S Ltd and P Ltd respectively on payment and receipt of the dividend would be:

### General journal of S Ltd

|  | Debit | Credit |
|---|---|---|
| Dividend Payable (Liability) | 10 000 | |
|     Cash | | 10 000 |
| (payment of final dividend) | | |

### General journal of P Ltd

|  | Debit | Credit |
|---|---|---|
| Cash | 10 000 | |
|     Dividend Receivable (Asset) | | 10 000 |
| (receipt of dividend) | | |

Hence, there are no balances in inter-entity dividend accounts relating to the dividend declared in the previous period and thus no consolidation eliminations are required.

However, if P Ltd had not recognised the dividend prior to receipt, the journal entry in the books of P Ltd on receipt of the dividend would be:

### General journal of P Ltd

|  | Debit | Credit |
|---|---|---|
| Cash | 10 000 | |
|     Dividend Revenue | | 10 000 |
| (receipt of dividend) | | |

The only dividend account open in either entity relating to the dividend is the Dividend Revenue account in P Ltd, as the Dividend Payable account in S Ltd was cleared when the dividend was paid.

*Consolidation elimination*
The consolidation adjustment entry required is:

**Consolidation journal**

|  | Debit | Credit |
|---|---|---|
| Dividend Revenue | 10 000 | |
| Retained Profits (Opening Balance) | | 10 000 |

The retained profits brought forward to the current year in S Ltd's individual accounts have been reduced by the dividend declared in the prior period. Because this dividend is not payable outside the group, opening retained profits are credited in the consolidation elimination entry to restore them to the amount applicable to the economic entity.

## TAX EFFECT OF DIVIDENDS

Section 46 of the *Income Tax Assessment Act 1936* provides, generally, that a parent entity which is a public company is entitled to a rebate of tax on dividends from a subsidiary. Therefore, for the purposes of this text, no tax-effect entry is required for elimination of dividend revenue on intra-group dividends.

## ILLUSTRATIVE EXAMPLE 6.2

# CONSOLIDATION USING VARIOUS INTRA-GROUP TRANSACTIONS

To reinforce the principles outlined in this chapter, the following is a comprehensive illustration of the consolidation process for a group comprising a holding company and a wholly-owned subsidiary where there have been intra-group transactions.

On 1 July 20X0, Chief Ltd acquired 100% of the issued shares of Sub Ltd for $30 000. At the date of acquisition, the shareholders' equity of Sub Ltd consisted of:

| | $ |
|---|---|
| Paid-up capital | 16 000 |
| General reserve | 6 000 |
| Retained profits | 4 000 |
| | $26 000 |

At 30 June 20X5, five years after acquisition, the accounts of the two companies appear as follows:

| | Chief Ltd | Sub Ltd |
|---|---|---|
| | $ | $ |
| Sales | 35 000 | 20 000 |
| Cost of goods sold | | |
| Opening stock 1 July 20X4 | 5 000 | 2 000 |
| Purchases | 23 000 | 12 000 |
| | 28 000 | 14 000 |
| Closing stock 30 June 20X5 | 4 000 | 2 000 |
| Cost of goods sold | 24 000 | 12 000 |
| Gross profit | 11 000 | 8 000 |
| Depreciation expense | 1 000 | 700 |
| Financial expenses | 600 | 800 |
| Other expenses | 640 | 1 000 |
| Total expenses | 2 240 | 2 500 |
| | 8 760 | 5 500 |
| Other income | | |
| Interest revenue | 240 | – |
| Dividend revenue | 2 000 | – |
| Total other income | 2 240 | – |
| Operating profit before tax | 11 000 | 5 500 |
| Income tax expense | 4 000 | 2 000 |
| Operating profit after tax | 7 000 | 3 500 |
| Retained profits 1 July 20X4 | 3 000 | 4 000 |
| Available for appropriation | 10 000 | 7 500 |
| Interim dividend paid | 1 000 | 800 |
| Final dividend proposed | 2 000 | 1 200 |
| Dividends paid and provided | 3 000 | 2 000 |
| Retained profits 30 June 20X5 | 7 000 | 5 500 |
| Paid-up capital | 30 000 | 16 000 |
| General reserve | 2 000 | 6 000 |
| 12% debentures (due 30 June 20X7) | – | 5 000 |
| Dividend payable | 2 000 | 1 200 |
| Other liabilities | 4 000 | 2 000 |
| | $45 000 | $35 700 |
| | | |
| Assets | | |
| Dividend receivable | 1 200 | – |
| Inventory | 4 000 | 2 000 |
| Non-current assets (depreciable) | 10 000 | 8 000 |
| Accumulated depreciation | (5 000) | (1 000) |
| Land | 5 000 | 15 000 |
| Investment in Sub Ltd | 26 000 | – |
| Debentures in Sub Ltd | 2 000 | – |
| Other assets | 1 800 | 11 700 |
| | $45 000 | $35 700 |

Additional information:
(a)  The identifiable net assets of Sub Ltd were recorded at fair value at the date of acquisition.
(b)  Any goodwill on acquisition is to be amortised over a ten-year period.
(c)  Immediately after acquisition, Sub Ltd declared and paid a dividend of $4000 from pre-acquisition profits. All other dividends have been from post-acquisition profits.
(d)  A non-current asset owned by Chief Ltd (cost $1000 and accumulated depreciation $500) was sold to Sub Ltd for $1000 on 1 July 20X3. Chief had depreciated this asset at 10% per annum straight line on original cost (i.e. $100 per annum), while Sub Ltd has applied a depreciation rate of 20% straight line (i.e. $200 per annum) from the date of transfer of the asset.
(e)  The opening stock of Chief Ltd includes unrealised profit of $1000 on stock transferred from Sub Ltd during the prior financial year. All of this stock had been sold to parties external to the group by Chief Ltd during the year ended 30 June 20X5.
(f)  During the current year, Chief Ltd had purchased inventory from Sub Ltd for $4000. This stock had previously cost Sub Ltd $3000. One-half of this stock had been sold to outsiders by Chief Ltd during the year.
(g)  Chief Ltd holds debentures in Sub Ltd amounting to $2000. Sub Ltd paid the 12% annual interest on debentures on 30 June 20X5.
(h)  Chief Ltd holds no investments in shares except for those held in Sub Ltd. Accordingly, examination of the Dividend Revenue and Dividend Receivable accounts in Chief Ltd's financial statements indicates that Chief Ltd has recognised dividend revenue prior to receipt.
(i)  The tax rate is 40%

*Required*
1  Prepare an acquisition analysis.
2  Prepare the consolidation elimination journal entries necessary to prepare consolidated accounts for the year ending 30 June 20X5 for the group comprising Chief Ltd and Sub Ltd.
3  Complete a detailed consolidation worksheet for the year ending 30 June 20X5.

**Solution**

**1  Acquisition analysis**

|  |  | $ |  |
|---|---|---|---|
| Fair value of identifiable net assets acquired | = | 16 000 | Paid-up capital |
|  |  | 6 000 | General reserve |
|  |  | 4 000 | Retained profits |
|  |  | $26 000 |  |

| Cost of acquisition | = $30 000 |
|---|---|
| Goodwill | = $4000 |
| Amortisation of goodwill | = $400 per annum |

**2  Consolidation journal entries**

**Consolidation journal**

|  | Debit $ | Credit $ |
|---|---|---|
| (1) Elimination of investment in subsidiary. |  |  |
| Retained Profits 1 July 20X4 | 4 000 |  |
| Paid-up Capital | 16 000 |  |
| General Reserve | 6 000 |  |
| Goodwill | 4 000 |  |
|     Investment in Sub Ltd |  | 30 000 |

|  | Debit | Credit |
|---|---|---|
|  | $ | $ |

**(2) Adjustment for dividend paid from pre-acquisition profits in year ended 30 June 20X1.**

| Investment in Sub Ltd | 4 000 |  |
| Retained Profits 1 July 20X4 |  | 4 000 |

**(3) Amortisation of goodwill.**

| Amortisation Expense (Other Expenses) | 400 |  |
| Retained Profits 1 July 20X4 | 1 600 |  |
| Goodwill |  | 2 000 |

**(4) Adjustment for unrealised profit on intra-group sale of non-current asset.**

| Retained Profits 1 July 20X4 | 500 |  |
| Accumulated Depreciation |  | 500 |
| Future Income Tax Benefit ($500 x 40%) | 200 |  |
| Retained Profits 1 July 20X4 |  | 200 |

**(5) Adjustment for depreciation on non-current asset sold.**

| Accumulated Depreciation | 200 |  |
| Retained Profits 1 July 20X4 |  | 100 |
| Depreciation Expense |  | 100 |
| Income Tax Expense ($100 x 40%) | 40 |  |
| Retained Profits 1 July 20X4 | 40 |  |
| Future Income Tax Benefit |  | 80 |

**(6) Elimination of unrealised profit in opening stock.**

| Retained Profits 1 July 20X4 | 1 000 |  |
| Opening Stock (P&L) |  | 1 000 |
| Income Tax Expense ($1000 x 40%) | 400 |  |
| Retained Profits 1 July 20X4 |  | 400 |

**(7) Elimination of intra-group sale of inventory.**

| Sales | 4 000 |  |
| Purchases |  | 4 000 |

**(8) Elimination of unrealised profit in closing inventory.**

| Closing Stock (P&L) ($1000/2) | 500 |  |
| Inventory (Balance Sheet) |  | 500 |
| Future Income Tax Benefit ($500 x 40%) | 200 |  |
| Income Tax Expense |  | 200 |

**(9) Elimination of intra-group debentures.**

| 12% debentures | 2 000 |  |
| Debentures in Sub Ltd |  | 2 000 |

|  | Debit | Credit |
|---|---|---|
| **(10) Elimination of intra-group interest on debentures.** | | |
| Interest Revenue ($2000 x 12%) | 240 | |
|     Financial Expenses (Interest Expense) | | 240 |
| | | |
| **(11) Elimination of interim dividend paid.** | | |
| Dividend Revenue (P&L) | 800 | |
|     Interim Dividend Paid (P&L) | | 800 |
| | | |
| **(12) Elimination of final dividend proposed.** | | |
| Dividend Payable (Liability) | 1 200 | |
|     Final Dividend Proposed (P&L) | | 1 200 |
| | | |
| Dividend Revenue (P&L) | 1 200 | |
|     Dividend Receivable (Asset) | | 1 200 |

## 3 Consolidation worksheet

| Account | Chief Ltd | Sub Ltd | Eliminations Debit | Eliminations Credit | Consolidation |
|---|---|---|---|---|---|
| | $ | $ | $ | $ | $ |
| Sales | 35 000 | 20 000 | 4 000 (7) | | 51 000 |
| Opening stock 1 July 20X4 | 5 000 | 2 000 | | 1 000 (6) | 6 000 |
| Purchases | 23 000 | 12 000 | | 4 000 (7) | 31 000 |
| | 28 000 | 14 000 | | | 37 000 |
| Closing stock 30 June 20X5 | 4 000 | 2 000 | 500 (8) | | 5 500 |
| *Cost of goods sold* | 24 000 | 12 000 | | | 31 500 |
| *Gross profit* | 11 000 | 8 000 | | | 19 500 |
| Depreciation expense | 1 000 | 700 | | 100 (5) | 1 600 |
| Financial expenses | 600 | 800 | | 240 (10) | 1 160 |
| Other expenses | 640 | 1 000 | 400 (3) | | 2 040 |
| *Total expenses* | 2 240 | 2 500 | | | 4 800 |
| | 8 760 | 5 500 | | | 14 700 |
| Interest revenue | 240 | – | 240 (10) | | – |
| Dividend revenue | 2 000 | – | 800 (11) | | |
| | | | 1 200 (12) | | – |
| *Total other income* | 2 240 | – | | | – |
| *Operating profit before tax* | 11 000 | 5 500 | | | 14 700 |
| Income tax expense | 4 000 | 2 000 | 40 (5) | 200 (8) | |
| | | | 400 (6) | | 6 240 |
| *Operating profit after tax* | 7 000 | 3 500 | | | 8 460 |
| Retained profits 1 July 20X4 | 3 000 | 4 000 | 4 000 (1) | 4 000 (2) | |
| | | | 1 600 (3) | 200 (4) | |
| | | | 500 (4) | 100 (5) | |
| | | | 40 (5) | 400 (6) | |
| | | | 1 000 (6) | | 4 560 |

**(continued)**

| Account | Chief Ltd | Sub Ltd | Eliminations Debit | Eliminations Credit | Consolidation |
|---|---|---|---|---|---|
| | $ | $ | $ | $ | $ |
| *Available for appropriation* | 10 000 | 7 500 | | | 13 020 |
| Interim dividend paid | 1 000 | 800 | | 800 (11) | 1 000 |
| Final dividend proposed | 2 000 | 1 200 | | 1 200 (12) | 2 000 |
| *Dividends paid and provided* | 3 000 | 2 000 | | | 3 000 |
| Retained profits 30 June 20X5 | 7 000 | 5 500 | | | 10 020 |
| Paid-up capital | 30 000 | 16 000 | 16 000 (1) | | 30 000 |
| General reserve | 2 000 | 6 000 | 6 000 (1) | | 2 000 |
| 12% debentures | – | 5 000 | 2 000 (9) | | 3 000 |
| Dividend payable | 2 000 | 1 200 | 1 200 (12) | | 2 000 |
| Other liabilities | 4 000 | 2 000 | | | 6 000 |
| *Total equities* | $45 000 | $35 700 | | | $53 020 |
| Dividend receivable | 1 200 | – | | 1 200 (12) | – |
| Inventory | 4 000 | 2 000 | | 500 (8) | 5 500 |
| Non-current assets (depreciable) | 10 000 | 8 000 | | | 18 000 |
| Accumulated depreciation | (5 000) | (1 000) | 200 (5) | 500 (4) | (6 300) |
| Land | 5 000 | 15 000 | | | 20 000 |
| Investment in Sub Ltd | 26 000 | – | 4 000 (2) | 30 000 (1) | – |
| Debentures in Sub Ltd | 2 000 | – | | 2 000 (9) | – |
| Goodwill | – | – | 4 000 (1) | 2 000 (3) | 2 000 |
| Future income tax benefit | – | – | 200 (4) | 80 (5) | |
| | | | 200 (8) | | 320 |
| Other assets | 1 800 | 11 700 | | | 13 500 |
| *Total assets* | $45 000 | $35 700 | $48 520 | $48 520 | $53 020 |

# Review

This chapter and the previous chapter examined the basic principles for the preparation of consolidated accounts for a group comprising a parent entity and a wholly-owned subsidiary. The consolidation adjustments required to eliminate the investment in subsidiary account in the parent entity's accounts were examined in chapter 5, while the present chapter discussed the adjustments required for intra-group transactions. Further aspects of the consolidation process relating to subsidiaries that are not wholly owned are discussed in the following two chapters.

# KEY TERMS

| | | |
|---|---|---|
| inter-entity transactions | intra-group inventory sales | intra-group services |
| intra-group borrowings | intra-group non-current asset sales | intra-group transactions |
| intra-group dividends | | unrealised profit or loss |

# REVIEW QUESTIONS

**6.1** What are inter-entity, or intra-group, transactions? Provide examples.

**6.2** What is the accounting treatment for intra-group transactions required by AASB 1024? What is the rationale for this accounting treatment?

**6.3** Explain the commonality between consolidation entries for intra-group services transactions and transactions involving the intra-group sale of inventory.

**6.4** Explain the difference in consolidation treatment for the intra-group sale of inventory where (a) all the inventory is sold to parties external to the group during the period, and (b) where all or a portion of the inventory remains on hand within the group at the end of the period. Explain the reason for this difference.

**6.5** Explain the difference in consolidation entries required for unrealised profit in closing inventory and for unrealised profit in opening inventory due to the intra-group sale of inventory.

**6.6** What consolidation adjustments are required for the intra-group sale of depreciable assets?

**6.7** In what circumstances is a tax-effect adjustment required when making an adjustment for an intra-group transaction? What is the rationale for this treatment?

**6.8** What are the consolidation adjustments required where there are borrowings owing between entities in a group and where interest is charged on those borrowings?

**6.9** What consolidation adjustments are required when a wholly-owned subsidiary declares a dividend from post-acquisition profits?

# EXERCISES

**Exercise 6.10**  **Intra-group services transactions**

Prepare the consolidation journal entries required for each of the following intra-group services transactions between Maggie Ltd and its wholly-owned subsidiary Twiggy Ltd.

(a) Twiggy paid $15 000 in management fees to Maggie.

(b) Maggie paid $5000 in computer maintenance fees to Twiggy.

(c) Twiggy paid $10 000 to Maggie for rental of a business premises. At the end of the accounting period, $1000 of this amount is recognised as prepaid rent expense in Twiggy's accounts and as unearned rent revenue in Maggie's accounts.

**Exercise 6.11  Intra-group sale of inventory**

Prepare the consolidation journal entries required for each of the following intra-group sale of inventory transactions between Zephyr Ltd and its wholly-owned subsidiary Ninja Ltd. Assume a tax rate of 40%.

(a) Zephyr sold inventory to Ninja for $10 000 during the accounting period. This inventory had an original cost to Zephyr of $8000. All of this inventory was sold by Ninja to parties outside the group during the accounting period.

(b) Ninja sold inventory to Zephyr for $12 000 during the accounting period. This inventory had an original cost to Ninja of $8000. One-half of this inventory was sold by Zephyr to parties external to the economic entity during the accounting period.

(c) Zephyr sold inventory to Ninja for $10 000 during the accounting period. This inventory had an original cost to Zephyr of $6000. Sixty per cent of this inventory was sold by Ninja to parties external to the economic entity during the accounting period.

**Exercise 6.12  Intra-group sale of inventory**

Bantam Ltd is a wholly-owned subsidiary of Lightning Ltd. During the financial year ended 30 June 20X2, Lightning sold inventory to Bantam for $50 000. This inventory had an original cost to Lightning of $40 000. During the accounting period, Bantam sold 40% of this inventory to parties external to the economic entity.

During the subsequent financial year (year ended 30 June 20X3), the remaining 60% of the above inventory was sold to parties external to the economic entity. In addition, Bantam sold inventory to Lightning for $30 000. This inventory had an original cost to Bantam of $25 000. Lightning still holds 20% of this inventory at 30 June 20X3. Assume a tax rate of 40%.

*Required*

1  Prepare the consolidation journal entries required as at 30 June 20X2.
2  Prepare the consolidation journal entries required as at 30 June 20X3.

**Exercise 6.13  Intra-group sale of depreciable assets**

Grimm Ltd sold an item of depreciable equipment to its subsidiary, Bronte Ltd, for $100 000 on 1 July 20X4. The equipment had originally been acquired by Grimm on 1 July 20X2 at a cost of $150 000. Grimm had been charging depreciation on this equipment at 20% straight line. On acquiring the asset, Bronte Ltd assessed that the equipment had a remaining useful life of four years and therefore commenced depreciating the equipment at 25% per annum straight line. Assume a tax rate of 40%.

*Required*

1  Prepare the consolidation journal entries required as at 30 June 20X5.
2  Prepare the consolidation journal entries required as at 30 June 20X6.

**Exercise 6.14**   **Intra-group sale of depreciable assets**
Kirkham Ltd sold a motor vehicle to its subsidiary, Alfred Ltd, for $35 000 on 30 June 20X2. The motor vehicle had originally been acquired by Kirkham on 1 July 20X1 at a cost of $40 000, and the company had been charging depreciation at the rate of 20% per annum straight line. On acquiring the asset, Alfred Ltd commenced depreciating the equipment at 25% per annum straight line. Assume a tax rate of 40%.

*Required*
1  Prepare the consolidation journal entries required as at 30 June 20X2.
2  Prepare the consolidation journal entries required as at 30 June 20X3.
3  Prepare the consolidation journal entries required as at 30 June 20X4.

**Exercise 6.15**   **Intra-group borrowings**
Chatwin Ltd borrowed $50 000 from its parent, Conrad Ltd, during the financial year ended 30 June 20X3. Chatwin paid $5000 interest on this loan during the year.
   During the subsequent financial year (year ended 30 June 20X4), Chatwin borrowed a further $30 000 from Conrad. Interest of $7000 on the two loans was paid by Chatwin during the year. In addition, a further $500 in interest was recognised as an accrued expense in Chatwin's accounts and as interest receivable in Conrad's accounts.

*Required*
1  Prepare the consolidation journal entries required as at 30 June 20X3.
2  Prepare the consolidation journal entries required as at 30 June 20X4.

**Exercise 6.16**   **Intra-group dividends from post-acquisition profits**
Williams Ltd is a wholly-owned subsidiary of Betts Ltd. On 15 January 20X2, Williams declared an interim dividend of $10 000 from post-acquisition profits. This dividend was subsequently paid to Betts on 5 February 20X2. Also, a final dividend of $15 000 from post-acquisition profits was declared and provided for by Williams on 15 June 20X2 to be paid on 1 August 20X2. This dividend was recognised as revenue by Betts in its accounts for the year ended 30 June 20X2.

*Required*
Prepare the consolidation journal entries required as at 30 June 20X2.

**Exercise 6.17**   **Intra-group dividends from post-acquisition profits**
Fulton Ltd is a wholly-owned subsidiary of Anderson Ltd. On 15 June 20X1, Fulton declared and provided for a final dividend of $20 000 from post-acquisition profits. This dividend was subsequently paid on 15 August 20X1, when it was recognised as revenue by Anderson. An interim dividend of $15 000 was declared and paid by Fulton on 15 January 20X2. A final dividend of $22 000 was declared and provided for by Fulton on 15 June 20X2 and subsequently paid on 15 July 20X2. This dividend was not recognised as revenue by Anderson prior to its receipt.

*Required*
Prepare the consolidation journal entries required as at 30 June 20X2.

**Exercise 6.18** **Consolidation — intra-group services, sale of inventory and sale of depreciable assets**

On 1 July 20X2, Titan Ltd acquired 100% of the issued shares of Cobra Ltd for $150 000. At the date of acquisition, the shareholders' equity of Cobra Ltd consisted of:

|  | $ |
|---|---|
| Paid-up capital | 120 000 |
| Retained profits | 30 000 |
|  | $150 000 |

At 30 June 20X4, two years after acquisition, the accounts of the two companies appear as follows:

|  | Titan Ltd | Cobra Ltd |
|---|---|---|
|  | $ | $ |
| Sales | 250 000 | 110 000 |
| Cost of goods sold |  |  |
| Opening stock 1 July 20X3 | 23 000 | 9 000 |
| Purchases | 135 000 | 47 000 |
|  | 158 000 | 56 000 |
| Closing stock 30 June 20X4 | 25 000 | 10 000 |
| Cost of goods sold | 133 000 | 46 000 |
| Gross profit | 117 000 | 64 000 |
| Depreciation expense | 25 000 | 15 000 |
| Rent expense | – | 4 000 |
| Other expenses | 42 000 | 30 000 |
| Total expenses | 67 000 | 49 000 |
|  | 50 000 | 15 000 |
| Other income |  |  |
| Profit on sale of equipment | 7 000 | – |
| Rent revenue | 4 000 | – |
| Total other income | 11 000 | – |
| Operating profit before tax | 61 000 | 15 000 |
| Income tax expense | 19 000 | 5 000 |
| Operating profit after tax | 42 000 | 10 000 |
| Retained profits 1 July 20X3 | 30 000 | 35 000 |
| Available for appropriation | 72 000 | 45 000 |
| Dividends paid | 35 000 | – |
| Retained profits 30 June 20X4 | 37 000 | 45 000 |
| Paid-up capital | 300 000 | 120 000 |
| Creditors & borrowings | 35 000 | 15 000 |
| Other liabilities | 60 000 | 5 000 |
|  | $432 000 | $185 000 |
| Assets |  |  |
| Cash at bank | 3 000 | 2 000 |
| Accounts receivable | 35 000 | 30 000 |
| Inventory | 25 000 | 10 000 |
| Investment in Cobra Ltd | 150 000 | – |
| Equipment | 115 000 | 70 000 |
| Accumulated depreciation | (60 000) | (21 000) |
| Land & buildings (net) | 144 000 | 79 000 |
| Other assets | 20 000 | 15 000 |
|  | $432 000 | $185 000 |

Additional information:

(a) The identifiable net assets of Cobra Ltd were recorded at fair value at the date of acquisition

(b) During the financial year, Cobra paid rent of $4000 to Titan.

(c) The opening stock of Cobra includes unrealised profit of $2000 on inventory transferred from Titan during the prior financial year. All of this inventory had been sold by Cobra to parties external to the group during the current financial year.

(d) Titan had sold inventory to Cobra for $15 000 during the year. This inventory had an original cost to Titan of $10 000. One-half of this inventory had been sold to outsiders by Cobra during the year.

(e) An item of equipment owned by Titan (cost $30 000 and accumulated depreciation $12 000) had been sold to Cobra for $25 000 on 1 July 20X3. Titan had depreciated this asset at 20% per annum straight line on original cost. Cobra has applied a 25% depreciation rate from the date of transfer of the asset.

(f) The tax rate is 40%.

*Required*

1 Prepare an acquisition analysis and the consolidation journal entries necessary to prepare consolidated accounts for the year ending 30 June 20X4 for the group comprising Titan Ltd and Cobra Ltd.

2 Complete a detailed consolidation worksheet for the year ending 30 June 20X4.

**Exercise 6.19** **Comprehensive**

On 1 July 20X4, Savage Ltd acquired 100% of the issued shares of Avenger Ltd for $200 000. At the date of acquisition, the shareholders' equity of Avenger Ltd consisted of:

|  | $ |
|---|---|
| Paid-up capital | 150 000 |
| General reserve | 20 000 |
| Retained profits | 10 000 |
|  | $180 000 |

At 30 June 20X8, four years after acquisition, the accounts of the two companies appear as follows:

|  | Savage Ltd | Avenger Ltd |
|---|---|---|
|  | $ | $ |
| Sales | 340 000 | 140 000 |
| *Cost of goods sold* | | |
| Opening stock 1 July 20X7 | 20 000 | 5 000 |
| Purchases | 200 000 | 73 000 |
|  | 220 000 | 78 000 |
| Closing stock 30 June 20X8 | 25 000 | 15 000 |
| *Cost of goods sold* | 195 000 | 63 000 |
| *Gross profit* | 145 000 | 77 000 |
| Depreciation expense | 32 000 | 23 000 |
| Interest expense | 9 000 | 1 000 |
| Management fees expense | – | 7 000 |

| | Savage Ltd | Avenger Ltd |
|---|---|---|
| | $ | $ |
| Other expenses | 43 000 | 34 000 |
| Total expenses | 84 000 | 65 000 |
| | 61 000 | 12 000 |
| *Other income* | | |
| Dividend revenue | 5 000 | – |
| Interest revenue | – | 3 000 |
| Management fees revenue | 7 000 | – |
| Total other income | 12 000 | 3 000 |
| Operating profit before tax | 73 000 | 15 000 |
| Income tax expense | 28 000 | 5 000 |
| Operating profit after tax | 45 000 | 10 000 |
| Retained profits 1 July 20X7 | 25 000 | 5 000 |
| Available for appropriation | 70 000 | 15 000 |
| Interim dividend paid | 10 000 | 2 000 |
| Final dividend proposed | 30 000 | 3 000 |
| Dividends paid and provided | 40 000 | 5 000 |
| Retained profits 30 June 20X8 | 30 000 | 10 000 |
| Paid-up capital | 400 000 | 150 000 |
| General reserve | 20 000 | 30 000 |
| Accounts payable | 40 000 | 20 000 |
| Dividend payable | 30 000 | 3 000 |
| 12% unsecured notes | 50 000 | – |
| Other liabilities | 16 000 | 15 000 |
| | $586 000 | $228 000 |
| | | |
| *Assets* | | |
| Accounts receivable | 50 000 | 26 000 |
| Inventory | 25 000 | 15 000 |
| Dividend receivable | 3 000 | – |
| Unsecured notes – Savage Ltd | – | 25 000 |
| Investment in Avenger Ltd | 190 000 | – |
| Other assets | 318 000 | 162 000 |
| | $586 000 | $228 000 |

Additional information:
(a) The identifiable net assets of Avenger Ltd were recorded at fair value at the date of acquisition
(b) Any goodwill on acquisition is to be amortised over a 20-year period.
(c) On 3 August 20X4, Avenger declared and paid a dividend of $10 000 from pre-acquisition profits. All other dividends have been from post-acquisition profits.
(d) During the current financial year, Avenger paid management fees of $7000 to Savage.
(e) During the year, Savage sold inventory to Avenger for $30 000. All of this inventory has been sold by Avenger to parties external to the group during the

year. This intra-group sale was made on credit terms, and $10 000 remains owing to Savage at balance date.

(f) Avenger holds one-half of the unsecured notes issued by Savage. Interest at the rate of 12% has been paid on these debentures during the year.

(g) On 25 January 20X8, Avenger paid an interim dividend of $2000 to Savage.

(h) Avenger declared a final dividend of $3000 on 20 June 20X8. Savage has recognised this dividend as a receivable at 30 June 20X8.

(i) The tax rate is 40%.

*Required*

1 Prepare an acquisition analysis.

2 Prepare the consolidation journal entries necessary to prepare consolidated accounts for the year ending 30 June 20X8 for the group comprising Savage Ltd and Avenger Ltd.

3 Complete a detailed consolidation worksheet for the year ending 30 June 20X8.

**Exercise 6.20** **Comprehensive**

On 1 July 20X1, Cyclone Ltd acquired 100% of the issued shares of Champion Ltd for $200 000. At the date of acquisition, the shareholders' equity of Champion Ltd consisted of:

|  | $ |
|---|---|
| Paid-up capital | 100 000 |
| General reserve | 30 000 |
| Retained profits | 20 000 |
|  | $150 000 |

At 30 June 20X4, three years after acquisition, the accounts of the two companies appear as follows:

|  | Cyclone Ltd $ | Champion Ltd $ |
|---|---|---|
| Sales | 290 000 | 105 000 |
| Cost of goods sold |  |  |
| Opening stock 1 July 20X3 | 25 000 | 11 000 |
| Purchases | 150 000 | 65 000 |
|  | 175 000 | 76 000 |
| Closing stock 30 June 20X4 | 20 000 | 10 000 |
| Cost of goods sold | 155 000 | 66 000 |
| Gross profit | 135 000 | 39 000 |
| Depreciation expense | 21 000 | 9 000 |
| Administrative expenses | 28 000 | 12 000 |
| Financial expenses | 30 000 | 8 000 |
| Selling expenses | 22 000 | 4 000 |
| Total expenses | 101 000 | 33 000 |
|  | 34 000 | 6 000 |
| Other income |  |  |
| Dividend revenue | 7 000 | – |
| Interest revenue | 2 000 | 3 000 |

| | Cyclone Ltd | Champion Ltd |
|---|---|---|
| | $ | $ |
| Rent revenue | 5 000 | – |
| Total other income | 14 000 | 3 000 |
| Operating profit before tax | 48 000 | 9 000 |
| Income tax expense | 17 000 | 3 000 |
| Operating profit after tax | 31 000 | 6 000 |
| Retained profits 1 July 20X3 | 25 000 | 15 000 |
| Available for appropriation | 56 000 | 21 000 |
| Interim dividend paid | 12 000 | 3 000 |
| Final dividend proposed | 28 000 | 4 000 |
| Dividends paid and provided | 40 000 | 7 000 |
| Retained profits 30 June 20X4 | 16 000 | 14 000 |
| Paid-up capital | 250 000 | 100 000 |
| General reserve | 20 000 | 40 000 |
| Creditors | 30 000 | 5 000 |
| Dividend payable | 28 000 | 4 000 |
| 10% debentures | – | 30 000 |
| Other liabilities | 60 000 | 5 000 |
| | $404 000 | $198 000 |
| | | |
| **Assets** | | |
| Cash at bank | 3 000 | 5 000 |
| Accounts receivable | 40 000 | 30 000 |
| Deposits | – | 60 000 |
| Inventory | 20 000 | 10 000 |
| Dividend receivable | 4 000 | – |
| Debentures – Champion Ltd | 20 000 | – |
| Investment in Champion Ltd | 180 000 | – |
| Plant & equipment | 106 000 | 80 000 |
| Accumulated depreciation | (64 000) | (15 000) |
| Land & buildings | 100 000 | – |
| Accumulated depreciation | (10 000) | – |
| Other assets | 5 000 | 28 000 |
| | $404 000 | $198 000 |

Additional information:
(a) The identifiable net assets of Champion Ltd were recorded at fair value at the date of acquisition
(b) Any goodwill on acquisition is to be amortised over a ten-year period.
(c) On 1 August 20X1, Champion Ltd declared and paid a dividend of $20 000 from pre-acquisition profits. All other dividends have been from post-acquisition profits.
(d) During the year, Champion paid rent of $5000 to Cyclone. This expense is recorded in Champion's accounts under the 'Administrative expenses' heading.
(e) An item of plant and equipment owned by Cyclone (cost $20 000 and accumulated depreciation $4000) had been sold to Champion for $18 000 on 30 June 20X3. Cyclone had depreciated this asset at 20% per annum straight line on original cost. Champion has also applied a 20% depreciation rate from the date of transfer of the asset.

(f) The opening stock of Cyclone includes unrealised profit of $1000 on inventory transferred from Champion during the prior financial year. All of this inventory had been sold by Cyclone to parties external to the group during the year ended 30 June 20X4.

(g) During the current financial year, Cyclone had sold inventory to Champion for $20 000. This inventory had previously cost Cyclone $16 000. One-half of this inventory has been sold by Champion to parties external to the group during the year.

(h) Cyclone holds two-thirds of the debentures issued by Champion. Interest at the rate of 10% has been paid on these debentures during the year. Interest expense is recorded in Champion's accounts under the 'Financial expenses' heading.

(i) On 15 January 20X4, Champion paid an interim dividend of $3000 to Cyclone.

(j) Champion declared a final dividend of $4000 on 15 June 20X4. Cyclone has recognised this dividend as a receivable at 30 June 20X4.

(k) The tax rate is 40%.

*Required*

1 Prepare an acquisition analysis.

2 Prepare the consolidation journal entries necessary to prepare consolidated accounts for the year ending 30 June 20X4 for the group comprising Cyclone Ltd and Champion Ltd.

3 Complete a detailed consolidation worksheet for the year ending 30 June 20X4.

**Exercise 6.21** **Comprehensive**

On 1 July 20X1, Dominator Ltd acquired 100% of the issued shares of Atlas Ltd for $320 000. At the date of acquisition, the shareholders' equity of Atlas Ltd consisted of:

|  | $ |
|---|---|
| Paid-up capital | 200 000 |
| General reserve | 50 000 |
| Retained profits | 30 000 |
|  | $280 000 |

At 30 June 20X5, four years after acquisition, the accounts of the two companies appear as follows:

|  | Dominator Ltd | Atlas Ltd |
|---|---|---|
|  | $ | $ |
| Sales | 360 000 | 195 000 |
| Cost of goods sold |  |  |
| Opening stock 1 July 20X4 | 45 000 | 20 000 |
| Purchases | 225 000 | 130 000 |
|  | 270 000 | 150 000 |
| Closing stock 30 June 20X5 | 40 000 | 30 000 |
| Cost of goods sold | 230 000 | 120 000 |
| Gross profit | 130 000 | 75 000 |

| | Dominator Ltd | Atlas Ltd |
|---|---|---|
| | $ | $ |
| Depreciation expense | 11 000 | 7 000 |
| Financial expenses | 9 000 | 9 000 |
| Selling expenses | 8 000 | 10 000 |
| Total expenses | 28 000 | 26 000 |
| | 102 000 | 49 000 |
| *Other income* | | |
| Interest revenue | 3 000 | 5 000 |
| Dividend revenue | 14 000 | – |
| Total other income | 17 000 | 5 000 |
| *Operating profit before tax* | 119 000 | 54 000 |
| Income tax expense | 48 000 | 20 000 |
| *Operating profit after tax* | 71 000 | 34 000 |
| Retained profits 1 July 20X4 | 30 000 | 10 000 |
| *Available for appropriation* | 101 000 | 44 000 |
| Interim dividend paid | 10 000 | 6 000 |
| Final dividend proposed | 30 000 | 10 000 |
| *Dividends paid and provided* | 40 000 | 16 000 |
| Retained profits 30 June 20X5 | 61 000 | 28 000 |
| Paid-up capital | 350 000 | 200 000 |
| General reserve | 30 000 | 50 000 |
| Creditors | 45 000 | 5 000 |
| Dividend payable | 30 000 | 10 000 |
| Accrued interest – Dominator Ltd | – | 1 000 |
| Loan – Dominator Ltd | – | 40 000 |
| Other liabilities | 40 000 | 10 000 |
| | $556 000 | $344 000 |
| | | |
| *Assets* | | |
| Cash at bank | 2 000 | 1 000 |
| Deposits | – | 65 000 |
| Inventory | 40 000 | 30 000 |
| Interest receivable – Atlas Ltd | 1 000 | – |
| Loan – Atlas Ltd | 40 000 | – |
| Investment in Atlas Ltd | 290 000 | – |
| Plant & equipment | 110 000 | 180 000 |
| Accumulated depreciation | (45 000) | (40 000) |
| Land & buildings | 120 000 | 102 000 |
| Accumulated depreciation | (5 000) | (14 000) |
| Other assets | 3 000 | 20 000 |
| | $556 000 | $344 000 |

Additional information:
(a) The identifiable net assets of Atlas Ltd were recorded at fair value at the date of acquisition
(b) Any goodwill on acquisition is to be amortised over a 20-year period.
(c) On 15 August 20X1, Atlas Ltd declared and paid a dividend of $30 000 from pre-acquisition profits. All other dividends have been from post-acquisition profits.

(d) An item of plant and equipment owned by Atlas (cost $30 000 and accumulated depreciation $6000) had been sold to Dominator for $22 000 on 1 July 20X2. Atlas had depreciated this asset at 10% per annum straight line on original cost, while Dominator has applied a depreciation rate of 20% straight line from the date of transfer of the asset.

(e) The opening stock of Atlas includes unrealised profit of $2000 on inventory transferred from Dominator during the prior financial year. All of this inventory had been sold by Atlas to parties external to the group during the year ended 30 June 20X5.

(f) During the current financial year, Atlas had purchased inventory from Dominator for $30 000. This inventory had previously cost Dominator $24 000. One-third of this inventory had been sold to outsiders by Atlas during the year.

(g) Atlas borrowed $40 000 from Dominator during the financial year. Atlas paid $2000 interest on this loan during the year. In addition, a further $1000 in interest has been recognised as an accrued expense in Atlas Ltd's accounts and as interest receivable in Dominator Ltd's accounts. Interest expense is included in Atlas Ltd's accounts under the 'Financial expenses' heading.

(h) On 15 July 20X4, Atlas paid a final dividend of $8000 to Dominator from profits for the prior financial year.

(i) Atlas has also paid an interim dividend of $6000 to Dominator on 1 February 20X5. In addition, Atlas has provided for a final dividend amounting to $10 000. Dominator has not recognised this dividend as a receivable prior to receipt.

(j) The tax rate is 40%.

*Required*

1 Prepare an acquisition analysis.

2 Prepare the consolidation journal entries necessary to prepare consolidated accounts for the year ending 30 June 20X5 for the group comprising Dominator Ltd and Atlas Ltd.

3 Complete a detailed consolidation worksheet for the year ending 30 June 20X5.

chapter

# 7

# CONSOLIDATION: OUTSIDE EQUITY INTERESTS

# introduction

**direct outside equity
interest**

**indirect outside
equity interest**

This chapter discusses the fifth step in the consolidation process listed in chapter 5, the calculation and disclosure of direct outside equity interests. Chapter 8 will introduce the concept of accounting for indirect outside equity interests.

The discussion and examples used in chapters 5 and 6 examined economic entity situations where the subsidiary is wholly owned by the parent. However, it is common for a parent to own less than 100% of a subsidiary and, in accordance with AASB 1024, may have control of a subsidiary with less than 50% ownership of the subsidiary.

The portion of the equity of a subsidiary not owned by a parent is known as outside equity interest and is defined in AASB 1024, para 9, as 'the equity in the economic entity other than that which can be attributed to the ownership group of the parent entity'. Therefore, in accordance with the entity concept of consolidation, equity to the economic entity or group is provided by members of the parent entity and by the equity interest in a subsidiary owned by other than the parent.

# Outside equity interests illustrated

This concept is demonstrated in Figures 7.1 and 7.2. Figure 7.1 shows the equity provided to the group in an economic entity with the subsidiary owned 60% by the parent.

**Figure 7.1**

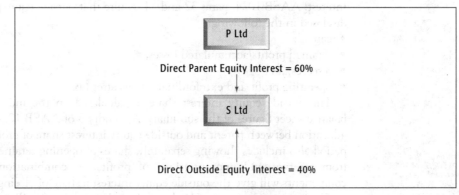

**Figure 7.2**

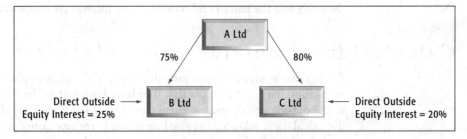

In the situation where a parent company owns 100% of the shares in a subsidiary company, clearly, 100% of the assets and liabilities of the subsidiary company are consolidated with the assets and liabilities of the parent company. Here, shares in S Ltd are eliminated against 100% of the equity acquired in S Ltd. This elimination entry enables the assets and liabilities of S Ltd to be added to the assets and liabilities of P Ltd. The cost of the investment is always substituted against the equity acquired **date of acquisition** at the date of acquisition. If the date of consolidation is after the date of acquisition, any increases in the equity (and therefore the net assets) of S Ltd remain in the consolidated accounts and represent a return on the investment originally made in S Ltd by P Ltd.

Where P Ltd owns less than 100% of the paid-up capital in S Ltd (say, 80%), there exists a direct outside equity interest. In this situation only the percentage of shares owned by P Ltd are eliminated against the equity acquired, even though 100% of S Ltd's assets and liabilities are consolidated with the assets and liabilities of P Ltd. This would create an imbalance if the direct outside equity interest was not shown. That is, the 20% direct outside equity interest must be accounted for in the consolidation accounts or they will not balance. This concept is based on the notion of control of S Ltd by P Ltd and conforms with the entity concept of consolidation adopted by AASB 1024. If consolidation of S Ltd's assets and liabilities was based on ownership and not control, this would be a form of proportional consolidation which is prohibited by AASB 1024.

**allocation**

After the consolidated accounts are prepared, the outside equity interest in the group, through an interest in the equity of each subsidiary, is calculated and shown separately in the financial statements. The consolidated shareholders' equity accounts are allocated between the parent entity interest and the outside equity interest. AASB 1024, paras 32 and 34 require that outside equity interest should be disclosed in the following:

- capital;
- retained profits/accumulated losses;
- reserves; and
- operating profit and extraordinary items after tax.

The outside equity interest share is calculated on the income statement and balance sheet figures of the subsidiary. Appendix 3 of AASB 1024 suggests that the allocation between parent and outside equity interest share of profits of a group for a period also includes showing separately, shares of opening retained profits, transfers from reserves and appropriations of profits. A combination of all of these components will give the outside equity interest a share of closing retained profits.

The income statement and balance sheet demonstrated in Illustrative example 7.2 show the way the parent and outside equity interest are disclosed.

# Calculation of outside equity interest

As the outside equity interest provides equity to the group, only a share of the profits of the subsidiary to the extent that they have been realised by the group are included in the outside equity interest share (see AASB 1024, para 33). Before carrying out the calculation, adjustments need to be made for any unrealised profits and losses made by the subsidiary when dealing with any other entities in the group.

## INTRA-GROUP TRANSACTIONS

There are essentially two types of intra-group transactions — those which involve only the profit and loss statement (eg service fee revenue and expenses and interest revenue and expense) and those which involve the transfer of assets (eg inventory and depreciable assets).

Intra-group items which involve only the profit and loss statement, such as interest revenue and expense, will never directly involve an outside party and it is difficult to discern at which point the revenue or expense is realised outside the group. To solve this problem, it is sometimes suggested that these transactions are realised from a group point of view at the time of the transaction and that no adjustment to a share of profits of the subsidiary for these items is necessary when calculating outside equity interest. This is incorrect because the outside equity interest is only entitled to a share of the profit the subsidiary has contributed to the economic entity. Therefore, both types of transactions mentioned above must be adjusted for when calculating the outside equity share of a subsidiary's equity.

Any unrealised profits or losses in the subsidiary's accounts, as a result of intra-group transactions, are not profits/losses from a group perspective. Therefore, the effects of such transactions must be eliminated before the outside equity interest is given a share of its subsidiary's equity. This means that the outside equity interest for consolidation purposes may be different to the outside equity interest in a subsidiary for legal purposes. That is, the subsidiary's legal accounts have to be adjusted for consolidation purposes if intra-group transactions have occurred.

Similarly, any goodwill that arose on consolidation has to be amortised in the consolidation process as per AASB 1013: Accounting for Goodwill. The amortisation expense is charged entirely against the parent company's share of the subsidiary company's equity, because only goodwill purchased by the parent is recorded in the consolidated statements. This means that the outside equity interest share of the subsidiary's equity is not adjusted for goodwill amortisation.

## TRANSFER OF ASSETS

The entity in the group now holding the depreciable asset will calculate depreciation on the cost to it rather than the original cost to the group at the time of transfer. The entity holding the asset earns income to offset this depreciation. Therefore, the approach taken is to treat the initial gain or loss on transfer of the depreciable asset as not being realised and to realise this gain or loss at the rate at which the entity now holding the asset charges depreciation.

For example, assume that a subsidiary sells a depreciable asset to its parent for a gain of $5000 before tax (tax rate 40%) and the parent depreciates the asset at 10% per annum upon transfer. The initial gain is treated as unrealised at the time of transfer and is then realised at 10% per annum over the next ten years. In this case the unrealised gain after tax is $3000 ($5000 gain – $2000 tax expense) at the time of transfer and the gain is realised to the group at $300 per annum ($3000/10 years), and therefore included in the outside equity interest share of profits.

**ILLUSTRATIVE EXAMPLE** `7.1`

# CALCULATION OF OUTSIDE EQUITY INTEREST

Assume that, on 1 July 20X4, P Ltd acquired 80% of the paid-up capital of S Ltd. At the date of acquisition all of the identifiable net assets of S Ltd were recorded at fair value. At 30 June 20X6, the date of the preparation of the consolidated accounts of the economic entity, the financial statements of S Ltd were as follows:

| Income Statement for the year ended 30 June 20X6 | |
|---|---|
| | $ |
| Operating profit before income tax | 60 000 |
| Income tax expense | 20 000 |
| Operating profit after income tax expense | 40 000 |
| Retained profits 1 July 20X5 | 35 000 |
| Total available for appropriation | 75 000 |
| Dividends paid | 10 000 |
| Dividends proposed | 10 000 |
| Transfer to general reserve | 2 000 |
| | 22 000 |
| Retained profits 30 June 20X6 | $53 000 |

### Balance Sheet as at 30 June 20X6

| | $ |
|---|---|
| Paid-up capital | 120 000 |
| Asset revaluation reserve | 4 000 |
| General reserve | 26 000 |
| Retained profits | 53 000 |
| 12% mortgage debentures | 85 000 |
| Dividends payable | 10 000 |
| Trade creditors | 20 000 |
| Provision for income tax payable | 10 000 |
| | $328 000 |
| | |
| Trade debtors | 13 000 |
| Inventory | 57 000 |
| Plant & machinery | 76 000 |
| Accumulated depreciation | (26 000) |
| Land | 208 000 |
| | $328 000 |

Transactions during the current year between P Ltd and S Ltd included the following:
(a) The opening inventory at 1 July 20X5 includes inventory sold by S Ltd to P Ltd at a profit of $1000 and inventory sold by P Ltd to S Ltd at a profit of $3000. All of this inventory had been sold outside the group by 30 June 20X6.
(b) The closing inventory of P Ltd includes inventory purchased from S Ltd during the year at a profit of $1500. All other inventory sold intra-group had been resold by the end of the year in which it was transferred.
(c) S Ltd received a $1000 fee from P Ltd for some management services provided to P Ltd.
(d) The tax rate is 40%.

The outside equity interest (OEI) share of the equity of S Ltd, after adjusting for unrealised profit and loss items, may be calculated as follows:

### OEI share of operating profit after tax

| | $ |
|---|---|
| Operating profit after tax | 40 000 |
| Add Profit in opening inventory after tax now realised ($1000 – $400) | 600 |
| Less Unrealised profit in closing inventory ($1500 – $600) | (900) |
| Less Management fee from P Ltd $1000 * | (1 000) |
| | $38 700 |
| Outside equity interest (20% of $39 100) | $7 740 |

* No tax effect because it is a permanent difference, not a timing difference.

The adjustment for realisation of profit in opening inventory sold from S Ltd to P Ltd is made because the inventory has now been sold outside the group and the profit is therefore realised from a group point of view. No adjustment is made for the inventory sold from P Ltd to S Ltd as the unrealised/realised profit on this sale does not affect the profit of S Ltd – that is, P Ltd made the profit, not S Ltd, and the outside equity interest is in S Ltd.

The deduction for unrealised profit on inventory sold this year from S Ltd to P Ltd is made because the inventory is still held in the group and no profit on the sale has been made from a group point of view. Because S Ltd's accounts contain unrealised profit from a group perspective, the outside equity interest share must be adjusted. Remember that the outside equity interests are allocated a share of the subsidiary company's profit *contributed to the economic group as a whole*. This is why the inter-company management fee also has to be adjusted.

**OEI share of retained profits at 1 July 20X5**

|  | $ |
|---|---|
| Retained profits 1 July 20X5 | 35 000 |
| *Less* Unrealised profit in opening inventory after tax | |
| ($1000 – $400) | (600) |
|  | $34 400 |
| Outside equity interest (20% of $34 400) | $6 880 |

The adjustment for the unrealised profit on inventory sold from S Ltd to P Ltd last year is made because the inventory is still held in the group at the beginning of the current year and no profit was realised last year from a group point of view. Therefore, the opening retained profits of S Ltd are overstated from the group view.

**OEI share of dividends paid**

| (20% of $10 000) | $2 000 |
|---|---|

**OEI share of dividends proposed**

| (20% of $10 000) | $2 000 |
|---|---|

**OEI share of transfer to general reserve**

| (20% of $2000) | $400 |
|---|---|

In accordance with Appendix 3 of AASB 1024, the figures calculated above would be shown in the consolidated income statement as the amounts applicable to the outside equity interest. The sum of these figures is also the amount of the outside equity interest in retained profits shown in the consolidated balance sheet and is calculated as follows:

**Summary of outside equity interest**

|  | $ |
|---|---|
| Operating profit after tax | 7 740 |
| *Add* Retained profits 1 July 20X5 | 6 880 |
| *Less* Dividends paid | (2 000) |
| Dividends proposed | (2 000) |
| Transfer to general reserve | (400) |
| OEI share of retained profits in balance sheet | $10 220 |

**OEI share of paid-up capital**

| (20% of $120 000) | $24 000 |
|---|---|

**OEI share of asset revaluation reserve**

| (20% of $4000) | $800 |
|---|---|

**OEI share of general reserve**

| (20% of $26 000) | $5 200 |
|---|---|

Thus the OEI is allocated a share of the pre- and post-acquisition equity of the subsidiary after the elimination of the effects of intra-group transactions.

ILLUSTRATIVE EXAMPLE **7.2**

# OUTSIDE EQUITY INTEREST – VARIOUS TRANSACTIONS

A comprehensive example follows to demonstrate the process of carrying out a consolidation for an economic entity containing a parent and a single subsidiary with an outside equity interest. The consolidated accounts with separate parent and outside equity interest information shown in the financial statements are also illustrated.

On 1 July 20X2, P Ltd acquired 60% of the issued shares of S Ltd for $18 000 when the shareholders' equity of S Ltd was:

| | |
|---|---|
| Paid-up capital | $18 000 |
| General reserve | 4 000 |
| Retained profits | 6 000 |

Immediately after acquisition, S Ltd declared and paid a dividend of $4000. All other dividends since have been from post-acquisition profits. At the date of acquisition, all identifiable net assets of S Ltd were recorded at fair value.

The accounts of the two companies disclosed the following at 30 June 20X4.

| Income Statements for the year ended 30 June 20X4 | | |
|---|---|---|
| | P Ltd | S Ltd |
| | $ | $ |
| Sales | 28 000 | 16 500 |
| Opening stock 1 July 20X3 | 5 000 | 2 000 |
| Purchases | 23 000 | 12 000 |
| | 28 000 | 14 000 |
| Closing stock 30 June 20X4 | 5 000 | 2 000 |
| | 23 000 | 12 000 |
| Gross profit | 5 000 | 4 500 |
| Depreciation and other expenses | 1 200 | 1 500 |
| | 3 800 | 3 000 |
| Dividend revenue | 1 200 | – |
| Operating profit before tax | 5 000 | 3 000 |
| Income tax expense | (2 000) | (1 200) |
| Operating profit after tax | 3 000 | 1 800 |
| Retained profits 1 July 20X3 | 3 000 | 6 000 |
| | 6 000 | 7 800 |
| Interim dividend paid | (1 000) | (800) |
| Final dividend declared | (2 000) | (1 200) |
| Transfer to general reserve | – | (2 000) |
| Retained profits 30 June 20X4 | $3 000 | $3 800 |

**Balance Sheets as at 30 June 20X4**

|  | P Ltd $ | S Ltd $ |
|---|---|---|
| Paid-up capital | 30 000 | 18 000 |
| General reserve | 2 000 | 6 000 |
| Retained profits | 3 000 | 3 800 |
| Dividend payable | 2 000 | 1 200 |
| Other liabilities | 4 000 | 2 000 |
|  | $41 000 | $31 000 |
|  |  |  |
| Dividend receivable | 720 | – |
| Inventory | 4 000 | 3 000 |
| Investment in S Ltd | 15 600 | – |
| Non-current assets (depreciable) | 10 000 | 7 000 |
| Accumulated depreciation | (5 000) | (1 000) |
| Land | 5 000 | 9 000 |
| Other assets | 10 680 | 13 000 |
|  | $41 000 | $31 000 |

Additional information:
(a) The transfer to reserves in the current year is from post-acquisition profits.
(b) A non-current asset owned by S Ltd (cost $1000, accumulated depreciation $500) was sold to P Ltd for $1000 on 1 July 20X2. P Ltd applies a depreciation rate of 20% per annum from the date of transfer of the asset.
(c) Inter-company sales of inventory totalled $6000 for the year.
(d) During the current year, P Ltd has purchased inventory from S Ltd at a profit of $800. Half of this inventory had been sold by P Ltd outside the group at the end of the year. At 30 June 20X4, S Ltd also holds inventory purchased from P Ltd at a profit of $500.
(e) The opening inventory of P Ltd includes unrealised profit of $1000 on inventory transferred from S Ltd in the previous year. All of this inventory had been sold by P Ltd by 30 June 20X4.
(f) P Ltd holds no investment in shares except for that held in S Ltd.
(g) The tax rate is 40% and P Ltd has a policy of amortising any goodwill on consolidation over ten years.

*Required*
Prepare the consolidated accounts for the economic entity at 30 June 20X4.

**Solution**

|  |  |  | $ |  |
|---|---|---|---|---|
| Fair value of identifiable net assets | = | | 18 000 | Capital |
|  |  | | 4 000 | General reserve |
|  |  | | 6 000 | Retained profits |
|  |  | | $28 000 |  |
| Fair value purchased (60% × $28 000) | = | $16 800 | | |
| Purchase consideration | = | $18 000 | | |
| Goodwill | = | $1 200 | | |
| Amortisation of goodwill ($1200/10 years) | = | $120 per annum | | |

## Consolidation journal

| | Debit $ | Credit $ |
|---|---|---|
| **(1)** Write-back of the pre-acquisition dividend received by P Ltd. (This results in the cost of the investment and retained profits being the same at acquisition date.) | | |
| Shares in S Ltd (60% × $4000) | 2 400 | |
| Retained profits 1 July 20X3 | | 2 400 |
| **(2)** Elimination of investment in subsidiary. | | |
| Retained profits 1 July 20X3 ($6000 × 60%) | 3 600 | |
| Paid-up capital ($18 000 × 60%) | 10 800 | |
| General reserves ($4000 × 60%) | 2 400 | |
| Goodwill | 1 200 | |
| Shares in S Ltd | | 18 000 |
| **(3)** Amortisation of goodwill. | | |
| Other expenses (amortisation of goodwill) | 120 | |
| Retained profits 1 July 20X3 | 120 | |
| Goodwill | | 240 |
| **(4)** Elimination of unrealised profit on the sale of a non-current asset. | | |
| Retained profits 1 July 20X3 ($1000 – $500) | 500 | |
| Accumulated depreciation | | 500 |
| Future income tax benefit ($500 × 40%) | 200 | |
| Retained profits 1 July 20X3 | | 200 |
| **(5)** Elimination of excess depreciation on non-current assets. | | |
| Accumulated depreciation | 200 | |
| Retained profits 1 July 20X3 | | 100 |
| Depreciation expense ($500 × 20%) | | 100 |
| Income tax expense ($100 × 40%) | 40 | |
| Retained profits 1 July 20X3 | 40 | |
| Future income tax benefit | | 80 |

(Recall that the asset was transferred two years before the date of consolidation. Therefore, retained profits, as well as this year's current profit, will be affected.)

| | Debit $ | Credit $ |
|---|---|---|
| **(6)** Elimination of intra-group sales. | | |
| Sales | 6 000 | |
| Purchases | | 6 000 |
| **(7)** Elimination of unrealised profit in closing inventory. | | |
| Closing stock ($400 + $500) (P&L) | 900 | |
| Inventory (balance sheet) | | 900 |
| Future income tax benefit ($900 × 40%) | 360 | |
| Income tax expense | | 360 |
| **(8)** Elimination of unrealised profit in opening inventory. | | |
| Retained profits 1 July 20X3 | 1 000 | |
| Opening stock (P&L) | | 1 000 |
| Income tax expense | 400 | |
| Retained profits 1 July 20X3 | | 400 |

|  | Debit | Credit |
|---|---|---|
|  | $ | $ |

(9) Elimination of interim dividend paid in current year.

| | Debit | Credit |
|---|---|---|
| Dividend revenue ($800 × 60%) | 480 | |
| Interim dividend paid (P&L) | | 480 |

(10) Elimination of intra-group final dividend.

| | Debit | Credit |
|---|---|---|
| Dividend revenue ($1200 × 60%) | 720 | |
| Dividend receivable | | 720 |
| Dividend payable (B/S) | 720 | |
| Final dividend declared (P&L) | | 720 |

These consolidation journal entries are now posted to the worksheet, as shown below.

## Consolidated income statement worksheet

| Account | P Ltd | S Ltd | Eliminations Debit | Eliminations Credit | Consolidation |
|---|---|---|---|---|---|
| | $ | $ | $ | $ | $ |
| Sales | 28 000 | 16 500 | 6 000 (6) | | 38 500 |
| Opening stock 1 July 20X3 | 5 000 | 2 000 | | 1 000 (8) | 6 000 |
| Purchases | 23 000 | 12 000 | | 6 000 (6) | 29 000 |
| | 28 000 | 14 000 | | | 35 000 |
| Closing stock 30 June 20X4 | 5 000 | 2 000 | 900 (7) | | 6 100 |
| Cost of goods sold | 23 000 | 12 000 | | | 28 900 |
| Gross profit | 5 000 | 4 500 | | | 9 600 |
| Depreciation & other expenses | 1 200 | 1 500 | 120 (3) | 100 (5) | 2 720 |
| | 3 800 | 3 000 | | | 6 880 |
| Dividend revenue | 1 200 | – | 480 (9) | | – |
| | | | 720(10) | | |
| Operating profit before tax | 5 000 | 3 000 | | | 6 880 |
| Income tax expense | (2 000) | (1 200) | 40 (5) | 360 (7) | (3 280) |
| | | | 400(8) | | |
| Operating profit after tax | 3 000 | 1 800 | | | 3 600 |
| Retained profits 1 July 20X3 | 3 000 | 6 000 | 3 600 (2) | 2 400 (1) | 6 840 |
| | | | 120 (3) | 200 (4) | |
| | | | 500 (4) | 100 (5) | |
| | | | 40 (5) | 400 (8) | |
| | | | 1 000 (8) | | |
| | 6 000 | 7 800 | | | 10 440 |
| Interim dividend paid | (1 000) | (800) | | 480 (9) | (1 320) |
| Final dividend declared | (2 000) | (1 200) | | 720(10) | (2 480) |
| Transfer to general reserve | – | (2 000) | | | (2 000) |
| Retained profits 30 June 20X4 | $3 000 | $3 800 | | | $4 640 |

## Consolidated balance sheet worksheet

| Account | P Ltd | S Ltd | Eliminations Debit | Eliminations Credit | Consolidation |
|---|---|---|---|---|---|
| Paid-up capital | 30 000 | 18 000 | 10 800 (2) | | 37 200 |
| General reserve | 2 000 | 6 000 | 2 400 (2) | | 5 600 |
| Retained profits 30 June 20X4 | 3 000 | 3 800 | | | 4 640 |
| Dividend payable | 2 000 | 1 200 | 720(10) | | 2 480 |
| Other liabilities | 4 000 | 2 000 | | | 6 000 |
| | $41 000 | $31 000 | | | $55 920 |
| Dividend receivable | 720 | – | | 720(10) | – |
| Inventory | 4 000 | 3 000 | | 900 (7) | 6 100 |
| Investment in S Ltd | 15 600 | – | 2 400 (1) | 18 000 (2) | – |
| Non-current assets | 10 000 | 7 000 | | | 17 000 |
| Accumulated depreciation | (5 000) | (1 000) | 200 (5) | 500 (4) | (6 300) |
| Land | 5 000 | 9 000 | | | 14 000 |
| Other assets | 10 680 | 13 000 | | | 23 680 |
| Future income tax benefit | – | – | 200 (4) | 80 (5) | |
| | | | 360 (7) | | 480 |
| Goodwill on acquisition | – | – | 1 200 (2) | 240 (3) | 960 |
| | $41 000 | $31 000 | $32 200 | $32 200 | $55 920 |

Outside equity interest is calculated as follows:

### OEI share of operating profit after tax

| | $ |
|---|---|
| Operating profit after tax | 1 800 |
| *Less* Unrealised profit in closing inventory after tax ($400 – $160) | (240) |
| *Add* Realisation of 20% of profit on sale of non-current asset after tax ($100 – $40) | 60 |
| *Add* Profit in opening inventory after tax now realised ($1000 – $400) | 600 |
| | $2 220 |
| Outside equity interest (40% of $2220) | $888 |

### OEI share of retained profits 1 July 20X3

| | |
|---|---|
| Retained profits 1 July 20X3 | 6 000 |
| *Less* Unrealised profit in opening inventory after tax ($1000 – $400) | (600) |
| *Less* Unrealised profit on sale of non-current assets ($500 – $200) | (300) |
| *Add* Realisation of 20% of profit on sale of non-current asset after tax ($100 – $40) | 60 |
| | $5 160 |
| Outside equity interest (40% of $5160) | $2 064 |

### OEI share of dividend paid
(40% of $800) — $320

### OEI share of dividend declared
(40% of $1200) — $480

### OEI share of transfer to general reserve
(40% of $2000) — $800

Using the above calculations, the outside equity interest share of retained profits at 30 June 20X4 is calculated as follows:

**OEI share of retained profits at 30 June 20X4**

(888 + 2064 – 320 – 480 – 800)                                                    $1 352

**OEI share of paid-up capital**

(40% of $18 000)                                                                        $7 200

**OEI share of general reserve**

(40% of $6000)                                                                          $2 400

A consolidated income statement and balance sheet for the economic entity of P Ltd and its subsidiary S Ltd can now be prepared using the consolidation column of the worksheet and the OEI share of equity calculated above. The parent entity interest is simply the difference between the consolidated equity accounts (right-hand column of the worksheet) and the OEI share already calculated.

| P Ltd Economic Entity | | | |
|---|---|---|---|
| Consolidated Income Statement as at 30 June 20X4 | | | |
| | | | $ |
| Sales | | | 38 500 |
| Cost of goods sold | | | |
| Opening stock | | | 6 000 |
| Purchases | | | 29 000 |
| | | | 35 000 |
| Closing stock | | | 6 100 |
| Cost of goods sold | | | 28 900 |
| Gross profit | | | 9 600 |
| Depreciation & other expenses | | | 2 720 |
| Operating profit before tax | | | 6 880 |
| Income tax expense | | | (3 280) |
| Operating profit after tax | | | 3 600 |
| | Parent entity interest | Outside equity interest | |
| | $ | $ | |
| Operating profit after income tax | 2 712 | 888 | 3 600 |
| Retained profits 1 July 20X3 | 4 776 | 2 064 | 6 840 |
| Total available for appropriation | 7 488 | 2 952 | 10 440 |
| Dividends paid | 1 000 | 320 | 1 320 |
| Dividends declared | 2 000 | 480 | 2 480 |
| Transfer to reserves | 1 200 | 800 | 2 000 |
| | 4 200 | 1 600 | 5 800 |
| Retained profits 30 June 20X4 | $3 288 | $1 352 | $4 640 |

**P Ltd Economic Entity**
**Consolidated Balance Sheet as at 30 June 20X4**

|  | $ |
|---|---|
| *Assets* | |
| Current assets | |
| Inventory | 6 100 |
| *Total current assets* | 6 100 |
| Non-current assets | |
| Non-current assets (depreciable) | 17 000 |
| Accumulated depreciation | (6 300) |
| Land | 14 000 |
| Other assets | 23 680 |
| Future income tax benefit | 480 |
| Goodwill on acquisition | 960 |
| *Total non-current assets* | 49 820 |
| *Total assets* | 55 920 |
| *Liabilities* | |
| Current liabilities | |
| Dividends payable | 2 480 |
| *Total current liabilities* | 2 480 |
| Non-current liabilities | |
| Other liabilities | 6 000 |
| *Total non-current liabilities* | 6 000 |
| *Total liabilities* | 8 480 |
| *Net assets* | $47 440 |

| *Shareholders' equity* | Parent entity interest $ | Outside equity interest $ | |
|---|---|---|---|
| Paid-up capital | 30 000 | 7 200 | 37 200 |
| General reserve | 3 200 | 2 400 | 5 600 |
| Retained profits | 3 288 | 1 352 | 4 640 |
|  | $36 488 | $10 952 | $47 440 |

# Review

This chapter has examined the concept and calculation of *direct* outside equity interest. Chapter 8 will introduce *indirect* outside equity interest. When calculating the outside equity interest share of the subsidiary company's equity, all unrealised profits/losses must be taken into account. Transactions that have occurred in previous years, such as the transfer of assets at a profit/loss and the sale of inventory, must be adjusted in the current year of consolidation if any unrealised profit/loss is still in the subsidiary's accounts. Remember that the outside equity interest is only given a share of the subsidiary's profit that has been contributed to the economic entity.

# KEY TERMS

| | |
|---|---|
| allocation | direct outside equity interest |
| date of acquisition | indirect outside equity interest |

# REVIEW QUESTIONS

**7.1** If a parent company owns less than 100% of the shares of a subsidiary, why is it correct to consolidate 100% of the assets and liabilities of the subsidiary?

**7.2** Why is the outside equity interest not affected by goodwill amortisation?

**7.3** 'The effects of all intra-group transactions must be adjusted for when calculating the outside equity interest share of a subsidiary's equity.' Explain.

**7.4** Are consolidated financial statements relevant to outside equity interests? Explain.

**7.5** If parent entity shareholders and outside equity interests are considered to be equal contributors of capital to the group, why is the outside equity interest disclosed separately to the parent equity interest?

**7.6** Explain, with journal entries, why the outside equity interest is affected when the subsidiary has sold inventory at a profit to a parent company in the year before consolidation and the inventory is on hand at the beginning of the year of consolidation.

# EXERCISES

**Exercise 7.7** **Outside equity interests — balance sheet**

On 1 July 20X4, J Ltd acquired 75% of paid-up capital of K Ltd for $150 000. At that date, shareholders' equity of K Ltd was:

| | |
|---|---|
| Paid-up capital | $100 000 |
| General reserve | 50 000 |
| Retained profits | 12 000 |

At 1 July 20X4 the net assets of K Ltd were at fair value and any goodwill is amortised straight line over five years.

Account balances at 30 June 20X6 were:

| | J Ltd $ | K Ltd $ |
|---|---|---|
| **Credit balances** | | |
| Paid-up capital ($1 shares) | 200 000 | 100 000 |
| General reserve | 194 000 | 60 000 |
| Retained profits | 26 000 | 14 000 |
| Trade creditors | 24 000 | 44 000 |
| Debentures | 200 000 | 50 000 |
| | $644 000 | $268 000 |

|  | J Ltd | K Ltd |
|---|---|---|
|  | $ | $ |
| **Debit balances** |  |  |
| Bank | 45 000 | 50 000 |
| Accounts receivable | 76 000 | 51 000 |
| Inventory | 95 000 | 50 000 |
| Investment in K Ltd | 150 000 | – |
| Land & buildings | 278 000 | 117 000 |
|  | $644 000 | $268 000 |

*Required*
Prepare the consolidated balance sheet of K Ltd as at 30 June 20X6.

**Exercise 7.8**   **Outside equity interest after payment of a pre-acquisition dividend**
On 1 July 20X2, V Ltd acquired 75% of the paid-up capital of X Ltd for $100 000.
Shareholders' equity of X Ltd at that date was:

| Paid-up capital | $100 000 |
|---|---|
| General reserve | 12 000 |
| Retained profits | 11 000 |

Immediately after the acquisition, X Ltd declared and paid a 10% dividend. Net
assets acquired were at fair value, and goodwill on acquisition is to be written off over
five years.

*Required*
1  Prepare the journal entries in V Ltd's accounts for the above transactions.
2  Prepare the journal entry for the elimination of the above dividend when
   consolidating the accounts of V Ltd and X Ltd for the year ended 30 June 20X3.
3  Prepare the entry for the elimination of the item 'Shares in X Ltd' when
   consolidating the accounts of both companies for the year ended 30 June 20X3.
4  Calculate the outside equity interest immediately after the payment of the pre-
   acquisition dividend.

**Exercise 7.9**   **Intra-group sale of a non-current asset**
A Ltd owns 80% of the paid-up capital of B Ltd. On 1 July 20X3, B Ltd purchased
an asset for $200 000. This asset has a five-year life and is depreciated straight line
for both accounting and taxation purposes. B Ltd sold this asset to A Ltd on 1 July
20X5 for $150 000. The company tax rate is 36%. For the year ended 30 June 20X7,
B Ltd made an after-tax profit of $500 000.

*Required*
1  Prepare the consolidation journal entries for 20X6 and 20X7 to adjust for this
   asset sale.
2  Calculate the outside equity interest share of B Ltd as at 30 June 20X7.

**Exercise 7.10**   **Outside equity interest — unrealised profits in inventory**
A Ltd purchased 80% of the paid-up capital ($1 shares) in B Ltd for $65 000 on
1 July 20X3. At the date of acquisition the balance sheet of B Ltd was as follows:

|  | $ | $ |
|---|---|---|
| Current assets |  |  |
| Accounts receivable | 18 680 |  |
| Inventory | 21 000 | 39 680 |
| Non-current assets |  | 64 520 |
|  |  | $104 200 |
| Trade creditors |  | 27 200 |
| Paid-up capital ($1 shares) |  | 50 000 |
| General reserves |  | 10 000 |
| Retained profits |  | 17 000 |
|  |  | $104 200 |

Immediately following the purchase, B Ltd declared a dividend of 10%. At 1 July 20X3 the net assets of B Ltd were at fair value.

At 30 June 20X6 the balance sheets of the two companies were as follows:

|  | A Ltd $ | B Ltd $ |
|---|---|---|
| Inventory | 47 160 | 22 000 |
| Other current assets | 50 500 | 19 750 |
| Advance to B Ltd | 9 000 | – |
| Investment in B Ltd | 61 000 | – |
| Non-current assets | 111 540 | 65 250 |
|  | $279 200 | $107 000 |
| Trade creditors | 34 660 | 20 200 |
| Advance by A Ltd | – | 9 000 |
| Paid-up capital | 200 000 | 50 000 |
| General reserve | 25 000 | 12 800 |
| Retained profits | 19 540 | 15 000 |
|  | $279 200 | $107 000 |

Inventory held at 30 June 20X6 by A Ltd includes inventory transferred from B Ltd at a profit of $2000. All other inventory held had been supplied from outside the group. Any goodwill on acquisition is to be amortised evenly over five years. The company tax rate is 36%.

*Required*
Prepare a consolidated balance sheet for A Ltd and B Ltd.

**Exercise 7.11** **Calculation of outside equity interest**
World Ltd has an 80% interest in Series Ltd which it acquired on 1 July 20X2. At 30 June 20X3, World Ltd held inventory of $50 000 which had been purchased from Series Ltd at a profit of $10 000.

The following transactions relate to the year ended 30 June 20X4.
(a) Series Ltd sold inventory to World Ltd for $200 000 which had cost Series Ltd $170 000. World Ltd has all of this inventory on hand at year end.

(b) World Ltd sold inventory to Series Ltd for $75 000 which had cost World Ltd $50 000. Series Ltd has half of this inventory on hand at year end.

(c) The operating profit after tax of World Ltd is $800 000 and for Series Ltd $700 000.

The company tax rate is 36%. Goodwill on acquisition is being amortised at $12 000 per annum.

*Required*

1  Prepare the consolidation journal entries for all the above transactions.

2  Calculate the outside equity interest in Series Ltd's operating profit after tax and World Ltd's share of consolidated profit after tax.

**Exercise 7.12  Outside equity interest — income statement**

On 1 July 20X4, C Ltd purchased 90% of the paid-up capital of D Ltd for $150 000. At that date, shareholders' equity of D Ltd was:

| | |
|---|---:|
| Paid-up capital ($1 shares) | $90 000 |
| General reserve | 30 000 |
| Retained profits | 10 000 |

Abridged income statements of both companies for the year ended 30 June 20X5 were as follows:

| | C Ltd $ | D Ltd $ |
|---|---:|---:|
| Retained profits 1 July 20X4 | 14 000 | 10 000 |
| Net profit | 18 000 | 16 000 |
| | 32 000 | 26 000 |
| Interim dividends paid | (14 000) | (8 000) |
| Proposed dividend | (7 000) | (4 500) |
| | 21 000 | 12 500 |
| Retained profits 30 June 20X5 | $11 000 | $13 500 |

Additional information:

(a) The closing stock of C Ltd included goods $5000 bought from D Ltd. This stock originally cost D Ltd $4000.

(b) C Ltd had included in its final accounts the dividend provided by D Ltd.

(c) All dividends are from post-acquisition profit.

(d) Any goodwill on acquisition is to be amortised evenly over a ten-year period.

(e) The company tax rate is 36%.

*Required*

Prepare a consolidated income statement of C Ltd for the year ended 30 June 20X5.

**Exercise 7.13** **Outside equity interest — balance sheets**

The summarised balance sheets of X Ltd and its two subsidiaries, Y Ltd and Z Ltd, at 30 June 20X6 were as follows:

|  | X Ltd | Y Ltd | Z Ltd |
|---|---|---|---|
|  | $ | $ | $ |
| Other current assets | 30 000 | 50 000 | 50 000 |
| Inventory | 40 000 | 30 000 | 40 000 |
| Non-current assets | 40 000 | 20 000 | 30 000 |
| Debentures in Z Ltd | 20 000 | – | – |
| Debentures in X Ltd | – | 10 000 | – |
| 60 000 shares in Y Ltd | 80 000 | – | – |
| 45 000 shares in Z Ltd | 70 000 | – | – |
|  | $280 000 | $110 000 | $120 000 |
| Sundry liabilities | 44 000 | 9 000 | 21 000 |
| Paid-up capital ($1 shares) | 150 000 | 80 000 | 60 000 |
| Debentures (secured) | 40 000 | – | 20 000 |
| General reserve | 40 000 | 15 000 | 17 000 |
| Retained profits | 6 000 | 6 000 | 2 000 |
|  | $280 000 | $110 000 | $120 000 |

The shareholders' equity of the two companies on 30 June 20X5, when the shares were acquired, was:

|  | Y Ltd | Z Ltd |
|---|---|---|
|  | $ | $ |
| Paid-up capital ($1 shares) | 80 000 | 60 000 |
| General reserve | 10 000 | 3 000 |
| Retained profits | 11 000 | 8 000 |

At 30 June 20X5 the net assets of Y Ltd and Z Ltd were at fair value.

Additional information:

(a) A 10% pre-acquisition dividend was paid by both Y Ltd and Z Ltd immediately after acquisition.
(b) Inventory at 30 June 20X6 included the following:
 • inventory supplied by X Ltd to Y Ltd at $1200 above cost; and
 • inventory supplied by Y Ltd to Z Ltd at $2400 above cost.
(c) Goodwill on acquisition is to be written off evenly over five years. The company tax rate is 36%.

*Required*
Prepare a consolidated balance sheet for the X Ltd group as at 30 June 20X6.

**Exercise 7.14**  **Outside equity interest — income statement, balance sheet**

On 1 July 20X2, John Ltd paid $96 000 for 80% of the paid-up capital of Doe Ltd. The shareholders' equity of Doe Ltd at that date was:

| | |
|---|---|
| Paid-up capital | $80 000 |
| Retained profits | 20 000 |

At date of acquisition the assets were recorded at fair value. One year later, the financial statements of the two companies were as follows:

| Income Statement for the year ended 30 June 20X3 | | |
|---|---|---|
| | John Ltd | Doe Ltd |
| | $ | $ |
| Sales | 112 000 | 100 000 |
| Stock 1 July 20X2 | 12 000 | 20 000 |
| Purchases | 84 000 | 70 000 |
| Stock 30 June 20X3 | 8 000 | 10 000 |
| Cost of goods sold | 88 000 | 80 000 |
| Gross profit | 24 000 | 20 000 |
| Expenses | (12 400) | (10 850) |
| Other income | 1 500 | |
| Operating profit before tax | 13 100 | 9 150 |
| Income tax expense | (5 200) | (4 150) |
| Net profit after tax | 7 900 | 5 000 |
| Retained profits 1 July 20X2 | 24 000 | 20 000 |
| Proposed final dividend | (1 000) | (500) |
| Retained profits 30 June 20X3 | $30 900 | $24 500 |

| Balance Sheet as at 30 June 20X3 | | |
|---|---|---|
| | John Ltd | Doe Ltd |
| | $ | $ |
| Bank | 12 500 | 27 300 |
| Receivables | 28 000 | 31 000 |
| Inventory | 8 000 | 10 000 |
| Investment in Doe Ltd | 96 000 | – |
| Office equipment | 6 200 | 2 300 |
| Other non-current assets | 37 300 | 55 400 |
| | $188 000 | $126 000 |
| | | |
| Creditors | 26 100 | 21 000 |
| Debentures | 30 000 | – |
| Provision for dividend | 1 000 | 500 |
| Paid-up capital ($1 shares) | 100 000 | 80 000 |
| Retained profits 30 June 20X3 | 30 900 | 24 500 |
| | $188 000 | $126 000 |

The following transactions occurred during the year:
(a) Inventory of $40 000 was sold to Doe Ltd by John Ltd.
(b) John Ltd leased to Doe Ltd a showroom for $900.
(c) Doe Ltd paid John Ltd interest of $200.
(d) The closing stock of John Ltd included $4000 obtained from Doe Ltd. The cost of this inventory to Doe Ltd was $3000.
(e) John Ltd recognises dividends as income when such dividends are declared.

Additional information:
Any goodwill on acquisition is to be written off straight line over five years. The company tax rate is 36%.

*Required*
Prepare the consolidated financial statements for the year ended 30 June 20X3.

**Exercise 7.15** **Calculation of parent and outside equity interest**
A Ltd purchased 80% of the paid-up capital of B Ltd on 1 July 20X4. A Ltd paid $250 000 more than the equity it acquired in the fair value of B Ltd's net assets. At the date of acquisition the depreciable assets of B Ltd were $50 000 below their fair value. These assets have a remaining economic life of five years. The decision was made to revalue these assets as part of the consolidation process. Goodwill is to be amortised over a 20-year period.

A Ltd earned an after-tax profit of $150 000 and B Ltd $80 000 for the year ended 30 June 20X5. At 30 June 20X4 the retained profits of A Ltd and B Ltd were $300 000 and $175 000 respectively. The company tax rate is 36%.

*Required*
1 Calculate consolidated profit for the year ended 30 June 20X5.
2 Calculate parent entity and outside equity interests in the consolidated profit.
3 Calculate consolidated retained profits at 30 June 20X5, showing the parent and outside equity interest.

**Exercise 7.16** **Comprehensive — multiple intra-group transactions**
On 1 July 20X1, P Ltd acquired control of S Ltd by purchasing 75% of the paid-up capital of S Ltd. At the date of acquisition the shareholders' equity of S Ltd consisted of:

| | |
|---|---|
| Paid-up capital | $30 000 |
| Retained profits | 6 000 |

At 1 July 20X1 all the identifiable net assets of S Ltd were recorded at fair value and any goodwill is amortised evenly over a ten-year period.
Trial balances of the two companies at 30 June 20X6 were:

| | P Ltd | S Ltd |
|---|---|---|
| | $ | $ |
| Sales | 50 000 | 80 000 |
| Opening stock 1 July 20X5 | 11 000 | 14 000 |
| Purchases | 35 000 | 60 000 |
| | 46 000 | 74 000 |
| Closing stock 30 June 20X6 | (12 000) | (15 500) |
| Cost of goods sold | (34 000) | (58 500) |

|  | P Ltd | S Ltd |
|---|---|---|
|  | $ | $ |
| Gross profit | 16 000 | 21 500 |
| Financial expenses | (1 500) | (2 000) |
| Other expenses | (5 500) | (7 500) |
|  | (7 000) | (9 500) |
|  | 9 000 | 12 000 |
| Interest revenue | 250 | – |
| Dividend revenue | 1 800 | – |
| Operating profit before tax | 11 050 | 12 000 |
| Income tax expense | (5 000) | (5 500) |
| Operating profit after tax | 6 050 | 6 500 |
| Retained profits 1 July 20X5 | 19 000 | 14 500 |
|  | 25 050 | 21 000 |
| Proposed final dividend | (2 400) | (2 400) |
| Retained profits 30 June 20X6 | 22 650 | 18 600 |
| Paid-up capital | 40 000 | 30 000 |
| Provision for income tax | 6 100 | 500 |
| Dividend payable | 2 400 | 2 400 |
| 10% debentures | – | 5 000 |
|  | $71 150 | $56 500 |
| Inventory | 12 000 | 15 500 |
| Other current assets | 14 650 | 1 500 |
| Plant | 30 000 | 65 000 |
| Accumulated depreciation | (17 000) | (30 500) |
| Debentures in S Ltd | 2 500 | – |
| Investment in S Ltd | 27 000 | – |
| Future income tax benefit | 2 000 | 5 000 |
|  | $71 150 | $56 500 |

Additional information:

(a) All dividends have been from post-acquisition profits except for a $4000 dividend paid by S Ltd in the year ended 30 June 20X2.

(b) During the financial year ended 30 June 20X6, P Ltd sold inventory to S Ltd for $9000 and S Ltd sold inventory to P Ltd for $10 000.

(c) The opening inventory of P Ltd at 1 July 20X5 included inventory sold by S Ltd at a profit of $800.

(d) At 30 June 20X6, P Ltd held $2500 of inventory purchased from S Ltd at a profit of $1200.

(e) Other current assets do not include any investments. All other inventory sold inter-company had been resold by the end of the year in which it was transferred.

(f) P Ltd purchased the debentures from S Ltd for par at the time of issue on 1 July 20X5.

(g) Goodwill is amortised evenly over a five-year period.

(h) The tax rate is 40%.

*Required*

Prepare the consolidated income statement and balance sheet for the economic entity at 30 June 20X6, showing a consolidated worksheet and all calculations.

# chapter 8

CONSOLIDATION: INDIRECT
OUTSIDE EQUITY INTERESTS

# introduction

The previous chapters on consolidation have considered situations where control is exercised via a direct equity holding by the parent entity in the subsidiary entity. This chapter is concerned with accounting for indirect ownership interests. Indirect ownership interests arise when the parent entity controls the subsidiary via an intermediate entity or company. Where the parent entity indirectly holds less than 100% of the share capital of the subsidiary, there will be both indirect parent entity interests and indirect outside equity interests to account for on consolidation.

This chapter illustrates three examples of consolidation that contain direct and indirect outside equity interests. This is the final chapter on consolidation and probably the most complex. Working through the illustrations and the questions at the back of the chapter is the best way to become familiar with the material.

# Examples of indirect outside equity interests

Indirect control of another entity may take a variety of forms. Figure 8.1 illustrates both direct and indirect ownership interests for a simple three-company group. Indirect ownership interests are shown by a dotted line.

**Figure 8.1**

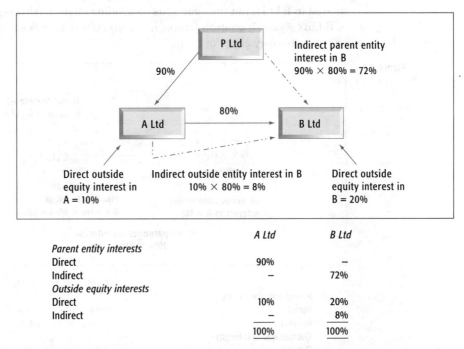

|  | A Ltd | B Ltd |
|---|---|---|
| *Parent entity interests* |  |  |
| Direct | 90% | – |
| Indirect | – | 72% |
| *Outside equity interests* |  |  |
| Direct | 10% | 20% |
| Indirect | – | 8% |
|  | 100% | 100% |

The above table demonstrates how the various ownership interests have been calculated. Calculation of P Ltd's interest in the directly owned A Ltd is straightforward. P Ltd owns 90% of the share capital of A Ltd, so there is a (100% – 90%) = 10% direct outside equity interest in A Ltd. For the indirectly controlled entity B Ltd, there is an indirect parent entity interest, as well as both direct and indirect outside equity interests. P Ltd's indirect parent entity interest arises through the intermediate entity A Ltd, which owns 80% of B Ltd's share capital. Because P Ltd controls A Ltd in terms of AASB 1024, P Ltd controls A Ltd's 80% interest in B Ltd. P Ltd's indirect interest in B Ltd is 90% × 80% = 72%. Since A Ltd owns only 80% of B Ltd's share capital, there is also a (100% – 80%) = 20% direct outside equity interest in B Ltd. Finally, there is a (10% × 80%) = 8% indirect outside equity interest in B Ltd, representing A Ltd's outside equity interest's share of A Ltd's 80% investment in B Ltd.

The indirect outside equity interest in B Ltd of 8% does not own shares in B Ltd but arises because of the direct outside equity interest of 10% in A Ltd's 80% investment in B Ltd — that is, 10% × 80% = 8%. In giving the direct outside equity interest in A Ltd of 10% a share of the equity of A Ltd (because they own shares in A Ltd) they are receiving a share of the equity relating to the assets of A Ltd, which includes the investment in B Ltd. Therefore, the indirect outside equity interest of 8% in B Ltd is only given a share of the post-acquisition profits of B Ltd contributed to the economic entity.

Recall from the discussion of control in chapter 5 that a parent entity may control a subsidiary even if their shareholding is less than 50%. In the case illustrated in Figure 8.2, P Ltd controls B Ltd, even though its indirect shareholding is only 42% (70% × 60%). A line of control exists because P Ltd controls A Ltd, which in turn controls B Ltd. Hence, the ultimate parent entity's (in this case, P Ltd) ownership interest in B Ltd is not the same as its controlling interest. Although P Ltd owns 42% of B Ltd's equity, it controls (through A Ltd) 60% of B Ltd's equity, and therefore B Ltd is a subsidiary entity of P Ltd.

**Figure 8.2**

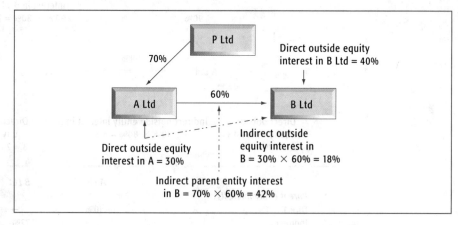

|  | A Ltd | B Ltd |
|---|---|---|
| Parent entity interests |  |  |
| Direct | 70% | – |
| Indirect | – | 42% |
| *Outside equity interests* |  |  |
| Direct | 30% | 40% |
| Indirect | – | 18% |
|  | 100% | 100% |

A parent entity can hold both direct and indirect ownership interests in a subsidiary. In Figure 8.3, P Ltd directly owns 20% of B Ltd's share capital and indirectly owns a further 48% (80% × 60%) through its holdings in A Ltd. P Ltd's total ownership interest in B Ltd is therefore 68%.

**Figure 8.3**

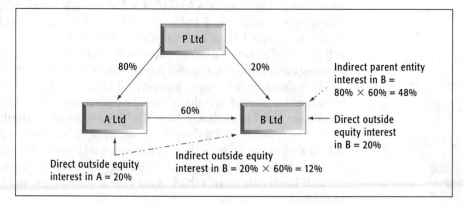

|  | A Ltd | B Ltd |
|---|---|---|
| *Parent entity interests* | | |
| Direct | 80% | 20% |
| Indirect | – | 48% |
| *Outside equity interests* | | |
| Direct | 20% | 20% |
| Indirect | – | 12% |
| | 100% | 100% |

# Accounting for indirect interests

There are two ways to proceed in accounting for indirect interests. The first is to sequentially consolidate so that in the example shown above, in Figure 8.3, A Ltd would consolidate the accounts of B Ltd, then P Ltd would consolidate the accounts of the A–B group. However, sequential consolidation is unwieldy, particularly for large group structures. The alternative is to use multiple consolidation so that the accounts of all subsidiary entities in the group are consolidated with those of the ultimate parent entity simultaneously. Sequential consolidation and multiple consolidation both generate exactly the same results. However, the multiple consolidation method is less cumbersome to apply.

**post-acquisition profits and changes in reserves**

The most important principle underlying the multiple consolidation method is that indirect ownership interests are relevant only to post-acquisition profits and changes in reserves. Hence, pre-acquisition capital and reserves are eliminated on the basis of direct ownership interests of the immediate parent entity, while post-acquisition profits and changes in reserves are allocated to the ultimate parent entity on the basis of both direct and indirect ownership interests. Why this is necessary may be seen by remembering that multiple consolidation is equivalent in outcome to sequential consolidation. In sequential consolidation the direct ownership interest of the immediate parent entity would be used to eliminate pre-acquisition capital and reserves; and the direct ownership interest of the ultimate parent entity would be used for allocating post-acquisition profits and reserves.

Three illustrative examples are used in this chapter. The level of complexity increases with each example.

## ILLUSTRATIVE EXAMPLE 8.1

## BALANCE SHEET, COMMON ACQUISITION DATE

On 1 July 20X4, A Ltd purchased 70% of the paid-up capital of B Ltd for $140 000 and 80% of the paid-up capital of C Ltd for $210 000. On the same date, C Ltd purchased the remaining 30% of B Ltd for $80 000. At the date of acquisition all assets were stated at their fair value.

The group may be depicted diagrammaticaly as in Figure 8.4.

**Figure 8.4**

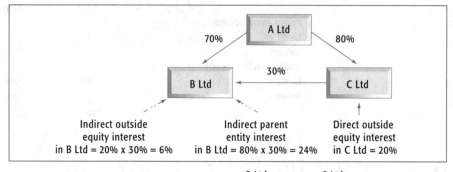

|  | B Ltd | C Ltd |
|---|---|---|
| *Parent entity interest* | | |
| Direct | 70% | 80% |
| Indirect | 24% | – |
| *Outside equity interest* | | |
| Direct | – | 20% |
| Indirect | 6% | – |
|  | 100% | 100% |

The shareholders' equity for each of the subsidiaries at acquisition date is as follows:

|  | B Ltd | C Ltd |
|---|---|---|
|  | $ | $ |
| Paid-up capital ($1 fully paid) | 160 000 | 200 000 |
| Retained profits | 14 000 | 20 000 |
| Reserves | 22 000 | 36 000 |

The balance sheets as at 30 June 20X6 for each of A Ltd, B Ltd and C Ltd are on the following consolidation worksheet. Any goodwill on acquisition is amortised on a straight-line basis over 20 years.

### Consolidation worksheet — balance sheets as at 30 June 20X6

| Account | A Ltd | B Ltd | C Ltd | Eliminations Debit | Eliminations Credit | Consolidation |
|---|---|---|---|---|---|---|
|  | $ | $ | $ | $ | $ | $ |
| *Shareholders' equity* | | | | | | |
| Paid-up capital | 320 000 | 160 000 | 200 000 | 320 000 (1) | | 360 000 |
| ($1 shares fully paid) | | | | | | |
| Retained profits | 22 000 | 20 000 | 24 000 | 30 000 (1) | | |
|  | | | | 2 920 (2) | | 33 080 |
| Reserves | 60 000 | 26 000 | 40 000 | 50 800 (1) | | 75 200 |
| *Liabilities* | | | | | | |
| Current liabilities | 100 000 | 54 000 | 16 000 | | | 170 000 |
| Total shareholders' | | | | | | |
| equity & liabilities | $502 000 | $260 000 | $280 000 | | | $638 280 |
| *Assets* | | | | | | |
| Investment in C Ltd | 210 000 | – | – | | 210 000 (1) | – |
| Investment in B Ltd | 140 000 | – | 80 000 | | 220 000 (1) | |
| Non-current assets | 87 000 | 145 000 | 105 000 | | | 337 000 |
| Current assets | 65 000 | 115 000 | 95 000 | | | 275 000 |
| Goodwill on acquisition | | | | 29 200 (1) | 2 920 (2) | 26 280 |
| Total assets | $502 000 | $260 000 | $280 000 | $432 920 | $432 920 | $638 280 |

The following consolidation journal entries are required.

(1) Elimination of the cost of investment against paid-up capital and pre-acquisition reserves.

|  | B Ltd (70%) | B Ltd (30%) | C Ltd (80%) |
|---|---|---|---|
|  | $ | $ | $ |
| Paid-up capital acquired | 112 000 | 48 000 | 160 000 |
| Retained profits | 9 800 | 4 200 | 16 000 |
| Reserves | 15 400 | 6 600 | 28 800 |
|  | 137 200 | 58 800 | 204 800 |
| Cost of investment | 140 000 | 80 000 | 210 000 |
| Goodwill on acquisition | 2 800 | 21 200 | 5 200 |

Each elimination entry is as follows:

## Consolidation journal

|  | Debit | Credit |
|---|---|---|
|  | $ | $ |
| Paid-up Capital | 112 000 |  |
| Retained Profits | 9 800 |  |
| Reserves | 15 400 |  |
| Goodwill on Acquisition | 2 800 |  |
| Investment in B Ltd |  | 140 000 |
| (A Ltd's investment in 70% of B Ltd) |  |  |
|  |  |  |
| Paid-up Capital | 48 000 |  |
| Retained Profits | 4 200 |  |
| Reserves | 6 600 |  |
| Goodwill on Acquisition | 21 200 |  |
| Investment in B Ltd |  | 80 000 |
| (C Ltd's investment in 30% of B Ltd) |  |  |
|  |  |  |
| Paid-up Capital | 160 000 |  |
| Retained Profits | 16 000 |  |
| Reserves | 28 800 |  |
| Goodwill on Acquisition | 5 200 |  |
| Investment in C Ltd |  | 210 000 |
| (A Ltd's investment in 80% of C Ltd) |  |  |

Combining the above three journal entries results in the following summarised journal entry.

|  | | |
|---|---|---|
| Paid-up Capital | 320 000 |  |
| Retained Profits | 30 000 |  |
| Reserves | 50 800 |  |
| Goodwill on Acquisition | 29 200 |  |
| Investment in B Ltd |  | 220 000 |
| Investment in C Ltd |  | 210 000 |

Note that this combination journal entry has been used to minimise the number of entries in the consolidation worksheet.

(2) Amortisation of goodwill.

$29 200/20 years = $1460 per annum
= $2920 for two years

## Consolidation journal

|  | Debit $ | Credit $ |
|---|---|---|
| Retained Profits | 2 920 | |
| Goodwill on Acquisition | | 2 920 |

Outside equity interests are calculated as follows:

|  | B Ltd $ | C Ltd $ |
|---|---|---|
| *Interest in share capital* | | |
| Share capital at acquisition | | 200 000 |
| Outside equity interest | | **(20%) 40 000** |
| *Interest in retained profits* | | |
| Pre-acquisition profits | | 20 000 |
| Outside equity interest | | **(20%) 4 000** |
| Post-acquisition profits | (20 000 – 14 000 | (24 000 – 20 000 |
| | = 6000) | = 4000) |
| Outside equity interest | **(Indirect OEI × 6%)** | **(20%) 800** |
| | **360** | |
| *Interest in reserves* | | |
| Pre-acquisition reserves | | 36 000 |
| Outside equity interests | | **(20%) 7 200** |
| Post-acquisition reserves | (26 000 – 22 000 | (40 000 – 36 000 |
| | = 4000) | = 4000) |
| Outside equity interests | **(Indirect OEI × 6%) 240** | **(20%) 800** |
| *Summary of outside equity interests* | | |
| In share capital of C Ltd | | 40 000 |
| In retained profits of C Ltd (4800) | | |
| and B Ltd (360) | | 5 160 |
| In reserves of C Ltd (8000) and B Ltd (240) | | 8 240 |
| *Total outside equity interests* | | $53 400 |

Total outside equity interests may also be calculated as a percentage of the net assets of C Ltd and B Ltd at 30 June 20X6. This also enables a check of the above calculation to be made.

|  | B Ltd $ | C Ltd $ |
|---|---|---|
| Share capital | 160 000 | 200 000 |
| Retained profits | 20 000 | 24 000 |
| Reserves | 26 000 | 40 000 |
| Value of net assets 30 June 20X6 | $206 000 | $264 000 |

Note that the retained profits of both B Ltd and C Ltd would have to be adjusted (as shown in the following two illustrative examples) for the effects of any unrealised profit/losses when calculating the value of the net assets at 30 June 20X6. This must be done, as the outside equity interests only receive a share of the subsidiary company's profits contributed to the economic entity.

| **Outside equity interests** | | |
|---|---|---|
| In C Ltd (direct) | $264\,000 \times 20\% =$ | 52 800 |
| **In B Ltd (indirect interest in** | $(20\,000 + 26\,000) -$ | |
| **post-acquisition profits and reserves)** | $(14\,000 + 22\,000) \times 6\% =$ | 600 |
| **Total outside equity interests** | | $53\,400 |

### A Ltd Economic Entity
### Consolidated Balance Sheet as at 30 June 20X6

| | | | $ |
|---|---|---|---|
| *Assets* | | | |
| Current assets | | | 275 000 |
| Non-current assets | | | 337 000 |
| Goodwill on acquisition | | | 26 280 |
| *Total assets* | | | 638 280 |
| *Liabilities* | | | |
| Current liabilities | | | (170 000) |
| *Net assets* | | | $468 280 |

| | Parent entity interest $ | Outside equity interest $ | |
|---|---|---|---|
| *Shareholders' equity* | | | |
| Paid-up capital | 320 000 | 40 000 | 360 000 |
| Retained profits | 27 920 | 5 160 | 33 080 |
| Reserves | 66 960 | 8 240 | 75 200 |
| *Total shareholders' equity* | $414 880 | $53 400 | $468 280 |

Note the following points:

1 Direct outside equity interests (DOEI) are given a share of equity of the relevant subsidiary where the DOEI is located. DOEI must be given a share of both pre- and post-acquisition equity.

2 The DOEI share of operating profit and retained profits must be adjusted for unrealised profits/losses caused by intra-group transactions. That is, the DOEI can only be given a share of the subsidiary's contribution to the economic entity. This will not always be the same as the subsidiary's separate entity operating profit and retained profits because of intra-group transactions.

3 Indirect outside equity interests (IDOEI) only receive a share of post-acquisition profits adjusted for the effects of intra-group transactions. Here post-acquisition equity means increases since the date of acquisition, as shown in Illustrative example 8.1. IDOEI are not given a share of paid-up capital because they do not own shares in the entity where the IDOEI is located.

4 Also, the subsidiary's operating profit and retained profits are *not* adjusted (written down) for goodwill amortisation when calculating outside equity interest. This is because only goodwill purchased by the parent company is recorded in the consolidated financial statements. Therefore, the goodwill amortisation expense is charged entirely against the parent company's share of the subsidiary's earnings.

## ILLUSTRATIVE EXAMPLE 8.2

# INCOME STATEMENT, BALANCE SHEET, INTRA-GROUP TRANSACTIONS, PROPOSED DIVIDENDS

This example is a sequential series of acquisitions, and the consolidation proceeds as if the acquisitions occurred on the same date.

Pluto Ltd acquired 75% of the issued share capital of Venus Ltd for $2 000 000 cash on 1 July 20X3. Exactly one year later, Venus Ltd purchased a 60% interest in Mars Ltd for $800 000 cash.

The group may be depicted diagrammatically as in Figure 8.5.

**Figure 8.5**

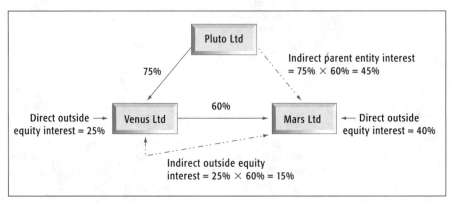

The direct and indirect equity interests in Venus Ltd and Mars Ltd may be summarised as follows:

|  | Venus Ltd | Mars Ltd |
|---|---|---|
| *Parent entity interest* | | |
| Direct | 75% | – |
| Indirect | – | 45% |
| *Outside equity interest* | | |
| Direct | 25% | 40% |
| Indirect | – | 15% |
|  | 100% | 100% |

The shareholders' equity section of the respective balance sheets at acquisition date was:

|  | Venus Ltd at 1 July 20X3 $ | Mars Ltd at 1 July 20X4 $ |
|---|---|---|
| Share capital | 1 800 000 | 900 000 |
| Retained profits | 500 000 | 300 000 |
|  | $2 300 000 | $1 200 000 |

At the dates of acquisition, all assets were stated at their fair values.

Other relevant information:
(a) Goodwill is amortised on a straight-line basis over 20 years.
(b) Mars Ltd sold inventory to Pluto Ltd during the current year at a profit of $2000. All of this inventory is on hand at 30 June 20X6.
(c) All three companies accrue dividends as income on declaration.
(d) Proposed dividends are from post-acquisition profits.
(e) The company tax rate is 40%.
(f) The balance sheets for Pluto Ltd, Venus Ltd and Mars Ltd for the year ended 30 June 20X6 are shown below in the consolidation worksheet.

## Consolidation worksheet — balance sheets as at 30 June 20X6

| Account | Pluto Ltd | Venus Ltd | Mars Ltd | Eliminations Debit | Eliminations Credit | Consolidation |
|---|---|---|---|---|---|---|
| | $ | $ | $ | $ | $ | $ |
| Operating profit after tax | 450 000 | 100 000 | 50 000 | 17 750 (2) 2 000 (3) 94 500 (4) | 800 (3) | 486 550 |
| Retained profits 1 July 20X5 | 2 500 000 | 750 000 | 400 000 | 555 000 (1) 31 500 (2) | | 3 063 500 |
| Proposed dividend | | (90 000) | (45 000) | | 94 500 (4) | (40 500) |
| Retained profits 30 June 20X6 | 2 950 000 | 760 000 | 405 000 | | | 3 509 550 |
| Paid-up capital | 4 000 000 | 1 800 000 | 900 000 | 1 890 000 (1) | | 4 810 000 |
| | 6 950 000 | 2 560 000 | 1 305 000 | | | 8 319 550 |
| Liabilities | | | | | | |
| Dividend payable | – | 90 000 | 45 000 | 94 500 (4) | | 40 500 |
| Non-current liabilities | 1 050 000 | 350 000 | 150 000 | | | 1 550 000 |
| Total shareholders' equity & liabilities | $8 000 000 | $3 000 000 | $1 500 000 | | | $9 910 050 |
| Assets | | | | | | |
| Cash | 50 000 | 20 000 | 20 000 | | | 90 000 |
| Receivable | 3 500 000 | 750 000 | 500 000 | | 94 500 (4) | 4 655 500 |
| Inventory | 50 000 | 30 000 | 10 000 | | 2 000 (3) | 88 000 |
| Future income tax benefit | | | | 800 (3) | | 800 |
| Investment in subsidiaries | 2 000 000 | 800 000 | – | | 2 800 000 (1) | – |
| Non-current assets (depreciable) | 1 000 000 | 550 000 | 280 000 | | | 1 830 000 |
| Accumulated depreciation | (100 000) | (60 000) | (50 000) | | | (210 000) |
| Land | 1 500 000 | 910 000 | 740 000 | | | 3 150 000 |
| Goodwill on acquisition | | | | 355 000 (1) | 49 250 (2) | 305 750 |
| Total assets | $8 000 000 | $3 000 000 | $1 500 000 | $3 041 050 | $3 041 050 | $9 910 050 |

The following consolidation journal entries are required.

(1) Elimination of the cost of the investment against share capital and pre-acquisition reserves.

|  | Venus Ltd<br>at 1 July 20X3<br>$ | Mars Ltd<br>at 1 July 20X4<br>$ | Total<br><br>$ |
|---|---|---|---|
| Paid-up acquired | (75%) 1 350 000 | (60%) 540 000 | 1 890 000 |
| Retained profits | (75%) 375 000 | (60%) 180 000 | 555 000 |
|  | 1 725 000 | 720 000 | 2 445 000 |
| Cost of investment | 2 000 000 | 800 000 | 2 800 000 |
| Goodwill on acquisition | $275 000 | $80 000 | $355 000 |

## Consolidation journal

|  | Debit<br>$ | Credit<br>$ |
|---|---|---|
| Share Capital | 1 350 000 |  |
| Retained Profits | 375 000 |  |
| Goodwill on Acquisition | 275 000 |  |
| Investment in Venus Ltd |  | 2 000 000 |
| (Pluto Ltd's 75% investment in Venus Ltd) |  |  |
|  |  |  |
| Share Capital | 540 000 |  |
| Retained Profits | 180 000 |  |
| Goodwill on Acquisition | 80 000 |  |
| Investment in Mars Ltd |  | 800 000 |
| (Pluto Ltd's 60% investment in Mars Ltd) |  |  |

Combining these two entries results in the following summarised journal entry.

| Share Capital | 1 890 000 |  |
|---|---|---|
| Retained Profits | 555 000 |  |
| Goodwill on Acquisition | 355 000 |  |
| Investment in Venus Ltd |  | 2 000 000 |
| Investment in Mars Ltd |  | 800 000 |

(2) Current and prior period goodwill amortisation charges on a straight-line basis over 20 years.

|  | Venus Ltd<br>$ | Mars Ltd<br>$ |
|---|---|---|
| Current amortisation charge | 13 750 | 4 000 |
|  | (275 000/20) | (80 000/20) |
| Prior period charges | 27 500 | 4 000 |
|  | (1.7.20X3 to 1.7.20X5 | (1.7.20X4 to 1.7.20X5) |
|  | = 13 750 × 2) |  |
| Total | $41 250 | $8 000 |

### Consolidation journal

|  | Debit | Credit |
|---|---|---|
|  | $ | $ |
| Amortisation Expense | 13 750 |  |
| Retained Profits 1 July 20X5 | 27 500 |  |
|   Goodwill on Acquisition |  | 41 250 |
| (Pluto Ltd's 75% investment in Venus Ltd) |  |  |
|  |  |  |
| Amortisation Expense | 4 000 |  |
| Retained Profits 1 July 20X5 | 4 000 |  |
|   Goodwill on Acquisition |  | 8 000 |
| (Pluto Ltd's 60% investment in Mars Ltd) |  |  |

Combining the two entries results in the following consolidation journal entry.

| | Debit | Credit |
|---|---|---|
| Amortisation Expense | 17 750 |  |
| Retained Profits 1 July 20X5 | 31 500 |  |
|   Goodwill on Acquisition |  | 49 250 |

(3) Elimination of unrealised profit in inventory and related tax effects.

| | Debit | Credit |
|---|---|---|
| Operating Profit after Tax | 2 000 |  |
|   Inventory |  | 2 000 |
| Future Income Tax Benefit | 800 |  |
|   Income Tax Expense (Operating Profit after Tax) |  | 800 |

(4) Elimination of proposed dividends (Venus → Pluto 90 000 × 75% = 67 500) (Mars → Venus 45 000 × 60% = 27 000).

| | Debit | Credit |
|---|---|---|
| Operating Profit after Tax | 94 500 |  |
|   Receivable |  | 94 500 |
| Dividend Payable | 94 500 |  |
|   Proposed Dividend |  | 94 500 |

Outside equity interests are calculated as follows:

**Interests in operating profit after tax**

|  | Venus Ltd | Mars Ltd |
|---|---|---|
|  | $ | $ |
| Operating profit after tax | 100 000 | 50 000 |
| *Less* Unrealised profit in closing inventory |  |  |
|   sold to Pluto Ltd (net of $800 tax) | – | (1 200) |
| *Less* Dividend revenue from Mars Ltd |  |  |
|   (no tax effect) | (27 000) |  |
| **Operating profit after tax contributed to** |  |  |
| **the economic entity** | 73 000 | 48 800 |
| Outside equity interest – direct | (25%) 18 250 | (40%) 19 520 |
|             – indirect |  | (15%) 7 320 |

In this case, *both the direct and indirect outside interests are considered because all current period profit is post-acquisition*. Hence, the outside equity interest in Mars Ltd is the total of the direct outside equity interest (40%) and the indirect outside equity interest (15%).

**Interest in retained profits 1 July 20X5**

|  | Venus Ltd | Mars Ltd |
|---|---|---|
|  | $ | $ |
| Pre-acquisition profits | 500 000 | 300 000 |
| Outside equity interest – direct | **(25%) 125 000** | **(40%) 120 000** |
| Post-acquisition profits to | (750 000 – 500 000) | (400 000 – 300 000) |
| 1 July 20X5 | 250 000 | 100 000 |
| Less Proposed dividends | (90 000) | (45 000) |
|  | 160 000 | 55 000 |
| Outside equity interest – direct | **(25%) 40 000** | **(40%) 22 000** |
| – indirect |  | **(15%) 8 250** |

There is no need to separately calculate the DOEI share of both pre- and post-acquisition equity for Venus Ltd. If the DOEI is given a share of the retained profits as at 1 July 20X5, this automatically includes the pre-acquisition amount. In Venus Ltd 25% × 660 000 = 165 000 is the same result as above (retained profits 750 000 – 90 000 proposed dividend = 660 000).

Only post-acquisition profits are allocated on the basis of both direct and indirect outside equity interests. For pre-acquisition profits, only direct outside equity interests are relevant.

**Interest in share capital**

|  | Venus Ltd | Mars Ltd |
|---|---|---|
|  | Venus Ltd | Mars Ltd |
| Share capital at acquisition | $1 800 000 | $900 000 |
| Outside equity interest | **(25%) 450 000** | **(40%) 360 000** |

(Recall that the IDOEI do not own any share capital in the subsidiary in which the IDOEI is located, here Mars Ltd.)

**Summary of outside equity interests**

|  | $ |
|---|---|
| In operating profit after tax of Venus Ltd ($18 250) |  |
| and Mars Ltd ($26 840) | 45 090 |
| In retained profits at 1 July 20X5 of Venus Ltd ($165 000) |  |
| and Mars Ltd ($150 250) | 315 250 |
| In the share capital of Venus Ltd ($450 000) |  |
| and Mars Ltd ($360 000) | 810 000 |
| **Total outside equity interests** | $1 170 340 |

Total outside equity interests can also be calculated as a percentage of the net assets of Venus Ltd and Mars Ltd at 30 June 20X6. This can also act as a check on the calculation of outside equity interests.

|  | Venus Ltd | Mars Ltd |
|---|---|---|
|  | $ | $ |
| Share capital | 1 800 000 | 900 000 |
| Retained profits 30 June 20X6 |  |  |
| (adjusted) (760 000 – 27 000 |  |  |
| dividend revenue) | 733 000 | 403 800 |
|  |  | (405 000 – 1200 unrealised profit in inventory (AT)) |
| Value of net assets at 30 June 20X6 | $2 533 000 | $1 303 800 |

## Outside equity interests

| | | |
|---|---|---|
| In Venus Ltd (direct) | 2 533 000 × 25% | 633 250 |
| In Mars Ltd (direct) | 1 303 800 × 40% | 521 520 |
| In Mars Ltd (indirect interest in post-acquisition profits) | (403 800 – 300 000) × 15% | 15 570 |
| **Total outside equity interests** | | **$1 170 340** |

### Pluto Ltd Economic Entity
### Consolidated Income Statement as at 30 June 20X6

| | Parent entity interest $ | Outside equity interest $ | $ |
|---|---|---|---|
| Operating profit after tax | 441 460 | 45 090 | 486 550 |
| Retained profits 1 July 20X5 | 2 707 750 | 355 750 | 3 063 500 |
| Proposed dividends | – | (40 500) | (40 500) |
| Retained profits 30 June 20X6 | $3 149 210 | $360 340 | $3 509 550 |

### Pluto Ltd Economic Entity
### Consolidated Balance Sheet as at 30 June 20X6

| | $ | $ | $ |
|---|---|---|---|
| *Assets* | | | |
| Current assets | | | |
| Cash | 90 000 | | |
| Receivable | 4 655 500 | | |
| Inventory | 88 000 | | 4 833 500 |
| Non-current assets | | | |
| Depreciable | 1 830 000 | | |
| Accumulated depreciation | (210 000) | 1 620 000 | |
| Land | | 3 150 000 | 4 770 000 |
| Future income tax benefit | | | 800 |
| Goodwill on acquisition | | | 305 750 |
| Total assets | | | 9 910 050 |
| *Liabilities* | | | |
| Current liabilities | | | |
| Dividend payable | | 40 500 | |
| Non-current liabilities | | 1 550 000 | |
| Total liabilities | | | (1 590 500) |
| Net assets | | | $ 8 319 550 |

| | Parent entity interest $ | Outside entity interest $ | |
|---|---|---|---|
| *Shareholders' equity* | | | |
| Paid-up capital | 4 000 000 | 810 000 | 4 810 000 |
| Retained profits | 3 149 210 | 360 340 | 3 509 550 |
| | $7 149 210 | $1 170 340 | $8 319 550 |

ILLUSTRATIVE EXAMPLE 8.3

# DIFFERENT ACQUISITION DATES, INTRA-GROUP TRANSACTIONS, DIVIDENDS

This example is more complex because Alpha Ltd has acquired its direct ownership interest in Beta Ltd *after* Beta Ltd acquired its controlling interest in Omega Ltd. For the purposes of calculating any discount or goodwill on acquisition, the cost of Alpha's investment in Beta is eliminated against the *consolidated* share capital and reserves of the Beta–Omega sub-group. In other words, Alpha's interest in Beta must include Beta's share of Omega's post-acquisition profits and changes in reserves.

On 1 April 20X4, Alpha Ltd paid $1 200 000 cash for 80% of the issued share capital of Beta Ltd. Beta Ltd controls one subsidiary entity, Omega Ltd, through a 90% shareholding that Beta acquired on 1 July 20X2 for $800 000. At the date of acquisition, all assets were stated at their fair value.

Figure 8.6 shows the diagrammatic representation of the group.

**Figure 8.6**

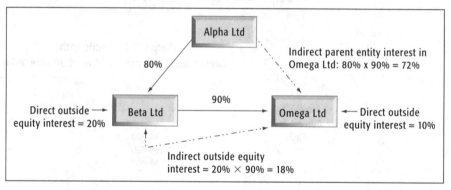

The respective interests in Beta Ltd and Omega Ltd may be summarised as follows:

|  | Beta Ltd | Omega Ltd |
|---|---|---|
| **Parent entity interests** |  |  |
| Direct | 80% |  |
| Indirect | – | 72% |
| **Outside equity interests** |  |  |
| Direct | 20% | 10% |
| Indirect | – | 18% |
|  | 100% | 100% |

The shareholders' equity balances for each of the subsidiaries at their respective acquisition dates are as follows:

|  | Beta Ltd at 1 April 20X4 $ | Omega Ltd at 1 July 20X2 $ |
|---|---|---|
| Share capital | 1 100 000 | 600 000 |
| Retained profits | 200 000 | 200 000 |
|  | $1 300 000 | $800 000 |

Other relevant information:

(a) The following intra-group sales of inventory occurred:
  • On 1 January 20X6, Beta Ltd sold inventory to Alpha Ltd for $50 000 for a profit of $6000. One-third of this inventory was still held by Alpha Ltd at 30 June 20X6.

- On 30 May 20X6, Omega Ltd sold inventory to Beta Ltd for $20 000 for a profit of $4000. Eighty per cent of this inventory was still held by Beta Ltd at 30 June 20X6.
- At 30 June 20X5, Omega Ltd had $2000 of unrealised profits in its closing inventory which had resulted from an inter-company sale of inventory from Beta Ltd.

(b) Alpha Ltd paid an interim dividend of $50 000 on 1 January 20X6 and declared a final dividend of $100 000. Beta Ltd paid an interim dividend of $20 000 on 1 April 20X6 and declared a final dividend of $50 000. Omega Ltd declared a final dividend of $40 000. Omega did not pay an interim dividend. All three companies accrue dividends as income *on declaration*. All dividends are from post-acquisition profits. .

(c) The retained profits of Omega Ltd at 1 April 20X4 were $250 000.

(d) Goodwill on acquisition is amortised straight line over 20 years.

(e) The company tax rate is 40%.

(f) The income statements and balance sheets of Alpha Ltd, Beta Ltd and Omega Ltd as at 30 June 20X6 are as per the following consolidation worksheets.

*Required*

Prepare a consolidated income statement and consolidated balance sheet for the financial year ending 30 June 20X6 for the Alpha–Beta–Omega group.

The consolidation worksheets are as follows:

## Consolidation worksheet — income statement for the year ended 30 June 20X6

| Account | Alpha Ltd | Beta Ltd | Omega Ltd | Eliminations Debit | Eliminations Credit | Consolidation |
|---|---|---|---|---|---|---|
| | $ | $ | $ | $ | $ | $ |
| Sales | 900 000 | 750 000 | 300 000 | 70 000 (5) | | 1 880 000 |
| Opening inventory 1 July 20X5 | 50 000 | 60 000 | 30 000 | | 2 000 (7) | 138 000 |
| Purchases | 650 000 | 420 000 | 180 000 | | 70 000 (5) | 1 180 000 |
| Closing inventory 30 June 20X6 | (40 000) | (64 000) | (28 000) | 5 200 (6) | | (126 800) |
| Cost of goods sold | (660 000) | (416 000) | (182 000) | | | (1 191 200) |
| Gross profit | 240 000 | 334 000 | 118 000 | | | 688 800 |
| Depreciation & other expenses | (60 000) | (80 000) | (70 000) | 4 000 (2) 6 480 (4) | | (220 480) |
| Dividend revenue | 56 000 | 36 000 | – | 16 000 (8) 76 000 (9) | | – |
| Operating profit before tax | 236 000 | 290 000 | 48 000 | | | 468 320 |
| Income tax expense | (75 000) | (92 000) | (15 000) | 800 (7) | 2080 (6) | (180 720) |
| Operating profit after tax | 161 000 | 198 000 | 33 000 | | | 287 600 |
| Retained profits 1 July 20X5 | 584 000 | 350 000 | 250 000 | 180 000 (1) 12 000 (2) 160 000 (3) 30 400 (3) 8 100 (4) 2 000 (7) | 800 (7) | 792 300 |
| Interim dividend paid | 50 000 | 20 000 | – | | 16 000 (8) | 54 000 |
| Final dividend declared | 100 000 | 50 000 | 40 000 | | 76 000 (9) | 114 000 |
| Retained profits 30 June 20X6 | $595 000 | $478 000 | $243 000 | | | $911 900 |

## Consolidation worksheet — balance sheet as at 30 June 20X6

| Account | Alpha Ltd | Beta Ltd | Omega Ltd | Eliminations Debit | Eliminations Credit | Consolidation |
|---|---|---|---|---|---|---|
| | $ | $ | $ | $ | $ | $ |
| Retained profits 30 June 20X6 | 595 000 | 478 000 | 243 000 | | | 911 900 |
| Paid-up capital | 5 000 000 | 1 100 000 | 600 000 | 540 000 (1) 880 000 (3) | | 5 280 000 |
| Shareholders' equity | 5 595 000 | 1 578 000 | 843 000 | | | 6 191 900 |
| Dividends payable | 100 000 | 50 000 | 40 000 | 76 000 (9) | | 114 000 |
| Other liabilities | 1 800 000 | 740 000 | 210 000 | | | 2 750 000 |
| Total liabilities | 1 900 000 | 790 000 | 250 000 | | | 2 864 000 |
| Total equities | $7 495 000 | $2 368 000 | $1 093 000 | | | $9 055 900 |
| Cash | 10 000 | 5 000 | 5 000 | | | 20 000 |
| Dividends receivable | 40 000 | 36 000 | – | | 76 000 (9) | – |
| Other receivable | 400 000 | 260 000 | 75 000 | | | 735 000 |
| Inventory | 40 000 | 64 000 | 28 000 | | 5 200 (6) | 126 800 |
| Investment in subsidiaries | 1 200 000 | 800 000 | – | | 800 000 (1) 1 200 000 (3) | |
| Non-current assets (depreciable) | 3 000 000 | 720 000 | 800 000 | | | 4 520 000 |
| Accumulated depreciation | (200 000) | (144 000) | (65 000) | | | (409 000) |
| Land | 3 005 000 | 627 000 | 250 000 | | | 3 882 000 |
| Future income tax benefit | | | | 2 080 (6) | | 2 080 |
| Goodwill on acquisition | | | | 80 000 (1) 129 600 (3) | 16 000 (2) 14 580 (4) | 179 020 |
| Total assets | $7 495 000 | $2 368 000 | $1 093 000 | $2 278 660 | $2 278 660 | $9 055 900 |

(1) Elimination of Beta Ltd's cost of investment against Omega's share of capital and pre-acquisition reserves.

| | $ | $ |
|---|---|---|
| Cost of investment | | 800 000 |
| Less Share of Omega Ltd's net assets at 1 July 20X2: | | |
| Share capital (600 000 × 90%) | 540 000 | |
| Retained profits (200 000 × 90%) | 180 000 | (720 000) |
| Goodwill on acquisition | | $ 80 000 |

### Consolidation journal

| | Debit $ | Credit $ |
|---|---|---|
| Share Capital (Omega Ltd) | 540 000 | |
| Retained Profits 1 July 20X5 (Omega Ltd) | 180 000 | |
| Goodwill on Acquisition | 80 000 | |
| Investment in Omega Ltd | | 800 000 |

(2) Amortisation of goodwill on acquisition of Omega Ltd over the four years from 1 July 20X2 to 30 June 20X6 (80 000/20 years = $4000 amortisation per year). The amortisation expense for the 20X6 financial year is charged against current expenses. The remaining $12 000 is debited to opening retained profits.

**Consolidation journal**

|  | Debit $ | Credit $ |
|---|---|---|
| Amortisation Expense | 4 000 | |
| Retained Profits 1 July 20X5 | 12 000 | |
| Goodwill on Acquisition | | 16 000 |

(3) The cost of Alpha Ltd's investment in Beta Ltd can now be eliminated against the pre-acquisition share capital and reserves of Beta Ltd, which includes Beta's share of Omega's post-acquisition profits.

|  | $ | $ |
|---|---|---|
| Cost of investment | | 1 200 000 |
| Less Share of Beta Ltd's net assets at 1 April 20X4: | | |
| Share capital (1 100 000 × 80%) | 880 000 | |
| Retained profits (200 000 × 80%) | 160 000 | 1 040 000 |
| | | |
| Less Alpha Ltd's share of the post-acquisition profits | | |
| of Omega Ltd to 1 April 20X4 | | |
| (250 000 – 200 000) × 80% × 90% | 36 000 | |
| Less Goodwill amortisation from acquisition date 1 July 20X2: | | |
| 4000 per year for 1.75 years × 80% (to 1 April 20X4) | 5 600 | (30 400) |
| Goodwill on acquisition | | $129 600 |
| | | |
| Share Capital (Beta Ltd) | 880 000 | |
| Retained Profits 1 July 20X5 (Beta Ltd) | 160 000 | |
| Retained Profits 1 July 20X5 (Omega Ltd) | 30 400 | |
| (Post-acquisition profits of Omega Ltd | | |
| less Goodwill amortisation to 1 April 20X4) | | |
| Goodwill on Acquisition | 129 600 | |
| Investment in Beta Ltd | | 1 200 000 |

(4) Amortisation of goodwill on acquisition of Beta Ltd from 1 April 20X4 to 30 June 20X6.

| | | |
|---|---|---|
| Amortisation Expense | 6 480 | |
| Retained Profits 1 July 20X5 | 8 100 | |
| (Amortisation from 1 April 20X4 to 30 June 20X5 = | | |
| 1.25 years × (129 600/20)) | | |
| Goodwill on Acquisition | | 14 580 |

(5) Elimination of inter-company sales.

**Consolidation journal**

|  | Debit $ | Credit $ |
|---|---|---|
| Sales | 70 000 | |
| Purchases | | 70 000 |

|  | Debit | Credit |
|---|---|---|
|  | $ | $ |

(6) Elimination of unrealised inventory profits in closing inventories and associated tax effects.

| | | |
|---|---|---|
| Closing Stock (P&L) | 5 200 | |
|     Inventory (B/S) | | 5 200 |
|     (5200 = 6000 × 33.3% + 4000 × 80%) | | |
| Future Income Tax Benefit | 2 080 | |
|     Income Tax Expense | | 2 080 |
|     (5200 × 40% = 2080) | | |

(7) Elimination of unrealised profits in opening inventory and associated tax effects.

| | | |
|---|---|---|
| Retained Profits 1 July 20X5 | 2 000 | |
|     Opening Inventory (P&L) | | 2 000 |
| Income Tax Expense | 800 | |
|     Retained Profits 1 July 20X5 | | 800 |
|     (2000 × 40% = 800) | | |

(8) Elimination of interim inter-company dividends paid.

| | | |
|---|---|---|
| Dividend Revenue (20 000 × 80%) | 16 000 | |
|     Dividend Paid | | 16 000 |

(9) Elimination of final dividends declared. Here, the amount payable to Beta Ltd from Omega Ltd (90% × 40 000 = 36 000) plus the amount payable to Alpha Ltd from Beta Ltd (80% × 50 000 = 40 000) is eliminated.

| | | |
|---|---|---|
| Dividend Revenue | 76 000 | |
|     Dividends Receivable | | 76 000 |
| Dividend Payable | 76 000 | |
|     Final Dividend Declared | | 76 000 |

Outside equity interests are calculated as follows:

### Outside equity interests in Beta Ltd

| | $ | | |
|---|---|---|---|
| Operating profit after tax | 198 000 | | |
| *Add* Unrealised profit in inventory | | | |
|     sold to Omega Ltd and realised in | | | |
|     current year (net of $800 tax) | 1 200 | | |
| *Less* Unrealised profit in closing | | | |
|     inventory sold to Alpha Ltd and | | | |
|     deferred until 20X7 (net of $800 tax) | (1 200) | | |
| *Less* Intercompany dividend revenue | | | |
|     from Omega Ltd (no tax effect) | (36 000) | | |
| **Operating profit after tax** | | | |
|     **contributed to the economic entity** | $162 000 | × 20% = | $32 400 |
| **Interest in retained profits 1 July 20X5** | | | |
| Retained profits 1 July 20X5 | 350 000 | | |
| *Less* Unrealised profit in opening | | | |
|     inventory sold to Omega Ltd and | | | |
|     realised in the current year | | | |
|     (net of $800 tax) | (1 200) | | |
| *Less* Interim dividend paid | (20 000) | | |
| *Less* Proposed dividends | (50 000) | | |
| **Retained profits 1 July 20X6** | | | |
|     **contributed to the economic entity** | 278 800 | × 20% = | 55 760 |
| **Interest in share capital** | 1 100 000 | × 20 % = | 220 000 |
| **Total outside equity interest in Beta Ltd** | | | $308 160 |

## Outside equity interests in Omega Ltd

| | $ | | | | |
|---|---|---|---|---|---|
| Operating profit after tax | 33 000 | | | | |
| *Less* Unrealised profit in closing inventory sold to Beta Ltd and deferred until 20X7 (net of $1280 tax) | (1 920) | | | | |
| **Operating profit after tax contributed to the economic entity** | 31 080 | × 10% (Direct OEI) | = | 3 108 | |
| | | × 18% (Indirect OEI) | = | 5 594.40 | 8 702.40 |

## Interest in retained profits 1 July 20X5

| | $ | | | | |
|---|---|---|---|---|---|
| Pre-acquisition profit | 200 000 | × 10% (Direct OEI) | = | 20 000 | |
| Post-acquisition profit | 50 000 | | | | |
| Proposed dividend | (40 000) | | | | |
| | 10 000 | × 10% (Direct OEI) | = | 1 000 | |
| | | × 18% (Indirect OEI) | = | 1 800 | |
| **Retained profits 1 July 20X6 contributed to the economic entity** | | | | | 22 800 |
| **Interest in share capital** | 600 000 | × 10% (Direct OEI) | = | | 60 000 |
| **Total outside equity interest in Omega Ltd** | | | | | **$ 91 502.40** |

## Summary of outside equity interests

| | $ |
|---|---|
| In operating profit after tax of Beta Ltd ($32 400) and Omega Ltd ($8702.40) | 41 102.40 |
| In retained profits at 1 July 20X6 of Beta Ltd ($55 760) and Omega Ltd ($22 800) | 78 560 |
| In the share capital of Beta Ltd ($220 000) and Omega Ltd ($60 000) | 280 000 |
| **Total outside equity interests** | **$399 662.40** |

Another way of looking at total outside equity interests is to calculate them as a percentage of the adjusted net assets of Beta Ltd and Omega Ltd. This can also act as a check on the calculation of outside interests.

| | Beta Ltd | | | Omega Ltd |
|---|---|---|---|---|
| | $ | | | $ |
| Share capital | 1 100 000 | | | 600 000 |
| Retained profits 1 July 20X5 (adjusted) | 278 800 | | | 210 000 |
| Operating profit after tax (adjusted) | 162 000 | | | 31 080 |
| Adjusted value of net assets at 30 June 20X6 | $1 540 800 | | | $841 080 |
| **Outside equity interests** | | | | |
| In Beta Ltd (direct) | 1 540 800 | × | 20% | 308 160 |
| In Omega Ltd (direct) | 841 080 | × | 10% | 84 108 |
| In Omega Ltd (indirect) | (841 080 − 800 000) × 18% | | | 7 394.40 |
| Total outside equity interests | | | | $399 662.40 |

**Alpha Ltd Economic Entity**
**Consolidated Income Statement as at 30 June 20X6**

|  | | | $ |
|---|---|---|---|
| Sales revenue | | | 1 880 000 |
| Cost of sales | | | (1 191 200) |
| Gross profit | | | 688 800 |
| Expenses | | | (220 480) |
| Operating profit before income tax | | | 468 320 |
| Income tax expenses | | | (180 720) |

|  | Parent entity interests | Outside equity interests |  |
|---|---|---|---|
|  | $ | $ |  |
| Operating profit after tax | 246 497.60 | 41 102.40 | 287 600 |
| Retained profits 1 July 20X5 | 695 740 | 96 560 | 792 300 |
| Dividends paid | (50 000) | (4 000) | (54 000) |
| Dividends proposed | (100 000) | (14 000) | (114 000) |
| Retained profits 30 June 20X6 | $792 237.60 | $119 662.40 | $911 900 |

**Alpha Ltd Economic Entity**
**Consolidated Balance Sheet as at 30 June 20X6**

|  | $ | $ | $ |
|---|---|---|---|
| *Assets* | | | |
| Current assets | | | |
|   Cash | | 20 000 | |
|   Other receivables | | 735 000 | |
|   Inventory | | 126 800 | 881 800 |
| Non-current assets | | | |
|   Depreciable | 4 520 000 | | |
|   Accumulated depreciation | (409 000) | 4 111 000 | |
|   Land | | 3 882 000 | 7 993 000 |
| Future income tax benefit | | | 2 080 |
| Goodwill on acquisition | | | 179 020 |
|    *Total assets* | | | 9 055 900 |
| *Liabilities* | | | |
| Current liabilities | | | |
|   Dividend payable | | | (114 000) |
| Non-current liabilities | | | |
|   Other | | | (2 750 000) |
|    *Total liabilities* | | | (2 864 000) |
|    *Net assets* | | | $ 6 191 900 |

|  | Parent entity interests | Outside equity interests |  |
|---|---|---|---|
|  | $ | $ |  |
| *Shareholders' equity* | | | |
| Paid-up capital | 5 000 000.00 | 280 000.00 | 5 280 000 |
| Retained profits | 792 237.60 | 119 662.40 | 911 900 |
|  | $5 792 237.60 | $399 662.40 | $6 191 900 |

Illustrative example 8.3 illustrated the situation where Alpha Ltd acquired its interest in Beta Ltd after Beta Ltd had acquired control of Omega Ltd. If Beta Ltd had acquired its controlling interest in Omega Ltd at the time that it was a subsidiary of Alpha Ltd, the same general principles for allocating direct and indirect interests would apply. That is, direct interests are used to allocate pre-acquisition share capital and reserves, while both direct and indirect interests are the basis for allocating post-acquisition changes in reserves.

# Review

This chapter completes our discussion of consolidation accounting by demonstrating the accounting treatment for indirect equity interests, using the multiple consolidation method. The most important principle underlying the correct accounting for indirect equity interests is that indirect interests are relevant only for the allocation of post-acquisition changes in reserves, while pre-acquisition share capital and reserves are allocated on the basis of direct ownership interests. The following end-of-chapter exercises are intended to reinforce this principle, as well as the principles of consolidation in general, in a variety of situations.

## KEY TERMS

direct equity holding

indirect ownership interests

post-acquisition profits and changes in reserves

## REVIEW QUESTIONS

**8.1** Discuss the multiple and sequential consolidation methods.

**8.2** How does an indirect outside equity interest arise? Explain, using a diagram.

**8.3** What are the differences between direct and indirect outside equity interests?

**8.4** Explain why an indirect outside equity interest is only given a share of post-acquisition equity.

## EXERCISES

**Exercise 8.5** **Determination of ownership interests**
Use a diagram to calculate the various OEIs in each of the following cases. Identify in each case exactly what the separate OEIs are entitled to.
(a) A owns 85% of X and 60% of Y. X owns 40% of Y.
(b) A owns 90% of B1 and 40% of B2. B1 owns 40% of B2.
(c) H owns 80% of S1, and S1 owns 80% of S2.
(d) H owns 75% of B1, and B1 owns 60% of B2.

**Exercise 8.6** **Direct/indirect OEI, balance sheet**

On 1 July 20X1, Z Ltd purchased 70% of the paid-up capital of A Ltd for $110 000. On the same date, A Ltd purchased 60% of the paid-up capital of B Ltd for $60 000. At that date, shareholders' equity of A Ltd and B Ltd was as follows:

|  | A Ltd | B Ltd |
|---|---|---|
| Paid-up capital ($1 shares) | $100 000 | $50 000 |
| Reserves | 40 000 | 30 000 |
| Retained profit | 8 000 | 10 000 |

At the date of acquisition, all assets were stated at their fair value. Balance sheets at 30 June 20X6 are as follows:

|  | Z Ltd | A Ltd | B Ltd |
|---|---|---|---|
|  | $ | $ | $ |
| Paid-up capital ($1 shares) | 400 000 | 100 000 | 50 000 |
| Reserves | 250 000 | 70 000 | 60 000 |
| Retained profit | 30 000 | 10 000 | 12 000 |
| Liabilities | 410 000 | 96 000 | 67 000 |
|  | $1 090 000 | $276 000 | $189 000 |
| Investment in A Ltd | 110 000 | – | – |
| Investment in B Ltd | – | 60 000 | – |
| Non-current assets | 980 000 | 216 000 | 189 000 |
|  | $1 090 000 | $276 000 | $189 000 |

Goodwill on acquisition is to be written off evenly over five years.

*Required*

Prepare the consolidated balance sheet of Z Ltd as at 30 June 20X6.

**Exercise 8.7** **Direct/indirect OEI, inter-company transactions**

On 1 July 20X5, O Ltd acquired 80% of the paid-up capital of H Ltd for $23 000 and H Ltd acquired 75% of the paid-up capital of J Ltd for $13 000. At that date the shareholders' equity of H Ltd and J Ltd was as follows:

|  | H Ltd | J Ltd |
|---|---|---|
| Paid-up capital ($1 shares) | $20 000 | $10 000 |
| Retained profit | 6 000 | 5 000 |

At the date of acquisition, all assets were stated at fair value. The company tax rate is 40%.

One year later the shareholders' equity of the three companies was as follows:

|  | O Ltd | H Ltd | J Ltd |
|---|---|---|---|
| Paid-up capital | $50 000 | $20 000 | $10 000 |
| Reserves | 8 000 | – | – |
| Retained profit | 16 000 | 10 000 | 9 000 |

Additional information:

(a) J Ltd sold inventory to H Ltd for $14 000 which had cost J Ltd $12 000.

(b) O Ltd sold inventory to H Ltd for $10 000 which had cost O Ltd $8000.

All of this inventory was on hand at year end.

*Required*
Calculate the total outside equity interests in the O Ltd, H Ltd and J Ltd group.

**Exercise 8.8** **Direct/indirect OE, balance sheet**
On 1 July 20X1, C Ltd purchased 80% of the paid-up capital of D Ltd for $220 000 and 10% of the paid-up capital of E Ltd for $24 000. On the same date, D Ltd purchased 60% of the paid-up capital of E Ltd for $128 000. The shareholders' equity of D Ltd and E Ltd at that date was:

|  | D Ltd | E Ltd |
| --- | --- | --- |
| Paid-up capital ($1 shares) | $160 000 | $120 000 |
| Reserves | 80 000 | 60 000 |
| Retained profits | 20 000 | 20 000 |

At the date of acquisition, all assets were stated at their fair value.
Balance sheets at 30 June 20X2 are as follows:

|  | C Ltd | D Ltd | E Ltd |
| --- | --- | --- | --- |
|  | $ | $ | $ |
| Paid-up capital ($1 shares) | 300 000 | 160 000 | 120 000 |
| Reserves | 200 000 | 100 000 | 80 000 |
| Retained profits | 32 000 | 28 000 | 24 000 |
| Liabilities | 600 000 | 280 000 | 200 000 |
|  | $1 132 000 | $568 000 | $424 000 |
| Investment in D Ltd | 220 000 | – | – |
| Investment in E Ltd | 24 000 | 128 000 | – |
| Other assets | 888 000 | 440 000 | 424 000 |
|  | $1 132 000 | $568 000 | $424 000 |

Goodwill on acquisition is to be written off evenly over five years.

*Required*
Prepare the consolidated worksheet and balance sheet of C Ltd as at 30 June 20X2.

**Exercise 8.9** **Multiple OEI in profit**
P Ltd owns 70% of the paid-up capital of R Ltd. R Ltd owns 80% of the paid-up capital of S Ltd. S Ltd owns 75% of the paid-up capital of T Ltd. The net profits of the four companies for the year ended 30 June 20X9 are as follows:

- P Ltd — $60 000 000
- R Ltd — $40 000 000
- S Ltd — $20 000 000
- T Ltd — $24 000 000

*Required*
1 Draw a diagram representing the group and identify the various outside equity interests.
2 Calculate the outside equity interests' share of consolidated net profit.

**Exercise 8.10**  **Direct/indirect OEI, inter-company transactions**

The following information has been taken from the books of three related companies as at 30 June 20X6 — Alfa Ltd, Beta Ltd and Gamma Ltd.

| | Alfa Ltd | Beta Ltd | Gamma Ltd |
|---|---|---|---|
| Retained profits as at 30 June 20X5 | $10 000 | $3 800 | $5 000 |
| Gross profit for year ended 30 June 20X6 | 29 000 | 16 000 | 17 000 |
| Selling expenses | 9 000 | 7 000 | 6 500 |
| Administration expenses | 8 000 | 4 500 | 3 900 |
| Dividend income | 4 980 | 1 920 | – |
| Dividends paid (from current profits) | 15 000 | 2 800 | 4 800 |
| Income tax expense | 5 000 | 2 100 | 2 500 |

Additional information:
(a)  The three companies are related in the following way:
  • Beta Ltd is owned 75% by Alfa Ltd and 25% by outside shareholders.
  • Gamma Ltd is owned 60% by Alfa Ltd and 40% by Beta Ltd.
(b)  The retained profits on acquisition of shares were as follows:
  • Retained profits of Beta Ltd when Alfa Ltd acquired its shares — $2200.
  • Retained profits of Gamma Ltd when Alfa Ltd and Beta Ltd acquired their shares — $2700. There was no goodwill or discount on acquisition.
(c)  Unrealised profits in inventories transferred and still on hand at 30 June 20X6:
  • $1000 in inventories transferred from Beta Ltd to Alfa Ltd.
  • $500 in inventories transferred from Gamma Ltd to Beta Ltd.
(d)  The tax rate is 40%

*Required*
Prepare a consolidated profit and loss statement for the year ended 30 June 20X6.

**Exercise 8.11**  **Profit and loss account, inter-company transactions**

The following information was taken from the books of A Ltd, B Ltd and C Ltd as at 30 June 20X6.

| | A Ltd | B Ltd | C Ltd |
|---|---|---|---|
| Retained profits 1 July 20X5 | $3 000 | $3 400 | $2 800 |
| Interim dividends paid | 2 000 | 2 800 | 1 200 |
| Debenture interest received from C Ltd | 100 | 150 | – |
| Dividends received | 2 100 | 960 | – |
| Income tax expense | 2 000 | 2 400 | 1 900 |
| Financial expenses | 1 500 | 1 800 | 600 |
| Inventory 1 July 20X5 | 10 000 | 12 000 | 8 000 |
| Purchases | 40 000 | 36 000 | 32 000 |
| Sales | 64 000 | 56 000 | 48 000 |

Additional information:
(a)  A Ltd acquired 75% of the share capital of B Ltd, and B Ltd acquired 80% of the share capital of C Ltd on 1 July 20X4, at which date the retained profits of B Ltd and C Ltd were as follows:
  • B Ltd — $2000
  • C Ltd — $1000
There was no goodwill or discount on acquisition.

(b) Inventory on hand at 30 June 20X6 (A Ltd — $7500; B Ltd — $8000; C Ltd — $6000) includes unrealised profits on inter-company sales as follows:
- A Ltd — profit of $2000 on goods obtained from C Ltd.
- B Ltd — profit of $1000 on goods obtained from A Ltd.

(c) Sales during the year include:
- C Ltd to A Ltd — $16 000
- A Ltd to B Ltd — $14 000

(d) The tax rate is 40%.

*Required*
Prepare a consolidated profit and loss statement of A Ltd and its subsidiaries as at 30 June 20X6.

**Exercise 8.12**  **Multiple interests, inter-company transactions, pre-acquisition dividend**
Following are the summarised balance sheets of three related companies as at 30 June 20X7.

| | A Ltd $ | B Ltd $ | C Ltd $ |
|---|---|---|---|
| Plant & machinery | 80 000 | 23 000 | 20 000 |
| Current assets | 90 000 | 19 500 | 31 500 |
| Inventory on hand | 60 000 | 32 500 | 15 000 |
| Debentures in C Ltd | – | 20 000 | – |
| 45 000 shares in B Ltd | 65 000 | – | – |
| 20 000 shares in C Ltd | – | 50 000 | – |
| | $295 000 | $145 000 | $66 500 |
| Paid-up capital ($1 shares) | 100 000 | 75 000 | 20 000 |
| Reserves | 30 000 | 16 250 | 2 250 |
| Retained profits | 39 000 | 36 000 | 14 000 |
| Liabilities | 26 000 | 17 750 | 5 250 |
| Debentures (due 30 June 2010) | 100 000 | – | 25 000 |
| | $295 000 | $145 000 | $66 500 |

A Ltd and B Ltd acquired their holdings in B Ltd and C Ltd respectively on 30 June 20X5, at which date the shareholders' equity was as follows:

| | B Ltd | C Ltd |
|---|---|---|
| Paid-up capital ($1 shares) | $75 000 | $20 000 |
| Reserves | 10 000 | 1 000 |
| Retained profits | 16 000 | 4 500 |

At the date of acquisition, all assets were stated at their fair value.

In August 20X5, C Ltd declared and paid a pre-acquisition dividend of 10%. Inventory on hand at 30 June 20X7 included goods obtained from within the group and incorporated in the books at invoice prices which exceeded cost to the following extent:
- Goods supplied by B Ltd to A Ltd at $2500 above cost.
- Goods supplied by C Ltd to A Ltd at $1500 above cost.
- Goods supplied by C Ltd to B Ltd at $1200 above cost.

The tax rate is 40% and goodwill on acquisition is to be written off straight line over ten years.

*Required*
Prepare a consolidation worksheet and a consolidated balance sheet for the group. Show all workings.

**Exercise 8.13**  **Direct/indirect OEI, no worksheet**
X Ltd owns 75% of Y Ltd. Y Ltd owns 40% of Z Ltd. X Ltd also owns 30% of Z Ltd. The ownership interests in Z Ltd were acquired when Z Ltd was incorporated.

The retained profits of the three companies at 1 July 20X6 and 30 June 20X7 are as follows:

|  | X Ltd | Y Ltd | Z Ltd |
|---|---|---|---|
|  | $ | $ | $ |
| Retained profit 1 July 20X6 | 50 000 | 15 000 | 10 000 |
| Retained profit 30 June 20X7 | 60 000 | 20 000 | 16 000 |

During the year, Z Ltd did not pay any dividends and there were no transfers between reserves. Inventory on hand at 1 July 20X6 includes unrealised profit on an intercompany sale by Z Ltd to Y Ltd. The unrealised profit was $2000. Inventory on hand at 30 June 20X7 includes unrealised profits on intercompany sales as follows:
- X Ltd — profit of $1000 on goods obtained from Z Ltd.
- Y Ltd — profit of $3000 on goods obtained from Z Ltd.

The company tax rate is 40%.

*Required*
1 Calculate the OEI in the opening retained profit of Z Ltd.
2 Calculate the OEI in the operating profit of Z Ltd.

**Exercise 8.14**  **Direct/indirect OEI, allocation to parent company**
Ell Ltd purchased 80% of the paid-up capital of MIMI Ltd on 1 July 20X4. Ell Ltd paid $500 000 more than the equity it acquired in the fair value of MIMI Ltd's net assets. At the date of acquisition the depreciable assets of MIMI Ltd were $100 000 below their fair value. These assets have a remaining economic life of four years. The revaluation of these assets was to be undertaken in the consolidation process.

On the same date, MIMI Ltd purchased 70% of the paid-up capital of MAC Ltd and paid $200 000 more than the equity it acquired in the fair value of MAC Ltd's net assets.

Goodwill is to be amortised over a ten-year period straight line.

Ell Ltd earned an after-tax profit of $200 000, MIMI Ltd $100 000 and MAC Ltd $150 000 for the year ended 30 June 20X5. At 30 June 20X4 the retained profits of the three companies were as follows:
- ELL Ltd — $400 000
- MIMI Ltd — $300 000
- MAC Ltd — $280 000.

The company tax rate is 40%.

*Required*

Calculate the following:

(a) Consolidated profit for the year ended 30 June 20X5.

(b) Individual outside equity interests (both direct and indirect) in the consolidated profit.

(c) Outside equity interests in the consolidated opening retained profit.

(d) Outside equity interests in the consolidated closing retained profit.

(e) The parent company's share of consolidated closing retained profit.

**Exercise 8.15** **Different acquisition dates, inter-company transactions**

On 1 July 20X4, A Ltd paid $2 000 000 cash for 80% of the paid-up capital of B Ltd. B Ltd controls one subsidiary company, C Ltd, through a 90% shareholding that B Ltd acquired on 1 July 20X2 for $1 000 000. The shareholders' equity balances for each of the subsidiaries at their respective acquisition dates are as follows:

|  | B Ltd<br>at 1 July 20X4 | C Ltd<br>at 1 July 20X2 |
| --- | --- | --- |
| Paid-up capital | $1 500 000 | $750 000 |
| Retained profits | 400 000 | 150 000 |

At the dates of acquisition, all assets were stated at their fair value.

The following are the summarised balance sheets of the A Ltd group as at 30 June 20X6.

|  | A Ltd<br>$ | B Ltd<br>$ | C Ltd<br>$ |
| --- | --- | --- | --- |
| Paid-up capital ($1 shares) | 2 500 000 | 1 500 000 | 750 000 |
| Retained profits | 800 000 | 600 000 | 220 000 |
| Asset revaluation reserve | 75 000 | 100 000 | – |
| Non-current liabilities | 100 000 | 50 000 | 30 000 |
| Current liabilities | 80 000 | 60 000 | 40 000 |
| Proposed dividend | 100 000 | 40 000 | 20 000 |
|  | $3 655 000 | $2 350 000 | $1 060 000 |
| Current assets | 125 000 | 75 000 | 70 000 |
| Non-current assets | 1 530 000 | 1 275 000 | 990 000 |
| Investment in B Ltd | 2 000 000 | – | – |
| Investment in C Ltd | – | 1 000 000 | – |
|  | $3 655 000 | $2 350 000 | $1 060 000 |

Goodwill on acquisition is amortised straight line over 20 years, and all three companies accrue dividends as revenue on declaration. The retained profits of C Ltd at 1 July 20X4 were $200 000. Assume a tax rate of 40%.

*Required*

Prepare a consolidation worksheet and a consolidated balance sheet for the A Ltd group as at 30 June 20X6. Show clearly the calculation of the various outside equity interests.

# chapter 9

## ACCOUNTING FOR ASSOCIATED COMPANIES

# introduction

In previous chapters the consolidation process was examined whereby if a company controls one or more other companies then it is obliged to prepare a set of consolidated financial statements. The emphasis was on control, this being the trigger for consolidation.

This chapter deals with accounting for investments in companies where the investor has significant influence, but not control. These investee companies are referred to as associates rather than subsidiaries. The current accounting standard on accounting for investments in associated companies is AASB 1016: Disclosure of Information about Investments in Associated Companies. AASB 1016 requires disclosures to be made about the financial performance of investments in associated companies in the notes to the accounts of the investor. This approach was adopted by AASB 1016 because of a legal impediment to integrating the equity accounting information into the investor's accounts, or the consolidated accounts in cases where consolidation is required.

Interestingly, ED 71: Accounting for Investments in Associates has been prepared in anticipation of the legal impediment being removed. The Second Corporate Law Simplification Bill Exposure Draft, issued by the Attorney-General in June 1995, includes proposals to remove the legal impediment. The legal impediment was identified in 1972 when the Victorian Corporate Affairs Commission, following legal advice, stated that the use of the equity method in the consolidated financial statements was not allowable as the definition of group accounts only allows the merging of the existing accounts of the holding or parent company and its subsidiaries. Hence, AASB 1016 required note disclosure in the investor's accounts.

ED 71 proposes that the equity method of accounting be used for investments in associates in:

- consolidated financial statements; or
- the financial statements of an entity which is not required to prepare consolidated financial statements.

Importantly, the principles of equity accounting remain the same, irrespective of how and where the equity accounted information is to be disclosed. The chapter proceeds on the basis that AASB 1016 is the current standard and is discussed in detail. A later section deals with the proposed changes under ED 71. The explanations offered about the technicalities of equity accounting, including a worksheet approach, will remain the same if and when ED 71 replaces AASB 1016.

# Significant influence

significant influence

investor

investee

AASB 1016.10 defines significant influence as 'the capacity of an investor to affect substantially either or both, of the financial and operating policies of the investee'. Recall that for consolidation where an investor has control over an investee, the investor has the capacity to control both the financial and operating policies of the investee. AASB 1016 states that significant influence normally arises from the investor's voting power in the investee. This power is normally related to the percentage of shares held.

AASB 1016, commentary, para (vi) lists the following factors that may indicate significant influence:

- representation on the investee's board of directors;
- participation in the investee's dividend decisions; and
- participation in the investee's policy-making decisions.

Whilst these factors help to establish if significant influence exists, AASB 1016 gives more concrete guidance when it states in the commentary that where an investor holds 20% or more of the voting power in the investee, this leads, in the absence of evidence to the contrary, to a presumption that the investor has significant influence over the investee.

# The cost method of accounting

cost method

Both AASB 1016 and ED 71 require an investment in an associate company to be recorded at cost of acquisition in the investor's separate financial statements. Under the cost method of accounting an investment is recorded at its cost of acquisition. Any dividends received from the investee are recorded as dividend income provided they are paid from post-acquisition profits of the investee. If paid from pre-acquisition profits or reserves, the dividends represent a return of capital (investment) and are credited against the Investment in Associated Company investment account rather than recorded as income. This is the same principle as that adopted in consolidation accounting.

The original cost of the investment will remain unchanged (except as noted above) unless the investment account is revalued in accordance with AASB 1010: Accounting for the Revaluation of Non-current Assets to record any changes in the underlying value of the investment.

The major limitation of the cost method is that the investment account only reflects the worth of the investment at acquisition date. For example, an investee company may be earning acceptable profits for many years but either paying low dividends per share or no dividends. In this case the investor's asset, at original cost, bears no relationship to its underlying worth. That is, the stream of dividend income which represents a return on the original investment does not provide an accurate indication of the investee's performance.

# The equity method of accounting

**equity method**

An investment is recorded at the acquisition cost and adjusted each period for changes in the net assets of the investee. That is, the amount of the investment is increased or decreased by the investor's percentage ownership interest in post-acquisition changes in all shareholder equity accounts.

On the other side of the accounting equation, the investor's share of an associated company's profit/losses is recorded. To avoid double counting, dividends received or receivable from an investee are deducted from the carrying amount of the investment account. This is because the profits from which the dividends are paid have already been accrued as income and as increases in the investment account.

**ILLUSTRATIVE EXAMPLE** 9.1

## DIFFERENCES BETWEEN COST AND EQUITY METHODS OF ACCOUNTING

Assume Richard Ltd acquired 40% of the shares of Green Ltd on 1 July 20X1 for $200 000. This investment gives Richard Ltd significant influence over Green Ltd. At that date the shareholders' equity of Green Ltd was.

| | |
|---|---|
| Paid-up capital | $440 000 |
| Retained profits | 60 000 |

For the year ended 30 June 20X2, Green Ltd records an after-tax profit of $120 000 and pays a dividend of $50 000. During this year Green Ltd also revalues its land by $50 000. Under both the cost and equity methods, the following journal entries would be recorded in the accounts of the investor, Richard Ltd.

| | | Debit | Credit |
|---|---|---|---|
| 20X1 | | $ | $ |
| July 1 | Investment | 200 000 | |
| | Cash | | 200 000 |
| | (to record the acquisition of the investment at cost) | | |
| | On receipt | | |
| | Cash | 20 000 | |
| | Dividend Income | | 20 000 |
| | (receipt of dividend from the investment − 50 000 × 40%) | | |

The following equity journal entries are recorded in the worksheet only of the investor, Richard Ltd.

| | | Debit | Credit |
|---|---|---|---|
| 20X2 | | | |
| June 30 | Investment | 48 000 | |
| | Share of Associated Company's | | |
| | Operating Profit after Tax | | 48 000 |
| | (equity accounting 40% of associated company's profits of 120 000) | | |

|  | Debit | Credit |
|---|---|---|
|  | $ | $ |
| 20X2 | | |
| June 30  Dividend Income | 20 000 | |
| Investment | | 20 000 |
| (equity accounting to reduce the investment by dividends received) | | |
| | | |
| Investment | 20 000 | |
| Asset Revaluation Reserve | | 20 000 |
| (equity accounting 40% of associated company's revaluation of 50 000) | | |

The balance in the investment account using equity accounting is calculated as follows:

|  | Debit | Credit | Balance |
|---|---|---|---|
|  | $ | $ | $ |
| Cash | 200 000 | | |
| Share of Associated Company's Profit | 48 000 | | |
| Dividend Income from Associated Company | | 20 000 | |
| Asset Revaluation Reserve | 20 000 | | 248 000 |

Note that the owners' equity of Green Ltd at date of acquisition (1 July 20X1) and increases in equity in the following year are:

|  | $ | $ |
|---|---|---|
| Paid-up capital | 440 000 | |
| Retained profits 1 July 20X1 | 60 000 | 500 000 |
| Net profit for year ended 30 June 20X2 | 120 000 | |
| *Less* Dividend paid | (50 000) | |
|  | 70 000 | |
| Asset revaluation reserve | 50 000 | 120 000 |
| Total equity | | $620 000 |
| Richard Ltd's 40% share is ($620 000 × 40%) | | $248 000 |

This is the same as the balance in the investment account (in the investor's books) as above. This occurs because the investment account is adjusted to reflect the investor's interest (here 40%) in the net assets of the associated company. This equality will not occur if adjustments have been made for any goodwill or discount on the acquisition of the investment, or for unrealised profits from inter-company trading.

The journal entries above for the equity method highlight two problems with the method. First, it has been suggested that the equity method breaches the revenue recognition principle in accounting. That is, the recognition of equity income in the investor's accounts should not occur as no external transaction has taken place and the investor does not control the investee. There is no guarantee that the investor will automatically share in the profits of the investee. For example, the investee may decide not to pay any dividends. In this case, none of the investee's profits will be distributed to the investor even though the investor has taken up a share of those profits.

Second, the balance in the investor's investment account reported using the equity method (above $248 000) is neither cost nor market value. It is only an amount that results from applying equity accounting procedures.

# Other methods of accounting for investments in associated companies

There are a number of problems inherent in both the cost and equity methods of accounting for investments in associated companies. Other methods of accounting for associated companies include proportional consolidation, full consolidation and the market value method.

**proportional consolidation**

Proportional consolidation involves an investor consolidating its proportional interest on a line-by-line basis of each amount in an associate's income statement and balance sheet. In the example used above, Richard Ltd would consolidate 40% of Green Ltd's assets, liabilities, revenues, expenses and equity. No outside equity interest is reported because proportional consolidation only consolidates the investor's ownership interest. The problem with this method is that whilst an investor holds a percentage of an associate's net assets it does not control the associate; rather, the investor has only significant influence. Financial statements prepared on this basis could be misleading to the investor's shareholders.

**full consolidation**

The same problem exists if full consolidation accounting is used. The investor would be reporting in its accounts net assets which it does not control. Here 100% of the associate's income statement and balance sheet items are consolidated and the proportion of the associate's equity not owned by the investor is reported as an outside equity interest.

**market value method**

The market value method records the investment account at its net market value at balance date. Any dividends received during the period and any changes in the market value between balance sheet dates are included in income and the investor's accounts. The major problem with the method is that a market to value the investment in the associate may not exist — for example, the shares may not be listed. Further, AASB 1010: Accounting for Revaluation of Non-current Assets prohibits recording revaluation increases to non-current assets as income.

# Applying the equity method

## GOODWILL ON ACQUISITION

In the example above, there was no goodwill or discount on acquisition when the cost of the investment was compared with the percentage of the equity acquired. As the investment account is recorded at cost of acquisition, any goodwill component is not recorded separately. The cost of acquisition must be compared with the fair value (the amount for which an asset could be exchanged between a knowledgeable willing buyer and a knowledgeable willing seller in an arm's length transaction) of assets acquired. Any resulting goodwill or discount on acquisition must be accounted for in accordance with AASB 1013: Accounting for Goodwill. Any goodwill must be amortised against income over a period not exceeding 20 years. Using equity accounting, the share of the associated company's profit and the carrying value of the investment need to be reduced by any goodwill amortisation. Prior period adjustments for goodwill amortisation also need to be recorded in the current year because a worksheet is used to implement equity accounting and previous adjustments and balances have not been carried forward (the same as consolidation). Any discount on acquisition must be written off against the non-monetary assets acquired.

For example, assume C Ltd acquires 25% of the paid-up capital of D Ltd for $2 000 000 on 1 July 2001. The shareholders' equity of D Ltd at that date was:

| | |
|---|---|
| Paid-up capital | $3 000 000 |
| Retained profits | 2 000 000 |

The assets of D Ltd were recorded at fair value. Goodwill is to be amortised over ten years, straight line. In C Ltd's accounts the investment will be recorded at its cost, $2 000 000. This acquisition cost must be compared to the percentage of net assets acquired to identify any goodwill or discount on acquisition.

| | $ |
|---|---|
| Net assets acquired | 1 250 000 (5 000 000 × 25%) |
| Cost of shares | 2 000 000 |
| Goodwill on acquisition | $ 750 000 |
| Therefore, amortisation expense | $ 75 000 per annum  (750 000/10 years) |

The equity journal entries are as follows:

| 2002 | | Debit | Credit |
|---|---|---|---|
| June 30 | Share of Associated Company's | | |
| | Operating Profit before Tax | 75 000 | |
| | Investment in D Ltd | | 75 000 |
| | (current year's goodwill amortisation) | | |

| 2005 | | | |
|---|---|---|---|
| June 30 | Share of Associated Company's | | |
| | Operating Profit before Tax | 75 000 | |
| | Opening Retained Profits | 225 000 | |
| | Investment in D Ltd | | 300 000 |
| | (current year's goodwill amortisation plus prior periods) | | |

| 2015 | | | |
|---|---|---|---|
| June 30 | Opening Retained Profits | 750 000 | |
| | Investment in D Ltd | | 750 000 |
| | (prior period's amortisation of goodwill) | | |

Because a new equity worksheet is compiled at each balance sheet date, all prior period adjustments must be incorporated in the new worksheet.

## IMPLEMENTING EQUITY ACCOUNTING

The techniques of applying equity accounting are similar to those of the consolidation process. The following steps are taken sequentially:

1  Equity journal entries are prepared.
2  The above entries are posted to an equity worksheet and balanced.
3  Equity financial statements are prepared.

4 From the equity financial statements the amounts required to be disclosed by AASB 1016 are identified.

5 Disclosure is made by way of notes to the accounts of the investor.

The above procedures mean that the accounting records of the investor are unaffected by equity accounting.

Disclosure by way of notes to the accounts means that the investee's results are not integrated with the investor's accounts as they are in the consolidation process. Note that disclosure only is required because the definition of group accounts does not allow the introduction of information into the consolidation process which was not already in the accounts of those entities comprising the group.

## PRO FORMA EQUITY JOURNAL ENTRIES

The pro forma equity journal entries are as follows:

(1) Record goodwill amortisation (if any).

|  |  | Debit | Credit |
|---|---|---|---|
| Year 1 | Share of Associated Company's | | |
| | Operating Profit before Tax | XXX | |
| | Investment in Associated Company | | XXX |
| | (current year's goodwill amortisation) | | |
| Year 2 | Opening Retained Profits | XXX | |
| | Share of Associated Company's Operating | | |
| | Profit before Tax (Current Year) | XXX | |
| | Investment in Associated Company | | XXX |
| | (current year's goodwill amortisation plus prior periods) | | |

As the investment is recorded in the investor's account at the cost of acquisition, goodwill is not recorded separately. Therefore, when implementing equity accounting, goodwill is calculated in the equity journal and written off against the investment because the goodwill is contained in the investment account.

(2) Take up a share of the associated company's current operating results.

|  | Debit | Credit |
|---|---|---|
| Investment in Associated Company | XXX | |
| Share of Associated Company's Income Tax | XXX | |
| Share of Associated Company's Operating | | |
| Profit before Tax | | XXX |
| Share of Associated Company's Extraordinary Items | | XXX |

(3) Record dividends paid by associated company during the current year.

|  | Debit | Credit |
|---|---|---|
| Dividend Income | XXX | |
| Investment in Associated Company | | XXX |

As (2) above takes up a share of the associated company's current operating profit, this journal entry prevents double counting as the dividend was paid from current profits.

(4) Record share of post-acquisition profits of associated company from date of acquisition to the beginning of the current year.

|  | Debit | Credit |
|---|---|---|
| Investment in Associated Company | XXX | |
|     Opening Retained Profits | | XXX |

(5) Record previous dividends received from the associated company from date of acquisition to the beginning of the current year.

| | | |
|---|---|---|
| Opening Retained Profits | XXX | |
|     Investment in Associated Company | | XXX |

Entries (4) and (5) could be combined — that is:

| | | |
|---|---|---|
| Investment in Associated Company | XXX | |
|     Opening Retained Profits | | XXX |

This entry takes up the investor's net share of post-acquisition profits to the beginning of the current year.

(6) Take up a share of post-acquisition increases in other reserves of the associated company.

| | | |
|---|---|---|
| Investment in Associated Company | XXX | |
|     Reserves | | XXX |
|     (say, asset revaluation reserve) | | |

## ILLUSTRATIVE EXAMPLE 9.2

## APPLICATION OF EQUITY ACCOUNTING

A Ltd acquired 25% of the paid-up capital of B Ltd for $1 500 000 on 1 July 20X1. At that date the shareholders' equity of B Ltd was as follows:

| | $000 |
|---|---|
| Paid-up capital | 3 000 |
| Asset revaluation reserve | 500 |
| Retained profits | 600 |
| | $4 100 |

For the two years to 30 June 20X3, B Ltd earned the following profits and paid the indicated dividends.

| | Operating profit and extraordinary items after tax | Dividends paid |
|---|---|---|
| | $000 | $000 |
| Year ended 30 June 20X2 | 420 | 200 |
| Year ended 30 June 20X3 | 375 | 180 |
| | $795 | $380 |

Therefore, retained profits of B Ltd at 1 July 20X3 must be:

|  | $000 |
|---|---|
| Retained profits 1 July 20X1 | 600 |
| + next 2 years' profits | 795 |
| – dividends paid | (380) |
| Retained profits 1 July 20X3 | $1 015 |

The income statements and balance sheets of A Ltd and B Ltd for the year ended 30 June 20X4 are shown below.

| Income Statements for the year ended 30 June 20X4 | | |
|---|---|---|
|  | A Ltd | B Ltd |
|  | $000 | $000 |
| Sales | 6 140 | 7 450 |
| Less Cost of goods sold | (2 150) | (3 200) |
| **Gross profit** | 3 990 | 4 250 |
| Expenses | (1 200) | (2 565) |
| Dividend revenue | 45 | – |
| **Operating profit before tax** | 2 835 | 1 685 |
| Income tax expense | (1 020) | (825) |
| Operating profit after tax | 1 815 | 860 |
| Extraordinary items (nil tax) | (200) | 250 |
| **Operating profit and extraordinary items after tax** | 1 615 | 1 110 |
| Retained profits 1 July 20X3 | 800 | 1 015 |
| Interim dividend paid | (200) | (180) |
| Final proposed dividend | (250) | (220) |
| **Retained profits 30 June 20X4** | $1 965 | $1 725 |

| Balance Sheets as at 30 June 20X4 | | |
|---|---|---|
|  | A Ltd | B Ltd |
|  | $000 | $000 |
| Plant & equipment | 3 415 | 3 895 |
| Inventory | 950 | 850 |
| Other current assets | 1 700 | 1 500 |
| Investment in B Ltd | 1 500 | – |
| *Total assets* | $7 565 | $6 245 |
| Paid-up capital | 4 000 | 3 000 |
| Asset revaluation reserve | 600 | 800 |
| Retained profits | 1 965 | 1 725 |
| Dividend payable | 250 | 220 |
| Non-current liabilities | 750 | 500 |
| *Total liabilities* | $7 565 | $6 245 |

When A Ltd acquired the shares in B Ltd, the assets of B Ltd were recorded at fair value. A Ltd records dividend revenue only on receipt of cash. Any goodwill on acquisition is to be amortised over ten years using the straight-line method.

The equity journal entries are as follows:

(a) Record goodwill amortisation.

| | $000 |
|---|---|
| Net assets acquired | 1 025 (4100 × 25%) |
| Cost of shares | 1 500 |
| Goodwill on acquisition | $ 475 |

Therefore, amortisation expense   =   $47.50 per annum (475/10 years)

| | Debit $ | Credit $ |
|---|---|---|
| Retained Profits 1 July 20X3 | 95 000 | |
| Share of Associated Company's Profit before Tax | 47 500 | |
|    Investment in B Ltd | | 142 500 |

Recall that a new equity journal is completed each year and no entries appear in either the investors' or the investees' financial statements. Hence the debit above of $95 000 against opening retained profits accounts for the annual amortisation expense charged in previous years and not carried forward.

(b) Record 25% share of B Ltd's operating results.

| | Debit $ | Credit $ |
|---|---|---|
| Investment in B Ltd (1 110 000 × 25%) | 277 500 | |
| Share of Associated Company's Income Tax (825 000 × 25%) | 206 250 | |
| Share of Associated Company's Operating Profit before Tax (1 685 000 × 25%) | | 421 250 |
| Share of Associated Company's Extraordinary Items (250 000 × 25%) | | 62 500 |

(c) The entry in (b) above took up a 25% share of B Ltd's operating profit. This means that any dividends paid during the year by B Ltd to A Ltd must reduce the asset Investment in B Ltd (in A Ltd's books) or the dividend would be counted twice.

| | | |
|---|---|---|
| Dividend Revenue | 45 000 | |
|    Investment in B Ltd (180 000 × 25%) | | 45 000 |

(d) Any increases/decreases in post-acquisition retained profits to the beginning of the current year are adjusted against A Ltd's asset Investment in B Ltd.

| | | |
|---|---|---|
| Investment in B Ltd | 198 750 | |
|    Retained Profits 1 July 20X3 (795 000 × 25% ) | | 198 750 |

(e) Using the same principle as in (c) above, because A Ltd has taken up a share of post-acquisition profits, any dividends received from B Ltd must reduce the asset Investment in B Ltd.

|  | Debit $ | Credit $ |
|---|---|---|
| Retained Profits 1 July 20X3 | 95 000 | |
| Investment in B Ltd (380 000 × 25%) | | 95 000 |

Entries (d) and (e) could be combined — that is:

|  |  |  |
|---|---|---|
| Investment in B Ltd | 103 750 | |
| Retained Profits 1 July 20X3 | | 103 750 |

This entry records the net increase ($795 000 – $380 000 × 25%) in A Ltd's investment account from acquisition to the beginning of the current year. This combined entry has been used in the following worksheet.

(f) The asset revaluation reserve of B Ltd has increased from $500 000 at date of acquisition to $800 000 after three years. A Ltd's share of this increase is now recorded in the equity journal.

|  | Debit $ | Credit $ |
|---|---|---|
| Investment in B Ltd | 75 000 | |
| Asset Revaluation Reserve (300 000 × 25%) | | 75 000 |

The equity accounting worksheet appears below. Only the accounts of A Ltd, investor, are shown and the equity journal entries above are recorded under the heading 'Equity accounting adjustments'.

## Equity accounting worksheet

| | A Ltd | Equity accounting adjustments Debit | Equity accounting adjustments Credit | Equity statements |
|---|---|---|---|---|
| | $ | $ | $ | $ |
| Sales | 6 140 000 | | | 6 140 000 |
| *Less* Cost of goods sold | (2 150 000) | | | (2 150 000) |
| **Gross profit** | 3 990 000 | | | 3 990 000 |
| Expenses | (1 200 000) | | | (1 200 000) |
| Dividend revenue | 45 000 | 45 000 (c) | | – |
| **Operating profit before tax** | 2 835 000 | | | 2 790 000 |
| Share of associated company's operating profit | | 47 500 (a) | 421 250 (b) | 373 750 |
| Income tax expense | (1 020 000) | | | (1 020 000) |
| Share of associated company's income tax | | 206 250 (b) | | (206 250) |
| **Operating profit after tax** | 1 815 000 | | | 1 937 500 |
| Extraordinary items (nil tax) | (200 000) | | | (200 000) |
| Share of associated company's extraordinary items | | | 62 500 (b) | 62 500 |

|  |  | Debit | Credit |  |
|---|---|---|---|---|
|  | $ | $ | $ | $ |
| **Operating profit and** | | | | |
| **extraordinary items after tax** | 1 615 000 | | | 1 800 000 |
|  | | | (d) | |
| Retained profits 1 July 20X3 | 800 000 | 95 000 (a) | 103 750 (e) | 808 750 |
| Interim dividend paid | (200 000) | | | (200 000) |
| Final dividend proposed | (250 000) | | | (250 000) |
| **Retained profits 30 June 20X4** | 1 965 000 | | | 2 158 750 |
| Paid-up capital | 4 000 000 | | | 4 000 000 |
| Asset revaluation reserve | 600 000 | | 75 000 (f) | 675 000 |
| Dividend payable | 250 000 | | | 250 000 |
| Non-current liabilities | 750 000 | | | 750 000 |
|  | $ 7 565 000 | | | $ 7 833 750 |
|  | | | | |
| Plant & equipment | 3 415 000 | | | 3 415 000 |
| Inventory | 950 000 | | | 950 000 |
| Other current assets | 1 700 000 | | | 1 700 000 |
| Investment in B Ltd | 1 500 000 | 277 500 (b) | 142 500 (a) | 1 768 750 |
|  | | 103 750 (d) | 45 000 (c) | |
|  | | (e) | | |
|  | | 75 000 (f) | | |
|  | $ 7 565 000 | $ 850 000 | $ 850 000 | $ 7 833 750 |

### Equity Income Statement for the year ended 30 June 20X4

|  | $ | $ |
|---|---|---|
| Operating profit before income tax | | |
| A Ltd | 2 790 000 | |
| Share of associated company | 373 750 | 3 163 750 |
| Income tax expense | | |
| A Ltd | (1 020 000) | |
| Share of associated company | (206 250) | (1 226 250) |
| **Operating profit after income tax** | | |
| **of A Ltd and its associated company** | | 1 937 500 |
| Extraordinary items (nil tax) | | |
| A Ltd | (200 000) | |
| Share of associated company | 62 500 | (137 500) |
| **Operating profit and extraordinary items** | | |
| **of A Ltd and its associated company** | | 1 800 000 |
| Retained profits 1 July 20X3 | | 808 750 |
| Interim dividend paid | | (200 000) |
| Final dividend proposed | | (250 000) |
| **Retained profits 30 June 20X4** | | $ 2 158 750 |

## Equity Balance Sheet at 30 June 20X4

| Assets | $ | Liabilities | $ |
|---|---|---|---|
| Plant & equipment | 3 415 000 | Dividend payable | 250 000 |
| Inventory | 950 000 | Non-current liabilities | 750 000 |
| Other current assets | 1 700 000 | | |
| Investment in B Ltd | 1 768 750 | Shareholders' equity | |
| | | Paid-up capital | 4 000 000 |
| | | Asset revaluation reserve | 675 000 |
| | | Retained profits | 2 158 750 |
| | $7 833 750 | | $7 833 750 |

The items required to be disclosed in note form by AASB 1016 may be identified from the above.

$

AASB 1016.22(a)

Share of associated company's operating profit and
extraordinary items after tax      *230 000
Less Dividend received from associate      (45 000)
Less Amounts already reflected in the
carrying amount of the investment
in the investor's accounts      (−)

     $185 000

* [277 500 − Goodwill 47 500 = 230 000]

AASB 1016.22(b)

Dividend revenue from associated company brought
forward to account during year      45 000

AASB 1016.22(c)

Share of associated company's increases/decreases
in reserves other than those already reflected in the
carrying amount of the investment      75 000

AASB 1016.22(d)

Share of associated company's retained profits to the
extent not reflected in the carrying amount
of the investment      **138 750
Add Share of dividend proposed by associated
company but unpaid at year end      55 000

     $193 750

** Retained profits 30 June 20X4      1 725 000
Less Pre-acquisition retained profits      600 000

     $1 125 000

A Ltd's share × 25%      281 250
Less Goodwill amortised      (142 500)

     $138 750

| | $ |
|---|---|

**AASB 1016.22(e)**

Share of associated company's reserves
(other than retained profits/losses)
to the extent not reflected in the
carrying amount of the investment — 75 000

**AASB 1016.22(f)**

Amount of investment as determined
under the equity method of accounting — ***1 768 750

*** Cost of investment — 1 500 000
*Plus:*
Share of retained profit (d) above — 193 750
Share of asset revaluation reserve — 75 000

**AASB 1016.22(g)**

Carrying amount of investment (cost method) — 1 500 000

In addition, AASB 1016, para .60 requires the following to be disclosed:

| Name of associated company | Principal activity | Ownership interest | Balance date of associated company | Post-balance date entries | Dissimilar accounting policies |
|---|---|---|---|---|---|
| B Ltd | (describe) | 25% | 30 June | nil | nil |

# Inter-company sales of inventory

AASB 1016, para .30 requires adjustments to be made to the investor's share of an associated company's profit or loss for the effects of any unrealised profits or losses on transactions between the investor and its associated company. Such transactions include sale of inventory and other assets. Profits or losses on these transactions are unrealised when such assets have not been sold to unrelated parties before balance date.

Only the amount of profit/loss on an inter-company transaction that relates to the percentage of shares held in the investee company is treated as unrealised. If there was unrealised profit on an inventory transaction of, say, $20 000 and the percentage of shares owned in the associated company was 40%, then $8000 would be subject to adjustment. This treatment contrasts with consolidation accounting where 100% of the profit or loss is considered unrealised and is eliminated.

## UNREALISED PROFIT IN INVENTORY SOLD BY AN INVESTOR TO AN ASSOCIATED COMPANY

*unrealised profit*

As the equity worksheet does not contain the accounts of the associated company, the adjustment must be made against the investor's sales and purchases account. The unrealised profit reduces the carrying amount of the investment; related tax-effect accounting entries are also made.

Assume Don Ltd owns 25% of the shares of Pooley Ltd and sold inventory to Pooley Ltd during the year ended 30 June 20X1. At year end, Pooley Ltd had $200 000 of this inventory on hand. The inventory had cost Don Ltd $150 000. The company tax rate is 33%.

The equity journal entry is as follows:

| | Debit | Credit |
|---|---|---|
| Sales (200 000 × 25%) | 50 000 | |
| Purchases (150 000 × 25%) | | 37 500 |
| Investment in Pooley Ltd (50 000 × 25%) | | 12 500 |
| Future Income Tax Benefit (12 500 × 33%) | 4 125 | |
| Income Tax Expense | | 4 125 |

This example assumes that Don Ltd has a detailed income statement. If this is not the case, the $12 500 unrealised profit is debited to operating profit before tax. The inventory of the associated company is overstated by $12 500 at balance date; hence a credit adjustment is made against the investment account because this represents the investor's percentage interest in the net assets of the associated company.

In the following year the inventory would have been sold to unrelated third parties; hence the unrealised profit of $12 500 is now realised. At balance date the journal entry is as follows:

| | Debit | Credit |
|---|---|---|
| Retained Profits | 12 500 | |
| Purchases | 37 500 | |
| Sales | | 50 000 |
| Income Tax Expense | 4 125 | |
| Retained Profits 1 July 20X1 | | 4 125 |

If a summarised form of income statement was provided, the entry would be a debit to retained profits of $12 500 and a credit to operating profit before tax of $12 500. Either entry has the effect of transferring the unrealised profit on inventory from last period to the current period as realised profit.

## UNREALISED PROFIT IN INVENTORY SOLD BY AN ASSOCIATED COMPANY TO ITS INVESTOR

Unrealised profit from the sale of inventory of an associated company to its investor must be removed from the investor's share of the associated company's profit or loss for the period. In this case the investor's ending inventory will also be overstated by the amount of the unrealised profit.

Assume Craig Ltd owns 25% of the shares of Stadler Ltd. The latter sold inventory to Craig Ltd during the year ended 30 June 20X1. At year end, Craig Ltd had $100 000 of this inventory on hand. The inventory had cost Stadler Ltd $60 000. The company tax rate is 33%.

The equity journal entry is as follows:

| | Debit | Credit |
|---|---|---|
| Share of Associated Company's | | |
| Operating Profit before Tax (40 000 × 25%) | 10 000 | |
| Closing Inventory | | 10 000 |
| Future Income Tax Benefit (10 000 × 33%) | 3 300 | |
| Share of Associated Company's | | |
| Income Tax Expense | | 3 300 |

In the following year the unrealised profit would be realised as the inventory would have been sold to unrelated third parties. At balance date the journal entry is as follows:

| | Debit | Credit |
|---|---|---|
| Retained Profits (net of tax, 10 000 – 3 300) | 6 700 | |
| Share of Associated Company's Income | | |
| Tax Expense | 3 300 | |
| Share of Associated Company's | | |
| Operating Profit before Tax | | 10 000 |

## LOSSES OF AN ASSOCIATED COMPANY

AASB 1016, para .100 requires that where an associated company incurs losses, the investment account should be reduced by the investor's share of those losses until the carrying amount is zero. The investment account should not be reduced below zero (a credit balance). AASB 1016, para .101 states that if the associated company returns to profitability, the investment in the associated company should only be increased after the unrecorded losses have been recouped.

## DISCLOSURE REQUIREMENTS (AASB 1016)

AASB 1016, para .22 requires the investor to disclose by way of notes the following information:
- the investor's share of the associated company's operating profits and losses and extraordinary items after income tax, and net of preference dividends to the extent that such share of profits and losses has neither been brought to account by the investor as dividend revenue nor is otherwise reflected in the carrying amount of the investment;
- dividend revenue from associated companies brought to account during the current financial year;
- the investor's share of any increments/decrements in other reserves of associated companies arising during the financial year, other than increments/decrements already reflected in the carrying amount of the investment;
- the investor's share at the end of the current financial year of the retained profits/accumulated losses not reflected in the carrying amount of the investment;
- the equity-accounted amount for investments in associated companies, as determined under the equity method of accounting; and
- the carrying amount for investments in associated companies as included in the consolidated accounts of the investor or, where group accounts are not prepared, in the accounts of the investor (as determined under the cost method of accounting less any pre-acquisition dividends received).

AASB 1016, para .60 also requires the following disclosures:
- the name and principal activities of the associated company;
- the investor's ownership interest in the associated company as at the associated company's balance date and, if different, at the investor's balance date;
- the balance date of the associated company;
- any material post-balance date events; and
- the nature of dissimilar accounting policies if adjustment to the associated company's results has not been made.

AASB 1034, para 6.1(f) requires that where an investment in an entity which is not a subsidiary or an associate is material, the following information is disclosed:
(i) the name of the entity;
(ii) its principal activities;
(iii) the percentage ownership interest held in the entity; and
(iv) the carrying amount of the investment.

# Accounting for investments in associates by the equity method (ED 71)

This exposure draft proposes that the equity method of accounting be applied to determine the carrying amounts of investments in associates in:
• consolidated financial statements; and
• the investor's separate financial statements, when the investor is not required to prepare consolidated financial statements.

The cost method of accounting would continue to be applied in determining the carrying amounts of investments in associates in the investor's separate financial statements, when the investor is also required to prepare consolidated financial statements. ED 71 would apply to general purpose financial reports of:
• all private reporting entities and each public sector reporting entity employing any accrual basis of accounting; and
• other public sector reporting entities to the extent practicable.

The exposure draft recommends that all associated entities, whether a current or non-current asset (in the investor's accounts) and whether incorporated or in some other legal form (but excluding unincorporated joint ventures) should be equity accounted. It also recommends that the carrying amount of an investment in an associate must not exceed its net market value. Where the net market value of an investment has fallen below its carrying amount, the carrying amount must be written down to that net market value. The amount of the reduction must be recognised in the profit and loss or other operating statement in the reporting period in which the reduction occurs.

## AASB 1016 AND ED 71

The major differences are as follows:
• Equity accounting will be applied to certain public sector entities.
• Rather than disclosing equity accounting information in notes to the accounts, it will be 'booked' in either the consolidated financial statements or the investor's financial statements where consolidated statements are not required.
• The carrying amount of an investment in an associate must not exceed its net market value.

Under ED 71, consolidated groups of companies will include a parent, subsidiaries *and* associates. The latter were excluded under AASB 1016 because of the requirement for note disclosure as a result of the legal impediment discussed earlier.

The example of A Ltd and B Ltd used previously to illustrate equity accounting principles under AASB 1016 is the same under ED 71 except for the disclosure requirements. The equity journal entries, equity accounting worksheet, equity income statement and equity balance sheet are prepared in the same way. However, whereas under AASB 1016 the equity income statement and balance sheet were used to identify the information required in notes to A Ltd's financial statements, the equity income statement and balance sheet are now what is required.

ILLUSTRATIVE EXAMPLE  9.3

# CONSOLIDATION AND EQUITY ACCOUNTING

This example will assume the same facts as A Ltd and B Ltd used earlier in the chapter but also include a subsidiary company, Z Ltd. This will illustrate the use of equity accounting where consolidated financial statements are prepared.

In addition to the facts given previously about A Ltd and B Ltd, A Ltd also acquired 100% of the paid-up capital of Z Ltd. The acquisition date was 1 July 20X1 and cost was $3 250 000. The shareholders' equity of Z Ltd at that date was:

| | |
|---|---|
| Paid-up capital | $2 000 000 |
| Retained profits | 1 000 000 |

The above example of a parent company A Ltd, its subsidiary company Z Ltd and A Ltd's associated company B Ltd illustrates the ED 71 requirement that the equity method of accounting be used for investments in associates in consolidated financial statements. The earlier example of A Ltd (investor) and B Ltd (associate) illustrates the use of the method in the financial statements of an entity which is not required to prepare consolidated financial statements.

The assets of Z Ltd were at fair value, and any goodwill on acquisition is amortised over ten years using the straight-line method. The income statements and balance sheets of A Ltd and Z Ltd for the year ended 30 June 20X4 are shown below.

| Income Statements for the year ended 30 June 20X4 | | |
|---|---|---|
| | A Ltd | Z Ltd |
| | $000 | $000 |
| Sales | 6 140 | 4 000 |
| Less Cost of goods sold | (2 150) | (1 200) |
| **Gross profit** | 3 990 | 2 800 |
| Expenses | (1 200) | (1 400) |
| Dividend revenue | 45 | |
| **Operating profit before tax** | 2 835 | 1 400 |
| Income tax expense | (1 020) | (600) |
| **Operating profit after tax** | 1 815 | 800 |
| Extraordinary items (nil tax) | (200) | |
| **Operating profit and extraordinary items after tax** | 1 615 | 800 |
| Retained profits 1 July 20X3 | 800 | 1 200 |
| Interim dividend paid | (200) | – |
| Final proposed dividend | (250) | (200) |
| **Retained profits 30 June 20X4** | $1 965 | $1 800 |

| Balance Sheets as at 30 June 20X4 | | |
|---|---|---|
| | A Ltd | Z Ltd |
| | $000 | $000 |
| Plant & equipment | 3 415 | 3 500 |
| Inventory | 950 | 500 |
| Other current assets | 1 700 | 1 100 |
| Investment in B Ltd | 1 500 | – |
| Investment in Z Ltd | 3 250 | – |
| | 10 815 | 5 100 |
| | | |
| Paid-up capital | 7 250 | 2 000 |
| Asset revaluation reserve | 600 | 100 |
| Retained profits | 1 965 | 1 800 |
| Dividend payable | 250 | 200 |
| Non-current liabilities | 750 | 1 000 |
| | 10 815 | 5 100 |

The first step is to consolidate A Ltd and Z Ltd. The consolidation journal entries are as follows:

(1) Record elimination of the investment against paid-up capital and retained profits acquired.

| | Debit | Credit |
|---|---|---|
| | $ | $ |
| Paid-up Capital | 2 000 000 | |
| Retained Profits | 1 000 000 | |
| Goodwill on Acquisition | 250 000 | |
| Investment in Z Ltd | | 3 250 000 |

(2) Record amortisation of goodwill (3 years @ $25 000 per annum).

| | | |
|---|---|---|
| Retained Profits 1 July 20X3 | 50 000 | |
| Expenses (Goodwill Amortisation) | 25 000 | |
| Goodwill on Acquisition | | 75 000 |

(3) Record elimination of proposed dividend of subsidiary, Z Ltd.

| | | |
|---|---|---|
| Dividend Payable | 200 000 | |
| Final Proposed Dividend | | 200 000 |

The consolidation worksheet appears as follows:

## Consolidation worksheet

| | A Ltd | Z Ltd | Eliminations Debit | Eliminations Credit | Consolidated statements |
|---|---|---|---|---|---|
| | $ | $ | $ | $ | $ |
| Sales | 6 140 000 | 4 000 000 | | | 10 140 000 |
| *Less* Cost of goods sold | (2 150 000) | (1 200 000) | | | (3 350 000) |
| **Gross profit** | 3 990 000 | 2 800 000 | | | 6 790 000 |
| Expenses | (1 200 000) | (1 400 000) | 25 000 (2) | | (2 625 000) |
| Dividend revenue | 45 000 | – | | | 45 000 |
| **Operating profit before tax** | 2 835 000 | 1 400 000 | | | 4 210 000 |
| Income tax expense | (1 020 000) | (600 000) | | | (1 620 000) |
| **Operating profit after tax** | 1 815 000 | 800 000 | | | 2 590 000 |
| Extraordinary items (nil tax) | (200 000) | – | | | (200 000) |
| **Operating profit and extraordinary items after tax** | 1 615 000 | 800 000 | | | 2 390 000 |
| Retained profits 1 July 20X3 | 800 000 | 1 200 000 | 1 000 000 (1) 50 000 (2) | | 950 000 |
| Interim dividend paid | (200 000) | – | | | (200 000) |
| Final dividend proposed | (250 000) | (200 000) | | 200 000 (3) | (250 000) |
| **Retained profits 30 June 20X4** | 1 965 000 | 1 800 000 | | | 2 890 000 |
| Paid-up capital | 7 250 000 | 2 000 000 | 2 000 000 (1) | | 7 250 000 |
| Asset revaluation reserve | 600 000 | 100 000 | | | 700 000 |
| Dividend payable | 250 000 | 200 000 | 200 000 (3) | | 250 000 |
| Non-current liabilities | 750 000 | 1 000 000 | | | 1 750 000 |
| | 10 815 000 | 5 100 000 | | | 12 840 000 |
| Plant & equipment | 3 415 000 | 3 500 000 | | | 6 915 000 |
| Inventory | 950 000 | 500 000 | | | 1 450 000 |
| Other current assets | 1 700 000 | 1 100 000 | | | 2 800 000 |
| Investment in B Ltd | 1 500 000 | – | | | 1 500 000 |
| Investment in Z Ltd | 3 250 000 | – | | 3 250 000 (1) | – |
| Goodwill on acquisition | | | 250 000 (1) | 75 000 (2) | 175 000 |
| | $10 815 000 | $5 100 000 | $3 525 000 | $3 525 000 | $12 840 000 |

The next step is to apply equity accounting to the consolidated totals to account for A Ltd's investment in B Ltd. The following worksheet uses the same elimination entries as were used in the example of A Ltd and B Ltd.

**Equity accounting worksheet**

| | Group consolidated | Equity accounting adjustments | | Economic group |
|---|---|---|---|---|
| | | Debit | Credit | |
| | $ | $ | $ | $ |
| Sales | 10 140 000 | | | 10 140 000 |
| Cost of goods sold | (3 350 000) | | | (3 350 000) |
| Gross profit | 6 790 000 | | | 6 790 000 |
| Expenses | (2 625 000) | | | (2 625 000) |
| Dividend revenue | 45 000 | 45 000 (c) | | – |
| Operating profit before tax | 4 210 000 | | | 4 165 000 |
| Share of associated company's operating profit | | 47 500 (a) | 421 250 (b) | 373 750 |
| Income tax expense | (1 620 000) | | | (1 620 000) |
| Share of associated company's income tax | | 206 250 (b) | | (206 250) |
| Operating profit after tax | 2 590 000 | | | 2 712 500 |
| Extraordinary items (nil tax) | (200 000) | | | (200 000) |
| Share of associated company's extraordinary items | | | 62 500 (b) | 62 500 |
| Operating profit and extra-ordinary items after tax | 2 390 000 | | | 2 575 000 |
| Retained profits 1 July 20X3 | 950 000 | 95 000 (a) | 103 750 (d)(e) | 958 750 |
| Interim dividend paid | (200 000) | | | (200 000) |
| Final dividend proposed | (250 000) | | | (250 000) |
| Retained profits 30 June 20X4 | 2 890 000 | | | 3 083 750 |
| Paid-up capital | 7 250 000 | | | 7 250 000 |
| Asset revaluation reserve | 700 000 | | 75 000 (f) | 775 000 |
| Dividend payable | 250 000 | | | 250 000 |
| Non-current liabilities | 1 750 000 | | | 1 750 000 |
| | 12 840 000 | | | 13 108 750 |
| Plant & equipment | 6 915 000 | | | 6 915 000 |
| Inventory | 1 450 000 | | | 1 450 000 |
| Other current assets | 2 800 000 | | | 2 800 000 |
| Investment in B Ltd | 1 500 000 | 277 500 (b) | 142 500 (a) | 1 768 750 |
| | | 103 750 (d)(e) | 45 000 (c) | |
| | | 75 000 (f) | | |
| Goodwill on acquisition | 175 000 | | | 175 000 |
| | $12 840 000 | $850 000 | $850 000 | $13 108 750 |

Note that a single worksheet incorporating the consolidation and the application of equity accounting techniques could be used. The economic group now shows the results of the consolidation of A Ltd and Z Ltd, as well as the results of A Ltd's investment in its associate B Ltd.

## DISCLOSURE REQUIREMENTS (ED 71)

Where the equity method of accounting is applied to investments in associates, the following must be disclosed separately:

(a) in respect of each associate:
   (i) its name and principal activities,
   (ii) the investor's ownership interest as at the associate's reporting date and, if different, at the investor's reporting date,
   (iii) the proportion of voting power held in the associate where different from the proportion of ownership interest held;

(b) the investor's share of associates':
   (i) operating profits and losses before income tax,
   (ii) income tax expense,
   (iii) extraordinary items (net of income tax);

(c) the extent to which retained profits or accumulated losses as at the beginning and end of the reporting period are attributable to associates;

(d) the extent to which other reserves are attributable to associates;

(e) investments in associates at their aggregate carrying amount;

(f) a schedule setting out the movements in the carrying amount of investments in associates, separately identifying new investments, disposals, equity share of profit or loss, dividends, and other movements;

(g) where investments in associates, either individually or in aggregate, are material to an evaluation of the financial performance and financial position of the investor, the recorded amounts of assets, liabilities and profits or losses of associates either individually, or in aggregate, as appropriate;

(h) where the reporting dates of the associate and the investor differ, any change since the previous reporting period;

(i) events or transactions which have occurred after the reporting date of an associate and which could materially affect the financial position or operating performance of that associate;

(j) where adjustments to eliminate the effect of dissimilar accounting policies cannot be made, the nature of the dissimilarities;

(k) the investor's share of contingent liabilities and capital expenditure commitments of an associate for which it also has a contingent liability;

(l) those contingent liabilities that arise because the investor is severally liable for all the liabilities of the associate;

(m) where an associate holds equity in the investor:
   (i) the amount of the dividend declared by the investor during the current financial year, reduced, to the extent of the investor's ownership interest in the associate, by the amount of dividends paid by the investor to the associate,
   (ii) the percentage of equity held by the associate;

(n) an explanation of and reasons for making adjustments to the quoted market price in determining net market value.

# Review

This chapter has examined accounting for associated companies using the equity method of accounting. It is important to realise that the principles of the equity method do not change under new or updated accounting standards on the method. Rather, the disclosure requirements may change but not the method's fundamentals. Various methods of accounting for inter-company investments were examined as an alternative to the equity method.

The current accounting standard AASB 1016, which requires note disclosure in the investor's accounts, is still the current accounting standard on equity accounting. This situation will not change until the Second Corporate Law Simplification Bill Exposure Draft becomes law.

## KEY TERMS

| | | |
|---|---|---|
| cost method | investor | significant influence |
| equity method | market value method | unrealised profit |
| investee | proportional consolidation | |

## REVIEW QUESTIONS

**9.1** What is the difference between significant influence and control?

**9.2** Explain why the directors of an investor company may wish to use equity accounting techniques to account for an investment rather than to consolidate the company in which it holds an investment.

**9.3** What are the limitations of using the cost method of accounting for an investment in another company?

**9.4** The equity accounting method has been described as 'one-line consolidation'. Explain the meaning of this terminology.

**9.5** What are the differences between AASB 1016 and ED 71?

**9.6** Discuss two criticisms that have been made about the equity method of accounting.

**9.7** Name and describe the methods available for accounting for an investment in another company.

# EXERCISES

**Exercise 9.8**  **Cost and equity methods**

On 1 July 20X3, XYZ Ltd acquired a 40% interest in ABC Ltd at a cost of $200 000. There was no goodwill involved in this transaction. For the year ended 30 June 20X4, ABC Ltd earned a net profit after tax of $75 000 and paid a dividend of $30 000. ABC Ltd's asset revaluation reserve increased from $40 000 to $60 000 in the same year.

*Required*

Prepare journal entries to account for the investment by XYZ Ltd for the year ended 30 June 20X4 using the cost and equity methods.

**Exercise 9.9**  **Cost and equity methods, dividends paid**

David Ltd purchased a 25% interest in Gleeson Ltd on 1 July 20X3 for $100 000. At this date the shareholders' equity of Gleeson Ltd was as follows:

| | |
|---|---|
| Paid-up capital | $200 000 |
| General reserve | 100 000 |
| Retained profits | 50 000 |

The assets of Gleeson Ltd were at fair value and any goodwill is to be amortised over ten years. For the year ended 30 June 20X4, Gleeson Ltd earned an operating profit after tax of $80 000. It also paid an interim dividend of $20 000.

*Required*

Prepare journal entries to record the investment made by David Ltd and the receipt of the dividend. Also prepare journal entries to account for the investment using the equity method of accounting.

**Exercise 9.10**  **Equity inter-company transactions**

Shane Ltd holds a 25% interest in Tait Ltd. During the year ended 30 June 20X3, Shane Ltd acquired $75 000 of inventory from Tait Ltd. The inventory had cost Tait Ltd $50 000. One half of this inventory was on hand at year end. Assume a tax rate of 33%.

*Required*

1 Prepare the equity accounting entries to account for the unrealised profit in inventory sold to Shane Ltd by Tait Ltd.
2 Prepare the equity accounting entries to account for the unrealised profit in inventory assuming the same facts but Shane Ltd sold the inventory to Tait Ltd.

**Exercise 9.11**  **Equity investment account**

Bob Ltd acquired 40% of the paid-up capital of Charles Ltd on 1 July 20X3 for $160 000. The following information gives selected accounts for each company.

*Charles Ltd*

| | |
|---|---|
| (a)  Paid-up capital and reserves at 1 July 20X3 | $300 000 |
| (b)  Interim dividend paid 31 December 20X3 | $20 000 |

(c)  Operating profit before tax for year ended 30 June 20X4     $250 000
(d)  Income tax expense for 20X4                                          $90 000

*Bob Ltd*
(a)  Goodwill on acquisition is amortised over five years, straight line.
(b)  Inventory on hand at 30 June 20X4 includes inventory purchased during the year from Charles Ltd at a profit of $15 000.
(c)  The tax rate is 36%.

*Required*
1  Prepare journal entries recording the acquisition in Bob Ltd's accounts.
2  Prepare equity journal entries to account for the investment in Charles Ltd.

**Exercise 9.12**    **Equity method with pre- and post-acquisition dividends**
On 1 July 20X6, Hoch Ltd acquired 40% of the shares of Scott Ltd for cash $238 000. At this date the shareholders' equity of Scott Ltd was as follows:

| | |
|---|---|
| Issued and paid-up capital | $350 000 |
| Retained profits | 50 000 |
| General reserve | 20 000 |

The assets and liabilities of Scott Ltd were at fair values. There have been no transfers to or from reserves. Profits and dividend payments of Scott Ltd for the next three years were as follows:

| Years ended 30 June (balance dates) | Profit after tax $ | Dividends paid $ |
|---|---|---|
| 20X7 | 130 000 | 40 000 (pre-acquisition) |
| 20X8 | 160 000 | 25 000 (post-acquisition) |
| 20X9 | 150 000 | 60 000 (post-acquisition) |

Goodwill is to be amortised over five years using the straight-line method.

*Required*
1  Prepare equity journal entries to record the investment in Scott Ltd and the receipt of the pre-acquisition dividend.
2  Calculate goodwill on acquisition and, assuming equity accounting is used, the balance of the Investment in Scott Ltd account as it would appear at 30 June 20X9 together with the relevant equity journal entries.

**Exercise 9.13**    **Equity method, asset revaluations, current year's profits**
Carla Ltd acquired 40% of the issued shares of Catherine Ltd for $125 000 on 1 July 20X4. On 1 September 20X4, Catherine Ltd paid the proposed dividend of $30 000 which appeared in its balance sheet at 30 June 20X4. In addition, on 1 February 20X5, the company paid an interim dividend in respect of current profits, amounting to $15 000.
   On 1 July 20X4, land was recorded in the books of Catherine Ltd at fair value. The fair value of the asset has since risen by $20 000 and this increment was recognised and credited to an Asset Revaluation Reserve account by Catherine Ltd on the company's balance date, 30 June 20X5.

As at 30 June 20X5, the following relates to Catherine Ltd:

| | |
|---|---|
| Operating profit before income tax | $75 000 |
| Income tax expense | 28 000 |
| Operating profit | 47 000 |
| Extraordinary items (net of tax) | 3 000 |
| Operating profit and extraordinary items | 50 000 |

*Required*

Prepare equity journal entries to record the above transactions.

**Exercise 9.14**

### Consolidation and equity accounting

On 1 July 20X1, Nick Ltd acquired all the issued shares of Faldo Ltd for $2 000 000. At that date the shareholders' equity of Faldo Ltd was:

| | |
|---|---|
| Paid-up capital | $1 000 000 |
| Retained profits | 890 000 |

All acquired assets were at fair value, and goodwill on acquisition is to be amortised over five years, straight line.

On the same date, Nick Ltd acquired 25% of the issued shares of Zoeller Ltd for $500 000. The shareholders' equity of Zoeller Ltd was:

| | |
|---|---|
| Paid-up capital | $800 000 |
| Retained profits | 250 000 |

The income statements and balance sheets of Nick Ltd, Faldo Ltd and Zoeller Ltd for the year ended 30 June 20X3 were as follows:

| Income Statements for the year ended 30 June 20X3 | | | |
|---|---|---|---|
| | Nick Ltd | Faldo Ltd | Zoeller Ltd |
| | $000 | $000 | $000 |
| Operating profit after tax | 1 250 | 840 | 900 |
| Retained profits 1 July 20X2 | 4 000 | 1 200 | 400 |
| Interim dividend paid | (200) | (150) | (100) |
| Retained profits 30 June 20X3 | 5 050 | 1 890 | 1 200 |

| Balance Sheets at 30 June 20X3 | | | |
|---|---|---|---|
| | Nick Ltd | Faldo Ltd | Zoeller Ltd |
| | $000 | $000 | $000 |
| Paid-up capital | 2 500 | 1 000 | 800 |
| Asset revaluation reserve | 400 | 200 | 100 |
| Retained profits | 5 050 | 1 890 | 1 200 |
| General reserve | 750 | – | 100 |
| | $ 8 700 | $ 3 090 | $ 2 200 |
| Property | 3 250 | 2 000 | 1 000 |
| Plant & equipment | 2 150 | 690 | 1 150 |
| Inventory | 800 | 400 | 50 |
| Investment in Faldo Ltd | 2 000 | – | – |
| Investment in Zoeller Ltd | 500 | – | – |
| | $ 8 700 | $ 3 090 | $ 2 200 |

For the year ended 30 June 20X2, Zoeller Ltd earned an operating profit after tax of $300 000 and paid a dividend of $150 000.

*Required*

1  Prepare consolidation journal entries for Nick Ltd and Faldo Ltd as at 30 June 20X3.
2  Prepare equity accounting journal entries for Nick Ltd and Zoeller Ltd as at 30 June 20X3.
3  Using a worksheet, show the results for the economic group.

**Exercise 9.15**  **Comprehensive under ED 71**

On 1 July 20X7, Major Ltd acquired 25% of the issued shares of Minor Ltd for $3 000 000. At that date the shareholders' equity of Minor Ltd was:

| | |
|---|---|
| Paid-up capital | $5 000 000 |
| Retained profits | 2 000 000 |

The next week Minor Ltd paid a pre-acquisition dividend of 10%. Minor Ltd's results for the following two years were:

| | Operating profit and extraordinary items after tax | Dividends paid |
|---|---|---|
| | $000 | $000 |
| Year ended 30 June 20X8 | 500 | 50 |
| Year ended 30 June 20X9 | 450 | 40 |

Both these dividends were post acquisition.

On 1 July 20X8, Major Ltd acquired 80% of the issued shares of Mitchell Ltd for $18 000 000. At that date the shareholders' equity of Mitchell Ltd was:

| | |
|---|---|
| Paid-up capital | $10 000 000 |
| Reserves | 3 000 000 |
| Retained profits | 5 500 000 |

Immediately after the acquisition, Mitchell Ltd paid a pre-acquisition dividend of 5%. The following transactions occurred during the year ended 30 June 20X9:

(a)  Minor Ltd sold inventory to Major Ltd. The profit component was $20 000 and Major Ltd has half of this inventory on hand at year end.
(b)  Major Ltd sold inventory to Mitchell Ltd. The profit component was $40 000 and Mitchell Ltd has all this inventory on hand at year end.
(c)  Minor Ltd revalued certain assets by $100 000.
(d)  Any goodwill on acquisition is to be amortised over ten years, straight line.
(e)  The tax rate is 40%.

The abridged balance sheets of the three companies for the year ended 30 June 20X9 are as follows:

|  | Major Ltd $000 | Mitchell Ltd $000 | Minor Ltd $000 |
|---|---|---|---|
| Paid-up capital | 38 000 | 10 000 | 5 000 |
| Reserves | 5 000 | 4 000 | 100 |
| Liabilities | 8 500 | 3 500 | 2 000 |
| Retained profits | 10 000 | 6 200 | 2 860 |
|  | $ 61 500 | $ 23 700 | $ 9 960 |
| Property, plant & equipment | 40 275 | 23 300 | 9 860 |
| Inventory | 750 | 400 | 100 |
| Shares in Mitchell Ltd | 17 600 | – | – |
| Shares in Minor Ltd | 2 875 | – | – |
|  | $ 61 500 | $ 23 700 | $ 9 960 |

*Required*

1  Prepare the general journal entries for the above transactions relevant to Major Ltd.
2  Prepare the equity journal entries to account for Minor Ltd's results.
3  Prepare consolidated journal entries for Major Ltd and Mitchell Ltd.
4  Prepare a worksheet (showing the consolidation and equity journal entries) for the economic entity of Major Ltd, Mitchell Ltd and Minor Ltd.

# chapter 10

# introduction

In general terms, a joint venture represents an arrangement between a number of participants who pool resources in a specific project or business undertaking. The distinctive feature is that participants to the joint venture jointly control and manage the project or undertaking for the mutual benefit of all the venture participants.

In practice, joint venture arrangements can be structured in a number of different ways. For example, a joint venture may be an incorporated body or may be unincorporated. This chapter examines the nature of joint venture arrangements in general, with particular reference to the true unincorporated joint venture. A number of specific accounting issues arise due to the nature of such arrangements. These accounting issues are addressed in AASB 1006: Accounting for Interests in Joint Ventures.

# Joint venture arrangements

**joint venture**
**joint control and**
**management**

A joint venture arrangement usually involves a number of participants pooling resources to jointly control and manage a specific project or business undertaking. For a wide variety of reasons, the individual participants in such arrangements have a preference to engage in the project jointly with other parties, rather than undertaking the project alone.

In general terms, a joint venture relationship can be described as 'an arrangement involving the cooperative efforts and utilisation of the resources of two or more separate entities working together to accomplish agreed-upon goals'.[1] The usual distinguishing features of joint ventures are that they involve a small number of participants engaging in a specific project or business undertaking that is carried on

**mutual benefit**
**shared risks**
**and rewards**

for the mutual benefit of all venture participants. The participants share in the risks and rewards of the joint venture undertaking.

The description above refers to joint venture arrangements in a general sense. However, a joint arrangement in practice can be structured in a number of alternative ways. One of the problems in attempting to define joint ventures is that such arrangements can take a variety of forms. For example, a joint undertaking may

**incorporated joint**
**undertaking**
**unincorporated joint**
**undertaking**

be incorporated or unincorporated. If incorporated, the joint arrangement would be structured within a separate company, with the share capital owned by the participating venturers. In such cases, as for investments in shares generally, the participants would account for their individual interest by the cost method. Depending on the degree of control of individual participants, consolidation or equity accounting principles may also be applicable.

An unincorporated joint arrangement may be structured as a trust, a partnership or what may be referred to as a true unincorporated joint venture. If structured as a trust, the arrangement will be established and governed by the provisions of the relevant trust deed. The distinction between a partnership and a true unincorporated joint venture, though, is not quite so clear.

AASB 1006 and AAS 19: Accounting for Interests in Joint Ventures specify accounting requirements applicable to participating venturers in a true unincorporated joint venture.[2] In AASB 1006, para .06, a joint venture is defined as 'an unincorporated contractual association, other than a partnership or trust, between two or more parties to undertake a specific business project in which the "venturers" meet the costs of the project and receive a share of any resulting output'. Hence, this definition specifically distinguishes an unincorporated joint venture from a partnership or trust arrangement. Given the definition, such

**contractual joint**
**venture**
**venturers**

arrangements are sometimes also referred to as contractual joint ventures.

Rather than pursuing a joint venture for joint or collective profitability, the individual joint venture participants, the venturers, receive their proportionate share of any resulting output. This is the key point which distinguishes a joint venture from a partnership. A partnership involves the partners carrying on a business in common with a view to profit. Accordingly, unlike a joint venture, a partnership has the opportunity to earn revenue, incur costs and derive a profit or loss. A venturer in a joint venture receives a proportionate share of the undertaking's output. This output may then be sold, or further processed for ultimate sale, with the profit being derived by the individual venturers rather than the joint venture itself.

Joint ventures are usually formed by the venturers entering into a written agreement, and the legal rights and obligations of the venturers will be determined by the exact terms of the agreement and any other subsequent contractual arrangements. The agreement will typically set out the terms of the joint control over the commercial undertaking, with each venturer usually participating in management without any party having unilateral control. The agreement may provide for appointment of a manager to oversee the day-to-day operations of the joint undertaking.

**unilateral control**

As the joint venture is not a separate legal entity, it cannot own assets or incur liabilities on its own behalf. The venturers usually hold assets jointly in agreed proportions as tenants in common, although some assets may remain the sole property of one venturer but be loaned to the joint venture undertaking. The venturers, in carrying on joint venture activities, may incur liabilities in common. This may involve the venturers being liable jointly, severally, or jointly and severally, depending on the terms of the borrowing or other liability.

Joint venture arrangements are common in such areas as the extractive industries (eg mineral, oil and gas exploration and/or development), real estate developments, long-term construction projects, primary production enterprises, and research and development activities. There are a number of reasons for structuring an individual project as a joint venture arrangement, these being:

- Joint ventures often involve undertakings of considerable size. Individual enterprises can pool their resources and jointly undertake projects that would be beyond the financial and managerial resources of the participants individually. This also enables the achievement of economies of scale.
- Joint ventures often involve speculative projects that face a high degree of risk. Conducting such activities through a joint venture allows the spreading of the risk between the joint venture participants.
- As different enterprises have different resources, skills and areas of expertise, it may be advantageous for these to be pooled in a joint venture. For example, one company may hold a registered patent, a second company may have development and manufacturing skills, and a third company may have surplus funds to invest. These resources could be combined to the mutual advantage of all three participants.
- A joint venture structure may allow the opportunity to invest in foreign countries and penetrate foreign markets. In many countries, individual enterprises may not be able to obtain the necessary clearances unless operations are structured in conjunction with a local enterprise or the host government.
- Joint ventures can be structured flexibly to suit the individual requirements of the different participants.
- Joint venture arrangements can provide taxation advantages for the participants.

The following articles reproduced from the *Australian Financial Review* provide two examples of joint venture undertakings. The first article describes a joint venture for the development of land in England, while the second describes plans for the building of a fibre cement production facility in the Philippines.

# Joint venture is a 'classic' move

**Robert Harley**

For Lend Lease chairman Mr Stuart Hornery the joint venture with Blue Circle Industries in south east England is 'classic Lend Lease'.

Strategically, the venture is part of the planned expansion of Lend Lease Europe, already underway with the $1.5 billion Bluewater shopping centre project and the 50 per cent interest in UK retail park developer Chelverton.

Beyond that, as Mr Hornery said yesterday, 'the BCI joint venture is another step in our strategy of developing long-term partnerships with major companies. Large-scale, complex urban regeneration is a growing market around the world'.

And beyond that again, the investment derives from a pioneering Lend Lease study into cities of the future which, for various reasons, identified Jakarta, Singapore, Bangkok, Shanghai, London, Barcelona and Warsaw as key targets for future investment. But the deal then has to be right. Shanghai, for example, is overheated.

And the deal with BCI — where the land is provided and Lend Lease adds the expertise — is classic. As Mr Hornery said: 'We provide the soft costs and we share profits.'

The key, Mr Hornery says, is 'unlocking value'. BCI's chief executive, Mr Keith Orrell-Jones, said he expected to realise 'full value' from the surplus land through the use of Lend Lease's 'considerable development skills'.

*Australian Financial Review,*
26 September 1996, p. 46

# James Hardie forms Philippines joint venture

**Duncan Craig**

James Hardie Industries Ltd has formed a joint venture with Jardine Davies Inc to build a $50 million fibre cement plant in the Philippines, as it embarks on a substantial investment program aimed at selling fibre cement products throughout Asia.

The company said yesterday construction would start next year on the Philippines fibre cement plant, located south of Manila, which will produce 20 million standard metres a year and be fully operational by mid-1998.

It would manufacture flatsheet, fibre-cement building boards for internal and external lining use.

James Hardie said it wanted to create a long-term fibre cement industry in the Philippines, to replace the traditional use of plywood and gypsum plasterboard.

The executive general manager of James Hardie International, Mr Ken Boundy, said the Manila project represented the first stage of its Asian growth strategy for fibre cement and related products.

Fibre cement has been the biggest success story for the group in the past two years, particularly in the US, and the group is flush with $385 million raised from the sale of its global irrigation business and its building services division.

Mr Boundy said yesterday that 500,000 new houses were built in the Philippines in 1996 and he expected the yearly rate to be between 400,000 and 600,000 in the next 10 years.

Mr Boundy said the Philippines housing sector's reliance on framed construction was ideal for Hardie's fibre cement siding board products, which aimed to capitalise on concerns about durability of plywood and gypsum plasterboard.

'There is current demand for 3 million units in the Philippines which can't be met and the government is trying to bridge the gap,' he said.

Mr Boundy said the new factory would exclusively supply the local housing market within four years.

Hardie could build a second fibre cement plant in Asia within two years if successful with its Asian-wide growth plans, he said.

'The big challenge is to knock off plywood. This Manila joint venture is more about pre-production marketing and the product prices will be more than 20 per cent lower than our US and Australian fibre cement prices.'

Mr Boundy said Hardie also planned to export product to the cladding market in Japan, the commercial facades business throughout South-East Asia, and enter the developer housing market in Indonesia and Malaysia.

'We will be pursuing those projects with a vigour at the start of next year,' he said. These projects would be largely supplied from Hardie's Aust-ralian and US factories.

In Indonesia, Hardie plans to enter the medium-cost tract (row-upon-row) housing market, in which lightweight concrete systems can be assembled quickly to meet growing demand for modern units.

In Japan and China, James Hardie would eventually aim to supply those masonry-based markets with 'building system' products, providing fibre cement products for partition walls and facade structures.

James Hardie owns two-thirds of the Philippines joint venture. Jardine Davies is a Philippines listed subsidiary of Jardine Pacific.

*Australian Financial Review,*
26 November 1996, p. 26

# Accounting issues related to joint ventures

The major accounting issues associated with unincorporated joint ventures relate to (a) accounting requirements for the joint venture itself, and (b) accounting by the venturers for their individual interests in a joint venture.

There are no statutory, professional or other requirements for a joint venture to prepare separate financial statements. The joint venture itself will rarely, if ever, be a reporting entity and will therefore not be required to prepare general purpose financial reports. The venturers will record their interest in respect of the joint venture individually in their own books of account. Nevertheless, a joint venture could keep its own financial records and prepare its own financial statements, and this will often be the case when a manager is appointed to coordinate the joint venture's activities.

With respect to accounting by venturers for their individual interest in a joint venture, the major issue is how such an interest should be recorded and disclosed in the financial statements. Is the nature of the interest similar to that of an investment in company shares, in which the appropriate accounting treatment is the recording of a one-line asset of the nature 'Investment interest in joint venture'? Alternatively, and similarly to a controlling interest in a subsidiary company, is the nature of a joint venture interest such that the underlying assets and liabilities of the joint venture should be consolidated into the individual venturers' financial statements? The issue of accounting by venturers for interests in joint ventures is addressed by AASB 1006. These provisions will be explained following a discussion of accounting by joint ventures.

# Accounting by the joint venture

As noted above, there are no statutory, professional or other provisions requiring joint ventures to prepare separate financial statements. Individual venturers will independently account for their interest in a joint venture in their own accounting records. Nevertheless, financial records and financial statements could be prepared for a joint venture, and this section outlines the broad principles underlying such preparation.

Assume that A Ltd, B Ltd and C Ltd enter into a joint venture agreement on 1 July 20X0 for the purpose of mining certain mineral deposits. To commence the project, A Ltd contributes $1 000 000 cash, B Ltd contributes $600 000, and C Ltd contributes $400 000, giving the venturers proportionate interests of 50%, 30% and 20% respectively. During the year, plant and equipment is purchased and the venture commences mining operations, incurring various expenses which are capitalised into work in progress and finished goods.

At 30 June 20X1, the balance sheet of the joint venture appears as below. This assumes that any inventory of finished goods has not been distributed to the venturers at balance date. A profit and loss statement is not required as (a) all operating costs have been capitalised into work in progress and finished goods inventory, and (b) the purpose of the joint venture is not to produce a profit but to mine mineral deposits for distribution to the venturers.

**ABC Joint Venture**
**Balance Sheet as at 30 June 20X1**

| | $000 | $000 |
|---|---|---|
| *Assets* | | |
| Current assets | | |
| Cash at bank | 50 | |
| Finished goods inventory | 500 | |
| Work in progress | 1 050 | 1 600 |
| Non-current assets | | |
| Plant & equipment | | 1 000 |
| *Total assets* | | 2 600 |
| *Liabilities* | | |
| Current liabilities | | |
| Creditors & borrowings | | 600 |
| *Net assets* | | $2 000 |
| | | |
| *Venturers' interests* | | |
| A Ltd – Contributions | | 1 000 |
| B Ltd – Contributions | | 600 |
| C Ltd – Contributions | | 400 |
| *Total venturers' interests* | | $2 000 |

If the finished goods inventory of $500 000 had been distributed to the venturers at the end of the financial year, the total and net assets of the joint venture would decrease by $500 000. The 'Venturers' interests' section of the balance sheet would then appear as below.

| | | $000 | $000 |
|---|---|---|---|
| *Venturers' interests* | | | |
| A Ltd | – Contributions | 1 000 | |
| | – Finished goods distributed | (250) | 750 |
| | | | |
| B Ltd | – Contributions | 600 | |
| | – Finished goods distributed | (150) | 450 |
| | | | |
| C Ltd | – Contributions | 400 | |
| | – Finished goods distributed | (100) | 300 |
| | *Total venturers' interests* | | $1 500 |

As there are no statutory or other regulations for the preparation of financial statements by the joint venture, various alternative accounting treatments to that illustrated above are possible. For example, depreciation on plant and equipment has not been charged. Also, it may be decided to recognise some tax-deductible operating expenses immediately rather than capitalise them into work in progress. Assuming plant and equipment is depreciated at 10% per annum straight-line and operating expenses of $200 000 are to be immediately expensed rather than capitalised, the balance sheet of the joint venture would appear as below.

**ABC Joint Venture**
**Balance Sheet as at 30 June 20X1**

|  | $000 | $000 |
|---|---:|---:|
| *Assets* | | |
| Current assets | | |
|   Cash at bank | 50 | |
|   Work in progress | 850 | 900 |
| Non-current assets | | |
|   Plant & equipment | 1 000 | |
|   *Less* Accumulated depreciation | (100) | 900 |
|     Total assets | | 1 800 |
| *Liabilities* | | |
| Current liabilities | | |
|   Creditors & borrowings | | 600 |
|   Net assets | | $1 200 |
| | | |
| *Venturers' interests* | | |
| A Ltd  – Contributions | 1 000 | |
|     – Finished goods distributed | (250) | |
|     – Share of depreciation expense | (50) | |
|     – Share of operating expenses | (100) | 600 |
| | | |
| B Ltd  – Contributions | 600 | |
|     – Finished goods distributed | (150) | |
|     – Share of depreciation expense | (30) | |
|     – Share of operating expenses | (60) | 360 |
| | | |
| C Ltd  – Contributions | 400 | |
|     – Finished goods distributed | (100) | |
|     – Share of depreciation expense | (20) | |
|     – Share of operating expenses | (40) | 240 |
|     Total venturers' interests | | $1 200 |

# Accounting by the venturers

## RECORDING OF INTERESTS IN JOINT VENTURES

### One-line method

In the ABC joint venture balance sheet as at 30 June 20X0, presented in the previous section, the venturers' interests — contributions for A Ltd, B Ltd and C Ltd were $1 000 000, $600 000 and $400 000 respectively. In originally contributing these cash amounts, the following accounting entries, shown in general journal format, would have been raised by the venturers in their own books of account.

|  | A Ltd | | B Ltd | | C Ltd | |
|---|---|---|---|---|---|---|
|  | Debit | Credit | Debit | Credit | Debit | Credit |
| Interest in Joint Venture | 1 000 000 | | 600 000 | | 400 000 | |
| Cash at Bank | | 1 000 000 | | 600 000 | | 400 000 |
| (cash contributed to joint venture) | | | | | | |

To account for the finished goods distributed to venturers and the share of depreciation and operating expenses for the year (refer to the second ABC joint venture balance sheet as at 30 June 20X1 presented in the previous section), the venturers would raise the following entries in their own books of account.

|  | A Ltd | | B Ltd | | C Ltd | |
|---|---|---|---|---|---|---|
|  | Debit | Credit | Debit | Credit | Debit | Credit |
| Finished Goods | 250 000 | | 150 000 | | 100 000 | |
| Depreciation Expense (JV)* | 50 000 | | 30 000 | | 20 000 | |
| Operating Expenses (JV)* | 100 000 | | 60 000 | | 40 000 | |
| Interest in Joint Venture | | 400 000 | | 240 000 | | 160 000 |
| (joint venture transactions) | | | | | | |

* For purposes of clarity, any accounts representing expenses or other items of the joint venture itself are followed by the notation (JV). In the example above, this is not applicable to the finished goods as these are not held by the joint venture but have been distributed to the venturers.

Corresponding with the ABC joint venture balance sheet as at 30 June 20X1, the Interest in Joint Venture account balances in the books of A Ltd, B Ltd and C Ltd would amount to $600 000, $360 000 and $240 000 respectively following posting of the above entries. In the absence of any further journal entries, the account Interest in Joint Venture would be disclosed as an asset in the venturers' balance sheets. This method of accounting by venturers for their interests in joint ventures is referred to as the one-line method. However, without further disclosures, this method does not provide full information on the proportionate interest in assets owned, and liabilities incurred, by the venturers in consequence of participation in the joint venture. For this reason, the one-line method is not permitted by AASB 1006. It is considered that this method overlooks the fact that 'the joint venture involves direct ownership of assets and direct incurrence of liabilities by the venturer' (AAS 19, para 12).

**one-line method**

## Line-by-line method

AASB 1006, para .10 requires a venturer's interests in joint ventures to be brought to account by including, in the respective financial statement classification categories, the following:

- the venturer's share in each of the individual assets employed in the joint ventures;
- liabilities incurred by the venturer in relation to joint ventures, including the venturer's share of any liabilities for which the venturer is jointly, severally, or jointly and severally liable; and
- the venturer's share of expenses incurred by the venturers in relation to joint ventures.

**line-by-line method**

This method of accounting for interests in joint ventures is referred to as the line-by-line method, as the venturer's proportionate share in each of the assets, liabilities and expenses of the joint venture is included within the venturer's financial

**pro-rata or proportionate consolidation** statements on a line-by-line basis. This method is also referred to as pro-rata or proportionate consolidation. However, these terms are deliberately not used here as they may cause confusion through use of the term 'consolidation', implying control, which is not applicable in a joint venture situation.

Proponents of the line-by-line method 'argue that it reflects both the nature and legal status of a joint venture in that it is the venturers that directly own the assets and incur the liabilities' (AAS 19, para 10). The method's advantage is that it provides a more complete picture of the operations, resources and obligations of the entity and more information on the risks faced by the entity. However, a potential disadvantage is that, in the absence of further disclosures, it could mislead financial statement users by conveying a view that the proportions of joint venture assets and liabilities recognised are under the direct and absolute control of the venturer.

To recognise, in accordance with the line-by-line method, the assets and liabilities of the ABC joint venture in the earlier example, the following additional journal entries in the venturers' books would be required. After posting of these entries, the venturers' Interest in Joint Ventures accounts will be closed off and their proportionate share of joint venture assets and liabilities will be recognised in the financial statements.

| | A Ltd | | B Ltd | | C Ltd | |
|---|---|---|---|---|---|---|
| | Debit | Credit | Debit | Credit | Debit | Credit |
| Cash at Bank (JV) | 25 000 | | 15 000 | | 10 000 | |
| Work in Progress (JV) | 425 000 | | 255 000 | | 170 000 | |
| Plant & Equipment (JV) | 500 000 | | 300 000 | | 200 000 | |
| Accum. Depreciation (JV) | | 50 000 | | 30 000 | | 20 000 |
| Creditors & Borrowings (JV) | | 300 000 | | 180 000 | | 120 000 |
| Interest in Joint Venture | | 600 000 | | 360 000 | | 240 000 |
| (joint venture assets and liabilities) | | | | | | |

An issue which arises is whether the substitution entry recording the venturer's proportionate share of joint venture assets and liabilities should be made in the actual books of the venturer or in a consolidation-type worksheet. AASB 1006, para .10 requires a venturer's interests in a joint venture to be 'brought to account' in accordance with the line-by-line method. This presumably allows either recording method. The journal entries illustrated in this chapter assume posting in the actual books of the venturer. However, the broad principles, and in many cases the actual entries themselves, are identical if a consolidation-type worksheet is used.

## ILLUSTRATIVE EXAMPLE  10.1

## LINE-BY-LINE METHOD

D Ltd and E Ltd enter into a joint venture agreement involving cooperative development of a potential new product for the computer industry. This development represents an extension of earlier research work carried out by each of the venturers individually. Rather than separately continue in competition with each other, the venturers have decided that it will be to their mutual advantage to combine their efforts. Each venturer contributes $250 000 cash to commence joint venture operations on 1 July 20X1. As the initial development work carried out by the joint venture yields promising results, a further $350 000 cash is contributed by each of the venturers on 1 February 20X2. At 30 June 20X2, the balance sheet of the joint venture appears as on the following page.

**D & E Joint Venture**
**Balance Sheet as at 30 June 20X2**

|  | $000 | $000 |
|---|---|---|
| *Assets* | | |
| Current assets | | |
| Cash at bank | 40 | |
| Investments | 140 | 180 |
| Non-current assets | | |
| Plant & equipment | 500 | |
| Development costs* | 670 | 1 170 |
| Total assets | | 1 350 |
| *Liabilities* | | |
| Current liabilities | | |
| Creditors & borrowings | 100 | |
| Provisions | 50 | 150 |
| Net assets | | $1 200 |
| | | |
| *Venturers' interests* | | |
| D Ltd – Contributions | | 600 |
| E Ltd – Contributions | | 600 |
| Total venturers' interests | | $1 200 |

\* It is assumed that these capitalised development costs satisfy the recognition criteria specified in AASB 1011: Accounting for Research and Development.

To recognise the venturers' contributions of $250 000 and $350 000 on 1 July 20X1 and 1 February 20X2 respectively, D Ltd and E Ltd would each record the following journal entries.

|  | Debit | Credit |
|---|---|---|
|  | $ | $ |
| Interest in Joint Venture | 250 000 | |
| Cash at Bank | | 250 000 |
| (cash contributed to joint venture) | | |
| | | |
| Interest in Joint Venture | 350 000 | |
| Cash at Bank | | 350 000 |
| (cash contributed to joint venture) | | |

To recognise the assets and liabilities of the D & E joint venture at 30 June 20X2 in accordance with AASB 1006, each venturer would record the following journal entry.

|  | Debit | Credit |
|---|---|---|
|  | $ | $ |
| Cash at Bank (JV) | 20 000 | |
| Investments (JV) | 70 000 | |
| Plant & Equipment (JV) | 250 000 | |
| Development Costs (JV) | 335 000 | |
| Creditors & Borrowings (JV) | | 50 000 |
| Provisions (JV) | | 25 000 |
| Interest in Joint Venture | | 600 000 |
| (joint venture assets and liabilities) | | |

### Arguments for and against the alternative methods

Some of the advantages and disadvantages of the alternative approaches to accounting for interests in joint ventures have been introduced in the preceding sections. The purpose of this section is to analyse the alternative methods in more detail.

*One-line method*

The major arguments in support of the one-line method are:

- A separate line item in the balance sheet, entitled 'Interest in joint venture' or similar, makes financial statement readers aware that the company has an interest in a joint venture. This signifies that the company has entered into arrangements with other entities to commit resources to a project over which the venturers individually do not have absolute control, and hence that these resources will not be available for other areas of the venturer's operations.[3]
- The one-line method may more accurately reflect the effective nature of the joint venture arrangement, in that each venturer's interest represents an aggregate interest in the total assets of the venture less any joint and separate liabilities incurred in connection with the venture. Hence, the interest is portrayed under the one-line method as a separate asset in the same way as for other investments.[4]

The major arguments against this method can be summarised as:

- Information is lost through aggregation of the joint venture interest into a single line item.[5]
- Any joint and separate liabilities incurred in connection with the joint venture may be netted off against the venturer's share of assets employed in the venture. In this way, 'it is possible to avoid presenting these liabilities as such in the balance sheet' (AAS 19, para 12).
- The one-line method does not reflect the fact that a joint venture involves the direct ownership of assets and the direct incurrence of liabilities by the venturers (AAS 19, para 12).

*Line-by-line method*

The major arguments supporting use of the line-by-line method are:

- This method reflects the nature and legal status of a joint venture. The venturers directly own the assets and incur the liabilities, and the method reflects this by recording the venturer's share of each of the individual assets employed and any liabilities incurred (AAS 19, para 10).
- It seems appropriate for each venturer to record its proportionate share of joint venture assets and include them with other similar assets that it owns, and likewise for liabilities.[6]

The major arguments against use of the line-by-line method are:

- Since control of the assets employed in joint ventures is shared with other participants, it would be misleading to include a share of those assets with other assets of the venturer (AAS 19, para 12).
- The line-by-line method can completely hide the existence of joint ventures in the absence of further disclosures.[7]

As already noted, AASB 1006 supports the line-by-line method. However, to address the arguments listed above against use of the method, various disclosures are required in the venturer's financial statements to highlight the existence of joint venture arrangements. These disclosure provisions are discussed later in this chapter.

## CONTRIBUTIONS OTHER THAN CASH

A venturer may contribute assets other than cash to a joint venture undertaking. AAS 19 requires a venturer's contribution to a joint venture, and any subsequent transfers of assets, to be viewed as transactions between the venturer and the other venturers (para 13). Implicit in this is the assumption that such transactions are at arm's length. The major implication is that, when a venturer contributes non-monetary assets to a joint venture, the transaction should be accounted for as a sale by the venturer to the other venturers of the relevant proportion of the asset. This requires the recognition of any profit or loss on sale of that proportion of the asset sold.

For example, assume that F Ltd and G Ltd enter into a joint venture agreement on 1 January 20X1 for the development of property. Each venturer has a 50% interest in the joint venture. To commence the development, F Ltd contributes $500 000 cash, while G Ltd contributes the land to be developed. This land, which has a current fair value of $500 000, had originally been purchased by G Ltd for $400 000. The joint venture agreement provides for the land to be held jointly by the venturers as tenants in common. The balance sheet of the joint venture at inception would appear as follows:

**F & G Joint Venture**
**Balance Sheet as at 1 January 20X1**

|  | $000 |
|---|---|
| *Assets* | |
| Current assets | |
| Cash at bank | 500 |
| Non-current assets | |
| Land | 500 |
| *Total assets* | 1 000 |
| *Liabilities* | |
| Current liabilities | – |
| *Net assets* | $1 000 |
| | |
| *Venturers' interests* | |
| F Ltd – Contributions | 500 |
| G Ltd – Contributions | 500 |
| *Total venturers' interests* | $1 000 |

To record its interest in the joint venture at 1 January 20X1, F Ltd would post the following journal entries.

| | Debit | Credit |
|---|---|---|
| Interest in Joint Venture | 500 000 | |
|   Cash at Bank | | 500 000 |
| (cash contributed to joint venture) | | |
| | | |
| Cash at Bank (JV) | 250 000 | |
| Land (JV) | 250 000 | |
|   Interest in Joint Venture | | 500 000 |
| (joint venture assets) | | |

In recording its interest in the joint venture, G Ltd must recognise the profit on the sale of the proportion of land sold to F Ltd. G Ltd has effectively sold a one-half interest in the land for $250 000, this one-half interest having an original cost of $200 000. Hence, G Ltd must record a profit on sale of the land amounting to $50 000. To recognise this profit and its interest in the joint venture, G Ltd would record the following journal entry.

| | Debit | Credit |
|---|---|---|
| Interest in Joint Venture | 250 000 | |
|   Land | | 200 000 |
|   Profit on Sale of Land | | 50 000 |
| (asset contributed to joint venture) | | |
| | | |
| Cash at Bank (JV) | 250 000 | |
|   Interest in Joint Venture | | 250 000 |
| (joint venture asset) | | |

After posting the above entries, G Ltd's accounts would reflect the company's 50% interest in the joint venture's cash balance. Also, as the sale of one-half of the land has been recorded, G Ltd's accounts would still reflect its ownership interest in the remaining one-half. In accordance with AASB 1010: Accounting for the Revaluation of Non-current Assets, the following journal entry could be recorded by G Ltd to revalue this remaining interest in the land to fair value.

| | Debit | Credit |
|---|---|---|
| Land (JV) | 50 000 | |
|   Asset Revaluation Reserve | | 50 000 |
| (revaluation of land) | | |

Following posting of this journal entry, G Ltd's ledger account for land, with a closing balance of $250 000, would appear as below. In accordance with AASB 1006 and the requirement for the line-by-line method of accounting for interests in joint ventures, it can be seen that G Ltd's financial statements reflect the company's 50% interest in the assets (cash and land) of the F & G joint venture.

| | | Debit $ | Credit $ | Balance $ |
|---|---|---|---|---|
| | **Land** | | | |
| Jan 1 | Opening Balance | | | 400 000 Dr |
| | Sale of Land | | 200 000 | 200 000 Dr |
| | Asset Revaluation Reserve | 50 000 | | 250 000 Dr |

ILLUSTRATIVE EXAMPLE **10.2**

# CONTRIBUTIONS OTHER THAN CASH

H Ltd, I Ltd and J Ltd enter into a joint venture agreement on 1 January 20X2. Each venturer has a one-third interest in the venture. To commence the development, H Ltd contributes $300 000 cash, I Ltd contributes patents having a fair value of $300 000 (original cost $150 000), and J Ltd contributes land having a fair value of $300 000 (original cost $210 000). In addition, the venturers jointly borrow a further $120 000 which is deposited in the joint venture's bank account. The balance sheet of the joint venture at inception would appear as follows:

| HIJ Joint Venture Balance Sheet as at 1 January 20X2 | | |
|---|---|---|
| | $000 | $000 |
| *Assets* | | |
| Current assets | | |
| Cash at bank | | 420 |
| Non-current assets | | |
| Land | 300 | |
| Patents | 300 | 600 |
| Total assets | | 1 020 |
| *Liabilities* | | |
| Non-current liabilities | | |
| Borrowings | | 120 |
| Net assets | | $900 |
| | | |
| *Venturers' interests* | | |
| H Ltd  – Contributions | | 300 |
| I Ltd  – Contributions | | 300 |
| J Ltd  – Contributions | | 300 |
| Total venturers' interests | | $900 |

To record its interest in the joint venture at 1 January 20X2, H Ltd would post the following journal entries.

| | Debit | Credit |
|---|---|---|
| | $ | $ |
| Interest in Joint Venture | 300 000 | |
| Cash at Bank | | 300 000 |
| (cash contributed to joint venture) | | |
| | | |
| Cash at Bank (JV) | 140 000 | |
| Land (JV) | 100 000 | |
| Patents (JV) | 100 000 | |
| Borrowings (JV) | | 40 000 |
| Interest in Joint Venture | | 300 000 |
| (joint venture assets and liabilities) | | |

I Ltd must recognise the profit on the sale of the two-thirds proportion of patents sold to H Ltd and J Ltd. Original cost of this two-thirds interest was $100 000 and sale consideration amounts to $200 000. Accordingly, the profit on sale amounts to $100 000. To recognise this profit and its interest in the joint venture, and to revalue to fair value its remaining one-third interest in the patents, I Ltd would record the following journal entries.

| | Debit $ | Credit $ |
|---|---|---|
| Interest in Joint Venture | 200 000 | |
| Patents | | 100 000 |
| Profit on Sale of Patents | | 100 000 |
| (asset contributed to joint venture) | | |
| Cash at Bank (JV) | 140 000 | |
| Land (JV) | 100 000 | |
| Borrowings (JV) | | 40 000 |
| Interest in Joint Venture | | 200 000 |
| (joint venture assets and liabilities) | | |
| Patents (JV) | 50 000 | |
| Asset Revaluation Reserve | | 50 000 |
| (revaluation of patents) | | |

Following posting of these journal entries, I Ltd's ledger account for patents would appear as below, the closing balance reflecting the company's one-third interest.

| | | Debit $ | Credit $ | Balance $ |
|---|---|---|---|---|
| | **Patents** | | | |
| Jan 1 | Opening Balance | | | 150 000 Dr |
| | Sale of Patents | | 100 000 | 50 000 Dr |
| | Asset Revaluation Reserve | 50 000 | | 100 000 Dr |

Similarly to the situation with I Ltd, J Ltd must recognise the profit on sale of the two-thirds proportion of land. Original cost of this two-thirds interest was $140 000 and sale consideration amounts to $200 000. Accordingly, the profit on sale amounts to $60 000. To recognise this profit and its interest in the joint venture, and to revalue to fair value its remaining one-third interest in the land, J Ltd would record the following journal entries.

| | Debit $ | Credit $ |
|---|---|---|
| Interest in Joint Venture | 200 000 | |
| Land | | 140 000 |
| Profit on Sale of Land | | 60 000 |
| (asset contributed to joint venture) | | |
| Cash at Bank (JV) | 140 000 | |
| Patents (JV) | 100 000 | |
| Borrowings (JV) | | 40 000 |
| Interest in Joint Venture | | 200 000 |
| (joint venture assets and liabilities) | | |
| Land (JV) | 30 000 | |
| Asset Revaluation Reserve | | 30 000 |
| (revaluation of land) | | |

Following posting of these journal entries, J Ltd's ledger account for land would appear as below.

| | Debit | Credit | Balance |
|---|---|---|---|
| | $ | $ | $ |
| **Land** | | | |
| Jan 1   Opening Balance | | | 210 000 Dr |
| Sale of Land | | 140 000 | 70 000 Dr |
| Asset Revaluation Reserve | 30 000 | | 100 000 Dr |

## CHANGES IN PROPORTIONATE INTERESTS

Subsequent to the establishment of a joint venture arrangement, the venturers may choose to vary their proportionate interests in the venture. Such changes can occur for a variety of reasons. For example, one venturer may sell all or a part of their interest to another venturer or a number of other venturers. Alternatively, a requirement for additional funds or other assets may be facilitated by an additional contribution from only one of the existing venturers or by the admission of an additional venture participant.

*restructuring*     These types of alterations represent a restructuring of the joint venture by means of commercial negotiation and settlement, and involve the transfer of rights and obligations between the contracting parties. In the course of negotiation, the participants will consider the worth of the net assets of the joint venture. Accounting for such restructuring will therefore involve consideration of the fair value of the assets exchanged and any resulting goodwill or discount on acquisition. This is illustrated in the following examples.

### Sale between existing venturers

The balance sheet below depicts a joint venture between K Ltd and L Ltd, with each venturer having a 50% interest.

| K & L Joint Venture<br>Balance Sheet as at 1 January 20X1 | | |
|---|---|---|
| | $000 | $000 |
| *Assets* | | |
| Current assets | | |
|     Inventories | | 600 |
| Non-current assets | | |
|     Property, plant & equipment | 1 800 | |
|     Patents | 300 | 2 100 |
|      *Total assets* | | 2 700 |
| *Liabilities* | | |
| Current liabilities | | |
|     Creditors & borrowings | | 300 |
|     *Net assets* | | $2 400 |
| *Venturers' interests* | | |
| K Ltd – Contributions | | 1 200 |
| L Ltd – Contributions | | 1 200 |
|     *Total venturers' interests* | | $2 400 |

Assume that K Ltd sells one-half of its 50% interest to L Ltd for $700 000 cash. After this transaction, the proportionate interests of K Ltd and L Ltd will amount to 25% and 75% respectively.

As a result of this market transaction, 25% of the joint venture has been valued at $700 000. The total market value of the joint venture (ie venturers' interests) can therefore be extrapolated as amounting to $2 800 000 (ie $700 000 / .25). As the total book value of the venturers' interests amounts to $2 400 000, and assuming that the book value of assets is equal to their fair value, this implies the existence of joint venture goodwill amounting to $400 000.

From the point of view of the books of the joint venture itself, the only necessary change would be to recognise K Ltd's interest in the joint venture as amounting to $600 000 after the sale (ie 25% of $2 400 000) and L Ltd's interest as amounting to $1 800 000 (ie 75% of $2 400 000). If the joint venture was also to recognise the goodwill in its own internal accounts, the interests of K Ltd and L Ltd would amount to $700 000 and $2 100 000 respectively.

In its own books, K Ltd would recognise a gain on the sale of the 25% interest amounting to $100 000. That is, its 25% interest, with a book value of $600 000, has been sold for $700 000. To recognise this gain on sale and to record the reduction in its interest in the assets and liabilities of the joint venture, K Ltd would record the following journal entry. This entry assumes that K's accounts already reflect the company's original 50% share of joint venture assets and liabilities in accordance with the line-by-line method.

| | Debit | Credit |
|---|---|---|
| Cash at Bank (sale proceeds) | 700 000 | |
| Creditors & Borrowings (JV) | 75 000 | |
| Inventories (JV) | | 150 000 |
| Property, Plant & Equipment (JV) | | 450 000 |
| Patents (JV) | | 75 000 |
| Gain on Sale | | 100 000 |
| (sale of interest in joint venture) | | |

From L Ltd's point of view, it has acquired net assets with a fair value of $600 000 for consideration of $700 000, implying goodwill on acquisition of $100 000. To record the increase in its interest in the joint venture and recognise this goodwill, L Ltd would record the following journal entries.

| | Debit | Credit |
|---|---|---|
| Interest in Joint Venture | 700 000 | |
| Cash at Bank (purchase consideration) | | 700 000 |
| (additional interest in joint venture) | | |
| | | |
| Inventories (JV) | 150 000 | |
| Property, Plant & Equipment (JV) | 450 000 | |
| Patents (JV) | 75 000 | |
| Goodwill (JV) | 100 000 | |
| Creditors & Borrowings(JV) | | 75 000 |
| Interest in Joint Venture | | 700 000 |
| (increase in joint venture assets and liabilities) | | |

The above entry records the goodwill on acquisition implicit in the acquisition by L Ltd of the 25% interest in the joint venture, and is in accordance with AASB 1015: Accounting for the Acquisition of Assets. This also theoretically means that goodwill is implicit in the remaining 75% interests (ie L Ltd's further 50% interest and K Ltd's 25% interest). As noted earlier in this example, the sale between the venturers implied the existence of total joint venture goodwill of $400 000. However, only $100 000 of this goodwill has been recognised in the individual venturers' accounts, this being the amount recorded in L Ltd's acquisition of the 25% interest from K Ltd. The additional $300 000 goodwill is implicit in L Ltd's further 50% interest and K Ltd's 25% interest. However, the recognition of this $300 000 of goodwill in the individual venturers' accounts is probably not allowed by AASB 1013: Accounting for Goodwill, as it has not resulted from an acquisition transaction and would equate to recognising internally generated goodwill. An alternative argument is that such recognition may be possible if the view is accepted that the old joint venture ceases to exist and a new joint venture is formed on the sale of the interest between the venturers. This view would be dependent on the exact terms of the agreement between the parties to the joint venture. In the present case, the view is taken that the sale of the interest between the venturers has not resulted in formation of a new joint venture.

## Introduction of a new venturer

Assume for the K & L joint venture illustrated in the previous example (and as depicted in the original balance sheet as at 1 January 20X1) that a new venturer enters the joint venture on 2 January 20X1. To provide further funds to facilitate planned expansion, the new venturer, M Ltd, contributes $1 200 000 cash in return for a one-third interest. It is assumed in this example that the book value of the joint venture assets represents their fair value.

Immediately after the entry of M Ltd, and based on the fact that a one-third interest has been valued at $1 200 000, the total worth of the joint venture can be valued at $3 600 000. This can be illustrated by recasting the balance sheet of the joint venture immediately after the entry of M Ltd to reflect M's contribution.

| KLM Joint Venture<br>Balance Sheet as at 2 January 20X1 | | |
|---|---|---|
| | $000 | $000 |
| *Assets* | | |
| Current assets | | |
| Cash at bank | 1 200 | |
| Inventories | 600 | 1 800 |
| Non-current assets | | |
| Property, plant & equipment | 1 800 | |
| Patents | 300 | 2 100 |
| *Total assets* | | 3 900 |
| *Liabilities* | | |
| Current liabilities | | |
| Creditors & borrowings | | 300 |
| *Net assets* | | $3 600 |

| | $000 | $000 |
|---|---|---|
| *Venturers' interests* | | |
| K Ltd – Contributions | | 1 200 |
| L Ltd – Contributions | | 1 200 |
| M Ltd – Contributions | | 1 200 |
| Total venturers' interests | | $3 600 |

To recognise its contribution to, and proportionate interest in, the joint venture, M Ltd would record the following journal entries.

| | Debit | Credit |
|---|---|---|
| Interest in Joint Venture | 1 200 000 | |
| Cash at Bank | | 1 200 000 |
| (cash contributed to joint venture) | | |
| | | |
| Cash (JV) | 400 000 | |
| Inventories (JV) | 200 000 | |
| Property, Plant & Equipment (JV) | 600 000 | |
| Patents (JV) | 100 000 | |
| Creditors & Borrowings (JV) | | 100 000 |
| Interest in Joint Venture | | 1 200 000 |
| (joint venture assets and liabilities) | | |

With respect to K Ltd and L Ltd, the table below illustrates their interests in the assets and liabilities of the joint venture before and after the admission of M Ltd.

| | Before (1/2 interest) | After (1/3 interest) | Difference |
|---|---|---|---|
| | $ | $ | $ |
| Cash | – | 400 000 | 400 000 (Dr) |
| Inventories | 300 000 | 200 000 | 100 000 (Cr) |
| Property, plant & equipment | 900 000 | 600 000 | 300 000 (Cr) |
| Patents | 150 000 | 100 000 | 50 000 (Cr) |
| Creditors & borrowings | (150 000) | (100 000) | 50 000 (Dr) |
| Venturer's interest | $1 200 000 | $1 200 000 | – |

To recognise the restructure, K Ltd and L Ltd would each record the following journal entry in their own accounts. The entry assumes that each of the individual companies' accounts already reflect the original 50% share of joint venture assets and liabilities in accordance with the line-by-line method.

| | Debit | Credit |
|---|---|---|
| Cash (JV) | 400 000 | |
| Creditors & Borrowings (JV) | 50 000 | |
| Inventories (JV) | | 100 000 |
| Property, Plant & Equipment (JV) | | 300 000 |
| Patents (JV) | | 50 000 |
| (restructure of joint venture) | | |

## JOINT VENTURE DISCLOSURE REQUIREMENTS

It was noted earlier in this chapter that a potential disadvantage of the line-by-line method is that it could mislead financial statement users by conveying a view that the proportions of joint venture assets and liabilities recognised are under the direct and absolute control of the venturer. Also, as the proportionate shares of joint venture assets, liabilities and expenses are aggregated with the entity's other financial statement items, it may be impossible to ascertain which items are subject to joint venture arrangements. Accordingly, various disclosures are required in the venturer's financial statements to highlight the existence of joint venture arrangements.

AASB 1006, para .20 requires disclosure of, if material, the venturer's share of the assets employed in joint ventures. This is to be shown in aggregate for all interests in joint ventures, and must be categorised as current or non-current and shown by class of asset within those categories. It is interesting to note that AASB 1006 does not require similar disclosure of the venturer's share of liabilities applicable to joint ventures although, of course, these liabilities will be aggregated with other liabilities in the venturer's balance sheet under the line-by-line method.

Also to be disclosed in aggregate for all interests in joint ventures are any contingent liabilities and capital expenditure commitments of the venturer, where these are material (AASB 1006, para .22).

The standard also requires disclosure of the following information in respect of a material interest in each joint venture:
- identification of the joint venture;
- a description of the principal activities of the joint venture; and
- the venturer's percentage interest in the output of the joint venture in the financial year. (AASB 1006, para .21)

## Review

The material in this chapter has provided a broad overview of the accounting principles applicable to unincorporated joint ventures, with particular reference to accounting standard AASB 1006. The chapter concentrated on accounting issues facing joint ventures and individual venturers, with particular reference to accounting principles for the recording of interests in joint ventures by venturers.

## Endnotes

1  JM Morris, *Joint Ventures: An Accounting, Tax, and Administrative Guide* (New York: John Wiley & Sons, 1987), p 1.

2  The accounting requirements specified in AASB 1006 and AAS 19 are essentially identical. However, AAS 19 provides a greater level of explanatory detail regarding the characteristics of unincorporated joint ventures and methods of accounting for interests in unincorporated joint ventures. References to AAS 19, rather than AASB 1006, are only provided in this chapter where there are no equivalent sections in the AASB standard.

3 PH Eddey, *Accounting for Interests in Joint Arrangements* (Discussion Paper No. 9, Australian Accounting Research Foundation, Melbourne, 1985), p 38.

4 ibid.

5 op cit., p 39.

6 op cit., p 35.

7 op cit., p 36.

## KEY TERMS

| | | |
|---|---|---|
| contractual joint venture | line-by-line method | shared risks and rewards |
| incorporated joint undertaking | mutual benefit | unilateral control |
| joint control and management | one-line method | unincorporated joint undertaking |
| joint venture | pro rata or proportionate consolidation | venturers |
| | restructuring | |

## REVIEW QUESTIONS

**10.1** Distinguish between an unincorporated joint venture to which AASB 1006 applies and other forms of joint arrangements.

**10.2** What are the advantages of structuring an undertaking as a joint venture?

**10.3** What are the disadvantages of structuring an undertaking as a joint venture?

**10.4** How may a joint venture hold assets and raise borrowings?

**10.5** What are the accounting issues and problems facing joint ventures?

**10.6** If a joint venture manager maintains the accounting records for a joint venture, what are generally the main records, calculations and reports required?

**10.7** Distinguish between the one-line method and the line-by-line method of accounting for interests in joint ventures. What are the advantages and disadvantages of each method? Which method is required by AASB 1006?

**10.8** What are the major accounting implications of a joint venturer contributing assets other than cash to a joint venture?

**10.9** Give examples of the types of events which can cause a change in proportionate interests in a joint venture. What are the major accounting implications?

**10.10** Summarise the disclosure requirements for joint ventures specified in AASB 1006.

# EXERCISES

**Exercise 10.11** **Joint venture balance sheet**
A Ltd and B Ltd enter into a joint venture agreement on 1 July 20X0 and commence operations by each contributing cash of $500 000 to the venture. Land and buildings (cost $350 000) and plant and equipment (cost $300 000) are purchased during the year (paid for from the joint venture's cash balances). Cash outlays of $300 000, comprising costs of production, were incurred by the joint venture during the financial year. Of these costs, 50% have been capitalised into work in progress and 50% into finished goods on hand.

*Required*
Prepare the balance sheet for the joint venture as at 30 June 20X1, assuming that no depreciation is to be charged on buildings or plant and equipment.

**Exercise 10.12** **Joint venture balance sheet**
For the joint venture between A Ltd and B Ltd outlined in Exercise 10.11 above, assume that the finished goods have been distributed to the venturers at balance date and that depreciation is to be charged, on a straight-line basis, in the joint venture's accounts. Assume that buildings, having a cost of $200 000, are to be depreciated at 1% per annum and that plant and equipment is to be depreciated at 10% per annum.

*Required*
Prepare the balance sheet for the joint venture as at 30 June 20X1 under the above assumptions.

**Exercise 10.13** **Recording of interest in joint venture**
Refer to Exercise 10.11. Prepare the journal entries for A Ltd and B Ltd to record their interests in the joint venture using the one-line and line-by-line methods.

**Exercise 10.14** **Recording of interest in joint venture**
Refer to Exercise 10.12. Prepare journal entries for A Ltd and B Ltd to record their interests in the joint venture in accordance with AASB 1006.

**Exercise 10.15** **Recording interests in joint venture — three venturers**
C Ltd, D Ltd and E Ltd have proportionate interests in a joint venture amounting to 50%, 30% and 20% respectively. The joint venture, which is engaged in the development and production of certain specialised computer components and has the registered business name Advanced Computer Products, was commenced on 1 July 20X0 with total cash contributions of $1 000 000. Finished goods with a cost of $100 000 were distributed to the venturers on 31 May 20X1. The balance sheet of the joint venture as at 30 June 20X1 appears on the following page.

**Advanced Computer Products**
**Balance Sheet as at 30 June 20X1**

|  | $000 | $000 |
|---|---|---|
| *Assets* | | |
| Current assets | | |
|    Cash at bank | 40 | |
|    Supplies | 140 | |
|    Work in progress | 200 | |
|    Finished goods | 160 | 540 |
| Non-current assets | | |
|    Plant & equipment | 500 | |
|    *Less* Accumulated depreciation | (50) | 450 |
|    Development costs | | 160 |
|    Patents & trademarks | | 50 |
|      *Total assets* | | 1 200 |
| *Liabilities* | | |
| Current liabilities | | |
|    Creditors & borrowings | | 350 |
|    *Net assets* | | $850 |
| | | |
| *Venturers' interests* | | |
| C Ltd  – Contributions | 500 | |
|       – Finished goods distributed | (50) | |
|       – Share of depreciation expense | (25) | 425 |
| | | |
| D Ltd  – Contributions | 300 | |
|       – Finished goods distributed | (30) | |
|       – Share of depreciation expense | (15) | 255 |
| | | |
| E Ltd  – Contributions | 200 | |
|       – Finished goods distributed | (20) | |
|       – Share of depreciation expense | (10) | 170 |
|      *Total venturers' interests* | | $850 |

*Required*

Prepare relevant journal entries for C Ltd, D Ltd and E Ltd to record their interests in the joint venture. Draft a disclosure note in compliance with the minimum requirements of AASB 1006 for C Ltd. (Assume that C Ltd does not have an interest in any other joint venture and that there are no material contingent liabilities or capital expenditure commitments related to the joint venture.)

**Exercise 10.16**  **Contributions other than cash — two venturers**

O Ltd and P Ltd entered into a joint venture agreement on 1 July 20X0. Each venturer has a 50% interest in the joint venture. To commence the development, O Ltd contributed $400 000 cash, while P Ltd contributed patents with an agreed fair value of $400 000. These patents were recorded in P Ltd's books at a value of $250 000.

*Required*

Prepare the journal entries for O Ltd and P Ltd to record their interests in the joint venture.

**Exercise 10.17**

### Contributions other than cash — three venturers

Q Ltd, R Ltd and S Ltd enter into a joint venture agreement on 1 July 20X1. Their proportionate interests in the venture amount to 40%, 30% and 30% respectively. To commence the venture, Q Ltd contributes $400 000 cash, R Ltd contributes plant and equipment having a fair value of $300 000 (original cost $500 000, accumulated depreciation $100 000), and S Ltd contributes land having a fair value of $300 000 (original cost $220 000).

*Required*

Prepare a balance sheet for the joint venture, as well as journal entries for Q Ltd, R Ltd and S Ltd to record their interests in the joint venture on its commencement.

**Exercise 10.18**

### Contributions other than cash — three venturers

Bing Ltd, Parker Ltd and Tan Ltd enter into a joint venture agreement on 1 January 20X0. To commence the venture, Bing Ltd contributes $600 000 cash, Parker Ltd contributes $100 000 cash and land having a fair value of $260 000 (original cost $150 000), and Tan Ltd contributes $40 000 cash in addition to plant and equipment having a fair value of $200 000 (original cost $240 000, accumulated depreciation $20 000). The joint venture operates under the business name Overseas Trading.

*Required*

Prepare a balance sheet for the Overseas Trading joint venture, as well as journal entries for Bing Ltd, Parker Ltd and Tan Ltd to record their interests in the joint venture on its commencement.

**Exercise 10.19**

### Sale between existing venturers

W Ltd sells one-half of its 40% interest in the joint venture depicted in the balance sheet below to V Ltd for $900 000 cash. The fair values of the individual joint venture assets are equal to book value, with the exception of land and buildings which have a fair value of $2 300 000. (Assume that the effect of this increase in the value of land and buildings has not been entered in the accounts of the individual venturers.)

| | **V & W Joint Venture** **Balance Sheet as at 30 June 20X2** | | |
|---|---|---|---|
| | | $000 | $000 |
| *Assets* | | | |
| Current assets | | | |
| | Cash | 200 | |
| | Inventories | 600 | 800 |
| Non-current assets | | | |
| | Property, plant & equipment | 1 700 | |
| | Land & buildings | 2 100 | 3 800 |
| | *Total assets* | | 4 600 |
| *Liabilities* | | | |
| Current liabilities | | | |
| | Creditors & borrowings | | 600 |
| | *Net assets* | | $4 000 |
| *Venturers' interests* | | | |
| V Ltd – Contributions (60%) | | | 2 400 |
| W Ltd – Contributions (40%) | | | 1 600 |
| | *Total venturers' interests* | | $4 000 |

*Required*

Prepare the journal entries required for W Ltd to record the sale of the joint venture interest and for V Ltd to record the acquisition of the interest.

**Exercise 10.20**  **Introduction of new venturer**

X Ltd and Y Ltd each have a 50% interest in the joint venture depicted in the following balance sheet.

| X & Y Joint Venture<br>Balance Sheet as at 1 January 20X2 | | |
| --- | --- | --- |
| | $000 | $000 |
| *Assets* | | |
| Current assets | | |
|    Cash at bank | 100 | |
|    Inventories | 600 | 700 |
| Non-current assets | | |
|    Plant & equipment | 2 500 | |
|    Land & buildings | 2 800 | 5 300 |
|      *Total assets* | | 6 000 |
| *Liabilities* | | |
| Current liabilities | | |
|    Creditors & borrowings | | 1 600 |
|      *Net assets* | | $4 400 |
| | | |
| *Venturers' interests* | | |
| X Ltd – Contributions (50%) | | 2 200 |
| Y Ltd – Contributions (50%) | | 2 200 |
|      *Total venturers' interests* | | $4 400 |

Z Ltd contributes $1 100 000 cash to the joint venture on 2 January 20X2 in return for a 20% interest in the venture.

*Required*

Prepare the journal entries necessary to record the changes in proportionate interests in the accounts of the individual venturers.

**Exercise 10.21**  **Comprehensive — sale between existing venturers**

Baz Ltd, Guy Ltd and Pam Ltd entered into a joint venture agreement on 1 January 20X3. Their proportionate interests in the joint venture are 50%, 30% and 20% respectively. To commence the joint venture, Baz Ltd contributed $500 000 cash, Guy Ltd contributed plant and equipment with a fair value of $300 000 (cost $400 000, accumulated depreciation $50 000), and Pam Ltd contributed cash of $100 000 and patents with a fair value of $100 000 (cost $60 000). The joint venture is carried on under the registered business name Explorations Mining.

The only transaction entered into by the joint venture in the six months to 30 June 20X3 was the payment of $500 000 cash for the right to mine in a particular area of South Australia. Also, depreciation calculated at the rate of 20% per annum was provided on the plant and equipment.

Subsequently, on 1 July 20X3, Baz Ltd sells one-half of its 50% interest in the joint venture to Pam Ltd for $260 000.

*Required*
Prepare the Explorations Mining balance sheet on commencement of the joint venture and the journal entries required for the venturers to record their share of joint venture assets and liabilities at commencement date. Also, prepare any journal entries required to record the above fact situation in the individual venturers' accounts on 30 June 20X3 and 1 July 20X3.

**Exercise 10.22**  **Comprehensive — introduction of new venturer**
Chester Ltd, Dan Ltd and Kate Ltd operate a joint venture under the business name Resdev. The venture was commenced on 1 July 20X1 with cash contributions of $1 200 000. The balance sheet for the joint venture as at 30 June 20X2 is given below.

|  | $000 | $000 | $000 |
|---|---|---|---|
| **Resdev** **Balance Sheet as at 30 June 20X2** | | | |
| *Assets* | | | |
| Current assets | | | |
| Work in progress | | 180 | |
| Finished goods | | 240 | 420 |
| Non-current assets | | | |
| Plant & equipment | 1 000 | | |
| *Less* Accumulated depreciation | (160) | 840 | |
| Patents | | 300 | |
| Development costs | | 600 | 1 740 |
| Total assets | | | 2 160 |
| *Liabilities* | | | |
| Current liabilities | | | |
| Creditors & borrowings | | | 960 |
| Net assets | | | $1 200 |
| | | | |
| *Venturers' interests* | | | |
| Chester Ltd – Contributions (25%) | | | 300 |
| Dan Ltd – Contributions (37.5%) | | | 450 |
| Kate Ltd – Contributions (37.5%) | | | 450 |
| Total venturers' interests | | | $1 200 |

On 1 July 20X2, Rawdyn Ltd contributes $300 000 cash to the Resdev joint venture in return for a 20% interest.

*Required*

1  Prepare journal entries for Chester Ltd, Dan Ltd and Kate Ltd to record their interests in the joint venture for the year ended 30 June 20X2.

2  Prepare the Resdev joint venture balance sheet on 1 July 20X2 subsequent to the introduction of Rawdyn Ltd (assuming the fair value of all assets equals their book value), and prepare the journal entries required to record the above fact situation in the individual venturers' accounts on 1 July 20X2.

# chapter 11

PUBLISHED FINANCIAL STATEMENTS

# introduction

Company financial statements comprise the profit and loss statement, balance sheet and statement of cash flows, together with various notes, declarations and reports. The general aim is for relevant and reliable information regarding the entity's financial affairs to be provided to shareholders and other interested parties.

Financial statements must comply with various legislative and other requirements and guidelines, some of which are detailed and involved. The Corporations Law requirements have also been affected, or will be affected, by the *First Corporate Law Simplification Act 1995* and the Second Corporate Law Simplification Bill 1996. The aim in this chapter is to provide a relatively concise overview of the major principles and requirements.

# Financial statements and financial reporting

Accounting has been defined as 'the process of identifying, measuring and communicating economic information to permit informed judgements and decisions by users of the information'.[1] This definition serves to emphasise that accounting involves (a) identifying transactions and events of an economic nature that are to be recognised and recorded, (b) measuring those transactions and events in financial terms, and (c) communicating or reporting that information to users. The broad objective is to enable those users to make informed judgments and decisions.

Financial information serves as an important input and guide for informed decision making in an economic environment. In the case of companies, as for many other types of entities, communication of the economic information required for user decision making is achieved by the preparation and dissemination of financial statements. These statements summarise the financial aspects of an economic entity's activities over a certain period of time, usually one *financial* year. They are designed to communicate information that will allow users to evaluate past performance and make decisions concerning the future. To enable effective communication, the information should be classified and summarised appropriately. In the case of corporations, the statements may be for an individual company or for a consolidated group (economic entity).

**users' information needs**

The financial statements are primarily addressed and directed towards the information needs of the members of the company, the shareholders. However, there are also many other potential user groups, or stakeholders, including:
- creditors, financial institutions, debenture holders and other lenders;
- prospective investors and financial analysts;
- employees, labour unions and employer groups;
- suppliers and customers;
- regulatory agencies and government departments; and
- special interest community groups and the public generally.

**accountability**

The publication of financial statements is one of the major means by which companies (or, more specifically, company directors) are made accountable. The *Oxford English Dictionary* defines *accountability* as 'The quality of being accountable; liability to give account of, and answer for, discharge of duties or conduct ...' Accountability exists where a social relationship involves investment which may be at risk and where such investment is undertaken conditional on the right to receive information and the right to have that information verified. Accountability is of particular importance in the case of corporations, as such entities embody a separate legal personality and their shareholders have the benefit of limited liability.

In the case of companies, particularly public companies, shareholders transfer resources to the control of managers, the directors, in the expectation of gain. However, as there is a risk that the shareholders may receive neither a gain on nor the return of their resources, such investment is made on certain conditions. The first is that directors report, from time to time, on the state of the resources under their control. This is done through the publication of financial statements. The second condition is that the information contained in these financial statements is auditors subject to verification by professional auditors who report their findings. Accordingly, the auditor's report is included as part of the financial statements.

# External reporting and general purpose financial reports

The above discussion highlights that the published financial statements of companies are primarily designed to fulfil the information needs of users and to discharge the company's accountability requirements. In this respect, the published financial statements of companies are often referred to as external reports. This is to distinguish them from internal reports which are provided to company management from within the organisation for planning and control purposes. While company management is able to request internal reports in any form desired and for any specific need, external users are not in such a position. It is therefore important that the financial statements prepared for external users disclose appropriate information to satisfy the informational needs of those users.

conceptual framework

External reporting by companies can be examined within the context of the Australian conceptual framework for financial reporting. The conceptual framework is designed to provide preparers, users, auditors and accounting standard setters with an explicit set of accounting concepts to guide financial reporting. While the primary purpose of the conceptual framework is to guide the standard setting Boards when developing and reviewing accounting standards and other authoritative documents, it is considered that knowledge of the concepts should also assist preparers, auditors and other parties to better understand the general nature and purpose of financial reports.[2] To date, four Statements of Accounting Concepts (SACs) have been issued as part of the Australian conceptual framework project.[3] While these concepts statements are non-mandatory for preparers of financial statements, they provide a theoretical background from which to examine company financial reporting. SAC 2 and SAC 3 are of particular relevance in any discussion of the objectives of external reporting.

general purpose financial reports

As company external reports are designed to satisfy the *general* informational requirements of a range of user groups, they are also referred to as general purpose financial reports. SAC 2: Objective of General Purpose Financial Reporting states that such reports focus on providing information to meet the common information needs of users who are unable to command the preparation of reports tailored to their particular information needs (para 7). The statement considers that such reporting is not an end in itself but is a means of communicating relevant and reliable information about a reporting entity to users (para 11). Hence, SAC 2 considers that general purpose financial reports should provide information useful to users for making and evaluating decisions about the allocation of scarce resources (para 43), and that managements of reporting entities should present these financial reports in a manner which assists in discharging their accountability (para 44). In discussing the types of information relevant to users' needs, the statement considers that general purpose financial reports should disclose information relevant to the assessment of performance, financial position, financing and investing, and information about compliance with any externally imposed requirements (para 45).

qualitative
characteristics

material information
relevance
reliability

SAC 3: Qualitative Characteristics of Financial Information identifies the attributes, or qualitative characteristics, that financial information should possess if it is to serve the objective specified in SAC 2. The statement considers that such reports should include all material information which satisfies the concepts of relevance and reliability (para 48). Thus, relevance and reliability are specified as primary qualitative characteristics. *Relevant* information will have value in terms of assisting users in making and evaluating decisions about the allocation of scarce resources and in assessing the rendering of accountability by the preparers of the financial information (para 8). *Reliable* information will, without bias or undue error, faithfully represent the transactions and events that have occurred and that have been measured and displayed in the financial reports (para 16). SAC 3 also specifies

timely basis
comparability
understandability

three secondary qualitative characteristics, stating that general purpose financial reports should be presented on a timely basis and in a manner which satisfies the concepts of comparability and understandability (para 49).

# Format of company financial statements

Financial statements must comply with various legislative and other requirements and guidelines. Prior to discussing these requirements, it is appropriate to provide an overview of the general format of company financial statements.

In order to comply with the legislative provisions of the Corporations Law and other sources of authority and guidance, company financial statements comprise the following reports:

- directors' report;
- financial report, comprising the profit and loss statement, balance sheet, statement of cash flows, notes to the financial statements and directors' declaration (where applicable, consolidated or group accounts must also be presented); and
- auditor's report.

While this chapter uses the term 'financial statements' in a general sense, it should be noted that s 295 of the Second Corporate Law Simplification Bill defines *financial statements* more narrowly as the profit and loss statement, balance sheet, statement of cash flows and, if required, consolidated statements. The financial statements for the year, together with the notes to the financial statements and the directors' declaration, make up the *financial report*.

annual report

The financial report, directors' report and auditor's report are usually presented as an integral part of the company's annual report. The earlier sections of the annual report, which often fulfil a general information and public relations role, usually comprise such matters as company background and structure, description of areas of business, highlights of the financial year, chairman's address, and review of the year's activities and operations. The later sections of the report then comprise the financial information presented in accordance with the applicable legislative and other provisions, standards and guidelines.

# Companies required to publish financial statements

The introduction of the *First Corporate Law Simplification Act 1995* (hereafter referred to as the First Simplification Act) has resulted in some fundamental changes in the provisions governing the categories of companies required to prepare accounts and publish financial statements. In this respect, we are referring to provisions requiring companies to (a) prepare financial reports in accordance with the Corporations Law and accounting standards, (b) have the reports audited, and (c) lodge the financial information with the Australian Securities Commission (ASC). Financial statements lodged with the ASC become public information and are available to interested parties.

## SAC 1: DEFINITION OF THE REPORTING ENTITY

reporting entity

Prior to the First Simplification Act, the question of whether a company needed to prepare financial statements was determined by the application of the reporting entity concept specified in SAC 1: Definition of the Reporting Entity. SAC 1 requires reporting entities to prepare general purpose financial reports (para 41). As noted earlier, general purpose financial reports are designed to satisfy the common information needs of a wide range of users who are unable to command the preparation of reports tailored to their particular information needs. SAC 1 defines reporting entities as those 'in respect of which it is reasonable to expect the existence of users dependent on general purpose financial reports for information which will be useful to them for making and evaluating decisions about the allocation of scarce resources' (para 40). Hence, the statement adopts a concept of the reporting entity 'which is tied to the information needs of users and the nature of general purpose financial reports' (para 12). An entity will be a reporting entity if there exists users who are dependent on general purpose financial reports for information to be relied on in making and evaluating resource allocation decisions. AASB 1025: Application of the Reporting Entity Concept and Other Amendments was issued to fully operationalise the reporting entity concept, the effect being to require reporting entities to comply with applicable AASB standards.

differential reporting

The rationale underlying the reporting entity concept, and differential reporting requirements generally, is that it may not be necessary for all entities to supply the same level of financial information, given the costs and benefits of providing that information. The costs of providing detailed financial information and disclosures may be justified for a public company having a large number of interested stakeholders. However, the costs of requiring the same level of financial information from small entities, such as small private companies, partnerships, family trusts or clubs, may exceed the benefits. The owners of small entities are usually closely involved in day-to-day operations and have access to the information they require on the entity's performance and financial position. Also, other users of financial information of small entities are usually able to request special purpose information to satisfy their individual needs. For example, a bank can directly request any information it may require from a small entity wishing to borrow funds.

## CORPORATIONS LAW AND THE FIRST CORPORATE LAW SIMPLIFICATION ACT 1995

The First Simplification Act, operative for financial years commencing after 9 December 1995, has introduced into the Corporations Law an alternative differential reporting concept to that outlined in SAC 1. The First Simplification Act has replaced the previous Corporations Law distinction between exempt and **size test** non-exempt proprietary companies with an objective test relying on company size. A company will now generally be required to prepare financial statements and have them audited and lodged with the ASC if it is a public company or is classified as a **large proprietary** large proprietary company. Additional disclosure requirements, to be discussed later **company** in this chapter, apply to companies that are classified as disclosing entities.

**small proprietary**    If classified as a small proprietary company, accounts will not generally be required **company** for external reporting purposes. Small proprietary companies will still be required to keep proper accounting records and registers and will obviously need to prepare accounts for internal management purposes and to satisfy taxation requirements. However, these accounts will not have to comply with Corporations Law and accounting standard requirements.

A proprietary company will be classified as small rather than large if it satisfies any two of the following three tests (s 45A(2)):
1  gross operating revenue of the company and any entities it controls of less than $10 million for the financial year;
2  gross assets of the company and any entities it controls of less than $5 million at the end of the financial year;
3  fewer than 50 full-time equivalent employees at the end of the financial year of the company or entities it controls.

Hence, a proprietary company with gross operating revenue of $9 million, gross assets of $6 million and 50 full-time equivalent employees would be classified as large as it has failed two of the three tests (the asset and employee tests). A proprietary company with gross operating revenue of $8 million, gross assets of $9 million and 49 full-time equivalent employees would be classified as small as it has satisfied two of the three tests (the revenue and employee tests).

In applying the size tests, the calculations of gross operating revenue, gross assets and number of employees must be made in accordance with accounting standards, even if the company is not a reporting entity. The calculations must be on a consolidated basis in accordance with AASB 1024: Consolidated Accounts. Hence, all controlled entities, even if they are not companies, are included and inter-company transactions are eliminated.

As noted earlier, a small proprietary company will generally not be required to prepare financial statements. However, financial statements will be required if:
• shareholders holding at least 5% of votes in the company request financial statements (s 293, Second Corporate Law Simplification Bill). The request may specify whether accounting standards are to be complied with, whether a directors' report is required and whether the statements are to be audited;

- the ASC directs the company to prepare a financial report (s 294, Second Corporate Law Simplification Bill). This direction may be for a complete financial report or may specify the particular requirements to be complied with;
- the company was under foreign control for all or part of the accounting period and was not consolidated in financial statements lodged by the foreign parent with the ASC (s 292(2)(b), Second Corporate Law Simplification Bill). In this case, audited financial statements must be lodged with the ASC in the same way as for large proprietary companies; or
- the company's memorandum or articles of association, or other requirements or agreements, require the preparation of financial statements. For example, a bank may insist on audited financial statements pursuant to a borrowing agreement.

All large proprietary companies, with two major exemptions, must prepare audited financial statements for lodgment with the ASC. The first exemption stems from *grandfathering* provisions introduced in conjunction with the First Simplification Act. These provisions are specified in s 320(4) of the Second Corporate Law Simplification Bill. They provide certain large proprietary companies that were exempt proprietary companies prior to the First Simplification Act with relief from the requirement to lodge accounts with the ASC, although audited financial statements must still be prepared. The provisions were introduced, as exempt proprietary companies under the previous legislation were not required to provide financial data to the ASC if their accounts were audited. The grandfathering provisions are designed to continue this exemption from lodgment. To take advantage of the grandfathering exemption, the company must have:

- been an exempt proprietary company on 30 June 1994;
- continued to meet the definition of exempt proprietary company, as in force at 30 June 1994, at all times since that date;
- been a large proprietary company at the end of the company's first financial year after 9 December 1995; and
- lodged an application for exemption with the ASC within four months of the end of the company's first financial year after 9 December 1995.

The second major exemption, stemming from ASC Class Order 96/1850, allows relief from the auditing requirements of the Corporations Law for certain large proprietary companies where an audit is considered to impose an unreasonable burden and to be not necessary to protect the public interest. The audit relief is available to large proprietary companies which are not grandfathered proprietary companies, disclosing entities, borrowing corporations or guarantors of borrowing corporations, and which have not been audited since 1993. Broadly, the relief is available on condition that:

- the directors and shareholders pass unanimous resolutions that the financial statements should not be audited;
- both the directors' statement and the company's annual return for each year contain unqualified solvency statements that, in the directors' opinion, there are reasonable grounds to believe that the company will be able to pay its debts as and when they fall due;

- various corporate governance requirements are complied with, including the preparation of quarterly management accounts available to shareholders if requested;
- for either the relevant financial year or the immediately preceding financial year the company must have made an operating profit after abnormal items and tax;
- liabilities do not exceed 70% of tangible assets at the end of the financial year and at the end of each quarter;
- the annual financial statements have been compiled by a professional accountant;
- copies of financial statements and annual returns are lodged with the ASC by the due dates; and
- the directors' report states that the financial statements have not been audited and that the requirements of the class order have been complied with.

There is one further exemption from the reporting requirements applicable to certain companies. ASC Class Order 95/1530 provides relief from accounting and audit requirements to wholly-owned subsidiaries whose accounts are included in the consolidated accounts of the parent entity and lodged with the ASC, provided the company is not a borrowing corporation or a disclosing entity. The relief is available subject to a number of conditions relating to the parent and its subsidiaries entering into a deed of cross-guarantee.

## THE PRESENT SITUATION

The above discussion highlights that there is some conflict between the SAC 1 reporting entity concept and the Corporations Law provisions subsequent to the First Simplification Act. The AASB had originally adopted the SAC 1 reporting entity concept in prescribing the entities required to prepare financial statements in accordance with AASB accounting standards. However, the First Simplification Act did not adopt the reporting entity concept and enacted the objective tests based on company size and the small/large distinction. This raised the question of exactly which entities are required to comply with AASB standards. For example, consider the following classes of companies:

- small proprietary companies required to lodge accounts with the ASC;
- large proprietary companies, not being reporting entities, that are permitted to lodge *unaudited* financial statements with the ASC; and
- public companies that are not reporting entities.

To address these uncertainties, the AASB in April 1996 issued Exposure Draft (ED) No. 72: Changes to the Application of AASB Standards to Reflect the First Corporate Law Simplification Act 1995. The exposure draft proposes to extend the application of AASB standards to all entities required to lodge financial statements on the public record, irrespective of whether they are reporting entities.

Opposition to the ED 72 proposal has been expressed by a number of parties, including the professional accounting bodies. Also, the introduction of the size test in the First Simplification Act has not been without some controversy and debate, and there is some inconsistency between ED 72 and the Second Corporate Law Simplification Bill 1996. Accordingly, the transition to the new reporting provisions may take some time and may result in further amendments in the future.

# Sources of authority and guidance

## CORPORATIONS LAW AND THE SECOND CORPORATE LAW SIMPLIFICATION BILL 1996

form

content

The Corporations Law, representing legislative authority administered by the ASC, is the most powerful influence prescribing the form and content of company financial statements. The Second Corporate Law Simplification Bill 1996 (hereafter referred to as the Second Simplification Bill) will result in some simplification to the wording of the Corporations Law requirements when enacted. In this section of the chapter, the major Corporations Law provisions relating to the form and content of published financial statements, as modified by the Second Simplification Bill, will be outlined. However, it should also be noted that company financial statements must also comply with any applicable Corporations Regulations and ASC Policy Statements and Practice Notes. Also, individual companies may be able to take advantage of ASC Class Orders which allow relief from certain Corporations Law requirements in particular specified situations.

### General requirements

financial reports

audits

The general requirements for financial reports and audits are specified in Chapter 2M of the Second Simplification Bill. The provisions relating to the classes of companies required to publish financial statements were summarised in a prior section of this chapter.

financial records

Sections 286 to 291 of the Second Simplification Bill prescribe requirements for financial records. Section 286 requires a company to keep written financial records that:
- correctly record and explain its transactions and financial position; and
- would enable true and fair financial statements to be prepared and audited.

true and fair view

The Corporations Law requires the accounts of a company to convey a true and fair view. In particular, s 297 of the Second Simplification Bill requires the financial statements and notes for the financial year to give a true and fair view of the entity's financial position. Also, if a company's financial statements, despite being prepared in accordance with applicable regulations and accounting standards, would not otherwise give a true and fair view, s 295(3)(c) requires any additional information necessary to give such a view to be included in the notes to the financial statements. Auditors are required to report whether or not, in their opinion, the financial statements give a true and fair view (s 309).

The term 'true and fair' is not defined in the Corporations Law or elsewhere in legislation or regulation, and has been subject to much debate as to its exact meaning. The term itself, and earlier terms such as 'full and fair', have been in use for a number of centuries and have become an enduring part of UK company legislation since the mid-1800s. The true and fair view requirement was introduced in Australia in the Victorian *Companies Act* of 1958 and in the Uniform Companies Acts of 1961 in the other states.

While there has been considerable debate and controversy on the exact nature of the term, the starting point for conveyance of a true and fair view requires compliance of the accounts with relevant statutory provisions, regulations and accounting standards. The accounting policies adopted should be appropriate to the company's business, and the accounts taken as a whole should provide adequate disclosure of all material matters, including any additional information required to give a true and fair view. Various requirements and recommendations in accounting standards and concepts statements are persuasive in considering whether accounts convey a true and fair view. In particular, AASB 1001: Accounting Policies requires accounting policies to be 'selected and applied in a manner which ensures that the resultant financial information satisfies the concepts of *relevance* and *reliability*, thereby ensuring that the *substance* of the underlying transactions and other events is reported' (para 4.1). SAC 3 states that, for information to be relevant and reliable, it is necessary for the substance, rather than the form, of transactions or events to be reported (para 24). This requires the genuine economic nature and effect of the transaction or event to be reported. Truth and fairness also presumably involves the financial information being useful to users for decision-making purposes, as specified in SAC 2. While the courts have the ultimate say in determining whether accounts are true and fair in individual situations and have the right to find the profession's standards and generally accepted accounting principles lacking, they have tended to look towards professional pronouncements and commercial accounting principles and practice for guidance.

**concise financial report**

With respect to annual reporting to members, some changes are contemplated in the Second Simplification Bill. The Bill will permit a concise financial report to be sent to a shareholder, rather than the complete annual report, if the shareholder so requests (ss 316 and 317). The required content of a concise financial report will be addressed in a forthcoming accounting standard.

## Profit and loss statement, balance sheet and notes to the financial statements

A profit and loss statement, balance sheet and notes to the financial statements are required pursuant to s 295 of the Second Simplification Bill. *Profit or loss* is defined in the Corporations Law as the 'profit or loss resulting from operations' of the company or economic entity (s 9). The term 'balance sheet' is not defined in the Corporations Law. Obviously, though, both the terms 'balance sheet' and 'profit and loss' as referred to in the law are subject to their normal accounting meaning. The notes to the financial statements comprise disclosures required by the Corporations Regulations, notes required by accounting standards, and any other information necessary to give a true and fair view (s 295(3)).

The former Schedule 5 to the Corporations Regulations, operative for financial years ending before 30 June 1997, prescribed a required format for the presentation of the profit and loss statement and the balance sheet. However, accounting standard AASB 1034: Information to be Disclosed in Financial Reports, which replaced Schedule 5, does not prescribe a standard format, instead stating that the 'most appropriate format should be developed having regard to the particular circumstances of the entity and the presentation of relevant and reliable information about its performance, financial position, and financing and investing activities' (para 3.1). AASB 1034 does require information in the balance sheet and the notes to the accounts to be condensed into relevant and comparable categories, with assets, liabilities and equity items classified according to their nature or function (para 4.1). Although standard formats are not prescribed, Appendix 1 of AASB 1034 does present suggested example formats for the profit and loss account and the balance sheet.[4] These sample formats are reproduced below.

### XYZ Consolidated Limited
### Example Profit and Loss Account
### for the financial year ended 30 June 19X7

| | Note | Consolidated 19X7 $000 | Consolidated 19X6 $000 | Company 19X7 $000 | Company 19X6 $000 |
|---|---|---|---|---|---|
| **Sales Revenue** | 2 | X | X | X | X |
| Cost of Sales | | (X) | (X) | (X) | (X) |
| **Gross Profit** | | X | X | X | X |
| Selling, general and administrative expenses | | (X) | (X) | (X) | (X) |
| | | X | X | X | X |
| **Other Revenue** | 2 | X | X | X | X |
| **Operating Profit Before Abnormal Items** | | X | X | X | X |
| Abnormal items | 3 | X | X | X | X |
| **Operating Profit Before Income Tax** | | X | X | X | X |
| Income tax expense | 4 | (X) | (X) | (X) | (X) |
| **Operating Profit After Income Tax** | | X | X | X | X |
| Profit on extraordinary items after income tax | 5 | X | X | X | X |
| **Net Profit** | | X | X | X | X |
| Outside equity interests in net profit | | (X) | (X) | – | – |
| **Net Profit Attributable to Members of the Parent Entity** | | X | X | X | X |

*Note:* If this format is adopted for presentation of the profit and loss account, the notes to the financial report would need to include a reconciliation of retained profits/accumulated losses in accordance with the requirements of para 9.1 in this Standard and the requirements of Accounting Standard AASB 1018: Profit and Loss Accounts.

*Source:* AASB 1034: Information to be Disclosed in Financial Reports, Australian Accounting Standards Board, December 1996, Appendix 1. Reproduced with the permission of the Institute of Chartered Accountants in Australia and the Australian Society of Certified Practising Accountants.

## XYZ Consolidated Limited
## Example Balance Sheet as at 30 June 19X7

| | | Consolidated | | Company | |
|---|---|---|---|---|---|
| | | 19X7 | 19X6 | 19X7 | 19X6 |
| | Note | $000 | $000 | $000 | $000 |
| **Current Assets** | | | | | |
| Cash | | X | X | X | X |
| Inventories | 6 | X | X | X | X |
| Receivables | 7 | X | X | X | X |
| Property, Plant and Equipment | 8 | X | X | X | X |
| Other | 9 | X | X | X | X |
| **Total Current Assets** | | X | X | X | X |
| **Non-Current Assets** | | | | | |
| Investments | 10 | X | X | X | X |
| Property, plant and equipment | 8 | X | X | X | X |
| Intangibles | 11 | X | X | X | X |
| Future income tax benefits | 12 | X | X | X | X |
| Research and development | | | | | |
| Expenditure capitalised | 13 | X | X | X | X |
| Other | 14 | X | X | X | X |
| **Total Non-Current Assets** | | X | X | X | X |
| **Total Assets** | | X | X | X | X |
| **Current Liabilities** | | | | | |
| Accounts payable | 15 | X | X | X | X |
| Borrowings | 16 | X | X | X | X |
| Provisions | 17 | X | X | X | X |
| Other | 18 | X | X | X | X |
| **Total Current Liabilities** | | X | X | X | X |
| **Non-Current Liabilities** | | | | | |
| Borrowings | 16 | X | X | X | X |
| Provisions | 17 | X | X | X | X |
| Other | 18 | X | X | X | X |
| **Total Non-Current Liabilities** | | X | X | X | X |
| **Total Liabilities** | | X | X | X | X |
| **Net Assets** | | X | X | X | X |
| **Equity** | | | | | |
| Parent entity interest issued capital | 19 | X | X | X | X |
| Reserves | 20 | X | X | X | X |
| Retained profits/accumulated losses | | X | X | X | X |
| **Parent Entity Interest in Equity** | | X | X | X | X |
| Outside equity interest | | | | | |
| Issued capital | 19 | X | X | - | - |
| Reserves | 20 | X | X | - | - |
| Retained profits/accumulated losses | | X | X | - | - |
| **Outside Equity Interest** | | X | X | - | - |
| **Total Equity** | | X | X | X | X |

*Source:* AASB 1034: Information to be Disclosed in Financial Reports, Australian Accounting Standards Board, December 1996, Appendix 1. Reproduced with the permission of the Institute of Chartered Accountants in Australia and the Australian Society of Certified Practising Accountants.

In examining the example formats, the following should be noted:
- Both company (parent entity) and consolidated (economic entity) figures are shown.
- Current and prior years' figures are shown, as required by AASB 1034 (para 14).
- The figures in the accounts have been rounded to the nearest $1000. Amounts may be rounded off in accordance with Corporations Regulations and ASC Class Orders. Regulation 3.6.05 allows rounding to the nearest $1000 where the total assets of the company or the economic entity exceed $10 million.
- References to notes to the accounts are included for various individual items. The notes provide further disclosure details for that item, often in compliance with accounting standard requirements.

## Statement of cash flows

Balance sheets, depicting an entity's financial position, and profit and loss statements, reflecting the performance of the entity, are prepared on the basis of accrual accounting. Accrual accounting involves the recognition of revenues and expenses of a financial period as they are earned or incurred, irrespective of the time at which any cash is received or paid. While the balance sheet and profit and loss statement are usually presented as the two major financial reports, the statement of cash flows is considered necessary to provide a more complete representation of an entity's financial position and performance. The requirement for a cash flow statement to be presented as a component of the financial statements is specified in s 295 of the Second Simplification Bill. A statement of cash flows for a reporting period indicates an entity's opening cash balance, inflows and outflows of cash during the period, and the closing cash balance. Information on the sources of an individual entity's cash balances during the period, and the manner in which that cash was utilised, is considered to provide relevant and reliable information for financial statement users.

As the detailed requirements for cash flow statements are specified in accounting standard AASB 1026: Statement of Cash Flows, discussion of this statement is left until the 'Accounting Standards' section later in this chapter.

## Directors' declaration

directors' declaration   A directors' declaration is an integral part of the financial report. The declaration is defined in s 295(4) to be a declaration by directors:
- that the financial statements and notes comply with accounting standards;
- that the financial statements and notes give a true and fair view; and
- whether, in the directors' opinion, there are reasonable grounds to believe that the entity will be able to pay its debts as and when they become due and payable.

The declaration must be made in accordance with a resolution of directors, specify the day on which the declaration was made, and be signed by a director (s 295(5)).

## Directors' report

directors' report   In addition to the directors' declaration, a directors' report must be included with the financial report. As with the directors' declaration, the directors' report must be made in accordance with a directors' resolution, specify the day on which it was made, and be signed by a director (s 301). The annual directors' report must include:

- a general management discussion (unless all members agree in writing that this is not necessary); and
- certain specific information.

The general management discussion involves a discussion and analysis of the matters about which members need to be informed if they are to understand the overall financial position of the entity (s 299). This is specified to include:
- results of operations (both overall and in key industry and geographical segments);
- key strategic initiatives adopted;
- major commitments entered into and sources of funding for those commitments;
- unusual or infrequent events or transactions;
- likely future developments in the business (unless this represents prejudicial information); and
- trends or events, both internal and external, that have had a significant effect, or are likely to have a significant effect, on the business (unless this represents prejudicial information).

The major specific items of information required, pursuant to s 300, include:
- dividends or distributions paid or provided for during the year;
- directors' names;
- options granted to any of the directors, or any of the five most highly remunerated officers of the company, where these are granted as part of remuneration;
- unissued shares or interests under option;
- shares or interests issued as a result of the exercise of an option; and
- indemnities given and insurance premiums paid for a person who is or has been a company officer or auditor.

Section 300(9) specifies additional rules for public companies. Unless the public company is a wholly-owned subsidiary of another company, the directors' report must include details of:
- directors' qualifications, experience and any special responsibilities;
- the number of meetings of the board of directors and board committees held during the year and each director's attendance at each of those meetings.

Section 300(10) also specifies additional requirements for listed companies. Unless the public company is a wholly-owned subsidiary of another company, the directors' report must include the following details for each director:
- their interests in shares and debentures of the company;
- their rights or options over shares in, or debentures of, the company; and
- contracts to which the director is a party, or under which the director is entitled to benefit, that confer a right to shares or debentures made available by the company.

**Auditor's report**
The auditing requirements for companies are prescribed in ss 309–315 of the Second Simplification Bill. The auditor is required to form an opinion and then report that opinion to company members. The auditor must form an opinion about:

- whether the financial report is in accordance with the Corporations Law (s 309(a));
- whether the financial report is in accordance with accounting standards (s 309(b));
- whether the financial report gives a true and fair view (s 309(c));
- whether the auditor has been given all information, explanation and assistance necessary (s 309(d));
- whether the entity has kept financial records sufficient to enable a financial report to be prepared and audited (s 309(e)); and
- whether the entity has kept other records and records required by the Corporations Law (s 309(f)).

For an audit of financial statements, s 310 requires a report to members on whether the auditor is of the opinion that the financial report is in accordance with the Corporations Law and accounting standards and whether the financial report gives a true and fair view. If the auditor is not of that opinion, the report must state why. The report must specify the date on which it was made.

The auditor's report must also disclose any of the following if they apply:

- the quantified financial effect of any departure from accounting standards (if this is not practicable, the report must say why);
- any defect or irregularity in the financial report; and
- any deficiency, failure or shortcoming in respect of the matters referred to in s 309(d), (e) or (f).

### Disclosing entities

enhanced disclosure requirements

disclosing entities

half-yearly reporting

continuous disclosure

The *Corporate Law Reform Act 1994* introduced enhanced disclosure requirements into the Corporations Law for companies and other entities classified as disclosing entities. The enhanced disclosure requirements entail half-yearly reporting (s 111AO) and the continuous disclosure of material information (s 111AP).

Disclosing entities are those which issue enhanced disclosure (ED) securities. Definitions of disclosing entities and ED securities are contained in ss 111AB to 111AM of the Corporations Law. Broadly, the following companies are regarded as disclosing entities:

- listed companies;
- companies issuing securities, other than debentures, pursuant to a prospectus;
- companies which offer securities, other than debentures, as consideration for the acquisition of shares pursuant to a takeover; and
- companies issuing debentures where a trustee for debenture holders has been appointed.

The continuous disclosure requirements with which listed and unlisted disclosing entities must comply are specified in ss 1001A and 1001B respectively. Listed disclosing entities are required to comply with the listing rules of the relevant securities exchange requiring the notification of significant new developments and other information as they arise. For publicly-listed companies, the appropriate authority is the Australian Stock Exchange (ASX), and the continuous disclosure requirements are tied into the ASX Listing Rules, particularly Listing Rule 3A(1).

**price-sensitive information**

With certain exceptions relating to confidential information, this listing rule requires the immediate notification to the exchange of any information concerning the company of which it becomes aware and which a reasonable person would expect to have a material effect on the price or value of the company's securities. This information is often referred to as price-sensitive information. Unlisted disclosing entities must notify such information to the Australian Securities Commission, unless the information is included in a supplementary or replacement prospectus.

In addition to the continuous disclosure provisions, disclosing entities are also subject to half-yearly reporting (ss 303 to 308). The Second Simplification Bill specifies the following requirements for the half-yearly statements and reports:

- a profit and loss statement, balance sheet, statement of cash flows, notes to the financial statements and, if applicable, consolidated accounts;
- a directors' declaration as to whether the financial statements and notes comply with accounting standards and give a true and fair view, and whether, in the directors' opinion, there are reasonable grounds to believe that the disclosing entity will be able to pay its debts as and when they become due and payable;
- a directors' report containing the names of the directors, a review of operations and the results of those operations; and
- an auditor's report on the half-yearly audit or review, requirements for which are specified in s 311. A half-yearly review can be less extensive than an audit of the annual financial statements.

## ACCOUNTING STANDARDS

Pursuant to the Corporations Law, directors must ensure that the company's financial statements are made out in accordance with applicable accounting standards approved by the Australian Accounting Standards Board (AASB) and its predecessor, the Accounting Standards Review Board (ASRB). In the circumstance where it is considered that compliance with a standard does not result in the presentation of a true and fair view, the standard's provisions must still be applied. However, as noted earlier in this chapter, directors are required in such circumstances to present such additional information and explanations as are necessary to give a true and fair view (s 295(3)(c)).

The Corporations Law only provides relatively general guidance as to the required form and content of the accounts. The accounting standards issued by the AASB aim to provide more detailed guidance, mainly by prescribing allowable accounting policies and requiring the disclosure of certain details of various transactions and balances. The provisions of a number of accounting standards have specifically been discussed in previous chapters. For example, AASB 1020: Accounting for Income Tax (Tax-effect Accounting) and AASB 1015: Accounting for the Acquisition of Assets were discussed in chapters 3 and 4 respectively, and AASB 1024: Consolidated Accounts was referred to in chapters 5 to 8. The major additional standards relating to financial statements generally, and for which a general, introductory overview is presented in the following sections of this chapter, are:

- AASB 1001: Accounting Policies;
- AASB 1002: Events Occurring after Balance Date;
- AASB 1004: Disclosure of Operating Revenue;
- AASB 1005: Financial Reporting by Segments;
- AASB 1017: Related Party Disclosures;
- AASB 1018: Profit and Loss Accounts;
- AASB 1026: Statement of Cash Flows;
- AASB 1031: Materiality; and
- AASB 1034: Information to be Disclosed in Financial Reports.

### AASB 1001: Accounting Policies

Knowledge of the accounting policies selected and applied by the company in preparing the financial statements is of importance to users. Such information enables an understanding of the basis of the financial statements; in turn, this enables a better appreciation of the figures themselves. The purpose of AASB 1001 is to:

- prescribe the concepts that guide the *selection* and *application* of accounting policies;
- prescribe the general *criteria* for the *disclosure* of accounting policies; and
- require certain *disclosures* in respect of the accounting policies adopted in the preparation and presentation of the financial report (para 3.1).

AASB 1001 defines accounting policies as 'the specific accounting principles, bases or rules adopted in preparing and presenting the financial report' (para 7). It was highlighted earlier in this chapter that the standard specifies that accounting policies must be selected and applied in a manner which ensures that the financial information is *relevant* and *reliable*, thereby ensuring that the *substance* of the underlying transactions and other events is reported (para 4.1).

With respect to the criteria for the disclosure of accounting policies, AASB 1001 states that accounting policies must be disclosed in a manner which ensures that the financial information is *comparable* and *understandable* (para 5.1). Comparability implies that the recognition, measurement and presentation of transactions and other events should be carried out in a consistent manner throughout an entity and over time, and that there should be consistency between entities (para 5.1.1). However, consistency should not impede the introduction of improved financial reporting. Understandability requires that the information should be presented in the most understandable manner but without sacrificing relevance or reliability (para 5.1.4). However, the standard assumes some level of competency on the part of users, in that it is 'assumed that users possess the proficiency necessary to comprehend the significance of contemporary financial reporting practices' (para 5.1.4).

**summary of accounting policies**

With respect to disclosures, AASB 1001 requires a summary of accounting policies to be presented in the initial section of the notes of the financial report (para 6.1). Such a summary must:

- state that the report is a general purpose financial report which has been prepared in accordance with accounting standards;

- identify the accounting policies adopted in preparing and presenting the report where (a) alternative accounting policies are permitted in an accounting standard, or (b) an accounting policy has been adopted in the absence of an accounting standard requirement; and
- if the report has not been prepared in accordance with the going concern or accrual accounting bases, this fact and the reason for non-application must be identified.

Guidelines in AASB 1001 also suggest that the following disclosures may be appropriate:

- that the report has also been prepared in accordance with Urgent Issues Group Consensus Views and relevant statutory and other requirements (para 6.1.2);
- the assumptions made in determining the policies applied and the methods adopted in applying them (para 6.1.3); and
- an explanation, if there is no accounting standard applicable to the item, of why the particular policy applied ensures that relevant and reliable information is presented (para 6.1.4).

AASB 1001 also requires appropriate disclosure of any changes to accounting policies from those applied in the preceding financial year (para 6.2) if such changes have a material effect in the current financial year or are expected to have a material effect in a subsequent year. Disclosure must be made of:

- the nature of the change;
- the reasons for the change; and
- the financial effects of material changes.

## AASB 1002: Events Occurring after Balance Date

The financial statements present information on a company's profit or loss, financial position and other matters for a period ending on a particular reporting date. Based on records kept throughout the financial year, the financial statements are finalised over a period of time subsequent to balance date. A potential problem is that events may occur during this post-balance date period that provide further information of relevance to the financial statements. These events may have particularly material consequences and, if so, will be of interest to financial statement users.

AASB 1002, para .03 requires the effect of material events occurring after balance date to be included in the accounts so that users are not misled. An event occurring after balance date is defined in the standard as a circumstance that has arisen, or information that has become available, after balance date but prior to the time of completion of the directors' statement (para .10). These events are also referred to as *subsequent* events or *post-balance date* events. AASB 1002 (commentary, para (ii)) distinguishes between two types of post-balance date events:

- those which provide evidence of, or further elucidate, conditions which existed at balance date; and
- those which create new conditions, as distinct from any that may have existed at balance date.

The first category of events occurring after balance date can provide additional evidence which assists in determining the amount of an item which was uncertain at balance date. Alternatively, it may reveal for the first time a condition that existed at balance date, thereby leading to the recognition of a new item or the correct measurement or valuation of an existing item (para .21). For example, post-balance date information may provide evidence that an existing provision for doubtful debts or provision for obsolete inventory is understated. In these circumstances, AASB 1002, para .21 requires an adjustment to the financial statements to be made if the financial effect is material. Hence, this requires the financial statements to be restated, involving an increase in the doubtful debts or obsolete inventory provisions to the higher amount suggested to be appropriate by the subsequent information. A further example of this type of subsequent event would be the withdrawal of a necessary line of credit by a bank to a company facing financial difficulties. This subsequent event may require the whole basis of the financial statements to be amended as the going concern assumption may no longer be appropriate. This may require the write-down of assets to net realisable value and the recognition of additional liabilities.

The second category of events occurring after balance date involves new conditions created after balance date. For example, a fire may destroy a major uninsured asset, or a major legal action against the company may be commenced. In these circumstances, disclosure of the event by way of a note to the accounts is required. AASB 1002, para .30 requires the following disclosures in the note:

- a description of each event and an estimate, where possible, of the financial effect of the event;
- a statement that each event occurred after balance date; and
- a statement that the financial effect of the event has not been recognised.

### AASB 1004: Disclosure of Operating Revenue

operating revenue Calculation of a company's profit or loss commences with the operating revenue figure. As operating revenue is one of the major factors impacting on a company's financial performance, disclosure of this item in the financial statements is considered to be particularly relevant. AASB 1004, para .10 requires disclosure of operating revenue, divided between sales revenue (or its equivalent) and other revenue. Individual components of other revenue must be disclosed separately if material. Operating revenue is defined as the amount of revenue after deducting any returns, allowances, duties, taxes and other amounts collected on behalf of third parties (para .06). If operating profit includes gains or losses from the sale of non-current assets, the gross proceeds of the disposal must be included in items of other revenue, and hence must be separately disclosed if material (commentary, para (vi)). With respect to items of other revenue, AASB 1034: Information to be Disclosed in Financial Reports requires dividend revenue and interest revenue to be separately disclosed.

## AASB 1005: Financial Reporting by Segments

**segment reporting**

Segment reporting involves the disaggregation of an entity's financial data by its major industry and geographical areas of activity. The disclosure of disaggregated information is considered to provide relevant information as it enables financial statement users to make better assessments of both past performance and future prospects. The various industry or geographical segments within which an enterprise operates may have differing profit prospects and risk exposures. AASB 1005 considers that the operations and results of different industry and geographical segments may be subject to a variety of special risks, such as the effects of technological change, the degree of government assistance, exchange rate fluctuations, international trade competition and political instability (commentary, para (i)).

**industry and geographical segments**

The purpose of AASB 1005 is to require the disclosure of information about the material industry and geographical segments in which a company operates in order to provide users with information necessary to gain an understanding of the risks and conditions facing the company or group (para .03). The standard only applies to listed companies and subsidiaries of listed foreign companies (para .02). Segments are defined as distinguishable industry and geographical components of the entity (para .06). An industry segment is engaged in providing a particular product or service or a collection of related products or services. A geographical segment represents operations in individual countries or groups of countries (para .06).

A company may operate predominantly in only one industry. In this case, AASB 1005, para .20 merely requires the disclosure of this circumstance together with a general description of the products and services from which revenue is derived. Likewise, if a company's operations are predominantly in one geographical segment, disclosure of that circumstance and the geographical location is all that is required (para .22).

To determine whether an industry or geographical segment is reportable under the standard, it is necessary to decide whether that segment is sufficiently material to warrant separate disclosure. In the absence of other factors, this will be the case where at least one of segment revenue, segment result or segment assets is 10% or more, respectively, of the total revenue, result or assets of all segments (commentary, para (ix)). Hence, if a company earned 75% of its revenue from Australia and 25% from New Zealand, segment information for these two geographical segments would be required.

For each material industry and geographical segment, the following information must be disclosed:

- segment revenue;
- segment result;
- the carrying amount of segment assets; and
- the basis of inter-segment pricing (if applicable).

As an example of these requirements, the segment reporting disclosures of Amcor Ltd for the year ended 30 June 1996 are reproduced on the following page.

## Segment Reporting: Amcor Ltd

| | Operating profit before income tax | | Sales revenue | | Total assets | |
|---|---|---|---|---|---|---|
| | 1996 $ million | 1995 $million | 1996 $ million | 1995 $ million | 1996 $ million | 1995 $ million |
| **NOTE 28.** | | | | | | |
| **SEGMENT REPORTING** | | | | | | |
| **Industry segments** | | | | | | |
| **Packaging** | | | | | | |
| Containers Packaging (1) | 235.0 | 239.5 | 2 571.1 | 2080.2 | 2 318.6 | 2 129.9 |
| Amcor Fibre Packaging (1) | 129.9 | 159.6 | 2 251.3 | 2 101.7 | 1 774.8 | 1 831.7 |
| Total Packaging | 364.9 | 399.1 | 4 822.4 | 4 181.9 | 4 093.4 | 3 961.6 |
| **Paper** | | | | | | |
| Amcor Paper Group (1) | 241.4 | 239.6 | 1 429.9 | 1 411.9 | 1 952.6 | 1 708.4 |
| Amcor Merchanting and | | | | | | |
| Trading (1) | 21.3 | 31.8 | 948.4 | 913.5 | 372.9 | 393.0 |
| Total Paper (1) | 262.7 | 271.4 | 2 378.3 | 2 325.4 | 2 325.5 | 2 101.4 |
| Investments/Other (1)(2) | 20.1 | 58.7 | – | 1 008.2 | 546.9 | 1 002.2 |
| Profit before interest and | | | | | | |
| income tax | 647.7 | 729.2 | | | | |
| Net interest | (128.0) | (113.1) | | | | |
| Profit before income tax | 519.7 | 616.1 | | | | |
| Abnormal items | (20.9) | (42.4) | | | | |
| Inter-segment sales (3) | | | (776.9) | (919.8) | | |
| | **498.8** | **573.7** | **6 423.8** | **6 595.7** | **6 965.8** | **7 065.2** |
| **Geographic segments** | | | | | | |
| Australia (1) (2) | 475.3 | 546.8 | 3 403.5 | 3 701.2 | 4 142.0 | 4 282.8 |
| New Zealand (1) (2) | 51.2 | 72.6 | 436.5 | 527.1 | 345.2 | 462.2 |
| North America (1) (2) | 66.6 | 79.0 | 1 237.6 | 1 491.2 | 936.1 | 1 102.8 |
| Europe (1) | 37.3 | 19.3 | 1 156.4 | 673.4 | 1 213.6 | 936.0 |
| Asia (1) | 17.3 | 11.5 | 189.8 | 202.8 | 328.9 | 281.4 |
| Profit before interest and | | | | | | |
| income tax | 647.7 | 729.2 | | | | |
| Net interest | (128.0) | (113.1) | | | | |
| Profit before income tax | 519.7 | 616.1 | | | | |
| Abnormal items | (20.9) | (42.4) | | | | |
| | **498.8** | **573.7** | **6 423.8** | **6 595.7** | **6 965.8** | **7 065.2** |

(1) Profit before interest and income tax
(2) Spicers consolidated in 1995 only. Dividend from Spicers included in 1996.
(3) Inter-segment sales mainly comprise sales of paper and paperboard which are priced on an arms length basis.

*Source:* Amcor Ltd, 1996 Annual Report.

## AASB 1017: Related Party Disclosures

related parties    The purpose of AASB 1017: Related Party Disclosures is to:

> require disclosure in the accounts and consolidated accounts of information relating to the relationships of the reporting entity with related parties and transactions with related parties, including the remuneration and retirement benefits of directors, loans received by directors and other director-related transactions. (para 7)

Related parties to an entity include persons or entities who may be in a position to enter into transactions on a non-arm's-length basis. AASB 1017 (commentary, para (iv)) states:

> The existence of a related party relationship may expose a reporting entity to risks, or provide opportunities, which would not have existed in the absence of the relationship. Related party transactions may, therefore, have a material effect on the performance, financial position, and financing and investing of a reporting entity... Transactions involving related parties cannot be presumed to be carried out on an arm's-length basis, as the requisite conditions of competitive, free-market dealings may not exist.

Related parties are defined in detail in para 9 of AASB 1017. Broadly, related parties include directors and director-related entities, entities which have control or significant influence over the company, entities over which the company has control or significant influence, and entities subject to common control. Related parties are divided into the following groups for disclosure purposes:
- directors and director-related entities (including spouses of directors, relatives of directors or spouses, and any other entity under the control or significant influence of such directors, spouses or relatives);
- wholly-owned group entities; and
- other related parties.

The disclosures required for director and director-related entity transactions are specified in paras 10 to 27. The following represents a brief summary of the disclosure requirements:
- names of directors;
- the total amount of income directly or indirectly received (or due and receivable) by all directors;
- for the total income figure described above, the number of directors receiving remuneration dissected into $10 000 bands (ie the number of directors receiving income below $10 000, $10 000 to below $20 000, $20 000 to below $30 000, etc);
- retirement benefits of directors;
- loans to directors; and
- other transactions of directors, prescribed so widely as to require the disclosure of virtually any transaction between the director and the company or group.

The director-related disclosures required by AASB 1017 'are deemed material regardless of the quantum of the amounts involved' (para 8). This is because the standard adopts the view that 'all director-related transactions are material by reason of their nature...' (commentary, para (viii)).

The disclosures relating to the wholly-owned group are prescribed in paras 28 to 30. The following represents a brief summary of the disclosure requirements:

- a description and the nature of the terms and conditions of each different type of transaction between related parties in the wholly-owned group;
- aggregate amounts of interest revenue, dividend revenue, interest expense, and provisions for doubtful receivables and write-downs of receivables in respect of transactions with related parties;
- aggregate amounts receivable from and payable to related parties;
- aggregate amounts of provisions for doubtful receivables from related parties;
- any ownership interest in each related party; and
- disclosure is not required of any of these transactions that have been eliminated for consolidation purposes.

The disclosures relating to other related parties are prescribed in paras 31 to 37. Broadly, these disclosures are similar to those required for other transactions of directors. These include transactions concerning shares or share options, interest, dividends, amounts receivable and payable, and provisions for doubtful receivables.

### AASB 1018: Profit and Loss Accounts

**profit and loss account**

AASB 1018: Profit and Loss Accounts specifies the approach to be used in determining profit or loss for a financial year and various disclosure requirements for profit and loss items. The required approach to determining profit and loss for a financial year is referred to as the all-inclusive approach. This requires that all items of revenue and expense must be taken into account in determining profit or loss, irrespective of whether or not they relate to the ordinary operations of the entity and even though they may relate to prior financial years (para 10). The only exception is for entries that give retroactive effect on a change of accounting policy pursuant to a statutory requirement (including accounting standards) or a Consensus View of the Urgent Issues Group (para 11). In these circumstances, the entry must be adjusted directly against retained profits or accumulated losses and adequate disclosure made.

AASB 1018 requires the following items to be disclosed:

- the operating profit or loss before and after tax (para 12);
- income tax recognised in arriving at the operating profit or loss after tax (para 13);
- the profit or loss (after all items) (para 14);

**abnormal items**
- abnormal items and any income tax applicable (para 15);

**extraordinary items**
- the aggregate amount of extraordinary items, and the nature and amount of each extraordinary item net of any income tax applicable (paras 16 and 17);
- the aggregate amount of transfers to and from reserves that affect retained profits or accumulated losses, to be shown after the profit or loss (paras 18 and 19); and
- comparative information for the preceding financial year (paras 20 and 21).

Abnormal items are any items included in the operating profit or loss after income tax which are considered abnormal by reason of their size and effect on the operating profit or loss for the year (para 9). Examples given in AASB 1018 of items that could fall within the abnormal definition include bad debts, inventory write-downs, write-offs of research and development expenditure, and profit or loss on the disposal of investments or properties (commentary, para (xii)).

Extraordinary items are attributable to transactions or other events of a type that are outside the ordinary operations of the entity and not of a recurring nature (para 9). AASB 1018 states that it is expected that items will fall within the definition of extraordinary items only on rare occasions (commentary, para (xv)). Examples given in the standard are the sale or abandonment of a significant business or all the assets associated with such a business, and the condemnation, expropriation or unintended destruction of a property.

### AASB 1026: Statement of Cash Flows

**Statement of cash flows**
AASB 1026: Statement of Cash Flows requires a cash flow statement to be included in financial statements. The purpose of a statement of cash flows is primarily to fulfil a liquidity analysis role. Cash is often referred to as the *life blood* of any business. Therefore, cash flow information is of particular interest in the analysis of a company's operations and its ability to pay its debts in the shorter term. More specifically, the following factors provide the rationale for the provision of cash flow information:
- profit does not necessarily equal cash flow;
- most financial statement users have an interest in cash flow in terms of the cash returns they can expect from their investments and the security of those investments;
- a positive cash flow is essential for an entity's financial viability and survival;
- as cash flow is the medium whereby access can be gained to resources through acquisition and rental, cash flow information enables users to judge the entity's ability to command resources; and
- information about the generation and use of cash flows is necessary to accompany information on profits and financial position to ensure managerial accountability.

AASB 1026 (commentary, para (v)) states that the information provided in a statement of cash flows, together with other information in the accounts, may assist in assessing the ability of the entity to (a) generate positive net cash flows in the future, (b) meet its financial commitments as they fall due, including the servicing of borrowings and the payment of dividends, (c) fund changes in the scope and/or nature of its activities, and (d) obtain external finance where necessary.

In broad terms, the standard requires a reconciliation of the opening and closing balances of cash. Cash is defined as 'cash on hand and cash equivalents' (para 9). Cash on hand is defined generally as notes, coins and deposits with financial institutions. The term 'cash equivalents' refers to highly liquid investments which are readily convertible into cash and which are used by the firm in its cash management function on a daily basis. Examples would include bank and non-bank bills, money market deposits close to maturity, borrowings in the form of money market funds, and bank overdrafts which are repayable on demand. A reconciliation of the actual balance sheet items comprising the opening and closing cash balances must be included in the statement (para 13).

In the cash flow statement itself, the cash flows are presented according to whether they relate to operating, investing or financing activities. Operating activities are those 'which relate to the provision of goods and services'; investing activities are those 'which relate to the acquisition and disposal of non-current assets ... and investments'; and financing activities are those 'which relate to changing the size and composition of the financial structure of the entity ... and borrowings' (para 9). The standard gives some guidance as to the types of transactions that fit into each of these three categories, but there is some discretion given to the preparer of the statement in this respect. Nevertheless, it is necessary for cash flows 'to be classified in a consistent manner over time' (commentary, para (xx)).

The importance of distinguishing between cash flows from operating, investing and financing activities can be illustrated by way of example. Consider an entity which discloses an increase in its net cash balance over the reporting period. Further analysis may reveal that the entity has negative cash flows from its operating activities and that the increase in its net cash position is entirely due to increased borrowings. Further analysis may reveal that these borrowings are at a high rate of interest and that they have resulted in the company's balance sheet exhibiting an extremely high level of gearing. This scenario would be completely different if the increase in the entity's net cash balance was due to healthy cash inflows from operating activities, particularly if the entity had been able to use these funds to retire debt or invest excess funds at a favourable rate. Accordingly, it is important to distinguish between cash flows from operating, investing and financing activities to provide a complete picture of the entity's cash flow performance and position.

AASB 1026 requires cash flows from operating activities to be presented using the direct method, involving the relevant cash inflows and outflows being reported in gross terms (para 17). The indirect method, which commences with net profit and adds or subtracts non-cash items to arrive at cash flows from operations, is not allowable. A reconciliation of cash flows from operating activities to operating profit or loss after income tax is required in a note (para 18). Also, the following cash flows must be disclosed separately (para 15):
- interest and other items of a similar nature received;
- dividends received;
- interest and other costs of finance paid;
- dividends paid; and
- income taxes paid.

As an example of the requirements of AASB 1026, the cash flow statement for Amcor Ltd for the year ended 30 June 1996 is reproduced on the following page.

## Amcor Ltd
## Statement of Cash Flows

| For year ended 30 June | Consolidated | | Amcor Limited | |
|---|---|---|---|---|
| | 1996 $ million | 1995 $ million | 1996 $ million | 1995 $ million |
| **Cash flows from operating activities** | | | | |
| Receipts from customers | 6 562.5 | 6 380.0 | 2 237.1 | 2 202.3 |
| Payments to suppliers and employees | (5 876.9) | (5 701.2) | (2 058.5) | (1 814.8) |
| Dividends received | 28.6 | 22.3 | 90.7 | 80.8 |
| Interest received | 10.8 | 7.2 | 39.8 | 36.0 |
| Interest paid | (157.5) | (126.0) | (112.7) | (90.8) |
| Income taxes paid | (173.9) | (144.8) | (106.0) | (60.0) |
| Dividends paid | (230.8) | (212.5) | (230.8) | (212.5) |
| Other income received | 27.0 | 29.1 | 7.3 | 6.0 |
| **Net cash from operating activities (1)** | **189.8** | **254.1** | **(133.1)** | **147.0** |
| **Cash flows from investing activities** | | | | |
| Loans – controlled entities | – | – | 20.8 | (463.7) |
| Loans to associated companies | (10.5) | (21.9) | – | – |
| Loans repaid by associated companies and other persons | 3.4 | 22.3 | 3.4 | 3.6 |
| Additional investment in controlled entities | (52.5) | (5.0) | – | – |
| Acquisition of: | | | | |
| • Controlled entities and businesses | (112.9) | (200.5) | (9.5) | – |
| • Investments | (9.3) | (1.2) | – | – |
| • Property, plant and equipment | (640.3) | (549.1) | (199.4) | (118.4) |
| Proceeds on disposal of: | | | | |
| • Controlled entities and businesses | 230.1 | 20.3 | – | – |
| • Investments | 33.8 | 11.3 | – | – |
| • Property, plant and equipment | 41.7 | 48.0 | 3.5 | 2.5 |
| **Net cash from investing activities** | **(516.5)** | **(675.8)** | **(181.2)** | **(576.0)** |
| **Cash flows from financing activities** | | | | |
| Proceeds from share acquisition scheme | 88.0 | 77.8 | 88.0 | 77.8 |
| Proceeds from issue and call on partly-paid shares | 5.3 | 5.1 | 5.3 | 5.1 |
| Loans from associated companies and other persons | 4.6 | – | 0.3 | – |
| Loans repaid to associated companies and other persons | (9.1) | (6.9) | – | (0.6) |
| Proceeds from borrowings | 744.0 | 430.4 | 405.7 | 343.3 |
| Repayment of borrowings | (396.7) | (83.6) | (177.0) | – |
| Principal lease repayments | (14.7) | (11.0) | (3.2) | (3.1) |
| **Net cash from financing activities** | **421.4** | **411.8** | **319.1** | **422.5** |
| **Net increase/(decrease) in cash held** | **94.7** | **(9.9)** | **4.8** | **(6.5)** |
| Cash at the beginning of the year | 64.2 | 64.4 | (12.1) | (5.6) |
| Less cash in entities deconsolidated as at 1 July 1995 | (27.6) | – | – | – |
| Exchange rate changes on foreign currency cash flows and cash balances | (6.1) | 9.7 | – | – |
| **Cash at the end of the year (2)** | **125.2** | **64.2** | **(7.3)** | **(12.1)** |

| | Consolidated | | Amcor Limited | |
|---|---|---|---|---|
| For year ended 30 June | 1996 | 1995 | 1996 | 1995 |
| | $ million | $ million | $ million | $ million |
| **(1) Reconciliation of operating profit after income tax** | | | | |
| **to net cash provided by operating activities** | | | | |
| Operating profit after income tax | 339.0 | 366.9 | 247.1 | 268.4 |
| Depreciation of property, | | | | |
| plant and equipment | 198.9 | 219.7 | 38.8 | 53.0 |
| Amortisation of leased assets | 7.6 | 6.0 | 5.6 | 7.3 |
| Amortisation of goodwill | 46.8 | 14.2 | 4.7 | 2.0 |
| (Profits)/losses on disposal of | | | | |
| non-current assets | (5.9) | (7.3) | (0.9) | 0.2 |
| Abnormal items from operational activities | 31.7 | 34.4 | 13.9 | 3.3 |
| Increase/(decrease) in current and | | | | |
| deferred taxes | (16.7) | 63.0 | (49.5) | 41.6 |
| Increase/(decrease) in provisions | (63.7) | 16.3 | (18.1) | (17.2) |
| Dividends paid | (230.8) | (212.5) | (230.8) | (212.5) |
| Cash flow from operations before | | | | |
| abnormal items | 306.9 | 500.7 | 10.8 | 146.1 |
| **Change in assets and liabilities** | | | | |
| **excluding acquisitions/disposals** | | | | |
| **of controlled entities and businesses:** | | | | |
| (Increase)/decrease in debtors, | | | | |
| prepayments and other items | (115.8) | (238.1) | (54.6) | (30.2) |
| (Increase)/decrease in inventories | 21.0 | (283.0) | (93.1) | (46.3) |
| (Increase)/decrease in creditors and accruals | (22.3) | 274.5 | 3.8 | 77.4 |
| **Net cash from operating activities** | **189.8** | **254.1** | **(133.1)** | **147.0** |

**(2) Reconciliation of cash**

For the purposes of the Statement of Cash Flows, cash includes cash on hand and at bank and short-term money market investments, net of outstanding bank overdrafts. Cash as at 30 June 1996 as shown in the Statement of Cash Flows is reconciled to the related items in the Balance Sheet as follows:

| | | | | |
|---|---|---|---|---|
| Cash – refer Note 6 | 125.2 | 95.8 | 0.2 | 0.2 |
| Short-term deposits – refer Note 7 | 65.3 | 33.6 | – | – |
| Bank overdrafts – refer Note 14 | (65.3) | (65.2) | (7.5) | (12.3) |
| | 125.2 | 64.2 | (7.3) | (12.1) |

**(3) Non-cash financing and investing activities**

During the year, the Economic Entity acquired property, plant and equipment with an aggregate value of $10.2 million by means of finance leases (1995 $7.7 million). These acquisitions are not reflected in the Statement of Cash Flows.

*Source:* Amcor Ltd, 1996 Annual Report.

## AASB 1031: Materiality

materiality    The concept of materiality, requiring financial reports to disclose all material information, is a basic feature of accounting. Consideration of materiality has implications for such questions as whether a particular item should be recorded in its own specific account or whether it is necessary for an individual item to be disclosed separately in the financial report. AASB 1031: Materiality states that consideration of materiality is an essential part of decisions about the information to be included in financial reports and how it is to be presented (para 3.1.2). This is because the inclusion of information that is not material, or the exclusion of information that is material, may impair the usefulness of the information provided to users.

AASB 1031 defines materiality, explains the role of materiality in making judgments in the preparation and presentation of the financial reports, and requires the standards specified in other accounting standards to be applied where their effect is material (para 3.1). Information is material if its omission, misstatement or non-disclosure has the potential to adversely affect (a) decisions about the allocation of scarce resources made by users of the financial report, or (b) the discharge of accountability by the management or governing body of the entity (para 4.1). In deciding whether an item or aggregate of items is material, the nature and amount of the items usually must be evaluated together, although individual items may be material solely due to their amount or solely due to their nature (para 4.1.3). An example of the latter would be related party transactions involving directors, which are required to be disclosed separately irrespective of amount pursuant to AASB 1017: Related Party Disclosures.

AASB 1031 emphasises that materiality is a matter of professional judgment. This is influenced by the characteristics of the entity and perceptions as to who are, or are likely to be, the users of the financial reports, and consideration of their information needs (para 4.1.6). However, arbitrary quantitative thresholds are included in the standard to guide professional judgment. These quantitative guidelines involve a comparison of the particular item with its base amount. Balance sheet items are compared with total equity or the appropriate asset or liability class, profit and loss items are compared with operating profit or loss or the appropriate revenue or expense amount, and cash flow statement items are compared with net cash provided by, or used in, the applicable operating, investing or financing activity (para 4.1.4). If the particular item is equal to or greater than 10% of the appropriate base amount, it would be presumed to be material unless there is evidence or convincing argument to the contrary (para 4.1.6(a)). Similarly, amounts equal to or less than 5% of the base amount would be presumed not to be material without evidence or convincing argument to the contrary (para 4.1.6(b)). Items between 5% and 10% of the base amount would obviously require the exercise of professional judgment in determining materiality.

## AASB 1034: Information to be Disclosed in Financial Reports

The former Schedule 5 to the Corporations Regulations, operative for financial years ending before 30 June 1997, required many individual disclosures in the financial reports. However, there was a degree of overlap between the disclosure requirements of Schedule 5 and the accounting standards. To avoid this duplication, Schedule 5 was repealed and AASB 1034 was promulgated to require the disclosure of various significant items not disclosed pursuant to other accounting standards.

The broad purpose of AASB 1034 is to:
- specify the manner in which assets, liabilities and equity items are to be classified;
- prescribe the presentation of particular assets, liabilities and equity items in the balance sheet and require certain details about them to be disclosed in the financial report; and
- prescribe specific disclosures additional to those required by other accounting standards.

The disclosure requirements specified in AASB 1034 are relatively detailed. The aim in this section of the chapter is to provide an overview of the major requirements. Some of the guidance provided by AASB 1034 has been referred to earlier in this chapter. This includes the example balance sheet and profit and loss formats (Appendix 1 of AASB 1034), the requirement for balance sheet information to be condensed into relevant and comparable categories (para 4.1), and the requirement for prior year comparative information (para 14).

AASB 1034 requires the financial report to be presented in the English language and in Australian currency, and to disclose the periods to which the report relates (para 13). For balance sheet amounts, the following items must be disclosed separately, classified between current and non-current amounts where applicable (para 5.1):

- cash
- inventories
- receivables
- investments
- property, plant and equipment
- intangibles
- accounts payable
- borrowings
- provisions
- issued capital
- reserves
- retained profits/accumulated losses.

The aggregate amounts of the following items must also be disclosed in the balance sheet (para 5.2):

- current assets
- non-current assets
- total assets
- current liabilities
- non-current liabilities
- total liabilities
- net assets
- total equity.

Various other detailed disclosure requirements for assets, liabilities and equity items are specified in paras 6 to 9 of AASB 1034. In addition, the amount of the following items recognised in the profit and loss statement must be disclosed in the financial report (para 10.1):

- dividend revenue;
- interest revenue;
- borrowing costs;
- net gains or losses on the disposal of assets;
- any net increment and/or decrement arising from the revaluation of assets;
- bad and doubtful debts; and
- amortisation, depreciation and diminution in the value of non-current assets.

Other disclosures required by AASB 1034 (paras 11 and 12) relate to:

- auditor's remuneration, divided between fees for the audit and for other services and between the parent entity and subsidiaries;
- where the entity is dependent on another entity for a significant volume of business or financial support, the name of the entity on which there is an economic dependence and the nature of that dependency;
- the extent to which dividends paid and proposed have been franked;
- the amount of franking credits available for the subsequent financial year; and
- details of executive remuneration. Details include: (a) the aggregate remuneration of all executive officers earning $100 000 or more; and (b) the number of executive officers whose total remuneration falls within each successive $10 000 band, commencing at $100 000. This information is only required for disclosing entities.

## STOCK EXCHANGE LISTING REQUIREMENTS

Companies listed on the Australian Stock Exchange must comply with its listing rules. Major requirements are for the continuous disclosure of price-sensitive financial information and half-yearly reporting. These were specified in the ASX's listing requirements prior to the Disclosing Entity provisions of the Corporations Law. A further major requirement is for companies to provide, in their annual reports, a statement of the main corporate governance practices that the company had in place during the reporting period.

The listing rules also specify certain disclosure requirements for financial statements additional to those required by the Corporations Law and accounting standards. These include details of substantial shareholders, distribution of shareholders (by number of shares), voting rights, the 20 largest shareholders and the percentage of the company's shares held by these shareholders, principal registered office, share registries, and the stock exchange or exchanges on which the company's shares are listed.

# Review

The material in this chapter has provided a broad overview of the authoritative principles that must be complied with in preparing and reporting financial information. The Corporations Law, including the First Simplification Act and the Second Simplification Bill when enacted, together with accounting standards represent the principal sources of authority and guidance. While some of the requirements are detailed and complex, a perusal of a public company's annual report will provide an appreciation of how the various provisions and guidelines interact in specifying the form and content of financial statements in practice.

# Endnotes

1 American Accounting Association (1966), *A Statement of Basic Accounting Theory*, American Accounting Association, Evanston, Illinois, p 1.
2 Australian Accounting Research Foundation and Australian Accounting Standards Board (1995), *Policy Statement 5: The Nature and Purpose of Statements of Accounting Concepts*, March, AARF and AASB, paras 5 and 6.

3 The Statements of Accounting Concepts (SACs) have been prepared jointly by the Public Sector Accounting Standards Board of the Australian Accounting Research Foundation and the Australian Accounting Standards Board (or the latter body's predecessor, the Accounting Standards Review Board). The four SACs issued to date are: SAC 1: Definition of the Reporting Entity (August 1990); SAC 2: Objective of General Purpose Financial Reporting (August 1990); SAC 3: Qualitative Characteristics of Financial Information (August 1990); and SAC 4: Definition and Recognition of the Elements of Financial Statements (March 1992, revised and reissued March 1995).

4 The Corporations Law prior to the Second Simplification Bill referred to the profit and loss *account*, and this is the term also used in AASB 1034. However, the Second Simplification Bill refers to the profit and loss *statement*.

## KEY TERMS

| | | |
|---|---|---|
| abnormal items | extraordinary items | related parties |
| accountability | financial records | relevance |
| annual report | financial reports | reliability |
| auditors | general purpose financial reports | reporting entity |
| audits | | segment reporting |
| comparability | half-yearly reporting | size test |
| conceptual framework | industry and geographical segments | small proprietary company |
| concise financial report | | statement of cash flows |
| continuous disclosure | large proprietary company | summary of accounting policies |
| differential reporting | material information | |
| directors' declaration | materiality | timely basis |
| directors' report | operating revenue | true and fair view |
| disclosing entities | price-sensitive information | understandability |
| enhanced disclosure requirements | profit and loss account | users' information needs |
| | qualitative characteristics | |

## REVIEW QUESTIONS

**11.1** (a) List the main categories of users of company financial statements.
(b) Provide examples of the purposes for which users might utilise the information conveyed in financial statements.

**11.2** The corporate form of organisation involves the separation of ownership and control and the principle of limited liability. Explain the relationship between these principles and the requirement for, and role of, company financial statements.

**11.3** Explain the concept of the reporting entity as outlined in SAC 1.

**11.4** Summarise the nature and content of the concepts outlined in SAC 2 and SAC 3.

**11.5** Outline the categories of companies required to prepare and lodge audited financial statements pursuant to the Corporations Law.

**11.6** Summarise the general requirements for financial records specified in the Second Corporate Law Simplification Bill 1996.

**11.7** Explain the meaning of the term *true and fair*, and summarise the Corporations Law requirements relating to a true and fair view.

**11.8** What are the required components of company financial statements pursuant to the Corporations Law?

**11.9** Outline the relationship between the Corporations Law and AASB accounting standards.

**11.10** Why is a statement of cash flows considered to represent an important component of a company's financial statements?

**11.11** (a) Outline the requirements for the directors' declaration specified in the Second Corporate Law Simplification Bill 1996.
(b) Outline the requirements for the directors' report specified in the Second Corporate Law Simplification Bill 1996.

**11.12** Summarise the requirements for the audit of company financial statements pursuant to the Corporations Law.

**11.13** When will an entity be classified as a disclosing entity? What are the additional reporting requirements with which disclosing entities must comply, and why is it considered that these entities should be subject to additional reporting requirements?

# EXERCISES

**Exercise 11.14**  **Objective of general purpose financial reports**
If general purpose financial statements are designed to satisfy the common information needs of a wide range of users and potential users, they will inevitably be prepared on the basis of compromise. Accordingly, financial statements prepared according to this objective will not successfully fulfil the needs of any individual user group.

*Required*
Critically evaluate the above statement.

**Exercise 11.15**  **Reporting entity tests**
The size test specified in the Corporations Law represents a more objective and workable concept than the reporting entity concept specified in SAC 1. Hence, the size test is the more preferable for the purpose of determining whether an individual company is required to prepare and publish financial statements.

*Required*
Explain what is meant by the term 'differential reporting', and critically evaluate the above comment.

**Exercise 11.16**

**Profit and loss — determination and disclosure**

AASB 1018 requires use of the all-inclusive approach for the determination of profit and loss for a financial period and requires the separate disclosure of abnormal and extraordinary items.

*Required*

Explain the meaning of each of these terms and provide examples of each. Explain why, in the context of the purpose of financial statements, the all-inclusive approach to profit determination is considered to be appropriate and why it is considered necessary to separately disclose abnormal and extraordinary items.

**Exercise 11.17**

**Abnormal and extraordinary items**

Hopkins Ltd manufactures and retails fashion clothing. For the year ended 30 June 20X4, and prior to the finalisation of the accounts for the items listed below, the company calculates its operating profit before tax as $500 000 and profit after tax as $320 000.

*Required*

State whether the following items, resulting from transactions or events occurring during the financial year, require separate classification and disclosure in the profit and loss statement as abnormal or extraordinary items (treat each item independently). Provide reasons for your answers.

(a) Hopkins earned a profit of $40 000 from the sale of shares held in a public company listed on the Australian Stock Exchange. As Hopkins is not a share trader and as the shares were originally acquired prior to the introduction of capital gains tax, none of the profit on sale is assessable to company tax. Hopkins continues to hold an investment portfolio, accumulated over a period of 15 years, with a market value at balance date of approximately $200 000. The sale of the shares during the year was the first ever undertaken by Hopkins. The company has no immediate plans for further share sales.

(b) A block of land held by Hopkins was compulsorily acquired by the federal government to allow for a future freeway. As a result of the compulsory acquisition, the company earned a profit amounting to $40 000. This transaction is liable to capital gains tax of $6000. The land had originally been acquired seven years ago to allow for a planned expansion. As Hopkins still plans to undertake this future expansion, the company intends to acquire another property with the proceeds from the sale.

(c) Due to various factors, including a particularly bad storm during the year, Hopkins writes off damaged inventory amounting to $45 000. This write-off is tax deductible at the company tax rate of 36%. The company's inventory write-offs have been relatively consistent over the past ten years, averaging 4.5% of the company's operating profit after tax.

(d) Hopkins has reviewed the useful life of its plant and equipment at balance date and determined that the life of some items should be revised downwards from six years to four years. This results in an adjustment to depreciation amounting to $42 000. Assume that this amount is deductible for tax purposes at the company tax rate of 36%.

(e) Hopkins received a payment of $58 500 on the liquidation of Moyne Pty Ltd. Moyne had been a major customer of the company, and this payment represented settlement of a receivable amounting to $120 000. This receivable had been written off as a bad debt in a prior financial year. The company does not usually have a high level of bad debt recoveries, with these averaging less than 1% of the company's annual operating profit after tax. Assume the amount received is subject to tax at the company tax rate of 36%.

(f) A small warehouse owned by Hopkins was destroyed by fire. The warehouse had been revalued in the accounts to $250 000, but was only insured to the extent of its original cost of $180 000. The warehouse contained a small amount of inventory, but this damage was covered by a general insurance policy held by the company. Assume that the uninsured amount of $70 000 is deductible for tax purposes at the company tax rate of 36%.

**Exercise 11.18**

**Various accounting standards**

Explain the general nature of the disclosures required by the accounting standards listed below. Why are these disclosures considered to be necessary in meeting the information needs of financial statement users?

(a) AASB 1001: Accounting Policies;
(b) AASB 1004: Disclosure of Operating Revenue;
(c) AASB 1005: Financial Reporting by Segments; and
(d) AASB 1017: Related Party Disclosures.

**Exercise 11.19**

**Profit and loss statement**

Wimmera Ltd, a company incorporated on 1 January 20X0, has prepared the following profit and loss statement for the year ended 30 June 20X4.

| Wimmera Ltd | |
|---|---|
| **Profit and Loss Statement for the year ended 30 June 20X4** | |
| | $000 |
| Operating revenue | $1 464 |
| Operating profit before abnormal items and tax | 365 |
| Abnormal items (after income tax of $38) | (68) |
| Income tax expense | (93) |
| Operating profit after income tax | 204 |
| Profit on extraordinary items after income tax | 77 |
| Net profit | $ 281 |
| Dividends paid and provided | $15 |
| Retained profits at the end of the financial year | $431 |

*Required*

Indicate the respects in which the above profit and loss statement should be amended, or additional notes added, to comply with the provisions of AASB 1001, AASB 1004, AASB 1018 and AASB 1034.

**Exercise 11.20**   Profit and loss statement

The trial balance for Wannon Ltd as at 30 June 20X3, prepared prior to the posting of closing journal entries, is presented below.

| | Debit $000 | Credit $000 |
|---|---:|---:|
| Sales revenue | | 997 |
| Dividend revenue | | 7 |
| Interest revenue | | 3 |
| Cost of sales | 355 | |
| Amortisation of goodwill | 5 | |
| Auditor remuneration | 36 | |
| Depreciation – motor vehicles | 25 | |
| Depreciation – plant & equipment | 66 | |
| Doubtful debts | 8 | |
| Interest expense | 32 | |
| Office expenses | 92 | |
| Rental | 15 | |
| Salaries | 104 | |
| Selling expenses | 97 | |
| Bad debt recovered (abnormal) | | 26 |
| Loss on destruction of building (extraordinary) | 42 | |
| Income tax expense | 61 | |
| Cash on hand (current) | 13 | |
| Inventories | 298 | |
| Receivables | 192 | |
| Provision for doubtful debts | | 12 |
| Deposits | 40 | |
| Future income tax benefits | 24 | |
| Franchises (cost) | 95 | |
| Goodwill | 100 | |
| Accumulated amortisation – goodwill | | 20 |
| Motor vehicles | 150 | |
| Accumulated depreciation – motor vehicles | | 50 |
| Plant & equipment | 460 | |
| Accumulated depreciation – plant & equipment | | 147 |
| Shares in listed companies (cost) | 62 | |
| Accounts payable | | 102 |
| Bank loan | | 100 |
| Bank overdraft | | 35 |
| Provision for deferred income tax | | 24 |
| Provision for income tax | | 59 |
| Unsecured notes | | 150 |
| Paid-up capital (500 000 ordinary shares) | | 400 |
| General reserve 1 July 20X2 | | 15 |
| Retained profits 1 July 20X2 | | 225 |
| | $2 372 | $2 372 |

Additional information:

(a) Included in auditor remuneration is $16 000 in fees for management consulting services.

(b) The bad debt recovered is subject to tax at the company tax rate of 36%. The loss on destruction of the building, caused by fire, is deductible for tax purposes.

(c) Directors have recommended a dividend of $65 000. This dividend, franked for income tax purposes at the rate of 36%, will utilise all the company's franking credits already in existence and those which will arise from income tax payable as at the end of the financial year.

(d) Directors also propose a transfer to general reserve of $25 000.

*Required*

Prepare a profit and loss statement and related notes for Wannon Ltd for the year ended 30 June 20X3. These should be in accordance with AASB 1018 and AASB 1034 (ignoring the requirement for prior period comparative figures).

**Exercise 11.21**  **Balance sheet**

Woomera Ltd, a company incorporated on 1 January 20X0, has prepared the following balance sheet as at 30 June 20X3.

**Woomera Ltd**
**Balance Sheet as at 30 June 20X3**

| | $000 |
|---|---|
| *Assets* | |
| Current assets | |
| Cash | 24 |
| Receivables & inventories (net) | 360 |
| Other | 190 |
| Non–current assets | |
| Shares in listed companies (at cost) | 57 |
| Plant & equipment (net) | 397 |
| Land & buildings (at valuation) | 560 |
| Intangibles (net) | 145 |
| Future income tax benefits | 34 |
| Research & development expenditure | 84 |
| *Total assets* | 1 851 |
| | |
| *Liabilities* | |
| Current liabilities | |
| Accounts payable & provisions | 82 |
| Borrowings | 86 |
| Provisions | 75 |
| Non–current liabilities | |
| Debentures (secured pursuant to trust deed) | 400 |
| Unsecured notes | 200 |
| Provisions | 54 |
| *Total liabilities* | 897 |
| | |
| *Net assets* | $954 |
| | |
| *Shareholders' equity* | |
| Ordinary & preference share capital | 700 |
| Retained profits & reserves | 254 |
| *Total shareholders' equity* | $954 |

*Required*

Indicate the respects in which the above balance sheet should be amended, or additional notes added, to comply with the provisions of AASB 1001 and AASB 1034.

**Exercise 11.22**  **Balance sheet**

Refer to Exercise 11.20 (Wannon Ltd). The following additional information is provided:

(a) All assets other than cash on hand, inventories and receivables are non-current. All liabilities other than accounts payable, bank overdraft, provision for income tax, and provision for dividend are non-current.

(b) Paid-up capital comprises 500 000 fully paid shares. No new shares were issued during the financial year.

(c) The company has a continuing dispute with the Australian Taxation Office following a tax audit held during the prior financial year. The dispute relates to repairs to plant and equipment claimed during the 20X1 and 20X2 financial years. The company believes that these deductions were correctly claimed and has received legal opinion from its solicitor to support this view. Accordingly, none of the disputed amount has been recognised in the accounts as a liability. The maximum amount of tax and penalties that would be likely to become payable, if the company was ultimately to be unsuccessful in the dispute, is estimated at approximately $15 000.

*Required*

Prepare a balance sheet and related notes, based on the above information, for Wannon Ltd as at 30 June 20X3. These should be in accordance with AASB 1034 (ignoring the requirement for prior period comparative figures).

**Exercise 11.23**  **Statement of cash flows**

A summary of Skene Ltd's cash account for the year ended 30 June 20X5 is provided below.

• Cash on hand at 1 July 20X4 is $9495 and at 30 June 20X5 is $12 292.

• Cash receipts for the year comprise the following items.

|  | $ |
|---|---|
| Issue of ordinary shares | 60 000 |
| Cash sales | 41 641 |
| Receipts from debtors | 65 288 |
| Bank loan | 30 000 |
| Sale of land | 75 600 |
| Sale of listed shares | 32 640 |
| Dividends | 1 275 |
| Interest | 2 384 |
|  | $308 828 |

- Cash payments for the year comprise the following.

|  | $ |
|---|---|
| Property, plant & equipment | 67 141 |
| Long-term loan repayment | 60 000 |
| Suppliers, for inventory & expenses | 36 944 |
| Dividends | 12 605 |
| Interest | 3 425 |
| Income tax | 31 167 |
| Wages | 42 777 |
| Research & development | 51 972 |
|  | $306 031 |

*Required*
Prepare a statement of cash flows for Skene Ltd for the year ended 30 June 20X5 in accordance with AASB 1026. Prior period comparative figures and a reconciliation of cash flows from operating activities to operating profit after tax are not required.

**Exercise 11.24**  **Comprehensive**
The trial balance for Foster Ltd as at 30 June 20X2, prepared prior to the posting of closing journal entries, is presented below.

|  | Debit | Credit |
|---|---|---|
|  | $000 | $000 |
| Sales revenue |  | 1 106 |
| Interest revenue |  | 8 |
| Profit on sale of plant & equipment |  | 10 |
| Purchases | 529 |  |
| Administrative & selling expenses | 153 |  |
| Amortisation of goodwill | 5 |  |
| Auditor remuneration | 18 |  |
| Bad debts | 5 |  |
| Depreciation – plant & equipment | 68 |  |
| Doubtful debts | 6 |  |
| Interest expense | 21 |  |
| Miscellaneous expenses | 28 |  |
| Rent | 17 |  |
| Salaries | 187 |  |
| Proceeds from insurance claim (extraordinary) |  | 20 |
| Income tax expense | 39 |  |
| Accounts receivable | 118 |  |
| Provision for doubtful debts |  | 11 |
| Cash on hand | 4 |  |
| Inventories 1 July 20X1 | 87 |  |
| Deposits | 130 |  |
| Future income tax benefits | 18 |  |
| Franchise (cost) | 220 |  |
| Accumulated amortisation – franchise |  | 20 |
| Goodwill | 100 |  |
| Accumulated amortisation – goodwill |  | 25 |

| | Debit $000 | Credit $000 |
|---|---|---|
| Plant & equipment | 472 | |
| Accumulated depreciation – plant & equipment | | 203 |
| Accounts payable | | 114 |
| Bank overdraft | | 13 |
| Provision for income tax | | 37 |
| Bank loan | | 200 |
| Provision for deferred income tax | | 22 |
| Paid-up capital (ordinary) | | 400 |
| Retained profits 15 December 20X1 | | 36 |
| | $2 225 | $2 225 |

Additional information:
(a) Inventory on hand at 30 June 20X2 amounts to $92 000.
(b) Included in auditor remuneration is $6000 in fees for various management consulting services.
(c) The profit on sale of plant and equipment is not considered to be abnormal. The written-down value of the item sold was $77 000.
(d) The proceeds from the insurance claim (extraordinary item) relate to a fire in one of the company's stores. The amount received is subject to taxation at the company rate of 36%.
(e) An interim dividend of $16 000 (2 cents per share) was paid on 15 December 20X1.
(f) Directors have recommended a final dividend of $32 000 (4 cents per share).
(g) All dividends are fully franked for income tax purposes at the rate of 36%. After payment of the above dividends, and taking into account franking credits that will arise from income tax payable as at the end of the financial year, the balance of the franking account will be $36 920.
(h) All assets other than accounts receivable, cash on hand and inventories are non-current. All liabilities other than accounts payable, bank overdraft, provision for income tax, and provision for dividend are non-current.
(i) Share capital comprises 800 000 fully paid ordinary shares. No new shares were issued during the financial year.

*Required*
Prepare a profit and loss statement and related notes for Foster Ltd for the year ended 30 June 20X3. These should be in accordance with AASB 1004, AASB 1018 and AASB 1034 (ignoring the requirement for prior period comparative figures).

**Exercise 11.25** Comprehensive
The trial balance for Banyan Ltd, a computer consulting firm, as at 30 June 20X3 is presented on the following page.

|  | Debit | Credit |
| --- | ---: | ---: |
|  | $000 | $000 |
| Sales revenue |  | 712 |
| Contract fees revenue |  | 645 |
| Dividend revenue |  | 12 |
| Interest revenue |  | 9 |
| Cost of sales | 362 |  |
| Administrative expenses | 77 |  |
| Amortisation of goodwill | 9 |  |
| Auditor remuneration | 33 |  |
| Bad debts | 15 |  |
| Depreciation – motor vehicles | 28 |  |
| Depreciation – office furniture & fittings | 36 |  |
| Depreciation – office equipment | 45 |  |
| Doubtful debts | 8 |  |
| Interest expense | 55 |  |
| Miscellaneous expenses | 34 |  |
| Profit on sale of property, plant & equipment |  | 16 |
| Salaries | 207 |  |
| Selling expenses | 95 |  |
| Depreciation adjustment (abnormal) | 44 |  |
| Profit on sale of copyright (extraordinary) |  | 62 |
| Income tax expense | 132 |  |
| Accounts receivable | 239 |  |
| Provision for doubtful debts |  | 17 |
| Cash on hand | 2 |  |
| Inventories | 141 |  |
| Deposits | 100 |  |
| Future income tax benefits | 34 |  |
| Goodwill | 80 |  |
| Accumulated amortisation – goodwill |  | 12 |
| Land & buildings (directors' valuation) | 600 |  |
| Motor vehicles (cost) | 150 |  |
| Accumulated depreciation – motor vehicles |  | 44 |
| Office equipment (cost) | 224 |  |
| Accumulated depreciation – office equipment |  | 55 |
| Office furniture & fittings (cost) | 182 |  |
| Accumulated depreciation – office furniture & fittings |  | 25 |
| Research & development expenditure (capitalised) | 107 |  |
| Shares in listed companies (cost) | 230 |  |
| Accounts payable |  | 66 |
| Bank overdraft |  | 45 |
| Provision for income tax |  | 70 |
| Provision for deferred income tax |  | 31 |
| Unsecured notes |  | 300 |
| Paid-up ordinary capital (400 000 shares) |  | 800 |
| Paid-up preference capital (200 000 shares) |  | 200 |
| Asset revaluation reserve |  | 100 |
| General reserve 1 July 20X2 |  | 31 |
| Retained profits 31 December 20X2 |  | 17 |
|  | $3 269 | $3 269 |

Additional information:
(a) Included in auditor remuneration is $13 000 in fees for taxation services.
(b) The profit on sale of property, plant and equipment is not considered to be abnormal. The written-down value of the item sold was $104 000.
(c) The abnormal item relates to a prior year adjustment of depreciation. This item is deductible for tax purposes at the company tax rate of 36%.
(d) The extraordinary profit on sale of the copyright is subject to capital gains tax of $20 000.
(e) Interim dividends of $6000 on preference shares (3 cents per share) and $4000 on ordinary shares (1 cent per share) were paid on 31 December 20X2.
(f) Directors have recommended a final dividend of $8000 on preference shares (4 cents per share) and $9000 on ordinary shares (2.25 cents per share).
(g) All dividends are fully franked for income tax purposes at the rate of 36%. After payment of the above dividends, and taking into account franking credits that will arise from income tax payable as at the end of the financial year, the balance of the franking account will be $112 240.
(h) Directors propose a transfer to general reserve of $50 000.
(i) All assets other than accounts receivable, cash on hand and inventories are non-current. All liabilities other than accounts payable, bank overdraft, provision for income tax and provision for dividend are non-current.
(j) Land and buildings were revalued by the directors on 30 June 20X3 on the basis of their estimate of current market value. The written-down value of the land and buildings at the date of revaluation was $500 000 ($200 000 for land and $300 000 for buildings). The land was revalued to $275 000 and the buildings to $325 000. No other revaluations were made during the year.
(k) Share capital comprises 400 000 fully paid ordinary shares and 200 000 fully paid cumulative 7% preference shares. No new shares were issued during the financial year.

*Required*
Prepare a profit and loss statement, balance sheet and related notes for Banyan Ltd for the year ended 30 June 20X3. These should be in accordance with AASB 1004, AASB 1018 and AASB 1034 (ignoring the requirement for prior period comparative figures).

chapter

# 12

# EXTERNAL ADMINISTRATION, INCLUDING LIQUIDATION

# introduction

This chapter deals with the various forms of external administration of a company as set out in the Corporations Law. External administration means that a company comes under the control of outside managers as opposed to its directors. Usually the responsibility for the control of a company is vested in directors who are appointed by shareholders. In a normal operating situation a company's directors are authorised to act in accordance with the company's constitution and the Corporations Law. Due to changing circumstances, which normally include the inability of the company to meet its liabilities as they fall due, directors may lose many of their powers and the control of the company is passed to an external administrator. Therefore, external administration is usually a response to company failure or distress. Such external administration includes the appointment of a receiver, an administrator or a liquidator. Each of these situations will be discussed. Companies subject to external administration must publicise this fact in all their dealings with external parties.

# Responses to financial difficulties

While the emphasis in this chapter will be on the various accounting issues, the legal implications will also be discussed because the accounting issues are guided by various provisions of the Corporations Law and case law. Before considering the various issues raised in this chapter, it is worth reviewing the basic structure of a balance sheet and the importance of cash flows in meeting the company's obligations as they fall due. A company's assets are funded by both owners' equity and external liabilities. As a **debt levels** general rule, the higher the debt levels or leverage, the greater the risk that a company **leverage** may not be able to meet its debts as they fall due. These liabilities are legally enforceable obligations which must be paid, as opposed to payments to shareholders via dividends which are at the discretion of directors' recommendations and approved by shareholders. Thus, it may be seen that liabilities are appropriately called primary claims against assets and shareholders' equity residual claims against assets.

In diagrammatic form:

| Liabilities | + | Owners' equity | = | Assets |
|---|---|---|---|---|
| **Primary** | | **Residual** | | |
| claims | | claims | | |
| against | | against | | |
| assets | | assets | | |
| ↓ | | ↓ | | |
| First to be paid | | Only paid after all liabilities have been satisfied | | |

If a company is to be liquidated, the assets must be sold and liabilities paid off in a strict order of repayment. Depending on their nature, assets may be difficult and costly to sell. In some circumstances it may be better if the assets are sold as a productive unit or a going concern, as this will provide a greater return to those with claims against the company. For example, selling a group of assets that produce a product would generally result in better cash proceeds than selling off the assets individually.

When assets have been disposed of, some liabilities rank higher for repayment than others, due to certain provisions of the Corporations Law and agreements previously entered into by the company. The liability structure of a company must therefore be **liquidator** carefully considered by the liquidator in order to ensure creditors are afforded their appropriate priority. Finally, the rights and obligations of shareholders must be carefully examined to ensure equitable treatment of all classes of shareholders.

**external administrator** The steps involved in the appointment of an external administrator are as follows:

Company A Ltd

Experiences trading difficulties and/or a shortfall in cash reserves to meet obligations or some other financial distress.

↓

Company A may enter into a:
• receivership,
• voluntary administration, or
• scheme of arrangement,

in order to achieve profitability, or to ensure the best return to creditors and shareholders. All of the above are therefore possible avenues for Company A Ltd to recover to profitability once more. If these avenues fail:

↓

**Company A enters liquidation, which may be:**
- members' voluntary,
- creditors' voluntary, or
- court-ordered.

↓

Upon completion of liquidation, Company A is struck off the register of companies and ceases to exist.

It should also be noted that under the Corporations Law, ss 572 to 574, a company which 'is not carrying on a business or is not in operation' may be struck off the register of companies. This may occur when a parent company has an inoperative subsidiary company which it no longer requires. The parent company simply applies to the Australian Securities Commission (ASC) for deregistration of the subsidiary. This procedure is much cheaper than formal liquidation proceedings.

**Australian Securities Commission**

# Receivership

**receiver**  A receiver must be a registered liquidator. The duties and responsibilities of a receiver are governed by the Corporations Law, ss 416 to 434.

A receiver is usually appointed by debenture (debt) holders under the terms of a debenture trust deed (essentially a loan agreement). A debenture trust deed is a document which states, amongst other things, what is to happen if interest or principal repayments are not paid on time. Non-payment may result in the appointment of a receiver by the debenture holders. Other secured creditors also have this right to protect their interests. Some secured creditors have a fixed charge against specific assets of a company. This is analogous to purchasing a house and borrowing money from a lending institution. The institution always has a charge against the property in case loan repayments are not met; thus, the house may be sold to protect the lending institution's investment.

**debenture trust deed**

**secured creditors**

A receiver's appointment is usually because of the following circumstances:
- failure of a company to make a loan repayment or interest payment to a secured creditor; or
- failure to adhere to any covenants contained in a debenture trust deed.

**covenants**

The major role of a receiver is to protect the interests of a secured creditor. This includes the protection of a company's assets over which the security has been given, receiving income from the secured assets, or arranging the sale of the assets to repay the secured creditor(s). If a company in receivership is forced into liquidation (say, by other creditors), the receiver must hand any surplus funds to the liquidator after the secured liability is discharged. Under certain circumstances a receiver may also be appointed by the court.

# Voluntary administration

**administrator**

As a result of the *Corporate Law Reform Act 1992*, the Corporations Law provides for an administrator to be appointed to take charge and investigate the affairs of a company in financial difficulties. The provisions covering voluntary administration came into effect on 25 June 1993 and replace official management provisions. Where company directors believe that the company is insolvent or may become insolvent (that is, unable to meet its debts as they fall due), an administrator may be appointed by a resolution of the board of directors. The aim of voluntary administration is to maximise the chances of the company remaining in existence, or if this is not possible, to produce a better return for the creditors and shareholders than would result from an immediate liquidation.

The major role of an administrator is to investigate the company's financial position and make appropriate recommendations to creditors. In effect, an administrator assumes control from the board of directors and is able to manage the company and dispose of assets if considered appropriate.

Following an administrator's investigation, which must be completed within 28 days of appointment, recommendations are made to creditors. These are either to:
- Enter into a deed of arrangement. (A deed of arrangement is an arrangement that binds all creditors of the company.) This will normally assist the company to return to a sound financial position, or provide for the best possible return to creditors in the circumstances.
- Liquidate the company.
- Terminate the administration and return control of the company to the board of directors (Corporations Law, s 439A).

During a voluntary administration, creditors may not take action against the company without leave of the court (Corporations Law, s 440). The intention of this section is to provide protection from creditors who may move to appoint a receiver or liquidator to safeguard their interests. Such action may not be in the best interests of all the company's creditors. There are two exceptions to this embargo:
1 A secured creditor with charges over all, or substantially all, of a company's property may enforce their charge if they do so within ten business days of the appointment of a voluntary administrator (Corporations Law, s 441A).
2 If a secured creditor has begun proceedings to enforce a charge before the commencement of voluntary administration, it may be continued (Corporations Law, s 441B).

In summary, this new form of administration enables directors to appoint an insolvency expert to advise on recovery strategies and hopefully avoid the need for liquidation.

The first large company to use the new provisions of the Corporations Law dealing with voluntary administration was Brash Pty Ltd (the Brash's group). In June 1994, Brash's creditors voted 820 to 7 in favour of a proposal made by Hotel Properties and Reef Holdings Ltd. Under the proposal a Deed of Company Arrangement was entered into by creditors so that unsecured creditors would receive approximately 38 cents in the dollar and secured creditors 75 cents in the dollar. This arrangement meant that creditors would lose approximately $74 million of the total outstanding amount of $155 million. At the end of the voluntary administration period, Brash's survived and creditors were better off than if the company had been liquidated.

Another example of a successful voluntary administration is that of a Queensland company called Aromas Pty Ltd, which ran a number of up-market coffee shops. Mr David Cassidy, a partner in the Chartered Accountancy firm of Grant Thornton, was appointed to Aromas Pty Ltd in mid-April 1995 under the voluntary administration scheme. The company was experiencing cash flow problems due to its expansion policies and strong competition. It was unable to pay its legal obligations as they became due. With the assistance and cooperation of Aromas' directors, secured and unsecured creditors executed a Deed of Company Arrangement. This deed involved the implementation of a reconstruction strategy comprising the following steps:

1 An administrator was appointed and a moratorium with all unsecured creditors established.
2 The administration department of the company was rationalised and restructured as a much more efficient and cost-effective unit.
3 A major marketing program was developed and implemented to increase retail sales and realise the company's potential.
4 Selected company assets were sold.

As a result of these actions, the following results were achieved:

• Cost savings of over $500 000 a year were achieved through rationalisation, whilst trading improved from the marketing and administration measures implemented.
• The sale of selected assets generated immediate cash flows which facilitated further trading and the repayment of secured and some partly secured creditors.

It is noteworthy that all creditors have since been repaid and Aromas Pty Ltd is trading profitably.

A director of the company praised the concept of voluntary administration by saying that 'without the availability of legislation and without the reconstruction strategy of Grant Thornton the business would probably not be here today'. Mr Cassidy noted that the focus of business recovery is changing to a more constructive and preventative role, with organisations more prepared to ask for help in time to save the company from liquidation.

# Scheme of arrangement

Schemes of arrangement are governed by the Corporations Law, ss 410 to 415A. A scheme of arrangement is an opportunity for both creditors and shareholders to receive a better return under the scheme than if the company was liquidated. Such a scheme requires:

• approval by a special resolution of creditors and shareholders;
• approval by the court; and
• approval by the ASC.

Specific schemes of arrangement may include:

• creditors agreeing to accept some cash and shares or debentures in full settlement of their claims;

- preference shareholders accepting new shares, preference or ordinary, instead of receiving arrears of dividends which the company is unable to pay; and
- creditors agreeing not to pursue their claims for a specified time period.

Clearly, the various groups of claimants view such schemes of arrangement as being preferable to a liquidation where very little, if any, funds may be available to them. From a practical perspective, however, schemes of arrangement are seldom used due to the high associated costs.

# Liquidation

Liquidation is a process in which the affairs of the company are wound up, and the company is dissolved and ceases to be a legal entity. There are three types of liquidation:
(a) a members' (shareholders') voluntary liquidation;
(b) a creditors' voluntary liquidation; and
(c) a court-ordered liquidation.

Whilst the accounting treatment is the same in each case, there are different regulations attached to each type of liquidation. Part 5.4 of the Corporations Law governs a court-ordered liquidation, while Part 5.5 governs members' and creditors' voluntary liquidations.

## MEMBERS' VOLUNTARY LIQUIDATION

solvent
special resolution

A company must be solvent to be liquidated at the discretion of its shareholders. The process requires a special resolution which must be approved by three-quarters of the shareholders present at a meeting of shareholders (s 253). In this type of liquidation the directors are required to make a written declaration that they believe the company will be able to pay its debts in full within a period not exceeding 12 months after the commencement of the liquidation. This declaration of solvency is set out as Form 520 in Schedule 2 to the Corporations Regulations.

In a members' voluntary liquidation, the shareholders appoint the liquidator, who must be registered with the ASC. The company directors must prepare a statement of assets and liabilities of the company, showing the assets at their realisable amounts and a schedule of liabilities due and payable.

The liquidator is then able to take control of and sell the assets, pay out liabilities and return any surplus to shareholders. Following a final meeting of shareholders, the ASC is notified of the completion of the liquidation and the company is struck off the register of companies.

## CREDITORS' VOLUNTARY LIQUIDATION

If a company is insolvent and therefore directors are unable to make a declaration of solvency, shareholders may agree to liquidate the company in favour of creditors. Whilst the shareholders appoint a liquidator at this meeting, creditors at their subsequent meetings may nominate an alternative liquidator if they wish. In this situation the creditors are in charge of the liquidation, rather than the shareholders.

## COURT-ORDERED LIQUIDATION

The court may order a liquidation upon a petition of creditors, shareholders or the ASC. The grounds for a court-ordered liquidation include the following:

- The company is unable to pay its debts.
- The company has by special resolution resolved that it be wound up by the court.
- Directors have been acting in their own interests rather than in the interests of the company.
- The company has not lodged reports or held meetings required by the Corporations Law, or other technical requirements have not been satisfied.

When the court orders a liquidation it appoints an official liquidator. The liquidator's duties are set out in the Corporations Law and include the following:

- take possession of the company's assets;
- realise the assets or continue the business if it will result in larger proceeds on sale of the assets in the future;
- ascertain the creditors and order of payment;
- pay the creditors; and
- distribute any residual funds to shareholders.

From the above discussion it may be observed that the degree of financial distress and availability of cash to repay creditors and shareholders tends to vary over the three types of liquidation as follows:

| Financial distress | Type of liquidation | Cash availability |
|---|---|---|
| Least | Members' voluntary | Most |
| ↓ | Creditors' voluntary | ↓ |
| Most | Court-ordered | Least |

These factors are usually dependent on the degree of solvency of the company.

Under each of the three types of liquidation, *A Report as to Affairs* is compiled by the directors and given to the liquidator. Form 507 of Schedule 2 is the *pro forma* report as to affairs. This report lists the assets of the company, separating secured and unsecured assets and the estimated realisable values of each asset class. The liabilities of the company are listed in the order of repayment described below. Total liabilities are deducted from the total estimated realisable asset values to ascertain if a cash surplus exists. Any contingent assets, such as unpaid share capital, and contingent liabilities are also listed.

**contingent assets**
**contingent liabilities**

## ORDER OF PAYMENT TO CREDITORS

As a general rule, debts which are secured must be paid before unsecured debts. A secured creditor may be paid by the liquidator, or the asset which is subject to the fixed charge may be claimed by the secured creditor and sold. If there is a surplus (asset proceeds exceed the secured creditor's debt), the balance is paid to the liquidator. If the sale proceeds are less than the debt, the unpaid balance ranks as an unsecured creditor.

For example, assume A Ltd is in liquidation. It owns property with a book value of $130 000. The NBA Bank holds a fixed charge over the land as security for a loan of $100 000. The bank elects to seize and sell the property to repay the loan. Sale proceeds are $150 000 and the residual is given to the liquidator. The journal entry in the books of the liquidating company is:

|  | Debit | Credit |
|---|---|---|
| Cash | 50 000 |  |
| Loan | 100 000 |  |
| Property |  | 130 000 |
| Liquidation Account |  | 20 000 |
| (gain on sale of land) |  |  |

All creditors must be paid in full before shareholders receive any return of capital. A ranking of creditors is contained in the Corporations Law (s 556) and this has to be followed strictly as there may be insufficient funds to meet all creditors' claims.

The order of payment is as follows:

1 *Secured creditors*

**fixed charge**      (a) creditors secured by a registered fixed charge over specific assets;

**floating charge**      (b) creditors secured by a registered floating charge over circulating assets, such as inventory and accounts receivable.

Floating charges rank below certain preferred creditors, as noted below.

2 *Preferred creditors*

The Corporations Law, s 556, allows certain creditors to have preferential status. After secured creditors, these are paid next in the following order:

(a) costs of liquidation, including the liquidator's fees;

(b) accrued wages and salaries, but with a maximum of $2000 for each 'excluded employee';

(c) workers' compensation obligations;

(d) accrued annual leave, long service leave and sick leave, with a maximum of $1500 for each 'excluded employee';

(e) retrenchment payments.

Note that (b), (d) and (e) above have priority over a floating charge (Corporations Law, s 561).

3 *Unsecured creditors*

These include:

(a) trade creditors, usually suppliers of inventory;

(b) uncovered portion of secured claims (noted above);

(c) unpaid directors' fees, and directors' salaries in excess of $2000;

(d) company income tax and PAYE deductions payable and other debts owing under Commonwealth laws, such as sales tax and telephone charges;

(e) debts under state laws, such as local rates and payroll tax;

(f) dividends declared but unpaid;

(g) contingent creditors' claims.

All unsecured creditors rank equally (Corporations Law, s 559). This means that in the absence of sufficient funds, *all* unsecured creditors receive an equal proportion of their debt (eg 10 cents for each dollar owed to them).

Note that an 'excluded employee' means a company employee who has been a director of the company during the 12 months before the liquidation date.

## PAYMENTS TO SHAREHOLDERS

All outside liabilities must be repaid in full before shareholders receive any repayment of capital. In a court-ordered liquidation there are rarely any funds available for shareholders after creditors are paid. The liability of shareholders is limited to the issued value of their shares. If such shares are not fully paid and there is a shortage of funds to repay creditors, the liquidator may make calls on the partly paid shares. In the case of liquidation of a company, the issued value sets the limit of liability. It should be noted that the price originally paid for the shares by shareholders is irrelevant (assuming a listed company). For example, a shareholder may have paid $2.50 via the stock exchange for a $1 ordinary share fully paid. If the company is liquidated, the shareholder loses $1.50 immediately and can only be refunded a maximum of $1 if sufficient funds are available.

**company's constitution**  If there are a number of share classes, the company's constitution should be examined to determine their rights. If the constitution is silent, all share classes are treated the same. Further, any special rights attached to preference shares must be documented in the constitution or they are not preferential in a return of capital. Depending on the constitution, there may be a ranking of shareholder classes. For example, the order of repayment may be:

1 preference shareholders;
2 'A' ordinary shareholders;
3 'B' ordinary shareholders.

Here the preference shareholders must be repaid before the 'A' ordinary shareholders, and the latter must be repaid before the 'B' ordinary shareholders. If there is insufficient cash to repay the preference shareholders and there is no uncalled capital available on the 'A' and 'B' ordinary shares, the preference shareholders receive the remaining cash and the 'A' and 'B' ordinary shareholders receive nothing.

Another variation may be:

1 preference shareholders;
2 'A' ordinary shareholders;
  'B' ordinary shareholders;
3 'C' ordinary shareholders.

In these cases the liquidator may make calls on shares that are partly paid to make payments to higher-ranking share classes. The liability of shareholders to contribute to meet any capital deficiency is described in ss 514 to 530 of the Corporations Law.

### Deficiency of capital

**deficiency of capital**  Any deficiency of capital must be borne by shareholders in proportion to the issued value of the shares held, not in proportion to the amounts paid up on those shares

(*Re Hodges Distillery Co. Ltd; Ex parte Maude* (1870) 6 Ch App 51). Thus, shareholders who have fully paid shares are not at a disadvantage compared to those who hold partly paid shares of the same issued value. This will mean that each shareholder loses the same proportionate amount per share when there is a deficiency, irrespective of how much has been paid up. For example, Tiger Ltd has the following issued capital:

|  | $ |
|---|---|
| 200 000 $1 'A' ordinary shares fully paid | 200 000 |
| 50 000 $1 'B' ordinary shares paid to 40 cents | 20 000 |
|  | $220 000 |

Assume that after creditors are repaid there is cash left of $120 000 to repay shareholders and the two share classes rank equally. A simple table helps in the calculation.

| Share class | Issued value | Paid-up capital | Share of deficiency | | Refund | Call |
|---|---|---|---|---|---|---|
| A | 200 000 | 200 000 | (200/250 × 100 000) | 80 000 | 120 000 | – |
| B | 50 000 | 20 000 | (50/250 × 100 000) | 20 000 | – | – |
|  | 250 000 | 220 000 |  | 100 000 | 120 000 | – |
| Cash available |  | 120 000 |  |  |  |  |
| Deficiency |  | 100 000 |  |  |  |  |

Here the paid-up capital is compared with the share of deficiency to determine a refund, or whether the liquidator will make a call. A call will be made if the share of loss is greater than the paid-up capital (assuming uncalled capital is available). In this example the 'A' class shareholders receive 60 cents in the dollar and the 'B' class shareholders receive no payment. However, each share class loses 40 cents per share — that is, the *same* proportionate amount per share.

If the $30 000 in uncalled capital on 'B' ordinary shares was called up, the result using the rule established by *Maude's* case would be the same. Paid-up capital of the 'B' ordinary shares would change from $20 000 to $50 000.

| Share class | Issued value | Paid-up capital | Share of deficiency | | Refund | Call |
|---|---|---|---|---|---|---|
| – | 200 000 | 200 000 | (200/250 × 100 000) | 80 000 | 120 000 | – |
| – | 50 000 | 50 000 | (50/250 × 100 000) | 20 000 | 30 000 | – |
| – | 250 000 | 250 000 |  | 100 000 | 150 000 | – |
| Cash available |  | 150 000 |  |  |  |  |
| Deficiency |  | 100 000 |  |  |  |  |

This simply means that the call of $30 000 made on 'B' ordinary shareholders is returned to them which, of course, would be impractical but illustrates the fairness to shareholders established in *Maude's* case.

### Surplus on liquidation

If there is a surplus on liquidation (more cash available than the paid-up amount on shares) and there are no special provisions in the company's constitution, the surplus is distributed using the above rule. This will usually only be the case with a members' voluntary liquidation where the company is solvent.

Where dividends have been declared but are unpaid at the time of liquidation, they rank equally with other unsecured creditors. Where a company in liquidation has cumulative preference shares as part of its capital structure, there may be arrears of preference dividends. Such arrears will only be paid if the constitution provides for such payment on liquidation. These dividends are shown in the balance sheet as a note to the accounts. If the constitution does provide for the payment of these dividends, the journal entry is:

|  | Debit | Credit |
|---|---|---|
| Liquidation | XXX | |
|     Preference Dividend Payable | | XXX |
| Preference Dividend Payable | XXX | |
|     Cash | | XXX |

This treatment is the same as other unrecorded liabilities.

Finally, calls in advance on a particular share class are repaid before any return of capital to that share class. However, the ranking established by the constitution must be maintained. For example, if preference shares were ranked first for repayment above 'A' ordinary shares (which had calls in advance), preference shareholders would be repaid in full before the 'A' ordinary calls in advance.

## CLOSING THE COMPANY'S BOOKS

### Journal entries

The *pro forma* entries to close the books are as follows:

- If there are calls in arrears and the liquidator is unable to recover this money, the shares are usually forfeited. The journal entry is:

|  | Debit | Credit |
|---|---|---|
| Paid-up Capital | XXX | |
|     Call | | XXX |
|     Forfeited Shares | | XXX |

- Transfer the balances in all asset accounts (except cash) and other debit balances such as goodwill and preliminary expenses to the Liquidation account.

|  | Debit | Credit |
|---|---|---|
| Liquidation | XXX | |
|     Assets | | XXX |

(Any cash balances will remain in the cash account.)

- Transfer any provision accounts relating to assets, such as accumulated depreciation and allowance for doubtful debts, to the credit of the Liquidation account.

|  | Debit | Credit |
|---|---|---|
| Accumulated Depreciation | XXX | |
| Liquidation | | XXX |

- Cash proceeds on sale of assets:

| | | |
|---|---|---|
| Cash | XXX | |
| Liquidation | | XXX |

- Any additional liabilities which are not recorded in the company's records but are legitimate liabilities, such as interest on overdraft accounts, should be established by a debit to the Liquidation account.

| | | |
|---|---|---|
| Liquidation | XXX | |
| Interest Payable | | XXX |
| | | |
| Interest Payable | XXX | |
| Cash | | XXX |

Further, preference dividends that are undeclared but payable under the company's constitution in the event of liquidation should also be established by a debit to the Liquidation account.

| | | |
|---|---|---|
| Liquidation | XXX | |
| Preference Dividend Payable | | XXX |
| | | |
| Preference Dividend Payable | XXX | |
| Cash | | XXX |

- Any discounts received on the payment of creditors is a gain on liquidation and is credited to the Liquidation account.

| | | |
|---|---|---|
| Creditors | XXX | |
| Cash | | XXX |
| Liquidation (Gain on Creditors) | | XXX |

- Liquidation expenses and the liquidator's remuneration are debited to the Liquidation account.

| | | |
|---|---|---|
| Liquidation | XXX | |
| Cash | | XXX |

At this point the balance in the Liquidation account represents either a loss or a gain on liquidation which will be borne or distributed to shareholders.

- Creditors and other debt holders should now be paid (not shareholders at this point).

| | | |
|---|---|---|
| Creditors | XXX | |
| Cash | | XXX |

- Shareholder reserves, including the Retained Profits and Forfeited Shares Reserve accounts, are now closed to the Liquidation account.

| | | |
|---|---|---|
| Retained Profits | XXX | |
| Forfeited Shares Reserve | XXX | |
| General Reserve | XXX | |
| Liquidation | | XXX |

If the balance sheet contains accumulated losses, which is highly likely in a creditors' or court-ordered liquidation, the balance is also transferred to the Liquidation account.

|  | Debit | Credit |
|---|---|---|
| Liquidation | XXX | |
| Accumulated Losses | | XXX |

The Liquidation account is now closed to the Shareholders' Distribution account. Assuming a loss on liquidation:

|  | | |
|---|---|---|
| Shareholders' Distribution | XXX | |
| Liquidation | | XXX |

Note that the shareholder accounts (Retained Profits, Forfeited Shares Reserve, Other Reserves, and Accumulated Losses) could also be transferred to the Shareholders' Distribution account as an alternative. If this method is used, the gain or loss on liquidation (above) should also be transferred to the Shareholders' Distribution account.

• Paid-up capital is transferred to the Shareholders' Distribution account.

|  | Debit | Credit |
|---|---|---|
| Paid-up Capital | XXX | |
| Shareholders' Distribution | | XXX |

• Finally, refunds to shareholders are paid from the Cash account and this will close that account.

|  | | |
|---|---|---|
| Shareholders' Distribution | XXX | |
| Cash | | XXX |

The share of deficiency borne by shareholder groups and cash payments to shareholders are all calculated using the table mentioned previously. Where losses are involved, the Shareholders' Distribution account will have paid-up capital on the credit side, and the debit side will have a combination of cash and each shareholder class's share of the deficiency.

## Ledger accounts

Liquidation, Cash and Shareholders' Distribution accounts are shown in ledger form as follows:

| Liquidation | Debit | Credit | Balance |
|---|---|---|---|
| Book values of assets transferred (excluding cash) | XXX | | |
| Unrecorded liabilities | XXX | | |
| Provision accounts transferred | | XXX | |
| Proceeds of sale | | XXX | |
| Gain on disposal of secured asset after payment of secured creditor (if any) | | XXX | |
| Discounts from creditors | | XXX | |
| All reserves and retained profits (note that accumulated losses would be a DR) | | XXX | |
| Balance now transferred to shareholders' distribution account (loss assumed) | | XXX | — |

|  | Debit | Credit | Balance |
|---|---|---|---|
| **Cash** | | | |
| Opening balance (if any) | | | XXX |
| Net amounts from secured creditors | XXX | | |
| Proceeds of asset sales | XXX | | |
| Any calls on shareholders | XXX | | |
| Payments to liquidator and other creditors | | XXX | |
| Payments to shareholders | | XXX | – |
| **Shareholders' Distribution** | | | |
| Paid-up capital | | XXX | |
| Transfer of deficiency from liquidation account | XXX | | |
| Payment of cash to shareholders | XXX | | – |

The following two examples illustrate these procedures.

## ILLUSTRATIVE EXAMPLE  12.1

# CASH AND SHAREHOLDERS' DISTRIBUTION ACCOUNTS

Allenby Ltd (in liquidation) had the following share capital at the commencement of the liquidation:
- 200 000 8% $1 cumulative preference shares, preferential both as to capital and arrears of dividends. These shares were fully paid, but dividends were three years in arrears.
- 200 000 $1 'A' ordinary shares paid to 50 cents each.
- 160 000 $1 'B' ordinary shares paid to 60 cents each.

The constitution provided that both 'A' ordinary and 'B' ordinary shares ranked equally except for voting rights. Assets realised $279 938, and debts proved totalled $76 986. Liquidator's remuneration and expenses totalled $8352.

During the course of the liquidation, the liquidator made the following calls:
- on 'A' ordinary shares, 25 cents per share; and
- on 'B' ordinary shares, 15 cents per share.

It was found impossible to recover calls on 10 000 'A' ordinary shares and 6000 'B' ordinary shares and the shares were forfeited.

### Required
Prepare the liquidator's Cash account and the Shareholders' Distribution account.

### Solution
The first step is to calculate the preference dividend, which is three years in arrears.

$$200\ 000 \quad \times \quad \frac{8}{100} \quad \times \quad 3 \quad = \quad \$48\ 000$$

Now calculate the amount received on the two calls and forfeit the shares on which calls were not paid.

Call on 'A' ordinary shares:

$$200\ 000 \quad - \quad 10\ 000 \quad = \quad 190\ 000 \times 25 \text{ cents}$$
$$= \quad \$47\ 500$$

Forfeiture of 10 000 'A' ordinary shares:

|  | Debit $ | Credit $ |
|---|---|---|
| Paid-up Capital – 'A' Ordinary | 7500 | |
| Calls in Arrears | | 2500 |
| Forfeited Shares | | 5000 |

Call on 'B' ordinary shares:

160 000    –    6000    =    154 000 × 15 cents

=    $23 100

Forfeiture of 6000 'B' ordinary shares:

|  | Debit $ | Credit $ |
|---|---|---|
| Paid-up Capital – 'B' Ordinary | 4500 | |
| Calls in Arrears | | 900 |
| Forfeited Shares | | 3600 |

| | Debit $ | Credit $ | Balance $ |
|---|---|---|---|
| **Cash** | | | |
| Proceeds of asset sale | 279 938 | | |
| Call – 'A' ordinary | 47 500 | | |
| Call – 'B' ordinary | 23 100 | | 350 538 |
| Liquidation expenses and remuneration | | 8 352 | |
| Creditors | | 76 986 | 265 200 |
| Preference dividend | | 48 000 | |
| Preference shareholders | | 200 000 | 17 200* |
| 'A' ordinary shareholders | | 9 500 | |
| 'B' ordinary shareholders | | 7 700 | – |

\* After the preference dividend and capital is repaid to preference shareholders there is $17 200 remaining for the 'A' ordinary and 'B' ordinary shareholders. A table is used to allocate these funds.

## Share Deficiency

| Share class | Issued value | Paid-up capital | | Share of deficiency | Refund | Call |
|---|---|---|---|---|---|---|
| 'A' ordinary | 190 000 | 142 500 | (190/344 × 240 800) | 133 000 | 9 500 | – |
| 'B' ordinary | 154 000 | 115 500 | (154/344 × 240 800) | 107 800 | 7 700 | – |
| | 344 000 | 258 000 | | | | |
| Cash available | | 17 200 | | 240 800 | 17 200 | – |
| Deficiency | | 240 800 | | | | |

Note:

| | | |
|---|---|---|
| Paid-up capital, 'A' ordinary | = | 190 000 × 75 cents |
| | = | 142 500 |
| Paid-up capital, 'B' ordinary | = | 154 000 × 75 cents |
| | = | 115 500 |

|  | Debit | Credit | Balance |
|---|---|---|---|
|  | $ | $ | $ |
| **Shareholders' Distribution** |  |  |  |
| Paid-up capital |  |  |  |
| Preference |  | 200 000 |  |
| 'A' ordinary |  | 142 500 |  |
| 'B' ordinary |  | 115 500 | 458 000 |
| Cash |  |  |  |
| Preference | 200 000 |  |  |
| 'A' ordinary | 9 500 |  |  |
| 'B' ordinary | 7 700 |  |  |
| Share of deficiency |  |  |  |
| 'A' ordinary | 133 000 |  |  |
| 'B' ordinary | 107 800 |  | – |

Note that the 'A' ordinary and 'B' ordinary shareholders bear the same share of loss.

| 'A' ordinary | 133 000/190 000 | = | 70 cents |
|---|---|---|---|
| 'B' ordinary | 107 800/154 000 | = | 70 cents |

That is, each class will receive a 5 cents per share refund.

| 'A' ordinary | 9 500/190 000 | = | 5 cents |
|---|---|---|---|
| 'B' ordinary | 7 700/154 000 | = | 5 cents |

# ILLUSTRATIVE EXAMPLE 12.2

## COMPREHENSIVE

Woods Ltd went into liquidation on 30 June 20X4 with the following balance sheet at the commencement of the liquidation.

**Woods Ltd**
**Balance Sheet as at 30 June 20X4**

|  | $ | $ | $ |
|---|---|---|---|
| *Assets* |  |  |  |
| Current assets |  |  |  |
| Inventory |  | 36 400 |  |
| Accounts receivable |  | 28 900 |  |
| Cash |  | 400 | 65 700 |
| Non-current assets |  |  |  |
| Land & buildings |  | 41 200 |  |
| Plant | 48 000 |  |  |
| *Less* Accumulated depreciation | 19 800 | 28 200 | 69 400 |
| Intangible assets |  |  |  |
| Goodwill |  |  | 23 200 |
| *Total assets* |  |  | 158 300 |
| *Liabilities* |  |  |  |
| Current liabilities |  |  |  |
| Bank overdraft |  | 20 000 |  |
| Trade creditors |  | 14 000 | 34 000 |

| | $ | $ | $ |
|---|---|---|---|
| Non-current liabilities | | | |
| Debentures | | | 13 000 |
| Total liabilities | | | 47 000 |
| Net assets | | | $111 300 |
| Shareholders' equity | | | |
| Authorised capital | | | |
| 50 000 preference shares of $1 each | | 50 000 | 180 000 |
| 50 000 'A' ordinary shares of $1 each | | 50 000 | |
| 40 000 'B' ordinary shares of $2 each | | 80 000 | |
| Issued and paid-up capital | | | |
| 20 000 preference shares of $1 each fully paid | | | 20 000 |
| 36 000 'A' ordinary shares called to | | | |
| 75 cents per share | | 27 000 | |
| Less Calls in arrears (6000 at 25 cents) | | 1 500 | 25 500 |
| 40 000 'B' ordinary shares called to $1.50 per share | 60 000 | | |
| Less Calls in arrears (8000 at 25 cents) | | 2 000 | 58 000 |
| | | | 103 500 |
| Asset revaluation reserve | | 12 600 | |
| Less Accumulated losses | | 4 800 | 7 800 |
| Total shareholders' equity | | | $111 300 |

Additional information:
(a) The arrears on 2000 'A' ordinary shares and on 4000 'B' ordinary shares were found to be irrecoverable and were forfeited by the liquidator.

(b) Expenses of winding up were $3600, and the liquidator was entitled to a remuneration of $3000.

(c) Assets realised the following:
| | |
|---|---|
| Land & buildings | $50 000 |
| Plant | 17 200 |
| Inventory | 27 800 |
| Accounts receivable | 25 000 |

(d) The creditors were paid off, less 5% discount.

(e) Preference shareholders were preferential as to return of capital.

*Required*
Prepare the Liquidation account, the Shareholders' Distribution account and the Cash account. Show how any deficiency is borne by the different shareholder classes.

### Solution

| | Debit | Credit |
|---|---|---|
| | $ | $ |
| **Forfeiture of shares** | | |
| Paid-up Capital – 'A' Ordinary | 1 500 | |
| Calls in Arrears | | 500 |
| Forfeited Shares | | 1 000 |
| (forfeiture of 2000 'A' ordinary shares) | | |

|  | $ | $ |
|---|---|---|
| Paid-up Capital – 'B' Ordinary | 6 000 | |
| Calls in Arrears | | 1 000 |
| Forfeited Shares | | 5 000 |
| (forfeiture of 4000 'B' ordinary shares) | | |

Note here that if 2000 'A' ordinary shares are forfeited, cash for the calls in arrears on 4000 at 25 cents must have been received by the liquidator. Similarly, cash for the calls in arrears on 4000 at 25 cents on the 'B' ordinary shares must have been paid to the liquidator. Further, these share forfeitures will change the paid-up capital on both share classes and therefore will affect the table showing the distribution of any deficiency.

|  | Debit | Credit | Balance |
|---|---|---|---|
|  | $ | $ | $ |
| **Liquidation** | | | |
| Inventory | 36 400 | | |
| Land & buildings | 41 200 | | |
| Plant | 48 000 | | |
| Accumulated depreciation | 19 800 | | |
| Accounts receivable | 28 900 | | |
| Liquidator's expenses | 3 600 | | |
| Liquidator's remuneration | 3 000 | | |
| Goodwill | 23 200 | | |
| Cash proceeds of sale | | 120 000 | |
| Discount on creditors* | | 700 | 43 800 Dr |
| Accumulated losses | 4 800 | | |
| Asset revaluation reserve | | 12 600 | |
| Forfeited shares | | 6 000 | |
| 'A' ordinary – share of loss | | 9 623 | |
| 'B' ordinary – share of loss | | 20 377 | – |

* $14 000 x .05 = $700

| **Cash** | | | |
|---|---|---|---|
| Cash (opening balance) | 400 | | |
| Call on 'A' ordinary (4000 × 25 cents) | 1 000 | | |
| Call on 'B' ordinary (4000 × 25 cents) | 1 000 | | |
| Proceeds of sale | 120 000 | | |
| Liquidation expenses | | 3 600 | |
| Liquidation reservation | | 3 000 | |
| Bank overdraft | | 20 000 | |
| Debentures | | 13 000 | 95 800 Dr |
| Trade creditors | | 13 300 | |
| Preference shareholders | | 20 000 | 49 500 Dr |
| 'A' ordinary | | 15 877 | |
| 'B' ordinary | | 33 623 | – |

|  |  | Debit $ | Credit $ | Balance $ |
|---|---|---|---|---|
| **Shareholders' Distribution** |  |  |  |  |
| Paid-up capital | – Preference |  | 20 000 |  |
|  | – 'A' ordinary |  | 25 500 |  |
|  | – 'B' ordinary |  | 54 000 | 99 500 |
| Share of deficiency | – 'A' ordinary | 9 623 |  |  |
|  | – 'B' ordinary | 20 377 |  |  |
| Cash | – Preference | 20 000 |  |  |
|  | – 'A' ordinary | 15 877 |  |  |
|  | – 'B' ordinary | 33 623 |  | – |

Note: Paid-up capital of 'A' ordinary is 34 000 3 75 cents = $25 500 and of 'B' ordinary is 36 000 3 $1.50 = $54 000.

## Share Deficiency

| Share class | Issued value | Paid-up capital | Share of deficiency | Refund | Call |
|---|---|---|---|---|---|
| 'A' ordinary $1 | 34 000 | 25 500 | 34/106 × 30 000 = 9 623 | 15 877 | – |
| 'B' ordinary $2 | 72 000 | 54 000 | 72/106 × 30 000 = 20 377 | 33 623 | – |
|  | 106 000 | 79 500 | 30 000 | 49 500 | – |
| Cash available |  | 49 500 |  |  |  |
| Deficiency |  | 30 000 |  |  |  |

Here both 'A' and 'B' ordinary shareholders bear the same relative apportionment of loss, based on the total issued value of capital.

| 'A' ordinary | 9623/34 000 | = | 28 cents (rounded) |
|---|---|---|---|
| 'B' ordinary | 20 377/72 000 | = | 28 cents (rounded) |

The per share apportionment of loss of 'A' and 'B' ordinary shareholders is therefore:

| 'A' ordinary | 9623/34 000 shares | = | 28 cents (rounded) |
|---|---|---|---|
| 'B' ordinary | 20 377/36 000 shares | = | 56 cents (rounded) |

As the 'A' ordinary shares are paid to 75 cents, the refund will be 47 cents per share. 'B' ordinary shareholders will receive a refund of 94 cents per share because the issue value is $2 rather than $1. That is, the per share loss is 28 cents x 2 = 56 cents and the paid-up value is $1.50, hence a refund of 94 cents (1.50 − 0.56).

The important point to note is that the same proportionate loss is borne by each share class.

Note that the distribution of cash to shareholders would vary if the rankings were different. If the preference, 'A' ordinary and 'B' ordinary shareholders all ranked equally, the deficiency would be borne as follows:

| Share class | Issued value | Paid-up capital | Share of deficiency* | | Refund | Call |
|---|---|---|---|---|---|---|
| | $ | $ | $ | | $ | |
| Preference $1 | 20 000 | 20 000 | 20/126 × 30 000 = | 4 762 | 15 238 | – |
| 'A' ordinary $1 | 34 000 | 25 500 | 34/126 × 30 000 = | 8 095 | 17 405 | – |
| 'B' ordinary $2 | 72 000 | 54 000 | 72/126 × 30 000 = | 17 143 | 36 857 | – |
| | 126 000 | 99 500 | | 30 000 | 69 500 | – |
| Cash available | | 69 500 | | | | |
| Deficiency | | 30 000 | | | | |

* These share of deficiency amounts have been rounded to the nearest $.

# Review

This chapter has examined external administration, including liquidation. Whilst the emphasis has been on the accounting issues associated with a liquidation, it is important to realise that a scheme of voluntary administration may greatly benefit a company in financial distress. This comparatively new scheme has certainly enabled many companies, both large and small, to trade out of their difficulties and hence avoid liquidation.

An emphasis was also placed on the amount lost by each class of shareholders in a liquidation. This illustrated that the same proportionate loss is borne by each share class.

# KEY TERMS

administrator

Australian Securities Commission

company's constitution

contingent assets

contingent liabilities

covenants

debenture trust deed

debt levels

deficiency of capital

external administration

fixed charge

floating charge

leverage

liquidator

receiver

secured creditors

solvent

special resolution

## REVIEW QUESTIONS

**12.1** The following is an extract from a Queensland provincial city's daily newspaper, *The Beaudesert Times*, 9 October 1996.

---

# First dividend paid to Kooralbyn's creditors

The creditors of Kooralbyn Hotel Resort have received their first dividend since the operation went under voluntary administration earlier this year.

Creditors were paid their first dividend of 10 cents in the dollar this week, which was promised under a deed of company arrangement after the resort suffered financial problems.

Administrator John Greig of Deloitte Touche Tohmatsu said creditors could be paid up to 50 cents in the dollar by early next year.

The next dividend will come primarily from the sale of the resort's 56 Augusta Terraces apartments.

'The deed provides specifically for the sale of the Augusta Terraces,' Mr Greig said.

'At this time there is no contract for the Augusta Terraces and we cannot make the next dividend until that is signed.

'But I assume they will be sold and settled by either late this year or early next year.'

Had the deed of company arrangement not been accepted by creditors and the company placed into liquidation, creditors would have stood to receive only 7.5 cents in the dollar.

'The voluntary administration has resulted in an increased return to creditors, many of whom are locals in the immediate Beaudesert area, which has experienced difficult times recently,' Mr Greig said.

Kooralbyn Hotel Resort's Committee of Creditors Chairperson Neville Black said the outlook for Kooralbyn was 'coming together'.

'The management agreement had guaranteed us 40 cents in the dollar and now they are talking about 50 cents,' Mr Black said.

'I'm quietly confident as the company picks up so too will Kooralbyn, it is too nice a place not to.

'The management plan is getting rid of the surplus land and assets and aligned with the top management, which is in place, I have no doubt things have turned around.

'If the resort had gone into liquidation we would have got about 7 cents in the dollar, so to be looking at 50 cents now we are way in front.

'Liquidation would also have been a lot more trauma for the whole district.'

Mr Greig said management emphasis had been on restoring the profitability of the resort by improving operating efficien-

cies, financial controls and focusing marketing on the key market segments of conference, inbound, leisure and golf.

Mr Greig said it was anticipated that the reorganisation would take about 12 to 18 months to work through.

He said when the administration was first adopted the resort was having difficulty obtaining supplies from creditors.

But the company has now obtained added funding and supply lines are again open, helping the resort run smoothly.

'We've had a very good September and things are looking bright,' Mr Greig said.

'Obviously it takes some time to restore profitability when you have been making a $4 million a year loss.

'Once the Augusta Terraces are sold, us as administrators retire and the detailed strategy, which is being worked out as the plan for the overall resort, takes over.

'The ownership of the resort stays with the Japanese [Towa Kohmuten Co Ltd] company which has owned it all along and the management is envisaged not to change with Jenny Cronin and Fortland Hotels doing a very good job.'

---

Using this case and other examples you are aware of, discuss the reasons why voluntary administration may be preferable to liquidating a company.

**12.2** Discuss the reasons why a company may be liquidated.

**12.3** Place the following creditors in the correct order of repayment as discussed in the chapter. The company has been placed into a court-ordered liquidation.

(a) Directors' fees owing.

(b) Telephone bill owing.

(c) Arrears of dividend on cumulative preference shares.

(d) Fees owing to auditors.

(e) Provision for deferred income tax.

(f) Principal and interest on a branch loan secured by a fixed charge over property.

(g) PAYE income tax deductions withheld.

(h) Council rates for the past year.

(i) Costs of the liquidator.

# EXERCISES

**Exercise 12.4** **Order of payment and share of deficiency**

The capital of a limited company consisted of 1500 preference shares (preferential as to both capital and dividends) $10 fully paid, 4000 ordinary shares $10 fully paid and 6500 ordinary shares of $10 paid up to $9. The constitution of the company provides that, in the event of liquidation, subject to prior claims of preference shareholders, losses are to be borne according to the issued value of shares.

The liquidator has realised all the assets, paid all liabilities and has $25 000 in hand. The liquidator's commission of 5% on this sum has still to be provided.

*Required*
Prepare a statement showing the order of payment and the amount payable to each class of shareholders.

**Exercise 12.5** **Share of deficiency**

The capital of Company Z Ltd is as follows:

|  | $ |
| --- | --- |
| 10 000 preference shares of $2 each fully paid | 20 000 |
| 100 000 'A' ordinary shares of $1 each fully paid | 100 000 |
| 20 000 'B' ordinary shares of $2 each paid to $1 | 20 000 |
| Paid-up capital | $140 000 |

The company's constitution provided that in the event of liquidation, losses are to be borne equally by all classes of shareholders. The cash available after all assets have been realised and liabilities and expenses paid is $40 000.

*Required*
Prepare a table showing the amount payable to each shareholder and the per share apportionment of loss and refund.

**Exercise 12.6** **Liquidator's cash available and share of deficiency**

Esmeralda Ltd went into voluntary liquidation on 30 June 20X2, its shareholders' equity being as follows:

|  | $ |
|---|---|
| 30 000 6% preference shares of $2 each paid to $1.50 | |
| (preferred as to return of capital in the event of liquidation) | 45 000 |
| 20 000 first issue 'A' ordinary shares of $1 each fully paid | 20 000 |
| 15 000 second issue 'A' ordinary shares of $1 each | |
| fully paid to 75 cents | 11 250 |
| 5000 'B' ordinary shares of $1 each paid to 25 cents | 1 250 |
| | 77 500 |
| | |
| General reserve | 8 200 |
| Retained profits | 4 000 |
| | $89 700 |

*Note*: The last preference dividend was paid to 30 June 20X0.

To adjust the rights of shareholders the liquidator made the following calls:
- 25 cents per share on second issue 'A' ordinary shares; and
- 25 cents per share on 'B' ordinary shares.

All amounts due on these calls were received except those in respect of 400 second issue 'A' ordinary shares and 200 'B' ordinary shares. These proved to be irrecoverable and were forfeited.

Debts due by the company amounted to $15 820, assets realised $80 100, and liquidation expenses were $929.

The liquidator's remuneration was fixed at 1% on the proceeds of assets.

*Required*
1  Prepare the liquidator's final statement of receipts and payments (ie work out the cash available — the liquidator's Cash account).
2  Prepare a statement showing the loss of capital and how it was borne by the shareholders.

**Exercise 12.7** **Liquidator's cash available and share of deficiency**

Meadowbank Ltd is in voluntary liquidation. The balance sheet as at the date of liquidation is as follows:

**Meadowbank Ltd**
**Balance Sheet as at date of liquidation**

| | $ | | $ | $ |
|---|---|---|---|---|
| Issued and paid-up capital | | Non-current assets | | 59 310 |
| Preference | | Current assets | | |
| 10 000 $4 shares fully paid | 40 000 | Bank | 1 500 | |
| 'A' ordinary | | Accounts receivable | 4 300 | 5 800 |
| (First issue) | | | | |
| 25 000 $1 shares fully paid | 25 000 | | | |
| (Second issue) | | | | |
| 25 000 $1 shares paid to 50 cents | 12 500 | | | |
| 'B' ordinary | | | | |
| 5000 $1 shares paid to 75 cents | 3 750 | | | |
| | 81 250 | | | |
| Accumulated losses | (32 140) | | | |
| Total shareholders' equity | 49 110 | | | |
| Trade creditors | 16 000 | | | |
| | $65 110 | | | $65 110 |

The order of priority provided in the company's constitution for repayment of capital is: (1) preference; (2) 'A' ordinary; and (3) 'B' ordinary.

The fixed assets realised $55 000, and accounts receivable were collected, less $800; the latter amount proved to be irrecoverable.

In order to adjust the rights of shareholders, the liquidator made the following calls:
- 25 cents per share on the 'A' ordinary shares (second issue); and
- 25 cents per share on the 'B' ordinary shares.

With the exception of the call on 1000 'A' ordinary shares which the liquidator was unable to recover, all calls were duly received.

Liquidator's remuneration was fixed at 1% on gross proceeds of assets (excluding bank balance) and liquidation expenses amounted to $105.

*Required*
1 Prepare the liquidator's statement of receipts and payments.
2 Prepare a worksheet showing the calculation of amounts due to the various shareholder classes.

**Exercise 12.8 Liquidator's cash available and share of deficiency**
On 30 November 20X6, Donnington Ltd, a company specialising in selling used cars, went into voluntary liquidation and the liquidator prepared a statement showing the financial position as follows:

| Assets | | $ |
|---|---|---|
| Trade debtors | | 5 400 |
| Inventory | | 85 500 |
| Land & buildings | | 32 500 |
| Furniture & fittings | | 2 000 |
| Plant & tools | | 1 800 |
| Liabilities | | |
| Bank (secured by floating charge) | | 32 800 |
| Trade creditors | | 15 300 |
| Wages | | 1 550 |
| Income tax | | 4 700 |
| Council rates | | 1 123 |
| Issued and paid-up capital was as follows: | | |
| 20 000 fully paid 5% preference shares of $1 each | | |
| (dividend paid to 30 June 20X0) | 20 000 | |
| 60 000 'A' ordinary shares of $1 each | | |
| paid to 75 cents | 45 000 | |
| 20 000 'B' ordinary shares 50 cents each | | |
| fully paid | 10 000 | |
| Total paid-up capital | $75 000 | |
| Calls in advance on 6000 'A' ordinary shares at | | |
| 10 cents per share | | 600 |
| Accumulated losses (debit) | | 1 429 |

Preference shares are preferential as to return of capital. This is the only reference in the constitution to the rights of shareholders in the event of liquidation.

The assets realised the following amounts:

| | $ |
|---|---|
| Trade debtors | 4 560 |
| Stocks | 52 000 |
| Land & buildings | 15 040 |
| Plant & tools | 1 350 |
| Furniture & fittings | 1 450 |

The uncalled capital was called up, but the amount due on 2000 shares was found to be irrecoverable. The liquidator's remuneration amounted to 5% on the proceeds of asset sales. Liquidation expenses were $500.

*Required*
1  Prepare the liquidator's statement of receipts and payments.
2  Prepare a statement showing how the loss of capital is calculated and borne by the shareholders.

**Exercise 12.9   Cash, liquidation and shareholders' distribution accounts**
Stricken Ltd went into liquidation on 1 April 20X5 and presents the following trial balance.

## Stricken Ltd
### Trial Balance as at 1 April 20X5

|  | $ | $ |
|---|---:|---:|
| Accounts receivable | 75 000 | |
| Inventory | 196 000 | |
| Motor vehicles | 16 000 | |
| Plant & equipment | 92 000 | |
| Land & buildings | 80 000 | |
| Preliminary expenses | 3 000 | |
| Accumulated losses (debit) | 200 000 | |
| Bank | | 58 000 |
| Trade creditors | | 69 000 |
| Accrued expenses | | 2 000 |
| Unsecured notes | | 100 000 |
| Paid-up capital ($1 shares) | | |
|   – Preference (fully paid) | | 150 000 |
|   – Ordinary class 1 (fully paid) | | 150 000 |
|   – Ordinary class 2 (called to 50 cents) | | 100 000 |
| Accumulated depreciation – motor vehicles | | 5 000 |
|   – plant & equipment | | 28 000 |
| | $662 000 | $662 000 |

Additional information:

(a) Proceeds from sale of assets:

| | |
|---|---:|
| Accounts receivable | $74 000 |
| Inventory | 160 000 |
| Motor vehicles | 9 000 |
| Plant & equipment | 52 000 |
| Land & buildings | 100 000 |

(b) Payments:

| | |
|---|---:|
| Interest on overdraft | $900 |
| Trade creditors | 67 800 |
| Accrued expenses | 2 100 |
| Unsecured notes & interest thereon | 102 200 |
| Liquidator's expenses & remuneration | 5 500 |

(c) Rights of shareholders: Preference shareholders were preferential as to return of capital, and ordinary shareholders ranked equally.

*Required*

Prepare the Cash account, the Liquidation account and the Shareholders' Distribution account.

**Exercise 12.10**   **Cash, liquidation and shareholders' distribution accounts**

Bredalbane Ltd went into voluntary liquidation on 30 September 20X4. At that date the following details were extracted from the books of account.

| | $ |
|---|---|
| Motor vehicles | 8 000 |
| Land & buildings | 124 000 |
| Plant & machinery | 29 490 |
| Inventory | 26 520 |
| Accounts receivable | 24 750 |
| Calls in arrears on 'A' shares, 25 cents per share | 480 |
| | $213 240 |
| | |
| *Issued capital and paid-up capital* – $1 shares | |
| 'A' shares called to 75 cents | 24 000 |
| 'B' shares called to 60 cents | 18 000 |
| Preference shares fully paid | 10 000 |
| Paid-up capital | 52 000 |
| Calls in advance 'B' shares | 180 |
| *Less* Accumulated losses | 4 800 |
| Shareholders' equity | 47 380 |
| Unsecured creditors | 27 640 |
| Mortgage on land & buildings | 113 240 |
| Bank overdraft secured by a floating charge | 10 500 |
| Unsecured notes | 8 000 |
| Debentures secured on plant & machinery | 6 000 |
| Forfeited shares reserve | 480 |
| | $213 240 |

Additional information:

(a) The estimated realisation amounts were:

| | |
|---|---|
| Motor vehicles | $6 500 |
| Land & buildings | 135 500 |
| Plant & machinery | 25 000 |
| Inventory | 23 292 |
| Accounts receivable | 22 000 |

(b) It is expected that 1200 of the 'A' ordinary shares with calls in arrears will pay the amount due.

(c) The item 'unsecured creditors' includes the following:

| | |
|---|---|
| Directors' fees | $1 600 |
| Long service leave | 2 527 |
| Income tax assessment | 990 |
| Wages | 700 |

Subsequent to the preparation of the statement of affairs, the liquidator realised on the assets at the amounts estimated. The liquidator's expenses and commission amounted to $800. A final distribution was made on 15 December 20X4.

*Required*
Prepare the Liquidation account, the Cash account and the Shareholders' Distribution account.

**Exercise 12.11**  **Cash, liquidation and shareholders' distribution accounts**

On 1 July 20X3, Downer Ltd went into voluntary liquidation and its assets and liabilities at that date were:

|  | $ | $ |
|---|---:|---:|
| *Issued and paid-up capital* | | |
| 20 000 6% preference shares of $1, each fully paid | | 20 000 |
| 30 000 ordinary shares of $1 each, called to 75 cents | 22 500 | |
| Less Calls in arrears of 25 cents per share | 500 | 22 000 |
| Paid-up capital | | 42 000 |
| Less Accumulated losses | | 25 000 |
| Shareholders' equity | | 17 000 |
| Unsecured notes | | 10 000 |
| Mortgage on property | | 15 000 |
| Trade creditors | | 3 400 |
| Outstanding liabilities | | 1 600 |
| | | $47 000 |
| Property | | 16 000 |
| Plant & equipment | | 12 000 |
| Cash at bank | | 300 |
| Accounts receivable | | 7 000 |
| Bills receivable | | 1 500 |
| Inventory | | 10 200 |
| | | $47 000 |

The outstanding liabilities comprised:

|  | |
|---|---:|
| Sales tax | 435 |
| Wages | 505 |
| Income tax deducted from employees' wages and salaries not yet remitted | 445 |
| Income tax for year ended 20X0 (the last year in which a a profit was made) | 215 |
| | $1 600 |

The company's constitution provided that in the event of liquidation, preference shares would be entitled to all arrears of preference dividends, whether earned, declared or not, up to 30 June immediately preceding the date on which liquidation commences.

This was the only reference made in the constitution to the rights of shareholders in the event of winding up. Dividends were in arrears for two years.

Assets realised the following amounts: property, $14 700; plant and equipment, $10 000; accounts receivable, $5000; bills receivable, $500; inventory, $8000; calls in arrears, $300.

*Required*

Prepare the Cash account, the Liquidation account and the Shareholders' Distribution account.

**Exercise 12.12** Comprehensive — liquidation

Alistair Ltd went into liquidation on 1 July 20X3 and presents the following balance sheet.

**Alistair Ltd**
**Balance Sheet as at 30 June 20X3**

| | $ | $ | $ |
|---|---|---|---|
| *Assets* | | | |
| Current assets | | | |
| Accounts receivable | | 3 000 000 | |
| Inventory | | 500 500 | 3 500 500 |
| Non-current assets | | | |
| Land & buildings | | 5 120 000 | |
| Furniture & fittings | 2 300 000 | | |
| *Less* Accumulated depreciation | 420 000 | 1 880 000 | 7 000 000 |
| Total assets | | | $10 500 500 |
| *Liabilities* | | | |
| Current liabilities | | | |
| Accrued expenses | | 75 200 | |
| Overdraft | | 57 000 | |
| Trade creditors | | 180 000 | 312 200 |
| Non-current liabilities | | | |
| Debentures | | | 1 000 000 |
| Total liabilities | | | 1 312 200 |
| Net assets | | | $9 188 300 |
| *Shareholders' equity* | | | |
| Authorised capital | | | |
| 500 000 preference shares of $1 each | | 500 000 | |
| 10 000 000 'A' ordinary shares of $1 each | | 10 000 000 | |
| 1 000 000 'B' ordinary shares of $2 each | | 2 000 000 | 12 500 000 |
| Paid-up capital | | | |
| 500 000 preference shares of $1 each | | | 500 000 |
| 10 000 000 'A' ordinary shares paid to 75 cents | | 7 500 000 | |
| *Less* Calls in arrears (50 000 at 25 cents) | | 12 500 | 7 487 500 |
| 1 000 000 'B' ordinary shares paid to $1 each | | | 1 000 000 |
| | | | 8 987 500 |
| Asset revaluation reserve | | 2 000 000 | |
| *Less* Accumulated losses | | 1 799 200 | 200 800 |
| Total shareholders' equity | | | $9 188 300 |

Additional information:

(a) Proceeds from the sale of assets and collections:

| | |
|---|---|
| Accounts receivable | $400 000 |
| Inventory | 1 900 000 |
| Land & buildings | 4 500 000 |
| Furniture & fittings | 1 220 000 |
| Calls in arrears | 11 500 |

(b)  Payments:

| | |
|---|---|
| Interest on overdraft | $1 782 |
| Trade creditors | 178 200 |
| Accrued expenses | 77 500 |
| Interest on debentures | 100 000 |
| Liquidator's expenses and fees | 350 000 |

(c)  Preference shareholders were preferential as to the return of capital, and ordinary shareholders ranked equally.

*Required*
Prepare the Cash account, the Liquidation account and the Shareholders' Distribution account.

# chapter 13

## CAPITAL REORGANISATION

# introduction

**capital structure**

When a company is formed, a particular capital structure is planned and put in place. That is, the price of shares to be issued and share classes (usually ordinary and possibly preference shares) are determined. Over time and as circumstances change, this structure may need to be amended. This chapter discusses four areas of change, each of which is subject to the authority of the Corporations Law. They are:

(a) alteration of share capital (s 193);

(b) reduction of share capital (s 195);

(c) redemption of preference shares (s 192); and

(d) share buy-backs (Division 4B).

A case study of Foster's Brewing Group Ltd in Appendix 13.1 is used to illustrate the relevance and practicality of a capital reorganisation.

# The direct method

The major changes in a capital reorganisation concentrate on the shareholders' equity section of the balance sheet and its components which are:

[Paid-up capital + Reserves and retained profits]  =  Assets − Liabilities
↓

Components are:
↓

Authorised capital

*Less* Unissued capital

Issued capital

*Less* Uncalled capital

Paid-up capital

**direct method**
**indirect method**

There are two methods used in accounting for a capital reorganisation, direct and indirect. The journal entries required in a capital reorganisation are easier to implement under the direct method, which is used in this text. The indirect method requires debit and credit entries to the components that make up paid-up capital. Using the direct method, journal entries are not required when there is no change to the amount of paid-up capital. Where paid-up capital is changed, only four accounts in the shareholders' equity section may be affected. These are the:

(a) Paid-up Capital account;

(b) Forfeited Shares account;

(c) Share Premium account; and

**capital redemption**
**reserve**

(d) Capital Redemption Reserve account.

A capital reorganisation deals with issued share amounts in a purely accounting sense. The accounting treatment does not directly affect the market price of shares. For example, in a subdivision of shares, converting say 100 000 $1 shares to 200 000 50 cent shares will halve the original issued price from $1 to 50 cents. The market price of the shares will also halve, but no overall value is added to market capitalisation. To illustrate, BHP Ltd's ordinary shares have an issued price of $1, whilst the market price is about $18 (May 1997). Any of the changes to paid-up capital discussed in this chapter could affect the issued price ($1) of BHP Ltd shares. However, from an accounting perspective, the market price ($18) is of no importance.

# Alteration of share capital

The reasons for altering share capital include the following:

- The present authorised and paid-up capital may be insufficient for current and future operations.
- The issued price of the shares may discourage disposal, and if the issued price is reduced investor activity may be increased.
- Some unissued shares may no longer be required as the company has no plans that require additional funds through an issue of shares.

Section 193 of the Corporations Law allows a company, if authorised by its constitution, by resolution in a general meeting to:

- increase authorised share capital;
- consolidate issued shares by increasing their dollar value and therefore reducing the number issued;
- convert shares into stock and stock into shares;

subdivision of issued shares

- subdivide issued shares by reducing their value and therefore increasing the number issued; and
- cancel unissued shares.

All of the above may be made through an ordinary resolution at a general meeting. These changes *do not affect the value of paid-up capital* and therefore creditors and other debt holders are not affected. The accounting treatment of each is now considered.

## INCREASING AUTHORISED SHARE CAPITAL

Increasing authorised share capital enables a company to issue more shares and therefore increase its asset base (cash) for additional projects. Both authorised capital and unissued shares are increased, but no journal entry is required, only alterations in subsidiary records. For example, a company with authorised capital and paid-up capital of $100 000 may wish to increase its authorised capital to $1 000 000 so that it may issue more shares.

## CONSOLIDATING ISSUED SHARES

Issued shares may be consolidated by reducing the number issued and therefore increasing their original issued price. As there is no change to paid-up capital, once again, no journal entry is required.

If a company's issued shares consisted of 100 000 $1 shares, these could be consolidated into 50 000 $2 shares or 25 000 $4 shares. Note that the value of paid-up capital does not change from a total of $100 000.

## CONVERTING SHARES INTO STOCK

This procedure is now rare for Australian companies; hence, it is only of historical interest. The idea is to convert fully paid shares into a number of stock units. If a company had 100 000 $1 shares — that is, a paid-up capital of $100 000 — this could be converted into, say, five stock units worth $20 000 each or any combination worth a total of $100 000. Once again, no journal entries are required, only changes in the share register.

## SUBDIVIDING SHARES

The issued price of shares may be reduced, and consequently the number of shares on issue will be increased. Whilst the total paid-up capital does not change, the market price of the shares would change in the same proportion. This may have the effect of making the shares more attractive to investors, particularly small investors. A company may have 100 000 $1 shares as paid-up capital. The market price at a particular date may be, say, $8. If the company decides to subdivide the shares into

200 000 50 cent shares, the paid-up capital remains the same but the market price of the shares will fall to approximately $4. This does not increase share value; rather, it could make the shares more attractive to investors. (Interestingly, News Corporation Ltd recently subdivided their shares and the market price fell in proportion to the subdivision.)

No journal entries are required, as again, there is no change to the paid-up capital.

## CANCELLING UNISSUED SHARES

As there is no effect on paid-up capital, no journal entries are required. A company simply cancels shares that have not been issued. Clearly, the directors would consider that such shares would not be issued in future.

The following example illustrates the procedures described above, as well as the practice of having different classes of ordinary shares — here, 'A' ordinary and 'B' ordinary class shares.

Example:

### Alteration of share capital
### Greg Ltd

|  | $ | $ |
|---|---|---|
| Authorised capital |  |  |
| 100 000 'A' $2 ordinary shares | 200 000 |  |
| 50 000 'B' $1 ordinary shares | 50 000 |  |
|  |  | $250 000 |
| Paid-up capital |  |  |
| 75 000 'A' ordinary shares paid to $1.50 | 112 500 |  |
| 50 000 'B' ordinary shares fully paid | 50 000 |  |
|  |  | $162 500 |

Greg Ltd's shareholders approved the following alterations to capital at a general meeting:
• cancel 'A' ordinary unissued shares;
• subdivide 'A' ordinary shares into $1 shares paid to 75 cents; and
• consolidate 'B' ordinary shares to $4 issued price.
No journal entries are required, only adjustments in the share register.

After the above changes have been made, the share capital of Greg Ltd is:

|  | $ | $ |
|---|---|---|
| Authorised capital |  |  |
| 150 000 'A' $1 ordinary shares | 150 000 |  |
| 12 500 'B' $4 ordinary shares | 50 000 |  |
|  |  | $200 000 |
| Paid-up capital |  |  |
| 150 000 'A' $1 ordinary shares paid to 75 cents | 112 500 |  |
| 12 500 'B' $4 ordinary shares fully paid | 50 000 |  |
|  |  | $162 500 |

Note that the paid-up capital of $162 500 has not changed. Further, the former $2 'A' ordinary shares are now $1 shares, which means that the issued 'A' ordinary shares must double in number. (Recall that 25 000 $2 'A' ordinary unissued shares were cancelled.)

# Reduction of share capital

The effect of changes in this section is to reduce the amount of paid-up capital and/or to change shareholders' liability for uncalled capital. This could adversely affect creditors and other debt holders, as there would be less money available to repay creditors in the event of a liquidation of the company. There are two main reasons why a company may wish to reduce its share capital:

1 Capital may have been lost or is no longer represented by assets.
2 Excess cash is held and the company has no use for this asset and decides to return cash to shareholders.

In the first instance, the before/after effects on the accounting equation are:

| BEFORE | Paid-up capital | = | Assets − Liabilities |
|---|---|---|---|
| | $200 000 | = | $250 000 − 100 000 |
| accumulated losses | (50 000) | | |
| | $150 000 | | |

Here the paid-up capital of $200 000 is overstated by $50 000 as a result of accumulated losses of $50 000. This has the effect of reducing owners' equity by the same amount. Appropriate journal entries result in the following:

| AFTER | Paid-up capital | = | Assets − Liabilities |
|---|---|---|---|
| | $150 000 | = | $250 000 − 100 000 |

A balance sheet that legally shows a net amount of paid-up capital of $150 000 looks far better than showing paid-up capital of $200 000 and accumulated losses of $50 000.

In the second instance, where a company has cash resources that are no longer required, the overall effect on the accounting equation is to reduce assets and owners' equity (paid-up capital) by the same amount.

For the protection of creditors under s 195, a scheme to reduce a company's capital must be authorised by the constitution, approved by special resolution of members and be confirmed by a court order. Section 195 describes three methods of reducing capital:

(a) reduce uncalled capital;
(b) cancel paid-up capital; or
(c) return paid-up capital via the cash account.

## REDUCING UNCALLED CAPITAL

In the late 1980s and 1990s it became more common for share issues to require full payment of the issued price. Before this period, shares generally required a payment of a proportion of the issue price upon application — say, 80 cents application on a $1 issue price. The difference of 20 cents represents uncalled capital. The amount of uncalled capital represents potential cash which a company is able to call up from shareholders. Clearly, if this is reduced, it benefits shareholders but may have adverse effects on creditors, as will be shown in the example below. Whilst no journal entry is required, authorised capital is reduced, but paid-up capital remains the same.

**Example:**

**Norman Ltd**

|  | $000 |
|---|---|
| Authorised capital | |
| 20 000 000 $1 ordinary shares | 20 000 |
| Paid-up capital | |
| 20 000 000 $1 ordinary shares | |
| (paid to 80 cents) | 16 000 |

Following court approval to extinguish uncalled capital, the new capital structure would appear as follows:

|  |  |
|---|---|
| Authorised capital | |
| 20 000 000 80 cent ordinary shares | 16 000 |
| Paid-up capital | |
| 20 000 000 80 cent ordinary shares (fully paid) | 16 000 |

Paid-up capital remains the same, $16 000 000, but notice that authorised capital is reduced by $4 000 000 (20 000 000 × 20 cents). This could affect creditors in the event of a liquidation of the company because that $4 000 000 can no longer be called up as the shares are now fully paid.

## CANCELLING PAID-UP CAPITAL

Section 195(1)(b) of the Corporations Law allows a company to cancel paid-up capital where it is lost due to past operating losses (accumulated losses brought forward) or where assets are overstated and need to be written down against paid-up capital. There are therefore two cases.

**capital reduction account**

1 *Lost paid-up capital:* Here a specific-purpose account called a Capital Reduction account is used. The journal entries are:

|  | Debit | Credit |
|---|---|---|
| Paid-up Capital | XXX | |
| Capital Reduction | | XXX |

The brought-forward losses are then written off against the new credit balance in the Capital Reduction account.

|  | | |
|---|---|---|
| Capital Reduction | XXX | |
| Accumulated Losses/Retained Profits | | XXX |

These two journal entries effectively eliminate losses brought forward. The Foster's Brewing Group Ltd recently used this procedure to write off accumulated losses of $1300 million.

2 *Assets overstated*: When writing down the value of assets, the amounts involved must go through the current period's profit and loss account. First, a Capital Reduction account is established by the following entry:

|  | Debit | Credit |
|---|---|---|
| Paid-up Capital | XXX | |
| Capital Reduction | | XXX |

Next, any existing accumulated depreciation is written off as follows:

|  |  |  |
|---|---|---|
| Accumulated Depreciation | XXX | |
| Asset | | XXX |

The write-down of the asset is then journalised as follows:

|  |  |  |
|---|---|---|
| Loss on Asset Revaluation | XXX | |
| Asset | | XXX |

The loss on asset revaluation is closed to the Profit and Loss Summary account at the end of the year.

|  |  |  |
|---|---|---|
| Profit and Loss Summary | XXX | |
| Loss on Asset Revaluation | | XXX |

This amount is then transferred to the Retained Profits account.

|  |  |  |
|---|---|---|
| Retained Profits | XXX | |
| Profit and Loss Summary | | XXX |

(loss on asset revaluation; this entry transfers the loss on asset revaluation via a closing entry to retained profits)

Finally, the write-down of assets is written off against the capital being reduced.

|  |  |  |
|---|---|---|
| Capital Reduction | XXX | |
| Retained Profits | | XXX |

In both the above cases, paid-up capital is reduced with a debit entry and a Capital Reduction account is created with the credit. This credit is then used to write off losses or absorb the write-down in the value of assets. Where assets are overstated, the extra journal entries are needed because of the requirements of AASB 1018: Profit and Loss Accounts and AASB 1010: Accounting for the Revaluation of Non-current Assets.

### Example:

The balance sheet of Nick Ltd showed the following:

**Nick Ltd**

|  | $ | $ | $ |
|---|---|---|---|
| *Shareholders' equity* | | | |
| Authorised capital | | | |
| 100 000 $1 ordinary shares | | | $100 000 |
| | | | |
| Paid-up capital | | | |
| 100 000 $1 ordinary shares | | | 100 000 |
| (fully paid) | | | |
| Retained profits/Accumulated losses | | | (2 000) |
| | | | $98 000 |

| | $ | $ | $ |
|---|---|---|---|
| *Assets* | | | |
| Equipment | 50 000 | | |
| *Less* Accumulated depreciation | (5 000) | 45 000 | |
| Goodwill | | 3 000 | |
| Land | | 245 000 | |
| | | | 293 000 |
| *Liabilities* | | | 195 000 |
| Net assets | | | $98 000 |

Following the necessary approvals, the shareholders of Nick Ltd decide to reduce paid-up capital by 20 cents per share and use the amount made available to write off accumulated losses, write down the net value of equipment to $35 000, and write off the asset account Goodwill.

The effect of the reduction of paid-up capital is best looked at by examining the change to one share and then multiplying by the number of issued shares.

| | Issued price | = | Paid-up | + | Uncalled |
|---|---|---|---|---|---|
| BEFORE | 1.00 | = | 1.00 | + | 0 |
| AFTER | 0.80 | = | 0.80 | + | 0 |
| | 0.20 | | 0.20 | | |

The total amount involved is then 20 cents × 100 000 shares = $20 000. The journal entry is therefore:

| | Debit | Credit |
|---|---|---|
| Paid-up Capital | 20 000 | |
|     Capital Reduction | | 20 000 |

The credit balance in the Capital Reduction account enables the other changes to be made.

Next, the existing accumulated depreciation against equipment is written off by the following entry:

| | | |
|---|---|---|
| Accumulated Depreciation | 5 000 | |
|     Equipment | | 5 000 |

To reduce the equipment to $35 000 (now at $45 000):

| | | |
|---|---|---|
| Loss on Asset Revaluation | 10 000 | |
|     Equipment | | 10 000 |

To write off existing goodwill:

| | | |
|---|---|---|
| Loss on Asset Revaluation | 3 000 | |
|     Goodwill | | 3 000 |

A closing entry then transfers the total loss on asset revaluation to retained earnings ($10 000 + $3000).

| | | |
|---|---|---|
| Retained Profits | 13 000 | |
|     Profit and Loss Summary | | 13 000 |

The Capital Reduction account is then used to write off this debit adjustment of $13 000 plus the $2000 balance of accumulated losses.

|  | Debit | Credit |
|---|---|---|
| Capital Reduction | 15 000 | |
| Retained Profits | | 15 000 |

Note that there is $5000 left in the Capital Reduction account ($20 000 − $15 000). The balance sheet of Nick Ltd now appears as follows:

|  | $ | $ |
|---|---|---|
| *Shareholders' equity* | | |
| Authorised capital | | |
| 100 000 80 cent ordinary shares | 80 000 | |
| Paid-up capital | | |
| 100 000 80 cent ordinary shares | 80 000 | |
| (fully paid) | | |
| Capital reduction reserve | 5 000 | |
| | | $85 000 |
| | | |
| *Assets* | | |
| Equipment at valuation | 35 000 | |
| Land | 245 000 | 280 000 |
| | | |
| *Liabilities* | | 195 000 |
| *Net assets* | | $85 000 |

There is no legal requirement to fully use any balance in the Capital Reduction account; hence, it will show as a shareholder reserve as above.

## RETURNING PAID-UP CAPITAL

If a company decides to return paid-up capital, by a cash payment to shareholders, the constitution must authorise the reduction, approval must be given by special resolution and confirmation is needed by the court.

It would be most unusual for a listed public company to utilise this part of s 195. Rather, the company would probably elect to purchase its own shares, thereby cancelling the issued shares purchased (s 205).

The journal entries are as follows:

|  | Debit | Credit |
|---|---|---|
| Paid-up Capital | XXX | |
| Shareholders' Distribution | | XXX |
| | | |
| Shareholders' Distribution | XXX | |
| Cash | | XXX |

A complication arises here in that there are three variations in the way paid-up capital may be returned to shareholders. In each variation, cash is returned to shareholders, but the company may elect to make changes in either uncalled capital or unissued shares.

1 Permanently reduce the issued value of the paid-up shares. That is, say a $1 fully paid ordinary share becomes 80 cents fully paid when 20 cents is returned.
2 Increase uncalled capital per share by an amount equal to the reduction in paid-up capital per share (here the issued price remains the same). That is, say, a share with an issued price of $1 paid to 60 cents has 20 cents returned, but at the same time 20 cents is added to uncalled capital.
3 Maintain the issued price by returning the shares to the balance of unissued shares.

**Example:**
Price Ltd has the following share capital:

| | |
|---|---|
| Authorised capital | |
| 200 000 $2 ordinary shares | $400 000 |
| Paid-up capital | |
| 100 000 $2 ordinary shares | $200 000 |
| (fully paid) | |

1 Assume the shares are to be reduced to $1 issue price and cash is to be returned to the shareholders.

| | Debit | Credit |
|---|---|---|
| Paid-up Capital | 100 000 | |
| Shareholders' Distribution | | 100 000 |
| | | |
| Shareholders' Distribution | 100 000 | |
| Cash | | 100 000 |

2 Assume that $1 per share is to be returned to shareholders and uncalled capital is increased by the same amount. This allows the company to recall the cash refunded to shareholders at a further date if necessary. The journal entries are the same as above. This results in paid-up capital being reduced to $100 000 and uncalled capital being increased by $100 000.
3 In the case where a company returns paid-up capital to shareholders, it may increase unissued capital by the same amount provided all of the paid-up capital in that class is being returned *and* any uncalled capital is also cancelled. For example, assume Corey Ltd has (in part) 100 000 $1 ordinary shares paid to 80 cents. Uncalled capital is therefore 20 cents per share. All paid-up capital is returned to shareholders on these shares and the shares are returned to unissued capital. The journal entry is:

| | Debit | Credit |
|---|---|---|
| Paid-up Capital | 80 000 | |
| Shareholders' Distribution | | 80 000 |
| | | |
| Shareholders' Distribution | 80 000 | |
| Cash | | 80 000 |

# Other issues

## REDUCTION OF STATUTORY RESERVES

The Corporations Law specifies that the Share Premium account and Capital Redemption Reserve may be treated as paid-up capital in a reduction scheme (s 192(5)). This means that any balance in these accounts may be used to return paid-up capital to shareholders via the cash account.

|  | Debit | Credit |
|---|---|---|
| Share Premium | XXX | |
| Capital Redemption | XXX | |
|    Shareholders' Distribution | | XXX |
|  |  |  |
| Shareholders' Distribution | XXX | |
|    Cash | | XXX |

Also, these balances may be transferred to a Capital Reduction account to write off accumulated losses and/or write down the value of assets.

## FORFEITURE OF SHARES

Where a company has decided to undertake a capital reorganisation and has calls in arrears, these calls should be forfeited as a first step. This changes the number of shares and dollar amounts of unissued and issued shares. The Corporations Law gives authority to use the balance in the Forfeited Shares account for a capital reduction. That is, the amount paid on these shares is forfeited by the company and is credited to a gain on the Forfeited Shares account. This applies to a listed public company where usually on resale the balance in the Forfeited Shares account must be returned to the former owner of the shares. Here the shares are cancelled and no resale occurs.

The journal entry is:

|  | Debit | Credit |
|---|---|---|
| Gain on Forfeited Shares | XXX | |
|    Profit and Loss | | XXX |
| Profit and Loss | XXX | |
|    Capital Reduction | | XXX |

## ARREARS OF PREFERENCE DIVIDENDS

It is often the case that companies which undertake a capital reorganisation have cumulative preference shares as part of their share capital. This means that any dividends payable on the preference shares will accumulate (hence the term 'cumulative') over time if insufficient cash is available to pay this liability.

The liability 'dividend payable' may well appear as *a note* to the balance sheet, rather than as a liability incorporated into the balance sheet. The note will show as 'arrears of preference dividend'.

In a typical capital reorganisation, preference shareholders may elect to receive, say, ordinary shares in the company as some compensation for their arrears of preference dividends which are unlikely to be paid in the foreseeable future.

For example, arrears of preference dividends of Colin Ltd were $25 000 on the date a capital reorganisation was commenced. The preference shareholders elected to receive 10 000 $1 ordinary shares as compensation for the $25 000 arrears of dividends.

Because the $25 000 arrears have not been incorporated into the accounts, the journal entry is simply:

|  | Debit | Credit |
|---|---|---|
| Capital Reduction | 10 000 | |
| Paid-up Capital | | 10 000 |

The difference between the two amounts, $15 000, does *not* have to be accounted for.

# Redemption of redeemable preference shares

Redemption of the above shares is discussed in this chapter as the accounting treatment may be part of a capital reorganisation. Recall that a company issuing redeemable preference shares has the right to redeem them on a particular date (maturity) or at the company's option beforehand. Companies are continually looking at savings in financing expenses — for example, interest costs on redeemable preference shares are a cost that can be managed and minimised. Assume a company issued preference shares with a 12% dividend payable. If the market rate falls to, say, 10%, the company is then paying a premium (an amount above the market price) of 2%.

If the preference shares are redeemable, they may be exchanged for other shares to reduce financing costs. This could take the form of preference shares paying lower dividends or ordinary shares. Usually if such shares are redeemed before their maturity date, a premium is paid to the shareholders. Section 192 of the Corporations Law guides the accounting procedure in this area. The major focus of s 192 is to ensure that capital is *not reduced* through redemption. Other important parts of s 192 are that the shares must be fully paid-up before they may be redeemed, redemption must not reduce authorised capital and, where shares are redeemed at a premium, the premium must be from profits or a share premium account.

Capital redemption of redeemable preference shares is carried out using one of the following methods:
- funding the redemption with profits that would otherwise be available for the payment of dividends;
- funding the redemption with a new issue of preference or ordinary shares; or
- funding the redemption by exchanging new shares for old.

The first method involves transferring an amount equal to the redeemed shares to a capital redemption reserve. This has the effect of preserving capital.

## REDEMPTION OUT OF PROFITS

Pavin Ltd had share capital of 100 000 fully paid $1, 10% redeemable preference shares. Assume that Pavin redeems the shares at par. The journal entries are:

|  | Debit | Credit |
|---|---|---|
| Paid-up Capital | 100 000 | |
|     Shareholders' Redemption | | 100 000 |
| Retained Profits | 100 000 | |
|     Capital Redemption Reserve | | 100 000 |
| Shareholders' Redemption | 100 000 | |
|     Cash | | 100 000 |

If Pavin Ltd redeems the shares at a 10% premium, the journal entries are:

| | | |
|---|---|---|
| Paid-up Capital | 100 000 | |
| Shareholders' Redemption | | 100 000 |
| Retained Profits | 110 000 | |
|     Capital Redemption Reserve | | 100 000 |
|     Shareholders' Redemption* | | 10 000 |
| Shareholders' Redemption | 110 000 | |
|     Cash | | 110 000 |

* If the $10 000 premium is payable from a share premium reserve, the above entry is:

| | | |
|---|---|---|
| Retained Profits | 100 000 | |
| Share Premium Reserve | 10 000 | |
|     Capital Redemption Reserve | | 100 000 |
|     Shareholders' Redemption | | 10 000 |

## REDEMPTION FROM A NEW ISSUE

John Ltd wants to redeem 1 000 000 preference shares of $1 fully paid by issuing 2 000 000 ordinary shares of 50 cents each, payable in full on application. As in the previous example, assume a premium is not paid and then a premium of 10% is paid. In the first instance, the journal entries are:

|  | Debit | Credit |
|---|---|---|
| Bank Trust | 1 000 000 | |
|     Application – Ordinary | | 1 000 000 |
| Application – Ordinary | 1 000 000 | |
|     Paid-up Capital – Ordinary | | 1 000 000 |
| Paid-up Capital – Preference | 1 000 000 | |
|     Shareholders' Redemption | | 1 000 000 |
| Shareholders' Redemption | 1 000 000 | |
|     Cash | | 1 000 000 |

With a 10% premium, the above amounts must be increased to include the extra 100 000 premium and this premium is set aside from retained profits as follows:

| | Debit | Credit |
|---|---|---|
| Bank Trust | 1 000 000 | |
| Application – Ordinary | | 1 000 000 |
| Application – Ordinary | 1 000 000 | |
| Paid-up Capital – Ordinary | | 1 000 000 |
| Paid-up Capital – Preference | 1 000 000 | |
| Shareholders' Redemption | | 1 000 000 |
| Retained Profits | 100 000 | |
| Shareholders' Redemption | | 100 000 |
| Shareholders' Redemption | 1 100 000 | |
| Cash | | 1 100 000 |

## REDEMPTION BY EXCHANGE

Daley Ltd has 1 000 000 $1, 15% preference shares and wants to redeem them with ordinary shares because the market rate has fallen. The company opts to redeem these shares before maturity and pays a 10% premium on redemption. The premium will be paid from profits. The journal entries are:

| | Debit | Credit |
|---|---|---|
| Paid-up Capital – Preference 15% | 1 000 000 | |
| Paid-up Capital – Ordinary | | 1 000 000 |
| Premium on Redemption | 100 000 | |
| Cash | | 100 000 |
| Profit & Loss (Premium on Redemption) | 100 000 | |
| Premium on Redemption | | 100 000 |

# Share buy-backs

Under the Corporations Law, Part 2.4, Division 4B, a company is able to buy back its own shares. A company may have excessive liquidity and instead of paying cash dividends, opts to buy back its shares. Depending on individual circumstances, this may be more beneficial to shareholders as capital gains tax may be paid on the shares rather than income tax, which is generally at higher rates.

The Corporations Law (s 206) defines a number of buy-back arrangements, including:

1  An odd-lot purchase where the number of issued shares purchased is less than one market parcel. Here the company purchases the shares and then cancels them. This may work the other way as well. For example, the National Australia Bank Ltd offers discounted prices to shareholders to increase their shareholding to a marketable parcel. Such a marketable parcel may consist of 300 shares. A shareholder, when issued shares as part of a dividend reinvestment plan, may have 267 shares and is offered 33 shares at a 5% discount to the market to ensure the parcel is marketable.

2  An employee shares purchase where a company buys back shares from employees who received the shares as part of an employee share scheme.

3  A buy-back scheme. There are a number of legal requirements under Division 4B that apply to a buy-back, including the following:
- Only ordinary shares can be acquired.
- A company's constitution must authorise a buy-back.
- There is generally a limit of 10% of the issued share capital imposed on listed companies.
- When a buy-back takes place, there must be a solvency declaration signed by all directors. This places responsibility on directors for the company's solvency in the following 12 months.
- The solvency declaration must be accompanied by an auditor's report to give it credibility.

# Second Corporate Law Simplification Bill

The Second Corporate Law Simplification Bill Exposure Draft was issued by the Attorney General in June 1995. It contains a number of amendments to existing sections of the Corporations Law dealing with capital reorganisation. The following table shows the existing sections and the new section amendments in the bill.

| Topic | Current section | New sections |
|---|---|---|
| Alteration of share capital | 193 | 254H |
| | | 258D |
| Reduction of share capital | 195 | 256B |
| | | 256C |
| | | 256D |
| | | 258A |
| | | 258B |
| | | 258E |
| Redemption of preference shares | 192 | 254A |
| | | 254K |
| | | 254L |
| | | 254J |

At the time of writing, the progress of the Second Corporate Law Simplification Bill Exposure Draft is uncertain.

A brief summary of the new amendments follows.

### Alteration of share capital

A company may convert all or any of its shares into a larger or smaller number of shares by resolution passed at a general meeting. Any amount unpaid on such shares has to be divided equally among the replacement shares. A copy of the resolution must be lodged with the Australian Securities Commission.

Companies will also be permitted to cancel shares that have been forfeited.

## Reduction of share capital

A company may reduce its share capital if it is fair and reasonable to all shareholders, does not materially prejudice the company's ability to pay its creditors and is approved by shareholders. If it is an equal reduction, only an ordinary resolution is required; but for a selective reduction a special resolution is required.

A reduction is an equal reduction if it relates only to ordinary shares, applies to each holder of ordinary shares in proportion to the number of shares held, and the terms of the reduction are the same for all shareholders. If these factors do not apply, the reduction is a selective reduction. This presumably means a reduction is a particular class of shares rather than all classes.

A company may reduce its share capital by cancelling any paid-up capital that is lost or is not represented by available assets. This power does not apply if the company also cancels shares.

## Redemption of preference shares

A company may redeem redeemable preference shares only on the terms on which they are on issue. On redemption the shares are cancelled. A company may only redeem redeemable preference shares if the shares are fully paid-up and out of the profits of a new issue of shares made for the purpose of the redemption. If the company redeems the shares out of the proceeds of a new issue of shares made for the purpose of the redemption, a reduction in share capital is allowed. That is, an equivalent amount does not have to be credited to a Capital Redemption Reserve account.

## Share premium account

The new amendments also contain a discussion on removing the share premium account. That is, if the issue price of a share is, say, $2 and par value no longer exists, there will be no amount credited to a share premium account. This has a number of implications in an accounting sense, including the ways in which a share premium account may now be used — for example, paying the unpaid portion of a less than fully paid share.

**ILLUSTRATIVE EXAMPLE** 13.1

## COMPREHENSIVE

The following example highlights the main points discussed in the chapter.

**Montgomerie Ltd**
**Balance Sheet as at 30 June**

|  | $000 | $000 | $000 |
|---|---|---|---|
| *Assets* | | | |
| Current assets | | | |
| Accounts receivable | | 906 | |
| Bills receivable | | 24 | |
| Inventory | | 1 154 | 2 084 |
| Non-current assets | | | |
| Plant & machinery | 1 653 | | |
| *Less* Accumulated depreciation | 321 | 1 332 | |
| Motor vehicles | 32 | | |
| *Less* Accumulated depreciation | 12 | 20 | |
| Land & buildings | | 1 500 | 2 852 |
| Intangible assets | | | |
| Goodwill | | | 400 |
| Total assets | | | 5 336 |
| *Liabilities* | | | |
| Current liabilities | | | |
| Bank | | 700 | |
| Trade creditors | | 744 | 1 444 |
| Non-current liabilities | | | |
| 9% unsecured notes | | | 1 200 |
| Total liabilities | | | 2 644 |
| Net assets | | | $2 692 |
| *Shareholders' equity* | | | |
| Authorised capital | | | |
| 1 200 000 8% preference shares of $2 | | | 2 400 |
| 4 000 000 ordinary shares of $1 | | | 4 000 |
| | | | $6 400 |
| Issued and paid-up capital | | | |
| 400 000 8% preference shares of $2 fully paid | | | 800 |
| 3 200 000 ordinary shares of $1 called to 75 cents | | | 2 400 |
| | | | 3 200 |
| *Less* Accumulated losses | | | 508 |
| Total shareholders' equity | | | $2 692 |

*Note*: Arrears of preference dividend, $64 000.

On 1 July, the following scheme of reorganisation was implemented:
(a) Unissued preference shares were cancelled.
(b) Unissued ordinary shares were subdivided into shares of 75 cents each.
(c) Arrears of preference dividend were satisfied through the issue of 80 000 ordinary shares of 75 cents each credited as fully paid.
(d) The issued 8% preference shares were converted to 6% preference shares and then subdivided into shares of $1 each.
(e) Issued ordinary shares were reduced to shares of 75 cents each credited as paid to 50 cents each.
(f) The 9% unsecured notes were redeemed through the issue of 12 000 $100 7% debentures. These debentures were secured by a floating charge over the company's assets.
(g) Asset values were adjusted as follows:
 • Accounts receivable were valued at $876 000.
 • Plant and machinery were valued at $1 200 000.
 • Goodwill was written off.
(h) Any balance in the Capital Reduction account was applied to the reduction of accumulated losses.

*Required*
1 Prepare journal entries recording the reconstruction.
2 Prepare a balance sheet after the reconstruction.

**Solution**
Recall that under the direct method, journal entries are only required when paid-up capital is affected.
(a) No journal entry required.
(b) No journal entry required.

|  | Debit $ | Credit $ |
|---|---|---|
| (c) Capital Reduction | 60 000 | |
| Paid-up Capital – Ordinary | | 60 000 |

(80 000 ordinary shares of 75 cents each issued to satisfy arrears of preference dividends)

*Note:* There is no need to account for the $4000 difference, because the preference shareholders have agreed that the share issue will satisfy the outstanding arrears in full.

(d) No journal entry required.

(e) Issued price = Paid-up + Uncalled
BEFORE 1.00 = 0.75 + 0.25
AFTER 0.75 = 0.50 + 0.25
0.25    0.25    0.00
*Note:* Uncalled remains the same.

|  | Debit $ | Credit $ |
|---|---|---|
| Paid-up Capital | 800 000 | |
| Capital Reduction | | 800 000 |

(to reduce paid-up ordinary capital: 3 200 000 shares issued × 25 cents reduction per share)

| (f) 9% Unsecured Notes | 1 200 000 | |
|---|---|---|
| 7% Debentures | | 1 200 000 |

(to redeem unsecured notes by issuing 12 000 $100 debentures)

(g) The original accounts receivable figure is $906 000 with no provision for doubtful debts. The new figure is $876 000. Therefore, a provision for doubtful debts of $30 000 must be created.

|  | Debit $ | Credit $ |
|---|---|---|
| Loss on Asset Revaluation | 30 000 | |
| Provision for Doubtful Debts | | 30 000 |
| Profit and Loss Summary | 30 000 | |
| Loss on Asset Revaluation | | 30 000 |
| Retained Profits | 30 000 | |
| Profit and Loss Summary | | 30 000 |
| Capital Reduction | 30 000 | |
| Retained Profits | | 30 000 |

To value plant and machinery at $1 200 000, it must be written down by $132 000 – that is:

| | |
|---|---|
| Original cost | $1 653 000 |
| Accumulated depreciation | 321 000 |
| Net book value | 1 332 000 |
| New value | 1 200 000 |
| Therefore, write down by | 132 000 |

|  | Debit $ | Credit $ |
|---|---|---|
| Accumulated Depreciation | 321 000 | |
| Plant & Machinery | | 321 000 |
| Loss on Asset Revaluation | 132 000 | |
| Plant & Machinery | | 132 000 |
| Profit and Loss Summary | 132 000 | |
| Loss on Asset Revaluation | | 132 000 |
| Accumulated Losses/Retained Profits | 132 000 | |
| Profit and Loss Summary | | 132 000 |
| Capital Reduction | 132 000 | |
| Accumulated Losses | | 132 000 |

To write off goodwill:

|  | | |
|---|---|---|
| Loss on Asset Revaluation | 400 000 | |
| Goodwill | | 400 000 |
| Profit and Loss Summary | 400 000 | |
| Loss on Asset Revaluation | | 400 000 |
| Retained Profits | 400 000 | |
| Profit and Loss Summary | | 400 000 |
| Capital Reduction | 400 000 | |
| Retained Profits | | 400 000 |

(h) After the above entries, the balance in the Capital Reduction account is $178 000 – that is:

| Capital Reduction | Debit $ | Credit $ | Balance $ |
|---|---|---|---|
| Paid-up capital – ordinary | | 800 000 | 800 000 |
| Paid-up capital – ordinary | 60 000 | | |
| Retained profits | 30 000 | | |
| Retained profits | 132 000 | | |
| Retained profits | 400 000 | | 178 000 |

Therefore, $178 000 may be applied to accumulated losses by:

| | Debit $ | Credit $ |
|---|---|---|
| Capital Reduction | 178 000 | |
|     Accumulated Losses | | 178 000 |

### Montgomerie Ltd
### Balance Sheet (after reorganisation)

| | $000 | $000 | $000 |
|---|---|---|---|
| *Assets* | | | |
| Current assets | | | |
|   Accounts receivable | 906 | | |
|   *Less* Provision for doubtful debts | 30 | 876 | |
|   Bills receivable | | 24 | |
|   Inventory | | 1 154 | 2 054 |
| Non-current assets | | | |
|   Plant & machinery | | 1 200 | |
|   Motor vehicles | 32 | | |
|   *Less* Accumulated depreciation | 12 | 20 | |
|   Land & buildings | | 1 500 | 2 720 |
|     *Total assets* | | | $4 774 |
| *Liabilities* | | | |
| Current liabilities | | | |
|   Bank | | 700 | |
|   Trade creditors | | 744 | 1 444 |
| Non-current liabilities | | | |
|   7% debentures | | | 1 200 |
|     *Total liabilities* | | | 2 644 |
|     *Net assets* | | | $2 130 |
| | | | |
| *Shareholders' equity* | | | |
| Authorised capital | | | |
|   800 000 6% preference shares of $1 | | | 800 |
|   4 266 667 ordinary shares of 75 cents* | | | 3 200 |
| | | | $4 000 |

|  | $000 | $000 | $000 |
|---|---|---|---|
| Issued and paid-up capital | | | |
| 800 000 6% preference shares of | | | |
| $1 fully paid | | | 800 |
| 3 200 000 ordinary shares paid to 50 cents | | | 1 600 |
| 80 000 ordinary shares fully paid | | | 60 |
| | | | 2 460 |
| Less Accumulated losses (508 – 178) | | | 330 |
| Total shareholders' equity | | | $2 130 |

\* The number and dollar amounts of the authorised capital of 4 266 667 ordinary shares of 75 cents may be calculated as follows:

|  | Number | (75 cents each) | $ |
|---|---|---|---|
| Unissued | 986 667 | 740 000 / .75 | 740 000 |
| Issued | 80 000 | 60 000 / .75 | 60 000 (note (e) above) |
| | 3 200 000 | 2 400 000 / .75 | 2 400 000 |
| Authorised | 4 266 667 | | 3 200 000 |
| Alternatively, | $3 200 000 / .75 = 4 266 667 | | |

# Review

This chapter has examined the concept and, through a case study in the appendix, the application of capital reorganisation. The use of the direct method means that no journal entries are required where paid-up capital remains unchanged. An emphasis was also placed on the irrelevance of market share prices when undertaking a capital reorganisation. That is, the accounting numbers are the focal point. The relevance and practicality of a capital reorganisation is demonstrated in the appendix by examining Foster's Brewing Group Ltd's reduction of capital scheme. Here accumulated losses of $1.3 billion were eliminated through a series of journal entries.

# KEY TERMS

| | |
|---|---|
| capital redemption reserve | direct method |
| capital reduction account | indirect method |
| capital structure | subdivision of issued shares |

# REVIEW QUESTIONS

**13.1** A capital reorganisation does not affect the market price of the company's shares. Discuss.

**13.2** What are the *pro forma* journal entries, if any, in the following cases:
(a) cancellation of unissued shares;
(b) forfeiture and cancellation of both issued and unissued shares;
(c) cancellation of accumulated losses;
(d) reduction of any uncalled liability on shares;
(e) returning paid-up capital to shareholders?

**13.3** What are the advantages, if any, in subdividing shares?

**13.4** Describe the circumstances that would influence a company to undertake a capital reorganisation.

**13.5** Discuss the treatment of 'arrears of preference dividends' in a capital reconstruction if there are insufficient funds to pay the dividend.

**13.6** Refer to the case study on Foster's Brewing Group Ltd in Appendix 13.1 (pp. 416–22) What reasons would you suggest for the company's reorganisation?

**13.7** If arrears of preference dividend were $200 000 and preference shareholders agreed to accept 100 000 $1 ordinary shares fully paid in full satisfaction of their dividends, what is the accounting treatment for the $100 000 difference?

**13.8** A company proposes to reduce the value of its paid-up capital of $500 000. In what ways may this amount be used?

**13.9** Discuss the effects, if any, on creditors when a company decides to implement a capital reorganisation.

# EXERCISES

**Exercise 13.10** **Paid-up capital not changed**
The shareholders' equity of Davis Ltd as at 30 June 20X2 is as follows:

| | |
|---|---|
| Authorised capital | |
| 10 000 000 $2 ordinary shares | $20 000 000 |
| Issued and paid-up capital | |
| 4 000 000 $2 ordinary shares fully paid | $8 000 000 |

The directors proposed the following capital reorganisation:
(a) cancel 2 000 000 unissued shares; and
(b) subdivide 4 000 000 $2 shares into 8 000 000 $1 shares.

*Required*
Prepare the necessary accounting action and the shareholders' equity of the company after the above has been implemented.

**Exercise 13.11** **Redemption of redeemable preference shares**

Prepare the journal entries for each of the following unrelated transactions:

1 Redeem at a premium of 50 cents per share, 200 000 $12 preference shares. Redemption is to be funded out of profits and the premium payable is funded from the Share Premium account.

2 Redeem at par value 100 000 $1 preference shares. The redemption is funded by a new issue of 200 000 50 cent ordinary shares.

3 Redeem at a premium of 10 cents per share, 200 000 $2 preference shares. Both redemption and premium are funded from profits.

**Exercise 13.12** **Changes to paid-up capital**

Love Ltd had incurred substantial losses and the directors decided to implement a capital reorganisation. The shareholders' equity section of Love's balance sheet immediately prior to the reorganisation is as follows:

|  | $ |
|---|---:|
| *Authorised capital* | |
| 100 000 50 cent ordinary shares | 50 000 |
| 100 000 $1 deferred shares | 100 000 |
| 100 000 $2 preference shares | 200 000 |
| | $350 000 |
| *Issued and paid-up capital* | |
| 80 000 ordinary shares paid to 40 cents | 32 000 |
| 30 000 deferred shares paid to 50 cents | 15 000 |
| 50 000 preference shares paid to $1 | 50 000 |
| | 97 000 |
| *Less* Accumulated losses | (40 000) |
| | $57 000 |

The following capital reorganisation was implemented:

(a) A call was made for the balance outstanding on deferred shares. All call money was received, then the shares were reduced to shares of 50 cents each fully paid.

(b) Issued ordinary shares were reduced to shares of 20 cents, each credited as paid to 10 cents.

(c) All unissued shares were cancelled.

(d) Issued preference shares were reduced to shares of $1 each with 50 cents per share being returned to shareholders.

(e) Uncalled capital on preference shares was reduced by 50 cents per share.

(f) The surplus resulting was used to reduce the accumulated losses.

*Required*

1 Prepare journal entries recording the above scheme.

2 Prepare a balance sheet after the reconstruction.

**Exercise 13.13**  Comprehensive

| | $000 | $000 | $000 |
|---|---|---|---|
| **Maggert Ltd** | | | |
| **Balance Sheet as at 30 June 20X2** | | | |
| *Assets* | | | |
| Current assets | | | |
|    Accounts receivable | 190 | | |
|    *Less* Provision for doubtful debts | 6 | 184 | |
|    Bills receivable | | 18 | |
|    Inventory | | 121 | |
|    Government bonds | | 2 | 325 |
| Non-current assets | | | |
|    Land & buildings | | 150 | |
|    Plant & machinery | 210 | | |
|    *Less* Accumulated depreciation | 40 | 170 | |
|    Motor vehicles | 16 | | |
|    *Less* Accumulated depreciation | 6 | 10 | 330 |
| Intangible assets | | | |
|    Goodwill | | | 20 |
|       *Total assets* | | | $675 |
| *Liabilities* | | | |
| Current liabilities | | | |
|    Bank | | 150 | |
|    Sundry creditors | | 130 | |
|    8% debentures | | 100 | 380 |
| Non-current liabilities | | | |
|    Unsecured notes | | | 70 |
|       *Total liabilities* | | | 450 |
|       *Net assets* | | | $225 |
| *Shareholders' equity* | | | |
| Authorised capital | | | |
|    200 000 ordinary shares of $2 | | | 400 |
|    150 000 8% preference shares of $1 | | | 150 |
| | | | $550 |
| | | | |
| Issued and paid-up capital | | | |
|    150 000 ordinary shares of $2 | | | |
|      called to $1.50 | | | 225 |
|    100 000 8% preference shares of | | | |
|      $1 fully paid | | | 100 |
| | | | 325 |
| *Less* Accumulated losses | | | 100 |
|       *Total shareholders' equity* | | | $225 |

Notes to the balance sheet:
1  Arrears of preference dividend were $24 000.
2  Debentures were redeemable at a premium of 5%.

On 1 July 20X2 the following scheme was put into operation:
(a) Government bonds were sold for $1900.
(b) Bills receivable were discounted for $17 000.
(c) The company's trade debtors were factored for $181 500. The factoring company insisted on full recourse, so the directors created a provision of $12 000 to provide for the liability likely to arise from bad debts.
(d) Each issued ordinary share was reduced to $1, credited as paid to 50 cents.
(e) Unissued ordinary capital was divided into shares of $1 each.
(f) Arrears of preference dividend were satisfied by the issue of 15 000 ordinary shares credited as fully paid.
(g) Debentures were redeemed (see Note 2, above).
(h) Unissued preference shares were cancelled.
(i) The issued 8% preference shares were converted to 6% preference shares.
(j) Asset values were adjusted as follows:
  (i) Land and buildings written up to $170 000.
  (ii) Plant and machinery written down by $24 000.
  (iii) Goodwill written off.
(k) Any balance in the Capital Reduction account was applied to the reduction of accumulated losses.

*Required*
1  Prepare journal entries recording the reconstruction.
2  Prepare the balance sheet on completion of the scheme.

**Exercise 13.14  Comprehensive**

The shareholders' equity of Jeff Ltd at 31 December 20X2 was as follows:

| | $ | $ |
|---|---|---|
| Authorised capital | | |
| 50 000  8% 'A' preference shares of $1 each | 50 000 | |
| 50 000  6% 'B' preference shares of $1 each | 50 000 | |
| 100 000  'A' ordinary shares of $1 each | 100 000 | |
| 100 000  'B' ordinary shares of $1 each | 100 000 | |
| 200 000 deferred founders shares of $1 each | 200 000 | |
| | | $500 000 |
| Issued and paid-up capital | | |
| 40 000  8% 'A' preference shares fully paid | 40 000 | |
| 50 000  6% 'B' preference shares paid to 75 cents | 37 500 | |
| 80 000 'A' ordinary shares fully paid | 80 000 | |
| 100 000 'B' ordinary shares paid to 75 cents | 75 000 | |
| 200 000 deferred shares fully paid | 200 000 | |
| | | 432 500 |
| Reserves | | |
| General reserve | 200 000 | |
| Accumulated losses | (300 000) Dr | |
| | | (100 000) Dr |
| Share capital and reserves | | $332 500 |

In the last two years, a series of losses has resulted in serious interruption to business. The directors believed that a capital reorganisation was appropriate at this time. Accordingly, with the consent of the court and creditors, the following capital reorganisation was agreed to:
(a) Issued 'A' preference shares were reduced to shares of 75 cents each fully paid.
(b) 'B' preference shares were reduced to shares of 75 cents each paid to 50 cents.
(c) Issued 'A' ordinaries were reduced to shares of 75 cents each paid to 50 cents.
(d) 'B' ordinaries were reduced to shares of 75 cents each paid to 25 cents.
(e) Deferred shares were reduced to shares of 50 cents each fully paid.
(f) Amounts made available by the reorganisation were applied to reducing the accumulated losses of the company.
(g) The general reserve was also applied to reducing accumulated losses.

*Required*
1  Prepare journal entries to implement the scheme.
2  Prepare a statement of shareholders' equity after the reorganisation.

**Exercise 13.15**  Comprehensive

**Brooks Ltd**
**Balance Sheet as at 30 June 20X2**

| | $ | $ |
|---|---|---|
| *Assets* | | |
| Current assets | | |
| Bank | 2 000 | |
| Sundry debtors | 3 000 | |
| Stock | 4 920 | 9 920 |
| Non-current assets | | |
| Land & buildings | 10 000 | |
| Plant & machinery | 9 000 | |
| Goodwill | 1 000 | 20 000 |
| Total assets | | 29 920 |
| *Liabilities* | | |
| Current liabilities | | |
| Trade creditors | 3 000 | |
| Total liabilities | | 3 000 |
| Net assets | | $26 920 |
| *Shareholders' equity* | | |
| Authorised capital | | |
| 10 000 6% $1 preference shares | | 10 000 |
| 40 000 $1 ordinary shares | | 40 000 |
| | | $50 000 |
| Issued and paid-up capital | | |
| 10 000 preference shares paid to 50 cents | | 5 000 |
| 30 000 ordinary shares called to 80 cents | 24 000 | |
| Calls in arrears on 10 000 ordinary shares | 2 000 | 22 000 |
| | | 27 000 |
| *Less* Profit and loss appropriation (debit) | | 80 |
| Total shareholders' equity | | $26 920 |

The necessary legal requirements have been met for the following reorganisation:
(a) Preference capital to be reduced to 10 000 shares of 75 cents each, paid to 50 cents.
(b) Issued ordinary shares to be reduced to 30 000 shares of 70 cents each fully paid. (The calls in arrears were duly received by the company.)
(c) The amount available from capital reduction to be applied to writing off goodwill completely, providing $500 for doubtful debts, and writing off accumulated losses, and the balance to be written off plant and machinery.
(d) It was decided to revalue land and buildings at $12 000.

*Required*
1 Prepare the appropriate journal entries.
2 Prepare the balance sheet of Brooks Ltd immediately following the reorganisation.

**Exercise 13.16**  **Forfeiture of shares and statement of shareholders' equity**
The shareholders' equity of Phil Ltd as at 30 June 20X2 consisted of:

|  | $ |
|---|---|
| **Authorised capital** | |
| 1 000 000 preference shares of $1 each | 1 000 000 |
| 1 000 000 ordinary shares of $1 each | 1 000 000 |
| **Issued and paid-up capital** | |
| 400 000 9% preference shares of $1 each | |
| called to 65 cents | 260 000 |
| *Less* Calls in arrears, 25 cents | (3 000) |
| 500 000 ordinary shares of $1 each called to 75 cents | 375 000 |
| *Less* Calls in arrears, 15 cents | (2 400) |
| | 629 600 |
| *Less* Accumulated losses | 174 000 |
| *Total shareholders' equity* | $455 600 |

On 1 July 20X2 the following capital reorganisation is approved by the court:
(a) Shares on which a call is in arrears are forfeited.
(b) Authorised capital is changed to 2 000 000 shares of 75 cents each.
(c) Issued preference capital is reduced to shares of 75 cents each paid to 50 cents.
(d) Issued ordinary capital is reduced to shares of 75 cents each paid to 50 cents.
(e) The amount made available by the reorganisation and forfeiture is used to write off the accumulated losses and goodwill (balance = $19 600).

*Required*
1 Prepare journal entries to implement the scheme.
2 Prepare a statement of shareholders' equity after the reorganisation.

**Exercise 13.17**  **Identifying changes between two balance sheets**
The shareholders' equity of Steve Ltd as at 30 June 20X2 consisted of:

|  | $ | $ |
|---|---|---|
| Authorised capital |  |  |
| 2 000 000 $2 shares | 4 000 000 |  |
| Issued and paid-up capital |  |  |
| 1 000 000 ordinary shares paid to $1 each | 1 000 000 |  |
| 400 000 8% preference shares fully paid | 800 000 |  |
| 500 000 deferred shares paid to 25 cents each | 125 000 | 1 925 000 |
| *Less* Appropriation (accumulated losses) |  | (650 000) |
| *Total shareholders' equity* |  | $1 275 000 |

On 1 July, the directors of Steve Ltd called up the balance of uncalled deferred capital. Having obtained all the required approvals, the company then reduced its capital and applied the resultant surplus as follows:

(a) Accumulated losses were written off.
(b) The value of plant and machinery was reduced by $20 000.
(c) Patents with a carrying amount of $50 000 were written off.
(d) The balance in the Capital Reduction account was used to reduce the value of goodwill.

The shareholders' equity as at 1 July 20X2 consisted of:

|  | $ | $ |
|---|---|---|
| Authorised capital |  |  |
| 2 400 000 $1 shares | 2 400 000 |  |
| Issued and paid-up capital |  |  |
| 1 000 000 ordinary shares paid to 75 cents |  | 750 000 |
| 800 000 8% preference shares |  | 800 000 |
| 500 000 deferred shares |  | 500 000 |
| *Total shareholders' equity* |  | $2 050 000 |

*Required*
Prepare all the journal entries which would have been recorded by the company on 1 July 20X2, in order to produce the above statement of shareholders' equity.

# Appendix 13.1

## CASE STUDY: FOSTER'S BREWING GROUP LTD

### 3. Reduction of Capital

The resolution set out below will be proposed as a Special Resolution:

'Subject to:

(a) confirmation by the Court;

(b) the lodgment of an office copy of the order of the Court with the Australian Securities Commission and compliance with any gazetting and advertising requirements ordered by the Court; and

(c) Resolution 5 set out in the Notice of Meeting dated 25 September 1995 being passed by members,

that:

(d) the issued share capital of the Company be reduced:

FROM: $3,267,392,723.30 divided into 3,266,702,631 ordinary shares of $1.00 each, fully paid (the 'fully paid shares') and 69,009,230 ordinary shares of $1.00 each, paid to one cent (the 'partly paid shares').

TO: $1,960,711,670.90 divided into 3,266,702,631 ordinary shares of 60 cents each, fully paid and 69,009,230 ordinary shares of 60 cents each, paid to one cent.

BY:

(a) cancelling 40 cents of paid up capital in respect of each fully paid share;

(b) cancelling 40 cents of capital not paid up in respect of each partly paid share;

(c) crediting an amount of $3,227,994.40 to a 'Capital Reconstruction Reserve'; and

(d) crediting an amount of $1,303,453,058 to the Accumulated Losses account of the Company; and

(e) the unissued share capital of the Company be reduced:

FROM: $1,664,288,139 divided into 1,639,288,139 ordinary shares of $1.00 each and 250,000,000 preference shares of 10 cents each.

TO: $1,008,572,883.40 divided into 1,639,288,139 ordinary shares of 60 cents each and 250,000,000 preference shares of 10 cents each; and

(f) Clause 4 of the Memorandum of Association and Article 2 of the Articles of Association of the Company be replaced with the following:

'The capital of the Company is $3,010,000,000 which is divided into:

(a) 4,975,000,000 Ordinary Shares of 60 cents ($0.60) each; and

(b) 250,000,000 Preference Shares of 10 cents ($0.10) each.',

but so that:

(g) the reduction of the par value of the partly paid shares shall not reduce the amount payable in respect of those shares; and

(h) except to the extent that the Company has agreed otherwise in writing, each holder of partly paid shares shall be obliged to pay the amount payable in respect of the partly paid shares in accordance with their terms of issue and the Company's Articles of Association.'

### 4. Consolidation of Share Capital

Subject to Resolution 3 being passed by members, the resolution set out below will be proposed as an Ordinary Resolution:

'Subject to:

(a) Confirmation by the Court of the reduction of capital referred to in Resolution 3 set out in the Notice of Meeting dated 25 September 1995; and

(b) the lodgment of an office copy of the order of the Court with the Australian Securities Commission and compliance with any gazetting and advertising requirements ordered by the Court,

that:

(c) every five issued ordinary shares of 60 cents each be consolidated and divided into three issued ordinary shares of $1.00 each on the basis that, if that results in a fractional entitlement for any shareholder, that fractional entitlement will be rounded up to the next whole number on the basis that the share resulting from the rounding up of the fractional entitlement will be paid up to the extent of the fractional entitlement and the rights attaching to that share will be proportional to the amount paid up;

(d) every five unissued ordinary shares of 60 cents each be consolidated and divided into three unissued ordinary shares of $1.00 each (adjusted as required to give effect to the rounding up of fractional entitlements under paragraph (c), so that the total issued and unissued capital of the Company remains equal to the Company's authorised capital);

(e) in accordance with Article 134D of the Company's Articles of Association, immediately after the rounding up of fractional entitlements under paragraph (c), amounts standing to the credit of the Company's share premium account be applied in paying up any amount unpaid in respect of any shares resulting from the rounding up referred to in paragraph (c);

(f) the authorised capital of the company be increased to $5,000,000,000 by the creation of 1,990,000,000 new ordinary shares of $1.00 each; and

(g) Clause 4 of the Memorandum of Association and Article 2 of the Articles of Association of the Company be replaced with the following:
'The capital of the Company is $5,000,000,000 which is divided into:
(a) 4,975,000,000 Ordinary Shares of $1.00 each; and
(b) 250,000,000 Preference Shares of 10 cents ($0.10) each.',
but so that:

(h) the total amount payable in respect of each share resulting from the consolidation and division of the partly paid shares immediately prior to the consolidation and division shall be the same as the total amount payable in respect of the partly paid shares from which that share is derived;

(i) the proportion between the amount paid and the amount unpaid in respect of each share resulting from the consolidation and division of partly paid shares shall be the same as it was in the case of the partly paid shares from which that share is derived; and

(j) except to the extent that the Company has agreed otherwise in writing, each holder of a share resulting from the consolidation and division of partly paid shares shall be obliged to pay the amount payable in respect of that share in accordance with the terms of issue of the partly paid shares from which that share is derived and the Company's Articles of Association.'

## 5. Amendments to the Articles of Association – Reconstruction of Capital

Subject to Resolutions 3 and 4 being passed by members, the resolution set out below will be proposed as a Special Resolution:

'Subject to Resolutions 3 and 4 being passed by members, that the Articles of Association of the Company be amended by:

(a) Inserting the following as Articles 21A and 21B immediately after Article 21:
'21A Notwithstanding anything to the contrary in these Articles, if the Company reduces the par value of any shares at a time when any amount remains unpaid in respect of any of those shares (whether on account of the nominal value of the shares or by way of premium):
(a) the reduction of the par value of the shares shall not reduce the amount payable in respect of the shares; and
(b) except to the extent that the Company has agreed otherwise in writing, each holder of the shares shall be obliged to pay the amount payable in respect of the shares in accordance with their terms of issue and these Articles.
21B Notwithstanding anything to the contrary in these Articles, if the Company consolidates and divides or

sub-divides any of its shares at a time when any amount remains unpaid in respect of any of those shares (whether on account of the nominal value of the shares or by way of premium) then, subject to the Listing Rules:

(a) the total amount payable in respect of each share resulting from the consolidation and division shall be the same as the total amount that was payable in respect of the shares from which that share is derived;

(b) the proportion between the amount paid and the amount unpaid in respect of each share resulting from the consolidation and division or the sub-division shall be the same as it was in the case of the shares from which that share is derived; and

(c) except to the extent that the Company has agreed otherwise in writing, each holder of a share resulting from the consolidation and division or the sub-division shall be obliged to pay the amount payable in respect of that share in accordance with terms of issue of the shares from which that share is derived and these Articles.'

(b) In Article 52(a), inserting the words 'or any' after the words 'consolidate and divide all'.

(c) In Article 128, inserting the words 'and further subject to Article 134D' after the words 'special rights as to dividend' in the first sentence.

(d) In Article 133(1), inserting the words 'Subject to Article 134D, the' in place of the word 'The' at the beginning of the first sentence.

(e) Inserting the following as Article 134D immediately after Article 134C:

'134D Notwithstanding anything to the contrary in these Articles and subject to the Listing Rules, if:

(a) the Company consolidates and divides all or any of its share capital into shares of larger amount than its existing shares; and

(b) fractional entitlements under that consolidation and division are to be rounded up,

any amount available for distribution to members or available to be applied for the benefit of members under Article 134 may be applied in paying up any amount unpaid on any shares resulting from the rounding up referred to in paragraph (b).'

## Explanatory Notes
Resolutions 3, 4 and 5

### Indicative Timetable

If members pass Resolutions 3, 4 and 5, the dates below (except for the date of the Annual General Meeting) are indicative of the capital reconstruction process subsequent to the AGM. In particular, court dates may change depending on the level of business before the Court on a particular day and on the availability of the judge. The subsequent dates will depend on the date of the order of the Court confirming the reduction of capital.

| Event | Date |
|---|---|
| Annual General Meeting | 23 October 1995 |
| First Court Hearing | 31 October 1995 |
| Confirmation Court Hearing | 3 November 1995 |
| Lodgment of Court Order with Commission | Close of business on 10 November 1995 |
| Capital Reconstruction Takes Effect | 13 November 1995 |
| Quotation of Shares on ASX on Deferred Settlement Basis | 13–28 November 1995 |
| Despatch of Uncertificated Holdings Statements or Share Certificates | 22–28 November 1995 |

### Resolutions 3, 4 and 5
### Capital Reduction, Consolidation of Share Capital and Related Amendments to the Articles of Association

The principal activities of Foster's Brewing Group Limited are the brewing and marketing of beer. The Company continues to liquidate non-core assets in an orderly manner. This program has required write downs and provisions that resulted in the Company incurring substantial losses. While the Company's core brewing businesses have continued to generate profits, the Company's accumulated losses as at 30 June 1995 still totalled approximately $1,303 million (approximately $1,308 million on a consolidated basis). These losses reflect a permanent reduction in the value of the Company's assets.

In these circumstances, your Directors believe that it is appropriate to reconstruct the Company's share capital to eliminate the accumulated losses and bring the Company's share capital more closely into line with its total shareholders' equity.

Accordingly, it is proposed that the par value of the Company's ordinary shares (both issued and unissued) be reduced by 40 cents per share. This will reduce its issued capital by approximately $1,306 million. Of this amount, approximately $1,303 million will be applied in writing off the Company's accumulated losses and the balance of approximately $3 million will be credited to a Capital Reconstruction Reserve.

Following this reduction in the par value of the Company's ordinary shares, it is proposed that the Company's share capital be consolidated into shares of $1.00. The proposed terms of consolidation are that every five ordinary shares of 60 cents will be consolidated to become three shares of $1.00 each.

The reduction in the par value of the Company's ordinary shares and their subsequent consolidation will not involve either:

(a)  a diminution of liability in respect of unpaid share capital; or

(b)  the payment to any member of any paid up share capital.

Accordingly, it will have no adverse financial effect on the Company or its members or creditors. Further, the proportionate ownership interest of each member in the Company remains the same before and after the capital reconstruction (subject to rounding of fractions). However, it will be a reduction of capital for the purposes of section 195 of the Corporations Law and therefore must be authorised by a special resolution and confirmed by the Court.

The reduction of capital takes effect upon the lodgment of a copy of the Court order with the Australian Securities Commission and compliance with any gazetting and advertising requirements ordered by the Court. The consolidation takes effect immediately thereafter.

The reconstruction of the Company's share capital will be reflected in the financial statements of the Company as follows:

| | Pre-reconstruction | Post-reconstruction |
|---|---|---|
| | $m | $m |
| Share capital | 3,267 | 1,961 |
| Reserves | 642 | 642 |
| Accumulated losses | (1,303) | – |
| Capital Reconstruction Reserve | | 3 |
| Shareholders' Equity | 2,606 | 2,606 |

**Total shareholders' equity will remain unchanged.**

### Effect on Fully Paid Ordinary Shares

The company currently has on issue approximately 3,267 million fully paid ordinary shares of $1.00 each. The par value of each of these shares will initially be reduced to 60 cents.

However, these shares will then be consolidated into ordinary shares of $1.00 each on a three for five basis. Accordingly, after the proposed consolidation, the Company will have on issue approximately 1,960 million fully paid ordinary shares of $1.00 each and the number of shares held by each member will be reduced by 40 per cent.

### Unmarketable and Uneconomic Parcels of Shares

Recently, the Australian Stock Exchange Limited announced that one share will be a trading unit. Previously, the minimum number of shares that could be sold, other than as odd lots, was 100 shares and there were financial disadvantages for members selling a parcel of shares which was not divisible by 100. That disadvantage no longer exists. However, the matter of members being left with an uneconomic parcel of shares (that is, where the size of the parcel is such that the cost of selling is disproportionate to the proceeds of sale) after the proposed reduction and consolidation remains.

The Company has made arrangements with a stockbroker to assist members who, after the reconstruction hold less than 500 shares, with an on-market scheme to move up to 500 shares, or to sell their entire holding. Participation in the scheme will be voluntary. Details of the offer will be posted to members at an appropriate time after the reconstruction.

### Effect on Partly Paid Shares

The Company has on issue approximately 69,000,000 ordinary shares of $1.00 paid to one cent. These shares are proposed to be reconstructed in the same manner as the fully paid ordinary shares, but so that the total outstanding liability of holders of the partly paid shares before and after the reconstruction remains unchanged.

While the holders of the partly paid shares will remain obliged to pay the full amount outstanding in respect of their shares in accordance with the terms of issue and the Deed approved by members on 13 November 1991, the reduction in the par value of the Company's ordinary shares will reduce the amount of the uncalled capital which a liquidator of the Company would be able to call up in the event of a winding up of the Company. This is because a liquidator only has a statutory right to call up the uncalled par value of shares and not the uncalled premium.

### Share Fractions

Under the consolidation, share fractions will arise unless shareholdings are divisible by five into an integral number. Accordingly, the Company proposes to round up fractional entitlements at no cost to individual members. This will be done by applying the Company's reserves to pay up the additional fraction required to increase each member's resultant holding to an integral number. By way of illustration, if a member currently holds 101 fully paid ordinary shares of $1.00, the reconstruction would otherwise result in a holding of 60.6 ordinary shares of $1.00. This holding will first be rounded up to 61 shares (with the last share paid up to 60 cents, with 40 cents unpaid) and then the Company's share premium account will be applied to ensure that the share is fully paid up i.e. 40 cents will be paid up.

Rounding of fractions will only occur in respect of registered holdings. The Company will not issue shares to facilitate any other rounding of beneficial holdings.

### Tax Implications

These general comments are provided only to give a broad outline of the taxation implications for members and should not be relied on or used as a substitute for professional advice.

The Australian Taxation Office, in an advance opinion to the Company, has advised that:

- the reduction in the par value of shares;
- the consolidation of shares; and
- the rounding up of fractional entitlements arising on the consolidation

will not involve a disposal of any shares by members for Australian capital gains tax purposes.

Accordingly, the capital reduction and consolidation will not affect the taxation status of shares held. In particular, after the capital reduction and consolidation:

- members whose existing shares were acquired before 20 September 1985 for Australian capital gains tax purposes will have an equivalent post consolidation holding of shares which will have been acquired before 20 September 1985 and will not be subject to Australian capital gains tax on disposal of these shares; and

- members whose existing shares were acquired after 19 September 1985 for Australian capital gains tax purposes will have an equivalent post consolidation shareholding which will have been acquired at the same time and which will have the same cost base for Australian capital gains tax purposes when capital gains tax liability needs to be calculated on disposal of these shares.

Share traders, other professional members and non-residents should seek professional advice in relation to their position.

### Share Trading and Share Certificates

The Company's shares will be quoted on the Australian Stock Exchange Limited ('ASX') on a deferred settlement basis for the 11 business days immediately following the date the reconstruction takes effect. Between the 7th and 11th business days after the date of the reconstruction, the Company will dispatch uncertificated security holding transaction statements to members (or share certificates where required by overseas exchanges), together with a statement advising them of the number of securities they hold after the reconstruction. The statement will advise members of the procedures to be followed for uncertificated trading. Share certificates issued prior to the reconstruction will then no longer be valid. Uncertification is further explained below (in the explanatory notes to Resolution 6).

**Increase in Authorised Capital**
Finally, it is proposed that, after the reduction of capital, the Company's authorised share capital be

increased to $5,000 million so that the authorised capital remains at the same level as before the reconstruction.

**Articles of Association**
A number of amendments to the Company's Articles of Association are also proposed to facilitate the proposed reconstruction of capital. The major changes are proposed in order that:
(a) it is clear that the reconstruction will not affect the liability of holders of partly paid shares to pay the full unpaid issue price of their shares; and
(b) the Company's reserves may be applied other than on a pro-rata basis solely for the purposes of rounding up fractional entitlements.

## SUMMARY AND INTERPRETATION OF THE PROPOSAL

The following synthesises the above extract and attempts to simplify the accounting treatment required for this reduction of capital.

In the five years to 1995, Foster's had undertaken a major reconstruction of assets. This included the sale of non-core assets and various business segments that were not related to the company's main business — the brewing and marketing of beer. These sales incurred large book losses and, over a five-year period, resulted in approximately $1 303 000 000 in accumulated losses showing on the balance sheet. Directors decided to seek the permission of shareholders to undertake a reorganisation of capital to eliminate these losses from the balance sheet.

A notice of the annual general meeting to be held on 23 October 1995 was sent to shareholders and this notice detailed the reconstruction. As an overview, the changes to the share capital were shown as follows:

|  | Pre-reconstruction $m | Post-reconstruction $m |
|---|---|---|
| Share capital | 3 267 | 1 961 |
| Reserves | 642 | 642 |
| Accumulated losses | (1 303) | – |
| Capital reconstruction reserve | – | 3 |
| Shareholders' equity | $2 606 | $2 606 |

Note that shareholders' equity remained the same. A deduction of $1 306 000 000 from share capital was used to write off accumulated losses of $1 303 000 000, leaving a credit balance in the Capital Reconstruction Reserve of $3 000 000. ('Capital Reconstruction Reserve' is another name for the Capital Reduction account.)

Clearly, the post-reconstruction balance sheet looks far more 'healthy' than the pre-reconstruction balance sheet. Before the detail is discussed, note that this procedure did not affect the market price of Foster's shares and therefore did not change shareholder wealth. It was simply an accounting way of removing large accumulated losses from the balance sheet.

To achieve the above, Foster's initiated a reduction of capital followed by a consolidation of share capital as follows:

**Issued share capital**
1 Cancel 40 cents of paid-up capital of each fully paid $1 ordinary share.
2 Cancel 40 cents of uncalled capital of partly paid ordinary shares.
3 Credit an amount of $1 303 000 000 against accumulated losses.
4 Credit an amount of $3 000 000 (the remainder) to a Capital Reconstruction Reserve.
5 Reduce the unissued ordinary shares of $1 to 60 cents.

The above reduced the issued price of ordinary shares, both issued and unissued, from $1 to 60 cents. Following this reduction in issued price, Foster's then consolidated the ordinary shares into shares of $1 by changing every five ordinary shares of 60 cents into three shares of $1 each ($3 total in each case).

This reduction in the issued price of the ordinary shares and subsequent consolidation did not involve any return of paid-up capital; it merely provided a way of eliminating large accumulated losses from the balance sheet.

The consolidation of the ordinary shares into $1 each on a three for five basis resulted in the number of shares held by each shareholder being reduced by 40%. After these changes, because there was no change to shareholder wealth, the market price of the shares was virtually unaffected.

# chapter 14

## ACCOUNTING FOR FOREIGN CURRENCY

# introduction

Business activity has become increasingly international, with companies having transactions and investments across national boundaries and multinational companies being established in many different countries. This has caused a problem for accounting for these types of activity, as usually there are different currencies used. Thus, the basic monetary measuring unit acquires different dimensions and in order to record and report these activities some conversion of the foreign currency to the domestic currency is necessary. This chapter explains the problems that arise for international activities and the accounting treatment of them consistent with the appropriate regulation, AASB 1012: Foreign Currency Translation.

# Foreign currency translation

**exchange rate movements**

**spot rate**

**forward rate**

**buy**

**sell**

**hedging**

The main difficulties in accounting for foreign currency transactions and investments arise through time factors. First, transactions occur over a period, yet the need for reporting on those transactions occurs at a different time, by which time the rate at which the currencies involved can be translated has changed. That is, there have been exchange rate movements. A foreign exchange rate is the rate at which one currency is exchanged for another. Second, some transactions occur over lengthy periods of time during which there may have been substantial exchange rate movements. Therefore, there are differing exchange rates *during* the activity or investment. In discussions about change in exchange rates over time, the expressions 'spot rate' and 'forward rate' are used. The spot rate is the exchange rate for immediate delivery of currencies to be exchanged, and the forward rate is that at a specified date in the future. The difference between the spot rate and the forward rate is usually referred to as a discount (when the spot rate is higher than the forward rate) or premium (when the spot rate is lower than the forward rate). Third, foreign exchange transactions often involve additional parties — foreign exchange dealers operating in a foreign exchange market — such that there are a variety of exchange rates. Anyone who has travelled overseas will be aware that the rate at which they buy their foreign exchange is different to that for which they sell (back) their foreign exchange on their return. These rates also differ from those quoted in the daily media broadcasts and from institution to institution (not to mention on the 'black market', down some 'dark alley'). Therefore, rates vary according to supply and demand and are not necessarily related to the relative purchasing power of the currencies involved. There are entities, or divisions of entities such as banks, that exist purely to gain from dealing in foreign exchange — foreign exchange ('forex') dealers. Fourth, a company may plan for a foreign transaction and agree to 'purchase' foreign exchange at some date in the future, in which case they purchase at a future rate. Or, it may simply buy foreign exchange to protect against future possible losses resulting from exchange rate movements — this is called hedging. Sometimes, the activity does not involve any intended physical transfer of foreign exchange but is merely expressed in foreign currency terms (there is an artificial foreign currency contract). Similarly, the charge for depreciation of foreign-held assets does not involve any physical transfer of foreign exchange.

These and other factors have an impact on the business activities and will ultimately affect the profit and loss of the reporting entity. Therefore, it is important to attempt to measure and report on these activities as accurately and fairly as possible. For example, a report in the *Australian Financial Review* points out that the profit of Santos Ltd was significantly boosted by a change in the accounting treatment of foreign exchange movements (10 September 1996, p 17). It was merely a change in the accounting method used that led to the greater reported profit figure!

# Accounting for foreign currency transactions

When accounting for foreign currency transactions it is usual to distinguish between short-term and long-term monetary items. Short-term monetary items arise as a result of selling and purchasing goods and services for cash and on credit. Cash transactions are immediate and would be translated at the rates in effect at the date of the transaction. However, where the transaction is on credit, it will be important to know what the terms are, as there is likely to be a change in the exchange rate between the date of the transaction and the date of settlement. Thus, for example, if goods are purchased from overseas today with payment due in a month's time, it is important to know the terms of the settlement. If the settlement is to be made in foreign currency, then there may well be a profit or loss resulting from exchange rate movements from the date of the purchase and the date of the settlement — the payment is to be made in a fixed amount of foreign currency. If the payment is to be made in a fixed amount of the domestic currency, then there is no profit or loss resulting from the credit terms.

For example, an Australian computer trading company purchases two computers from a Hong Kong company for HK$18 000 each, the exchange rate being A$1 = HK$6. The company will record (in Australian dollars, of course) the purchase in the normal way, viz:

|  | Debit | Credit |
|---|---|---|
| Purchases | 6000 | |
| Accounts Payable | | 6000 |
| (purchase of two computers) | | |

If, by the time the company settles this account, the exchange rate has changed to A$1 = HK$5 and the terms are for settlement to be in Hong Kong dollars, the company is obliged to pay HK$18 000 for each computer. But what would have cost it A$6000 now costs it A$7200 (HK$36 000/5). The fall in the value of the Australian dollar has cost the company A$1200 — more Australian dollars are required to purchase the same number of Hong Kong dollars. The general journal entry to reflect this would have been:

|  | Debit | Credit |
|---|---|---|
| Accounts Payable | 6000 | |
| Exchange Loss | 1200 | |
| Bank | | 7200 |
| (settlement of Hong Kong account) | | |

The company has incurred an additional expense — exchange loss — solely due to its having a liability which has to be satisfied in a foreign currency. Of course, had the terms of the contract been for the payment of the Hong Kong equivalent of A$6000 (the contract was expressed in fixed units of domestic currency), the Australian company would have not lost from the fall in the exchange rate. The supplier (in Hong Kong) would have lost on the settlement (so it is unlikely to have agreed to these terms), receiving HK$15 000 for each machine and not the expected HK$18 000. However, had the exchange rate moved the other way, the Australian company would have gained and would have recorded an exchange profit (or exchange gain). For example, if the exchange rate at settlement had been A$1 = HK$6.40, the payment would have been recorded as:

|  | Debit | Credit |
|---|---|---|
| Accounts Payable | 6000 | |
| Bank | | 5625 |
| Exchange Profit | | 375 |
| (settlement of Hong Kong account) | | |

Accounting for foreign sales on credit is the converse of the above. So, if the Australian company makes sales of 30 tonnes of dried pasta to a client in Italy for A$3000, the general journal entry would be:

|  | Debit | Credit |
|---|---|---|
| Accounts Receivable | 3000 | |
| Sales | | 3000 |
| (sales on credit) | | |

When the payment is received, the accounts receivable will reflect this. However, it is common for such transactions to be invoiced in the foreign currency, so, if the exchange rate is 1000 lire = A$1 the invoice will be for 3 000 000 lire. Any movements in the exchange rates will affect the transaction. So, if the exchange rate changes (falls) to 900 lire = A$1, then the Australian company will receive an exchange profit — they receive more Australian dollars for the same number of Italian lire. The Italian client will have to pay the Australian company 3 000 000 lire and, whereas it was receiving A$1 for every 1000 lire, it now receives A$1 for every 900 lire. The entry, in the Australian company's books, would be:

|  | Debit | Credit |
|---|---|---|
| Bank | 3333 | |
| Accounts Receivable | | 3000 |
| Exchange Profit | | 333 |
| (receipt from Italian client) | | |

## UNREALISED TRANSACTIONS

So far we have assumed that the transactions are realised at the time of financial statement preparation. The exchange loss or profit would be shown in the profit and loss statement. However, if at balance date the transactions were unrealised it would be necessary to provide for any possible exchange loss or profit by using the foreign currency exchange rate at balance date. Thus, an Allowance for Exchange Loss account or an Allowance for Exchange Profit account would be created, with the corresponding amount being expensed or added to revenue, whatever the case might be. For example, an unrealised loss on exchange would be entered:

|  | Debit | Credit |
|---|---|---|
| Exchange Loss | XXX | |
| Allowance for Exchange Loss | | XXX |
| (provision for potential exchange loss) | | |

The allowance account would be shown in the balance sheet as a deduction from accounts receivable (in the case of foreign currency sales) in the same way as an allowance for doubtful debts.[1]

When the loss or profit is realised, it is written off against the allowance accounts. For example, an Australian company sells 1 000 000 tonnes of rice to a Japanese company, invoicing in yen the equivalent of A$50 000. At the date of the sale, the exchange rate is 70 yen = A$1, so the invoice is for 3.5 million yen.

The general journal entry in the Australian company's books is:

|  | Debit | Credit |
|---|---|---|
| Accounts Receivable | 50 000 | |
| Sales | | 50 000 |
| (sale of rice to Japanese client) | | |

The Australian company has a balance date before settlement is due, by which time the exchange rate has risen to 75 yen = A$1 (ie the Australian currency has risen in value against the yen). The company has incurred an exchange loss [(¥3 500 000/70) — (¥3 500 000/75) = A$3333] and would record the loss to balance date:

|  | Debit | Credit |
|---|---|---|
| Exchange Loss | 3 333 | |
| Allowance for Exchange Loss | | 3 333 |
| (provision for potential loss from exchange rate movements) | | |

The balance sheet would include in the current assets:

|  | $ | $ |
|---|---|---|
| Accounts receivable | 50 000 | |
| *Less* Allowance for exchange loss | 3 333 | 46 667 |

At the date of settlement the exchange rate is 80 yen = A$1. The company would have to record:

|  | Debit | Credit |
|---|---|---|
| Bank | 43 750 | |
| Allowance for Exchange Loss | 3 333 | |
| Exchange Loss | 2 917 | |
| Accounts Receivable | | 50 000 |
| (receipt of cash from Japanese client) | | |

## LONG-TERM MONETARY ITEMS

When companies borrow or lend foreign currency for periods longer than one year, there are issues of realisation and recognition of revenue and/or expense involved. AASB 1012 (commentary, para (vi)) requires all exchange differences relating to monetary items to be brought into account in the financial year in which the exchange rate changes. Therefore, if the exchange rate changes over the life of a loan, the consequent profits or losses should be accrued in the year the changes occur. For example, if, on 1 January Year 1, an Australian company were to borrow for three years 1 million Deutschmarks from a German bank when the exchange rate was A$1 = 1.60DM, the liability of the company at the date of the granting of the loan is A$625 000. If the exchange rate changes over the life of the loan, the company will bring into account any profit or loss at the next balance date. Let us assume, then, that the following exchange rates apply:

|  | 1 Jan Year 1 | 31 Dec Year 1 | 31 Dec Year 2 | 31 Dec Year 3 |
|---|---|---|---|---|
| A$1 = | 1.60DM | 1.55DM | 1.50DM | 1.47DM |

The liability at 31 December each year and the increase over the previous year would be:

|  | 1 Jan Year 1 | 31 Dec Year 1 | 31 Dec Year 2 | 31 Dec Year 3 |
|---|---|---|---|---|
| Liability | A$625 000 | 645 161 | 666 667 | 680 272 |
| Increase |  | 20 161 | 21 506 | 13 605 |

Therefore, the company would need to increase the liability at each balance date (31 December, in this case), recognising the expense of the exchange loss.

| Year 1 |  | Debit | Credit |
|---|---|---|---|
| Jan 1 | Bank | 625 000 |  |
|  | German Bank Loan |  | 625 000 |
|  | (loan from German bank raised) |  |  |
|  |  |  |  |
| Dec 31 | Exchange Loss | 20 161 |  |
|  | German Bank Loan |  | 20 161 |
|  | (recognition of exchange loss) |  |  |
| **Year 2** |  |  |  |
| Dec 31 | Exchange Loss | 21 506 |  |
|  | German Bank Loan |  | 21 506 |
|  | (recognition of exchange loss) |  |  |
| **Year 3** |  |  |  |
| Dec 31 | Exchange Loss | 13 605 |  |
|  | German Bank Loan |  | 13 605 |
|  | (recognition of exchange loss) |  |  |
|  | German Bank Loan | 680 272 |  |
|  | Bank |  | 680 272 |
|  | (repayment of loan) |  |  |

In the above example there has been a gradual deterioration in the Australian dollar in respect of the Deutschmark over the life of the loan. Had the exchange rate fluctuated, it could have been possible to have recorded an exchange profit, in which case the German Bank Loan account would have been debited and the Exchange Profit account credited.

## QUALIFYING ASSETS

Although referred to by a rather unusual term, certain items are classified as qualifying assets and the accounting treatment of them is different to other items. Basically, the term 'qualifying assets' refers to assets under construction either by the company or for the company (for future use). The cost of the acquisition of such assets requires certain exchange differences to be included as part of the cost. These costs are limited to those arising in respect of monetary items that can be reasonably attributed to qualifying assets. It is only for this class of 'assets' that exchange differences are to be included in the cost. However, the fundamental principle is that assets are not to be carried in the books at an amount in excess of their recoverable amounts.

# Accounting for hedging transactions

**hedging transactions**

In order to minimise the risk of exposure to movements in foreign currency rates, companies may enter into other transactions with a view to offsetting any potential losses — 'avoiding or minimising possible adverse financial effects or movements in exchange rates' (AASB 1012). These transactions are termed hedging transactions. Hedging transactions can relate to specific commitments or general commitments. As their names imply, a *specific* hedge is directly related to a specific transaction, and a *general* hedge is designed to cover overall net actual or anticipated currency exposure. Hedging should be distinguished from speculative dealings, which are defined in the standard as 'the taking of a position in a foreign currency . . . solely for the purpose of profiting from movement in the exchange rate for that currency'. To be effective, hedges create foreign currency assets or liabilities that produce returns opposite to the assets or liabilities being hedged. The easiest and most common form of hedge is to buy or sell currency at the date of the initial transaction. For example, an Australian company may purchase goods from a Hong Kong company and agree to pay HK$36 000 in one month's time. At the date of the purchase the exchange rate is A$1 = HK$6. As described above, the company would record the purchase as follows:

|  | Debit | Credit |
|---|---|---|
| Purchases | 6000 | |
| Accounts Payable | | 6000 |
| (purchase of goods from Hong Kong company) | | |

At the same date the company could purchase HK$36 000 and deposit it in a Hong Kong bank, such that it would record:

| | | |
|---|---|---|
| Hong Kong Bank | 6000 | |
| Bank | | 6000 |
| (deposit of foreign currency in foreign bank) | | |

Note that the deposit is, of course, expressed in the Australian dollar equivalent — the domestic currency of the company. Thus, in one month's time the Australian company would simply draw a cheque on its Hong Kong bank for HK$36 000 to settle the account with the Hong Kong supplier. Having done this, the Australian company has protected itself from possible losses that could have arisen from a change in the exchange rate. The company would record this as follows:

|  | Debit | Credit |
|---|---|---|
| Accounts Payable | 6000 | |
| Hong Kong Bank | | 6000 |
| (payment of supplier) | | |

Hedging contracts can take various forms and there are several different terms used to describe the different forms. In the simple example above, the Australian company may have borrowed rather than purchased the Hong Kong currency. Alternatively, it may have entered a transaction in the forward market by which it agrees to purchase from a third party foreign currency sometime in the future at a rate decided now. A similar form of contract is that on the futures market. This is an organised market in which transactions can take place and is less fixed than the forward market arrangement. A recent development is the swap market where, as its name implies, foreign currency commitments are exchanged (usually at an arrangement cost). The management of foreign currency transactions can become very complex and there are usually specialists within large companies who have responsibility for arranging and managing foreign currency transactions. As indicated, accounting for foreign transactions, including hedging, is regulated by AASB 1012. It sets out strict rules as to the recognition of a hedge transaction for a specific commitment, which distinguishes it from a hedge of a general commitment and a speculative transaction. Essentially, the principle is that there must continue to be a definite association between the hedge and the specific commitment.

**forward market**

**futures market**

**swap market**

### SPECIFIC HEDGE COMMITMENTS

Specific hedge commitments relate to various transactions, including:
(a)  the purchase or sale of goods or services;
(b)  foreign currency monetary items; and
(c)  investments in self-sustaining (see below) foreign operations.

Generally, any gain or loss resulting from a hedge transaction for a specific commitment is recognised in the profit and loss immediately. Any costs on the hedge of a purchase or sale of goods or services are to be included in the cost of goods or services. Any exchange revenues or expenses on the hedge of monetary items are to be recognised in the period in which they arise. Exchange gains or losses arising from a hedge on a net investment in self-sustaining foreign operations (see below) are to be transferred on consolidation to a foreign currency translation reserve.

**ILLUSTRATIVE EXAMPLE**  **14.1**

## SPECIFIC HEDGE ON PURCHASE OF GOODS

Australian Gourmet Foods Ltd, on 1 May 20X0, imported 10 000 tonnes of New Zealand lamb from New Trade (NZ) Ltd, payment due 31 July 20X0. The cost was NZ$120 000. On 1 May the spot rate was A$1 = NZ$1.20; the three-month forward rate was A$1 = NZ$1.15. Australian Gourmet Foods Ltd entered into a foreign currency contract with its bank for the purchase of NZ$115 000 for delivery on 31 July 20X0. At balance date, 30 June 20X0, the exchange rate was A$1 = NZ$1.10; on 31 July the spot rate was A$1 = NZ$1.08.

The general journal of Australian Gourmet Foods Ltd would include the following entries:[2]

| | Debit $ | Credit $ |
|---|---|---|
| **20X0** | | |
| **May 1** Foreign Currency Receivable | 100 000 | |
| Deferred Cost of Hedge Contract | 4 348 | |
| Hedge Contract Commitment | | 104 348 |
| (forward contract on NZ currency) | | |

*Note:* The company has agreed to accept NZ$120 000 in three months' time when the rate is expected to be A$1 = NZ$1.15, so the total cost will be (NZ$120 000/1.15 = A$104 348). This is the *cost* of the inventories at the date of purchase.

| | Debit $ | Credit $ |
|---|---|---|
| **May 1** Purchases | 104 348 | |
| Deferred Cost of Hedge Contract | | 4 348 |
| Accounts Payable | | 100 000 |
| (purchase of goods from New Trade (NZ) Ltd) | | |

The liability at this date is to pay NZ$120 000 with an exchange rate at this date of A$1 = NZ$1.20, which is A$100 000.

By balance date the exchange rate has changed, which has also changed the liability. The company is still committed to pay NZ$120 000, but this now would cost (NZ$120 000/1.10) A$109 091. Thus, the liability has to be increased.

| | Debit $ | Credit $ |
|---|---|---|
| **June 30** Exchange Loss | 9 091 | |
| Accounts Payable | | 9 091 |
| (loss arising from fall in exchange rate) | | |

However, the increase in the liability is offset by the gain on the foreign currency contract. That is, the 'value' of the receivable is now $109 091 (the right to receive NZ$120 000 with the current exchange rate being A$1 = NZ$1.10). Thus, the receivable has to be increased.

| | Debit $ | Credit $ |
|---|---|---|
| **June 30** Foreign Currency Receivable | 9 091 | |
| Gain on Foreign Currency Contract | | 9 091 |
| (gain on foreign currency contract) | | |

On settlement date the liability has further increased due to the change in the exchange rate. That is, there is a commitment to pay NZ$120 000 with an exchange rate of A$1 = NZ$1.08 (NZ$120 000/1.08 = A$111 111). Therefore, the payable has to be increased by A$2020. Similarly, the receivable has also increased.

|  | | Debit $ | Credit $ |
|---|---|---|---|
| July 31 | Exchange Loss | 2 020 | |
| | Accounts Payable | | 2 020 |
| | (loss arising from fall in exchange rate) | | |
| | | | |
| July 31 | Foreign Currency Receivable | 2 020 | |
| | Gain on Foreign Currency Contract | | 2 020 |
| | (gain on foreign currency contract) | | |

The company will have to pay the amount agreed in the hedging contract of 1 May.

| July 31 | Hedge Contract Commitment | 104 348 | |
|---|---|---|---|
| | Bank | | 104 348 |
| | (payment as agreed in foreign currency contract) | | |

The company will receive in return NZ$120 000 (measured in local currency as A$111 111).

| July 31 | Bank (Foreign Currency Held) | 111 111 | |
|---|---|---|---|
| | Foreign Currency Receivable | | 111 111 |
| | (NZ$120 000 at rate of A$1 = NZ$1.08) | | |

The company will have to settle its account with the supplier by paying NZ$120 000 (once again, measured in local currency as A$111 111).

| July 31 | Accounts Payable | 111 111 | |
|---|---|---|---|
| | Bank (Foreign Currency Held) | | 111 111 |
| | (payment of New Trade (NZ) Ltd) | | |

Note that if the contract had *not been hedged,* the entries would have been:

| 20X0 | | | |
|---|---|---|---|
| May 1 | Purchases | 100 000 | |
| | Accounts Payable | | 100 000 |
| | (goods purchased on credit from overseas supplier) | | |
| June 30 | Foreign Exchange Loss | 9 091 | |
| | Accounts Payable | | 9 091 |
| | (increased liability due to change in exchange rate) | | |
| July 31 | Foreign Exchange Loss | 2 020 | |
| | Accounts Payable | | 2 020 |
| | (increased liability due to change in exchange rate) | | |
| July 31 | Accounts Payable | 111 111 | |
| | Bank | | 111 111 |
| | (settlement of liabiity) | | |

A similar treatment is accorded specific hedges for foreign currency monetary assets. That is, exchange losses and profits are recognised in the period in which they arise. As indicated earlier, if the hedge is on the net investments in a self-sustaining operation and is accounted for using the current rate method (explained in the following section), any profit or loss arising from a hedge also would be taken to a foreign currency translation reserve.

## GENERAL HEDGE COMMITMENTS

The treatment of losses and profits resulting from hedges for general commitments is the same as that described for specific monetary items hedges — viz, they are recognised in the period in which they arise. Also, initial costs are amortised over the life of the hedge.

# Financial statement translation

## DEFINING THE NATURE OF FOREIGN OPERATIONS

The treatment of foreign currency transactions in Australia has not been without controversy, indicating that there have been some very differing views as to the best ways to incorporate the results of international transactions. So far we have been discussing 'one-off' transactions. However, Australian companies often have foreign subsidiaries and/or branches and the problem is how to incorporate the results of these entities with the Australian reporting entity which, of course, is reporting in Australian dollars. The standard, AASB 1012: Foreign Currency Translation has settled many of these disputes by requiring certain treatments in certain situations. In respect of foreign operations the standard distinguishes between those that are

**integrated foreign operations** regarded as integrated and those that are self-sustaining. Integrated foreign operations are those foreign operations that are 'financially and operationally inter-dependent, either directly or indirectly, with the company and whose day-to-day operations normally expose the company or group to foreign exchange gains or

**self-sustaining foreign operation** losses'. On the other hand, a self-sustaining foreign operation is a foreign operation that is 'not an integrated foreign operation, being an operation that is independent, financially and operationally, of the company and whose operations do not normally expose the company or group to foreign exchange gains or losses'.

The aim of the standard is to reflect the underlying relationships between a company and its foreign operations and to ensure the disclosure of all material information which would enable users relying on the accounts to assess the significance of the foreign operations. Thus, the distinction between self-sustaining and integrated operations is important because the standard requires different accounting treatment of each. The definitions are clearly designed to distinguish operations on the basis of the extent to which they expose the reporting entity to exchange gains and losses. The standard provides illustrations (in para (xi)) of situations that can be described as self-sustaining:

(a) The cash flows of the company are largely unaffected by the activities of the foreign operation.

(b) The sale prices of the foreign operation's products or services are not materially influenced by domestic conditions and such prices are primarily determined by factors other than changes in exchange rates.

(c) The foreign operation's major markets do not include the company's country.

(d) The foreign operation's costs are not materially affected by domestic prices.

(e) The foreign operation's day-to-day financing is not supplied by the company.

(f) here are no material inter-company transactions or other interchanges with the foreign operation in the course of normal activities.

Having described self-sustaining operations, all other operations are regarded as integrated operations.

## METHODS OF FOREIGN CURRENCY TRANSLATION

Over the years there have been several suggested methods for translating foreign currency transactions for reporting in financial statements. For example, all items could be translated at the rate current at the date of the transactions giving rise to them. This is known as the *historical rate method*. Or, all items could be translated at the date current at the preparation of the financial statements. This method is known as the *closing rate method*. Although having the attraction of simplicity, both of these methods have been regarded as not reflecting the real economic significance of foreign operations. (The closing rate method is still used in New Zealand.) The Australian standard describes two methods for translating foreign currency transactions — namely, the temporal method and the current rate method. Consequently, these are the methods most employed in Australia today and they are defined in AASB 1012 (para .06) in the following terms:

**temporal method**

**current rate method**

*The temporal method* is a method of translating the accounts or group accounts of a foreign operation whereby:

(a) (i) Monetary items are translated at the exchange rate current at balance date; and

(ii) non-monetary items are translated at exchange rates current at the transaction dates, or, where a non-monetary item has been revalued, at the exchange rate current at the date of revaluation.

(b) Owner's equity at the date of investment, including in the case of a corporation, share capital at acquisition and pre-acquisition reserves, is translated at the exchange rate current at that date.

(c) Post-acquisition movements in owner's equity, other than retained profits or accumulated losses, are translated at the exchange rates current at the dates of those movements, except that where a movement represents a transfer between items within owner's equity, the movement shall be translated at the exchange rate current at the date that the amount transferred was first included in owner's equity.

(d) Distributions from retained profits (ie dividends paid or proposed, or their equivalent) are translated at the exchange rates current at the dates when the distributions were proposed (or, where the approval of equity holders is not sought, at the dates when the distributions were declared).

(e) Post-acquisition movements in retained profits or accumulated losses, because of transfers from the profit and loss account, are brought to account as a result of applying (f) below for each financial year.

(f) Revenue and expense items are translated at the exchange rates current at the transaction date, except that non-monetary items are translated at the rates used to translate those non-monetary items.

In short, the temporal method utilises the principle that balance sheet or profit and loss items which have a current value at balance date are translated at the current exchange rate, while all other balance sheet and profit and loss items are translated at their respective historical rates.

*The current rate method* is a method of translating the accounts or group accounts of a foreign operation, whereby:

(a) Assets and liabilities are translated at the exchange rate current at balance date.

(b) Owner's equity at the date of investment, including in the case of a corporation, share capital at acquisition and pre-acquisition reserves, is translated at the exchange rate current at that date.

(c) Post-acquisition movements in owner's equity, other than retained profits or accumulated losses, are translated at the exchange rates current at the dates of those movements, except that where a movement represents a transfer between items within owner's equity, the movement shall be translated at the exchange rate current at the date that the amount transferred was first included in owner's equity.

(d) Distributions from retained profits (ie dividends paid or proposed, or their equivalent) are translated at the exchange rates current at the dates when the distributions were proposed (or, where the approval of equity holders is not sought, at the dates when the distributions were declared).

(e) Post-acquisition movements in retained profits or accumulated losses, because of transfers from the profit and loss account, are brought to account as a result of applying (f) for each financial year.

(f) Revenue and expense items are translated at the exchange rates current at the transaction date.

Unfortunately, the current rate method is somewhat ad hoc and is difficult to defend conceptually. However, it is the most popular method in practice.

The rates to be used by these two methods can be summarised (using the paragraph subheadings from the above):

|        | Temporal          | Current rate      |
|--------|-------------------|-------------------|
| (a) (i)  | balance date      | balance date      |
| (ii)   | recognition date  | balance date      |
| (b)    | acquisition date  | acquisition date  |
| (c)    | recognition date  | recognition date  |
| (d)    | date paid         | date paid         |
| (e)    | transaction date  | transaction date  |
| (f)    | transaction date  | transaction date  |

## ILLUSTRATIVE EXAMPLE 14.2

## TEMPORAL AND CURRENT RATE METHODS

Perrin Ltd, an Australian company, incorporated a foreign subsidiary, Laing Inc, on 1 January 20X1 with an issued capital of 2 000 000 units of foreign currency (FC). At the same time, Laing Inc borrowed on the foreign financial market 500 000 FC at 10% per annum. Laing Inc purchased non-current assets at a cost of 2 000 000 FC. At that date, 1 January 20X1, the exchange rate was A$1 = FC6. By the end of the year, 31 December 20X1, the exchange rate was A$1 = FC8 and Laing Inc had balances in its ledger which included the following:

|  | FC |
|---|---|
| Sales | 3 000 000 |
| Purchases | 1 000 000 |
| Wages and salaries | 400 000 |
| Inventories (purchased 31 December 20X1) | 350 000 |
| Interest | 50 000 |
| Other expenses | 550 000 |
| Depreciation | 300 000 |
| Non-current assets | 2 000 000 |
| Loan | 500 000 |

The financial statements for Laing Inc can be translated as set out below, which shows the results of employing first the temporal method and then the current rate method. The amount for retained profits will be a balancing figure (the difference between the assets and the equities, including the liabilities).

## Translation of financial statements

|  | Foreign currency | | Temporal method | | | Current rate method | | |
|---|---|---|---|---|---|---|---|---|
| (31 December 20X1) | | FC000 | Transl. rate | A$000 | A$000 | Transl. rate | A$000 | A$000 |
| *Assets* | | | | | | | | |
| Bank | | 1 500 | 0.125 | | 187.50 | 0.125 | | 187.50 |
| Inventories | | 350 | 0.125 | | 43.75 | 0.125 | | 43.75 |
| Non-current assets | | 2000 | 0.167 | | 334.00 | 0.125 | | 250.00 |
| Depreciation | | −300 | 0.167 | | −50.10 | 0.125 | | −37.50 |
| | | 3 550 | | | 515.15 | | | 443.75 |
| Loan | | 500 | 0.125 | | 62.50 | 0.125 | | 62.50 |
| Paid-up capital | | 2 000 | 0.167 | | 334.00 | 0.167 | | 334.00 |
| Retained profits | | 1 050 | | | 118.65 | | | |
| Reserves | | | | | | | | 47.25 |
| | | 3 550 | | | 515.15 | | | 443.75 |
| Sales | | 3 000 | 0.146 | | 438.00 | 0.146 | | 438.00 |
| Purchases | 1000 | | 0.146 | 146.00 | | 0.146 | 146.00 | |
| Closing inventory | −350 | 650 | 0.125 | −43.75 | 102.25 | 0.125 | −43.75 | 102.25 |
| | | 2 350 | | | 335.75 | | | 335.75 |
| Wages | 400 | | 0.146 | 58.40 | | 0.146 | 58.40 | |
| Interest | 50 | | 0.146 | 7.30 | | 0.146 | 7.30 | |
| Other expenses | 550 | | 0.146 | 80.30 | | 0.146 | 80.30 | |
| Depreciation | 300 | 1 300 | 0.167 | 50.10 | 196.10 | 0.146 | 43.80 | 189.80 |
| | | 1 050 | | | 139.65 | | | |
| Translation loss | | | | | 21.00 | | | |
| Operating profit | | | | | 118.65 | | | 145.95 |
| Forex translation reserve | | | | | | | | 98.70 |
| Retained profits & FCTR | | | | | | | | 47.25 |

In the example, the exchange rates used to translate the figures are:
Start of year (1:6)     0.167     End of year (1:8)     0.125
Average rate ((0.167 + 0.125)/2)     0.146

The translation loss is the amount by which this closing retained earnings is less than the profit calculated from the profit and loss account. Thus, employing the temporal method, the translation loss is:

| | A$000 |
|---|---|
| Profit (in profit and loss account) | 139.65 |
| Retained profits balance | 118.65 |
| Translation loss | $21.00 |

Had the balance in the retained profits been greater than the profit calculated in the profit and loss account, there would have been a translation gain. In the example this is not the case, because there has been a loss due to holding net monetary assets (in the foreign subsidiary) in a period in which the Australian dollar has increased in value relative to the foreign currency (FC). A reconciliation of the translation loss for the temporal method is given below.

When using the current rate method, the difference is regarded as a movement in the Foreign Exchange (Currency) Translation Reserve (FCTR). Therefore, in the example:

| | A$000 |
|---|---|
| Profit (in profit and loss account) | 145.95 |
| Retained profits & FCTR balance | 47.25 |
| Foreign exchange translation reserve | |
| (decrease) | $ 98.70 |

(Note that the balance sheet indicates the $47.25 as a residual item.)

## Calculation of translation loss (temporal method)

| | 1 Jan 20X1 | | 31 Dec 20X1 | | |
|---|---|---|---|---|---|
| | FC | | FC | | |
| Monetary assets | 2 500 | | 1 500 | | |
| Monetary liabilities | 500 | | 500 | | |
| | 2 000 | | 1 000 | | |
| | FC | Rate | A$ | A$ | |
| Net monetary assets | 2 000 | 0.167 | | 334.00 | |
| Add increase in monetary items from: | | | | | |
| Sales | 3 000 | 0.146 | | 438.00 | |
| | 5 000 | | | 772.00 | |
| Less decrease in monetary items from: | | | | | |
| Purchases | 1 000 | | 0.146 | 146.00 | |
| Wages | 400 | | 0.146 | 58.40 | |
| Interest | 50 | | 0.146 | 7.30 | |
| Other expenses | 550 | | 0.146 | 80.30 | |
| Non-current assets | 2 000 | 4 000 | 0.167 | 334.00 | 626.00 |
| Net monetary assets | | 1 000 | | | 146.00 |
| Net monetary assets at end × Rates | | | | | 146 |
| Net monetary assets at end × Current rate (1000*0.125) | | | | | 125 |
| Translation loss | | | | | −21 |

Remember that monetary assets are cash or near cash, so at 1 January 20X1, these are the cash from the share issue (FC2 000 000) and the loan (FC500 000). By 31 December 20X1, these are cash at bank indicated in the balance sheet (FC1 500 000). Monetary liabilities are commitments to be met in cash or cash equivalents – the loan (FC500 000).

## THE TRANSLATION LOSS (OR GAIN)

*translation loss* Note the different treatments of the translation loss. In the temporal method, the loss (or gain if there had been one) is an expense (or gain), whereas when using the current rate method the loss (or gain) is transferred to the foreign exchange (currency) translation reserve.

The temporal method attempts to show the loss (or gain) calculated on net monetary assets, while the current rate method calculates the loss (or gain) based on net assets. Thus, the temporal method suggests that the change in exchange rates has resulted in a current period loss (or gain).

# Review

Accounting for currency transactions and translations is an increasingly important area given the increase in international and transnational business activities. As indicated above, it can be a highly complex area and the setting of standards was not without controversy. However, there is now general agreement that the methods of accounting for such activities are best described in the accounting standard. The techniques described here have been kept uncomplicated in order to explain the basic procedures. The controversies and the theoretical debates are more properly found in an accounting issues or theory text. A more advanced practical exposition would include the consolidation of more than one foreign subsidiary, some of which could be integrated operations, others self-sustaining. The accounting standard AASB 1012 has two extensive appendices illustrating many of these more complex aspects.

# Endnotes

1  Some people suggest that there is no need for an allowance account being created in which case the accounts receivable (in this example) could have been credited. However, the treatment described here, although slightly longer, is preferred because extra information is provided — that is, there is a signal that the loss is unrealised at balance date.  Similarly with an exchange profit.
2  The method used here is known as the gross method. Another method, the net method, offsets the asset and liability amounts for convenience rather than 'theoretical' purposes.

# KEY TERMS

| | | |
|---|---|---|
| buy | futures market | sell |
| current rate method | hedging | spot rate |
| exchange rate movements | hedging transactions | swap market |
| forward market | integrated foreign operations | temporal method |
| forward rate | self-sustaining foreign operation | translation loss |

# REVIEW QUESTIONS

**14.1** In what way does the time factor affect economic activity that is transacted in different currencies?

**14.2** Distinguish between the spot rate and the forward rate in respect of foreign currency transactions. Why are they different?

**14.3** How do foreign currency exchange rate movements affect the buying and selling of goods transactions?

**14.4** What are the problems in accounting for foreign currency long-term monetary items? Are the accounting problems the same as those for the short-term transactions of buying and selling goods?

**14.5** What are the characteristic differences in operations considered integrated and those considered self-sustaining? What possible reasons are there for making such a distinction?

**14.6** Distinguish between the temporal method of foreign currency translation and the current rate method. Is it likely that there would be a translation loss under one method but a translation gain under the other?

**14.7** What is foreign currency hedging? Why is it used in business?

**14.8** Briefly describe the following in respect of foreign currencies and indicate their relevance:
(a) the forward market;
(b) the futures market; and
(c) the swap market.

**14.9** Why is hedging for specific (foreign currency) commitments different from hedging for general commitments?

**14.10** Ozzie Ltd buys goods from Pomme Ltd, a UK company, and receives an invoice for £50 000 at which time the exchange rate is £1 = A$2. When the payment is due for the goods, the exchange rate is £1 = A$1.90. Does Ozzie Ltd gain or lose by the exchange rate fluctuations, first, if the settlement was to be in pounds sterling and, second, if it is to be in Australian dollars?

# EXERCISES

**Exercise 14.11**  **Foreign purchase transaction**

On 30 March 20X8 a food retail chain, Australian Pancakes Ltd, purchased from a Canadian company pure maple syrup at a cost of C$30 000. On this date the exchange rate was A$1 = C$0.90. The agreement required settlement on 30 June. By the date of settlement the exchange rate had changed such that on 30 June it was A$1 = C$0.95.

*Required*
Prepare general journal entries to record the purchase and the payment in the books of Australian Pancakes Ltd.

**Exercise 14.12**  **Foreign sale transaction**

Australian Meat Packers Ltd, on 31 August 20X9, sold 100 000 tonnes of beef to Hillbilly Hamburger & Hash, Inc, a US retail food chain, for $1000 a tonne. At that date the exchange rate was A$1 = US$0.75. The terms of the sale were for payment in two months, and on 30 October the US company settled its account. The exchange rate at this date was A$1 = US$0.80.

*Required*
Prepare general journal entries in the books of Australian Meat Packers Ltd, assuming:
(a) the transaction is in Australian dollars;
(b) the transaction is in US dollars, the invoice date being 31 August 20X9;
(c) as in (b), except that the balance date of Australian Meat Packers Ltd is 30 September, at which date the exchange rate is A$1 = US$0.78.

**Exercise 14.13**  **Foreign long-term and sales transactions**

Australian Bean Growers Ltd balances its books on 30 June 20X4. Prior to balance date the following transactions occurred:

| 20X4 | |
|---|---|
| May 2 | Purchased electronic bean counter from a Swiss company for 300 000 Swiss francs; the exchange rate is A$1 = 1.60 Swiss francs. |
| May 20 | Sold soya beans on credit to an Indonesian company for 122 000 000 rupiah; the exchange rate is 980 rupiah = A$1. |
| June 21 | Settled account with the Swiss company, the exchange rate being A$1 = 1.65 Swiss francs. |
| June 30 | Exchange rate is A$1 = 1015 rupiah. |
| August 1 | Received payment from the Indonesian company for the sale on 20 May. The exchange rate at this date is A$1 = 1010 rupiah. |

*Required*
Prepare general journal entries in the books of Australian Bean Growers Ltd to record the above.

**Exercise 14.14**    **Long-term monetary transaction**

An Australian company borrows, for three years, 2 000 000 Deutschmarks from a German bank when the exchange rate was A$1 = 1.60DM on 1 January 20X3. The following exchange rates existed over the life of the loan:

|  | 1 Jan 20X3 | 31 Dec 20X3 | 31 Dec 20X4 | 31 Dec 20X5 |
|---|---|---|---|---|
| A$1 = | 1.60DM | 1.65DM | 1.50DM | 1.62DM |

*Required*

1   Indicate at what amount the loan would be reported in the balance sheet prepared at 31 December each year.
2   Prepare general journal entries that would be made in relation to the loan over the life of the loan, assuming it is duly repaid at the due date.

**Exercise 14.15**    **Foreign transactions and hedging**

Kaidonis Sweets Ltd, an Australian wholesale confectionery company, purchased on credit from The Cornelius Peanut Products Company Inc, a US company, reeses pieces (an American confectionery) costing US$75 000, with payment due in three months. The following exchange rates existed:

| At date of purchase, 30 April 20X2 | A$1 = US$0.75 |
|---|---|
| At balance date, 30 June 20X2 | A$1 = US$0.80 |
| At date of settlement, 31 July 20X2 | A$1 = US$0.84 |

*Required*

1   Prepare general journal entries, in the books of Kaidonis Sweets Ltd, to record the above transactions, including any entry necessary at balance date.
2   Assuming Kaidonis Sweets Ltd wished to minimise the loss from potential exchange rate movements and entered into a foreign currency contract for the purchase, at a forward rate of A$1 = US$0.73, of US$75 000 for delivery on 31 July 20X2, prepare all general journal entries associated with the purchase and payment of the goods.

**Exercise 14.16**    **Translation of foreign currency financial statements**

Spasich Ltd operated as producers of sundried vegetables. After some years of success the company decided to expand and formed a New Zealand subsidiary, C & T (NZ) Ltd, on 1 January 20X0. The subsidiary was formed with a paid-up capital of NZ$500 000. It purchased plant and equipment at a cost of NZ$560 000, some of which was bought on credit so that there were accounts payable of $100 000, leaving a balance at the bank of NZ$40 000.

By the end of the year the summarised financial statements of C & T (NZ) Ltd appeared as follows:

## C & T (NZ) Ltd
### Profit and Loss Statement for the year ended 31 December 20X0

|  | NZ$ | NZ$ |
|---|---|---|
| Sales |  | 400 000 |
| Less Cost of goods sold |  | 80 000 |
|  |  | 320 000 |
| Cash expenses | 100 000 |  |
| Depreciation | 40 000 | 140 000 |
| Profit before tax |  | 180 000 |
| Taxation expense |  | 80 000 |
| Net profit |  | 100 000 |

*Note:* Revenue was earned and expense incurred evenly through the year.

## C & T (NZ) Ltd
### Balance Sheet as at 31 December 20X0

|  | NZ$ | NZ$ |
|---|---|---|
| Plant & equipment | 560 000 |  |
| Accumulated depreciation | 40 000 | 520 000 |
| Investments |  | 120 000 |
| Bank |  | 140 000 |
|  |  | 780 000 |
| Paid-up capital | 500 000 |  |
| Retained profits | 100 000 | 600 000 |
| Accounts payable |  | 100 000 |
| Income tax payable |  | 80 000 |
|  |  | 780 000 |

The following exchange rates are relevant; A$1 was equal to:

|  | NZ$ |
|---|---|
| 1 January 20X0 | 1.00 |
| Average for year | 1.10 |
| 31 December | 1.20 |
| At date of purchase of non-monetary investments | 1.08 |

*Required*

Prepare the financial statements for C & T (NZ) Ltd in Australian dollars using:
(a) the temporal method; and
(b) the current rate method.

**Exercise 14.17**  **Translation of foreign currency financial statements**
The following are comparative financial statements for 20X6 and 20X7 of Superfun
Ltd, which operates in Japan. Superfun Ltd was established on 1 July 20X6 and is an
integrated subsidiary of Killjoy Ltd, an Australian company.

### Superfun Ltd
### Profit and Loss Statement for the year ended 30 June 20X7

|  | Yen | Yen |
|---|---|---|
| Sales |  | 2 000 000 |
| Less Cost of goods sold |  | 700 000 |
| Gross profit |  | 1 300 000 |
| Other income |  | 100 000 |
|  |  | 1 400 000 |
| Other expenses |  |  |
| Depreciation | 150 000 |  |
| Wages & salaries | 700 000 |  |
| Other expenses | 400 000 | 1 250 000 |
| Profit |  | 150 000 |

### Superfun Ltd
### Balance Sheet as at 30 June 20X7

|  | 1 July 20X6 Yen | 30 June 20X7 Yen |
|---|---|---|
| Accounts receivable | – | 150 000 |
| Inventory | – | 50 000 |
| Investments | 700 000 | 700 000 |
| Plant & equipment | 1 500 000 | 2 150 000 |
| Less Accumulated depreciation |  | (150 000) |
| Cash | 1 000 000 | 200 000 |
|  | 3 200 000 | 3 100 000 |
| Accounts payable | – | 100 000 |
| Loan payable | 2 200 000 | 1 850 000 |
| Paid-up share capital | 1 000 000 | 1 000 000 |
| Retained profits | – | 150 000 |
|  | 3 200 000 | 3 100 000 |

Additional information:
(a) The accounts are in Japanese yen.
(b) Other income consisted of two equal interest payments made on 31 December
and 30 June.
(c) Additional plant and equipment was purchased on 30 June.

(d) During the above financial year the exchange rate moved steadily from 1 July: A$1 = ¥90 to 30 June: A$1 = ¥70.
(e) Inventory was acquired at year end.
(f) Investments are described as monetary.

*Required*
1 Calculate the foreign exchange translation profit/loss for the 20X7 financial year.
2 Assume Superfun is a self-sustaining operation and calculate the foreign currency translation reserve as at 30 June 20X7.

**Exercise 14.18  Translation of foreign currency financial statements**
Trellis Ltd is an Indonesian subsidiary of Plant Ltd, an Australian retailer of specialist garden products. Trellis was incorporated on 1 July 20X3. Financial information available is listed below:

|  | 1 July 20X3 Rupiah (000) | 30 June 20X4 Rupiah (000) |
|---|---|---|
| Paid-up share capital | 1 000 000 | 1 000 000 |
| Accounts receivable |  | 240 000 |
| Shop fittings | 400 000 | 400 000 |
| Accumulated depreciation on shop fittings |  | 40 000 |
| Depreciation expense |  | 65 000 |
| Cash at bank | 500 000 | 900 000 |
| Motor vehicles | 100 000 | 100 000 |
| Accumulated depreciation on motor vehicles |  | 25 000 |
| Accounts payable |  | 120 000 |
| Sales |  | 3 000 000 |
| Cost of goods sold |  | 1 000 000 |
| Other expenses |  | 1 200 000 |
| Inventory 30 June |  | 280 000 |

Additional information:
(a) Exchange rates: at 1 July 20X3, rupiah 1000 = A$0.75; at 30 June 20X4, rupiah 1000 = A$0.95.
(b) The rates moved steadily during the above period. Inventory was acquired at year end.

*Required*
For the year ended 30 June 20X4:
1 Assume that Trellis Ltd is a self-sustaining operation and calculate the foreign exchange translation gain/loss and prepare the translated financial statements.
2 Assume that Trellis Ltd is an integrated operation and prepare the translated financial statements. Indicate the foreign exchange translation gain/loss and where it would be disclosed in the financial statements of Plant Ltd.

**Exercise 14.19  Translation of foreign currency financial statements**
Chreamy Ltd is a Swiss-based manufacturer of speciality cheeses. On 1 July 20X3 it was taken over by Craiburn Ltd, an Australian dairy products distributor. The financial statements of Chreamy Ltd as at 30 June 20X4 were as follows:

## Chreamy Ltd
### Profit and Loss Statement for the year ended 30 June 20X4

|  |  | Swiss Francs |
|---|---|---|
| Sales |  | 1 200 000 |
| Less Cost of goods sold |  |  |
| Opening inventory | 300 000 |  |
| Purchases | 600 000 |  |
|  | 900 000 |  |
| Closing inventory | 250 000 | 650 000 |
| Gross profit |  | 550 000 |
| Other expenses |  |  |
| Administrative & selling | 150 000 |  |
| Depreciation | 40 000 | 190 000 |
| Operating profit before income tax |  | 360 000 |
| Income tax expense |  | 160 000 |
| Operating profit after tax |  | 200 000 |
| Retained profits 1 July 20X3 |  | 90 000 |
| Retained profits 30 June 20X4 |  | 290 000 |

## Chreamy Ltd
### Balance Sheet as at 30 June 20X4

|  | 1 July 20X3 Swiss Francs | 30 June 20X4 Swiss Francs |
|---|---|---|
| Assets |  |  |
| Current assets |  |  |
| Cash at bank | 40 000 | 180 000 |
| Accounts receivable | 110 000 | 170 000 |
| Inventory | 300 000 | 250 000 |
| Total current assets | 450 000 | 600 000 |
|  |  |  |
| Non-current assets |  |  |
| Plant & equipment | 360 000 | 320 000 |
| Buildings | 100 000 | 100 000 |
| Total non-current assets | 460 000 | 420 000 |
| Total assets | 910 000 | 1 020 000 |
|  |  |  |
| Liabilities |  |  |
| Current liabilities |  |  |
| Accounts payable | 70 000 | 50 000 |
|  |  |  |
| Non-current liabilities |  |  |
| Loan | 400 000 | 330 000 |
| Total liabilities | 470 000 | 380 000 |
| Net assets | 440 000 | 640 000 |
|  |  |  |
| Represented by: |  |  |
| Paid-up capital | 350 000 | 350 000 |
| Retained profits | 90 000 | 290 000 |
|  | 440 000 | 640 000 |

The relevant exchange rates were:

| | |
|---|---|
| At 1 July 20X3: | A$1 = 5.6 Francs |
| Average for period 1 July 20X3 to 30 June 20X4: | $A1 = 6.0 Francs |
| Ending inventory acquired: | A$1 = 6.2 Francs |
| At 30 June 20X4: | A$1 = 6.4 Francs |

*Required*

1 Translate the financial statements of Chreamy Ltd in accordance with the provisions of AASB1012, assuming:
 (a) Chreamy Ltd is an integrated foreign operation; and
 (b) Chreamy Ltd is a self-sustaining foreign operation.
2 Highlight the translation gain/loss and its disclosure.

**Exercise 14.20** **Translation of foreign currency financial statements**

Due to an expanding market, Australian gemstone manufacturer Moonstone Ltd established a subsidiary in New Zealand, Greengem Ltd, on 1 July 20X8. Moonstone Ltd contributed A$900 000 in capital which was combined with borrowings of NZ$500 000 from a New Zealand financial institution. To start the new company, Greengem Ltd purchased new plant and equipment on 2 July 20X8 worth NZ$800 000.

During the year, the following foreign currency rates applied: at 1 July 20X8, NZ$1 = A$0.8; at 30 June 20X9, NZ$1 = A$0.6. The rate changed steadily during the year.

The financial statements of Greengem Ltd for the year ended 30 June 20X9 were as follows:

**Greengem Ltd**
**Profit and Loss Statement for the year ended 30 June 20X9**

| | NZ$ | NZ$ |
|---|---|---|
| Sales | | 600 000 |
| *Less* Cost of goods sold | | |
| Purchases | 450 000 | |
| Closing inventory | 210 000 | 240 000 |
| Gross profit | | 360 000 |
| Administrative & selling expenses | 120 000 | |
| Depreciation | 60 000 | 180 000 |
| Operating profit | | 180 000 |

**Greengem Ltd**
**Balance Sheet as at 30 June 20X9**

| | NZ$ | | NZ$ |
|---|---|---|---|
| Accounts payable | 40 000 | Cash | 300 000 |
| Loan | 370 000 | Accounts receivable | 60 000 |
| Issued capital | 720 000 | Inventory | 210 000 |
| Retained profits | 180 000 | Plant & equipment | 740 000 |
| | 1 310 000 | | 1 310 000 |

Assume that closing inventory was acquired in the last half of the year and that loan repayments were made evenly during the year.

*Required*
Translate the New Zealand statements into Australian dollars, assuming that the New Zealand subsidiary is fully integrated.

# Index